After service as a Royal Marine Commando Officer and a commander of a Special Boat Service unit in the Far East, Paddy Ashdown served as a diplomat in the Foreign Office before, in due course, being elected as the Member of Parliament for Yeovil, serving in that capacity from 1983 to 2001. In 1988 he became leader of the Liberal Democrats, standing aside eleven years later. He was appointed as the international community's High Representative for Bosnia and Herzegovina, serving from 2002 to 2006. He is the author of many books, including *A Brilliant Little Operation*, which won the British Army Military History prize for 2013.

From the reviews for *The Cruel Victory*:

'[Ashdown's] career as a soldier and politician have equipped him to tell [this story] well. The fighting is described briskly and without excessive military jargon. The first-hand sources make it vivid'

EDWARD STOURTON, *The Times*

'Written with pace, the detail is fine … There are also moving domestic details, inspirational accounts of bravery, brilliant command, occasional mercy and good fortune, and the necessary but appalling stories of the retributions and atrocities that marked the end of the Free Republic of the Vercors'

CLARE MULLEY, *Spectator*

'Excellent in showing how men across France mobilized … for Ashdown, Vercors is the "hidden story of D-Day"'

MARCO GIANNANGELI, *Sunday Express*

'This is an epic story of heroism by ordinary people and high-level bungling, containing a wealth of detail from German as well as Resistance and Allied sources'

GWYN GRIFFITHS, *Morning Star*

THE CRUEL VICTORY

THE FRENCH RESISTANCE, D-DAY AND THE BATTLE FOR THE VERCORS 1944

PADDY ASHDOWN

WILLIAM
COLLINS

William Collins
An imprint of HarperCollins*Publishers*
1 London Bridge Street
London SE1 9GF
WilliamCollinsBooks.com

First published in Great Britain by William Collins in 2014
This William Collins paperback edition published 2015

1

A catalogue record for this book is
available from the British Library

ISBN 978-0-00-752081-7

Maps by Harriet McDougall

Printed and bound in Great Britain by
Clays Ltd, St Ives plc

MIX
Paper from
responsible sources
FSC® C007454

FSC is a non-profit international organisation established to promote
the responsible management of the world's forests. Products carrying the
FSC label are independently certified to assure consumers that they come
from forests that are managed to meet the social, economic and
ecological needs of present or future generations,
and other controlled sources.

Find out more about HarperCollins and the environment at
www.harpercollins.co.uk/green

To the boy in the white shirt

CONTENTS

In war, young men go out to die for old men's dreams

Anon

A NOTE ON USAGES

In this text I have not included dialogue unless it comes from a source who I have reason to believe might have been present at the time or it has been noted down as dialogue in the course of taking testimony from a living witness.

Since this story concerns primarily military operations, I have used the twenty-four-hour clock throughout. In 1943 and 1944 all British forces in the European theatre used Greenwich Mean Time (GMT) plus one hour (UK Single Summer Time) from 16 August to 3 April, and GMT plus two hours from 4 April to 15 August (UK Double Summer Time). The time used in all German-occupied western European territories was Central European Time (CET), which in that era was UK Single Summer Time plus two hours. Since this story takes place primarily in France, all times in the text are given in, or adjusted to be consistent with, CET.

For a similar reason, units of measurement have been converted, where appropriate, to the metric scale.

Readers may want to know what the wartime franc was worth. Prices more than doubled during the four years of the German occupation of France, and inflation was very much worse on the black market. But one can get a rough idea of money values if one thinks of 1,000 francs in 1943–4 as the equivalent of 250 euros or £200 today.

Except where otherwise stated the translations of French source documents into English are those of the author. Where the original French was in a written formal document I have tried to make the translation as precise as possible. Where the original source is oral (for example, the oral evidence of witnesses) I have allowed myself greater latitude to cope with the differences in sentence formation between spoken French and English in an attempt to preserve the original sense and colour, while conveying this to the English reader in the most readable fashion.

The word 'maquis' has subtly different meanings in English and French. The word originates from the Corsican term for the dry scrub which covers the hills of southern and Mediterranean France, but even more so from a Corsican expression *prendre le maquis*, which means to shelter in the woods to escape the authorities or a vendetta (to go underground). Even today, the word is used by the French primarily to describe those who resisted the Germans by going into the countryside and especially the wilder places. They formed into groups which sometimes took the name of the area they operated in – for instance, *le maquis du Vercors*. The term *maquisard* in French denotes someone who belonged to a *maquis* cell, usually in a rural area. In French the term is not normally taken to apply to those who belonged to urban Resistance groups (for example, in Paris or Lyon). In modern English usage, however, the word Maquisard has become, for all practical purposes, synonymous with that of a Resistant, whether urban or rural. Since this is an English book the word Maquis is used in the English sense, except where it is plainly inappropriate to do so.

One of the problems with writing this book has been the story's high degree of complexity and detail. In an attempt not excessively to confuse the reader, I have tried to keep the personal names of those who played a minor role in the story out of the main text. For those interested, these, where known, are given in the Notes. Similarly, I have removed from the main text as many of the military unit names as possible; these too can be found in the Notes. And finally, in the same endeavour, I have submerged some of the myriad organizations involved in both London and Algiers. Thus the main directing French organization in London, the Bureau Central de Renseignements et d'Action (BCRA), is referred to simply as 'London' or 'de Gaulle's headquarters in London', while the main Algiers organization for directing the Resistance in southern France, the Special Projects Operations Centre (SPOC), becomes just 'Algiers'.

For the same reason and in the hope it will make them more accessible to the reader, I have tried to simplify the references by providing abbreviations for the main archives which I have consulted (such as TNA for the British National Archives at Kew, and NARA for the US National Archives and Records Administration). A key giving each of these abbreviations can be found at the start of the Notes section.

PREFACE

I first became fascinated by the wartime epic of the Vercors in the early 1970s when I worked in the United Kingdom Mission to the United Nations in Geneva. I was drawn to it because of the tragedy and the horror of the story. But also because it struck me as a powerful example of a subject that has always fascinated me: the consequences for those on the front lines of conflict when those at the top know too little about the harsh realities of war, or think too little about what their decisions mean on the ground.

This is a French story, of course. But it is also a very human epic which has lessons for us all. The strong are not always wise. The simple not always stupid. The weak do not always lose. In most cases, the final determiner of outcomes rests, not with machines, or might, or well-laid plans, but with how individuals behave at the moment of trial.

This story has another function too. In this, the year of the seventieth anniversary of D-Day, it is as well to remember that the Normandy invasion was about more than what happened on the Normandy beaches, most of which is minutely documented and recorded. This is the hidden story of D-Day, when thousands of ordinary, untrained and in most cases crudely armed French men and women put their lives at risk quite as much as those who stormed the beaches, because they were determined to help throw out a hated occupier and join the fight to liberate their country.

DRAMATIS PERSONAE

BENNES, Robert (BOB)*
Zeller's radio operator and commander of La Britière radio house.

BILLON, Francis (TARTANE)
Parachuted in with Tournissa. Injured. One of those shot at the Grotte de la Luire.

BLAIN, Léa
Cipher and coding assistant to Eucalyptus. Runner for Jean Prévost.

BLANC, Paul (JEAN-PAUL)
Commander of the Trièves Maquis unit on the Pas de l'Aiguille.

BOIRON, Victor
Tractor driver in Vassieux.

BOISSIÈRE, Gustave (BOIS)
Speleologist and liaison officer to the Eucalyptus Mission.

BORDENAVE, André (DUFAU)
Commander of 6th BCA.

BOURDEAUX, Louis (FAYARD)
Commander of a Maquis company in Royans.

BOURGEOIS, Maurice (BATAILLE)
Maquis leader who accompanied Vernon Hoppers on the Lus-la-Croix-Haute ambush.

BOURGÈS-MAUNOURY, Maurice (POLYGONE)
Military delegate of R1, then National Military delegate.

* Aliases in brackets.

BOUSQUET, René (CHABERT)
Huet's deputy.

BUCKMASTER, Colonel Maurice
Head of SOE's F Section.

CAMMAERTS, Francis (ROGER)
SOE F Section Organizer of Jockey circuit.

CATHALA, Gaston (GRANGE)
Maquis leader in the west of the plateau.

CHAMBONNET, Albert (DIDIER)
Commander of the Secret Army in the Lyon area.

CHAMPETIER DE RIBES, Maude (DANIELLE)
Milice spy and mistress of Dagostini.

CHAVANT, Eugène (CLÉMENT)
(*Le Patron*) Political leader of the Vercors.

CONSTANS, Jean (SAINT-SAUVEUR)
Responsible for assistance to the Vercors in Algiers.

CONUS, Adrien (VOLUME)
Member of Eucalyptus Mission. Sent by Huet to get help from Bauges
Maquis on 21 July.

COSTA DE BEAUREGARD, Roland (DURIEU)
Responsible for the northern sector of the Vercors.

COULANDON, Émile (GASPARD)
Resistance leader on the Mont Mouchet.

CROIX, Yves (PINGOUIN)
Eucalyptus Mission radio operator.

CROUAU, Fernand (ABEL)
Commander of Compagnie Abel.

DAGOSTINI, Raoul
Milice Chief.

DALLOZ, Pierre (SENLIS)
Conceived Plan Montagnards in 1942.

D'ANGLEJAN (ARNOLLE)
One of Huet's staff officers. He organized the counter-attacks in Vassieux.

D'ASTIER DE LA VIGÉRIE, Emmanuel (BERNARD)
Senior French Resistance official in London and Algiers.

DARIER, Albert (FÉLIX)
Member of the Mens section of the Compagnie de Trièves.

DELESTRAINT, Charles (VIDAL)
General. Head of the Secret Army in southern France. Captured and died in Dachau.

DESCOUR, Jacques (LA FLÈCHE)
Marcel Descour's son. Killed at Vassieux, 21 July 1944.

DESCOUR, Marcel (BAYARD and PÉRIMÈTRE)
Chief of Staff of the Secret Army in R1 and FFI Commander of Region 1.

DESMAZES, Marie Alphonse Théodore René Adrien (RICHARD)
Secret Army conspirator with Delestraint in Bourg-en-Bresse.

DROUOT, Jean (HERMINE)
FFI leader in the Drôme.

EYSSERIC, Gustave (DURAND)
Maquis commander at Malleval.

FARGE, Yves (GRÉGOIRE and BESSONNEAU)
Commissioner of the Republic.

FISCHER, Dr Ladislas
Doctor in Saint-Martin and Grotte de la Luire. He sometimes used the false identity Lucien Ferrier while in the Vercors.

GANIMÈDE, Dr Fernand
Doctor in Saint-Martin and Grotte de la Luire.

GARIBOLDY, Paul (VALLIER)
First leader of Groupe Vallier.

BLUM-GAYET, Geneviève (GERMAINE)
Early Vercors Resistant activist.

GAGNOL, Abbé
The priest of Vassieux.

GEYER, Narcisse (THIVOLET)
Maquis commander. Responsible for the southern sector of the Vercors.

GODART, Pierre (RAOUL)
Maquis commander at Malleval.

GRANVILLE, Christine (née Krystyna SKARBEK) (PAULINE)
SOE F Section courier for Jockey circuit.

GUBBINS, Brigadier Colin
The operational head of SOE.

GUÉTET, Dom (LEMOINE)
Marcel Descour's counsellor/monk.

HAEZEBROUCK, Pierre (HARDY)
Commander of the defence of Vassieux. Killed 21 July 1944.

HOPPERS, Vernon G.
Commander of the US Justine Mission.

HOUSEMAN, John (RÉFLEXION)
Member of Eucalyptus Mission.

HUET, François (HERVIEUX)
Commanded the Maquis on the Vercors.

HUMBERT, Jacques
Retired General who walked to the Vercors to join the battle on 21 July 1944.

JACQUIER, Paulette (MARIE-JEANNE and LA FRETTE)
Leader of Maquis group in the Chambarand forest.

JOUNEAU, Georges (GEORGES)
Garage owner and head of the Motor Transport Depot on the Vercors.

KALCK,* Louis (ANDRÉ and JOB-JOB)
Commander of Compagnie André defending the eastern passes.

KNAB, Werner
Commander German Sipo/SD Lyon area.

KOENIG, Marie Joseph Pierre François (known as Pierre)
Appointed by de Gaulle as CO of FFI.

LASSALLE, Pierre (BENJAMIN and BOLIVIEN)
Descour's radio operator at La Matrassière and La Britière.

LE RAY, Alain (BASTIDE and ROUVIER)
Vercors military commander until January 1944 and then FFI
commander of Isère Department.

LONGE, Desmond (RÉFRACTION)
Leader of Eucalyptus Mission.

MARTIN, Léon Dr
One of the founders of Grenoble resistance in the Café de la Rotonde.

MAYAUD, Charlotte (CHARLOTTE)
Early Vercors Resistant and organizer in Villard de Lans. Also a courier
and liaison agent.

MOCKLER-FERRYMAN, Eric
Director for SOE operations in western Europe.

MONTEFUSCO, Mario (TITIN and ARGENTIN)
Radio operator at La Britière.

MOULIN, Jean (REX, MAX and RÉGIS)
De Gaulle's representative in southern France and the architect of the
unified southern Resistance.

MYERS, Chester L.
Hoppers' second-in-command on the Justine Mission.

NIEHOFF, Heinrich
German military commander southern France.

---

* There are several versions of this name, including Calke and Calk. I have used the
one given in the journal of the 11th Cuirassiers and Robert Bennes' memoirs.

ORTIZ, Peter Julien (CHAMBELLAN and JEAN-PIERRE)
US Marine parachuted in with the Union Mission and subsequently
the head of Union II.

PECQUET, André Édouard (BAVAROIS and PARAY)
Eucalyptus Mission radio operator.

PFLAUM, Karl Ludwig
Commander 157th Reserve Division.

PINHAS, France
Nurse at the second Battle of Saint-Nizier.

PRÉVOST, Jean (GODERVILLE)
Writer and friend of Dalloz. Commander of Compagnie Goderville in
the north of the Vercors.

PROVENCE, Mireille
Milice spy.

PUPIN, Aimé (MATHIEU)
Early Vercors Resistance leader.

RAYNAUD, Pierre (ALAIN)
An agent of Cammaerts and commander of a Drôme Maquis unit.

REY, Fabien (MARSEILLE and BLAIREAU)
Expert in and author of Maquisard guide to the the flora and fauna of
the Vercors.

REY, Sylviane
Nurse and friend of Francis Cammaerts.

RITTER, Stefan
Commander No. 8 Company Reserve Gebirgsjäger Battalion II/98.

ROMANS-PETIT, Henri (ROMANS)
Resistance leader in the Jura.

ROUDET, Marcel (RAOUL)
Corrupt Lyon policeman who led his own 'Raoul Maquis'.

SALLIER, Ferdinand (CHRISTOPHE)
Maquis leader in the west of the Vercors.

SAMUEL, Dr Eugène (JACQUES and RAVALEC)
Early founder of the Resistance movement in Villard-de-Lans.

SCHÄFER, Friedrich
Commander Kampfgruppe Schäfer.

SCHWEHR, Franz
Commander Kampfgruppe Schwehr.

SEEGER, Alfred
Commander Kampfgruppe Seeger.

SOUSTELLE, Jacques
Confidant of de Gaulle and head of the French Directorate for
Intelligence and Special Forces.

STÜLPNAGEL, Carl-Heinrich
German military commander for all France.

TANANT, Pierre (LAROCHE)
Huet's Chief of Staff.

THACKTHWAITE, Henry (PROCUREUR)
British member of the Union Mission.

TOURNISSA, Jean (PAQUEBOT)
Landing-ground expert sent in to build an airstrip at Vassieux.

ULLMAN, Henri (PHILIPPE)
Commander of Compagnie Philippe.

ULLMANN, Dr Marcel
Doctor in Saint-Martin and Grotte de la Luire.

VILLEMAREST, Pierre FAILLANT de (FRANTZ)
Maquis intelligence expert and later commander of the Groupe Vallier.

VINCENT, Gaston (AZUR and PIERRE)
OSS agent in Saint-Agnan.

VINCENT-BEAUME, André (Capt. VINCENT and SAMBO)
Head of Huet's 2nd Bureau (intelligence).

WINTER, Anne
Nurse at the Grotte de la Luire.

ZABEL
Commander Kampfgruppe Zabel.

ZELLER, Henri (FAISCEAU and JOSEPH)
Chief of Resistance in south-east France.

LIST OF MAPS

PROLOGUE

Above the city of Grenoble, at Saint-Nizier-du-Moucherotte, the sun rose into a perfect sky at 04.48 on the morning of 13 June 1944. For the 700 young men who had spent the previous night under the summer stars, strung out along a 3-kilometre defensive line on the Charvet ridge, it bought a welcome warmth against the damp early-morning chill. Bees hummed among the flowers and grasses and everywhere little birds darted from clump to bush, seeking out insects. High above the early lark let down her string of liquid notes. Below them, the Grésivaudan valley, bounded by the Chartreuse massif on one side and the Bauges and Oisans ranges on the other, glowed with the colours of high summer. And in the distance, like a great white whale, the snow-covered hump-back of Mont Blanc sparkled in the sunlight. In normal times this would have been good day for lovers – and country walks – and family picnics. But this was not a normal time – and this would not be a normal day.

Modern-day soldiers almost always fight and die miles from home. But these young men – many little more than boys – looked down that morning to see their home city laid out as plain as a street map. They knew its every nook and cranny. There was the park where they had played football with friends. There the school they had attended. There the square in which they had hung around, watching the girls go by. There the café where they had met a lover. And there the rented flat where wives and children still slept this summer morning, as they lay out in the dew-soaked grass, waiting for the enemy to come.

Whatever politicians say, soldiers do not die for their country. They die, mostly, for the man next to them – the comrade they know will lay down his life for them. And for whom they, too, will lay down theirs in their turn – if required to do so. But most of these young Maquisards lying out this warm summer's morning on the Charvet hill, in the same clothes – even the same white shirts – in which they had left home only days previously, were different. Young, naive, unpractised in the use of arms, inexperienced in the terrors of war, they had come to the plateau out of a genuine sense of patriotism mixed with romance and adventure. Their youthful enthusiasm remained undimmed by the dull, mind-numbing routines of the professional soldier. How were they to know that their proudly acquired Sten guns would be little more than pop-guns against the steel-clad might and majesty of the world's finest army, now massing invisibly below them? How were they to know, plucked so suddenly out of comfortable city lives, what it would be like to watch a friend cough out his life's blood on the grass next to them? These things were literally beyond their imaginings.

And so, in ways unknown to the common soldier, they lay there, wait-ing for their enemy – apprehensively of course – but in their innocence also proudly, bravely, determinedly, ready to carry out what they believed was a glorious duty on behalf of their long-oppressed country. 'It's the morning of Austerlitz!' declared one, referring to Napoleon's great victory over the Austrians in 1805.

Suddenly, there was a new noise punctuating the early-morning hum of the city, drifting up to them on a light summer breeze. It was the insistent thump of a German heavy machine gun somewhere in the woods and meadows below them. Little flowers of dirt started sprouting among them in the long grass where they lay. Looking to the foot of the hill, they could make out tiny dots of field grey spreading out as they started to move slowly up towards them.

'They're coming!' someone shouted.

1

THE VERCORS BEFORE THE VERCORS

For those who live around the Vercors massif – from the ancient city of Grenoble lying close beneath its north-eastern point to the vineyards of Valence scattered around its south-western slopes – the forbidding cliffs of the plateau are the ramparts of another country. To them, this is not just a mountain. It is also a state of mind. Even when hidden behind a curtain of summer rain or with its summits covered by the swirling clouds of a winter tempest, the great plateau is still there – offering something different from the drudgery and oppressions of ordinary life down below. Best of all, on still, deep-winter days, when the cold drags the clouds down to the valleys, up there on the Vercors looking down on the sea of cloud, all is brilliant sunshine, deep-blue skies, virgin snow and a horizon crowded with the shimmering peaks of the Alps.

Today, this is a place of summer escape and winter exhilaration. But its older reputation was as a place of hard living and of refuge from retribution and repression.

The historical importance of the Vercors lies in its strategic position dominating the two major transport corridors of this part of France: the Route Napoleon which passes almost in the shadow of the plateau's eastern wall and the valley of the River Rhône, which flows through Valence some 15 kilometres away from its south-western shoulder.

The Romans came this way fifty years before the birth of Christ. Pliny, writing in AD 50, referred to the people of the plateau as the Vertacomacori, a word whose first syllable may have been carried forward into the name 'Vercors' itself. Eight centuries later, the Saracens followed the Romans, implanting themselves in Grenoble for some years. According to local legend, they even sent a raiding party towards the Pas de la Balme on the eastern wall of the plateau, but were beaten back by local inhabitants rolling rocks down on the invaders. Less than a hundred years later, towards the end of the tenth century, the Vikings came here too, but from the opposite direction – south down the Rhône in their longships. And 400 years after that, the Burgundian armies followed them on their own campaign of conquest and pillage. Then in March 1815, Napoleon, after landing on the Mediterranean coast from Elba, marched his growing army north along the route which still bears his name under the eastern flank of the Vercors, towards Grenoble, Paris and his nemesis at Waterloo.

Napoleon excepted, what is most significant about these invaders is that, though there are signs enough of their passing in the countryside below, there are few on the Vercors itself. It is as though these foreigners were content to pass by in the valleys without wishing to pay much attention to the cold, poverty-stricken and inhospitable land towering above them. One consequence of this passage of armies and occupiers is, however, more permanent. The historian Jules Michelet, writing in 1861, commented: 'There is a vigorous spirit of resistance which marks these provinces. This can be awkward from time to time; but it is our defence against foreigners.'

The plateau itself is shaped like a huge north-pointing arrowhead some 50 kilometres long and 20 wide. It covers, in all, 400,000 hectares, about the same size as the Isle of Wight. An Englishman who will play a small part in this history described it, in his prosaic Anglo-Saxon way, as a great aircraft-carrier steaming north from the middle of France towards the English Channel.

This extraordinary geological feature is the product of the the shrinking earth and the faraway press of the African continent, whose northward push against the European mainland generates the colossal pressures which wrinkle up the Alps and squeeze the Vercors limestone massif straight up in vertical cliffs, 1,000 metres above the surrounding plain.

No concessions are found here to accommodate the needs of man. The Vercors offers nothing in the way of easy living. Extreme difficulty of access made the plateau one of the poorest areas, not just of France, but of all Europe, until new roads were blasted up the cliff faces in the nineteenth century. The forbidding bastion of the eastern wall of the plateau, stretching from Grenoble to the plateau's southern extremity, is accessible only by goats, sheep and intrepid walkers. For vehicles, there are just eight points of access to the plateau, one on its southern flank, five spread out along its western wall and two on its north-eastern quar-

THE VERCORS

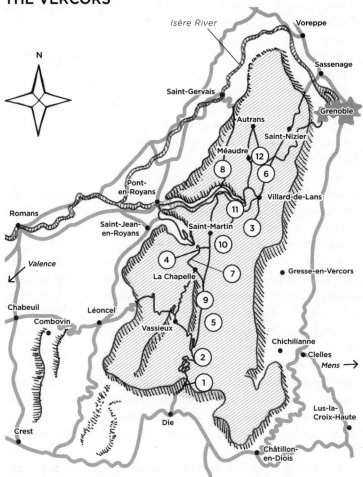

① Chamaloc	⑤ Grotte de la Luire	⑨ Saint-Agnan
② Col de Rousset	⑥ Lans	⑩ Tourtres
③ Corrençon	⑦ Les Barraques	⑪ Valchevrière
④ Grands Goulets	⑧ Rencurel	⑫ Col de la Croix Perrin

ter. Of these, all bar one involve either deep gorges into which the sun hardly ever penetrates or roads which rise dizzily through a tracery of hairpin bends to run along narrow ledges and through dark tunnels blasted from vertical rock faces.

Only the road on the plateau's north-eastern edge offers something different. Here the slope rises placidly from the back gardens of the Grenoble suburbs and is served by a moderately engineered road, supplemented, until 1951, by a small funicular tramway, at the top of which is the little town of Saint-Nizier. This sits on its own natural viewing platform, looking out over the city to the mountain-flanked valley of the Isère (known as the Grésivaudan valley) and the white mass of Mont Blanc in the distance.

The Vercors plateau itself is dominated by three rolling ridges which run along its length from north to south like ocean breakers. Their tops are above the treeline, rock-strewn and so sparsely covered with mountain grasses that on bright summer days the white from the limestone below seems to shimmer through the thin air and dazzle the eyes. In some high, very exposed areas, where the hot summer winds have whipped off all the soil, the limestone rock is laid bare and fissured into deep cracks, some large enough for a man – or several men – to stand up in. These are wild and terrible places, known to the locals as *lapiaz*. Their only gentleness lies in the strange lichens and alpine plants which make their homes in the cracks and survive by straining moisture from the dew-laden air of summer mornings.

Further down, there are cool conifers and one of the largest stands of hardwood in western Europe. Further down still, cradled in the valleys, are the little towns, villages and hamlets of the Vercors community – many of them, such as Saint-Martin, Saint-Julien, Saint-Agnan, La Chapelle, speaking of a past where an attachment to the right God was as important to survival as skill at animal husbandry and knowing the right time to plant the crops. Here, though the bitter snow-filled winters remain tough, there is good grazing and comfortable summer living.

One essential ingredient of life, however, is not easily available – water. This is a limestone plateau and every drop that falls as rain or seeps away from melting snow drops down through the limestone into hidden channels, underground rivers and a still-undiscovered network of chambers and caverns which honeycomb the whole Vercors plateau. Some say a drop of moisture captured in a snowflake which falls on the summit of the plateau's highest peak, the 2,341-metre Grand Veymont, will take three years to pass in darkness through the hidden channels under the mountains before it sees the light of day again, tumbling down through the plateau's gorges on its way to the Rhône and the warm waters of the Mediterranean far away to the south. Surface water across the whole plateau is rare and wells and springs even more so. All of them are widely known and meticulously marked on every Vercors map.

This is the unique topography and meteorology which has played such an important part in shaping both the Vercors, and the lives of those who have struggled to live and take refuge there, not least during the years of France's agony in the Second World War.

But it is not just the topography that makes the Vercors unique. The plateau lies at the precise administrative, architectural, cultural and meteorological dividing line between northern, temperate, Atlantic France and that part of France – Provence – which looks south to the Mediterranean. The frontier between the departments of the Isère and of the Drôme divides the plateau into two halves: the northern Vercors is in the Isère and the southern Vercors is in the Drôme.

At least until the Second World War, these two Vercors were quite different. Indeed, as late as the nineteenth century, the rural folk of the plateau spoke two different and mutually incomprehensible languages, the *langue d'oc* and the *langue d'oïl*. The northern Vercors took its lead from sophisticated Grenoble. Here, at Villard-de-Lans, was established one of the first – and one of the most fashionable – Alpine resorts in France, frequented in the 1930s by film stars, the fashionable, the *sportif* and the nouveau glitterati of Paris. During pre-war summers, the area became one of the favourite Alpine playgrounds for those with a passion for healthy and sporty living; it teemed with hikers, climbers, bikers and even practitioners of Robert Baden-Powell's new invention from England, *le scouting*. The southern Vercors on the other hand – the 'true Vercors' according to its inhabitants – remained virtually unchanged: still agricultural, still largely isolated, still taking its lead more from Provence and the south than the styles and sophistications of Paris and the north.

This division is visible even in the vegetation and architecture of the two halves. Travel just a few tens of metres south through the short tunnel at the Col de Menée at the south-eastern edge of the plateau and there is a different feel to almost everything. Even the intensity of the light seems to change. Pine trees, temperate plants and solid thick-walled houses, whose roofs are steeply inclined for snow, give way almost immediately to single-storey houses with red-tiled roofs crouching against the summer heat, tall cypresses as elegant as pheasant feathers, the murmuring of bees and the scent of resin in the air. Here the hillsides are covered with wild thyme, sage and the low ubiquitous scrub called *maquis*, from which the French Resistance movement took its name.

Many factors and many personalities shaped the events which took place on the Vercors during the Second World War. One of them was the extraordinary, secluded, rugged, almost mythical nature of the plateau itself.

2

FRANCE FROM THE FALL TO 1943: SETTING THE SCENE

It is only the French themselves who understand fully the depth of the wounds inflicted by the fall of France in 1940. They had invested more in their Army than any other European nation with the exception of Germany. With around 500,000 regular soldiers, backed by 5 million trained reservists and supported by a fleet of modern tanks which some believed better than the German Panzers, the French Army was regarded – and not just by the French – as the best in the world.

It took the Germans just six weeks to shatter this illusion and force a surrender whose humiliation was the more excruciating because Hitler insisted that it took place in the very railway carriage where Germany had been brought to her knees in 1918. It is not the purpose of this book to delve in detail into how France fell. But one important element of those six weeks in the summer of 1940 is often overlooked. Not all of France's armies were defeated.

The French Army of the Alps – the Armée des Alpes – never lost a battle. They held the high Alpine passes against a numerically superior Italian assault. And they stopped the German Army too, at the Battle of Voreppe, named for the little town just outside Grenoble which guards the narrows between the Vercors and the Chartreuse massifs. Indeed the Battle of Voreppe ended only when the French artillery, wreaking havoc on German tanks from positions on the northern tip of the Vercors plateau, were ordered to return to barracks because the ceasefire was about to come into force. Thanks to this action, Grenoble and the Vercors remained in French hands when the guns fell silent. But this was small comfort to the victorious French Alpine troops who now found that they were part of a humiliated army. They regarded themselves as undefeated by the Germans but betrayed by the Armistice and ached to recover their lost honour.

The French rout and the German columns pushing deeper and deeper into France set in train a flood of internal refugees who fled south in search of safety. It was estimated that some 8 to 9 million civilians – about a quarter of the French population – threw themselves on to the roads, seeking to escape the occupation. They were later referred to as *les exodiens*. Among them were 2 million Parisians, French families driven out of Alsace-Lorraine and many Belgians, Dutch and Poles who had made their homes in France.

The ceasefire between German and French troops came into force at 09.00 on 24 June 1940 and was followed by the Armistice a day later. Under the terms of this peace, France was divided in two. The northern half, known as the Zone Occupée or ZO, was placed under General Otto von Stülpnagel, named by Hitler as the German Military Governor of France. The southern half, the Zone Non-Occupée or ZNO, comprising about two-fifths of the original territory of metropolitan France, was to be governed by Marshal Pétain, who set up his administration in the central French town of Vichy. The two were separated by a Demarcation Line, virtually an internal frontier, which ran from the border with Switzerland close to Geneva to a point on the Spanish border close to Saint-Jean-Pied-de-Port.

There was another France created by the nation's defeat and humiliation, but very few knew about it at the time. It had left with General Charles de Gaulle in a British plane from Mérignac airport outside Bordeaux not long before the Armistice was signed. On 18 June 1940, just two days after he arrived in London, de Gaulle made the first of his famous broadcasts to the French people: 'has the last word been said? … Is defeat final? No! Believe me, I who am speaking to you from experience … and who tell you that nothing is lost for France … For France is not alone! She is not alone! She is not alone! … This war is a world war. Whatever happens, the flame of the French resistance must not be extinguished and will not be extinguished.' The sentences were stirring enough. The problem was, almost no one in France heard them. In the early 1940s there were only 6 million radios in France and, since a quarter of France's population were in captivity, or fighting, or on the roads fleeing the invader, there were not many who had the time to sit at home with their ears glued to the radio, even if they had one.

With almost 70,000 casualties, 1.8 million of her young men in German prisoner-of-war camps and *la gloire française* ground into the dust alongside the ancient standards of her army, France's first reaction to her new conqueror was stunned acquiescence. Early reports arriving

OCCUPIED TERRITORIES 1942

Dunkerque

Lille

Territories annexed by the Reich

Cherbourg

Paris
⊙

Occupied Zone

Northern Zone

Closed Zone

Demarcation Line

Geneva

Vichy ⊙

River Rhône

Bordeaux

Grenoble

Lyon

Vercors

Free Zone

Southern Zone

Italian border

Italian occupation zone (after Nov. 1942)

Toulouse

Nice

Saint-Jean-Pied-de-Port

Marseille

Toulon

Spanish border

Corsica

N

in London from French and British agents all speak of the feeble spirit of resistance in the country. In these first days, many, if not most, of the French men and women who had heard of de Gaulle saw him as a rebel against the legitimate and constitutional government in Vichy. They trusted Pétain to embody the true spirit of France and prepare for the day when they could again reclaim their country. After all, was he not the hero of Verdun, the great battle of 1916? Some believed fervently that the old warrior's Vichy government would become, not just the instrument for the rebuilding of national pride, but also the base for the fight back against the German occupier and that he, Pétain, the first hero of France, would become also the 'premier résistant de la France'.

There were, of course, some who wanted France to follow Germany and become a fascist state. In due course they would be mobilized and turn their weapons on their fellow countrymen. But these were a minority. For the most part, after the turbulence and the humiliation, the majority just wanted to return to a quiet life, albeit one underpinned by a kind of muscular apathy. The writer Jean Bruller, who was himself a Resistance fighter and used 'Vercors' as his *nom de plume*, clandestinely published his novel *Le Silence de la Mer* in 1942. In this he has one of his characters say of France's new German masters: 'These men are going to disappear under the weight of our disdain and we will not even trouble ourselves to rejoice when they are dead.'

There were many reasons why, in due course and slowly, the men and women of occupied France broke free of this torpor and began to rise again. But two were pre-eminent: the burning desire to drive out the hated invader, and the almost equally strong need to expiate the shame of 1940 and ensure that the France of the future would be different from the one that had fallen.

The formation of the earliest Resistance groups came organically – and spontaneously – from French civil society. Some were little more than clubs of friends who came together to express their patriotism and opposition to the occupier. Others were political – with the Communists being especially active after Operation Barbarossa, Hitler's invasion of Russia in June 1941. Almost all were strenuously republican in their beliefs. There were even Resistance organizations supporting the regime in Vichy, preparing for the day when they would help to recapture the Zone Occupée. Although the early Resistance groups concentrated mainly on propaganda through the distribution of underground news-papers, over time they evolved into clandestine action-based organiza-tions capable of gathering intelligence, conducting sabotage raids and carrying out attacks on German units and installations.

In London, too, France's fall changed the nature of the war that Britain now had to fight. Now she was utterly alone in Europe. Churchill knew that, with the British Army recovering after the 'great deliverance' of Dunkirk, the RAF not yet strong enough for meaningful offensives against German cities and the Royal Navy struggling to keep the Atlantic lifeline open, the only way he could carry the war to the enemy was by clandestine rather than conventional means.

On 22 July 1940, he created the Special Operations Executive (SOE), instructing it to 'set Europe ablaze'. SOE, headed by Brigadier Colin Gubbins and headquartered in Baker Street near Marylebone station, was organized into 'country sections' which were responsible for intelligence, subversion and sabotage in each of Europe's occupied nations. France, however, had two country sections: F (for France) Section and RF (for République Française) Section. The former, led by Colonel Maurice Buckmaster, was predominantly British run and was staffed mostly by British officers and agents. The latter, which acted as a logistical organization for Free French agents sent into France, was made up almost exclusively of French citizens. Although members of the same overall body, SOE's F and RF sections adopted totally different ways of doing business. The 'British' F Section operated through small autonomous cells, which were in most cases kept carefully separate from each other in order to limit the damage of penetration and betrayal. RF Section, on the other hand, tended to run much larger, centrally controlled agent networks.

But the organizational complexity and rivalry in London – which often seemed to mirror that on the ground in France – did not end there. De Gaulle, whose headquarters were at 4 Carlton Terrace overlooking the Mall, had his own clandestine organization too, headed by the thirty-one-year-old, French career soldier Colonel André Dewavrin. This acted as the central directing authority for all those clandestine organizations in France which accepted the leadership of Charles de Gaulle. However, as one respected French commentator put it after the war, 'General de Gaulle and most of those who controlled military affairs in Free France in the early days were ill-prepared to understand the specificities of clandestine warfare … [there was a certain] refusal of career military officers to accept the methods of [what they regarded as] a "dirty war". It was a long and difficult process to get [the French in] London to understand the necessities of the "revolutionary war".

For Churchill, who knew that a frontal assault on Festung Europa (Fortress Europe) was still years away, the strategic opportunities offered by the French Resistance, fractured and diffuse as it was, were much less appealing than those in the Balkan countries. The French Resistance may have been a low priority for Winston Churchill in these early years, but for General de Gaulle, who created the Forces Françaises Libres on 1 July 1940, it was the only means of establishing himself as the legitimate leader of occupied France. For him it was imperative to weld all this disparate activity into a unified force under his leadership, capable not only of effective opposition to the Germans, but also of becoming a base for political power in the future.

De Gaulle's opportunity to achieve this came in October 1941 when the charismatic forty-one-year-old Jean Moulin escaped from France over the Pyrenees and arrived in Lisbon. Here Moulin, who, as the Préfet of the Department of Eure-et-Loire had been an early resister against the Germans, wrote a report for London: 'It would be mad and criminal not to use, in the event of allied action on the mainland, those troops prepared for the greatest sacrifice who are today scattered and anarchic, but tomorrow could be able to constitute a coherent army … [troops] already in place, who know the terrain, have chosen their enemy and determined their objectives.'

Moulin met de Gaulle in London on 25 October 1941. The French General could be prickly and difficult, but on this occasion the two men instantly took to each other. On the night of 1/2 January 1942, Jean Moulin, now equipped with the multiple aliases of Max, Rex and Régis, parachuted back into France as de Gaulle's personal representative. His task was to unify the disparate organizations of the Resistance under de Gaulle's leadership. Thanks to Moulin's formidable energy, organizational ability and political skill, he managed to unify the three key civilian Resistance movements of the southern zone into a single body whose paramilitary branch would become the Secret Army, or Armée Secrète, the military arm of the Gaullist organization in France.

Among those with whom Moulin made contact on this visit was the sixty-one-year-old French General, Charles Delestraint, who de Gaulle hoped would lead the Secret Army. On the night of 13/14 February 1943, a Lysander light aircraft of the RAF's 161 Special Duties Squadron, which throughout the war ran a regular clandestine service getting agents into and out of France, flew from Tempsford airport north of London to pick up Moulin and Delestraint and fly them back to Britain.

Here, the old General, who had been de Gaulle's senior officer during the fall of France, met his erstwhile junior commander and accepted from him the post of head of the Secret Army in France under de Gaulle's leadership. His task was to fuse together all troops and paramilitary organizations, set up a General Staff and create six autonomous regional military organizations, each of which should, over time, be able 'to play a role in the [eventual] liberation of the territory of France'. Delestraint's first act was to write a letter under his new alias, 'Vidal', to 'The officers and men of all Resistance paramilitary units':

> By order of General de Gaulle, I have taken command of the Underground Army from 11 November 1942.
>
> To all I send greetings. In present circumstances, with the enemy entrenched everywhere in France, it is imperative to join up our military formations now in order to form the nucleus of the Underground Army, of which I hold the command. The moment is drawing near when we will be able to strike. The time is past for hesitation. I ask all to observe strict discipline in true military fashion. We shall fight together against the invader, under General de Gaulle and by the side of our Allies, until complete victory.
>
> The Commanding General of the Secret Army
> Vidal

On the night of 19/20 March, another Lysander flew Moulin and Delestraint back to France, where the flame of resistance was beginning to take hold. This change of mood was due, principally, to three factors.

The first was the increasing severity of German reprisals. In the beginning, hostages were taken at random, held against some required action by the French civil authorities and then released. But when Germans started to be assassinated, things took a much darker turn. On 20 October 1941 the German military commander of Nantes was shot dead.

The Germans responded by taking fifty hostages from the local community and summarily executed them. As this practice became more and more widespread French outrage and anger deepened and the ranks of the Resistance swelled.

The second event which transformed the nature of the Resistance movement in France began at dawn on 8 November 1942, when Allied troops stormed ashore on the beaches of French North Africa. The strategic consequences of Operation Torch were very quickly understood by the Germans. Now the defeat of their forces under Field Marshal Rommel and the Allied occupation of the whole of the North African coast were only a matter of time. Germany's hold on continental Europe could now be threatened not just from the Channel in the north, but also from the Mediterranean in the south. Three days after Torch, the Germans swept aside the barriers on the Demarcation Line and, amid squeals of protest from the Vichy government, sent their armoured columns surging south to complete their occupation of the whole of metropolitan France. This destroyed the Vichy government's constitutional legality and laid bare the bankruptcy of their claim to be the protectors of what remained of French pride and sovereignty.

It also had another, even more powerful effect. The Vichy Armistice Army, or Armée de l'Armistice, created from the broken elements of France's defeated armies, was immediately disbanded, causing some of its units to take to the *maquis*. Some dispersed individually and re-assembled under their commanders in the forests, taking with them their structures, their ranks, their customs and even their regimental standards. From about January 1943 onwards, senior ex-Armistice Army officers, including two who will be important in our story, Henri Zeller and Marcel Descour, began to work more closely with Delestraint's Secret Army. To start with, both forces, though co-operating closely with each other, maintained their separate autonomy. But in December 1943 they agreed to fuse together to form a single military structure, the FFI – the French Forces of the Interior, or Forces Françaises de l'Intérieur – under de Gaulle's command.

The third and arguably greatest factor which turned many French men and women from relative apathy to armed resistance was Germany's seemingly unquenchable appetite for resources and manpower. The Germans demanded 60 per cent of all France's agricultural production, amounting to some 600,000 tonnes of food and equipment a month, causing severe rationing and acute food shortages, especially in the cities. Inevitably this in turn gave birth to an extensive, all-pervasive (and all-providing) black market. It was, however, Germany's demand for labour which, more than anything else, provided the French Resistance with the recruits it needed to become a genuine popular movement.

It all began with a bargain which seemed, given the exigencies of war and France's position as a subjugated nation, reasonable enough. With so many of her male population under arms, Germany was desperate for labour to run her industries and work her farms. Programmes to attract workers from France were implemented. These included a Sauckel/Laval scheme initiated in June 1942 (known in France as *La Relève* – the levy) under which the Germans would exchange prisoners of war for special-ised volunteer workers on a ratio of 1 to 3. But by late summer 1942 *La Relève* had produced only some 40,000 new workers – nothing like enough for Germany's needs; Sauckel demanded more.

To fulfil these new German demands, Pétain and Laval signed a law on 4 September 1942 requiring all able-bodied men aged between eight-een and fifty and all single women between twenty-one and thirty-five 'to do any work that the Government deems necessary'. By these means the Sauckel/Laval deal was completed, albeit a month late, in November 1942. But this merely encouraged the Germans to demand even more. This time, in exchange for 250,000 French workers, an equal number of French PoWs would be given, not their freedom, but the status of 'free workers' in Germany. Laval agreed, but soon found that he could not keep his side of the bargain without adopting new measures of coercion. A law was passed on 16 February 1943 which required all males over twenty to be subject to the Compulsory Labour Organization (known as the STO after its French name – Service du Travail Obligatoire) and regulations governing the STO were issued the same day, calling up all those aged twenty to twenty-three for compulsory work in Germany. In March 1943, Sauckel again upped the stakes, demanding a further 400,000 workers, 220,000 of whom would go to Germany while the remainder would be handed over to Organisation Todt, the German-run labour force in France.

Of all the events in the early years of the German occupation which helped turn France against her occupiers, undermined the Vichy admin-istration and boosted the cause of the Resistance, none did so more, or more quickly, than the establishment of the STO. The German Ambassador in Paris, Otto Abetz, later remarked: 'If ever the Maquis were to erect monuments in France, the most important should be dedicated to "Our best recruitment agent, Gauleiter Sauckel".'

There were public demonstrations against the STO across France, one being in the little market town of Romans under the western edge of the Vercors. Here, on 9 and 10 March 1943, the entire population occupied the railway station shouting, 'Death to Laval! Death to Pétain! Long live de Gaulle!' and stood in front of the train taking their young men away to Germany. Huge numbers of young men, now known as *réfractaires*, took to the *maquis* to avoid being sent to Germany. SOE agents reported to London on 12 March 1943 that the number of young men who had gone into hiding in the Savoie and Isère departments alone had reached 5,000 and was rising at an increasing rate every week.

These young men fled to the *maquis* for a complex set of reasons, not all of them to do with patriotism. For some it was simply a matter of avoiding being sent to Germany. For others it was seen as a form of civil disobedience. For many it was the romance of living the clandestine life in the mountains and the forests. Down there on the plain, men and women lived lives which were inevitably tainted by the daily exigencies of coexistence with the enemy. But up there in the high places and the forests the air was clean and freedom was pure and uncompromised.

But whatever their motives, all now lived as outlaws who had to rely on the already established Resistance movements for their food, shelter and protection. London recognized the opportunity and sent huge sums of money, mostly through Jean Moulin, to pay for food and shelter for the *réfractaires*. The French Resistance movements now found themselves with a growing of pool of young men whom they quickly set about turning into fully trained, armed and committed Maquisards.

It was probably in response to the new threat posed by this rise of the Resistance that, on 30 January 1943, Vichy Prime Minister Pierre Laval created – with help from the Germans – a new and much hated paramilitary force, the black-shirted Milice Française or French Militia, whose exclusive task was to fight the Resistance. Made up chiefly of Frenchmen who supported fascism, but including many from the criminal fraternity, the Milice by 1944 achieved a total strength in Vichy France, including part-time members, of perhaps 30,000. Although they worked very closely with both the Italians and the Germans, they were largely autonomous from any Vichy authority outside their own line of command, often operating outside the law and beyond its reach when it came to the torture, summary execution and assassination of their fellow French men and women.

And so it was that, by the early months of 1943, the forests and fast-nesses of places like the Vercors had become home and refuge to a poly-glot collection of the broken elements of defeated France: its new generations, its old administrators, its competing political parties, its heterodox communities and the scattered fragments of its once proud army. With the United States now in the war, with the Allied landings in North Africa and, just ten days later, the German defeat before the gates of Stalingrad, de Gaulle knew, as did almost every thinking French man and woman, that a turning point had been passed. It was now inevitable that Germany would lose. Only three questions remained. How long would it take? How could the Resistance be welded together into a force strong enough to play a part in the liberation of their country? And what would be the best military strategy to follow?

3

BEGINNINGS

The notion that the Vercors might become a citadel of liberty against France's invaders began to take root in several places, among very different people and in very different ways, during the first half of 1941. According to Vercors legend it was first discussed one early-spring day in March 1941 when two old friends, both mountaineers, both writers and both members of France's intellectual elite, were cutting down a dead walnut tree in a meadow above a small villa called La Grande Vigne, near the town of Côtes-de-Sassenage, a few kilometres north-west of Grenoble.

La Grande Vigne, which lies so close under the northern flank of the Vercors that the plateau's slopes and woods seem to look in at every window, was – and remains still – the family home of the Dalloz family. In 1941, its occupants were the forty-one-year-old architect, writer, one-time government servant and ardent mountaineer Pierre Dalloz and his painter wife, Henriette Gröll. On this March day, the couple were entertaining two of their closest friends – and frequent visitors to La Grand Vigne – Jean Prévost and his doctor wife, Claude. Prévost, a year younger than Dalloz, was a startlingly handsome man with an arresting gaze and a character which combined love of action with a sturdy intellectual independence. A pacifist, an early and enthusiastic anti-fascist, Prévost had fiercely opposed the Munich settlement but had nevertheless heavily criticized the pre-war anti-German mood in France. He was best known as one of the foremost young writers in France, having written several well-received books, along with articles in the prestigious French magazine *Paris-soir*. Indeed it was writing which formed one of the major bonds between the two men – at the time of their tree-cutting exploit Dalloz was working on a translation of St Bernard's *Treatise on Consideration*, while Prévost was preparing a study on Stendhal which would be published to widespread acclaim in Lyon on 9 November 1942, just two days before the German invasion of France's 'free' southern zone.

According to Dalloz's account, the two men were busy cutting down the old walnut tree – with Prévost offering his friend unsolicited advice on the best way to accomplish the task – when Dalloz stopped, leant on his axe and looked up at the cliffs of the Vercors rising above them into the blue March sky. 'You could look at that up there as a kind of island on terra firma,' he said, 'a huge expanse of Alpine pasture protected on all sides by these vast Chinese walls of rock. The gates into it are few and carved out of the living rock. Once closed, paratroopers could be dropped clandestinely. The Vercors could then explode behind the enemy lines.'

There the conversation ended and the thought seemed to die. 'I thought that the idea was probably a bit naive,' Dalloz was later to explain. 'This was more the kind of thing that the military would be considering, rather than me.' It would take eighteen months, disillusion with the military leaders and a France more ready for resistance to bring it back to life.

A few kilometres away in Grenoble, General André Laffargue, a divisional commander in the Armistice Army, was also desperate to return to the struggle and spoke of the Vercors as 'a vast closed Alpine fortress protected by a continuous solid wall of limestone rock'. He even drew up plans to protect the plateau against all comers with fixed defences made up of a ring of 75mm mountain guns sunk into concrete casements – a sort of Alpine Maginot Line, as though the recent failure of the first one had not been enough.

Some of Laffargue's junior officers had a more realistic notion about what should be done to plan for the day when they would again take up their fight against the occupier and had begun to stockpile hidden weapons for future use. From late 1940 right through to the German invasion of Vichy France in November 1942, arms, ammunition and a wide range of matériel, including vehicles, fuel, optical equipment, engineering material, radios and medical stores, were spirited out of the city and into the surrounding countryside, and in particular on to the Vercors. All sorts of imaginative methods were used: lorries with false floors, carts loaded with hay, empty water and petrol bowsers, accumulator batteries emptied of acid and reserve petrol tanks on vehicles. They also made use of forged travel permissions so that the arms could be transported in official vehicles.

One of the chief smugglers who would in due course lead a local Resistance group in his own right, later described one of their hiding places: 'An office of one of the Justices of the Peace in Grenoble became a veritable arsenal: heavy, medium and light machine guns, rifles, revolvers, munitions, explosives and aircraft incendiary bombs were hidden under the protection of the sword of Justice. The Court clerk, assisted by his men, buried the ammunition and concealed the arms in the walls. The judges of the police tribunals never guessed that under the defendants' bench were hidden light machine guns, while sub-machine guns were piled up underneath the floorboard on which they sat holding court.'

By these means and many others, some thirty-five secret arms depots were established during the first months of 1941. At the time of the German invasion of Vichy, this number had increased to 135. These depots contained, it is estimated, 300 light and heavy machine guns, 3,000 revolvers together with a variety of other light arms, thirty 75mm mountain guns, four 81mm mortars, 4 tonnes of optical instruments such as binoculars, 5 tonnes of explosives, eight full petrol tankers and more than 200 vehicles of all types.

Another clandestine Armistice Army unit, meanwhile, forged false papers for military personnel imprisoned for breaking Vichy laws and those who had already gone underground.

On a fine August afternoon in 1941, five men sitting round a table in a working-class café behind Grenoble station took a decision which, though they did not know it, would link their fate indissolubly to the young military arms smugglers just up the road, even though their motives were entirely political and not military.

The Second World War had taken a surprising turn in June 1941 when Hitler launched Operation Barbarossa, the surprise invasion of Russia. Until this point, Hitler's 1939 non-aggression pact with Stalin had meant that the war had been largely located in the west. Now the full force of his armies would strike east. Widely recognized as the key military turning point (and Hitler's biggest mistake) of the early years of the war, Barbarossa had an effect on the populations of occupied western Europe that is often overlooked. Before Hitler's invasion, the fact that

Russia had stood aside from the struggle against fascism had constrained the attitude of the Communists in particular and the European left in general. Now, however, there was a common front against a common enemy. The French Communists and (though for very different reasons) their partners on the left, the French Socialist Party, shifted from an attitude of wait and see to one of activism – a process which greatly accelerated later in 1941 when, on 5 December, the Germans were beaten back from the gates of Moscow and, three days after that, following Pearl Harbor, the United States entered the war.

The five conspirators sitting in the Café de la Rotonde on the Rue du Polygone would have felt the ripples of these faraway events and would have known what they meant. Now there was hope; now there was a distant, dangerous possibility of liberation.

The Café de la Rotonde, set slightly back from the main thoroughfare, was a pink-stuccoed building on whose front façade three brown-shuttered windows functioned as a permanent prop for sheaves of bicycles. The area, just behind Grenoble freight station, was a working-class district, grimy with the soot of trains and permanently resonating with the clash of shunting engines, the hiss of steam and the day-round passage of lorries to and from the loading quays of the great station. Though graced by the name of café, La Rotonde was more like a bistro which depended for its custom on the railway workers at the station, the drivers of goods lorries and the workers at a nearby gas works, all of whom knew they could get a good cheap lunch here, washed down with the rough white wine of the nearby Grésivaudan valley.

At first sight, the five conspirators, all of whom held strong left-wing views, had nothing in common with the two intellectuals who had cut down a walnut tree at Sassenage four months earlier. They had even less in common with the young Army officers who, for months past, had been smuggling lorryloads of arms and ammunition past the front door of the café. But all three groups were in reality bound to a single purpose that would, in due course, bring them together in a common enterprise which would transcend their political differences: the distant but now growing possibility that some time – some time soon perhaps – their country might be free again.

Among those seated at the table that afternoon was a figure of medium height, round shoulders and powerful build whose face was underpinned by a sharply etched chin and enlivened by eyes which missed little that went on around him. Aimé Pupin, the *patron* of La Rotonde, was normally to be found behind its dark wooden counter, chatting to his customers and overseeing the service at the tables. Passionate about rugby – he had been a formidable hooker in his youth – Pupin had received, like so many of his class in pre-war France, only the bare minimum of education. But he had a force of personality, matched by firm opinions and a propensity for action, which made him a natural if at times obstinate and impetuous leader. He also had a marked sense of idealism for the brotherhood of man and the Socialist cause, and this was ardently shared by the four men sitting around him, all of whom were not only fellow members of the Socialist Party but also Masons.

Beside Pupin sat Eugène Chavant, forty-seven years old, stocky, pipe-smoking, taciturn, the haphazardly trimmed moustache on his upper lip complementing an unruly shock of hair greying at the temples. Chavant's quiet demeanour hid an iron will and unshakeable convictions. As a young man he had followed his father into the shoe-making trade. During the First World War he had been quickly promoted to sergeant and platoon commander in the 11th Dragoons and received the Médaille Militaire and the Croix de Guerre with four citations for bravery. When the First World War finished, he returned to Grenoble, became a leading member of the French Socialist Party and was elected on the first ballot with the entire Socialist list in the 1936 elections. For this he was summarily sacked from his post as foreman in a local shoe factory, forcing him to go into the café business in order to pursue his political convictions. He had later been elected Mayor of the Grenoble suburb of Saint-Martin-d'Hères and was now, like Pupin, the *patron* of a restaurant in a working-class district of the city.

Others round the table included a railway worker at the station, a garage owner and Léon Martin, who practised as a doctor and pharmacist in the city. At sixty-eight, Martin was the oldest of the five, a past Socialist Mayor of Grenoble city and a strong opponent of the Vichy government. He told his co-conspirators that he believed the time had come to set up a Resistance cell in the Grenoble area. The others enthusiastically agreed, and the meeting broke up – but not before the conspirators marked their passage into the shadows by distributing aliases. Chavant's clandestine name would henceforth be Clément and that of Pupin, Mathieu. Slowly, over the following months, the little group drew more and more supporters to their meetings in the back room of Dr Martin's pharmacy at 125 Cours Berriat, which lies under the rim of the Vercors at the western edge of the city.

Although the daily lives of those who lived on the Vercors itself were less affected by the fall of France and the establishment of the Vichy government than those in Grenoble, the plateau was by no means immune from its consequences.

On 28 September 1940, the prestigious Polish school in Paris, the Lycée Polonais Cyprian-Norwid, which had decamped from the capital shortly after the Germans arrived, formally re-established itself in Villard-de-Lans on the northern half of the plateau. A month later, on 28 October, it opened its doors to students – chiefly the children of Polish refugees from the north – in the Hôtel du Parc et du Château, a famous pre-war skiing establishment in the town.

On 23 May 1941, a trainload of French refugees, driven out of their homes in Alsace-Lorraine by incoming German families, arrived in the station at Romans, below the western edge of the Vercors. They were kept on the station for three days while the Vichy authorities found houses in the region, many of them in the Villard-de-Lans area. To add to these new arrivals, Jewish families soon started to arrive as well, fleeing the early round-ups in the northern zone, later replicated by the Vichy government in the south as well. Even by the standards of a town used to the annual influx of winter-sports visitors, life in Villard was becoming unusually cosmopolitan.

Some time during the late summer or early autumn of 1941, a quite separate group of conspirators, also Socialists and Masons, started meeting in secret in Villard-de Lans. The moving spirit of this group, who were initially unaware of their Grenoble co-conspirators, was another doctor/pharmacist called Eugène Samuel. A Rumanian by origin, Dr Samuel, who had come to Villard to join his wife after the fall of France in 1940, held his meetings in the back room of his pharmacy under the cover of a Hunting Committee. The Villard group was as varied as its Grenoble equivalent, consisting, apart from Samuel himself, of a hotelier, the local tax inspector, the director of the Villard branch of the Banque Populaire and the three brothers, Émile, Paul and Victor Huillier, who ran the local transport company. Not long after their formation, the Villard group began searching for other organized Resistants in the area.

Through the good offices of one of their number they were put in touch with Léon Martin in Grenoble.

On Easter Monday (6 April) 1942, 'the day the history of [the Resistance] in the Vercors started', according to Léon Martin, the two groups met together in Villard and agreed to form a single organization to promote the Socialist cause and foment resistance in the area. The journey had begun that would take this handful of idealistic plotters from furtive meetings in the back rooms of local pharmacies to a fully fledged, 4,000-strong partisan army ready to take on the full might of the German Wehrmacht.

Marcel Malbos, one of the teachers at the Polish school in Villard, summed up the mood of these early resisters: 'When the life of a whole people is mortally threatened, when the tyrant sets out to destroy a whole civilization along with both its culture and its people, when the shipwreck is upon you – then, just when all seems lost, suddenly a conjunction of events occurs, as is so often found in history, which offers the possibility of hope. [In our case] it was the creation on our mountain plateau of a patch of dry land above the flood – above the tumult – where a few men came together to create a kind of rebirth. And soon this tiny plot above the waves would become a rock, a refuge, a home and a fortress …'

4

THE ARMY GOES UNDERGROUND

All day and all night, General Laffargue stayed in his grand office with its heavy Empire desk in the Hôtel de la Division on one side of the Place Verdun in Grenoble. The date was 10 November 1942, two days after the Allied landings in French North Africa, and the General was expecting a telephone call from his superior which would set in train the plan already drawn up by Vichy military headquarters for mobilization of the Armistice Army against a German invasion in the south. All through the long day and night, into 11 November (the anniversary of the German surrender in 1918), the General waited. But the call never came.

The truth was that the government of Vichy had been thrown into complete confusion, not to say panic, by the Allied invasion of North Africa. The Vichy leaders knew what would come next, but should they oppose, or acquiesce? Anticipation and indecision came to an end at dawn on 11 November 1942, when Hitler's personal emissary arrived in Vichy and delivered a letter from the Führer to Marshal Pétain informing him that Axis troops were taking control of Vichy France. In fact, the Germans had already launched Operation Attila. Some hours previously Italian units had stormed across the French/Italian frontier with orders to occupy Grenoble. Meanwhile German columns under Generalleutnant Heinrich Niehoff, the newly appointed German Army commander for southern France, pressed at full speed towards Lyon where they swung south heading for the Mediterranean coast.

Early on the morning of that same day, 11 November 1942, a young cavalry officer, Lieutenant Narcisse Geyer, received orders to man the Pont de la Boucle in Lyon and maintain public order when the Germans arrived.

The thirty-year-old Geyer, known as 'Narc' to his friends, was in many ways a man born out of his time. Small in stature, dapper in dress, never other than a soldier, never out of uniform, ever impetuous of spirit, courageous to the point of folly and always in search of *la gloire*, he would have been far more at home among Dumas' Three Musketeers than in the dull, gloryless existence of a junior officer in a defeated army. He was the scion of a military family: his father's last words to the priest who comforted him as he lay dying of wounds in October 1918 had been 'It is a terrible shame that my son is too young. He could have replaced me.' Geyer, true to the family tradition, had fought with distinction under the then Colonel Charles de Gaulle before the fall of France, earning himself a Croix de Guerre for his bravery.

But it was not only the man who represented what was seen at the time as the forever vanished days of France's military glory. The unit he commanded in Lyon that day was itself one of the most illustrious of France's cavalry regiments. The 11th Cuirassiers (motto 'Toujours au chemin de l'honneur' – 'Forever the path of honour') was founded by Louis XIV in 1668, still carried the French royal insignia of the fleur de lys on its regimental standard and had fought with distinction in all the great battles of the Napoleonic Wars.

To ask such a man and such a regiment to guard a bridge in order to facilitate the entry of a hated occupier was too much for Geyer to bear. Wilful as ever and largely on a whim, he ignored his orders and, leading a troop of fifty-six of his troopers, mounted on horses and accompanied by eight machine guns and four mortars, headed north out of the city towards the forests of the Savoie. A few kilometres out of Lyon, Geyer appears to have had second thoughts – or at least to have concluded that going underground with his troops required more preparation than a spur-of-the-moment canter through the streets of Lyon. He turned his troops round and, rather ignominiously one imagines, led them back to barracks.

A few days after the occupation of Grenoble by the Italians, General Laffargue called his senior commanders together in the Mairie of Vizille, a small town south of Grenoble, to discuss what should be done. The meeting broke up in indecision. Aimé Pupin, one of the Café de la Rotonde plotters, rushed to Vizille and did his best to persuade Laffargue's men not to hand over their weapons to the Germans. But the officer in charge refused even to see Pupin and ordered his regiment to disarm, leaving Pupin to comment: 'We Resistants were left with just empty hands.' At Christmas 1942, Pupin listed the arms at his disposal as a revolver and a rubber hammer.

On 27 November the Germans disarmed the remaining French units, disconnected their telephones and emptied the French barracks in Lyon and Vienne.

Narcisse Geyer's second opportunity for a more considered escape came that day when the Germans burst into the Cuirassiers' barracks in the Lyon suburb of Part-Dieu and began to drive the regiment from their quarters. Geyer grabbed his unit's regimental standards and took them to the barracks guardroom, from where they were passed over the wall to a party waiting outside. Geyer's initial intention had been to leave Lyon for the forests by bicycle. But how could a cavalryman leave without his horse? So that night he led a small group back to the barracks where, having muffled his horse Boucaro's hooves to deaden the noise, he walked his mount to a nearby lorry and drove out of the city and into life as a Maquisard.

Geyer, his horse and two or three of his Cuirassiers took refuge in a fortified farm with thick walls and a massive iron-studded gate, attended by stables and substantial outbuildings in the Forêt de Thivolet, 8 kilometres west of the Vercors. It was from this farm that Geyer took the *nom de guerre* Thivolet by which he would from now on be known. Over the next months, Geyer, who had a disparaging view of non-military Maquisard units, referring to them as 'as civilians playing at soldiers', returned several times to see his old troopers, eventually persuading some fifty of them to join him. The 11th Cuirassiers was reborn as a clandestine unit of the French Resistance under a courageous but headstrong young officer, complete with its standards, its insignia, its uniforms, its ranks and its proud customs, such as the habit of saying the regimental grace before every dinner: 'Gloire et honneur à ce cochon de popotier' – 'Glory and honour to the pig of a cook (who made this)'.

On 28 November, another much loved commander of one of France's best Alpine units gathered his men in the square of the little town of Brié-et-Angonnes, 5 kilometres south-east of Grenoble, and asked them to sing the regimental song for one last time. Then he told them, with tears in his eyes, that he had just received the order for the battalion to be disbanded. But, he reassured them, 'one day soon the bell will toll again to call us to action … no power on earth can break the bonds which bind us together as a fighting unit'.

Another French officer central to this story was among the many who chose the clandestine life during these turbulent days of November 1942.

The forty-three-year-old Marcel Descour, one of the earliest organizers of secret resistance within the old Armistice Army, was, like Geyer, a decorated and courageous cavalry officer. Tall, and spare of build, Descour had a thin angular face adorned with a small military moustache and topped with carefully coiffed, lightly oiled, swept-back black hair. With an air of command that indicated that he expected instant obedience, Descour, conventionally military in his ideas, decidedly right wing in his political views and strongly Catholic in his beliefs, was always accompanied by his 'religious counsellor' and éminence grise, a Benedictine monk called Dom Guétet. Guétet's omnipresence, reinforced by a cadaverous frame and sombre monk's habit, made him look, according to one observer, 'A bit like one of those holy soldier monks of the Middle Ages who accompanied their feudal masters on the Crusades'. Descour's view of himself may be guessed at by his choice of alias, Bayard – after the fifteenth-century knight Pierre Terrail, the Chevalier de Bayard, famous as 'The knight without fear and without reproach'.

Pierre Dalloz, in his house at La Grande Vigne in Côtes-de-Sassenage, watched all the farce and tragedy of the days after 11 November with despair. He confided his fears and his concept of the Vercors as a guerrilla base behind enemy lines to a young friend, Jean Lefort, who was not only an enthusiastic caver, with a deep knowledge of the Vercors, but was also a decorated officer in a French Alpine regiment. Lefort was as enthusiastic about the idea as Dalloz, and encouraged the older man to put the concept down on paper.

That mid-December night in 1942, Dalloz made the first three-page draft of his plan. 'The project had ripened in me over the time [since he had first discussed it with Jean Prévost] and my thoughts flew easily off my pen on to the paper. After I had finished, I opened the door and breathed in the cool night air. The highest branches of the almond tree in the garden swayed in the wind, as though trying to sweep the stars from the sky, and the clamour of the local stream filled the silent darkness. The Vercors was there, very close – almost alongside me. I thought for a long moment. Secrecy suddenly seemed my co-conspirator; the moment was heavy with responsibility, resolution and hope.'

CAMPS AND PLANS

The bitter winter of 1942/3, which destroyed Hitler's armies before the gates of Stalingrad, also held the Vercors in an icy siege. The cold that Christmas cut like a knife. The plateau lay under a deep layer of snow which weighed down branches in silent pine forests, piled up thick white quilts on timbered roofs and gave an extra tinge of blue to the woodsmoke rising from farmhouse chimneys.

It was a bad time to be away from home. Yet this was the choice that many young men in France faced that December: to leave home for the forests or join the work transports to Germany. By December 1942, the number of fleeing *réfractaires* was causing severe administrative problems for Resistance movements such as the Martin/Samuel organization in Grenoble and Villard-de-Lans. In early December, a group of young railwaymen from Grenoble station approached one of Eugène Chavant's friends, Jean Veyrat, who had by now joined the Café de la Rotonde plotters in Grenoble. The young men told Veyrat that they wished to go underground to avoid having to leave for Germany. But where could they go?

In the second week of December, Eugène Samuel went to the little town of Pont-en-Royans, whose ancient houses cling impossibly to the vertical sides of the Gorges de la Bourne, guarding the narrow bridge which spans the river and the western entry to the plateau. Here he knocked on the door of one of his brothers-in-law, the café owner and town Mayor Louis Brun, and asked if he could help. Brun said he knew just the place.

On 17 December 1942, Brun, accompanied by Simon, Samuel's younger brother, struggled through deep snow to look at an isolated farmhouse with substantial outbuildings called La Ferme d'Ambel, which lay in a desolate and deserted valley in the south-western corner of the plateau. It was ideal. The farm, fed by a bountiful and permanently running spring, is tucked under a high ridge covered in woods, which sweep down almost to its back door. The main access for vehicles is by a rough track served by stone bridges, leading down through beechwoods which shield the area from the nearby mountain road. The house, together with the loft space above and its outbuildings, was capable of accommodating, the two men estimated, around fifty or so *réfractaires*.

To add to its advantages the Ferme d'Ambel lay at the heart of a large timber concession centred on the nearby Ambel forest, which provided good cover for human activity in the area – indeed the *réfractaires* could be employed as a useful local labour force. These timber concessions played an important part in the life (and especially black-market life) of wartime France. Timber produced charcoal and charcoal produced the gas which, in the absence of readily available petrol, was the main driving power of the *gazogène* lorries and cars which could be seen everywhere puffing and wheezing around the streets of Grenoble and struggling their way in a cloud of smoke up the steep roads of the plateau. It was for this reason that timber concessions were often closely linked with the haulage industry – and so it was with the concession at the Ambel forest, two of whose most active partners were members of the transport firm run by the three Huillier brothers who had helped to found the Villard-de-Lans group of early resisters.

On 6 January 1943, a dozen or so young men, made up chiefly of railway workers and Polish refugees from Villard, moved into the Ambel farm. That month, as the pressure of conscription grew, a clandestine system was established to deal with the increasing flood of young men seeking refuge from the transports to Germany. Would-be *réfractaires* would be asked to go to a hardware shop, run by two sympathizers just a couple of hundred metres from the Place Verdun in Grenoble. The shop was served by two entrances, one on the main street and a second leading on to a small street at the rear. Here, in a back room, they were interviewed by Eugène Chavant and, if found acceptable, were instructed to go home, pack a few necessaries in a rucksack and catch the little funicular railway run by the Huillier brothers to Villard-de-Lans. There they would transfer to a Huillier bus to Pont-en-Royans where they would go to Louis Brun's restaurant. From here they were guided across the mountains at night to Ambel. On arrival, they would be met by the site director of the Ambel forestry concession, Louis Bourdeaux, who had been appointed by the Villard group as the Ambel's camp commander.

Measures were also put in train to make Ambel as secure as possible. The lights in the Ferme d'Ambel, which depended on a single electric cable supplied from the hydroelectric plant at Pont-en-Royans, were left on all day and night. This enabled a Resistance sympathizer at the plant to warn of approaching danger by turning the supply (and therefore Ambel lights) on and off three times in quick succession. Ambel was now a properly structured Maquis camp. Some claim that it was the first to be established in all France.

Meanwhile, at Côtes-de-Sassenage, Pierre Dalloz was thinking of ways to pursue his own ideas about the use of the Vercors to fight back against France's occupiers. Encouraged by Jean Lefort's welcome for his plan (but still completely unaware of the existence of his co-conspirators in Grenoble and Villard-de-Lans), he decided to take matters further. He was advised by a left-wing friend at Grenoble University that the man to see was Yves Farge, the foreign affairs editor of the regional newspaper *Progrès de Lyon*, who was known to have high-level Resistance connections.

In late January 1943, Dalloz, with his plan carefully tucked into an inside pocket of his jacket, took the train to Lyon, calling a little after midday at the offices of *Progrès* where he asked for the foreign affairs editor. The two men went to a nearby restaurant, where over lunch Dalloz explained his idea. He left a copy of his paper with Farge, who expressed enthusiasm for the plan and promised to ensure that it would be seen by the 'appropriate people'. Farge must have briefed Jean Moulin very shortly after the lunch, for on 29 January Moulin sent a courier to de Gaulle in London with full details of the Dalloz plan and a personal recommendation that it should be supported.

On 31 January, Farge paid Dalloz a return visit in Grenoble to tell him that Moulin had seen the plan, approved it and agreed that 25,000 francs should now be assigned to Dalloz to develop the idea. Dalloz hurriedly typed a second, more comprehensive paper on his ideas. A few days later, he received a note which instructed him to join Farge and to 'Be in the waiting room at Perrache station in Lyon at 12h15 on 10 February where "Alain" will meet you.' The two men found their contact 'Alain' in deep contemplation of the window display of the station bookshop. 'The meeting place has been changed,' he instructed. 'Someone will be waiting for you at Bourg-en-Bresse station. There is a train at 16h20. When you arrive, stand in front of the station entrance and carry a copy of the newspaper *Signal* in a prominent place. General "Vidal" will approach you. He will be dressed in a grey overcoat with a white silk handkerchief displayed in the top pocket.'

The two men did not have to stand long outside the station entrance before they saw, in the light of a street lamp, a rather small man with a brisk military step displaying a most luxurious silk white handkerchief, which fluttered in the wind from his top pocket. After introductions, the old soldier led them away from the station, turning left into the main street of Bourg-en-Bresse and, 200 metres further on, passing a cake shop whose éclairs Dalloz remembered with great affection from his youth. The General stopped in front of the next-door building, a three-storey turn-of-the-century terraced town house. Here he took a step back to get a better look, as though checking he was in the right place, and then fumbled with his key for a moment in the lock of the heavy oak front door before it opened. Inside, the General lit a match to find the switch and turned the lights on. They were in a large room with closed shutters which turned out to be the offices of an insurance company. A moment later they were joined by a fourth, older man with a magnificent white moustache who introduced himself as General 'Richard'.

In fact, the two civilians were in the presence of the two most important military officers in the hierarchy of the Secret Army in France: the man de Gaulle had charged with heading up the Resistance's military wing, Charles Delestraint and his deputy General Desmazes. Dalloz ran through his three-page report, a copy of which he gave to Delestraint, together with an annotated map of the Vercors, a guidebook of the plateau and several supporting photographs. After asking Dalloz some searching questions, Delestraint pronounced his verdict: 'From now on the Vercors will be part of the national military plan for liberation. From today it will be known as the Plan Montagnards.'

Two days later, on the moonlit night of 12/13 February 1943, two Lysander light aircraft from the RAF's 161 Squadron landed in a field near Ruffey-sur-Seille in the Jura. Here they picked up Jean Moulin and Charles Delestraint, who carried a briefcase containing Dalloz's papers, maps and photos for Plan Montagnards, and flew them back to Britain. During his stay in London, Delestraint had several meetings with de Gaulle at which he discussed his plans for the Secret Army, including in the Vercors. Afterwards, according to de Gaulle, Delestraint 'was able to work usefully with the Allied leaders. Thereby, the operations of the

Secret Army during the landing in France would be linked as closely as possible to the plans of the Allied Command.'

On 25 February 1943, just under a fortnight after Delestraint had landed in Britain, Dalloz was listening to the 'personal' messages for France broadcast by the BBC in its nightly programme *Les Français parlent aux Français* when he heard the announcer say: 'Les montagnards doivent continuer à gravir les cimes.'* It was the code message that Dalloz had been given by Delestraint to indicate that his proposal had been agreed by London. Plan Montagnards was to proceed as discussed.

It has always been presumed that Plan Montagnards was a purely French affair, known only to the Free French authorities in London and specifically not shared with the British, either at this stage or later. But we now know that Dalloz's plan was in fact discussed with the British officer acting as French Regional Controller, who was directly responsible to the head of SOE, Brigadier Gubbins. A minute addressed to the Controller dated 10 April 1943 concluded that Montagnards could be 'of appreciable value in support of an operation directed against the Mediterranean coast of France'. Noting that Dalloz's plan 'provides for co-operation with Allied airborne troops', the minute makes it explicitly clear that 'It seems extremely unlikely that such co-operation could be provided, except possibly from Africa, and it is certain that we could not promise it. We therefore feel that even if the organisation is to be encouraged they should be told … that they must expect to work on their own.'

Back in the Vercors, Dalloz immediately set about assembling a small team to help him carry out a full-scale study of the plateau. This included the head of the Department for Water and Forests on the Vercors, whom Dalloz asked to make a record of the plateau's topography including its many caves and underground caverns, and an ex-commander of the Mountain Warfare School at Chamonix, whom he tasked with drawing up an inventory of all the huts, refuges, food resources, secret caches of arms and explosives and available vehicles on the plateau.

Dalloz, looking for a third member of his team, also sought out a young ex-Army officer whom he had not met, but had heard of as a skilled and courageous mountaineer. Alain Le Ray, who at thirty-two was Dalloz's junior by almost ten years, was also an ex-member of a now disbanded Alpine regiment and had a number of noted Alpine climbing

* 'The mountain men should continue to climb to the peaks.'

firsts to his credit. First captured by the Germans in 1940, he escaped, only to be recaptured and sent to the supposedly escape-proof PoW camp of Colditz Castle. But Colditz held him for only three weeks before he escaped again, this time making successful 'home run' back to France.

Le Ray, tall, athletic and striking to look at, was a most unusual Army officer for his time. Scrupulous about maintaining his political neutrality, meticulous in his analysis, cool in his judgements, he had, unlike most of his Army counterparts, a natural feel for irregular warfare, including an understanding of the need to make compromises in order to combine both the military and civilian elements of the French Resistance. Dalloz asked Le Ray to conduct a full-scale military study of the Vercors. Assisted by three fellow ex-officers, one of whom, Roland Costa de Beauregard, would later command a guerrilla unit on the plateau, Le Ray completed his study (see Annex B) while awaiting Delestraint's return from London.

While Dalloz's team were conducting their various surveys of the plateau, Dalloz and Farge were busy touring the shops in Grenoble and buying up all the available guidebooks and Michelin maps of the area. On the few days the two men were not scouring map shops they were criss-crossing the plateau in a taxi, looking for parachute and landing sites. On one such visit in early March, with the snow melting, Farge and Dalloz clambered over a forest-covered ridge to inspect one of the enclosed high mountain pastures which are a feature of the Vercors. The place was called Herbouilly and they immediately recognized it as an excellent parachute landing ground. There was only one problem. Right in the middle of the valley was a substantial, but unoccupied, farmhouse which was the property of someone suspected of being sympathetic to the Germans. Farge solved the problem by bringing in a special group of Resistants from Lyon one night to burn the place to the ground. By mid-March the two men felt they were ready for Delestraint's return from London and the next stage of Plan Montagnards.

Elsewhere on the plateau, however, things which had started so well for Eugène Samuel and his team working with the *réfractaires* suffered a serious setback.

6

EXODUS AND FOLLY

'So you do not wish to go and work in Germany?' Eugène Chavant asked abruptly, pulling his pipe out of his mouth for a moment.

'No, M'sieu.' The young man, no more than twenty or so, nervously twisted his beret between his fingers.

'Who told you to contact me about this?'

'My boss at the shoe factory, M. Blanc, told me you would be a good person to talk to, M'sieu.'

'So you want to join the Maquis?'

'Yes, M'sieu.'

'Are you aware that life in the Maquis is very hard?'

'Yes, M'sieu.'

'Do you understand the risks involved – great risks?'

'Yes, M'sieu.'

'And you know how to keep your tongue, do you?'

'Absolutely, M'sieu.'

'OK. Go to the Fontaine halt on the tramway which takes you up to Villard at five o'clock tomorrow evening. Ask for one of the Huillier brothers and tell him discreetly that you have come to see "Casimir" – that's the password. He will tell you what to do next. Follow his instructions closely and without any questions. Take a rucksack with what you need. But be careful. Don't take too much. You must look like a casual traveller.'

The young man nodded and left the room, closing the door behind him.

Eugène Chavant took out a small piece of paper and wrote a message for his friend Jean Veyrat: 'There will be one *colis* [package] to take up to Villard tomorrow evening.'

The following evening a Huillier bus set the young man down in the main square of the town of Méaudre on the northern half of the Vercors plateau. Here, following his instructions, he went to a café in one of the town's back streets where he found he was among a number of young men who likewise seemed to be waiting for something – or someone. A short time later an older man arrived. He was wearing hiking clothes and boots and carried a small khaki rucksack.

'Follow me,' he said, and led the way out of the café and into the darkness.

The little group walked north along back roads for forty minutes or so and then took a short break before starting to climb steeply up the mountain. Half an hour later they entered a forest and five minutes after that their guide stopped in the darkness and gave three low whistles. Out of the night came three answering whistles. A guide emerged from the trees and led the little group of newcomers to a shepherd's hut in a clearing in the forest. Though it is doubtful that any of them realized it, they had all taken an irreversible step out of normality, into the Maquis and a life of secrecy and constant danger. One way or another, their lives would never be the same again.

As German demands for manpower increased, the trickle of *réfractaires* turned into a flood. The numbers at the Ambel farm quickly rose to eighty-five. There was no more space. In Eugène Samuel's words, 'The young men coming up the mountain became more and more numerous. Now it was not just the specialists who were being called away, but whole annual intakes of young men whom Laval wanted to send to help Hitler's war effort. There was a mood of near panic among the young men, and the resources of the Gaullist resistance organizations were very soon swamped. We needed new camps; we needed more financial resources; we needed food; we needed clothes and above all we needed boots. We needed to organize some kind of security system to search out the spies who we knew the Milice were infiltrating with the *réfractaires*. We needed arms.'

New camps were soon found. And not just in the Vercors. Elsewhere in the region, other early Resistance groups were also establishing camps for fleeing *réfractaires* in the remote areas of the nearby Chartreuse Massif and the Belledonne and Oisans mountain ranges which bordered the Grésivaudan valley. Between February and May 1943, eight new *réfractaire* camps – housing some 400 men in all and numbered consecutively from Ambel (C1) – were established across the Vercors plateau under the direction of Aimé Pupin. To this total must be added two military camps, one set up in May by an ex-Military School in Valence, another established in November under the control of Marcel Descour.

Those who joined the camps between March 1943 and May 1944 (that is before the Allied landings in Normandy) were of differing ages and came from a wide area. In a sample of forty-four *réfractaires* in the initial influx between March and May 1943, almost half were over thirty years old, many of them married. As might be expected, the majority (60 per cent) were from the immediate locality (the region of Rhône-Alpes), but among the rest almost 10 per cent were Parisians, a further 10 per cent were born out of France and nearly 15 per cent came from the eastern regions of France. There was similar diversity when it came to previous employment. In C3, above Autrans, nearly half the camp members had been ordinary workers, almost a third technicians of one sort or another, some 12 per cent were students and nearly 10 per cent had been regular soldiers. Politically, too, there was a broad variety of opinions and views. The fact that the great majority of the Vercors' civilian camps were loyal to de Gaulle meant that the organized presence of the Communists and the French far right was almost non-existent on the plateau. Individually,

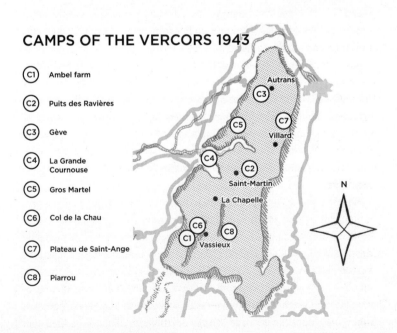

CAMPS OF THE VERCORS 1943

C1   Ambel farm

C2   Puits des Ravières

C3   Gève

C4   La Grande Cournouse

C5   Gros Martel

C6   Col de la Chau

C7   Plateau de Saint-Ange

C8   Piarrou

however, the camps included adherents to almost every political belief (except of course fascism). Political discussions round evening campfires were frequent, varied and at times very lively.

By autumn 1943, every community of any size on the plateau had a secret camp of one sort or another near by – and every inhabitant on the plateau would have been aware of the unusual nature of the new young visitors in their midst. For Samuel, Pupin, Chavant and their colleagues, the administrative burden of all this was immense. Pupin later said: 'We didn't have a moment of respite. Our eight camps occupied our time fully.' The biggest problem by far, however, was finding the money to pay for all this. Collections were made among family, well-wishers and work-places – two Jewish men contributed between them 20,000 francs a week which they had collected from contacts. But it was never enough.

London started providing huge subventions to support the *réfractaire* movement. During Jean Moulin's visit to London in February 1943, de Gaulle charged him with 'centralizing the overall needs of the *réfractaires* and assuring the distribution of funds through a special organization, in liaison with trades unions and resistance movements'. On 18 February, Farge delivered a second massive subvention amounting to 3.2 million francs to be used for Dalloz's Plan Montagnards alone. And on 26 February Moulin's deputy sent a coded message to London containing his budget proposals for March 1943. This amounted to a request for no less than 13.4 million francs for all the elements of the Resistance controlled by de Gaulle, of which some 1.75 million francs per month was designated for the Vercors. This was in addition to the private dona-tions pouring into Aimé Pupin's coffers by way of a false account in the name of a local beekeeper, 'François Tirard', at the Banque Populaire branch in Villard. This level of support made the Vercors by far the biggest single Resistance project being funded by London at this point in the war.

Despite these significant sums, money remained an ever-present problem for those administering the Vercors camps through 1943 and into the following year. A British officer sent on a mission to assess the strength and nature of the Maquis in south-eastern France visited the Vercors later in 1943 and reported that those in the camps 'have to spend much of their time getting food etc. They have to do everything on their own and are often short of money. In one case they stole tobacco and sold it back onto the Black Market to get money.'

Not surprisingly this kind of behaviour, though by no means common, caused tensions between the *réfractaires* and local inhabitants. With food so short, the proximity of groups of hungry young men to passing flocks of sheep proved to be an especially explosive flash-point. On 14 June 1943, the *réfractaires* of Camp C4, fleeing to avoid a raid on their camp by Italian Alpine troops, arrived on the wide mountain pasture of Darbonouse where they were met by a flock of sheep numbering some 1,500. Their commander told them: 'If there is any thieving I will take the strongest measures against the perpetrators. Remember that it is in our interests to make the shepherds our friends. Remember too that it is through our behaviour that the Resistance is judged.'

On the other hand, not far away at the Pré Rateau mountain hut above Saint-Agnan, another band of young *réfractaires* who had absconded from their original camp enjoyed a merry summer of pilfering and theft, to the particular detriment of the flocks of sheep in the area.

Tensions between local farmers were considerably eased when spring turned into summer and some camp commanders offered their young men as free labour to cut and turn grass and bring in the harvest. It was very common during the summer days of 1943 to see small armies of fit and bronzed young men among the peasant families in the fields and pastures of the Vercors. The easy habits of city living were being replaced by the calloused hands and sinewed bodies necessary for survival as a Maquisard.

This was not so everywhere. There was considerable variation between camps according to how and by whom they were run. By the middle of 1943, many camps had ex-military commanders and were run on military lines. Here, by and large, there was good order, effective security, discipline and good relations with the locals. In other camps, however, things had 'the appearance of a holiday camp [with] young men taking their siestas in the shade of the firs after lunch or lying out in the sun improving their tans'.

One feature dominated the daily routine of all the camps, whether well run or not – the routine of the *corvées*, or camp chores. There were *corvées* for almost everything from peeling potatoes to gathering water (which in some camps had to be carried long distances from the nearest spring), bringing in the food, collecting the mail, chopping and carrying the wood (especially in winter), cooking, washing up and much else besides. Some camps – the lucky ones – were able to use mules for the heavy carrying, but many relied for their victuals, warmth and water on the strong legs and sturdy backs of their young occupants alone.

Soon it was realized that work in the fields was not going to be enough to keep the minds of intelligent young men occupied – or prepare them for what everyone knew would come in due course. One of the organizations established by the Vichy government – and then dissolved shortly after the German invasion of the south – was a school to train 'cadres' or young professionals to run Vichy government structures. The École d'Uriage, many of whose students came from the Army, was located some 15 kilometres outside Grenoble. Following the lead of its commander, the École soon became a hotbed of Resistant sentiment. When the École d'Uriage was dissolved in December 1943, most of the students and staff swiftly reassembled in the old château of Murinais, just under the western rim of the Vercors. It was from here, at the suggestion of Alain Le Ray, who had by now become the effective military commander of all the camps, that flying squads, usually of three or four students and staff, were sent out to the camps to provide training for the *réfractaires*. Typically a Uriage flying squad would spend several days in a camp, following a set training programme which provided military training, cultural awareness and political education. The curriculum included instruction in basic military skills, training exercises, weapon handling, physical exercise, map reading and orientation, security, camp discipline, hygiene and political studies covering the tenets of the Gaullist Resistance movement and a briefing on the aims of the Allies and the current status of the war. One camp even received instruction in Morse code. In the evenings there were boisterous games and the singing of patriotic songs around the campfire. Study circles were established which continued to meet after the flying squad had moved on. In many cases camp members were required to sign the Charter of the Maquis, which laid out the duties and conduct expected of a Maquisard. The Uriage teams even produced a small booklet on how to be a Resistance fighter with a front cover claiming it was an instruction manual for the French Army.

There was also some less conventional training given by one of the Vercors' most unusual and remarkable characters. Fabien Rey was famous on the plateau before the war as a poacher, a frequenter of the shadowy spaces beyond the law, an initiate into the mysteries of the Vercors' forests and hidden caves and an intimate of the secret lives of all its creatures. During the summer and autumn months of 1943, when not striding from camp to camp to share his knowledge with the young men from the cities, his latest crop of trapped foxes swinging from his belt, he could always be found sitting in his cabin invigilating a bubbling stew of strange delicacies such as the intestines of wild boars and the feathered heads of eagles, which he would press on any unwary visitor who passed. He also wrote a small cyclostyled handbook on how to live off the land on the plateau. It too was widely distributed and eagerly read.

In February 1943, Yves Farge, who had by now become the chief intermediary between Jean Moulin, de Gaulle's emissary, and the Vercors Resistants, made the connection between Pierre Dalloz and Aimé Pupin's organization. From now on, the two organizations, which were soon joined by their military co-conspirators, were fused into a single Combat Committee which directed all Resistance activity on the plateau.

On 1 March 1943, at a meeting in the Café de la Rotonde, Yves Farge handed Aimé Pupin the first tranche of the money London had sent by parachute to pay for the camps. Farge stayed the following night with Pupin and then, on the morning of 3 March, the two men set off on a day's reconnaissance of the southern half of the plateau in a taxi driven by a sympathizer. They went first to La Grande Vigne to collect Pierre Dalloz and then continued their journey up the mountain to Villard-de-Lans, where they collected Léon Martin. From there the little group pressed on to Vassieux: 'What I saw in front of me was the wide even plain around Vassieux … The aerial approaches to the plain from both north and south were unencumbered by hills, especially to the south. Somehow I had known that we would find an airstrip and here it was – and even better than I could have dreamed of … all around were wide areas which appeared specially designed to receive battalions parachuted from the sky.'

The little group stopped for a drink in a small bistro in Vassieux, pretending that they were looking to buy a piece of land on which to construct a saw-mill. But according to Dalloz, no one in Vassieux was deceived and the whole town, from that day onwards, believed that General de Gaulle himself was about to descend from the sky at any moment. The impression that secrets were impossible on the Vercors was further reinforced at lunch when, despite their attempts to appear discreet, the waiter at the Hôtel Bellier in La Chapelle announced their entry into the hotel dining room with the words 'Ah! Here are the gentlemen of the Resistance.'

That afternoon, the party returned to Villard where they dropped off Léon Martin before taking a quick detour to look at Méaudre and Autrans in the next-door valley. Crossing back over the Col de la Croix Perrin, they were surprised to see Léon Martin standing in the middle of the road flagging them down urgently. It was bad news. The Italians had raided the Café de la Rotonde and arrested Pupin's wife and fourteen other core members of the Grenoble organization.

Pupin immediately went to ground in Villard but not before taking two precautions. He dispatched Fabien Rey to Ambel to tell the *réfractaires* to decamp until the coast was clear. And he sent a friend down to Grenoble to try to prevent his records from falling into the hands of the Italians (whose soldiers had often frequented La Rotonde). He needn't have bothered. The quick-witted Mme Pupin had burnt the records before they could be found. In the absence of any evidence, the Italians had to release all the detainees a few days later.

Aimé Pupin and his co-conspirators should have realized that they had been given two warnings that day. First that their activities were no longer secret. And second that keeping centralized records was dangerous folly. Sadly neither warning was heeded.

EXPECTATION, *NOMADISATION* AND DECAPITATION

Flight Lieutenant John Bridger, DFC, throttled down and watched the needle on his Lysander's air-speed indicator drop back. Almost immediately the little aircraft's nose dipped towards the three dots of light laid out ahead like an elongated 'L', the long stroke pointing towards him and the short one at the far end pointing to the right.

Bridger was one of the most experienced pilots in RAF's 161 Lysander Squadron. On a previous occasion he had burst a tyre while landing Resistance agents at a clandestine strip deep in France. Worried that, with one tyre out, his Lysander (they were known affectionately as 'Lizzies') would be unbalanced for take-off, he pulled out his Colt automatic, shot five holes in the remaining good tyre, loaded up his return passengers for the UK and took off on his wheel rims.

Maybe it was because of his experience that he had been chosen for Operation Sirène II. Tonight, 19 March 1943, he was carrying passengers of special importance – Charles de Gaulle's personal representative in France, Jean Moulin, the Secret Army's commander General Charles Delestraint and one other Resistance agent. In truth, with three passengers on board, the little plane was overloaded for it was designed to take only two. But 161 Squadron pilots were used to pushing the limits.

Bridger's destination this night was a flat field close to a canal a kilometre east of the village of Melay, which lies in the Saône-et-Loire valley 310 kilometres south-east of Paris and 700 from 161 Squadron's base at Tangmere on the English south coast. This meant a round trip in his unarmed Lysander of some 1,500 kilometres, most of which would be flying alone over enemy-occupied territory. With a cruising speed of 275 kilometres per hour and allowing for headwinds and turn-around time on the ground, Bridger would be flying single handed for the best part of seven unbroken hours.

Like all of the RAF's clandestine landings and parachute drops into France, tonight's operation was taking place in the 'moon period' – roughly speaking the ten nights either side of the full moon (sometimes known by the codeword Charlotte). The remaining ten nights of the month were known as the 'no moon period' when conditions were too dark for accurate parachuting or safe landings. The March 1943 full moon occurred two days after Bridger's flight, which meant that the moon's luminosity this night was 91 per cent of that of the full moon, enabling Bridger to see many of the main topographical features such as woods and towns of the area he would be flying over. Most visible of all would have been the great rivers of France, which were 161 Squadron's favourite navigational aids.

According to his logbook Bridger took off from 161 Squadron's base at RAF Tangmere at 22.44 hours, two and a half hours after sunset that day. His post-operational report of his route is laconic and sparse on detail: 'went via St Aubin-sur-Mer, Bourges, Moulins and direct to target. Apart from meeting a medium sized [enemy] aircraft 4 miles north of Moulin … the journey was uneventful.'

At Moulins, Bridger would have turned due east to pick up the River Loire, now turned by the gibbous moon into a great ribbon of silver, its little lakes and tributaries appearing as sprinkles of tinsel scattered across the darkened countryside. Here he swung south on the last leg of his journey – a lonely dot hidden in the vast expanse of the night sky. It is not difficult to imagine Jean Moulin and Charles Delestraint looking down on the moon-soaked fields and villages of occupied France and wondering about the task ahead and what it would take to free their country from the merciless grip of its occupiers.

The reception team waiting for Bridger at Melay that night was commanded by forty-year-old Pierre Delay, an experienced operator who had already received the Croix de Guerre from de Gaulle for his conduct of a previous SOE landing. He had been alerted that there was to be a landing on this site by a special code phrase broadcast during the six-minute 'Messages personnels' section of the BBC's *Les Français parlent aux Français*. Delay had chosen Melay for tonight's operation because he had a cousin who had a safe house 2 kilometres north of the landing site where the new arrivals could be put up, and a sympathetic local garage owner, whose Citroën was always available on these occasions.

According to Bridger's operational report he 'Reached target at 0140, signals given clearly & flare path good'. Delay's men, who had waited in the deepening cold for two hours before Bridger arrived, now watched as the plane – it seemed big to them now – glided in almost noiselessly to touch down on the dewy grass. Moulin and Delestraint were bundled into the waiting Citroën and spent the night in the safe house, leaving the following day for Macon. They had arrived back in France to take command of a Resistance movement which was in a high state of expectation that the Allied landings would take place some time during the summer of 1943.

An SOE paper marked 'MOST SECRET' and dated 13 March 1943, just a week before the return of Moulin and Delestraint, discussed the possible uses of the Resistance in the event of an Allied landing, but warned that 'the state of feeling in France has, after a gradual rise in temperature, suddenly reached fever pitch … there is a real danger that, if this … is allowed to pass unregarded, the French population … will subside into apathy and despair'. On 18 March, the night before Moulin and Delestraint landed, Maurice Schumann – who was for many the voice of Free France broadcasting on the BBC – was so inspired by news of the flood of *réfractaires* to the Haute-Savoie that he invoked the famous French Revolutionary force, the Légion des Montagnes, in one of his famous broadcasts, implying a Savoyard uprising. He was immediately rebuked by his London superiors for being premature – but he had accurately caught the feverish mood of excitement and expectation.

On 23 March, just three days after he arrived, Jean Moulin sent a coded telegram to London saying that the mood was so 'keyed up' that he had been 'obliged to calm down the [Resistance] leaders who believe that Allied action was imminent'. One local Resistance leader, however, was sure that the state of over-excitement was generated not in France, but in London: 'not a single one of us at the time was expecting an imminent landing. The truth was that the "over-excitement" of the [local] leaders reflected our intense preoccupation with the drama that was unfolding as a result of having Maquis organizations [in the field] without any support and our irritation over the attitude of de Gaulle and [the French] clandestine services.'

De Gaulle's personal instructions to Delestraint before his departure, a copy of which can still be found in the French military archives in the

Château de Vincennes in Paris, also give the impression that D-Day is fast approaching. Under the heading of 'immediate actions' to be taken 'In the present period, before the Allied landings', he instructed Delestraint to 'prepare the Secret Army for the role it is to play in the liberation of territory', including the 'delicate measures necessary to permit a general rising of volunteers after D-Day [referred to by the French as 'Jour J'] in the zones where this can be sustained because of the difficulty the Germans have in dominating the area' – a clear reference, it would seem, to Plan Montagnards and the Vercors.

Whatever the true cause of all this premature excitement, the Vercors was not immune from its effects. Aimé Pupin commented that in the camps on the plateau the Allied landings were expected daily and 'They were all burning for action …' Unfortunately it was not just the Resistance who were 'burning for action' in anticipation of an Allied landing soon. France's German and Italian occupiers were too.

By this stage of the war the British codebreakers at Bletchley Park had broken the Japanese diplomatic code and were able to provide SOE with the complete text of a cable sent by Japan's Ambassador to France giving his analysis of the state of the Resistance, following a visit to Vichy in the middle of 1943. This document revealed that the Gestapo had penetrated the entire Resistance movement and were also anticipating 'a hypothetical D Day which they feared might be imminent'. The Ambassador predicted that the Gestapo would soon unleash a 'heavy drive' against Resistance structures with the aim of emasculating them before any landing could take place. At the end of April agents in France were also reporting to London that the Germans were making detailed plans to combat an Allied invasion in the summer.

By the time of the Japanese Ambassador's visit to Vichy the 'heavy drive' had, in fact, already started. Following the arrest of Aimé Pupin's wife in the Café de la Rotonde on 3 March, the Italians raided the Ferme d'Ambel. But, warned by Fabien Rey, the young occupants fled before the enemy party got there. Then on 18 March Italian mountain troops tried to surprise the C4 *réfractaire* camp on La Grande Cournouse, the great forest-covered buttress of rock which overlooks the Gorges de la Bourne. Once again the Maquis were warned in time and managed to slip away in good order. By now similar operations were taking place against *réfractaire* camps across the whole of the region and even in Grenoble.

On 19 April the Italians tried again on the plateau, this time raiding C7 camp on the Plateau de Saint-Ange. 'The Italians arrived so quickly that our sentries didn't have time to warn us and everyone tried to find the best hiding place they could, some taking refuge in holes, others scrambling towards the nearest pine tree … No fewer than a dozen of us ended up sitting perched, rucksacks on our backs, in the branches of one especially large fir. "Now this really is what I call a Christmas tree," one wit remarked. The camp dog, thinking it was all some kind of game, tore after us yelping as we ran for our hiding place and then insisted on sitting down at the base of the tree staring intently at our merry pantomime, while we tried in vain to persuade it to go away. The Italians, the black feathers on their Alpine hats waving in the wind, ran past us not ten metres away.'

Alain Le Ray, who spent much of his time travelling from one camp to the other checking on wellbeing, security and training, saw the danger early and issued instructions: 'At the smallest sign of trouble, get out, cover your tracks and keep moving for as long as possible.'

By the beginning of May, the Maquisards of C4 camp arrived back at their original site on La Grande Cournouse after a long series of peregrinations, only to be woken in the early morning of 18 May by their sentry shouting 'Les Ritals! Les Ritals!' (slang for Italians). In a later coded message to London Aimé Pupin reported that a force of Italian Alpini 'three thousand' strong, guided by the Milice, had scaled the sheer slopes from the Gorges on to the plateau overnight. But again the attack appears to have been bungled for, of the eighty in the camp, at the time, the Alpini managed to catch only four, whom they surprised returning from collecting food. De Gaulle himself sent a message to the young Maquisards congratulating them on 'thwarting the attack'.

And so began what the Vercors fugitives called the 'summer of *nomadisation*' with the *réfractaires* and their leaders playing a game of cat and mouse with the Italian Army which the Maquisards almost invariably won. But it meant constant changes of camp, hurried last-minute exits and lengthy marches across the mountains often at dead of night. Uncomfortable as it was, the hardships of this period served to toughen soft city bodies and create a real sense of teamwork, comradeship and trust in their leaders.

On one occasion a troop of fleeing Maquisards (after two weeks of *nomadisation*) passed through the little settlement at Col de Rousset where the redoubtable Jeanne Bordat, known as Mémé Bordat, kept a bar/café/rest house for the refreshment of travellers crossing the Col. Hot on the fugitives' tail came a troop of Alpini led by an Italian officer who demanded to know where the Maquis were. Mémé Bordat denied any knowledge of the Maquis – indeed, she wanted to know what exactly were these mythical creatures, 'the Maquis', for she had never seen them. The Italian officer replied that they were the young men who lived in the mountains. Again Mémé Bordat professed ignorance. Again the Italian returned to the charge, demanding in more insistent terms to know where the fugitives were. Finally, according to Vercors legend, the good Mme Bordat lifted her skirt, pulled down her knickers and, pointing to her bottom, told the officer that if he really wished to know where the young men were, no doubt he could find them up there. The officer left, red faced, taking his Alpini with him.

The importance of this story lies not so much in its veracity as in the indication it provides that, although the disruption caused by *nomadisation* was uncomfortable, the French Resistance in the Vercors did not regard the Italian Army as a serious threat. As one Maquis leader put it 'The "Piantis"* were less troublesome and much easier to fool than their allies and friends [the Germans].' Francis Cammaerts, a British SOE agent in south-eastern France, had the same view: 'the morale of the Italian Army was so low that [they] … presented no difficulty to the French resistance movements, as nearly all their work was left to the French police'.

Meanwhile, progress continued to be made on the Montagnards plan. In April, Jean Moulin sent a further 1.6 million francs to Dalloz for Montagnards and asked London for a further 40 million to fund his work across France.

On 6 April 1943, just ten days after his return from London and right in the middle of the early Italian raids on the plateau, Delestraint, on Jean Moulin's instructions, attended a meeting of the Montagnards leaders in the main reception room of Pierre Dalloz's house at La Grande Vigne, looking out over Grenoble and the Alps on the other side of the Grésivaudan valley. It was a beautiful day, with early-spring light streaming through the windows and the brilliance of the snow on the distant mountains, reflecting in the gilt mirrors on the Villa's walls. Here,

---

* Another nickname for the Italian troops – perhaps a corruption of 'les Chiantis'.

protected by sentries posted at all the main points around the house and on the neighbouring roads, Delestraint was briefed in detail by Dalloz and his co-conspirators on the state of Montagnards. This included presentations on the camps, the Maquisards, the logistics, lorries and cars, mountain refuges, parachute sites and landing zones, resources and food.

Dalloz wrote: 'We told him that we had no doubt that the Allies would land on the beaches of Provence and that the Germans would try to reinforce their positions before the attack by moving their forces along the north–south line of the valley of the Rhône and the Route des Alpes. But they would be very concerned about their line of retreat. At this moment the Vercors would rise and block the access roads to the plateau at the ten points marked in red on the map. The Allies could then launch paratroop units with their full armament on to the plains of the Vercors at Vassieux, Autrans and Lans … This would be the signal for the whole region to rise. Lyon would fall.'

That night the whole company had a convivial dinner at the Restaurant des Côtes at Sassenage and the following day accompanied Delestraint on a tour of inspection of the plateau. They went first to Saint-Nizier, the gateway to the northern half of the plateau. Delestraint immediately identified this as the weak point in the Vercors' natural defences and warned prophetically, 'Without mountain artillery, or at least mortars, you cannot expect to hold the plain of Villard-de-Lans for very long. In these circumstances it might be best to defend instead the southern, more mountainous part of the Vercors.'

Over lunch in a restaurant at La Balme-de-Rencurel in the Bourne gorges, the old General turned to Aimé Pupin and asked, 'Why did you choose the Vercors?'

'Pure romanticism, mon Général,' Pupin replied. 'I was always fascinated by the fact that Mandrin [an eighteenth-century brigand with a Robin Hood reputation] was able to escape the police when he took refuge here.'

It had been a good day and Delestraint, who expressed himself well satisfied, thanked everyone for their work and promised that 'The Vercors will play an important role when eventually the Allies land in France.'

Throughout April and early May, despite Italian Army raids on the camps, the Montagnards preparations continued, including a plan to install a high-powered transmitter in Villard-de-Lans which could be used by General de Gaulle to broadcast to the whole of France when he set up his government on the plateau after the Allied landings. Chavant, Pupin and others even began to search for appropriate houses to be used as de Gaulle's personal accommodation when he arrived.

This high mood of hope and optimism was reflected in London. On 4 May, de Gaulle addressed a reception for young people at the Grosvenor House Hotel. He said 'France can return again to her force of arms and her hopes, waiting for the day when, her liberation accomplished and her victories achieved, she can escape from her pains and ruins to claim her greatness and her place among the ranks of the great nations again.'

Despite such intoxicating dreams, there were more prosaic problems which needed urgent solutions – the Maquisards in the camps lacked boots. A raid was duly mounted to appropriate a large number of boots and shoes from a nearby government depot, which were distributed for the comfort of blistered feet across the plateau. This success was followed by several other raids on the valley to obtain what the plateau lacked, attracting the attention of the Italian secret police, OVRA. Whatever the ineffectiveness of the Italian Army, the same could not be said of this organization which worked closely with the Gestapo. On 24 April OVRA agents arrested and tortured Dr Léon Martin, then imprisoned him in the Fort d'Esseillon in Modane close to the Italian border. 'I sent Benoit to see if it might be possible to spring him,' Aimé Pupin explained. 'But he came back saying it was hopeless.'

OVRA's next chance came not through their own work but through a mixture of complacency, braggadocio and stupidity on the part of the Maquisards. It began one day in mid-May when a garage owner with known Resistance sympathies was asked to hide two full ex-Army petrol bowsers in his garage until they could be collected. He was given a password and firm instructions that he should on no account allow the vehicles to be stolen or captured by the Italians. This was easier said than done since Italian soldiers were billeted in a house not fifty metres from his garage. He made the vehicles safe by chocking them up on bricks, removing their wheels and distributor heads, and repainting them in the livery of the Water and Forestry Department.

For a week or so, nothing happened. But then, when the owner arrived at his garage as usual on 27 May, he found the doors had been forced overnight. The vehicles were still there, though there had clearly been an attempt to replace their wheels. But the bowsers were empty. Two days later the garagist was arrested and questioned by OVRA and accused of providing petrol to the Maquis. Only then did it emerge that the break-in at his garage had been carried out by a team of eleven armed Maquisards from Villard-de-Lans who had attempted to 'liberate' the vehicles and take them on to the plateau, where the petrol was desperately needed to keep the Huillier buses running. On the way down from the plateau, the 'commandos' had stopped at a bar in Grenoble well known for its Resistance sympathies. Here they met a fellow Resistant leader who, hearing of the exploit, told them that it was extremely foolish, since he could easily get false papers to allow the vehicles to be driven up to the plateau without any risk. But the leader of the Villard commandos insisted on pressing ahead with his plans. Of course, since no warning had been given to the owner, the commando team had no option but to break into his garage, where they duly discovered that the vehicles were immovable. Realizing there was nothing further they could do, they set off to return to the plateau. But, breaking all the normal security rules, they chose to travel back by the same route by which they had come down. At the Pont de Claix just outside Grenoble they ran into an OVRA checkpoint in the early hours of the morning. A search of the back of the lorry revealed that it was full of quietly sleeping 'commandos', their arms stacked neatly by their sides. All ten were arrested, interrogated and in due course deported to Italy.

The next day, 28 May, the OVRA and the Milice swooped. A black OVRA car supported by a lorry full of Alpini arrived in Villard in mid-morning and arrested Victor Huillier, four other key Resistance organizers and finally, after a lengthy search, Aimé Pupin himself, hiding in a loft. At the same time, a Milice search of the village turned up a cache of some 6 tonnes of dynamite hidden near by. Almost the entire leadership of the Vercors Resistance had been decapitated in a single morning. Other arrests of those further down the chain swiftly followed. Thanks to fast footwork, Farge, Le Ray, Chavant and Dalloz among the main leaders managed to escape (Dalloz's wife Henriette Gröll fled her home in La Grande Vigne in the middle of a reception for forty guests moments before Italian troops roared in to take possession of the house). However, thanks to Pupin's habit of keeping neat centralized records, all were now hunted fugitives.

On 28 May London sent instructions to Delestraint to refrain from all military action. That afternoon Farge had a clandestine meeting with Dalloz in a grove of acacia trees on the Quai de France, alongside the Isère in Grenoble. 'My friend,' said Farge, 'you and I have the money in our pockets and the clothes we stand up in. We have nothing else now. No job, no home, no family, no name. From now on we live the clandestine life, or we don't live.' Chavant hurriedly left Grenoble to find refuge in a village west of Grenoble, Farge fled for Paris, Dalloz for Aix-les-Bains and Le Ray for the plateau.

On 2 June, Dalloz received instructions to meet Delestraint in a restaurant in Lyon, where the old General instructed him that Alain Le Ray and Jean Prévost were to take over the Vercors Resistance structures and Dalloz himself was to go to Paris where he should meet the General again on the terrace of the Chez Francis restaurant by the Alma-Marceau exit of the Métro at 18.00 on 6 June 1943. When the two conspirators met in Paris they found the restaurant too crowded for safe discussion, so they walked together to the house where Dalloz had found temporary refuge in Paris. Here Delestraint told Dalloz that, if anything happened to him, Dalloz should go to London where he would help to prepare the way for Plan Montagnards.

Dalloz may have been lucky. Three days after his meeting at Chez Francis, Delestraint was arrested emerging from another Métro station, La Muette, on his way to a meeting with another Resistance leader. He was handed over to the 'Butcher of Lyon', Klaus Barbie of the Gestapo, and interrogated for more than fifty no doubt terrible hours, before being sent, as a *Nacht und Nebel** prisoner, to Natzweiller-Struthof concentration camp in Alsace. He was shot in Dachau three weeks before the German surrender in 1945.

On 18 June, a message from Jean Moulin written before Delestraint's arrest arrived in London. Moulin's report warned: 'the safety of the Vercors has been compromised. Many arrests have taken place owing to indiscretions committed by some of them [the leaders of the Vercors]. The Commander of the Groups [Le Ray] and his Chief of Staff [Prévost] have had to go into hiding and the Vercors must therefore be left for the

---

* Literally 'Night and fog'. It meant he was allowed no contact with the outside world whatsoever. The purpose was to make people completely disappear so that no one knew their whereabouts or their fate.

moment and reconstituted later … No one is to take to the *maquis* until further orders. All direct wireless communications between the Vercors and London is to cease.' Moulin's decision to 'put the Vercors to sleep' was a wise one, for by now a wave of Gestapo arrests was sweeping the whole of France, north and south.

Despite these events, a meeting of the Directing Committee for the whole of the southern zone, chaired by Moulin himself, was held as planned on 21 June in the outskirts of Lyon. The location was betrayed and in a Gestapo swoop Moulin, together with seven other key Resistance leaders, was seized. Moulin was handed over to Klaus Barbie and tortured to death.

The leadership and structure of the Resistance in southern France now lay in ruins. It was not just the Vercors that had been decapitated. Similar operations had taken place in Isère, the Haute-Savoie and the Alpes-Maritimes. A British Cabinet paper of the day estimated that 'fifteen principals and several hundred subordinates of the Fighting French organisation were arrested' in the Gestapo swoops. An SOE paper quoting a secret French source put the figure much higher: 'some three thousand members of resistance groups were rounded up and put in prison by the Germans, the majority being in Fresnes [the notorious Gestapo prison in Paris]'.

One element, however, made the Vercors different from all others affected. While the Resistance structures on the plateau could be rebuilt, the crucial connection between Plan Montagnards and those at the very top of the Free French leadership, which had given the Vercors a prime position in French plans for the liberation of southern France, had been irretrievably broken.

8

RETREAT, RETRENCHMENT AND RECONSTRUCTION

For Alain Le Ray and Jean Prévost, standing now almost alone amid the wreckage of the Vercors Resistance, the first and most pressing problem was money and how to rebuild their organization. Le Ray managed to make contact with one of the few members of the Moulin organization in Lyon who had survived the summer purges and who was able to provide enough money to cover the plateau's immediate needs. His next task was to try to make contact with those who had survived the May arrests. Pierre Dalloz, with Delestraint's last words instructing him to go to London ringing in his ears, had already set out on what would be a long and hazardous odyssey out of France.

Eugène Chavant, however, seemed to have vanished. In fact Chavant, who had first taken refuge in the countryside outside Grenoble, soon decided he was safer with trusted friends in the city, one of whom ran the Perrin sports shop in the Place des Postes. One day, quite by chance it seems, Chavant spotted a young, impressive-looking man buying fishing tackle and asked who he was. He was told that the man was an Army officer connected with the Resistance. A meeting was arranged at which a personal bond was immediately established between the two. The forty-nine-year-old Chavant, whose socialist background made him instinctively suspicious of the military and their right-wing ways, found in Le Ray, thirty-two at the time, an energetic and politically sensitive partner. For his part, Le Ray, who had an understanding of the importance of close politico-military cooperation which was unusual for French officers of the day, saw the older man as a wise counsellor and effective political operator. A close working relationship was quickly established.

At the end of June a meeting of key leaders in the Vercors region was held at the Château de Murinais under the western edge of the plateau. Its purpose was to re-establish a functional organization in place of the one which had been destroyed by the May arrests. A second Combat Committee made up of five men and two women was created under the overall control of Eugène Chavant (now increasingly referred to as *le Patron*). The two military representatives on the Committee were Alain Le Ray and one of his lieutenants, Roland Costa de Beauregard.

Though there would be changes to the personnel at the top, this second Vercors Combat Committee, known throughout the Resistance simply as the 'Organisation Vercors', would form the basic structure responsible for the direction of all Resistance operations on the Vercors right through to the end of the war. It did not, however, have either the attention of the Free French leadership in London or the direct communication with them that its predecessor had enjoyed.

To start with, Chavant himself stayed in Grenoble, making regular visits to the plateau on the tram to Saint-Nizier and Villard. But in September he moved to take up permanent residence at Saint-Martin on the Vercors itself. By the end of the year effective civilian control of almost all Resistance activities on the Vercors had been established, with Chavant presiding over two administrative sub-units, one covering the northern and the other the southern half of the plateau. Given that this was all done under the noses of a seemingly alert enemy, Chavant's organization was astonishingly comprehensive. It incorporated the postal and telecoms services in the area, the co-ordination of friendly Gendarme units where these existed, the setting up of a system of 'sentinels' linked by phone and courier, the direction of the plateau's hydroelectric generating plants and a system of motorcycle couriers based at the western edge of the plateau at Saint-Nazaire-en-Royans, who were ready round the clock to carry messages and alert the plateau of impending danger.

Alain Le Ray, replicating Chavant's civilian structure, split his military 'command' in two as well, appointing Costa de Beauregard as commander of the north and another of his officers the south. Over the summer months and into the early autumn, Le Ray concentrated on reorganizing, training and, as far as he could, arming the Vercors camps, always ensuring that everything he did was coordinated with Chavant and his civilian partners. Far from lazing around in 'holiday camps', most of the Vercors *réfractaires* – when they weren't out in the fields helping to get in the harvest – spent this summer on forced marches, on learning to live off the land and on repeated military manoeuvres under the direction of professional military officers who had by now been appointed to command each of the camps on the plateau.

Le Ray himself embarked on a tireless round of the camps, checking on their security, seeing to their needs and instructing them about their role and importance. A flavour of these events is given in an account of Le Ray's visit to the Vercors' first camp, the Ferme d'Ambel. After a dinner sitting, quiet and unannounced, among the *réfractaires* around the rough wooden tables of Ambel's refectory, Le Ray called for silence and spoke: 'From today you will be a part of a new French force which General de Gaulle has created, with the support of our powerful Allies, to recover our independence and rediscover the true strength of our country. This is the great task which is before you, the glory which is yours to achieve. You have responded to this appeal even before it was made. You have taken your posts, even before they were assigned to you … The role you have already accepted to play is one of the most important in the battle for our freedom. This is what your leaders confirm today, placing their trust in your courage. Now you must wait for their orders – they will not be long in coming. In a few months – in a few weeks, perhaps – the signal will be given. You must be ready. I am here today to give you my assurance that the service you will give – the sacrifice you will perhaps have to make – will be fully recognized and will contribute decisively to the victory your courage will have delivered.'

After the war Le Ray outlined what he was trying to achieve during his push for better organization and coordination in the late spring and early summer of 1943:

We had to change our whole approach according to five principal aims:

1. The elimination of all the damaging distinctions between the military and the civilians. We were now united together under a single category: Resistance fighters.
2. A structure of command which was as simple and direct as possible.
3. The elimination of all embedded prejudices, especially where the lifestyles of the Maquis groups could have the effect of damaging relations with the local villages.

4. A dual role for those who remained in their own communities waiting for the call to action:* providing intelligence, early warning, food and supplies to the Maquis, putting together teams, quickly and on demand, for specific assignments.

5. The strengthening of the professional and leadership elements in each of the Maquis groups.

It was in pursuit of the fourth of these, 'A dual role for those who remained in their own communities', that a decision was taken which was to have a profound effect on all those who lived around the Vercors during the struggle ahead. Conscious that there would be a general mobilization of forces when the Allies landed, Le Ray proposed that a reserve force made up of four secret Maquisard companies should be raised from the young men of the communities lying outside the mountainous perimeter of the Vercors. Each of these would be led by a professional military officer who would provide them with training at the weekends. No doubt one of Le Ray's motives in proposing this reserve force was to help deepen the connection between the military and the local civil society. But it had strong military advantages too for it provided, not just reinforcement which could be called to the plateau when required, but also a kind of informal militarized cordon around its outside edge which would act both as a warning system and as a line of defence in case of attack.

One of these companies was founded by a Socialist professor of mathematics at the Romans Technical College, André Vincent-Beaume, and was constituted from young volunteers from the towns of Romans, Bourg-de-Péage and Saint-Donat-sur-l'Herbasse off the western edge of the plateau. A secret programme of recruitment to what was eventually to become Abel Company began in the three towns in June 1943, with recruits being drawn from factories, warehouses, offices, local clubs (especially the rugby club) and even the patient lists of a doctor and a dentist in the area. Provisioning and money for the clandestine unit was provided from local sources, chiefly by collections in factories, churches and clubs. A hundred pairs of boots were donated by a local factory

---

* They were called *sédentaires* – that is, Resistants who stayed in the farms and communities in which they lived and continued their work as normal during the day, but trained secretly as Maquisards at the weekends.

owner (this area is famous in France as the centre of the shoe industry) and funds were banked in the Romans branch of the Banque Populaire.

Serious training, conducted mostly by military professionals and consisting of long forced marches, military manoeuvres and occasional firing of weapons, began in July. At weekends the young men of Abel Company would quietly melt away from their communities and re-assemble in forest clearings or at mountain refuges on the high pastures of the plateau, returning on Sunday evening ready for work next day. In August, Abel Company, now numbering some 235 Maquisards and divided into four sections, was formally given its proposed area of oper-ation when full mobilization on 'Jour J' occurred – they were to help defend the whole of the south-west quadrant of the plateau.

The D-Day mobilization process itself was carefully planned. Special signs were prepared which would be nailed to trees and barn doors indi-cating where to find assembly points, there was a mass purchase of Michelin maps of the area, camping gear was requisitioned from local sporting and hardware shops and each Maquisard was required to have a rucksack ready packed for quick departure containing a candle, spare shoes, a blanket, a waterproof sheet, a set of mess-tins, eating utensils and a water bottle.

On the other side of the Vercors massif, in the little market town of Mens in the Trièves region, under the plateau's south-eastern corner, the same thing was happening.

'You free this evening after 8 p.m.?' asked Jacques, who owned a saw-mill at the entry to Mens. It was six o'clock in the evening and almost dark when he had knocked on the door of the Darier house. The evening light caught the last streaks of unmelted snow on the slopes of the Bonnet de Calvin, high above the little town.

'Sure. I can easily be free,' Albert Darier replied.

'Good.' Jacques continued, 'I know you believe in the Resistance. But we have nothing organized here. One of the key men in the Secret Army is coming tonight to see if we can set up a unit in the Trièves. If you would like, why not come along and meet him – and bring anyone else you think might be interested.'

When Albert Darier, who turned twenty-one that year, and six of his closest companions arrived at 20.00 precisely in the first-floor private room set aside in the Café de Paris, he found a brightly lit space with several chairs set around a table on which stood a small vase of spring flowers. His friend Jacques and a young stranger, who was introduced as 'Emmanuel, one of the local chiefs of the Secret Army', were already there. Otherwise the room was empty.

At first the stranger seemed a little disappointed that there were so few of them. But Albert Darier explained that he had known of the meeting only a couple of hours previously and had not had time for discreet contact with more of his friends. Reassured, the stranger spoke of the need to resist the enemy in organized groups and to play a part in the liberation and future of France. He continued, 'I warn you. It will be hard. Some of us will not return ... There will be few to help us. We will not be protected by the laws of war, because we will be "terrorists". And we will be fighting more than just men. We will be fighting the beast of the Nazi regime ... This beast will defend itself with blood and terrible savagery. And it will become even more terrible as its final agonies draw near.' The six young men sitting round the table hung on every consonant and syllable the mysterious stranger spoke. 'We will have not just to defend, but also to attack. We will certainly have to kill ... But to fight we shall need arms. And at present I have none ... I don't know when exactly the arms will come. But I do know they will come. They have been promised. Maybe not tomorrow, but in due course.'

By now it was late and the Café de Paris had already closed. One by one the new recruits slipped down the back stairs and out into the darkness to their homes, their warm beds and the comfort of their families. The Mens platoon of the Compagnie de Trièves had been formed. In due course they would be given the crucial task of defending the high passes on the south-east corner of the Vercors' eastern ramparts. Slowly but surely Alain Le Ray was creating a ragged but surprisingly capable guerrilla force – except of course for arms, of which they had none, apart from an occasional old hunting rifle and what little was left of the arms smuggled out of Grenoble that the Italians hadn't found.

On 10 and 11 August 1943 the leadership of the Organisation Vercors arranged a mass convocation of all the Vercors Maquis and those from the neighbouring areas, on the high pasture of Darbonouse, overlooked by the Grand Veymont which towers above the eastern plateau. Maquis groups and their leaders from across the plateau and beyond made their way up the mountain to a meeting point in a small natural amphitheatre in front of a shepherd's hut, located in a hidden dip in the middle of the Darbonouse pasture. Sentries were posted at strategic points around the area and each group were required to provide their names and give the password – 'Great Day'. The Maquis chiefs were accommodated in the shepherd's hut. Tents stolen from the valley were erected for the rest. Formal proceedings were opened on 10 August with a singing of the 'Marseillaise' and the raising of the national flag. Le Ray's original plan seems to have been to have two days of open-air discussions and then take the Organisation's leaders on a tour of inspection of key sites on the plateau. But the clouds swept in and it started to rain, so this was abandoned.

There is no reliable record of how many attended this gathering, which some have compared, rather grandly, with the great feast at the Fête de la Fédération of 14 July 1790, a key event in Revolutionary France. We do know, however, that all the main Vercors leaders were there, including Le Ray, Chavant, Samuel and Prévost, as well as many of the heads of the newly formed Maquisard companies and others among the second echelon of Vercors leaders, including a doctor from Romans, Dr Fernand Ganimède, who will feature later in our story.

Le Ray opened proceedings with a statement of intent: 'We have to eliminate all passive attitudes among our people. Our Maquis companies must be divided into highly mobile groups of thirty with the majority coming from those who have been in the camps already established. The danger lies in us becoming too settled in one place – too fixed. Mobility, speed and prudence – these are our best defences.'

He then outlined three possible future strategies. The first was a fortress strategy in which the Vercors would be held against all comers. The second, which he called the 'hedgehog' strategy, was to use the plateau as a base from which raids could be mounted on the Germans in the valley, with the raiders disappearing into the forests if they themselves were attacked. The third strategy was effectively Plan Montagnards – a proposal to turn the Vercors into an airbase to be held as an advanced bastion for a few days only, so as to enable airborne troops to fly in, consolidate and then begin attacking German lines of communications in the valley, while at the same time widening the secure base to other areas. It was this latter view which won the day, though some were worried it gave the starring role to the incoming paras, leaving the Maquisards as bystanders to the main action.

Despite the incessant rain, which caused the convocation to break up on 11 August, everyone realized that a watershed had passed. They had a united organization and a clear strategy to follow: 'Never had the Vercors been more confident. Never had it been more sure of itself. Never had it been so united.'

Some time in August 1943 a tall Englishman with unusually large feet came to the Vercors for a meeting with Eugène Chavant. The twenty-seven-year-old Francis Cammaerts, alias 'Roger', was arguably one of the most successful of all SOE agents in wartime France. He had been landed by Lysander on 21 March 1943, two days after Moulin and Delestraint had landed at Melay. Equipped with a false identity in the name of Charles Robert Laurent, he had orders to assess the work of an SOE 'circuit' run by Peter Churchill and his courier Odette Sansom near Annecy in the Savoie. But he soon realized that Churchill's security was so bad that it was only a matter of time before his organization was penetrated by the Gestapo. In fact Cammaerts only just managed to avoid the catastrophe when Churchill and many of his colleagues were arrested. Cammaerts duly set about constructing his own network under his SOE codename Jockey, which extended across the whole of the south and east of France. By the time 'Grands Pieds' (as he was quickly christened by Chavant) came to the Vercors he was, despite his youth, already respected even by hardened Maquis leaders twice his age and had become a marked man, much sought after by the Germans. One of the reasons for Cammaerts' success was the scrupulous attention he paid to security and to the welfare of his agents and the fact that he ran his network through a series of isolated and unconnected cells so as to limit the danger of total collapse if one was penetrated.

'I met ... Eugène Chavant ... and we walked up [the mountain] together and met a couple of the military chaps,'* Cammaerts said later of this visit. 'It was obvious that Plan Montagnards had an enormous amount to commend it and I backed it as much as I could ... The supposition was that after Normandy there would be either a sea landing in the south of France very shortly or an airborne landing where the troops, backed by the Resistance ... [would land in mountainous areas such as the Vercors] which we could have held ... against anything the Germans could put up ... for the forty-eight hours it would take them [the parachutists] to gather their material together and be in combat trim.'

* Probably Le Ray and de Beauregard.

What is striking about these events of July and August is that the Italians, who had caused so many problems for the Vercors Maquisards earlier in the year, seem effectively to have vanished from the scene, more concerned perhaps with events at home in Italy than with what happened in the country they were occupying. On 17 August, a week after the Darbonouse gathering broke up, the Allies declared Sicily (which had been invaded once North Africa had been secured) free of Axis troops. Allied forces were now poised only a stone's throw from the Italian mainland with an invasion expected any day.

Despite the easing of Italian pressure, the task facing leaders of the Organisation Vercors as they attempted to coordinate action on the plateau remained challenging. The temporary vacuum of local leadership caused by the May and June arrests had resulted in a climate of free-for-all when it came to forming new Resistance organizations. Now anyone could start their own Maquis – and they did. These newly formed Resistance groups varied greatly in quality – some good, many bad and a few deeply corrupt.

Among the latter category was a Maquis group led by an ex-policeman from Lyon called Marcel Roudet. A close collaborator of the equally dubious Chief of Police in Lyon, Roudet bought a café in La Chapelle some time in 1943 and started his own Maquis, which he used to 'legitimize' what was essentially a criminal gang specializing in theft, the black market and extortion. In due course Roudet, himself a heroin addict, became so powerful that he was even capable of terrorizing Eugène Samuel and was said by many to have 'the whole of the south in his pocket'. As Albert Darier recalled, 'He was big, strong and had the look of a real gangster chief about him. Roudet was impressive, even menacing, to look at. Always explosive, always on the edge, always prone to pulling out his revolver at the slightest provocation, he was at his most terrifying when he needed a "fix". Then he would go into the nearest chemist and demand an ampoule of morphine with menaces. As soon as he had left the shop, one of his men, whose job it was, would take out the syringe which he always carried, and inject Roudet's arm then and there on the street.'

Another 'freelance' Maquis, but one of a very different nature, was the Groupe Vallier, founded by the twenty-four-year-old Paul Gariboldy, a one-time draughtsman at the Merlin-Gerin engineering works in Grenoble. This group of audacious young desperadoes quickly became famous for their flamboyant dress, insouciance in the face of danger and expertise at assassinating collaborators even in broad daylight on the streets of Grenoble. Gariboldy himself was described by a Resistance comrade as 'An extraordinary man. Full of passion. He was afraid of nothing. He was maybe brave to the point of foolhardiness. He just didn't know where or how to stop.'

But when it came to assassination, no one was more feared on the plateau than 'Petit René' (his real name was René Lefèvre), who had been forced to watch when his mother and father had been summarily executed by the Germans. He had sworn implacable vengeance against the occupiers and all who collaborated with them. Small of stature, with finely drawn lips, a nervous rictus smile and a facial tattoo illustrating the four aces, he killed without pity – always, according to Vercors legend, downing a glass of undiluted anisette in one gulp to steady his nerves before each execution. René was rumoured, by mid-1944, to have executed more than fifty targets, chiefly collaborators of one sort or another, though this figure is certainly a gross exaggeration.

During the winter of 1943/4, Le Ray and Chavant did their best, with varying degrees of success, to bring these independent groups under central control. Chavant in particular was strongly opposed to summary executions and insisted, especially latterly, that the death penalty for traitors should be carried out only after due process – even though this was, initially at least, of a fairly rudimentary sort.

By this time, the social base of the local Resistance movement had widened. The Vercors women, involved right from the start in the first Resistance structures, were now playing a more important role. Alongside the domestic burdens of keeping families together while husbands and sons were in the forests and delivering bread, pails of milk or bags of pâté and cheeses to groups of desperate, hungry young men, the women of the Vercors also carried heavy loads when it came to more direct engagement in the active work of the Resistance. Some like Paulette Jacquier led a Maquis group in their own right. Others such as Charlotte Mayaud and Geneviève Blum-Gayet were closely involved from the start in the second Combat Committee which had been established in June. Gaby Lacarrière and Jacqueline Gröll from Sassenage, still in their teens, acted as spies and couriers, carrying out numerous sorties by bicycle through the checkpoints and into Grenoble on missions to gather information or carry vital packages and messages both to and from the plateau. Léa Blain, a young girl from the village of Chatte west of the Vercors Massif, came to the plateau to help with the coding and decoding of secret telegrams for London and subsequently paid for it with her life. As did Rose Jarrand, the schoolmistress at the little village of Les Chabottes close to Saint-Agnan on the plateau, whose classrooms were used for a period as an arms depot.

Pierrette Fave later wrote to her new husband Robert, who was already in the Resistance, explaining why she wanted to join him: 'The circumstances demanded that we young should be active, not passive … For some, I was just a young girl who ran off. But I was utterly committed – I wanted to join the Resistance as you had done. At 20 you want to change the world. Or at least you want to try. I regret none of it, but it was hard.' Pierrette Fave was not alone in rejecting passivity in favour of action.

Many local priests felt the same. The Catholic Church within France had initially responded to the Franco-German Armistice by recognizing the legitimacy of the Vichy government and declaring that armed resistance was a mortal sin. At the introduction of the STO the Church hierarchy, fearing civil war, ordered obedience to Laval's order and advised those called up to follow instructions and leave for Germany. The long-serving Bishop of Grenoble, Alexandre Caillot, known as the 'most Pétainist Bishop in France', retained this view till the end of the war. There was also at least one churchman suspected of passing information to the Germans.

But these 'collaborators' were the exception. By early 1944, the majority of ordinary priests adopted an increasingly militant, pro-Resistance stance. Some were leaders of Maquis groups – Abbé Pierre led one in the Vercors on the Sornin plateau – while many others served as ordinary footsoldiers. The beautiful twelfth-century abbey and convent at Léoncel, below the south-western edge of the plateau, was used by the wireless operators of at least two clandestine radios in direct communication with London. As one Vercors combatant, no lover of the Church and its ways, put it: 'The Vercors priests were a rugged breed, and not at all like the soft idiots in the Bishop's palace. They were deeply integrated into their villages and communities, where the leadership of the priest was much respected. Throughout the long period of suffering and pain of the occupation they never hesitated to show their commitment by publicly castigating from their pulpits, both the Nazis and the French who served them.' A British officer in the Vercors described one of the local priests bending down to pray over the body of a dead Maquisard, causing his surplice to lift up at the back, revealing 'the leather belt around his cassock, fixed onto which was a Colt 45 automatic pistol and about half a dozen [hand] grenades'.

Resistance sympathizers also included some who were supposed to be active servants of the Vichy state. Many town Gendarmeries were especially prone to turning a blind eye to Resistance activity – in some cases even participating themselves. By the end of the summer of 1943 most ordinary members of local communities were at least passively sympathetic to the Resistance, though, as we shall see, this may have had less to do with genuine commitment and more to do with the fact that there were almost no penalties attached to supporting or even assisting the Resistance. The Italian occupying forces did not, in the main, indulge in sanctions or reprisals against the civilian population. This was, however, about to change.

PRESSURE AND PARACHUTES

The Allies invaded Italy proper on 3 September 1943. Corsica rose the following day, thanks largely to the Communists but aided by the British. Peeved at being bypassed in the first French liberation victory, de Gaulle later commented sourly, 'British intelligence, which ordinarily did not go out of their way to be generous without ulterior motive, procured ten thousand machine guns [for the Communists].' Five days later, on 8 September, Marshal Badoglio (Mussolini had already been deposed on 25 July) signed an armistice between the Italian government and the Allies in Cassibile in Sicily.

The German response to the Italian surrender was pre-planned, swift and bloody. Since 15 July, ten days before the fall of Mussolini, French agents in the Savoie had reported to London that heavy German troop concentrations were seen moving south towards Grenoble. On 6 August, a German infantry division, redeployed from Brittany, was reported transiting the city, heading for the Italian border. On 30 August, the German 157th Reserve Division under the command of the fifty-two-year-old Generalleutnant Karl Ludwig Pflaum established its head-quarters in the city.

Within hours of the Italian surrender, German troops occupied Grenoble, forcibly ejecting the Italians from their barracks. There were running battles between Italian and German troops on the streets of the city and a 'massacre' of Italian officers at the Hôtel les Trois Dauphins in Place Grenette. Some Italian soldiers immediately joined the Resistance, but most fled for home. Desperate Italian troops were seen passing through the Trièves area heading for the Italian border 70 kilometres away.

With Grenoble under German control, it was not long before the Gestapo arrived in the city. Their headquarters were established in the Hôtel Moderne, while another building, 28 Cours Berriat, was converted into an interrogation centre. This address was soon to become infamous in the city as a place of torture. The Gestapo rapidly found their hands full, not because of the Vercors, but because of what was happening outside their own front door. On a bright afternoon in October Paul Gariboldy emptied a whole magazine from the window of a speeding car at the Milice headquarters in the Hôtel de l'Angleterre less than a kilometre from Gestapo headquarters, shouting, 'Get out. France is free,' as his vehicle sped away to the sound of tinkling glass and the echoes of gunfire reverberating from the nearby buildings. On 6 October, a jumpy German sentry shot dead a local engineer who was fumbling in his pocket for his house key. By now, tension was rising dangerously in the city. On 11 November, the anniversary of the signing of the 1918 Armistice, the call went out from Resistance circles for a strong show of defiance to 'raise our voices once more against the [German] oppression'.

At 10.00 on 11 November, more than 1,500 people turned out 'as if from a signal' and marched towards the Diables Bleus monument to the French Chasseurs Alpins to celebrate France's First World War victory over the Germans. The demonstrators were stopped by a massive show of force by the Vichy police, who herded them back to the city centre where they found themselves blocked by a troop of Germans with machine guns. Caught in a sandwich between the police behind and the machine guns in front, they were embroiled in a tense stand-off. The German officer's orders in these circumstances were to open fire, but the police intervened and, arresting many, dispersed the crowd. More than 600 protesters were subsequently tried and deported; 120 of them were never seen again.

Worse was to follow. Two days after the demonstrations at Les Diables Bleus, on the night of 13/14 November, Aimé Requet managed, single-handedly, to blow up 150 tonnes of ammunition at the old French artillery depot, the Polygone de l'Artillerie. The blast could be heard more than 50 kilometres away. German reaction was instantaneous and ferocious. On 15 November, reinforced by a troop of Miliciens drafted in from Lyon, they launched what has subsequently become known as the Grenoble St Bartholomew's Day massacre. It started with information given to the Gestapo by a French couple and was, as before, greatly assisted by the Resistance habit of keeping centralized records. By the time the massacre ended after some two 'weeks of blood', the Gestapo, assisted by the Milice, had cut a swathe through the Grenoble Resistance organization with arrests, deportations, summary executions and assassinations.

Denise Domenach-Lallich, who was nineteen in 1943, noted the new atmosphere of repression and fear in Lyon, writing in her diary in October: 'the curfew sounds at ten o'clock in the evening and no one gives us passes because of the reprisal troops, Mongol-types who shoot anything that moves … One grows quickly in the moment when one doesn't die … several of my friends have been caught and shot three days later.'

Paradoxically, with the Germans so busy in Grenoble and Lyon, these were relatively quiet weeks on the Vercors. On 11 October, the Gestapo arrested a Maquis leader in Saint-Jean-en-Royans. There was also a German raid on a camp on the south-western edge of the plateau, looking for a radio set which their *gonio* detection vans had identified in the area. (*Gonio* was an abbreviation of *voitures de radiogonio*.) But the camp's inhabitants were able to disperse into the forests quickly enough to avoid capture; 'we went three days with nothing to eat but artichokes which we found in a shepherd's garden', one complained afterwards, '… before finally ending up at the Grande Cabane [a mountain refuge] below the Grand Veymont'.

Although the Germans had so far mostly left the plateau alone, events in Grenoble caused some nervousness in the camps. The diary of Lieutenant Louis Rose in the Forêt de Thivolet records a number of false alerts in October, including an excitable sentry who called the unit to arms at 04.00 because he feared they were about to be attacked by what turned out to be a troop of badgers foraging in the woods.

And then, on 13 November 1943, just one day after the full moon and the same night that Aimé Requet blew up the ammunition store at the Polygone de l'Artillerie in Grenoble, the plateau received its first major parachute drop at Darbonouse, the isolated Alpine pasture on the eastern side of the plateau which had been the site of the Resistance gathering of 10/11 August. The arming of the Vercors had begun.

In fact there is good evidence that the original plan had been to begin this process a month earlier, during the moon period in October 1943. The logbook for one of the Tempsford RAF squadrons shows that on the night of 16/17 October a Halifax bomber took off from the airfield on a mission to parachute containers to a site identified as 'Trainer 96', a codeword which in relation to other missions refers to Vassieux. This supposition is supported by the list of code phrases for parachute drops to be carried out in the October 1943 moon period which were given out in the BBC's nightly broadcast to France on 30 September. This list contains one phrase whose main elements would later become indelibly linked with the Vercors: 'Le chamois bondit' ('The chamois leaps'). Unfortunately, however, if such a drop was planned, it never took place for the pilot's logbook notes that the mission had to be aborted because the 'A/c [aircraft] caught fire'.

In some ways the choice of the Darbonouse for this drop was a strange one, for access to this high pasture is by difficult, barely motorable forest tracks and mountain paths. A drop on the parachute sites previously identified by Dalloz, on the open plain near the village of Vassieux or in the wide valleys around Saint-Martin and Villard, would have been much easier for all. It may be, however, that the October German activity in the south-west of the plateau and in Grenoble made it wiser to choose somewhere further away from habitation and main roads.

André Valot, at the time the second-in-command at the Ferme d'Ambel, recalled this momentous drop on 13 November: 'It was a Sunday. Louis Bourdeaux and I were sitting ... in the dining room after dinner smoking and listening somewhat distractedly to the "Messages personnels" section [of the BBC] broadcast ... Suddenly I was transfixed. I felt myself go pale and the shock caused Bourdeaux to drop his cigarette. Had we not just heard our codeword "Nous avons visité Marrakech" ["We visited Marrakesh"]? Disbelieving, we listened again; the voice said it again – more insistently this time. The message we had been waiting for! The aircraft we had been longing for were at last coming! They were coming just as promised ... Now the voice was gone and they were playing some recorded music. We looked at each other, our eyes filled with tears, our spirits full of disbelieving laughter. We hugged each other. At last our hopes had been fulfilled; our resolution rewarded; our confidence confirmed. "Shall we go?" I said. "You bet," Louis replied. "I will telephone to make the arrangements."'

Valot and Bourdeaux quickly gathered their men and set off in trucks for the Darbonouse pasture. They were not alone. The entire plateau had either heard the BBC broadcast or heard of it and knew what it meant. As Valot's *gazogène* trucks wheezed up the steep tracks leading to the eastern plateau, threading their way through the forest, it seemed as if half the Vercors were there as well. Young men from other camps marching along, singing patriotic songs, groups of peasants driving pack mules, old carts drawn by oxen and, of course, more ubiquitous *gazogène* trucks, all making their way to the drop site – all intent on carrying away at least a share of the booty which the distant BBC voice had promised would fall from the sky that very night.

It was 22.00 by the time Valot and his team reached the shepherd's hut at Darbonouse. Here they joined a small crowd who had already arrived from other camps, milling around an assortment of trucks, carts and motorcycles. Around them a recent fall of snow had gathered in drifts at the edges of the forest and in the pasture's shallow undulations. And in the distance the great mass of the Grand Veymont looked down, its summit capped with snow, sparkling in the moonlight.

Eugène Samuel and Roland Costa de Beauregard had already taken charge of the drop site. Three-man sentry posts, each with a machine gun, had been placed on all the points of access and bonfires were already being prepared. There was plenty of time. H-hour – when the aircraft would arrive – was not until an hour after midnight. Valot described the scene:

By midnight, all was ready and there was nothing to do but wait …

… The moon slowly slipped towards the horizon threatening to leave us alone under a silent and empty sky.

And then suddenly, borne on the wind, there was a sound like a far-off whispering. Almost nothing. No more than the rustle leaves make in a breeze. But quickly it became more constant, heavier somehow and with a kind of strong underlying beat. Soon we could tell where it came from – the north-west. It was them – it was undoubtedly them!

We stood in the middle of the site and the Commander pulled out a large electric torch. Pointing it in the direction of the noise, he started to flash a series of dots and dashes in Morse code. Suddenly – there! – up there! A new star suddenly appeared and flashed back the same sequence at us! They had seen us …

'Light the fires!'

Immediately a lance of flame, fanned almost flat by the wind, leapt out of the darkness near by. Then another and another and another until a vast letter T was picked out in flames around us – four bonfires long and three across. Above us we heard the still invisible aircraft turning as though enclosing us in a wide circle of noise, holding us in an embrace of friendship. We suddenly felt – wonderfully – that we were not alone.

And then the miracle happened. One of the aircraft burst out of the darkness above us following the line of the long stroke of the T. And suddenly, beneath it, a great white flower blossomed against the darkness of the sky. It did not appear to us as something falling, but rather as something sprouting out of nothing – as though it was the product of magic conjured into existence by the black shape above and by the noise it made. And then there was another and another and another. The wind made them all dance as though in some fantastical aerial ballet. The spectacle was one of utterly intoxicating, utterly astonishing beauty. Now we could see the round circles of the parachutes jostling each other for position. Below each one swung a long black, cylindrical shape. At first we thought they were men. Then a dull heavy thud, then two, then three, then four, five, six, ten, twenty, thirty, repeated and repeated and repeated. The white flowers now lay deflated, exhausted, dead and lifeless on the ground around us. The miraculous cargo had arrived.

Everyone, even the sentries rushed to the landing ground – if an enemy had attacked us then we would all have been caught like rats in a feeding frenzy …

We rushed to the dark forms lying inert in the grass … and began to unpack our treasures. They were contained in long aluminium tubes shaped like torpedoes: rifles, stripped-down machine guns, wicker baskets covered in cloth containing bandages and surgical instruments. Here were heavy iron boxes containing ammunition and explosives and there were bundles of clothing and waterproof covers and woollen wear. No presents could have been more welcome … thank you, Father Christmas!

[In the end, however], the arms, the explosives, the equipment – though all were magnificent, our nocturnal visitors brought us an even more special gift. They brought us back our confidence, our enthusiasm and, with these, the sure knowledge that we were not, after all isolated, abandoned and alone.

What may be guessed at from Valot's lyrical account, but is not explicitly stated, is that the results of the Darbonouse parachute drop were less than optimal. The high wind distributed the parachutes and containers over a very large area and some were not found until years later hanging in the branches of fir trees or lying in the bottom of small depressions where they had plunged into deep snowdrifts. The contents of those that were found were enthusiastically pillaged, resulting in some groups having arms without ammunition, some ammunition without arms, some boxes of grenades, others the detonators, some surgical instruments which they didn't know how to use and more woollen socks than they could ever possibly wear. There would, in due course, be a price to pay for all this undisciplined brigandage.

Much of what could be recovered in an organized fashion was stored in a nearby cave, the Grotte de l'Ours, and distributed later. The Maquis unit which had established itself at Malleval on the east of the plateau went to collect its share ten days after the drop and came back with an entire lorry full of arms and ammunition, storing it in the village presbytery.

Two days after the Darbonouse parachute drop, on 15 November, Francis Cammaerts was recalled to London, where he explained in detail his plans to hold the Valensole, the Beaurepaire and the Vercors plateaux as bridgeheads for paratroops in the event of a landing in the south of France. It was a message which would have been welcome in the British capital for, at the Quebec Conference in August 1943, Churchill and Roosevelt had decided that 'Operations against southern France (to include the use of trained and equipped French forces) should be undertaken to establish a lodgement in the Toulon and Marseille area to exploit northward in order to create a diversion in connection with Overlord. Air-nourished guerrilla operations in the southern Alps will, if possible, be initiated.' Planning for the invasion of the Mediterranean coast of France began immediately under the codename Anvil. In a September minute to the Allied Supreme Commander General Dwight Eisenhower, it was proposed that Anvil should be a diversionary operation to be carried out simultaneously with Operation Overlord, the D-Day landings. Its primary aim was not to capture territory but to draw German troops south, away from the Normandy beaches.

The Vercors may have lost its direct line to the highest level of the Free French command in London, but events elsewhere were conspiring to give it a potentially important role to play in the much bigger game which the Supreme Allied Command was now planning – the invasion of the European mainland.

On the Vercors, however, the autumn of 1943 brought the Resistance more to worry about than the distant plans of the mighty. On 24 November, three German *gonio* radio-detector vehicles were seen in La Chapelle. It seemed that they found nothing, for they were reported at the end of the day returning home over the Col de Rousset 'empty handed'. The plateau breathed a sigh of relief. But it was premature.

The following day, the Gestapo descended on Saint-Martin in force and, seeming to know exactly what they were looking for, headed straight for a large farmhouse complex, Les Berthonnets, a kilometre or so east of the village. This housed two clandestine radios and their operators, Gaston Vincent and Pierre Bouquet, working to the Algiers office of the American equivalent of the SOE, the Office of Strategic Services (OSS). Warned just in time, the two men fled, Vincent carrying his heavy radio set. After a short chase, a German soldier who got within range of the weighed-down Vincent shot and wounded him. Helped by the owner of Les Berthonnets, Vincent hid in a pile of hay in a barn. Here he was subsequently found by a German search party, covered in blood. Presuming him to be dead, they left him alone.

Bouquet, however, was caught and held, but then – surprisingly – released by the Gestapo. He re-established contact with the Resistance but was placed under discreet observation. His former colleagues concluded that he had been 'turned' while in captivity. His body was found on 23 December, riddled with bullets as a result of an assassination that had all the hallmarks of a Resistance execution.

Though this raid was small in comparison with later incursions, it indicated the Germans' determination to ensure that the Vercors did not harbour activities against their interests. And it demonstrated their ability to invade the plateau and leave it again, whenever they chose to do so. The Vercors Resistants may have viewed the plateau as a safe area, but the Germans certainly did not.

The damage done by the Gestapo's 25 November raid was minor, however, compared with that done not much more than a week later by the French regional military commanders.

In the early autumn Marcel Descour – accompanied by his ever-present counsellor/monk Dom Guétet – took up a new post as the Military Chief of Staff for Region 1 of the Secret Army, within which the Vercors fell. He was therefore, in effect, Alain Le Ray's direct military commander. Descour's job was to unify the disparate elements of the Resistance in his region under an effective military command. Criticisms of the Vercors Maquisards for their lax ways had already reached him and he may have taken their independence of spirit as a challenge to his authority. He may also have been irked by the fact that, while he was trying to unify fighting structures under military control, in the Vercors it was a civilian in the form of *Patron* Chavant who was formally in charge, and Le Ray seemed content with this.

Whether there is substance in this or not, the question of the Vercors and Le Ray as its military chief came to a head at a meeting called by Descour and attended by all the military commanders in the Lyon area in early December. Not long into the meeting, Descour himself started openly criticizing Le Ray for 'feudalism' and especially for the mishandling of the parachute drop at Darbonouse. Le Ray described what followed as an 'Inquisition based on the unproven suspicions of the unidentified'. Finally unable to control himself, he exploded: 'Well, if it's my resignation you want, you have it.'

Descour returned fire with fire: 'Resignation accepted!'

Both men were later to say that they regretted their hotheadedness – though Le Ray regarded an eventual rupture as inevitable. 'The Vercors was seen as a trump card in the whole French Resistance organization. The authorities wanted to put someone there who they could be sure would be their man.'

However, even if both men had wanted to pull the moment back, they couldn't. The die had been cast, the damage done. The Vercors had lost its most able commander and the only one who understood that guerrilla warfare was about constant mobility and the closest possible military/civilian integration, not fixed defences and conventional military control. Some believe that many of the tragedies which would ensue would not have happened if these few testosterone-fuelled seconds could have been avoided. Chavant was furious when he heard and wanted to disband the whole Vercors structure immediately. But Le Ray, who had been instructed to leave his post at the end of the following January, persuaded him not to, saying that no purpose could be served by adding revenge to rancour.

Everyone presumed that, after the 'resignation' of Le Ray, his deputy, the much liked and admired Roland Costa de Beauregard, would take his place. But Descour, true to Le Ray's prediction that the Army wanted a man who would take the Army line, chose Narcisse Geyer, who was at the time still in the nearby Thivolet forest. Geyer, acknowledged by all to be a man of great courage, initiative and élan, had many qualities. Among them, however, were not tact, diplomacy, sensitivity or any kind of understanding of the role of the civilians in the struggle. Diminutive, right wing and haughty in his demeanour, Geyer was mostly to be seen in full uniform, complete with kepi and soft white cavalry gauntlets, riding around the plateau on his magnificent stallion Boucaro: Descour could hardly have chosen a person less likely to appeal to Eugène Chavant and his Socialist colleagues. It did not help that Geyer himself made it plain to all that he intended to marginalize the Combat Committee and place the plateau under overall military control.

The first meeting between Geyer and Chavant at a saw-mill near Saint-Julien-en-Vercors in the weeks before Christmas went as badly as might have been predicted. Chavant took an instant and intense dislike to his haughty new military partner, refusing to permit him to have any contact with the camps or give training to the Maquisards. Geyer reciprocated by making plain his distaste at having to discuss military matters with a civilian. This deep schism was widened by the different strategies followed by the Maquis fighters on the one hand and the professional military on the other. The military pursued a 'wait and see' policy whose aim was to avoid drawing German attention to themselves in order to gain the time and space to build up their units and train their men for the 'big moment' (D-Day) – when they could come out into the open and play a major part in the liberation of their country. The Maquisard leaders, however, pursued an activist policy which concentrated on small raids and sabotage designed to harry the Germans, make them feel insecure and deny them freedom of movement. This policy had the double advantage of hardening and professionalizing their guerrilla forces through action, while at the same time encouraging other young men to the cause.

The difference between these two approaches became evident in December 1943 when there was a sudden and sharp increase in the raids carried out from the Vercors plateau and the area around it. On the night of 1/2 December there was an attack on high-tension electricity lines near Bourg-de-Péage. At 08.20 the following day, an explosion rocked the Borne Barracks in Grenoble, killing twenty-three German and Italian soldiers and wounding 150 French civilians. In reprisal, the Germans shot thirteen hostages. On 10 December, railway locomotives were sabotaged at Portes-lès-Valence and, the following day, the Merlin-Gerin engineering works in Grenoble were attacked, causing an estimated 30 million francs' worth of damage. On 15 December the Maquis group in the Malleval valley in the north-west corner of the plateau sabotaged the Valence-to-Grenoble railway. On the 20th, the Mayor of Vilnay was assassinated for collaboration and, two days later, another train was sabotaged at Vercheny. On 27 December, in what it is tempting to think of as an attempt to make the old year go out with a bang, there were raids and reprisals at Vercheny, Sainte-Croix, Pontaix and Barsac.

This increased level of sabotage and raids seems not to have been set back by the early and ferocious arrival of 'General Winter'* on the plateau. On 6 November, unseasonably early, the first heavy snow fell on the Vercors. Two weeks later, there was an even covering of 30 centimetres of fresh snow, right down to the mid-levels of the plateau. By Christmas, the snow was a metre deep at the Ferme d'Ambel.

This was the first winter which most of the young *réfractaires* had spent away from home and they found it very hard. Even the simplest chores required super-human effort. Almost worse than the cold was the sheer unrelieved, bone-numbing boredom, with nothing to do but get on each other's nerves as the snow swirled outside their mountain refuges, while the days shortened and the nights, lit only by a single oil lamp, lengthened interminably. Morale plummeted and young men started slipping away for the comforts of their homes in the valleys. Of more than 400 *réfractaires* estimated to be in the camps in September, only 210 of the hardiest were left by Christmas. The camps at C8 and C11 fused together and descended to take refuge in the old, now deserted eleventh-century monastery of Our Lady of Esparron under the eastern ramparts of the plateau. Christmas, when it came, was celebrated by the young men in their mountain refuges and forest huts as best they could, given their conditions and heterogeneous beliefs. In Camp C3 above

---

* The phrase is a Russian one which is used to account for the fact that so many winter invasions of the country have failed. Russians also refer to 'General Snow' and 'General Mud'.

Méaudre, Christians gave readings from the Bible, the Jews from the Torah and the Communists from the texts of Karl Marx.

As early as October the camp at C2 had been abandoned when its inhabitants descended from the plateau to winter quarters in empty houses in the village of Malleval, nestling in a steep little bowl to which the only easy access was through the narrow gorge at Cognin, off the north-western quadrant of the plateau. Here the Maquisards under the leadership of Pierre Godart had an excellent relationship with all the local villagers, who despite the wartime restrictions still managed to organize a sumptuous Christmas for their young visitors. Godart sent one of his most devout men to Grenoble to ask the Bishop if he could provide a priest to take Christmas mass for the Maquisards in the little village church. But the answer was an abrupt no – 'those who put themselves outside the law, are also outside the law of God', as one later observer summed up the great churchman's response. Eventually, however a priest was found to take confession and mass. On Christmas Eve, a French traditional *réveillon de Noël** began.

The little Malleval church was first decked out in full winter finery. Then, soon after dark, processions of torches started to wind their way down the tracks leading from the outlying farms where each Maquis section of sixteen was housed. Soon their voices could be heard carrying across the valley and the little dots of men's figures could be picked out against the whiteness of the snow. In due course, each column arrived and filed into the church, Christian and Jew and Communist and atheist alike. 'It seemed as if all the world was there, in the little white church lit by carbide lamps which cast a flickering glow, making the shadows dance and shooting their beams into even the darkest corners. The old people sat quietly, their walking sticks between their knees, as others squeezed up to make room for the new arrivals. Even the women joined us, including the mothers, wives and some fiancées of the Maquisards, giving our little ceremony some of the sweetness of home.'

Then the feasting began: 'The menu would have dignified a prince … the food seemed to have come from every corner of the land. The baker at Cognin brought breads and cakes. A veal calf had been carried down from Rencurel and all the fish and fowl of the area seemed to have been gathered together in our church, especially to grace our Christmas.

* Festivities at Christmas.

There were even two cases of champagne freshly arrived from Reims. The feasting went on all the night. Songs were sung; an accordion was brought out – then more songs and more songs until finally the dawn burst in among us. On this night, for us, the men of the Maquis, life was wonderful.'

Surely, next year – 1944 – the Allies would land and France would be free again. And then life would be wonderful every year.

10

THE LABOURS OF HERCULES

As the men of the Malleval Maquis were celebrating the Christmas season waist deep in snow, Winston Churchill, dressed in his famous silk dressing gown emblazoned with a red dragon, was lying in bed in an airy room in General Eisenhower's villa in Carthage (prophetically called La Maison Blanche), recovering from pneumonia and a heart attack. Denied his customary cigar and restrained in his consumption of alcohol, he was tetchy and fulminating against 'the scandalous … stagnation' of the Italian campaign.

It is tempting to believe that his complaints about the slow progress in Italy might have been a displacement activity for the much bigger personal setback he had just suffered at the hands of his 'friend' President Roosevelt at the Tehran Tripartite Conference which had just ended. At Tehran, the American President had blindsided Churchill by teaming up with Stalin to defeat one of the Prime Minister's most ardent and long-favoured schemes, the invasion of what he called the 'soft underbelly of Europe' on a line which began on the Pisa–Rimini axis in Italy and ran through the Balkans to the oilfields of Rumania. Churchill had invested hugely in arms, supplies and support for Tito's Yugoslav guerrillas as a preparation for this assault, which was now, thanks to the US/Russian alliance, to be abandoned in favour of a simultaneous double invasion of France, one from the north across the Channel (Overlord) and the second from the south across the Mediterranean from Algiers (Anvil). It was easy to see why the Soviets were opposed to Churchill's Balkan plans – they saw this area as their sphere of post-war influence and did not want the British anywhere near it. Roosevelt's reasons were less understandable. He mistakenly believed he could establish a post-war strategic alliance with Stalin and needed Soviet support for what he saw as the cornerstone of this new relationship, the establishment of the United Nations. Churchill was left hurt and fuming at this first stark evidence of

Britain's coming weakness between the two superpowers in the post-war world. 'There I sat with the great Russian bear on one side of me, with paws outstretched, and on the other side the great American buffalo and, between the two, the poor little English donkey who was the only one ... who knew the right way home.'

The decisions of Tehran had now shifted the entire axis of the Allied European war effort from the south and the east (Italy and the Balkans), where Churchill had made his greatest investment, to the north and the west (the Russian front and Overlord). Despite these crushing disappointments, the British Prime Minister was not a man to mope for long. If the overall strategy had changed, his must too. Now France, a country he knew well and loved deeply, was to be the main stage, not the Balkans. Within days of leaving his sickbed he was meeting members of the French Resistance in North Africa and planning how Britain, which had so far largely ignored French partisans in favour of those of Yugoslavia and Italy when supplying arms, could help foster the growth of the Resistance movement.

It is often said that Churchill was a dewy-eyed romantic when it came to partisans. He was. But his attachment to the fostering of internal resistance had a hard-edged military rationale, too; it was a way to keep occupied countries in a ferment of opposition against the Germans and to prevent them from relapsing into apathetic torpor, as France had done after the Armistice; it was also a means by which the 'skill, dash and courage' of British agents behind enemy lines could influence the outcome of events in ways which compensated for the relatively meagre matériel resources the country was able to commit at this stage of the war, compared with those of the US and Russian colossi. There were also those in Whitehall (perhaps even including Churchill himself) who thought that, in terms of blood and loss, France's sacrifice during the war had so far been small. So it was no great thing to ask her now to risk a greater price for her own liberation.

Churchill had always admired de Gaulle, even if he did not like him. But up to now the French General had been just another leader-in-exile of a conquered European country and these were two to the penny in the London of 1941–3 – though, as Foreign SecretaryAnthony Eden ruefully admitted, de Gaulle stood out from the crowd because he caused 'us [the British government] more difficulties than all our other European allies put together'. Now, however, with France the main stage for the next phase of the war in the West, de Gaulle, the territory of France and the capabilities of the French Resistance took on new strategic importance.

De Gaulle himself had started 1943 with few assets and even fewer friends. Disliked by Roosevelt, disregarded by the British war leadership and personally irksome to Churchill, he had almost nothing going for him – and very little he could call his own in France or among the Free French either. Like the Pope, of whom Stalin famously asked 'How many Divisions does he have?', de Gaulle may have been the spiritual embodiment of the French Resistance, but of actual 'Divisions' he had few.

De Gaulle might have expected that Operation Torch, the Allied invasion of North Africa and the liberation of the French colony of Algeria (where Eisenhower had now set up his headquarters), would have strengthened his position as the French leader with whom the Allies had to deal. In fact the opposite happened.

The Americans chose instead Henri Giraud, a French general who had been captured at the fall of France, been imprisoned in Königstein Castle, escaped under curious circumstances and made his way to Toulon where an Allied submarine had picked him up and delivered him to Gibraltar. He arrived on the Rock only a few hours before the start of Operation Torch. Eisenhower promptly asked him to assume command of all French troops in North Africa. Giraud at first refused because he was not commanding the whole Allied operation, but eventually relented. When he left Gibraltar for Algiers on 9 November 1942, Giraud remarked, 'You may have seen something of the large De Gaullist demonstration that was held here last Sunday. Some of the demonstrators sang the Marseillaise. I entirely approve of that! Others sang the Chant du Départ [a military ballad]. Quite satisfactory! Others again shouted "Vive de Gaulle!" No objection. But some of them cried "Death to Giraud!" I don't approve of that at all.'

Giraud knew perfectly well that de Gaulle was his deadly rival for the leadership of the free and the fighting French. But he also knew who was in the dominant position – he was, and by far. With the personal support of Roosevelt and the practical support of Eisenhower, he was in the place that mattered most – Algiers – and he commanded not only more French troops but also the only formed French units at that time fighting alongside their Allied comrades.

Giraud's support inside France was less certain. But then so was de Gaulle's. At the beginning of 1943, the Resistance was quarrelsome, fragmentary, diverse and riven by political rivalry. There were Gaullists to be sure. But also Giraudists. And many whose loyalties were to neither of the above, but to the Communists, the Socialists and even (still) to the Pétainists. The Secret Army was by comparison more Gaullist, but by no means uniformly so. Meanwhile, as de Gaulle understood very well, when it came to the actual government of France the relative position of the potential French leaders was going to be irrelevant, because the American President was planning to impose an Allied Military Government in Occupied Territories – known as an AMGOT. France would be governed for a period at least, as Italy had been, by foreigners. That was Roosevelt's plan. That was what Giraud was acquiescing in. He, de Gaulle, would not.

But, at the start of 1943, de Gaulle's chances of fulfilling his aim of being the leader who took his country back to freedom, self-government and eventually great-power status seemed ambitious to say the least. To succeed, he had to make himself the unchallenged leader of the free and fighting French inside and outside France. That meant going head to head with the most powerful man in the world, President Roosevelt, and wresting power from his favourite, Giraud. Then he had to make himself and his supporters so indispensable to the liberation of France that a French government would follow, not a government of transition drawn up in Roosevelt's back office. And he had to achieve this with limited influence and only few assets to his name. These were the labours of Hercules indeed. But, remarkably, by the end of 1943, de Gaulle had accomplished all of them.

On 30 May 1943, de Gaulle arrived in Algiers, having finally negotiated terms for a partnership with Giraud. Five days after his arrival, on 4 June, de Gaulle took to the airwaves on Radio Algiers: 'Everything is now in play – our army and our navy are playing a key part in a drama of indescribable importance. Our sacred duty is to show again what great things can be accomplished by the arms of France.' Not since Lenin had been smuggled into Russia in a sealed train had such an insertion of poison been accomplished with such devastating consequences into the body politic of the ruling (in this case Giraudist) establishment. In a series of moves of cunning and ruthlessness, de Gaulle progressively sidelined and then summarily removed Giraud, leaving himself in sole charge. It would take until the D-Day landings of June 1944 for Roosevelt to come to terms with this reality, but there was little he could do. Giraud was the past. De Gaulle was now the future.

De Gaulle's success in gaining control of the power structures in Algiers was replicated inside France. Francis Cammaerts, who had a ringside seat in the key months, saw the shift of opinion and remarked on its speed. 'In March 1943, still, Gaullism was not necessarily the only salvation. By August 1943 it was. No one in the Resistance in France thought that there was any solution to the French future except through de Gaulle ...' This represented an astonishing success for the General for it gave him the means, not just to unseat Giraud, but to play a direct role alongside the Allies in his country's liberation. No government in France could now be formed without de Gaulle's consent and active participation. In short, if de Gaulle could build up the political effect of the Resistance and make it a potent military force, then Roosevelt's plan for a transitional government in France would be a dead letter.

Such a project, however, was not without its complications. On the one hand, the Resistance gave de Gaulle legitimacy, but, as one sharp-eyed commentator put it after the war, de Gaulle 'had to navigate between two contradictory pitfalls: on the one hand to convince the Allies of the necessity to support the armed struggle as a means of reinforcing the legitimacy of Gaullism; and on the other to control and channel the internal struggle in France in such a way as ... more effectively to integrate its activities into the plans of the Allies and, above all, prevent, within the metropolitan Resistance, the emergence of "counter-forces" capable of contesting [de Gaulle's] capacity to govern the country after the Liberation'.

De Gaulle's second problem was that the French Resistance was held in very low regard by the British and American authorities. Churchill loved France and recognized its claims to great-power status. But he was not averse to making unflattering comparisons between the French Resistance and Tito's Yugoslav partisans, who were tying down some twenty German divisions in bloody guerrilla warfare. Roosevelt, on the other hand, had something close to contempt for France, seeing it as a decadent imperial power which lacked the moral fibre Britain had shown in the early years of the war. On the question of the effectiveness of the 1943 French Resistance (or rather lack of it), the two leaders and their staffs were united: it could not in 1943, and would not in 1944, be able to deliver anything of weight to the coming battle on French soil. It was this opinion that de Gaulle had, by hook or by crook, to change.

Back in March 1943, the British War Cabinet had met to take the first of several decisions establishing the priorities for the supply of arms and equipment to partisan forces in Europe. It put France as third strategic priority behind the Italian-held islands, Corsica and Crete (taken as one) and Yugoslavia. These priorities were personally reconfirmed by Churchill himself in August and November of that year. A Cabinet paper at the end of March put total Resistance strength in France at 175,500. Yugoslavia, with a much smaller population, had partisans, they estimated, numbering 220,000. The paper included an annex showing Resistance strengths as a proportion of what it referred to as 'net male population'. This showed that 30 per cent of 'available' men were in the Resistance in Norway, 6 per cent in Denmark and Poland, whereas in France, no doubt because of its internal divisions, it was just 3 per cent.

An SOE assessment in May and June 1943 pronounced the French Resistance 'at its lowest ebb' and added that its forces 'could not be counted on to be a serious factor unless and until they were rebuilt on a smaller and sounder basis'. The paper ended by warning that this would require a 'total reorganisation and reformation'. London's reaction to the deficiencies in the Resistance organization was to send out tripartite 'missions' made up of representatives of France, Britain and the US with the task of assessing what needed to be done to mend the gaping holes left by Gestapo arrests and to create a new structure of organizational control. One of these missions in October 1943 estimated Resistance strength in the *maquis* of the Rhône-Alpes as 2,300 and described the Vercors camps they had visited as 'modestly equipped and armed, adequately turned out given the very difficult conditions, good morale'.

Having elbowed Giraud out of the way, de Gaulle was now free to take further steps to reform the command and control of the Resistance by setting up Committees of Liberation in all the French departments and naming military delegates for each of the three administrative levels of the country – national, zonal and regional. The General was beginning to assemble a government for France, though it would take long tortuous months before first the British and then, finally and reluctantly, Roosevelt gave formal recognition to this. Over succeeding months this structure was progressively strengthened, in large part prompted by the fact that, by the end of November 1943, it was clear that an invasion of France was being planned and that, citing security as the reason, the British and Americans were going neither to involve, consult nor indeed even inform de Gaulle about what they had in mind.

De Gaulle was predictably furious at the snub. But it also presented him with a real practical problem. If he knew nothing of Allied plans, how could he ensure that the Resistance would be in a position to assist when the great moment came? His answer was to set up a special planning unit in December 1943 to prepare a 'rational plan for the participation of Resistance activity in the eventuality of an Allied landing on French soil', without having the first idea where the landings would be, what form they would take or how they would be exploited. De Gaulle made his position clear in a speech given on 8 October 1943, in liberated Corsica: 'Victory is approaching. It will be the victory of liberty. How could such a victory not be the victory of France as well?'

One of the key staff in the planning unit de Gaulle had set up was an exceptionally able captain of Czech origin, Ferdinand Otto Miksche. On 20 January 1944, Miksche produced a study listing the options before the British and American planners, drawing conclusions about which in the end they would be most likely to choose. It was astonishingly accurate in predicting that one of the most likely landing points was Normandy – a conclusion which would have deeply worried France's allies, who were trying desperately to keep the location of Overlord secret. This study also proposed possible military actions which could be undertaken by the Resistance to assist the invasion, wherever it occurred. These were discussed with the British, who 'showed a great deal of interest and asked for a second ... detailed study of the conditions under which French resistance would help in the landing'.

In Miksche's second study he stressed (somewhat hopefully) that the Resistance 'although not an ensemble of regular military units [should] be looked upon as a regular Army obeying orders from the Allied High Command'. He also identified several territorial zones of France and how the Resistance might be employed as the Allied breakout from the beachhead developed. Among these were areas where 'redoubts of Resistance' would be established 'in districts geographically unsuitable for large scale military operations', such as the Alps (including the Vercors). Miksche's plan continued the drift towards something more ambitious and permanent than Dalloz's original Plan Montagnards (of which at this stage he had no knowledge). 'In these redoubts', he wrote, 'the Maquis would be organized and be in readiness for sabotage and guerrilla operation behind enemy lines ... the creation of *permanent* redoubts [emphasis added] would inevitably expand, even before D-Day, through the arrival of patriots who refused to accept forced labour for the enemy.'

The idea of 'Resistance redoubts' (*réduits* in French) was not a new one. On 13 November 1943, a secret meeting in Switzerland between British SOE representatives and a gathering of Resistance and Secret Army leaders (who were also unaware of the existence of Plan Montagnards) concluded with a recommendation that the Vercors (among other possible 'redoubt' areas) should be held 'as a fortress from which raids could be made' on German lines of communication. Two weeks later, on 29 November 1943, an experienced French agent, in London at the time, wrote a paper picking up on the fortress idea and proposing the establishment of 'geographic fortresses' manned by 'trained, disciplined, adequately armed and properly led forces' in places like the Vercors. The aim was 'to place at the disposition of the Allied High Command, forces under their direct control which could offer operational possibilities comparable with parachute troops dropped in advance. These should be kept hidden until after, or exceptionally a little before, D-Day.' Note the key proposition here. The Maquis would not create an area *for* paratroopers, but would instead take on the role *of* paratroopers dropped in advance.

On 31 December 1943, an SOE paper followed up this thinking and proposed that 'small controlled areas' should be created for the delivery of weapons and paratroops after D-Day. These would be established where 'the Maquis [could] occupy ground which can be comparatively easily defended and thus controlled'. This imprecise language left it open for some to believe that the Maquis could defend these controlled areas by themselves. In the fertile soil around this lacuna, muddled thinking, unclear orders and military *folie de grandeur* would take root, flourish and ultimately cost the lives of many hundreds of the young, the inexperienced and the innocent.

Pierre Dalloz arrived in Algiers on 25 November 1943 having completed a long and hazardous crossing of France under the false identity of René Brunet, an even more dangerous one over the snow-bound passes of the Pyrenees and a short stay in Gibraltar. He was horrified that no record of or interest in Plan Montagnards could be found in any quarter. He immediately sat down and reconstructed the plan from memory, dictating it to the personal secretary of one of de Gaulle's most senior advisers (see Annex B). It was to be to no avail. When Dalloz finally arrived in London at the end of January 1944, he was to find that those who should have been aware of his plan were as ignorant of its existence in the British capital as their counterparts had been in the North African one.

The truth was that when it came to deciding the fate of the Vercors, the template now being used was not Dalloz's carefully calibrated Plan Montagnards but something altogether more ambitious. Some among those, British and French, who were directing the Resistance from London were beginning to believe that the young men who had first taken refuge on the Vercors plateau and then been turned into a rough guerrilla fighting force might, in due course and with a little help, be able to take on a face-to-face defensive battle with the gathered might of the German Army.

Between Christmas and New Year – at about the same time that Churchill in his sickbed in Carthage was concluding he had to take the French Resistance more seriously – one of London's 'mission leaders', who had now teamed up with the Maquisards on another of the planned redoubts, the Glières plateau east of Geneva, sent a message to London: 'We consider that the Glières plateau is now an impregnable fortress.'

It would not be long before this boast, and with it the developing concept of the 'defendable redoubt', would be tested.

11

JANUARY 1944

Emmanuel d'Astier de La Vigérie, aristocrat, adventurer, libertine, Socialist, one-time self-proclaimed Communist, eternal optimist, Resistance leader and senior member of de Gaulle's government-in-exile in Algiers, was summoned to attend the British Prime Minister in the Villa Taylor in Marrakesh at 10.00 on 15 January 1944. De Gaulle himself had just flown back to Algiers, having been in Marrakesh for a morning parade of troops, over which he and Churchill had jointly presided as a show of unity between the two men. It may even have been that Churchill had deliberately waited for the General's departure before calling d'Astier to see him.

D'Astier records that when he arrived at the Villa Taylor 'Duff Cooper was there, as was Macmillan just back from Egypt ... Clementine and Mary Churchill were on the terrace together with Diana Cooper, who despite her straw hat and chiffon veil looked like a Rossetti painting. Although it was winter it was as warm as a May day on the Île de France. An ADC came for me and led me through darkened rooms to a modest door which opened to reveal Churchill sitting in a large bed, a cigar clamped between his teeth. The nurse attending him stood up and left; the chamber was as small, sparse and white as a hospital room. Somewhat intimidated I stumbled into my first words in English but was soon at my ease ... He was an accomplished verbal jouster – never quibbling over positions which he knew were untenable ... always knowing when to feint and when to riposte, jumping from word to word, barking with anger from time to time, but chiefly for effect (though it brought the nurse scurrying back in on one occasion to relieve him of his cigar and put it out).'

At the end of two hours, Churchill, dressed in air-force-blue silk pyjamas, finally allowed de La Vigérie to turn the subject to the matter of Britain's miserly approach to arming the French Resistance, about which d'Astier had complained publicly and vociferously. The Frenchman outlined the case for Britain to deliver something more than just warm words which, he claimed, was about all that had been given so far. Churchill appeared to listen and finally conceded, as though offering a great gift, 'OK, we'll give you what you need. I will give the orders myself. Come and see me in London and we will discuss it more.' It was a piece of typical Churchillian gamesmanship, designed to get the maximum out of graciously conceding a position which had in fact been decided upon even before d'Astier entered the room.

On the day before this piece of theatre, an apparently hale and hearty Churchill had chaired a meeting with his Chiefs of Staff Committee of the War Cabinet in the splendid surroundings of Government House in Gibraltar. All his key advisers and naval, military and air force leaders were there. This was the moment when he had to shift British policy to accommodate the demise of his Balkan enthusiasms in favour of a strategy based on a simultaneous pincer movement through France, from the English Channel in the north and the Mediterranean in the south. But Churchill was constitutionally incapable of taking defeat lying down. He had grumpily come to terms with the Overlord landings on the Normandy beaches, but the grand strategist in him still balked at the Anvil landings on France's Mediterranean coast. He would still have preferred to continue the Allies' northern push through Italy ending with a swing west across the Alpine passes into the Savoie, the Isère and the Haute-Savoie.

The War Cabinet minutes record: 'The Prime Minister … was inclined to agree that Overlord should be strengthened and that Anvil should revert to pre-Tehran dimensions' (that is, at most, a possible diversionary attack to draw troops from the north, if needed). Churchill would in fact make several determined attempts to divert Roosevelt and Eisenhower away from Anvil, each more desperate than the last, as the date for the Mediterranean landings approached. For the moment, however, he was content to prepare the ground for a return to his preferred strategy if and when the opportunity arose. The minutes of the War Cabinet meeting that day at Government House in Gibraltar reflect this change of course very clearly. Having spent the last year denying that the French Resistance had any strategic importance (and consequently refusing them priority in the supply of arms), Churchill and his key advisers now agreed that 'A vigorous plan should be worked out to stimulate guerrilla operations in the mountains of the Savoie and in the country between Ventimiglia and the Lake of Geneva.'

The implications of this decision for the Vercors and other possible Alpine redoubts were considerable. First, they would now have first place in the supply of arms they had so far been denied. And secondly, they had become key to whichever southern French strategy the Allies would finally decide on: to both Cammaerts' 'leapfrogging' plan in the case of Anvil, and to Churchill's Alpine passes plan if Anvil was dropped in favour of a push through Italy.

Miksche's study had proposed six possible areas for the establishment of redoubts: the Pyrenees, the Massif Central, the Morvan forest, the Vosges mountains, the Jura and the Alps. But of the options that were now being developed by the Allies (albeit unknown to the French) for the purpose of a southern invasion, only the Alps and the Jura would be relevant. If de Gaulle wanted the Resistance to coordinate its actions in a way which would make them most valuable to the Allies, it was in the Vercors and the other Alpine redoubts that he needed to invest. Unfortunately, he and his advisers had other ideas – ideas which, driven more by political considerations than military ones, would have profound implications for the Vercors.

The next substantive meeting between Churchill and d'Astier was at a conference chaired by Churchill in the Cabinet Room at 10 Downing Street on 27 January. Again, all the British Prime Minister's key advisers were there. First, Churchill played the Yugoslav card: 'I aided Mihailovic – they were brave men. Now I am helping Tito. The more the Germans slaughter his men, the more ferocious they get. That's what I am looking for.' Then he questioned d'Astier about the reliability of the Resistance: 'Can you assure me that you French will not use the weapons we provide to shoot each other? That you will follow strictly the orders of Eisenhower without question or considerations of a political nature?' Finally, he reverted once more to his master card – gracious generosity. 'I have decided', he said at the end of the meeting, with the air of a kindly uncle giving money to an impecunious relative, 'to help the French patriots.'

The minutes of the meeting, normally dry affairs, give a flavour of the event in which the Prime Minister's peculiarly personal cadences can be easily detected: 'The Prime Minster said that he wished and believed it possible to bring about a situation in the whole area between the Lake of Geneva and the Mediterranean comparable to the situation in Yugoslavia.

Brave and desperate men could cause the most acute embarrassment to the enemy and it is right that we should do all in our power to foster and stimulate so valuable an aid to the Allied strategy.' Perhaps more important than these fine words was the conclusion of the meeting, which was that the RAF's first priority – after the bomber offensive on German cities – should now be 'The French Maquis'. Churchill went on to stipulate that, as a start, arms sufficient to equip 8,000 Maquisards should be dropped into the Alpine region during the month of February 1944.

Though the Americans would also, in due course, throw their formidable weight behind the arming of the French Resistance, it was Churchill's decision of 27 January 1944 which began the process which would, in the end, deliver 13,000 tonnes of arms by air to France, sufficient to equip some 425,000 Maquisards. Churchill reinforced the decision he had taken at the meeting with d'Astier by establishing a British committee specifically tasked with coordinating government action to aid the French Resistance. But Eisenhower, rightly spotting an attempt by Churchill at unilateral action in support of his own strategic preferences, insisted that the British committee should be subsumed into his command. And matters did not end there. On 3 March, Eisenhower complained to Churchill that aid to the Resistance in south-east France was being sent at the expense of assistance to the Maquis in the Normandy/Brittany area, where it was needed in support of Overlord, the Allies' agreed first priority. In a typically terse handwritten note, Churchill rejected Eisenhower's request to change the priorities he had set in the meeting with d'Astier on 27 January: 'The Mountain people have had little enough. No alteration in my plans as arranged. WSC 4.3.44.' This was not romance; far less was it charity. It was Churchill keeping his strategic options open in case, as he hoped, Anvil would be abandoned.

But, whatever Churchill's motive, the effects for the Maquis in the Alps and the Jura was dramatic. Thanks to the Prime Minister's personal intervention and the strategic opportunities he saw along the Italian/ French Alpine border, the 'Mountain people' of south-east France had now leapt above those of central Bosnia as Britain's first priority for supply and reinforcement from the air. Probably more than any other place in south-east France, it was the Vercors which would benefit most from this largesse, becoming, over the ensuing months, a huge depot and distribution centre for arms and supplies dropped, not just for the

Vercors but for the Maquis in the neighbouring Belledonne, Chartreuse and Oisans ranges as well.

The first effects of the 1943 decision to encourage 'air-nourished guerrilla operations in the southern Alps' were felt in the Vercors on the night of 5/6 January 1944. In the early hours of 6 January, the Union Mission, together with twelve containers of arms and six packets containing 16.25 million francs, was parachuted to a landing site at Eymeux, under the western edge of the Vercors plateau. The three Union Mission members who parachuted into Eymeux that night were an ex-British schoolmaster turned SOE agent, Henry Thackthwaite, a US Marine called Peter Ortiz and a French radio operator.

The Union Mission's task was to assess the state of the Resistance in the Savoie, Isère and Drôme (especially in relation to the Maquis' needs in terms of weapons and clothing) and their possible deployment after D-Day. Although the Mission members dropped wearing civilian clothes, they brought uniforms with them and wore these for the rest of their visit – the first Allied officers to have been seen in uniform in metropolitan France since the fall in 1940.

The Mission's first visit was to the Ferme d'Ambel. André Valot was there. Though his description suffers from a number of inaccuracies and is characteristically over-coloured, the general impression – and especially in his account of how this event was seen by the Maquisards – is probably fairly accurate: '[One day] a huge yellow limousine arrived … magnificently decorated with three flags flying from its bonnet: the French Tricolour in the centre and the Union Jack and the Stars and Stripes fluttering proudly on either side. Even before the doors were fully open an extraordinary figure leapt out: a gangly red-haired giant with a lanky body, a bony face – sunburnt to the colour of coffee – and the expression of a child with a permanent grin on its face … "Hi, boys," he said, pulling a hip flask out of his back pocket. "You sure are up pretty high here, but great country, yeah! I'm Lieutenant Jean-Pierre [Ortiz carried false identity documents in the name of Jean-Pierre Sellier]. Here have a drink. It's whisky – the real McCoy. It came from the sky last night, like me. I would rather have broken my leg than break this. You bet!"'

Valot's narrative continued: 'In the back of the yellow limousine there was a coffer full of Chesterfield cigarettes and chocolates, whose distribution created an immediate, steadfast and unbreakable affection for the American Army in general and most particularly for its representative, who had so wonderfully fallen to us from the sky the previous night. Every time Ortiz met someone new he pulled out his indestructible hip flask, filled up a small drinking cup which also acted as its metal cap and ordered, "Here have a drink." He was rarely refused, roaring with laughter and slapping the poor unfortunate recipient on the back with a force sufficient to dislocate the collarbones of the unwary.'

The reports submitted to London by Thackthwaite, both by coded signal from France and on his return in May, were comprehensive. He recommended that 'The Vercors plateau offered the best strategic position on which the Maquis could be based. From here they would have the best chance of attacking and hindering the Germans, whether or not the expected invasion of the southern coast of France materialised.' For this reason he especially asked for heavy weapons to be sent to the Vercors – a plea which was to be repeated many times, always in vain.

Thackthwaite made other notable recommendations and observations: 'All sorts of expedients were … used [by the Maquisards] to obtain money, including stocks of tobacco … taken from shops [which] are sold on the black market, and … acts of brigandage … [We] found men in the Maquis barefoot and with one blanket between them … [there was a general] lack of equipment and especially transport … the Maquis surgeons need … surgical knives, scissors, forceps, anaesthetic masks, dissecting scissors, basins, amputating saws, morphine, quinine, permanganate of potassium, syringes, needles and tourniquets … The civilian population are very impatient for D-Day to come … Politically de Gaulle is the only head the people look to … morale is good and improving now the winter is over … The civilian soldiers [Maquis] show a great deal more bite than the ex-officers of the Armistice Army … Maquis lack of confidence in such men is easily understood … many officers … gave us the impression that all serious fighting can be left to the Allies … It might be possible to control places like the Vercors … but the numbers at present are insufficient … [they] would have to be reinforced by parachute troops … 7,000 men are necessary for the Vercors.'

The third week of January 1944 saw a spell of bright, settled and warm, almost spring-like, weather in the Vercors. The roads were suddenly free of snow – unusual in any January, but doubly so in a winter such as this.

Perhaps it was the good weather which, on 17 January, tempted Narcisse Geyer to move his troops from the Forêt de Thivolet off the west of the plateau to Les Combes, a large farmhouse in the woods above Saint-Martin-en-Vercors. He was preparing for his take-over of command from Alain Le Ray at the end of the month. His first action was to conduct a brief inspection of the Maquis camps which made up his new command. Afterwards, he returned to his base full of complaint about what he had seen in the camps: 'It is just not possible to take seriously a war with these people who seem incapable of even the smallest sign of discipline.'

Marcel Descour had also decided that the growing strength of the Vercors meant that he should establish his regional headquarters on the plateau. He chose a large farmhouse, Peyronnet, in the little village of La Matrassière, only 3 kilometres or so from Geyer. On 4 January he sent an advance party of staff and radio operators, one of whom was Pierre Lassalle, to begin preparations. Descour and his counsellor/monk Dom Guétet would follow later. Despite the relatively clement weather and the kindness of the inhabitants of Peyronnet farm, life was tough, especially for the operators working their radios and Morse keys in the farm's barns. 'For fifteen straight days', Pierre Lassalle recounted afterwards, 'my life was divided between brief visits from our hosts and long hours submerged under a mountain of blankets, listening to broadcasts, my headphones permanently clamped on my head and my numb fingers twiddling radio dials.'

Perhaps it was the same good weather that also tempted Herr Bold and Herr Schönfeld, both German officials from Valence, a Dutch journalist, Meneer Koneke, and an interpreter to take a drive through the middle of the Vercors the next day. The tourists requisitioned a car from a Valence garage and instructed the owner to drive them to the Vercors, approaching the heart of the plateau through the Gorges de la Bourne. They got as far as the narrow steep-arched bridge which crosses the Bourne torrent at the Pont de la Goule Noire (literally the Bridge of the Black Hole). The bridge is a perfect spot for an ambush position – which was exactly what it was that day. The 'tourists' were immediately taken prisoner and escorted to Geyer at Les Combes farm. Here they were politely but firmly interrogated and then incarcerated under armed guard in a shepherd's hut behind Geyer's headquarters.

The following day, fifteen-year-old Gilbert Carichon was walking down with his brother, having been collecting wood in the forest above Rousset – the village in which he lived – when he saw a requisitioned Peugeot 202 car with four German soldiers. The Germans were asking questions about the four who had gone missing the previous day – had anyone seen them? Gilbert and his brother walked quietly past the group being interrogated and slipped down a back alley to the small village grocer's shop. There they found Marcel Roudet, the corrupt ex-policeman who led the Maquis Raoul. As they watched, the German soldiers drove off north towards La Chapelle. Roudet suddenly pulled out a whistle and blew it hard just as the Germans were passing the cemetery on the outskirts of the village. Immediately eight to ten Maquisards popped up behind the graveyard wall and sprayed the enemy vehicle with machine-gun fire. The car immediately slewed into the ditch. Inside was one soldier wounded in the back who was quickly finished off (afterwards they said he had reached for a weapon). The other three got away. One vanished into the forest; a second, wounded in the foot, managed to struggle up the mountain to the Col de Rousset, where he phoned for help. A third reappeared some time later near La Chapelle and was quickly captured and imprisoned.

Everyone knew what would come next – and come it did. Early in the morning of 22 January, reports started arriving of a German column of 300 soldiers, equipped with heavy machine guns and two 37mm cannon, moving up the precarious mountain road leading from Sainte-Eulalie, at the mid-point of the western edge of the plateau, to the tunnels which give access to the Vercors at Les Grands Goulets. This vertiginous terrain is not difficult ground to defend. The Resistants first tried a blocking position above the little town of Échevis halfway up the valley along which the road runs. But this was quickly pushed aside by overwhelming German force. Next, Marcel Roudet overturned a lorry on the narrow road to block the Germans' passage. But this too was summarily destroyed by the 37mm cannon and the column, barely halted, swept on. Next came the most difficult part, the portion of the road running along a narrow ledge midway up a cliff face. Here, following a determined attempt made by the Resistance, the German column was halted – but only briefly. Soon Alpine troops could be seen swarming up the slopes to get above the Maquis positions, and the defenders had to pull back. A final attempt at defence was made at the tunnels, which open onto the plateau proper, but again the Maquis positions were quickly turned by Alpine troops suddenly appearing above them. The order to retreat was given. Within minutes the Germans were pouring through the tunnels and on to the plateau, burning the village of Les Barraques and pressing on to La Chapelle. Here they spared the village because they found their missing wounded soldier well cared for in the local Gendarmerie. Before leaving, however, they burnt a number of houses in Rousset in reprisal.

The day after the burning of Les Barraques and Rousset, a German Fieseler Storch light observation aircraft (the Maquisards called them *mouches* – flies) spent some time flying idly round the bowl in which the village of Malleval lay – but no one paid it much attention.

Although the Vercors had suffered during the German incursion of 22 January, the damage was by no means all one-sided. The Resistance campaign of sabotage continued apace, much of it the work of Pierre Godart's Maquis in Malleval. This progressive and destructive thumbing of Resistance noses at the German occupiers came to a head on the night of 27/28 January, when sixteen locomotives were blown up at the railway marshalling yards at Portes-lès-Valence, causing the divisional commander Generalleutnant Pflaum to announce that, from now on, he was taking personal charge of all anti-partisan operations.

Things were changing on the Resistance side as well. On 25 January there was a large meeting in the Hôtel de la Poste at Méaudre to establish, in accordance with de Gaulle's instructions, a Liberation Committee which would, among other things, coordinate all Resistance military and political action in the area. Exceptionally, Alain Le Ray was invited by Chavant to attend, despite the fact that he was about to leave the Vercors. Significantly Geyer was not. One of the conclusions of the conference was to confirm that the Vercors would not fall under either the Drôme or the Isère Resistance structures, but would have its own autonomous organization under Eugène Chavant's leadership, because 'the redoubt is supposedly under the control of the supreme Allied Command'.

During the meeting there was a heated discussion as to whether the best policy was to remain hidden until D-Day or to become active immediately. In the course of this one of the delegates warned, 'If, on the great day, I am asked to go to the Vercors, I shall immediately refuse. In my opinion the Vercors is nothing more than a trap.' Although no one at the meeting knew it, just the kind of trap he was warning about was already beginning to close.

In Malleval an attempt had been made by an ex-Alpine regimental commander to conscript the young men of the Malleval Maquis into a reconstituted version of his old unit. This caused serious tensions between the Maquisards and the French Alpine soldiers in the little closed valley. To the horror of the Maquisards, their much loved and trusted commander, Pierre Godart, was first effectively dismissed and then, on 20 January, replaced by Gustave Eysseric, an Alpine unit officer. When some of the Maquis attempted to raise a petition to express their concerns, they were cut short. 'This is the Army. You don't have personal opinions and we do not recognize petitions.' Disgusted, almost half the Maquisards left the Malleval valley. They were the lucky ones.

In the very early hours of 29 January, the day after Pflaum had announced he was taking personal charge of anti-partisan operations, German units arrived in the little town of Cognin, lying across the narrow mouth of the Gorges du Nant, which, at the time, provided the only properly motorable access to the steep-sided amphitheatre of the Malleval valley. A little after dawn, a German column set off up the winding, snow-covered road over one shoulder of the gorge, heading for Malleval village. They took a local man as hostage. They seemed to know exactly what they were aiming for, having been, some said, informed by a local spy. At 08.20, with the hostage walking in front of the first vehicle, the German column emerged out of the gorge and took Eysseric's guard post at the mill below Malleval village completely by surprise. The outpost's defenders were overrun after a brief but ferocious fight. The telephone line to Eysseric in the village was cut but not before a warning had been phoned through.

Eysseric tried desperately to rally his scattered and sleeping troops but he soon realized that he had no hope of holding the attack and ordered a withdrawal into the forest behind the village. As his men ran for cover, they were cut down by Alpine troops who had skied in over the high passes the previous night and, in their white camouflaged uniforms, taken up positions around the village, cutting off all the possible exits. Only very few got away from the slaughter. One who didn't was Gustave Eysseric himself. After the raid, all the wounded and some of the prisoners were shot, including some Yugoslav deserters who had arrived to join the Resistance in Malleval only days before. Later, the villagers were interrogated and beaten: six of them, including a Jewish woman refugee, were shoved into a nearby building and burnt alive. The village itself was sacked and burnt. In total at Malleval, thirty-three were killed and twenty-six buildings destroyed.

By the end of January 1944, it should have been clear to all from the burning of Les Barraques that the Germans could mount punitive expeditions on the plateau at will. And the disaster at Malleval illustrated their strategy for doing it. Surround – attack – annihilate the enemy – destroy their bases and the property of those who helped them. Unhappily even after these two January tragedies, too many of the Vercors commanders continued to act as though neither Les Barraques nor Malleval had ever happened.

And in this they were not alone. Even as Malleval was burning, young Maquisards were already gathering, on the 'impregnable fortress' of the Glières plateau, 200 kilometres north of the Vercors. They, too, believed they were in a fortress, when in fact they were in a trap.

12

OF GERMANS AND SPIES

One thing was clear from the string of setbacks suffered by the Organisation Vercors in January 1944. German knowledge of what was happening on the plateau was detailed and accurate. By late 1943 both the Germans and the Resistance had developed extensive networks for gathering intelligence on each other.

Right from the start the Vichy intelligence services, including the Milice, had managed to infiltrate many of the *réfractaires*' camps and build up a network of informers among the local French population. During the summer of 1943, the able young Resistance commander of Camp C2 near Villard-de-Lans, Pierre Faillant de Villemarest, was so concerned about infiltration that he suggested to the Vercors' civil and military leaders that a proper intelligence and security service be established on the plateau. It was agreed that he and a girl called Charlotte Mayaud from Villard should undertake the task. The two quickly established an intelligence network among local doctors and set up a rudimentary surveillance service and a warning system to sound the alert in the event of an approaching threat. Villemarest very soon realized that the problem was much worse than he had thought, and concluded that the whole of the Organisation Vercors was deeply penetrated.

In September 1943, a man called Henri Weiss suddenly appeared and took over the running of a café in Villard. Surveillance quickly revealed that he was in contact with a Belgian named Lecuy who appeared to have no visible means of support but was staying in Villard's most luxurious hotel, the Splendide. Further investigation uncovered a 'spy ring' which included two hotel owners and a groom called 'Mistigri', who was himself a member of one of the *réfractaires*' camps. It was obvious to Villemarest that, between them, they had perfect oversight of everyone who arrived and left the town. Further surveillance established that the Belgian, Lecuy, held regular clandestine meetings with a German official in

Grenoble who turned out to be none other than the infamous Gestapo chief Klaus Barbie. Villemarest gave a full report with supporting evidence to Chavant, but *le Patron* dismissed it all as 'too imaginative'. Not long afterwards, the body of the Belgian, Lecuy, was found in a wood outside Villard. Local rumour said that he had been tempted to the spot by a Villard lady of relaxed virtue and that Villemarest had had something to do with the death.

Disgusted by Chavant's naivety, Villemarest relinquished his job and left the plateau in February 1944. In the first half of 1944, however, Villemarest's worst suspicions were confirmed when several Maquisards deserted from the camps. Some of these were suspected of being Milice infiltrators. One, Cémoi (we know only his alias), who had joined one of the camps in February, deserted to the Milice on 24 April. He was later captured and executed. It was not until June 1944 that a proper system of security was finally established on the plateau.

Although the plateau itself was riddled with insecurity, there were active and successful Resistance intelligence networks operating in the Grenoble area which were able to provide the Vercors leaders with reliable information on German intentions. These included many in the Vichy civil administration and the local police as well as the Gendarmerie. Post offices were also a fruitful source of information, as were local telephone-exchange operators who turned their well-known habit of listening to conversations into a patriotic duty. Others on whom the Organisation Vercors could normally rely included especially the local restaurateurs, who formed an extensive intelligence network of their own. This included establishing an organization for stealing side-arms from Germans dining at local restaurants and smuggling these to the Resistance in the forests.

Alongside the local intelligence organizations operating in the Vercors during this period there were also a number of French and Allied secret services doing the same thing. These included the French intelligence services based in London, SOE, SIS (also known as MI6), MI9 (Britain's secret service dedicated to helping escaped PoWs and airmen), the intelligence service of the Polish government-in-exile and the American Office of Strategic Services, which ran, among other agents, Gaston Vincent, who was based in Saint-Agnan-en-Vercors until his death in June 1944.

On the other side, the German and Milice networks often made use of those involved in the black market and, it was said, brothel keepers, barbers and barmen. In his Union report, Thackthwaite added to this list waitresses in small-town and village restaurants, who were used as agents provocateurs. Apart from human sources, the Germans also put considerable effort into gathering signals intelligence and closing down secret radio stations. In one case a Milice agent who had been successfully infiltrated into one of the Vercors' clandestine radio teams had to be got rid of because, 'although he was assigned as a trustworthy person', further enquiries were made and 'It was discovered that his brother was a Milicien and his sister-in-law worked for the Gestapo.'

German intelligence even successfully took over some Resistance radio networks in their entirety. For example, a Greek called Guy Alexander Kyriazis was sent by the German secret service to work in a British-run SIS network called Alliance. Posted to Grenoble, he was paid 7,000 francs a month and appears to have operated until the end of the war, planting false messages and passing back codebooks to his masters. When subsequently interrogated by the Allies, he claimed that 'the Germans … knew the details of the wireless procedure which was being used at Grenoble [and] were intercepting messages'.

The job of German intelligence was made much easier by that fact that the radio security of both the Resistance in the field and their Free French controllers in London was very lax and their codes extremely insecure. The British government became very concerned about this, especially now that planning had started on the greatest secret of the war, the date and location of D-Day. On 13 January 1944, the British War Cabinet took the decision that, because of the insecurity of the French codes, all signals or messages sent by the French in London and Algiers had to be transmitted through the British communication systems or use British or US codes. De Gaulle was predictably furious, calling it 'an outrage and an insult'.

An SOE report on French radio security dated 29 January 1944, just a few days before the Malleval disaster, gives some indication of the scale of the problem: '[French] Security … is lamentable … Continual losses of [Resistance] chiefs, money, codes, archives, couriers, list of names which [were] unparalleled … we have continually pointed out *over a year* that [their] codes are fundamentally insecure and badly coded … We have finally been reduced to breaking them [the French codes] ourselves to prove [to the French] their insecurity … *It must be assumed that every [French] message code can be read by the Germans as easily as by ourselves* [emphasis in original].'

Closer to D-Day, the British went further, refusing to allow anyone of any nationality to leave Britain whom they believed knew anything, or thought they knew anything, about D-Day.

The approach of D-Day was beginning to concentrate German minds, too. As 1943 drew to a close without an invasion, it was clear to all that it must happen in the spring or summer of 1944. This time, however, the task for the Germans would not just be to disrupt the Resistance control networks, as in 1943, but to destroy the Maquis units themselves. And this would involve not individual arrests outside Métro stations or swoops on safe houses, but a series of bloody battles in which no quarter would be given to the 'terrorists'.

On 3 February 1944, the German Deputy Supreme Commander West, Luftwaffe Field Marshal Hugo Sperrle, set out the policy with chilling clarity in what has become known as the 'Sperrle-Erlass' order, prescribing the behaviour of German troops in the struggle ahead:

1. We are not in the occupied western territories to allow our troops to be shot at and abducted by saboteurs who go unpunished …
2. If troops are attacked … countermeasures [must be taken] immediately;

These include an … immediate return of fire. If innocent persons are hit this is regrettable but entirely the fault of the terrorists.

The surroundings of any such incident are to be sealed off … and all the civilians in the locality, regardless of rank and person, are to be taken into custody.

Houses from which shots have been fired are to be burnt down …

… A slack and indecisive troop commander deserves to be severely punished because he endangers the lives of the troops … and produces a lack of respect for the German armed forces.

Measures that are regarded subsequently as too severe cannot in view of the present situation, provide reason for punishment.

A week later, on 12 February, the German military commander of France, General Carl-Heinrich von Stülpnagel, also conscious of the impending invasion, issued an order calling for the urgent destruction of Maquis groups within the next months: '*The main task in the coming weeks and months is … fully to repacify the areas which are contaminated by bandits and to break up the secret resistance organizations and to seize their weapons* ... In areas where gang centres form, these must be combated with a *concentrated use of all available forces* ... The *objective* must be to break up all terrorist and resistance groups even before the enemy landing [emphasis in original].'

The Germans were moving on to the offensive and the main burden of their offensive in the northern Alps would fall on General Pflaum, who commanded 157th Reserve Division based in Grenoble. Pflaum's division was, as its name suggests, not a front-line unit. Its main task was not combat but training. But it was also charged with a military task – the maintenance of order, especially where this threatened key German communications routes. Pflaum's priority was to keep open at all costs the road and rail communications corridors running through the north and centre of his area of responsibility.

Karl Pflaum himself was a career officer with a good deal of active service as an infantry soldier on the eastern front where he had commanded a front-line division from the autumn of 1941 until he was relieved of his command because of heart disease. Pflaum's direct superior in France was the commander of the Military Zone of the South of France, Generalleutnant Heinrich Niehoff, whose reporting line ran through Stülpnagel to the Supreme High Command of the German Army in Berlin and thence to Hitler's bunker.

When it came to carrying the main burden of infantry fighting in Pflaum's area, the only troops of true front-line quality he could rely on were his elite Alpine Gebirgsjäger Regiment – it was these troops that had come in overnight on skis to take up positions behind Malleval, cutting off the Maquisards trying to flee from the valley. Well trained and well led, the Gebirgsjäger were exceptionally capable in mountainous areas and winter conditions. But not many of Pflaum's troops were of the same standard as his Alpine units. One experienced French officer in Grenoble in late 1943 and 1944 commented after the war that the units based in and around Grenoble were 'mainly troops under instruction, with the exception of the officers and a few more experienced soldiers'. In the German tactic of surround, attack, annihilate, destroy, these were troops who would be employed chiefly in the first and last phases – cordoning before the operation started and reprisals after the fighting had finished.

For many German soldiers, France, and especially the south of France, was regarded as an easy, even idyllic posting. A German historian of the period wrote that those stationed at Annecy, where the headquarters of one of the Gebirgsjäger regiments was housed in an old hotel, enjoyed 'A life lived in the midst of this jewel of nature. The fourteen-kilometre lake stretches its arms right into the centre of the city, making it into a veritable oasis designed to please the eye. The houses are beautifully maintained and surrounded by groves and vines, which also decorate the surrounding hills. And everywhere the sparkling lake with its canals crossed by many bridges seems to act as a silver adornment to the whole scene. The men of the Regiment saw themselves as the fortunate inhabitants of a paradise right in the middle of the Second World War.'

This paradise was, however, soon to turn into something far less pleasant. By the early months of 1944, the morale of many of the raw recruits who made up the majority of Pflaum's division was low and their steadiness under fire shaky. By now they would have known that the war would be over in the next year or so and that Germany was not going to win. Moreover, by this time they had become hated occupiers, facing an increasingly well-armed and capable insurrection, in a country which grew more hostile by the day. What was going to happen to them when they had to get out?

In a coded message to London on 11 February 1944, a French agent remarked on the jumpiness of German troops in the Annecy area: 'The Germans load their rifles when travelling through tunnels on the railway. In the streets in the evening, they keep turning round and are always careful to keep their distance from all active members of the Gestapo [for fear of being caught in a Resistance assassination attempt] … A German who had broken his leg at a winter sports station recently was to be taken to hospital … but the comrade who was to accompany him refused through fear of the Maquis.' In his report on the Union Mission, Henry Thackthwaite was more blunt, describing some of these rear-area German troops as 'corrupt and miserable'.

Beyond his own forces, Pflaum could also call on neighbouring units who, together with other specialized theatre units, supplied supporting troops for a number of anti-partisan operations carried out in his area. Finally, he could request assistance from outside the French theatre as well. In early spring 1944, experts in the conduct of anti-partisan operations in the Balkans were brought in to advise and train some key elements of Pflaum's forces. On the darker side, among these additional troops were units known as the Eastern Troops made up of captured prisoners of war and Russian deserters from the eastern front. These included Turkmens, Uzbeks, Kazakhs, Azerbaijanis and Georgians. They wore German uniforms with armbands showing their nation of origin. At their peak these Eastern Troops, totalling almost half a million, were chiefly used to carry out reprisals in the 'annihilation' phase of anti-partisan operations on the Russian front, Yugoslavia and subsequently France. The French christened them 'Mongols' because of their Asian features and their reputation for acts of horror and atrocity.

These were not the only troops of non-German origin under Pflaum's command. There were also some – perhaps up to 20 per cent – who came from other occupied countries. These included Slovenes and Poles. Thackthwaite's Union Mission report describes the quality of these troops as 'in general bad … [many] are … ready to join us on D-Day'.

On the face of it Pflaum himself was third in the German command hierarchy in France. But this is to give a false view of his true position. There were officers, especially within German security structures, who had at least as much influence as he did on anti-partisan operations. The most important of these was the head of the Sipo/SD, an umbrella organization which incorporated both the German Security Police and the Security Department. This body is often known as the 'Gestapo', though the Gestapo was in fact only one of the component units within the Sipo/SD. The chief of the Lyon Sipo/SD, which covered the Vercors area, was SS-Obersturmbannführer Werner Knab, one of whose subordinates was Klaus Barbie.

Knab had a huge influence on the conduct and command of all anti-partisan operations in the Lyon area. Following some previous disagreement with his superiors he had been posted to the Ukraine, where he was assigned to one of the most notorious of the so-called 'mobile killing units' to 'demonstrate his reliability'. This he succeeded in doing in quick order, gaining a reputation for the ruthless destruction of partisan units and unwanted elements such as Jews.

Pflaum himself, on the other hand, had first intended to wage a 'clean war' against the French Resistance. In fact, until around late April 1944 he believed (not perhaps without some justification) that the local population did not as a whole support the Resistance and that some were even hostile to it. By late spring 1944, however, Pflaum's opinion and that of his division had become much more aggressive as the casualties from guerrilla actions started to rise. In the first five months of 1944, the division lost fifty-five of its soldiers, killed or wounded by the Resistance. In the ten weeks from June to mid-August that figure rose to 650. The totals for Resistance and civilians killed by the Germans rose commensurately – from sixty in February 1944 to 840 in July.

13

FEBRUARY 1944

February 1944 saw the pace of events begin to quicken towards the great event which everyone knew was ahead – some time, somewhere – in the coming year: the Allied invasion of the northern European mainland.

On 5 February Pflaum launched 2,000 men against Maquis concentrations around the towns of Nantua and Oyonnax in the southern Jura. The Resistance in this area was led by a remarkably successful guerrilla leader called Henri Romans-Petit, who, like Alain Le Ray, understood that the art of guerrilla warfare was not to stand and fight, but to hit and run. Aided by an unusually heavy snowfall, he and his men melted away into the forests. The Germans called off the operation on 13 February. Although they had temporarily cleared the operational area of 'terrorists', Romans-Petit suffered few losses and was able to return to his old positions very soon afterwards.

This was to be the first of three major operations conducted by Pflaum in the ten weeks from 2 February to 18 April, all in the area immediately south and west of Lake Geneva (see map on page 139). At this stage the Germans believed, like Churchill, that the main threat was not a southern landing but an Allied push through Italy, over the Alps and down the two communication corridors which ran south-west of Lake Geneva: the southern railway corridor past Aix-les-Bains and the Lac du Bourget and the western road corridor through to Nantua and Oyonnax.

This is not to say, however, that the Germans could afford to ignore the Vercors completely, for the Maquis on the plateau were still highly active. On the night of 1/2 February, for example, the transformers at the Saint-Bel works in Grenoble were sabotaged and 2,700 kilograms of explosive were stolen. On 19 February, another sabotage attack on the station at La Mure, south of Grenoble, destroyed a train and winding gear. On 29 February, a dozen or so locomotives were blown up at Veynes station, 15 kilometres south of the Vercors.

At dawn on 3 February, the day after the start of Pflaum's operation in the Jura, Paul Adam was on guard duty in the deep snow, with a friend, a Sten gun, two grenades and a telephone. Their sentry post was positioned on a railway viaduct a kilometre or so north-east of the deserted thirteenth-century monastery of Our Lady of Esparron. Here, the previous November, he and his fellow Maquisards had taken refuge from the bitter winter. It was dark and one of Paul Adam's Maquisard friends had just left, hitching a lift to a meeting on a passing train. He was followed a little later by another on his way home to pick up some washing from his mother. '[Suddenly] the noise of some vehicles attracted our attention,' Paul Adam wrote later, 'but we thought it was only the lorries arriving at the nearby saw-mill. I was just in the process of telephoning the monastery to ask for a change of guard, when my mate, who had gone to stretch his legs on the viaduct, suddenly came dashing back shouting, "Les Boches! Les Boches!"'

The two men started to climb the slope towards the monastery, 'but halfway up we heard a shout which stopped us dead in our tracks. Thirty metres away, on the road leading up to the monastery, I saw vehicles. I got ready to fire on the ones in front of us which were full of troops, hoping to escape in the chaos which would ensue, when suddenly a huge German leading a patrol of twelve others came round the corner … beyond him there was an armoured car with machine guns mounted on a turntable which began to rotate towards us, its guns firing … Since it was clearly impossible to get back to the monastery where we could hear a fierce firefight already in progress … we went back to the viaduct through the woods. As we got there, a train arrived pulling cattle wagons. The doors were open and we could see that carriage after carriage was filled with Germans … After the train had passed, we saw, below the viaduct, some vehicles, one of which had a fat German leaning against his cab, chatting while he lit a cigarette. He took several deep pulls on his fag, stuck one hand in his pocket and began to admire the countryside. "It's all over for you my friend," I said to myself and, taking aim at some kind of badge he had on his chest, I fired. He dropped dead without even letting go of his cigarette … after a forced march over rocks and across mountain torrents we finally arrived at a station, where we knew a train would pass in an hour or so … The station master gave us each a blue denim working shirt and an old hat as disguise and let us board the train without tickets, our stripped-down Stens hidden in our haversacks.'

Back at the monastery, Jean Sadin was getting up when the German attack started: 'It was just getting light ... I was doing up my laces when suddenly I saw a signal maroon hanging in the sky ... then a second and a third ... We quickly woke everyone up. Suddenly a rattle of machine-gun fire hit the area round my window. I leapt to one side and took up a position where I was able to see some Germans enter a building not 30 metres away. After a brief attempt at resistance, our commander gave the order to disperse – every man for himself. My friend, not hearing my cries ... dashed out and was immediately cut down ... We managed to flee by a back door, taking refuge among the bushes and rocks near by. As we ran, a huge explosion rocked the monastery building behind us.'

Amazingly, only two of the Esparron Maquis were killed. If the German attack had been more efficiently prosecuted, if they had followed their normal practice and surrounded the monastery, many more would have died.

The unusually heavy February 1944 fall of snow also affected another gathering of Maquisards 60 kilometres to the north, on the 'impregnable fortress' of the Glières plateau, which dominates the main Geneva–Chamonix road and railway, some 15 kilometres north-east of Annecy. Many regarded this high plateau, which was an ideal site for the para-chuting of arms, as more impregnable and easier to defend than the Vercors. On 7 February, Churchill was shown an urgent telegram from one of London's agents describing the situation on the plateau: 'VERY urgent. We have given the order to take strong action in the Savoie. We ask for instant despatch of parachute troops and arms, above all machine guns – and also air support. We are ready for action but we urgently need aid and assistance.' The British Prime Minister was asked to give special priority to the plateau, whose fall would have 'severe repercussions for the whole of the Resistance'.

Over the previous weeks, encouraged by calls by the French service of the BBC, Maquisards had flooded on to the Glières plateau, including some fifty Spanish republicans and numerous retired soldiers from the area. By the end of February, it was reported that there were now '350 trained and experienced men [who are] occupying an exceptionally strong position on the ... plateau'. This was followed by a string of optimistic messages, which spoke of the 'citadel of the Glières' and 'The high morale of our Maquis who take on ... day by day, the semblance of regular troops who are disciplined and well led. If we can adequately supply them from the air, we will have here a body of men who can be used when D-Day comes.' On 19 February material was sent from the plateau for use in a BBC broadcast: 'We shall remain on this impregnable plateau with the banner: "Live in Freedom or Die".'

In the second half of February a clandestine meeting, attended by senior Resistance leaders in the region, was held in Lyon to discuss overall strategy. The concept of establishing 'redoubts of Resistance', as proposed by Ferdinand Miksche in his report of 20 January, was discussed. Henry Thackthwaite, the SOE agent leading the Union Mission, was there and strongly opposed the idea of fixed defence, preferring a mobile defence in which the Maquisards would retire before a German advance, while keeping them under fire during the day and then attacking them on the flanks and from behind at night. He was supported by the then head of the Secret Army in the area, Albert Chambonnet. When it came to guerrilla warfare, Chambonnet, who was not of the French Army but an ex-Air Force officer, held the same opinion as Romans-Petit and Alain Le Ray. On 9 February he had issued instructions to the Maquis in his area, 'Never accept frontal combat with the enemy. Pull back and attack his flanks without mercy.' A few days after the Lyon meeting Chambonnet wrote a prophetic letter expanding on his views: 'If we concentrate our forces in the most defendable mountainous areas, two possibilities will ensue; either the enemy will attack and destroy them, or they will be content to block them and our best forces will be locked up and neutralized.' Later still, in April, Chambonnet wrote a note on the specific subject of the Vercors: 'A vast apparatus [is being assembled] on the Vercors in order to strike a decisive and "brilliant" blow against key enemy positions along the main Alpine routes … I am firmly opposed.' Tragically, Chambonnet's warnings went unheeded.*

At the end of the second week of March the redoubt strategy was raised again when local Resistance leaders met in Annecy to decide what should be done about the Maquis groups now gathered in strength on the Glières plateau. Most of the local Resistance commanders were opposed to a fixed defence of the plateau. But their opinion was over-

* On 10 June, four days after D-Day, Albert Chambonnet was arrested by the Gestapo. He was shot on 27 July at Lyon.

ruled by a representative from London who attended the Annecy meeting. According to one of those close to these events, London's man told the gathering that they 'had to give London the proof that the Resistance is not just talk, but a considerable force which the Germans will have to reckon with'. In the end, despite heavy reservations, it was this opinion which prevailed.

London's message that the Resistance had to prove itself in the Glières was by no means an idle one. Churchill himself was becoming increasingly dissatisfied with what he saw as the reluctance of the French, despite all the arms he was dropping to them, to go on to the offensive. On 14 February, Desmond Morton, Churchill's personal assistant, wrote a note to Lord Selborne, the minister in charge of SOE: 'In general the PM thinks that we must make the French show much greater zeal in trying to remedy their own considerable defects.'

It was not long before the Annecy decision to defend the Glières as a redoubt was tested. On 26 March Pflaum launched a mixed force of 3,000 troops supported by artillery and aircraft against the plateau. Two battalions of Gebirgsjäger scaled the ramparts of the 'impregnable fortress' by night with relative ease. It was all over in less than four days and was followed by the usual shootings, burning of farms and an extensive programme of reprisals.

While most of the major Resistance actions in the month of February 1944 took place in and around the Glières plateau, the Vercors was not without its excitements. On 28 February, Peter Ortiz sent an urgent signal to London reporting that the Germans were about to mount an attack on the plateau with three mechanized battalions and some light tanks. In fact, the rumour (it was unsubstantiated) seems to have reached the Vercors a few days previously, for, on 25 February, Narcisse Geyer's regimental journal reported a 'Major alert: imminent powerful German attack' and described the unit's night flight to new positions. Elsewhere that night, across the plateau, other camps were hurriedly packing up kit, squirrelling away ammunition in nearby caves and then scurrying into the forest in small groups. The false alarm had a bad effect on morale, causing 'a profound disappointment, even real irritation in all the camps ... We had somehow waited for, even looked forward to, an attempt at a "heavy blow" [from the Germans], believing totally in the natural protection the plateau afforded us as the defenders. And now, at the first sign of serious threat, we were told to disperse and hide! It made us all feel very deflated,' said André Valot.

By this time Francis Cammaerts was already back in the area. He had parachuted into France on the night of 9/10 February after three months in which he had been rebriefed and had taken some holiday with his wife. His arrival, however, was less congenial than he might have hoped for: the parachute site chosen for that night was at Castellane, 170 kilometres south-east of the Vercors. But when the Halifax arrived in the area, after an uncomfortable journey through heavy flak, they found the site completely obscured by cloud. 'The dispatcher told me ... the mission was aborted. The next thing I knew was him saying we'd have to jump – the aircraft was on fire ... As I jumped I could see that it was ablaze. As I was descending I realised the huge canopy of the parachute fell more slowly through thick cloud than it would through clear sky. So I was going down very slowly. It was like being in a dense London smog virtually the whole time – I don't know how many minutes it took from 10,000 feet but it seemed an eternity ... When I finally came out of the cloud I had 25 metres to go! A potato patch is the softest part of a farm you could wish for and there one was, and I hit it. In that filthy weather I could have landed in the middle of Lyon, not on a lonely farm.'

Cammaerts' orders for this, his second mission, instructed him to pursue his leapfrog plan to use the Valensole, Vercors and Beaurepaire plateaux as 'bridgeheads' on which Allied paratroopers could land, adding that this had now been formally approved for consideration as part of Operation Anvil, the Allies' planned southern invasion on the Mediterranean coast. The strategic importance of the Vercors plateau in the event of either an invasion from the south or an attack across the Alpine passes had been confirmed.

14

MARCH 1944

The instructions given by Winston Churchill in February 1944 that arms drops to the Resistance should be doubled in the month of March produced swift results, most, but not all of them, welcome to the Vercors. On 4 March, in what seems a desperate measure to dispatch arms by any means, the RAF carried out a 'blind drop'* of containers near Romans. Peter Ortiz, who was in the area at the time, complained bitterly to London in an 'outspoken denunciation … As soon as he received the warning [of the drop] he left to try to stop the Germans recovering the material which had been dropped, but it was they who had the largest share. Such operations put the whole region into an excited state and expose the population to harsh reprisals as well as putting the reception committees to unjustifiable risks.'

On 10/11 March, the night of the March full moon, the first major parachute drop the plateau had received since Darbonouse four months previously took place when five Stirling heavy bombers success-fully parachuted containers at a site codenamed Gabin, 2 kilometres west of Saint-Martin-en-Vercors, in an open valley surrounded by woods.

Five days later, at 01.05 hours on 16 March 1944, a Halifax bomber captained by Pilot Officer Caldwell took off from RAF Tempsford on Operation Bob 149. His mission was to drop eighteen containers packed with arms and seven packages to the Gabin site. Caldwell crossed the Channel and, skirting Paris, continued south over Burgundy and Bourg-en-Bresse to his final landmark, the Lac de Charavines, 60 kilometres north-west of his target. The lake was not difficult to spot, its silver surface shimmering like a mirror in the moonlight. Here Caldwell started his twenty-minute 'dead reckoning' run in to his target. His

---

* A parachute drop for which no reception committee has been arranged.

after-action report is brief: 'Pinpointed lake WNW of Target & ground detail. Lights on when aircraft arrived'.

Judging from Caldwell's description, he overflew the target from the north in order to establish its precise location and exchange code signals with the reception team: 'Good reception and correct letter'. Banking his aircraft, he retraced his steps from the south, the moon now shining over his right shoulder. With the Gabin site visible, he reduced his height above the ground to a spine-tingling 120 metres. On his first run, he dropped nine containers and five packages before pulling out to avoid the high ground north of the Gorges de la Bourne, swinging the big Halifax round again and repeating the same procedure from the north to south, dispatching the remaining nine containers and two packages. Caldwell had arrived over Gabin at 04.02 hours and, twenty minutes later, his mission accomplished, he was heading home for Tempsford. He had an uneventful return journey, dropping leaflets over the little Burgundy town of Époisses, half hidden in the 'ground haze over northern France', and touching down at his home base a little before dawn at 07.10.

For the Gabin reception team on the ground, that night was cold with a sky spangle-full of stars and a moon of crystal brightness which illuminated every detail of woods and fields, sparkling under a recent heavy fall of snow. A deep frost had laid a hard crust over the snow and sheet ice on the roads, making the going difficult for the reception committees waiting patiently for Caldwell to arrive. The moon rose in the southeastern quarter at half an hour after midnight and would therefore have been hanging over the southern shoulder of the Grand Veymont when Caldwell arrived.

All eighteen containers were recovered from the snow that night. Of these, seven were filled with captured German Mauser rifles and machine pistols, one with Bren light machine guns, one with mortars, two with mortar bombs and a further two with grenades and explosives. In addition, there were three packages containing ammunition and four full of boots. On the same night, at a drop site called Cavalier near by, another drop was made of six mortars, eight Brens, ten rifles, fifty-six American carbines and 180 Sten guns, together with ammunition, boots and socks.

The inclusion of mortars in this parachute drop is intriguing, as it has always been assumed that no mortars were ever dropped to the Vercors. We do not know whether the weapons parachuted this night were the light 2-inch mortar, which was ineffective and little more than a small arm, or the medium 3-inch mortar – a much more useful weapon in heavy combat. However, given that Thackthwaite, in earlier signals, had requested the latter, it seems reasonable to conclude that these were the heavier mortars, in which case they were the first and last ever dropped on the plateau. The reason why no more mortars were dropped to the Vercors, despite urgent requests for them in the months to come, was that it was discovered that the mortar ammunition was unstable and had a habit of exploding on impact with the ground – though this was never explained to those who subsequently made increasingly desperate pleas for them from the plateau.

The morning after the drop was bright and clear. The men from Geyer's headquarters and other camps in the area spent almost the whole day gathering up the night's bounty and carrying it in carts, on mules and on their own backs to the nearby cave of Barme-Chenille, where it was stored away under lock and key. No one knows whether the events of the following day, 18 March, were connected with this drop (which the Germans would certainly have known about), or whether they had been informed of what was going on at La Matrassière by a local priest who was also a German spy, as many in the Vercors believed at the time.

Saturday 18 March 1944 was a cold, still morning with a thick fog which lay in the valleys and covered the lower pastures of the Vercors. At 06.00 hours, Denise Glaudas, a Resistance activist, was listening, as she always did, to the early-morning broadcast from the BBC when she heard the sound of heavy lorries approaching her house in Villard-de-Lans. At this time in the morning – before light – it had to be Germans. To her horror, the vehicles stopped outside her house. She froze, waiting for the knock on the door, and then sighed with relief as they drove off. When all was quiet she looked out of her window to see tyre tracks in the snow and the unmistakable signs that her wall had been used as a *pissoire* by several German soldiers in need of urgent relief. She gave the matter no further thought and returned to bed.

Half an hour later, at 06.30, the local bus to Grenoble turned a corner in the narrow winding road at the bottom of the Gorges de la Bourne to find itself bonnet to bonnet with the first truck in a long German convoy, accompanied by an armoured car and consisting of some tens of German troop-carrying lorries, each mounted with a machine gun. One of the passengers on the bus that morning was Denise Vallier, who was on her way to work in Grenoble: 'A German soldier leapt out of the front vehicle and ordered our driver to get off the road. It was a difficult manoeuvre for him since the edges of the narrow road were piled high with snow. He thought to himself, "No need to hurry. The longer I take, the more time will be gained for those on the plateau." The men on the bus were ordered to get out and were searched, but cursorily, I thought. After a little time they all got back on to the bus, though I noticed that one had lost his green lumber jacket* in the process. Our driver was ordered to get a move on and some of the passengers had to help shovel away the snow which blocked us.'

Eventually, the German convoy continued its journey up the steep road to Saint-Julien. Here, at the far end of the village, it turned right on to a smaller farm road. A little outside Saint-Julien, the troops disembarked, spread out and quickly made their way on foot over the fields to the little hamlet of La Matrassière. There had been no warning of the convoy's approach. It had come overnight and undetected by the Vercors telephone warning system, 40 kilometres from Grenoble, up the Vercors escarpment, through Saint-Nizier and Villard-de-Lans and right into the heart of the Vercors before anyone was aware of the threat. At the last minute, Geneviève Blum-Gayet, a Resistance liaison agent from Villard, accompanied by two companions, tried desperately to reach Saint-Julien ahead of the column but got her car shot up for her pains. She was lucky to get away with her life.

The Germans burst into the headquarters being prepared for Marcel Descour at Peyronnet farm at La Matrassière. As it happened, Pierre Lassalle had left just that morning to take up a new post as radio operator with Henri Zeller, the Resistance commander for the south-east. Lassalle was walking through the fog over the snowy fields to catch a mid-morning bus from Saint-Martin, when he heard the shooting and explosions behind him.

The Maquisards in the farm itself had no hope. Five were killed instantly, including the two officers. The two radio sets (one in contact with Algiers and the other with London), together with their codes, were captured and Peyronnet farm burnt to the ground. The raiders, who seemed to know precisely where they were going, then turned towards Geyer's headquarters in Les Combes Farm and the two nearby camps at

* Known as a 'Canadienne'.

Le Bouget, which they destroyed with explosive. Geyer and his men, hearing the explosions and shooting at La Matrassière, fled with as many of their bags and as much baggage as they could carry to the forests. All escaped but one, Marc-Henri Leroy, who hid in a pile of hay at the nearby Borel farm. Just before the Germans set fire to the farm, they found the Sten gun Leroy had dropped in his flight to the hay barn. The German officer in charge demanded that the farmer, Henri Borel, should hold the weapon. Sensing a trap, Borel refused. The officer repeated the order. When Borel refused again, the officer pulled out his pistol and shot him dead in front of his family. According to witnesses, Borel shouted 'Vive La France!' as he died. Leroy was burnt alive when the farm was put to flames.

The German column then reassembled and, taking two prisoners with them, left the plateau. The Maquisards, believing that the Germans would leave by the way they had come, placed ambushes on the road back through Villard, but instead of going up the Gorges de la Bourne, the Germans turned left at the Pont de la Goule Noire and went down to Pont-en-Royans without mishap.

In all, the raid had cost the lives of six Maquisards and three civilians and resulted in the destruction by fire of nine farms and numerous other buildings. Had the Germans not been in such a hurry to leave the plateau before nightfall, they could have had an even greater harvest. For that night the RAF came back for another parachute drop at the Cavalier site near Saint-Martin. Mistaking the burning farms from the German raid as the signal fires of the reception committee, the aircraft, flying very low, dropped their loads along the Saint-Martin–Saint-Julien road. On the ground the reception teams, camping in the open in case the Germans came back, were rather disorganized and managed to recover only four-teen containers and eight packages. These included three containers of .303 ammunition, one of Italian carbines, two of German Spandau machine guns, three of Stens and five of grenades and explosives. The drop also included one package of Mauser ammunition, one of shoes and six packages with yet more Stens.

On 5 April a former French military inspector for the region wrote a report for Albert Chambonnet in which he said, referring to the burning of Descour's future headquarters at La Matrassière, 'The destruction of a headquarters right in the middle of the Vercors does not give confidence in the strategic qualities of those currently in charge there.'

One way or the other, 18 March 1944 produced a bumper crop for German intelligence. Along with the wirelesses and codes from La Matrassière, seven high-ranking French officers visiting the Vercors that day were arrested on their way back to Lyon, along with their archives and the early plans for the BBC code phrases to be used for D-Day.

Though the German raid on La Matrassière was the largest of the Vercors actions in March, it was not the first or only one. There had also been what has been described as a 'skirmish' at the bridge at Pont-en-Royans on 9 March. In fact it was rather less than that. Four Maquisards were returning to recover material from their old camp on the plateau when they bumped into a German patrol searching for 'terrorists'. Although their papers appeared in order, a search of their truck revealed a pistol hidden in the back. Arrested and tortured, the four were summarily shot and their bodies left by the roadside near a village close to Romans.

Later in the month, what might more properly be called a skirmish occurred at the other end of the Vercors. On 22 March, Paul Gariboldy, the leader of the Groupe Vallier, who had a price on his head as a consequence of a raid on Grenoble Post Office earlier in the month, was caught in a Milice ambush at a garage in Fontaines, a suburb of Grenoble, and killed. He was twenty-three years old. His Groupe Vallier colleagues wanted to take his body to the morgue in the hospital at Villard, but Eugène Chavant got to hear of the scheme and put a stop to it. As a replacement act of honour to their dead chief, his men next planned to hoist a large tricolour on one of the Vercors' summits. On their way up to the plateau from Sassenage, they met some German officers and, not wishing to waste the opportunity, opened fire on them before dispersing to Villard-de-Lans. Here they bumped into the same officers again just outside the tram station. The Germans took refuge in a nearby hotel and, running up to a first-floor window, fired on the young Maquisards as they raced across an open space below, hitting two of them. A second burst mortally wounded a third and shattered the femur of a fourth just as he was throwing a grenade. The grenade rolled back and exploded close to the wounded men, killing both instantly. The battle ended, leaving two Maquisards dead and two wounded.

The Vercors Maquis had their successes too, of course. The raid on the Grenoble Post Office which ultimately led to the death of Paul Gariboldy netted the sum of 6 million francs, of which Chavant got half for the

Vercors. Narcisse Geyer was furious about this piece of 'gangsterism', which he regarded as below the standards required by members of his 'army', and complained to his chief, Marcel Descour, in the strongest possible terms. This was odd because, two days later, the diary of one of his own officers, Lieutenant Louis Rose, records that he was sent out on a reconnaissance for a raid which was subsequently carried out on a tobacco and shoe depot at Grand Lemp, 10 kilometres north-west of the Vercors. Perhaps what Geyer was really objecting to was not Gariboldy's 'gangster' hold-up but the subsequent division of the spoils in favour of the civilians rather than the military. Either way, the event did nothing to lessen tensions between the civilian and the military on the plateau.

Meanwhile the programme of sabotage, mostly carried out from the Vercors, continued unabated. Tanneries and leather factories in Pont-de-Claix, Fontaines and Grenoble were seriously damaged in a wave of Maquisard attacks on 17 March. Four days later, in a night of sabotage in the Valence area, there was an incendiary attack on the home of the Chief of Milice at Bourg-en-Valence, and agents of Cammaerts' Jockey network blew up eight locomotives at Portes-lès-Valence, another twenty in Valence itself, and threw in an attack on a local factory for good measure. On 24 March, Cammaerts' men struck again, destroying an engine and thirty-five trucks in Valence marshalling yards – and again two days later, destroying another twenty locomotives.

On 29 March, in response to another false alarm the Vercors leadership issued 'Order No. 3', calling on all camps on the plateau to adopt a state of 'dispersed defence'. All arms were hidden away in uninhabited farms and in the Vercors' caves, the camps were abandoned for the time being and the Maquis groups dissolved into small bands which took refuge in the forests or with families in isolated farmhouses. Once more morale on the plateau dropped – and not just on the Vercors. In a report written on 26 March, which was carried to London by Lysander on 10 April, Francis Cammaerts wrote: 'Passing very difficult days. Germans attacking all over … general acute disappointment due to delayed Allied arrival … strongly mounting current of Anglophobia everywhere, particularly among the Resistance movement. The SS [sic – there were no SS in the area. He was probably referring to the Sipo/SD] have been given charge of fighting Resistance with instructions to use same methods as in Russia. Result is a reign of terror, farms burnt, shootings and hangings.'

Altogether it had been a bad month for the French Resistance in the south-east of France. At La Matrassière, the Germans had shown once again that they could gain access to the Vercors plateau at will and destroy what they wished to destroy, unscathed. On the Glières plateau they had demonstrated that they had both the ability and the troops to take on large-scale operations aimed at encircling and destroying any fixed Maquisard defensive position, no matter what the terrain.

Despite this, many in London continued, throughout March and beyond, to plan for a strategy which the fall of the Glières plateau had just proved to be disastrous. On 6 March, Miksche in the French planning unit in London produced a paper predicting that in 'generally mountainous areas covered with large forests … where German supervision is much reduced … it is unlikely at the time of the Allied landing [that] the Germans will in these areas be able to place themselves in a stronger position than they are at present … the few enemy detachments [there] will be obliged to limit their activity to guarding vital communication centres [and] trying to prevent the descent of patriots from the mountains down to the valleys … In these regions of difficult access for the German invader, and of easy defence for the French patriots, firm strongholds can be established – operational bases of lasting value for the organization of the French Resistance.'

The British in SOE agreed. In an exercise which involved the triumph of limitless hope over recent bitter experience, they produced a paper on 22 March proposing 'To develop guerrilla activity to such an extent as to take large areas under patriot control, confining the enemy to populated areas and main routes, with the result that the Germans [will] find it necessary to concentrate their occupational troops on important Lines of Communication and strong points'.

On the wider political front, two decisions were made in March 1944 which would have profound implications for the Vercors.

On 22 March, Dwight Eisenhower, very unusually, attended a British War Cabinet meeting in Downing Street, with Churchill in the chair. The two leaders reviewed the plans for Anvil and Overlord and concluded that, because of a shortage of landing craft, the two operations could not be conducted simultaneously. Overlord would take centre stage and come first. Anvil would be relegated to the status of an 'add-on' (to Churchill's secret delight), which would come afterwards, as and when resources and circumstances permitted. Suddenly, what had always been understood (the Vercors would rise in the context of a simultaneous landing in the north and south of France) became open to misunderstanding (would it now have to wait for the southern invasion?). The operational timing and indeed purpose of playing the 'Vercors card' (and that of the other southern redoubts) had altered completely. This increased the likelihood that, whether through an excess of enthusiasm, muddled thinking or plain inadvertence (or a combination of all three), the redoubts would be told to rise too early, with tragic consequences.

Six days previously, on 16 March, the day of the second parachute drop above Saint-Martin, another decision already taken by Churchill and Eisenhower was communicated by telegram from the British and American planners in London to their opposite numbers in Algiers: 'SHAEF [Eisenhower's Supreme Headquarters] have laid down that the French shall be told nothing of operational plans before D-Day and probably for some time after D-Day.' De Gaulle, who was still refused recognition as the legitimate leader of France by both the British and the Americans, had sensed the way this decision was going even before it was made. But this did not diminish his fury: 'France, who brought freedom to the world and who has been, and still remains, its champion, does not need to consult outside opinions to reach a decision on how she will reconstitute liberty at home ... Wherever they may be and whatever may happen, Frenchmen must accept orders only from this Government from the moment they are no longer personally subjected to enemy coercion. No authority is valid unless it acts in the name of this Government.'

But, not content with just speaking out, he acted too. Fearing an Allied interim government in France and furious at being left out, he carried on preparing his own civil and military plans which, though running in parallel with those of the Allies, would have a distinctly French flavour. He was determined that, whatever the British and Americans thought, the French were going to play a substantial part in their own liberation and have sovereign control of the government of their country afterwards.

But this brought de Gaulle hard up against the old dilemma which would dog him until D-Day. Was he in favour of a 'national uprising' or not? On the one hand, a national uprising in his name would massively increase his legitimacy with the British and Americans. On the other it could lead to violent political turbulence over which he would lose control, so giving the Americans another reason for imposing an Allied interim government.

De Gaulle's ambivalence shows very clearly in his actions during March. He had already created the FFI, the French Forces of the Interior, in an attempt to bring the Resistance movements under formal military control, stipulating that 'Local clandestine activities had … to take on the character of a national effort … [and] had to lead the army out of the shadows to fuse with the rest of the single French Army.' But on 18 March he made a statement publicly confirming the utility of a spontaneous general national uprising, believing that it would have the effect of increasing his legitimacy in the face of the Americans. Then three days later, he sent out secret messages to his nominated delegates across France: 'use every means possible to put the brakes on a national uprising'.

De Gaulle was walking a tightrope between two seemingly contrary ends. He wanted a spontaneous national uprising, but he wanted also to control it. His answer was to send two secret couriers carrying microfilm to the Military Delegates for the northern and southern zones of France with detailed plans for action after D-Day. The instructions for the Military Delegate for the southern zone, which he was to pass on to his regions, stated, among other things, that 'in the Savoie and the Dauphiné [in which the Vercors lies] there are strong Maquis organizations which are to constitute rallying points for most of the effective forces in the area'. For the moment, de Gaulle could believe that he had created the theoretical mechanism to have an uprising, but a controlled one. But would it be strong enough to curb the hot-blooded in the heat of battle, when D-Day was actually announced?

Meanwhile in Algiers plans continued to be developed for a substantive role for French forces in the liberation of their country, along the lines which de Gaulle had set in train. These were based on the work already done in London which proposed, among other options, redoubts which could be 'controlled by the Maquis' in three possible areas: in the Pyrenees, in the Massif Central in central France and in the Alps – including, of course, the Vercors.

15

WEAPONS, WIRELESSES, AIR DROPS AND CODES

In the month of April 1944, the RAF carried out, in all, 403 parachute drops and thirty-four clandestine landings transporting agents out of and into occupied France. The weapons dropped in this month included 117,000 grenades, 72,000 rifles and sub-machine guns, 3,300 Bren light machine guns or Vickers medium machine guns, 138 (mostly light) mortars and 500 shoulder-fired anti-tank weapons, including bazookas. An increasing amount of this was flown, not from Britain, but from airfields in Corsica and North Africa. The area in France which received the greatest share of the tonnage dropped in April was R1 – Region 1, roughly from the Rhône valley to the Italian border and from the Jura mountains to a point some 50 kilometres south of the Vercors. Although we do not know the precise breakdown of arms dropped to the Vercors during the moon period of April 1944, we do know that it amounted in all to some 14 tonnes, making the plateau, which had by now become a distribution centre for the entire area, by some way the largest recipient in southern France of Churchill's sudden largesse from the sky.

Sometimes, containers were packed to fulfil specific requests from agents or commanders on the spot. For instance, in the case of the Vercors, these included medical instruments, boots, socks, or even (for Peter Ortiz) a specific kind of cigar, or a special hunting rifle to be purchased from a particular London shop. Getting the right equipment into the right container and the right containers into the right aircraft was, therefore, an important logistical task.

Packing was also a problem. A badly packed container often meant that all the effort and danger of getting the goods to the drop site would be wasted because the contents would be smashed on landing. Francis Cammaerts reported after one drop that the packing was so bad that 'at least three containers full of material … exploded and detonators were frequently loose', causing losses of 'at least 20% of … material in breakages

[just] through the parachutes not opening and a higher percentage through breakages'. It was not just the weapons which could be damaged by these mistakes. Living near a parachute drop site could also be a hazardous business. On 19 April 1944, Cammaerts sent a furious message to Algiers about a parachute operation on 14/15 March. There is no record of a drop on the Vercors that night, so this was probably an operation somewhere else in his area. Cammaerts had a habit of being unbuttoned when angry and on this occasion he was very angry: 'Delivery parachutes failed to open as usual. Containers fell on a house and crushed the back of the mother of one of reception committee. This bloody carelessness is absolutely inexcusable. You might as well drop bombs. Relatives didn't complain, but my God I do.'

The British insistence on night dropping also presented a problem. All the aircraft used by the British for this task had ranges that could cover the whole of France. But the need for aircraft to be back in friendly airspace by dawn meant that their effective dropping range was limited by the hours of darkness: the shorter the nights, the shorter the effective ranges of the aircraft. In order to overcome this problem, one of the RAF's Special Duty Squadrons which specialized in clandestine parachute drops to France – 624 Squadron, with eighteen Halifaxes – was moved to Blida airfield, 30 kilometres south-west of Algiers, on 16 February 1944.

By 1944, the pilots of these Special Duty Squadrons had had nearly four years' experience of night drops to the Resistance and were very good at it. Nevertheless, mistakes were made as, for instance, on the Saint-Julien drop of 19/20 March when, according to the reception party, the dropping aircraft released their loads at such a high altitude that the containers were scattered far and wide and it took days to recover them. Two containers landed about 15 kilometres away and nine were recovered only because they happened to land near a Maquis camp 'on the other side of the mountain'.

Such complaints were, however, rare where the British were concerned. But the Americans took more time to learn the techniques. Francis Cammaerts, viewing things from the ground and in typically acerbic mood again, wrote: 'The plane when it was British left quietly on its last pass after a little blinking of its lights. It was quickly done. If it was an American plane it was a little different. No feints on the approach, no detours over a neighbouring village to divert attention, no arrival at the site with the motors stilled and flying at low altitude in order to obtain a better grouping of the dropped items. No, as soon as the site was spotted, the plane went higher in order, one would say, to better survey the result; a dispersion area of four or five kilometres because the release was made at high speed, with the necessary results ... Then when everything was spoiled, quite satisfied with himself the pilot descended at speed ... doubtless to prove that he saw us and that if he had launched everything into nature, it wasn't his fault.'

For those on the ground, receiving a parachute drop was not just risky, it also required a high degree of logistical organization. Very often, when a large parachute drop was received, the male population of the neighbouring villages would turn out to help carry away the matériel, gather up the parachutes and hide the traces before first light the next morning. This often entailed using farmers' carts, *gazogène* lorries and mules. Some of the matériel was hidden in caves, but arms were also transported to depots for later dispersal, while ammunition was frequently placed in makeshift central magazines in a shed or a barn, for later distribution.

Most of the arms dropped to the Vercors were sent first to the stoutly constructed school house at Chabottes, near Saint-Agnan, which operated as an armoury where weapons that had arrived in a stripped-down state could be assembled and tested and and those which had been broken on the drop could be mended or cannibalized. One of the problems which the Maquisards faced was that new weapons were almost always dropped without their instruction manuals, so it was often the case that 'experts' had to find out how they worked before they could be distributed for use. That work too was done in the Chabottes school house.

Normally, each recognized and agreed parachute site was assigned a codename and an 'alert' code phrase chosen by the ground reception team. This was broadcast the night before by the BBC's French service. The reception team were then required to send back another agreed code phrase by wireless, indicating that they were ready to receive the drop and that the area was secure. Around April 1944, all of Dalloz's original parachute sites were reclassified and given new codenames, most of them based on items of stationery.

That same spring, the Vercors reception teams received a relatively new piece of SOE equipment, the Eureka or S-Phone. This was designed to assist in locating and guiding incoming aircraft and consisted of a

DROP SITES

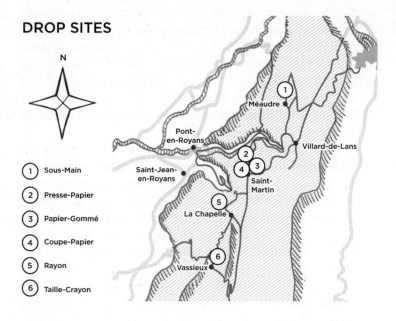

N

1 Sous-Main

2 Presse-Papier

3 Papier-Gommé

4 Coupe-Papier

5 Rayon

6 Taille-Crayon

small radio set with a directional aerial worn on the operator's chest. By pointing the aerial in the general direction of the incoming aircraft, the operator could speak to the pilot of the leading plane.

The weapons parachuted to the French Resistance came from a very wide variety of sources including those captured from the enemy. This caused problems as each weapon needed a different calibre of ammunition. Most Maquis bands had no means of resupply during a battle – so, when what the men carried ran out, the battle had to end.

Although the variety of arms used in the Vercors was wide, the staple weapons on the plateau were the British Lee-Enfield Mark 4 rifle, the American M1 carbine, the British Sten gun, the American Thompson sub-machine gun, the British Bren light machine gun, the British Mills grenade (or bomb), the British-made Gammon grenade and the American bazooka.

The single-shot, bolt-operated Lee-Enfield No. 4 rifle was the same as the standard-issue British Army rifle of the time. Though heavy, it was a robust, highly effective and well-tried weapon, which fired .303 ammunition from a magazine of ten rounds which could easily be 'recharged' (reloaded). Although cumbersome for close-quarter battle, the No. 4 rifle was ideal for accurate fire from a distance of up to 1,000 metres. This range gave the Maquis time to escape before the enemy could get close to them. The semi-automatic American M1 Winchester carbine was much more useful as an assault weapon. It was lighter than the British rifle, fired a smaller bullet (.30) and had a shorter range. But it had the advantage of being capable of firing either repeated single shots or as an automatic.

By far the most common weapon in the hands of the Maquis across France and in the Vercors was the British-made Sten gun, which became almost an unofficial symbol of the French Resistance. The Sten was a truly dreadful weapon, often as lethal to its owner as it was to the enemy. Cheap, mass-produced, badly designed, difficult to aim and prone to jamming, it was probably, despite these defects, responsible for killing more Germans than any other Resistance weapon in France. But its habit of going off and unleashing a whole magazine when dropped also caused the accidental death of a good number of Maquisards – at least three of them on the Vercors. Some 4.6 million Stens were manufactured during the Second World War.

The American Thompson machine gun, though also prone to jamming, was much more sought after. Robust and well built, the 'Tommy gun' carried the cachet of American pre-war gangster films. With a magazine carrying up to forty heavy, 0.5-inch body-stopping rounds, it was a most effective weapon for close-quarter fighting. The light machine gun most used by the French Resistance throughout the war was the British-made Bren. Based on a pre-war Czech design, this took the same .303 round as the Lee-Enfield Mark 4 rifle, had a similar range and was a robust and effective guerrilla weapon in the right hands.

The other British weapon in widespread use in the Vercors, as else-where in France, was the Mills bomb or grenade. Ideal for close-quarter fighting especially in confined spaces such as lorries or small rooms, it could, when detonated, be deadly to anyone within 25 metres. By far the most effective, most admired and most powerful of all the hand grenades used by the Resistance, however, was the Gammon bomb or grenade. This highly flexible weapon came as an empty stockingette to which a fuse was already attached. It could then be filled with plastic explosive to taste, depending on the target. Half a stick of plastic explosive, together with some shrapnel made from, say, nails or a broken cast-iron cooking pot, made a deadly anti-personnel weapon for use in enclosed spaces. When completely filled with explosive, it was lethal on armoured targets and to everyone else in the area, including the thrower if he was not behind good cover. It was especially prized by the Maquis because it was light to carry when empty, took up very little space and could be filled, on site, according to its intended task.

A brand-new weapon, which did not get into Vercors hands in any numbers until some time in June 1944, but which was greatly prized thereafter, was the American bazooka. This was light and could easily be carried by a single man. It fired a rocket-propelled projectile consisting of a shaped explosive charge capable of punching its way through all but the thickest armoured plate. It was accurate and lethal up to about 150 metres, especially against thin-skinned vehicles like troop-carrying lorries. The Maquisards loved it and the Germans hated it.

With D-Day approaching, it became increasingly necessary to have real-time, reliable communications between the Vercors, Algiers and London. From April and May 1944 onwards, the plateau housed, not just the command post for the Vercors, but also Marcel Descour's regional head-quarters, the headquarters of Henri Zeller, the commander of the Resistance in south-east France, and the wireless operators who served Cammaerts' Jockey circuit.

It was eventually decided to group together all the wireless sets and operators serving their different networks in an old creamery at La Britière on the road between Saint-Agnan and Saint-Martin. At the height of operations in the Vercors, there were no fewer than ten radios and their operators working for different parent organizations in London and Algiers, all transmitting from this one cramped building. The oper-ators (known as 'pianists') worked in Morse code, frequently for extremely long hours. It was not unusual to find a La Britière operator fast asleep, his headphones still clamped to his ears and his hand still resting on his Morse key.

SOE radio operators were expected to transmit and receive in Morse at twenty-five words a minute, but many could manage much more than that. The standard speed in the British Army was twelve. Such was the pressure of work that these 'pianists' were frequently assisted by a small team of local volunteers who helped with the coding and decoding of telegrams using one-time code pads. One operator who sent eighty-five coded messages to London in the first three weeks of July needed three assistants working shifts to keep up with the coding and decoding. While transmissions were in progress, sentries were posted outside La Britière to keep an eye open for threats, especially from passing aircraft and detector vans.

The average lifespan of a radio operator in France has been calculated as no more than six months. Francis Cammaerts' radio operator, Augustin Deschamps, was the exception. He operated continuously from October 1942 to the end of the war, sending 416 messages in all and becoming the longest-serving, surviving SOE operator.

Although there were a number of larger non-portable wireless sets in use at La Britière, the classic SOE set issued to most of their radio operators in the second half of the war was the British B Mark III wireless which could be carried around in a small suitcase. The B Mark III could be connected to the mains or to a 12-volt car battery. It could also in emergency be charged from a 'Pedalator' powered either by the feet or (in extreme cases) by hand.

One of the paradoxes of the Resistance forces on the Vercors and elsewhere throughout France was that, although they could communicate with London and Algiers in a matter of minutes, it could often take hours to get a message to one of their own units just a few kilometres away. Wirelesses enabled the Germans to operate as a modern army. But the Vercors commanders had to revert to the medieval practice of sending messages, almost literally, by runners on foot with forked sticks.

The pre-war years had been the heyday of radio and it was not long before the British and French found that ordinary radio broadcasts could also be used for clandestine communication. Very early in the war the BBC's French Service became a key channel for clandestine communication with Resistance circuits in France. The 'Messages personnels' section of the BBC French Service's magazine programme *Les Français parlent aux Français* was the main vehicle for transmitting messages to Resistance units by the use of agreed code phrases.

'Messages personnels' was broadcast four times a day on long, medium and short waves. However, the southern two-thirds of France could be reached only on short wave from London. Because of this, not long after the invasion of Italy, the BBC opened up a broadcasting station transmitting to the south of France in Bari in Italy. In early March 1944, small, robust, portable, short-wave wireless receivers were included in many parachute drops, so that Resistance fighters in southern France could more easily listen to operational messages.

The D-Day planners were not slow to realize the potential ability of the BBC to transmit operational messages to Maquis groups. Indeed this was so important that the Prime Minister himself became involved. On 12 March, the SOE asked Churchill to mediate in a dispute with the Ministry of Information, which was trying to limit SOE's use of broadcasting time. Explaining their case for more broadcast hours, the SOE letter stated: 'HQ SHAEF have confirmed that they will probably want … simultaneous action taken throughout France in order to obtain the maximum dislocation and chaos in the enemy rear.' Despite the fact that the Ministry of Information was run by his close friend Brendan Bracken, Churchill backed the SOE case.

In the last months of 1943, London began assembling a list of secret code phrases for D-Day. Each military region was to receive, in all, six code phrases. The first two related to D-Day and consisted of an 'alert' phrase, designed to tell people to listen closely to their radios at every broadcast over the coming days, and the second was an 'end of alert' phrase indicating that the alert period was over. The remaining four messages were phrases to initiate the pre-planned regional sabotage plans in support of operations on and after D-Day. The theory was that this would enable London to calibrate Resistance action precisely in each region.

But would it be strong enough to cope with the wave of euphoria, hope and dreams when the great day came?

16

APRIL 1944

On Good Friday, 7 April 1944, a pretty and well-dressed young woman claiming to be a student booked into the Hôtel Bellier in La Chapelle, causing something of a stir in the village. Her name was Maude Champetier de Ribes and she was the daughter of a cousin of the French Senator Auguste Champetier de Ribes, an early opponent of Marshal Pétain and, at the time, under arrest by the Germans. Judging from her fashionable clothes, everyone thought she had come from Paris for a short holiday. Tourism, based chiefly on winter sports, had continued on the plateau, but in much diminished form. Nevertheless, it was unusual in these wartime years to see visitors so late – and so smartly dressed.

Not unnaturally, the chic, well-connected and attractive Mlle Champetier de Ribes, who frequently left the hotel to take the air on long walks in the neighbourhood, became a centre of attraction, especially for the young Maquisards based in and around the town. One of them, seeking to impress, told her he was part of a huge force of Maquisards on the plateau, numbering some 5,000.

At about the same time, another attractive young tourist, Mireille Provence, booked into the Hôtel Virard in Saint-Jean-en-Royans at the western edge of the plateau. She claimed to be from Alsace-Lorraine and to have come for a few days' walking. Although dressed 'like a film star', she went out for long walks every day with her dog in the nearby Forêt de Lente, home to a number of Maquis camps. She too caught the eye of the local Maquisards, who, as young men will, went out of their way to strike up conversations with this unusual and alluring newcomer. But she also attracted the attention of others.

Mireille Rigoudy, *patronne* of the Hôtel Virard, mentioned her new guest to one of the Maquisard leaders in the area. Mlle Provence was put under discreet surveillance, presumably by the hotel staff, for it was soon reported that, as well as smart clothes, she had unusually luxurious underwear and spoke in German every night to a telephone number in Grenoble.

On Easter Sunday, the Milice occupied Saint-Jean-en-Royans and raided the Maquis camps in the Forêt de Lente. Meanwhile other Vichy security forces descended on the Ferme d'Ambel and, finding a small cache of arms in the house, burnt it to the ground. That night, the Milice withdrew from the plateau taking nine hostages with them. Thanks to the Maquis' early-warning system, all the camps' inhabitants were able to melt away into the forest long before the Milice raiding parties arrived. That night a slip of paper was secretly delivered under the door of the Milice Chief in Saint-Jean. It read: 'If you touch one hostage or arrest one member of the civil population, you will die.' The hostages were released next morning.

At lunchtime on Easter Monday, a crisis meeting was held in the Café Juge in Saint-Jean to discuss the Milice raid and 'the lady with the dog'. Most people in the town believed her to be a German spy whose information had helped the Milice go straight to the Forêt de Lente camps. Among those present were the most senior Resistance leaders on the plateau – including Jacques Huillier, Eugène Samuel, Louis Bourdeaux and André Valot. There was an intense discussion for an hour or so, at the end of which Bourdeaux summed up the meeting: 'We are not the Gestapo. We have no concrete proof against her. No further action. Leave it.'

In La Chapelle they took a more aggressive view. On that same day, Easter Monday, a small group from the village including Marcel Roudet, the ex-Lyon policeman, accompanied by one of Geyer's men, detained Maude Champetier de Ribes and, after questioning, took her to Valence, where she was released. Another of Geyer's men, who had been in the Hôtel Bellier when Mlle de Ribes booked in, was instructed to follow her discreetly. She went first to Valence and then to a hotel in Grenoble, where she gave him the slip.

These Milice raids, though no doubt disruptive and destabilizing, did not at first sight appear to have a long-term effect on the ability of the local Resistance to carry out operations, for that same night, 10 April 1944, four agents, fifteen containers of arms and six packages containing 90 million francs were parachuted into a site at Eymeux, just outside Saint-Jean-en-Royans.

Three days later, however, the Resistance leaders in La Chapelle received an urgent telephone call from a restaurant owner in Valence. He refused to talk on the telephone and demanded that someone should come to meet him urgently. Two Maquisards were sent down to Valence, where the café owner told them that the previous evening some senior Germans and Milice had had dinner in his restaurant, during which he overheard them discussing an operation involving 'major forces' which would be launched on the Vercors on 16 April – three days away.

On the night of 15 April, the order went out for the Maquisards to hide their weapon stocks, leave their camps and disperse into the forests. One camp near the Col de Rousset were late in pulling out and bumped into a Milice patrol coming over the Col by a forest track in the early morning of 16 April. There was a short firefight before both Milice and Resistants pulled back with only light casualties on each side.

At 16.00 that afternoon, a Milice convoy of twenty-five vehicles led by two infamous Miliciens, Jacques Dugé de Bernonville and Raoul Dagostini, rolled into Vassieux and installed themselves in the Hôtel Allard. Dagostini was accompanied by a smart girl in Milice uniform, referred to as 'Colonel Maude', who turned out to be his mistress. She was soon recognized as Maude Champetier de Ribes, the attractive and inquisitive 'student' who had been in La Chapelle just a week earlier. She was described during her time in Vassieux in terms which say as much about the voyeurism of the observer as they do about the nature of his subject: 'A veritable amazon. Her hips delicately moulded into a pair of Milice uniform trousers, her abundant mane of dark hair covered by an officer's flat cap, her firm bust under a loose-fitting jacket held in by the straps of her cross-belt, along with her haughty expression, her sensual mouth, her habit of leaping on to the saddle of her male colleagues' motorcycles in the manner of a cowboy mounting his thoroughbred horse …'

There was another eye-catching young French girl who also accompanied the Milice on their raid – 'Mireille Provence'. In fact we now know that her real name was Simone Waro, a nightclub singer from Paris. Married, divorced and with a child, 'Provence' was a clever, alluring and experienced adventuress. Unlike her compatriot Maude de Ribes, whose attachment to the Milice sprang from her passion for Dagostini, Mireille Provence seems to have been a genuine and enthusiastic fascist, who was said, according to one Vercors legend, to have participated in interrogation and torture sessions of captured Maquis. But there is no firm evidence to support this.

The Vichy security forces' raids that morning were not confined to Vassieux. They also occupied the town of Die, where Milice guards were placed on all bridges. In addition they took over the post offices in the main towns on and around the plateau, including Crest, Saint-Jean, Romans and La Chapelle (where a small detachment of Germans – probably observers – also set themselves up in the Hôtel Bellier).

It was however, Vassieux, seen by both the Germans and the Milice as the centre of Maquis activity on the plateau, which bore the brunt of the Milice action that day. Later, the town priest, Abbé Gagnol, wrote: 'It was Sunday at four o'clock. The celebration of the end of Easter week had just drawn to a close with the singing of Vespers followed by a gathering of parishioners outside the Mairie, when suddenly someone shouted that there was a long column of military vehicles and lorries approaching the town … In a trice, the village was encircled and there was a chatter of machine guns from positions set up around the town, even in the church tower! The village young men had no chance to escape and were quickly rounded up …'

Gagnol went to see Dagostini and told him, 'I will stand as guarantor for the young men of my parish whom you have arrested totally without reason. These are neither bandits nor criminals.'

'Monsieur le Curé, don't fool with me,' retorted Dagostini. 'I know there are these young shits here – and they are hidden in this village. It's no good trying to hide the truth from me. We are very well informed … It's 5.30 now. Come and see me again at 6 p.m. …'

'I went back at exactly 6 p.m. After another hour of discussion … he gave me his promise that my young men would be released. And indeed they were a little later. After spending some time peeling potatoes for the Milice's evening meal, they were all allowed to return home … except … two strangers whom I didn't know and for whom I could not speak.'

There followed a week of interrogations, torture, arrests, searches, the burning of farms and houses where weapons or ammunition were found and summary trials which handed down death sentences to a number of those who had fallen into Dagostini's hands. It must be added that there were also a depressing number of denunciations by local people both of individuals and of hidden arms dumps. Abbé Gagnol spent most of the next week visiting Dagostini and his fellow Milice chiefs, pleading for the lives of his parishioners, eventually succeeding in having them all released except for two from outside the Vassieux parish and for whom the Abbé could not vouch.

The following Sunday, the Vassieux villagers, along with some 200 Miliciens, crowded into the village church for Sunday mass. The Abbé's sermon was uncompromising: 'My brothers, it is first of all to you, my Vassieux parishioners, that I address my words. I urge you to be calm and have faith, despite the terrible and painful things that have been forced upon us … Now, members of the Milice, I want to speak to you … As a priest I say to you that it is my duty to remind you of what is meant by Christianity, which you Milice profess to defend. Is not the thirteenth article of the Milice code "To defend Christianity"? Christianity demands the practice of justice and charity! But these last few days justice and charity have been violated by you all. You say you are fighting terrorism. But with sorrow I have to say to you that you are the real terrorists here in our town. You say you have come here to preserve law and order, but I say you are in fact fomenting revolution …'

That afternoon, Gagnol was called to give the last rites to three condemned men, two of them the strangers he had been unable to speak for. An hour later the men were tied to posts set out in front of two haystacks and, in Gagnol's presence and that of most of the town, were executed by firing squad. Their bodies were thrown in the town rubbish pit. Before light the following morning, as Vassieux was still deep in troubled sleep, the Milice pulled out. The nightmare was over.

But its effects reverberated for some time afterwards. So far, supporting the Resistance on the plateau had been cost free. Now people had been shown in the most brutal terms that by doing so they placed their lives and property in danger. 'The Milice incursion cast a dark shadow over the plateau,' noted one commentator afterwards. 'Doubt began to infect the population and even the Maquisards too. Morale [among the Maquisards] had already taken a battering as a result of the rigours of a hard winter, repeated blows struck against them by the enemy and the decisions to disperse into the forests and avoid battle whenever they could. Now it plummeted even further.' The desertion rates began to rise again and many among the civil population started to blame the Maquis for having brought this catastrophe upon their heads. Relations between them started to cool.

Despite these terror tactics in Vassieux, the Germans, who had kept a close eye on the Vassieux operation, were very dissatisfied with the

Milice performance. Three executions, six prisoners deported to Dachau and a few farms burnt were a totally inadequate outcome, given the numbers everyone knew were on the plateau. The Germans concluded that the Milice could not be relied on when it came to serious operations to destroy Resistance concentrations. They would have to do the job themselves.

Meanwhile general German nervousness about an impending invasion was reaching fever pitch. A British intelligence summary published on 20 April, based on a captured German document passed to London from Berne in Switzerland, listed the actions the Germans were planning to take when D-Day happened. These included confining the French militia to barracks, taking over electricity-supply systems, seizing vehicles and horse-drawn carriages, controlling roads, and requiring French citizens on the street to wear a German-issued armband and to walk with their hands permanently clasped behind their back, at risk of being shot if either condition was not observed. The closing of shops and of some factories, together with the mass movement of populations in sensitive zones, was also planned.

Two days later, on 22 April, an event occurred in Nice on the French Mediterranean coast which added significantly to German jumpiness and was to have a profound impact on the future of the Vercors plateau.

Shortly after Francis Cammaerts had returned to France, he was joined by an American OSS agent, an expert on forward airfields and landing points, whose job was to assist with the project Cammaerts had been charged with in his orders – the creation of a string of Resistance strongpoints which could be used to leapfrog paratroops ahead of the advancing southern invasion forces. The first job assigned to Cammaerts' assistant was to survey the Valensole plateau, then to look at the Vercors and after that at the Beaurepaire massif. But before he could complete his work in Valensole, he was betrayed to the Germans and captured along with documents containing details of the Allied leapfrogging plans. Now the Germans knew – or thought they knew – the strategic importance of the Vercors in the context of a southern invasion.

It is possible that it was because of this information that, at about this time, Berlin suddenly shifted anti-partisan operations from the northern Geneva corridor to the area around Grenoble, ordering General Heinrich Niehoff to start planning an operation to destroy the Maquis on the Vercors plateau.

GERMAN OPERATIONS 1944

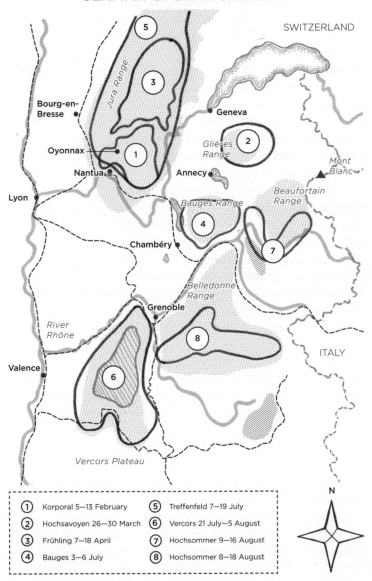

SWITZERLAND

Bourg-en-Bresse

Oyonnax

Nantua

Lyon

Geneva

Glières Range

Annecy

Bauges Range

Chambéry

Belledonne Range

Grenoble

River Rhône

Valence

Vercors Plateau

Mont Blanc

Beaufortain Range

ITALY

Jura Range

① Korporal 5—13 February
② Hochsavoyen 26—30 March
③ Frühling 7—18 April
④ Bauges 3—6 July
⑤ Treffenfeld 7—19 July
⑥ Vercors 21 July—5 August
⑦ Hochsommer 9—16 August
⑧ Hochsommer 8—18 August

N

At the time Pflaum's troops were engaged with another operation against Maquis units in the Jura. Once again, Romans-Petit's Jura Maquis simply melted back into the forests. On 18 April, Pflaum began slowly withdrawing his forces, moving them south to the area around Grenoble in preparation for the attack which Berlin had ordered against the Maquis on the Vercors plateau.

Elsewhere, the lessons from the Glières disaster were beginning to sink in, at least with Francis Cammaerts. On 16 April, the day the Milice occupied Vassieux, he wrote to London about his visit to the plateau some weeks previously. His report was flown back on a Lysander, reaching London on 30 April: 'Anglophobia referred to in my last report is increasing daily – all work is going to be very difficult until D-Day ... when that day comes there will be a change of attitude ... [But] if you want results, it must come quickly. [In the Vercors] have visited the big chief [Chavant] and confidence is established. There is a finely organised army who have contact with North Africa, but their supplies, though plentiful, are not what they need; they need long distance and anti-tank weapons. They have received an Anglo-American Mission visit, but this does not seem to have produced the results desired ... they can hang on for some time ... but it mustn't be too long or they may suffer an attack similar to that in Glières, though my impression is that they would not make the same mistakes.'

The folly of seeking to hold fixed positions in the face of a superior German army determined not to allow the Resistance to threaten their lines of communication was not, however, understood by all. On the same day that Cammaerts was warning of a repeat of the Glières tragedy, the Resistance leader of the Maquis in the Auvergne/Massif Central area in central France, started to plan a rising and a redoubt on the nearby Mont Mouchet.

For de Gaulle's colleague Emmanuel d'Astier de La Vigérie, back in London, the blame for the fall of Glières lay not in the wrong tactics, but in lack of British support. On 17 April he wrote a strong letter to Lord Selborne of SOE complaining: 'Our intelligence services signalled yours giving the details of German troops assembling to carry out the "cleansing" of Maquis in the Glières and asking for them to be bombed. SHAEF, sadly, did not think it appropriate to order these operations because they judged they were not worth the risks involved.'

D'Astier added: 'the Maquis are the avant garde of the invasion. Apart from the commandos, they are the only troops engaged on the Western front. The question of the morale of these troops must be considered in the same way as the morale of the rest of the Armies … An operation which may be regarded as not "worth it" in a direct strategic sense could nevertheless have a fortunate effect on the morale [of France] and because of this should be seen … as a good investment in the future … The French people as a whole and the Resistance in particular cannot see how Allied aircraft can mount almost daily attacks on industrial targets and railways which are often right next door to Maquis … while leaving German military targets nearby untouched and free to attack Resistance forces.'

Selborne took the point and promised to do better in future, replying on 1 May: 'I am happy to tell you that we agree with your view … I therefore believe that, in the future, when we receive these requests from the Resistance we will be able to satisfy them.' It was a promise which would be honoured more in the breach than in the observance over the coming months.

Meanwhile, on the plateau itself, there was more than the Milice to worry about. Relations between Eugène Chavant as civil head of the Vercors and Narcisse Geyer, the plateau's military commander, had become unworkable.

During April, a gaunt figure in civilian hiking clothes calling himself 'Hervieux' started paying mysterious visits to the camps on the plateau. His real name was François Huet. Tall, with piercing blue eyes, a spare, ungainly frame and an earnest, perhaps rather humourless personality, the thirty-nine-year-old Huet was a career French Army officer who had served with distinction during the fall of France and had been an early member of the Secret Army. He was the scion of a notable Grenoble family, and his views were those of the traditional French Army officer of his time – right wing, Catholic and in favour of the preservation of the traditional hierarchies in both the Army and the French state. Although in no way a deep or imaginative thinker, he was an intelligent man of measured views and sound military skills who could show extraordinary calmness in the face of crisis. Above all, Huet believed that, as an officer in the French Army, honour, obedience and duty should be the primary arbiters of his life and the frame for all his decisions.

Huet was later to claim that his mysterious April and May visits to military camps on the plateau were to prepare himself for the task he would soon be asked to undertake. But the fact that he was accompanied by the even more gaunt and cadaverous figure of Descour's monk-counsellor, Dom Guétet, leads to the suspicion that the purpose of these visits may rather have been to report to Descour on the state of the Vercors and especially the effectiveness of Geyer as a commander.

Chavant, excluded from all military councils, knew none of this and would anyway probably have concluded that a complaint about Geyer to Descour would only result in the military closing ranks and defending their own. He knew that he would have to go above military heads in France to Algiers if he wanted to be rid of the impetuous young cavalry commander. But how to get to the North African capital? As it happened, the Vercors' resident American spy, Gaston Vincent, who worked for the OSS, had, about this time, just acquired a German plan showing the enemy's entire defence system along France's Mediterranean coast. To Algiers, now deep into planning Anvil, this was, of course, gold dust.

It was arranged that Chavant and his friend Jean Veyrat should act as couriers and take the plan to Cap Camarat, at the southern end of the Bay of Saint-Tropez. Here a submarine would pick them both up and take them to Algiers. Chavant and Veyrat caught a train from Valence to Saint-Raphael, arriving in the Mediterranean coastal town in the early afternoon. But they were still 37 kilometres away from Cap Camarat and there were only six hours to go to their rendezvous time. They tried to procure bicycles but failed. So they set off on foot.

As Chavant later recorded: 'After some time we heard the rumbling of a vehicle engine and while it was still some distance away, made signs to it to stop for us … It was about two o'clock in the afternoon, and with bright sunlight reflecting on the vehicle's windscreen we could not see who the vehicle's occupants were. We simply walked on in our original direction until, when the lorry came to a halt a few metres up the slope from us, we suddenly realized that it was a German lorry carrying a load of sand. In its cabin were the driver and two armed men. What were we to do now? … [We climbed on board and] after a while the lorry rounded a bend in the road and swung in towards the closed gate of a German storage yard for materials. The driver stopped and sounded his horn to call for the gate to be opened. We took the opportunity to jump down and I moved forward to thank the driver for having taken us aboard. I shook hands with him somewhat vigorously and we slowly walked away along the road.'

They still had 25 kilometres to go. It was tough going in the heat. Chavant was thinking of giving up when 'I spotted a farm about 150 metres from the road, with a woman standing outside the farmhouse hanging up washing ... Veyrat and I made straight for the house where the woman, who was the owner, was ... shocked to see our bedraggled, exhausted condition, drenched as we were with sweat after having gone the best part of 30 kilometres on foot. Instead of giving us water, as we asked, she gave us the last of her litre of wine ... We offered her payment but she would not accept it ... Relieved and more comfortable after our visit, we found it quite easy to tackle the remaining distance to Ramatuelle, where we arrived at exactly 6.45 p.m. We just had time to refresh ourselves with a glass or two of mint-flavoured lemonade and then we were ready for our rendezvous ...'

But their contact never appeared. The two men had no option but to begin the long journey back to the Vercors. Passing through Ramatuelle they heard the sound of a BBC broadcast issuing from a small house in the village. The two threw themselves on the hospitality of the occupier: 'She gave us some eggs for our evening meal and then took us to the local café to introduce us to its landlord, who cooked the eggs for us. He also allowed us to bed down for the night on benches in his café. The lady even arranged to meet us next morning and drive us to Saint-Tropez in her bus, which she did, dropping us off right at the station ... At this point ... we took the decision to ask the lady if we could leave our "packages"* with her, with the intention of picking them up on a future visit. We told her absolutely nothing about their contents. She accepted. In spite of the fact that we gave her no information I have somehow ever since had the feeling that she understood perfectly ... what it was all about.'

---

* Containing the secret German defence plans.

A BASKET OF CRABS

President Roosevelt had originally planned that his closest military adviser, the US Chief of Staff General George C. Marshall, should take command of the Overlord invasion of northern France. But in the end he told Marshall, 'I didn't feel I could sleep at ease if you were out of Washington,' and chose Eisenhower for the job instead.

Before he left Algiers on 30 December 1943 to take up his new post, Eisenhower had a private meeting with de Gaulle. The two men got on well together. Eisenhower understood the sensitivities and pride of the French leader better than Roosevelt, who had no patience with de Gaulle's arrogance and his refusal to compromise in the face of the manifest power of the United States in comparison to the practically non-existent contribution that France could bring to winning the war. De Gaulle's meeting with Eisenhower ended rather emotionally, with the American confessing: 'I recognise that I have committed an injustice towards you [referring to the American preference for Giraud] and it is important to say it.' De Gaulle replied, 'You are a man' – in English. Relations between the two men were to remain cordial, even when de Gaulle had fallen out with almost every other Allied leader.

Unfortunately, however, American policy towards de Gaulle and the Free French was set not by General Eisenhower but by President Roosevelt, who regarded de Gaulle as a British stooge and refused implacably to recognize him or his 'government' as the legitimate representatives of the French nation. The British privately disagreed with Roosevelt and accepted the legitimacy of de Gaulle's claims. But they supinely followed the American lead. Most other London-based governments-in-exile, such as those of Czechoslovakia, Poland, Belgium, Luxembourg, Yugoslavia and Norway, had recognized de Gaulle's government by the end of May 1944. Roosevelt explained his position as deriving from a point of principle: he wanted the French people to decide who their leader and government should be after the war was over – not to have this thrust on them by an Allied wartime decision. 'We have no right to colour their views or to give any group the sole right to impose one side of a case on them,' he told the Secretary of State, Cordell Hull. However, Roosevelt's obdurate refusal to accept the obvious looked to de Gaulle suspiciously like preparing the way for an Allied Military Government in France which would be imposed over his head.

With Eisenhower and SHAEF planning Overlord in London and both de Gaulle's 'government' and Allied Force Headquarters (AFHQ) under the command of the British General Sir Henry 'Jumbo' Maitland Wilson, planning Anvil in Algiers, the scene was set for muddle, duplication and unclear command structures. This was greatly exacerbated by the fractured political mix in Algiers and the convoluted structures of the French 'government'. The palace coup that had ousted Giraud in March 1944 ended in the creation of a de Gaulle-led coalition of unlikely bedfellows which allied his own Gaullists with Communists and Socialists.

There was, however, a price to be paid for this jarring alliance. The French leadership echelons in Algiers were shot through with bitterness and anger on the part of the Giraudists who had lost, compounded by political conspiracy, rivalry and jockeying for power by everyone else. The Gaullists, who had the whip hand in the government, plotted constantly to outmanoeuvre and, if possible, exclude their rivals, especially their Communist colleagues such as the Minister for Air, Fernand Grenier, who was responsible for the FFI's very limited air assets (chiefly some superannuated training aircraft in Syria). The non-Gaullists counter-plotted to resist the erosion of their power and leverage.

The situation was not improved (except of course for the plotters) by the intestinal complexity of French decision-making mechanisms, both in Algiers and on the French mainland. These were headed by the French Committee for National Liberation, chaired by de Gaulle. Below this sat the Military Action Committee responsible for the direction of the Resistance in France. This committee, also chaired by de Gaulle, had as its secretary Jacques Soustelle, giving Soustelle, who was in addition the head of the French Special Forces Directorate, a key position at the centre of the decision-making web. De Gaulle's ministers for the Army, the Navy and the Air Force sat on a separate committee (again chaired by de Gaulle), the National Defence Committee, which could make recommendations, but could not itself initiate actions.

Whether by accident or not, this cumbersome structure, riven at every level by political infighting, provided the ideal conditions for de Gaulle to do what he did best – divide and rule. The consequence was that most of the important decisions were cobbled together in informal huddles, then validated in de Gaulle's private office and finally rubber-stamped in the formal committee structures of the 'government'. The committees which made up this 'government' were more a duelling ground for political sword-fighting than a structure for rational decision-making.

Complex structures and unclear command lines were, however, by no means the special preserve of Algiers. In March 1944, de Gaulle appointed the French hero of the North African campaign, General Marie-Pierre Koenig, to be the head of all French regular and irregular forces operating in France and the chief interlocutor with SHAEF in London. But Roosevelt intervened and refused to give Eisenhower permission to deal with Koenig, except on strictly defined military matters related to D-Day. This did nothing to foster either good relations or smooth decision-making.

There was also the question: how far did Koenig's writ run? Was he responsible for all of France or just the northern half, which would be affected by Overlord? The problem was solved by making Koenig responsible for operations in all of France up to the moment Anvil was launched, when command of operations in southern France would pass to Algiers. This arrangement at least had the benefit of theoretical clarity – but all would depend on whether it would work in practice, given that Algiers provided most of the resources going into southern France and made most of the decisions about what happened there. Koenig in London might will the ends, but it was Algiers who willed the means.

One of Eisenhower's first acts on arriving in London was to establish a single coordinating and directing body (special forces HQ – SFHQ)for all special forces operations in France under his personal control within SHAEF. On 23 May 1944 (just two weeks before D-Day), a North African equivalent was established in Algiers – the Special Projects Operations Centre (SPOC). This also had its own training and preparation facility for agents going into France at the Club des Pins, a collection of holiday huts on the beach at Sidi Ferruch 20 kilometres west of the city. In theory both the Algiers and London organizations charged with directing operations in occupied France were created as strictly Anglo/US/French tripartite organizations. But in reality, since the French had no resources to bring to the table, they were the constant *demandeurs* and thus always treated as the junior partners.

The French representative involved in directing Resistance operations from Algiers, Lieutenant Colonel Jean Constans, was the person whom the Vercors relied on to meet its needs. Though he had been personally appointed by Jacques Soustelle, Constans' exact position was never properly clarified by the French, greatly undermining his authority with his British and American partners alike. Koenig insisted that Constans should be his representative in Algiers, but this was never accepted by Soustelle or by any of those below him in the 'government'.

Constans' ability to do his job was further weakened by the fact that he had little influence with the *de facto* head of SPOC, the senior British SOE officer Francis Brooks Richards. 'Apparently just a member of the British section, Brooks Richards was more an autonomous liaison officer representing the whole Allied Command to whom we were subordinated,' Constans later noted, his frustration showing.

The feeling was mutual. In an interview given after the war, Brooks Richards offered not only his personal view of his French partner but also a glimpse of the poisonous atmosphere inside the Algiers organization which the Resistance in southern France – and the Vercors – depended on for help. 'Constans ... found it quite hard to carve out a job for himself. He was a perfectly nice man who hadn't really got very much of a job. Poor Constans waved about regarding himself as rather too senior to deal with me and was cold-shouldered by the others.'

British disdain was not only directed at their French partners. It also extended to their American colleagues in OSS, whose dedicated special forces units arrived in Algiers during April. An internal SOE minute of 6 March 1944 complained, 'This note will give you an idea of the difficulty we are having in working with OSS in Algiers as they are irresponsible and also underhand.'

Matters were not improved by the fact that physical arrangements in Algeria were almost as defective as the personal relationships. The new organization was housed in a complex of nine British Nissen huts, twenty-five tents and a wooden mess hall set up near the Villa Magnol, close to the centre of Algiers. One of the Nissen huts was fitted out with maps and charts giving the position of all agents and dropping sites across the whole of the southern zone. Another was dedicated to the writing, receiving and distribution of all messages. A third dealt with the encoding and decoding of messages. But the cramped conditions and limited resources in the two huts which dealt with signals to and from France ensured that the operators were very quickly swamped by the increasing volume of messages up to and after D-Day.

In Britain, French Resistance signals were received at the SOE station at Grendon Hall in Buckinghamshire and then sent on for decoding before being delivered, day and night, by dispatch rider to SOE headquarters in Baker Street. In Algiers, however, the decoding of incoming signals did not begin immediately on their receipt, but had to wait for the normal start of work on the morning after they were received. To begin with, all the signals from the previous night were spread out on a large table and the decoders, who preferred to work with the agents they were used to, made their own selections of which they would decode first. An attempt would then be made to assess the importance of each decoded signal and decide who should see it, after which the signal would pass into the convoluted structures of Maitland Wilson's Algerian headquarters. Here again, lack of clarity of command made the business of distribution very difficult. Communications with British SOE agents, like Francis Cammaerts, were an entirely British affair and therefore relatively straightforward. But signals to and from organizations like the Vercors, which were under direct French command, were the responsibility of Jacques Soustelle. These complexities meant that urgent messages from Resistance centres in France could often take as much as three or even four days to reach their final destination.

The spectacle of all this squabbling, infighting and dysfunctionality was astonishing to those who arrived in Algiers from occupied France. Soustelle himself recognized this, but not, it seems, his responsibility for making it so: 'Those arriving in Algiers having experienced the most terrible dangers in France were deeply shocked by what they saw … They could not forgive the spectacle of personal rivalry and structural dysfunctionality they witnessed which only served to undermine the assistance that our patriotic fighters were entitled to expect from those who were supposed to serve them.'

The French writer Antoine de Saint-Exupéry, at the time a fighter pilot in Algiers, put it more bluntly, describing the atmosphere in the city as like a 'pétaudière'* and a 'bain de haine'.† Eugène Chavant called it a 'panier de crabes'.‡

---

* Literally a fart chamber or more commonly, perhaps, a dung heap.

† A sink of wickedness and squabbling.

‡ A basket of crabs.

18

MAY 1944

With spring turning to summer, anticipation began to rise towards fever pitch as France and its occupiers sensed that the invasion must now be very near. On 1 May 1944, the BBC accidentally sent out a string of warning messages to sabotage teams across France instructing them to stand by – a landing was imminent. Dr Josef Götz, German intelligence's chief radio expert in France, immediately understood the significance of the broadcasts and sent out a warning that a landing was to be expected in days. When nothing happened, his credibility was critically damaged.

In early May, for reasons we do not know, the German attack on the Vercors ordered by Berlin, which was originally due to take place in May, was 'postponed for an indefinite period'. Some speculate that this was because Pflaum needed more intelligence on the Maquis dispositions on the plateau. This may have been one reason. But it seems more likely that two other factors were more important in forcing Pflaum to delay. The first was the strength of the Vercors Maquis, which was larger and better equipped than those either on the Glières or in the Jura; and the second was that, if the Germans were to follow their established strategy of surround, attack, annihilate, destroy, then the size of the Vercors meant that Pflaum would need more troops than he had under his own command. He would have to wait for reinforcements.

Allied plans for the invasion, however, continued apace. In the very early hours of 4 May, a Hudson light bomber landed at a clandestine strip near Macon, loaded eight passengers, including Henry Thackthwaite of the Union Mission, and flew them back to Britain. Thackthwaite was taken straight to SOE headquarters in Baker Street to give a 'fresh account at first hand of conditions'. It was probably as a direct result of Thackthwaite's information that, in early May, SOE took the decision that a second mission, codenamed Eucalyptus and dedicated entirely to the Vercors, should be sent in – though in the event they would not actually get there until the third week of June. Thackthwaite's report also stressed the plateau's urgent need for heavy weapons and especially mortars and anti-tank guns. It was a recommendation that would be repeated many times in the weeks to come – but always in vain.

On the same day that Thackthwaite left for Britain, a meeting took place between two senior representatives of the civilian and military Resistance organizations in the southern zone to try and find a way to resolve the growing tensions between the two. A 'charter' was drawn up designed to regulate civil/military relations. It declared, more in hope than expectation, that the divisions between the military and the civilian elements of the Resistance would henceforth 'cease to exist in the face of the great events which we will shortly face'. It also stipulated that 'to appoint the military commanders without the agreement of the political leaders will prolong reluctance, misunderstanding and obstruction,' a precise description of what had happened when Geyer had been imposed on the Vercors without Chavant's agreement.

Roland Costa de Beauregard, who commanded the northern half of the Vercors under Geyer, saw the problem at first hand and – at some risk – wrote a private report to Marcel Descour about conditions on the plateau. It was, but only by inference, highly critical of Geyer. 'There is without doubt a problem of personalities. The need to have effective military command, in principle, is no longer contested by senior elements on the civil side … But the person who could achieve this in practice does not yet exist – and could not be found on the civilian side, or at present on the military side either.'

Descour could not ignore the problem, not least because, his enthusiasm for redoubts undimmed, he had at the same time been pressing Algiers to turn the Vercors into 'a strong bridgehead which would enable a lightning advance of [Allied] forces from a landing in the south'. He turned immediately to François Huet.

Descour arranged to meet Huet on 6 May 1944 in the Rue du Plat in Lyon. It was raining softly as the two men walked down the busy street, chatting in low voices. 'The time has come, François,' the older man began. 'I want you to take command of the Vercors. The situation is rather delicate. This conflict [between Geyer and Chavant] has got to be stopped. But we can't afford to lose Geyer. It might be wise to point out that you're not actually superseding him but have been appointed to a kind of broader role above him.' Huet accepted, subject to obtaining

Chavant's agreement, adding: 'But conditions in the Grenoble area worry me. The Germans won't tolerate the situation on the Vercors for very long.' It seems, however, that Chavant was never consulted about the plan to remove Geyer, for within a few days of the meeting between Descour and Huet, *le Patron* had once again left the Vercors with Jean Veyrat to make a second attempt to reach Algiers.

In the North African capital and in London things were now moving swiftly towards the event everyone was waiting for. On 16 May, de Gaulle in Algiers issued a directive 'concerning the military operations to be carried out by the French Forces of the Interior with the aim of liberating the territory of metropolitan France'. Attached to this document was an annex entitled 'Plan Caïman'. This was the product of the process initiated by Miksche to come up with a French plan which, while seeking to assist the Allied invasion, would at the same time enable de Gaulle's forces to play a major part in their country's liberation.

This first iteration of the Caïman Plan proposed areas where French operations should be concentrated. The most ambitious and the most important proposal was that French airborne forces, working with the Resistance, should 'liberate' an area in western France centred on the Massif Central. The aim was to link up with an Allied invasion in northern France, while at the same time supporting an invasion on the Mediterranean coast by opening up the way to the Massif Central.

The second area of French action suggested by de Gaulle's study was in the Rhône valley, where Maquisards from bases like the Vercors would cut lines of communications, harry the enemy and assist an Allied southern invasion force by helping to free up a corridor to Grenoble. From here the Allies could choose between continuing either north-east to the Italian frontier or north-west towards Besançon and central France.

Two things are noteworthy about the study de Gaulle approved on 16 May. The first was that the Caïman Plan envisaged an 'air bridgehead' only in the Massif Central and not in places like the Vercors, as previously proposed by Cammaerts and agreed by Allied headquarters in Algiers. The second was that, while the French action proposed in the Rhône Valley (including the Vercors) was consistent with Allied plans, the Caïman Plan for an air landing in the Massif Central had no connection with Allied intentions whatsoever.

What de Gaulle was in effect suggesting, although it was never explicitly explained as such, was that after a seaborne landing in the north of

France commanded by the US and another led by the British in the south, there should be a French-led air invasion in the centre. Leaving aside whether or not this made military sense, its political advantages to de Gaulle were obvious. He would have a liberation 'front' all of his own. It would, moreover, be far easier for de Gaulle to have political control over post-D-Day France if he was in charge in the centre, rather than an also-ran to the Americans and British in the north and the south.

The implications for the Vercors in all this, however, were huge. Both in Eisenhower's plan for a Mediterranean coast invasion followed by a thrust north through Grenoble and Lyon, and in Churchill's preference for an invasion across the Italian frontier and a thrust west and south-west past Geneva, the Vercors and Plan Montagnards would have a real part to play. In de Gaulle's plan for an additional air assault on the Massif Central, they would have none.

On 20 May 1944, four days after de Gaulle had approved Caïman, 3,000 Maquisards gathered in the area around the Mont Mouchet in the Massif Central and erected a banner declaring 'Ici commence La France libre'. The Germans responded immediately and with overwhelming force. Three weeks later the rising was put down with great brutality and heavy local reprisals.

On the same day that the Mont Mouchet rose, a joint Anglo-French meeting was held in West Court, Finchampstead, outside London. Its purpose was 'To examine the support and employment of Resistance in France after D-Day'. The presumption accepted by all at the meeting was that the Resistance should be called to arms in two phases. Those in the northern half of France would take immediate action on D-Day. Those in the south would be launched into action later in the context of a southern invasion. An important conclusion of the meeting proposed the creation of 'Redoubts [in] those few mountainous areas where we can be sure we can securely build up forces ... [which] could be a firm base which could (protect an) "airhead" from which large-scale Allied airborne forces could operate'. Despite the opposition of many Resistance leaders on the ground in France and the clear and painful experience of Glières (soon to be repeated in the Mont Mouchet), the establishment of redoubts after D-Day had now become official Allied policy.

The next morning, 21 May, there was a meeting at Allied headquarters in Portsmouth to consider the conclusions of the Finchampstead discussions of the day before. The Allied military planners comprehensively

OPTIONS FOR THE SOUTHERN INVASION

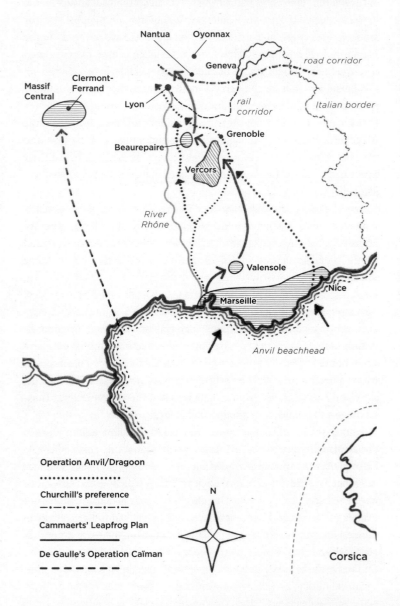

Nantua
Oyonnax
Geneva
road corridor

Massif Central
Clermont-Ferrand
Lyon
rail corridor
Italian border

Beaurepaire
Grenoble

Vercors

River Rhône

Valensole

Nice

Marseille

Anvil beachhead

Operation Anvil/Dragoon
....

Churchill's preference
—·—·—·—·—·—

Cammaerts' Leapfrog Plan
——————

De Gaulle's Operation Caïman
— — — — — — —

N

Corsica

rejected the possibility of redoubts. They insisted that the time was not yet right for projects which they would not have the resources to support until after the Normandy bridgehead had been secured, and ordered that Resistance operations in the context of D-Day should be confined to the sabotage plans already agreed. These were: a coordinated attack on the French railway system; an attack on underground long-distance tele-coms cables; the sabotage of electricity supply lines; attacks on Wehrmacht convoys and guerrilla actions against German command posts, petroleum facilities and ammunition dumps.

What is extraordinary is the extent to which this instruction from the Allied Supreme Command was subsequently simply ignored. It should have been the end of the entire *réduit* project. Instead, all sides blithely continued with their various redoubt plans, as though nothing whatever had changed.

The 21 May SHAEF meeting seems also to have decided to reverse the original plan to call the Resistance to action in two phases, with 'circuits' in the north being launched on D-Day, while those in the south waited for the southern invasion. SHAEF decided instead that the Resistance across all France, north and south, would be called to action together on D-Day. That night London sent a signal to Maitland Wilson in Algiers warning him of this significant change, which would carry heavy conse-quences for the Resistance in his area of responsibility (southern France): 'Action messages. These are to be sent to the field at H minus seven and a half hours.* They will instruct *all* resistance groups [emphasis added] within a maximum period of forty-eight hours of receipt of the message, to set off their rail demolitions, carry out their telecommunications sabotage and put their general guerrilla plan into effect.'

Four days after this order, a meeting took place in London between the British Brigadier Eric Mockler-Ferryman of SOE and General Koenig, the man appointed by de Gaulle as overall head of French forces in France. The purpose was to agree which elements of the Resistance would be called to arms on D-Day and how. Mockler-Ferryman did not trouble to explain to Koenig that these orders had in fact already been decided on. Although hesitant, Koenig eventually agreed on the princi-ple that the responsibility to issue orders to the Resistance would be Eisenhower's, but warned that a 'heavy responsibility [would lie with

---

* That is, seven and a half hours before the first Allied troops hit the beach.

those who initiated] a premature launch [of Resistance groups] that could not be supported by air'. Mockler-Ferryman left the meeting well satisfied, though he noted afterwards that he doubted that Koenig realized at the time the full implications of what he had agreed to.

The following day, 26 May, to the fury of Churchill and Roosevelt, de Gaulle decided that his government in Algiers would henceforth be publicly referred to as the Provisional Government of France. Later that day, Francis Cammaerts sent a message from his headquarters in Seyne-les-Alpes to London confirming that 'a small number of paratroops could hold air bridgeheads ... for some time' and asked for officers in uniform to be parachuted in soon after D-Day.

It was in this climate of feverish preparation, confused aims and wild schemes that, a day later, on 27 May, Eugène Chavant and John Veyrat finally arrived in Algiers after a journey which had included trains, buses, a US motor torpedo boat and an aircraft from Corsica. They were immediately taken to see Jean Constans, who, despite having arrived from London himself only a few days previously, acted as guide and host during their few days in the North African capital.

Paradoxically, just the day before Chavant's arrival in Algiers, a telegram he had sent before leaving the Vercors finally reached the desk of Francis Brooks Richards. Its subject was Plan Montagnards: 'Eugène Chavant begs to pass to his chiefs the following message: Measures taken last year by General Vidal and known to Dalloz, now in Algiers, can be fully carried out. German and Milice incursions have left resources intact ... [we have] prepared five companies of *sédentaires*.* Can assure protection for mobilisation of DZ [dropping zone] for regular paratroops provided further drops are received for 2 light and 1 heavy companies. Should we continue with project? If yes we need senior officer to take overall command of the organization. Await orders and instructions. Signed Chavant.'

Le Patron's first Algiers meeting was with Constans himself. Pointing out the dispositions of troops on the plateau and the positions of the various landing sites on a map, Chavant told Constans that to make Plan Montagnards work, the plateau would need to be reinforced by 2,500 regular paratroops. Constans didn't turn a hair and promised him 4,000. Chavant also explained the difficulties he had with Geyer and asked for

* 'Shadow' Maquis units continuing ordinary lives in their home communities until called up.

him to be replaced. Later Chavant met, among others, Soustelle who, at the end of *le Patron*'s visit, gave him two sealed brown envelopes to hand over to Descour on his return and the following written statement of approval and support on behalf of General de Gaulle:

Algiers 30 May 1944.

Decision.
The directives given by General Delestraint [Plan Montagnards] for the Vercors remain in force.

The execution of this plan shall be *conducted through the regional and departmental structures under the command of the Regional Military Delegate for the R1 Region* [emphasis in original] in liaison with … London on the one hand and Algiers on the other.

Signed on behalf of General de Gaulle.
Jacques Soustelle

What is astonishing about the encouragement which Chavant received for Plan Montagnards in Algiers – and especially the specific order given to enact it by Soustelle on behalf of de Gaulle – is that it came just nine days after SHAEF in London had decreed that post-D-Day action should be confined solely to sabotage and not include redoubts. On the face of it this looks like the Algiers French deliberately ignoring SHAEF's orders. But the real reason was probably, once again, not conspiracy but poor communication between London and Algiers.

On the day before Soustelle signed the paper for Chavant on behalf of de Gaulle, the French leader's Chief of Staff, General Antoine Béthouart, had a meeting with General 'Jumbo' Maitland Wilson, the British commander of Anvil. During this meeting the two men discussed how the Resistance might best be employed in conjunction with Allied strategy. They agreed that, in addition to the sabotage plans already envisaged, there would be 'guerrilla' operations undertaken from Maquis-dominated areas (in effect redoubts) in, among other regions, the Alps. The following day, instructions along these lines were sent by microfilm to the commanders of each of the key French regions, including Colonel Henri Zeller who was responsible for Resistance activity in south-east France (including the Vercors).

It seems inconceivable that Maitland Wilson would have gone directly against the orders of his superior, Eisenhower, had he known of them. It is much more likely that he was ignorant of SHAEF's instructions at the time. But, whatever the reason – failure to communicate, deliberate intent or misunderstanding – the fact remains that, at this moment, just days away from D-Day, the orders being sent to the Resistance in southern France by London and Algiers were fatally muddled and contradictory.

After the war, when people tried to assess the importance of the document Soustelle gave Chavant, some claimed that it did not really amount to a commitment of support and that Chavant, unused to the sophisticated ways of high-level headquarters, imagined the 'Decision' signed on behalf of de Gaulle to be something more than was in fact intended. There is, however, in the French military archives at Vincennes in Paris another document recording Chavant's visit. This reveals in detail, both what Chavant asked for and what was agreed, including:

The Vercors should be turned into a Resistance bastion with the aim of

a. Acting as a rallying point for the local people on D-Day
b. Serving as a base for parachute drops and for operations by airborne troops …

As a result of M. Chavant's requests, the following decisions have been taken …

… Arms sufficient for 4 Companies will be parachuted to the Vercors during the next 'moon period'.

A sum of 1 million francs will be provided to M. Chavant before his departure from Algiers …

A Mission order will be given to Mr Chavant confirming that he should continue with [Plan Montagnards] …

London will be advised of these decisions.

After the war there would also be those who would claim that Koenig in London, who was of course the person officially in charge of the Resistance in the whole of France, only heard of Chavant's visit some two weeks after the event and that Soustelle had therefore given undertakings he was not entitled to give without clearing them first with London and Koenig. The full Constans report did, indeed, not arrive in London until 8 June, but it seems difficult to believe, not least because of the line 'London will be advised of these decisions', that a summary of it was not sent much earlier.

Cammaerts, among others, would subsequently assert that the British in London were totally unaware of the promises made to Chavant. This, however, is also inaccurate. In the evening of 28 May, a coded telegram from Algiers, probably composed by Brooks Richards, was sent to SOE in London: 'Chavant arrived Algiers last night … On interview makes an excellent impression … Has made serious preparation to form redoubt. Stocking food supplies and preparing more … Does this concord [sic] with you over … redoubt plans …? It would seem excellent project …'

London replied swiftly. Their telegram, timed at 02.47 on the following day, said: 'We have consulted Thackthwaite who considers plan practicable and that an enduring base could be established with minimum initial reinforcement of 1,000 paratroops …' The Allies may not have been party to the specific promises made to Eugène Chavant, but they certainly knew what was planned and, what is more, broadly welcomed it.

This was not the only telegram sent from London to the North African capital that day. At 16.05, London sent a one-line coded message: 'Il y a de l'eau dans le gaz. Repeat. Il y a de l'eau dans le gaz.' Algiers was being informed of the code phrase which would shortly be broadcast by the BBC to instruct Resistance units in the R1 Region, including the Vercors, to listen carefully to their radios for further developments. Something big was about to happen.

THE FIRST FIVE DAYS
OF JUNE 1944

Although there were storms in the Channel in the first week of June 1944, there was sparkling weather and brilliant sunshine on the Vercors plateau. 'The sky was a resplendent, royal blue, and the air delicious to breathe, even at 1,000 metres. Up there on the summits, one felt totally free,' wrote Pierre Tanant, who had recently arrived on the plateau. Jean Prévost, now installed in a stout stone house called Valet farm near Saint-Agnan-en-Vercors with his wife, Claude, and his three children, Michel, Françoise and Alain, commented with the eye of a writer on the extraordinarily pure, 'vertical' quality of the light during these early June days. It was as though the whole plateau had decided to dress up in its very best to welcome the liberation which now seemed so near.

Although there was some guerrilla action during this first week of June 1944 (no less than 7 tonnes of tungsten was stolen from a factory in Saint-Béron north-west of the Vercors on the night of 1/2 June), it seemed that everyone was somehow holding their breath. Elsewhere, however, these were febrile days. On 1 June, 10 Downing Street wrote a letter to Miss M. P. Hornsby-Smith at SOE: 'The Prime Minister has seen [the SOE] minute on assistance to the French Resistance [and] … air operations during the May moon period. You may like to know that he noted on the latter: "Good. Press on."'

That morning there was another meeting in SOE's headquarters in Baker Street to finalize the details of Resistance action after D-Day. Despite SHAEF's clear 21 May instructions that this should be limited to sabotage and should *not* include the creation of redoubts, one of the meeting's chief conclusions dealt with the command of the redoubts already decided on at the Finchampstead meeting of 20 May. The word *réduit* had by this time gained such currency among Allied planners that it was now used even in English documents.

That night, the BBC (this time intentionally) broadcast 162 messages to Resistance organizations right across France, warning of action to come. Once again, Josef Götz warned his superiors that an invasion was near. But because of the previous false alarm, no one paid any attention.

That same day, Winston Churchill dispatched his envoy, Duff Cooper, by private plane to Algiers, carrying a personal invitation from the Prime Minister for de Gaulle to come to London. The French leader initially refused, declaring Roosevelt's intention to install an Allied Military Government in France as the reason. But over the next twenty-four hours he relented.

Meanwhile, in France, Pflaum reported on 3 June 1944: 'Of the five Departments of our region, it is the Department of the Isère which is the most active … The terrorists here operate chiefly against Wehrmacht soldiers … attacks against the railways continue without any reduction … Practically all the lines between Grenoble and Lyon and Grenoble and Chambéry are cut. Explosive attacks against factories and pylons are increasing constantly.' He was not making much of a success of keeping open the lines of communication through his area.

While Pflaum was telling his superiors how troublesome the Resistance in his area was proving, two senior officers, Brigadier Mockler-Ferryman and his OSS opposite number Joe Haskell, took the train to Portsmouth to call on Lieutenant General Walter Bedell Smith, Eisenhower's Chief of Staff, at Southwick House, the Supreme Commander's forward headquarters. The pair first briefed Bedell Smith, outlining the extensive Resistance networks throughout France, the kind of damage they could inflict and the severe dangers they would run if prematurely brought into action. They asked for guidance. Did the Supreme Commander still want the Resistance to rise all across France as had been agreed by SHAEF on 21 May? Or did he wish to revert to the plan for them to rise in phases starting with those closest to the Normandy beaches?

At the time, Eisenhower was away from his headquarters attending last-minute meetings with his key commanders at Bushy Park on the western outskirts of London. When he returned to Southwick House in the late afternoon, Bedell Smith asked for an answer to the question posed by the two visitors from London. The Supreme Commander's response was clear. He needed as much help as he could get, wherever he could get it. The whole Resistance should be called to arms across France and, wherever they were, they should do as much damage as they could. In the famous words of Marshal Foch, the order was 'Tout le monde à la bataille.'

It is not clear whether Eisenhower knew that this decision directly contradicted the earlier joint Anglo/French/US understanding that the Resistance should be called to action in two phases in order not to expose those furthest from the Normandy beaches to German retaliation at a time when the Allies could not help them. But even if he did know of this, it seems certain that he would still have made the same decision. This was the most important Allied action of the Second World War. If it failed, the war would be prolonged at huge cost in Allied lives, with perhaps many more European countries having to depend on the Russians for their 'liberation'. The Supreme Commander was only too well aware just how narrow the chances of success would be on the Normandy beaches. It was vital to keep the Germans guessing; vital to persuade them to keep their divisions in the south, against the possibility that Normandy was a feint (as many of them believed) and would swiftly be followed by an Allied invasion from the Mediterranean. If the cost Eisenhower had to pay to keep his enemy off-balance was the destruction of a few Resistance networks, then that was a price he was prepared to pay. There would, he knew, be more than enough blood to his account anyway, crossing the Normandy beaches and breaking out through the German lines behind them. For him, this was a tough but necessary military decision. But for many young Frenchmen in places like the Vercors, it would be a fatal one.

When Mockler-Ferryman and Haskell met Bedell Smith on 3 June, the presumption was that D-Day would take place as planned on 5 June. On this basis, Mockler-Ferryman decided that the French should be informed of Eisenhower's decision in the evening of the following day, 4 June, just hours before the BBC planned to broadcast the code phrases which would launch them to action. He therefore instructed that Colonel Dewavrin, the head of de Gaulle's Resistance directorate in London, and General Koenig should be called in for a briefing in the early evening of 4 June. However, at a meeting in Portsmouth at 04.00 on the morning of 4 June, Eisenhower made the dramatic decision that, because of the poor weather forecast in the Channel, D-Day would be delayed by twenty-four hours. Mockler-Ferryman hurriedly changed what was intended to be a briefing on the most important event of the war into an impromptu cocktail party.

De Gaulle finally arrived at Northolt Airport near London on the morning of 4 June, to be welcomed by a band playing the 'Marseillaise' and a personal letter from Churchill inviting him to lunch: 'My dear general! Welcome to these shores. Very great military events are about to take place.' De Gaulle was driven to meet Churchill at a railway siding at Droxford, north of Portsmouth, where the Prime Minister, who had been persuaded by the King not to watch D-Day from a ship off the Normandy beaches, had parked his private train as close to the action as he could get. Churchill walked down the tracks to meet the French leader, his arms outstretched in welcome. De Gaulle coldly rejected the gesture and, in the subsequent meetings between the two men, vented his anger against Roosevelt's refusal to recognize his government. When Churchill urged the General to meet Roosevelt to patch things up, the French leader demanded to know why he should 'lodge my candidacy for power in France with Roosevelt; the French government exists'. It was at this meeting that, according to de Gaulle, Churchill said that, if forced to choose between France and America, Britain would always choose America. The fact that de Gaulle was probably exaggerating to make his point did not prevent the claim from colouring the attitude of Gaullist France to Britain for many years to come, not least in the context of the early development of the European Community.

On his arrival at Northolt, de Gaulle had also been handed the speech that it was proposed he should broadcast on the morning of D-Day. The General flatly rejected the text on the grounds that it placed too much stress on French obedience to the Allied Command and made no mention at all of his 'Provisional Government'.

So began two days of disputes between Churchill and de Gaulle which, laden with tantrums, fits and wild threats, lurched between thunderous stupidity and common farce. De Gaulle called Churchill a 'gangster' while Churchill accused the General of 'treason at the height of battle' and issued instructions that he should be flown back to Algiers 'in chains if necessary'. Cables flew backwards and forwards between London and Washington on an almost hourly basis saying 'The General will speak' followed by 'The General will not speak.' Only the assiduous day-and-night scurrying of anxious diplomats on each side managed to pull the two men back from the brink, so, but only narrowly, averting a real tragedy.

Soon after midnight on 4 June, a few hours before the British and French leaders began their descent into schoolboy squabbling on a Hampshire railway siding, two Westland Lysanders dropped almost silently out of a moonlit sky on to a meadow 2 kilometres north of the little town of Saint-Vulbas, which lies on the west bank of the Isère 25 kilometres or so from the outskirts of Lyon. Four passengers were landed and five picked up for the return journey to Calvi in Corsica. Among the arrivals were Eugène Chavant and Jean Veyrat carrying new signal codes, a bag containing two sealed envelopes for Marcel Descour and 2.5 million francs in 500-franc notes. The two men were bundled into a car and taken to a safe house in the Villeurbanne district in Lyon. Here, on the morning of 5 June, they were joined by Marcel Descour, to whom Chavant showed the 'Décision' signed by Soustelle on behalf of de Gaulle and handed over the two sealed envelopes containing Descour's orders. Recalling this meeting after the war, Descour said: 'I remember very clearly my meeting with Chavant after his return from Algiers. With an air of triumph, he first gave me the paper signed by Soustelle. And then he told me of the verbal assurances he had received [in Algiers] that the Vercors would receive "important" reinforcements of both men and arms.'

Meanwhile, in London, late in the afternoon of 5 June Colonel David Bruce, the London Chief of the American Office of Strategic Services (OSS), accompanied by Brigadier Colin Gubbins, the head of SOE, called on General Koenig in his Duke Street offices in St James's. Gubbins announced: 'The Supreme Commander wants us to call out the South as well [for D-Day]. It is vital that the enemy should not know until the last possible moment exactly what assault he is facing and from what direction.' Bruce then elaborated: 'As a result of the report made by Thackthwaite on his return from France, we are very concerned that, if we send the messages calling the Maquis to arms, only to those Maquis groups in the north of France, the Germans will conclude that they face an attack only from the north.'

This time, Koenig understood precisely the implications of what he was being asked to agree to. French men and women were going to be told to launch into action prematurely and suffer the terrible consequences in order to make it easier for Allied troops to get across the Normandy beaches into mainland France. Despite his worries, however, Koenig did not believe he could, at this late hour, countermand the orders of the Supreme Commander. He responded: 'I hope that at the earliest opportunity I may be permitted to issue an order to the southern Maquis to withdraw from combat.' His two visitors, whose only thought was for what would happen in Normandy in the next few days, readily agreed. Dewavrin, who was also present at the meeting, was much less sanguine than his boss, expressing his concern at this sudden reversal of what had been long-established policy. Others on the French side, who heard of the decision later that day, were equally shocked and suspected the perfidious hand of the SOE behind a decision which they knew would result in the needless deaths of many Resistance fighters. Ironically, Pierre Dalloz, now back in London from Algiers, was also in Duke Street that day, warning Miksche of the tragic consequences which would ensue if the Vercors were called to arms too early.

As Koenig explained after the war, it was not only the Germans who were deceived by the call for universal mobilization – the Resistance were too: 'Our men in the R1 and R2 regions believed that, if they received the orders calling them to action, then it must mean that the invasion of Normandy would swiftly be followed by another on the south coast of France as well.' In fact, a date for Anvil had not yet even been set. And some, led by Churchill, were still trying to ensure that it never happened at all.

Although there was much going on at a high level in London, lower-level planning for what happened after D-Day continued as well. SHAEF produced instructions dated this day, 4 June, for post-D-Day operations. These completely ignored the Supreme Headquarters' earlier instructions to concentrate on sabotage only and called for Resistance activity '[in remote] areas [in order to create] diversionary threats the enemy cannot afford to neglect, thereby tying down a portion of his available forces'. In a section of this document listing 'Special Forces available' to carry out these tasks, there was included: 'French parachute troops from North Africa who can operate in conjunction with resistance elements and provide them with a stiffening framework'. This was just what Pierre Dalloz and Jean Prévost had envisaged when they had conceived the idea of Montagnards as they stood by a chopped-down walnut tree under the forbidding cliff face of the Vercors, all that time ago.

For Eugène Chavant and Jean Veyrat in Lyon, 5 June was another day of travelling. But they were not the only people heading for the Vercors that day. François Huet went up to the plateau by bus that morning from Grenoble, intending to call on the commander of the northern sector,

Roland Costa de Beauregard, before continuing to Saint-Martin and the delicate business of taking over from Geyer the following day.

The bus to Autrans took Huet past Pierre Dalloz's house, La Grande Vigne, in Sassenage, then up the narrow defile of the Furon gorge and through the Tunnel d'Engins which punched its way through a rock wall, giving sudden access to the plateau itself. Beyond this, the wide green Lans valley opened up, laid out to pasture and an occasional ploughed field already turning green with the shoots of young summer wheat. To his right and left, Huet would have seen the long arms of the Vercors' ridges running away from him to the south, clothed in forests and topped with rock-strewn crests. Cradled between them at the far end of the valley, the little town of Villard-de-Lans perched on a hilltop. This was a familiar landscape to Huet; he would have come here many times for family picnics in summer and for winter skiing expeditions. Now he looked at it with different eyes – the eyes of a military commander.

In Villard, with its cobbled square, substantial hotels, step-gabled houses and steep roofs staked to hold the winter snow, the bus halted to drop and take on passengers. Leaving Villard, the vehicle then plunged down the road through the Gorges de la Bourne to the Pont de la Goule Noire, dark and cool even on this early June day, and then on down the valley, the frothing torrent of the Bourne river on its left. After 4 kilometres in the gloom, Huet and his fellow travellers finally broke out into sunshine again at the village of La Balme-de-Rencurel. Here, turning right, they made their way north up another valley bordered by high north/south-running forest-clad ridges, to Rencurel, Méaudre and finally Autrans.

In Autrans, François Huet, still in his hiking clothes, hitched his rucksack on his back and started the two-hour ascent to Plénouse, a rockstrewn plateau covered in *lapiaz* – the deeply fissured limestone pavements. This was a desolate place, but not too desolate for sheep and shepherds and just the right hiding place for Maquisards. It did not take long for Huet to find de Beauregard's base, an old shepherd's hut hidden among trees close to one of the Vercors' rare permanent water supplies – the Fontaine de Plénouse. Huet's arrival, panting from the climb (as some of de Beauregard's men commented unkindly afterwards), was unexpected. A rough and unpractised guard of honour was hastily assembled for the new commander, which Huet inspected with due seriousness. Then the two commanders settled down to talk.

At just short of thirty-one, Roland Costa de Beauregard was the son of an aristocratic family from the Nièvre. On Francis Cammaerts' first visit to the plateau, he had been taken by Chavant up the mountain to meet de Beauregard. 'Now I will show you a real French aristocrat,' the Socialist ex-Mayor had told the Englishman just before they arrived. Unusually de Beauregard had not followed the normal practice of French aristocratic sons by seeking a commission in a cavalry regiment, but had chosen instead the much tougher life of a Chasseur Alpin. By the time he took command of the northern Vercors plateau, de Beauregard had already received the Légion d'Honneur for his part in repulsing an Italian attack with superior forces on a key Alpine pass during the first weeks of the war. A skilled military commander with an innate feel for the tactics of guerrilla warfare, he was much respected by those under his command, whether civil Maquis or ex-professional soldiers.

From the Plénouse heights, it is possible to see almost the entire Vercors plateau, running away to the south below. Although the valleys of the southern plateau are not easily distinguishable, the main features of the ridges which separate them can be picked out, as can, most prominently of all, the hunched shoulders and sharp peak of the Grand Veymont which crowns the plateau's eastern ramparts. On 5 June the sky was, as in the preceding days and those which followed, azure blue with a brilliant sun, though according to some witnesses there was a light dusting of snow lying on the highest summits and ridges. It is not difficult to imagine the two commanders looking down on the Vercors below, smoking and talking of the battles ahead and how they might be fought, as the last rays of the sun lit up the snow-covered peaks of the Alps to their east.

For those close to de Gaulle and Churchill, back in London, the night of 5/6 June was rather less congenial. It was spent in a seemingly endless scurrying of worried diplomats and anxious advisers between a volcanic Churchill and an obdurate de Gaulle, the latter still refusing to make any broadcast other than one of his own choosing the following morning. It was not just the content he objected to, however. It was the order of speaking. The plan was first for the heads of state of the governments-in-exile to speak to their people over the BBC: the King of Norway, the Queen of Holland, the Grand Duchess of Luxembourg. Then the Prime Minister of Belgium would speak for his government. Then Churchill, then Eisenhower and finally de Gaulle, to the people of France. The

General refused adamantly. If he came straight after Eisenhower it would look as though he was the Supreme Commander's subordinate in France. Churchill threatened to cut de Gaulle out altogether. De Gaulle counter-threatened to withdraw the 200 French liaison officers at that very moment embarking with Allied units all along the south coast of England. Eventually, with the Allies worn out by days of obduracy, de Gaulle got his way.

Eisenhower wrote of this battle of wills in carefully restrained terms in his memoirs: 'We particularly desired de Gaulle to participate with me in broadcasting on D-Day to the French people so that the population, avoiding uprisings and useless sacrifices at non-critical points, would still be instantly ready to help us where needed. We worked hard, within the limits of our instructions, to win de Gaulle to our point of view, but … he did not meet our requests.'

At 02.00 on 6 June, with the landing craft and ships now well on their way and the first airborne troops preparing to land on French soil, it was finally agreed that Eisenhower would speak at 10.30, followed by the heads of state. De Gaulle would then record his statement at the BBC at 13.30, giving time for his words to be checked by Anthony Eden, before they were transmitted in the regular 18.15 BBC magazine programme *Ici la France*, when his address would be followed by a French translation of Eisenhower's earlier words of that morning.

By the time this tortuous arrangement had been agreed, the BBC had already sent out the messages calling the Resistance to action all across France the previous evening. According to the BBC records held in its archive at Caversham, there were 187 of these in all – far more than on any previous night of the war. Dr Götz in Paris spotted what was happening immediately and identified no fewer than fifteen of the broadcast code phrases as action messages for agents who had already fallen into his hands. He immediately raised the alarm that the invasion was immi-nent. The German Fifteenth Army, responsible for the defence of the Pas de Calais, sent out a warning to all units that the invasion was expected within the next forty-eight hours. The German Seventh Army, guarding the Normandy beaches, initially ignored Götz's warning, but soon changed its mind and sent out a 'Level 2' warning (the highest alert level) to all its units. Walter Schellenberg, Heinrich Himmler's aide and Deputy Chief of the SS Main Security Office, also knew what the messages meant and warned Hitler's office. Contrary to popular belief, the German units

The Pioneers: Guillaume Dalloz (top left), Jean Prévost (top right), Léon Martin (middle left), Eugène Chavant (middle right), Aimé Pupin (bottom left)

Alain Le Ray

Ferme d'Ambel

Narcisse Geyer

Fabien Rey

Réfractaires at Camp C6 Summer 1943

Military training for young Maquisards

Gebirgsjäger in action

The winter of 1943–4: wood *corvée* (right); rations *corvée* returning to camp (below)

Peter Ortiz, USMC

Henry Thackthwaite, SOE

Dom Guétet and Marcel Descour

François Huet

Huet's Headquarters,
Villa Bellon, Saint-Martin

Milice with arrested Maquisards
(second and third from left),
Vassieux, April 1944

Proclamation of the
République Libre du Vercors

Geyer takes the parade,
Saint-Martin, 25 June 1944

République Française

LIBERTE EGALITE FRATERNITE

POPULATION DU VERCORS :

Le 3 Juillet 1944, LA RÉPUBLIQUE FRAN-
ÇAISE a été officiellement restaurée dans le Vercors.

A dater de ce jour les décrets de VICHY sont abolis
et toutes les lois Républicaines remises en vigueur.

LE COMITÉ DE LIBÉRATION NATIONALE DU VERCORS
investi dans ses fonctions par Monsieur le Commissaire de la République,
détient des pouvoirs très étendus.

Chargé de l'application de ces décisions, il désire administrer le pays avec le
plus grand esprit de JUSTICE, mais aussi avec FERMETÉ. Le Comité compte
sur le concours dévoué et sur le bon sens de toute cette population du Vercors,
qui pendant toute la parade de la résistance clandestine a manifesté en courage
et en attachement à la France au-dessus de tout éloge.

Notre région est en état de siège. Le Comité de Libération Nationale demande
donc à la population de faire l'impossible comme il le fera lui-même pour mettre
à la disposition du Commandement Militaire que la charge nécessaire de nous
protéger contre ceux encore toujours ces barbares, tous les moyens dont il dispose.

Habitants du Vercors, c'est chez vous que la grande
RÉPUBLIQUE vient de renaître. Vous pouvez en être
fiers. Nous sommes certains que vous saurez la défendre.
Nous voudrions que le 14 JUILLET 1944 soit pour
le Vercors une occasion de plus de manifester sa foi Ré-
publicaine et son profond attachement à la grande
Patrie.

VIVE LA REPUBLIQUE FRANÇAISE !

VIVE LA FRANCE !

VIVE LE GENERAL DE GAULLE !

Pour le Comité de Libération Nationale,
LE PRÉSIDENT : CLÉMENT

defending the Channel coastline were fully alert to the fact that the invasion was coming. They were surprised, not by the fact that it arrived at dawn on 6 June, but only by the fact that the huge invasion armada appeared off the beaches of Normandy and not those of the Pas de Calais where they had expected it.

Many legends have sprung up about the BBC messages sent out on the night of 5/6 June 1944. This is hardly surprising. It is almost impossible for us, so long afterwards, to imagine the emotional effect which these messages and the astonishing, longed-for news they carried must have had on those gathered round hidden radios in apartments in Lyon or Paris, or sitting round campfires in the forest, or crowded into a shepherd's hut, high in the mountains.

One of these legends, which almost every French man and woman is taught at school, is that there was a single message, drawn from a couplet of the French poet Verlaine, telling the whole of France that D-Day was happening. The first line in the couplet, 'Les sanglots longs des violons d'automne', was supposedly broadcast as the alert message several days before. And the second, 'Bercent mon coeur d'une langueur monotone', was broadcast at 22.15 on 5 June telling all France that their liberation was at hand. These lines from Verlaine were indeed broadcast – but they were not the action message for all France, only for one SOE circuit operating in the area around Tours. There was no countrywide message, only individual ones for each Resistance circuit or network.

The Vercors too has its own legend of what was broadcast that night. This has it that a specific message for the Vercors, instructing it to rise – 'Le chamois des Alpes bondit'* – was among those broadcast by the BBC on 5 June. There were even those who swore on their lives that they had heard this message themselves on their own radios. But there is no evidence whatever in any of the very comprehensive records held in the BBC archives in Caversham that any such phrase was either on the list of messages prepared for this night or among those which were actually broadcast. In fact, the only messages for the Vercors sent on the BBC transmission of 22.15 on 5 June were those which were designated for the whole of the R1 area – that is, four messages designed to unleash the first four of the sabotage plans already agreed.

A close study of the list of alert messages sent by the BBC on 1 June

* 'The Alpine Chamois leaps'.

and the action messages actually sent on 5 June reveals one further note-worthy fact. SOE's original plans for the actions which their British-run circuits would take in the southern half of France after D-Day envisaged, not just plans for sabotage, but also the establishment of what they referred to as *zones à contrôler*.* These were seen as locations rather simi-lar to redoubts, where SOE agents would come out into the open to take broad control of areas 'remote from enemy concentrations' which could be used as places where Resistance forces could gather and Allied para-chutists might land. The alert messages sent to SOE F Section's circuits in the south of France on 1 June included warnings that they should prepare to establish these *zones à contrôler*. But none of these were included in the action messages sent on 5 June. SOE had, it seems, taken account of SHAEF's decision to confine action strictly to clandestine sabotage and, changing its mind between 1 and 5 June, did not instruct its agents to come out into the open at this point. On D-Day itself, Cammaerts instructed his networks to stay hidden: 'it would be at least two months before they would be needed … he would notify everyone when the south of France D-Day took place'. Unfortunately, perhaps due to the British prohibition on any direct French radio communications with France before D-Day, this crucial message was not passed in the same way to the French-run Resistance networks in southern France, which included the Vercors.

All of this, along with the high-level squabbling in London, was of course totally unknown to François Huet and his comrades, sleeping under the stars in the pure air, high on the Plénouse plateau that historic night. But its consequences were about to become deeply woven into all their fates. Costa de Beauregard's radio operator, his ear pressed against his little short-wave radio, would have heard the messages somewhere between 22.30 and 23.00. He hurried to wake Huet and the others to give them the news. D-Day had arrived! There was great excitement and speculation. Eventually Huet tried to get back to sleep – but he could not. He decided to set off at first light the following morning to take over his command at Saint-Martin.

---

* Zones to be controlled (by our forces).

D-DAY: 6 JUNE 1944

For René Piron in the town of Romans, just below the western wall of the Vercors plateau, the night of D-Day was not a quiet one: 'It was midnight. A violent banging on my door made me wake up with a start. I had no weapons in the house and ... thought of what had happened to our chief Michel who had been suddenly arrested by the Germans with his driver the previous Sunday ... I was scared stiff. But I had no choice. I opened the door – and let out a sigh of relief! It was our Lieutenant Jeannot, dressed in hiking clothes and standing ironically to attention ... He told me, still half asleep, that the Allies would be landing at dawn this morning on the beaches of Normandy and that, as planned, the sabotage of the railway system in the Romans area had to be executed immediately. He had to repeat the message to me twice before I got it. It took my breath away ...'

The Maquisards, noted Piron, all had their duties to perform. 'We knew exactly what we had to do. Now we would have to come out into the open – now we would have to become "terrorists". I threw on my Maquisard clothes and started mentally to check how many men we had and how many would now not come with us. We had to remember that we were asking them to abandon their families, their work, their security ... My work that night was simple. I only had my deputy and two section chiefs to alert. They would then alert their own men ... I first woke up comrade Chartier ... gave him the good news and told him to empty our secret magazine of all equipment and ammunition ... I found my deputy already up and dressed, as were my section chiefs ... At 5 o'clock, my sack on my back, I said goodbye to my wife and left home. She was very brave and uttered no syllable of complaint, which made leaving much easier ...'

And so it was all over France. As Allied landing craft were using the final hours of darkness to manoeuvre into position for their dawn run in to the Normandy beaches, French men (and some women) were slipping through the darkness down silent streets to knock on neighbours' doors and tell them the hour had come; worried wives were saying goodbye to husbands they might never see again; and young men (and some not so young) were pulling on boots and hitching up rucksacks before quietly closing their front doors behind them and vanishing into the darkness.

In Saint-Donat, just west of the Vercors, a Maquisard whose alias was Yvon also had a disturbed night: '1 a.m. Suddenly the village exploded into unusual activity. Despite the black-out, lights suddenly burst on in the windows of apartments and houses in the town. Someone knocked on the door. The order for mobilization had been given. We were to report immediately to Headquarters. Right under the noses of the Germans, everyone was alerted. In the darkened streets, silhouettes flitted from door to door and shadows moved silently down walls and streets.'

Yvon remembered how his comrades responded: 'I can see their faces now, my comrades, on that morning of 6 June. Standing together in the darkness on the terrace in front of my house, waiting for the truck … I can see them still as they took their weapons out from the hiding places, assembled them and cleaned them for action, for all the world as if we were experienced soldiers … I can see their faces – serious and determined. No bravado. Just the cold resolution a man feels when he must leave behind all that he loves, all that he lives for. His wife, his children, his possessions. All left in danger, without either security or a sure means of living. All to be reduced to no more than dear memories held in the heart … all in the cause of doing our duty.'

It was the same for Jean Dacier in nearby Crest, close by the southwestern tip of the Vercors: 'On the evening of 5 June we were all … gathered round our little radio, which we had christened "Biscuit" because of the tin in which it was hidden … The Captain had the headphones on and I was almost lying on top of him trying to hear what was being said. Suddenly London announced that D-Day was happening in Normandy. We all jumped around, delirious with joy. After that I left … we had to blow up some pylons carrying high-tension electricity cables. That night I also blew up the railway line causing the derailment of an engine and its tender. Then we hurried back home.'

By the time they got back, 'the chiefs who had been alerted one by one had got the weapons out from their hiding places and distributed them among us … It seemed as though our days of darkness were over … of course the Boches would no doubt come soon. But the gates of Hitler's impregnable Festung Europa had been broken down ... A new wind of optimism was blowing ... [Later] a little man began going round announcing that the military command in the area wished the public to know that the French Fourth Republic had been proclaimed in the town and that all citizens should remain calm, close their windows but leave their shutters open. Only members of the Resistance had the right to use the roads except between 11 a.m. and 3 p.m. when people could get their food and provisions. A table was set up in the main square to enable those who wished to enrol. Lots came. No formalities, no name, just a forename or an alias which people could choose for themselves, together with an oath of allegiance, was sufficient.'

The Crest Maquis spent the morning of 6 June placing sentries on all the roads and preparing defensive positions. In the late afternoon, Jean Dacier was resting in the shade of a large vine when he heard the noise of an approaching motorcycle which screeched into the town square, its rider yelling at the top of his voice: 'The Boches are coming! The Boches are coming!' These words, recorded Dacier, 'hit us like a bolt of electricity', and everyone crowded round the messenger. 'They're in two columns coming from different directions.'

'How many vehicles?'

'At least twenty.'

The battle for the 'Fourth Republic of Crest' lasted about a quarter of an hour, with the Germans using artillery and heavy machine guns to drive the Maquis out. Then they burnt houses, indulged in some minor pillage and left. It was not a big event on this day of big events – except of course for the people of Crest.

The German action in Crest is an exception. In all other accounts of what happened in the Vercors area on 6 June, the Germans are curiously absent – as though they were for a moment stunned into inaction. In Bourg-de-Péage, a cavalcade of lorries filled with young volunteers and draped with tricolours passed through cheering streets, and in Sassenage, the northern gateway to the plateau, little groups of volunteers were seen in lorries and cars making their way up to the Vercors. South of the Vercors at Die, a new Maquis group formed spontaneously on D-Day and appointed themselves the guardians of the southern entry to the plateau, at the village of Chamaloc. They also took on the task of preparing to close off the road which crossed the Col de Grimone off the

Vercors' south-eastern corner, if asked to do so. Even more dramatic events were unfolding in the little Alpine town of Barcelonnette in the Ubaye valley 175 kilometres south-west of the Vercors. There the young Maquis chief had heard his BBC action message, 'Méfie toi du toréador',* and immediately sprang into action, arresting the small German garrison in the town, hoisting the tricolour above the Mairie and declaring the 'Free Republic of Barcelonnette'.

Things were a little less dramatic in Grenoble. Here, the Communists, quick off the mark as ever, confined themselves to the distribution of a political tract calling for the 'Creation of combat groups to sustain the Movement and defend against the Boches'. Elsewhere, D-Day sparked an outbreak of private celebrations, street parties and flags. In one or two places there was even some firing of weapons in spontaneous *feux de joie*. The Germans in the city were suspiciously quiet for some reason or other. Everyone felt that retribution would come later – that night perhaps.

Medical Professor Etienne Bernard found himself swept up in the mood too. Walking along a Grenoble street, he was suddenly approached by a young man who appeared from nowhere on a bicycle: 'I didn't know who he was, but he recognized me,' Bernard wrote after the war. 'He was obviously a member of the Maquis and shouted at me as he rode past, "Time to get up to the plateau." I knew what he meant. The Vercors was preparing for action and it seemed certain that there would be German searches and round-ups in Grenoble that night. I left immediately for my little house in Rencurel and the following morning, with another doctor called Ferrier, offered my services to the Maquis hospital at Saint-Martin.'

Paul Dreyfus, an author and journalist, caught the mood of that day perfectly, writing after the war: 'In Grenoble, Romans, Bourg-de-Péage, Valence, on this day of 6 June, the excitement was at a peak. From these towns, the Vercors was seen as a fantastic citadel encircled, above the dark wall of pines, by a white ring of limestone cliffs. The young had made a thousand visits there, walking and climbing. The older ones had hunted hares and grouse. One way or the other they all knew the footpaths of this grim, powerful massif. In those intoxicating hours it seemed impregnable.'

---

* Beware the toreador.

Up on the plateau too, the towns and villages were in festive mood. When the car carrying François Huet and Roland Costa de Beauregard passed through Autrans, Méaudre and Rencurel on its way to Saint-Martin, it was mobbed by cheering citizens. The same happened when the two men arrived in Saint-Martin itself, where a throng of people had gathered, cheering, kissing each other and dancing in the streets. To add to the drama, at 10.00, shortly after Huet had arrived, several squadrons of American Flying Fortresses flew over the plateau, leaving vapour trails in the clear blue sky as they headed north-west for the Normandy beaches. The ground trembled with the rumble of their engines, and the exultant crowds cheered them to the echo as they passed.

A meeting was hastily convened in the Hôtel Breyton, where de Beauregard introduced Huet to the assembled multitude as the new commander of the Vercors. Chavant – *le Patron* – had not yet arrived back on the plateau. There was more cheering and more hugging before Huet managed to quieten things down. One man asked why the plateau had not already been closed off for action. Others swore they had heard 'Le chamois des Alpes bondit' announced by the BBC. Huet, aware of the gravity and irreversibility of a premature move to shut off the plateau, tried to calm things down: 'Before we do anything, we have to have confirmation of what we have heard on the radio. I have had no orders to mobilize the plateau and you know as well as I do that if this is done too soon it could end in disaster. We must be sure that the paratroops are ready to leave Algiers.'

At this point his voice was drowned out by a clatter of hooves outside. Narcisse Geyer, mounted on his stallion Boucaro, had ridden into the town square accompanied by several of his officers. A moment later, Geyer – as always, dressed in full cavalry uniform, complete with kepi and soft white leather gloves – strode into the meeting, performed an exaggerated bow to Major Huet, sat down, lit a cigarette and declaimed: 'Bravo! C'est le grand boum!* Now we shall really have some sport!' Huet acknowledged the younger officer coolly and continued with his speech urging calm and caution.

At this juncture, someone brought in the message sent out that morning to the Resistance across France by General Koenig. Hoping it might help calm the excitement, Huet read it out. But Koenig's words were

---

* 'It's the big bang.'

designed to stir emotions, not quiet them. 'The battle for the liberation has been launched'; people should put aside their political differences and 'realize the need for total cooperation in the aim of driving the enemy from France'. Koenig's exhortation was greeted by a further outburst of clapping and cheering. Huet insisted, 'We are here the incarnation of the French army. We need to remember that we must be a proper army with all that that means. Above all we must have discipline and honesty.' Huet told everyone to get back to their tasks. And so the meeting broke up.

Huet's next job was his most difficult one – telling Geyer that he, Huet, was now in charge. The cavalry officer did not take it all well and remained unconvinced by Huet's attempt to explain that the role he had been asked to fulfil by Descour was a new one designed to provide oversight of the whole plateau; Geyer was not being demoted; he would still retain command of the southern half of the plateau. The cavalry Captain would have none of it. The bad blood generated during this meeting would poison relations between Huet and his junior commander for the remainder of their time together on the Vercors.

Huet spent the rest of the day setting up his headquarters on the ground floor of the Hôtel Breyton.

Others were also on the move on this day. Eugène Chavant and Jean Veyrat spent the night of 6/7 June in Pont-en-Royans where, according to some reports, Chavant intervened to stop the summary execution of a captured member of the Milice.

In Lyon, Marcel Descour met over lunch with his superior Henri Zeller. Descour announced that he was going to the Vercors to set up his R1 regional headquarters. He had in fact already chosen a site for his new HQ after the destruction of his original choice by the Germans during their March raid on La Matrassière. This time Descour seems to have taken some care to ensure that he would not again be surprised by unwelcome intruders. The site he chose was a large forestry building called Rang des Pourrets, perched 300 metres above Saint-Agnan, on a ledge from which it commanded a perfect view of everything which moved in the valley below. Other security features included an escape route which led on to empty mountain and forest and a single means of frontal access: an easily blocked forest track which rose in full view by way of tortuous bends from the valley below. Two wireless operators also received new orders that day. Pierre Lassalle and the twenty-three-year-old Captain Robert Bennes, who had parachuted into France in mid-March, were instructed to join Descour at Rang des Pourrets as soon as possible.

In fact quite a number of people were heading for the Vercors on 6 June. Georges Jouneau, a Parisian who ran a used-car depot and breakers' yard behind the city cemetery in Lyon, gathered up as many roadworthy vehicles and as many begged, borrowed and stolen (chiefly from the Germans) spare tyres, petrol cans and useful spare parts as he could muster and drove up to the plateau that day to form the beginning of the Vercors' own makeshift Motor Transport Depot.

Back at the BBC in London, staff were busy trying to manage the D-Day broadcasts. When de Gaulle turned up at Broadcasting House at 13.30 he claimed not to have a written version of his speech. So a harassed official was forced to take down his words verbatim. These were then rushed to Anthony Eden who approved them and the BBC was instructed that they could play the recording of his words on the 18.15 programme. In the event, de Gaulle's speech, lasting five minutes and twenty-two seconds, went out at 18.31.

The General was in characteristically rousing form. He began: 'The Supreme battle has been joined. After so many battles, so much fury, so much pain, this is the decisive moment, this is the blow for which we have for so long waited. It is the battle in France, and it is the battle of France … For the sons of France, wherever they are and whatever they are, the simple and sacred duty is to fight the enemy by every means in their power. To strike and destroy the enemy: the enemy who has pillaged and sullied our nation: the enemy who is so detested, so dishonourable. The enemy who has done everything he can to escape his just destiny and who will do all he can to hold on to our sacred soil for as long as possible. The orders given by the French Government and by their leaders which it has recognized must be followed precisely … From behind the clouds so heavy with our blood and tears, the sun of our greatness is now reappearing.'

The French translation of Eisenhower's broadcast in English at 10.30 that morning followed straight after de Gaulle at 18.39 and was a minute shorter and much less incendiary than that of the French leader. The Supreme Commander said that the 'the gallant forces of France' were participating in the D-Day landings in order to 'play a worthy part in the liberation of their homeland'. But then he went out of his way to warn people of the dangers of damaging reprisals if premature action was taken in those areas beyond the battle zone. 'A premature uprising of all Frenchmen may prevent you from being of maximum help to your country in the critical hour. Be patient, prepare.'

De Gaulle's broadcast was repeated in full on the 22.15 evening broadcast on 6 June, as was a cut-down version of Eisenhower's statement. The French leader's statement was then repeated again in full, but this time without the accompanying statement from Eisenhower at 01.30, 02.30 and 12.45 the following day, 7 June. In the end it was the French leader's clarion call to arms that the French people heard, not the more cautious words of the American Supreme Commander.

What is striking about these two addresses is the extent to which they represented a reversal in both tone and substance of the previous positions taken by the two men. Eisenhower, who only hours previously had overruled a phased call to arms in favour of simultaneous action in all corners of the country, was now publicly urging exactly the opposite. Meanwhile, de Gaulle's powerful message, which especially in the overcharged emotional context of D-Day could only be seen as a call to arms for every Frenchman and woman in every part of France, countermanded his earlier instructions to 'use every means possible to put the brakes on a national uprising'.

In his post-war memoirs, de Gaulle confirms that his nationwide call to arms was entirely intentional and not a misunderstanding on the part of those who heard it: 'The news of the landing gave the Maquis its cue for concerted action … However, the Allied Command regarded the extension of guerrilla warfare with a certain mistrust … Therefore [they] hoped that the resistance would not precipitate matters except in the region of the bridgehead [Normandy]. The proclamation General Eisenhower wanted to read on the radio on 6 June warned French patriots to stay on their guard [that is, remain hidden] … I however urged them to fight with all means in their power according to the orders given by the French Command.'

The truth was that the Allies seemed not to be able to agree, either between themselves or even between one day and another, exactly what they wanted the French to do. Indeed there were contradictions even within de Gaulle's speech itself, with the first half containing what was, in the General's words, an immediate 'concerted call to action', while the second warned that the action would be 'hard and long' and require extended perseverance. After four years of waiting, it would have been difficult enough, even in the best of worlds, to restrain an impatient France from taking impetuous action. But with messages so ill thought out and so contradictory as those they heard on 6 and 7 June, it is scarcely surprising that French men and women followed their instinct, which, whether wise or not, was to stand up and fight. And many of them paid unnecessarily with their lives in consequence.

And so it was de Gaulle's stirring D-Day 'concerted call to action', and not his warning of the long battle ahead, or his earlier calls for caution, or Eisenhower's measured tones advising the same, which would have echoed in the ears of Marcel Descour as he prepared to leave Lyon for the Vercors and his first meeting on the plateau with his newly appointed commander, François Huet.

21

MOBILIZATION

Some time during the morning of 7 June, Eugène Chavant, *le Patron*, finally reached Saint-Martin. As he and Jean Veyrat clambered down from the bus which had brought them up the mountain from Pont-en-Royans, people streamed out of the Hôtel Breyton and into the town square to greet the two heroes on their return from Algeria. Sitting round a table in the hotel café, Chavant related his visit, the assurances he had received from Soustelle, speaking for de Gaulle himself, and the orders he had brought back for Marcel Descour. The Vercors must now prepare for the arrival of the 4,000 paratroops promised by Constans. And that was not all: 'The General will almost certainly be establishing his headquarters here on the Vercors. We must find him a suitable house.'

Later that day, Chavant and Huet met for the first time. 'Good day,' Chavant opened. 'We are to work together. I should warn you straight away that I am Socialist, anti-clerical and anti-militarist.'

'I, Sir,' Huet replied, 'am a career soldier and, in consequence, completely uninterested in politics. But it is fair to tell you that I am a fervent and practising Catholic.'

There was a moment's silence as *le Patron* regarded his new military colleague closely. Then he took both Huet's hands in his and shook them warmly: 'I like men with convictions. We'll get on fine.'

So began a relationship which, despite the evident differences between the two men, was to prove close, trusting and enduring, even through the many difficult times that lay ahead.

Although 7 June 1944 was relatively quiet on the plateau, it was not so elsewhere. Some 225 kilometres west of the Vercors, the Maquis took over the Corrèze town of Tulle, home to a sizeable arms industry and some 20,000 inhabitants. The intention was to use liberated Tulle as a kind of urban redoubt which would act as a gathering point for the

Maquis and a base for future action. Meanwhile south-east of the Vercors, the Maquisards in the 'Free Republic of Barcelonnette' consolidated their grip on the town and set up a ring of defensive positions covering the narrow passes which give access to the Ubaye valley in which Barcelonnette lies. To the north of the Vercors, Romans-Petit's Maquis were also in action, declaring the foundation of the French Fourth Republic in the 'liberated' Jura towns of Nantua and Oyonnax.

Southern and central France was, in short, in uproar, with German garrisons from every corner reporting outbreaks of Resistance activity to the German Army headquarters in Toulouse: 'Impression growing that Maquis are a strictly organized military force and effective action against them possible only with heavy weapons …'; 'Tarbes infected with guerrillas …'; 'Vital importance to protect wolfram mines east of Limoges …'; 'Two trucks of 2nd Panzer pioneer battalion attacked by guerrillas in lorry with machine gun at approaches to Figeac. Enemy lorry destroyed by gunfire. 5 enemy killed, 2 SS killed, driver taken prisoner …'

At 11.15 that morning, after a crucial twenty-four hours of hesitation, Field Marshal Gerd von Rundstedt, Hitler's Commander in the West, finally sent orders to the Das Reich Division – only recently posted to the Toulouse area to recover from three years fighting on the Russian front – that they should prepare to move north to reinforce the German ring round the Normandy beaches.

At 14.00 that day, Marcel Descour began his journey up to the Vercors. Accompanied by his monk/counsellor Dom Guétet, his son Jacques and one of Geyer's men, he left Lyon by car for the plateau, spending that night in Valence before completing his journey the following day.

While Descour was leaving Lyon, Chavant, accompanied by Huet, was attending a meeting in Rencurel of the local Departmental Liberation Committee, which coordinated Resistance activity in the Isère. Chavant introduced the new Vercors commander and briefed the gathering on the results of his visit to Algiers. He took the opportunity to back Huet in urging caution. 'Calm your men,' Chavant told the meeting. 'Make sure that they do not take imprudent actions. Our time will come later.'

That night, the Resistance took advantage of the lull in German activity to mount a raid to steal explosives, detonators and fuses from four factories in the Grenoble area and another on a post office in the Grenoble suburb of Saint-Bel, walking away with 1,545,000 francs. In another raid on Crest station, 60,000 litres of industrial alcohol and a wagon full of tobacco destined for the Germans were 'appropriated' for Maquis use.

The following day, as the Das Reich Division began their long, lumbering blood-soaked journey north in a huge column of armoured vehicles, the German high command turned their attention to the guerrilla attacks which were spreading like wildfire across southern France. Von Rundstedt, under some pressure from Hitler's headquarters, issued an Order of the Day to all units in the south of France, which was to become the template for all future German anti-partisan operations: '[I] expect operations against the guerrilla gangs in southern France to proceed with extreme severity and without any leniency. These constant trouble spots must be finally eradicated … Partial successes are of no use … The forces of resistance are to be crushed by fast and all-out effort. For the restoration of law and order the most rigorous measures are to be taken to deter the inhabitants of these infested regions who must be discouraged as a warning to the entire population from harbouring resistance groups … Ruthlessness and rigour at this critical time are indispensable if we are to eliminate the danger that lurks behind the backs of the fighting troops and prevent even greater bloodshed among the troops and the civilian population in the future.'

In what some might regard as a rather forlorn attempt to limit reprisals against the Resistance, Eisenhower, under pressure from the Free French, also issued a statement that morning demanding that the Germans treat armed French Resistants operating behind German lines as, in effect, a part of his army and therefore entitled to be accorded full combat status under the terms of the Geneva Convention. The German response was swift and dismissive: 'The Supreme Command of the Wehrmacht has decided that members of the French resistance movement are to be treated as guerrillas.'

Later that evening, after a bitter fight with some German casualties, the forward units of the Das Reich Division finally took Tulle. The following morning, the bodies of forty German prisoners were found in the local school. They showed signs of having been executed and mutilated – at least this was the claim the Germans would later make in mitigation to explain why they picked ninety-nine young men from the town, many chosen almost at random, and hanged them from Tulle's lampposts and balconies.

Two days later, on 10 June, the Das Reich descended on Oradour-sur-Glane. By the time they left, 624 civilians including 190 children had been massacred, many burnt alive. Though it would not be long before the total number killed by the Germans in this horror would be exceeded elsewhere, the massacre in Oradour remains the signature atrocity of all the bitter years of the German occupation of France, to which the silent, ruined buildings of the village still bear terrible testimony.

As the Das Reich Division was consolidating its grip on Tulle on the evening of 8 June, Marcel Descour and his companions were making their way in the pouring rain through Pont-en-Royans on to the Vercors plateau. Passing through the tunnels at the Grands Goulets, the R1 commander was surprised to note that neither was guarded. His first words to Huet when they met at Saint-Martin that evening were: 'Have you mobilized the Vercors?'

'Mobilized? No. Not yet.'

'What do you mean not yet?'

'You know better than I that the Vercors is to mobilize only in the context of an Allied invasion in the south. At present they have not even consolidated a bridgehead eight hundred kilometres away to the north. I have had no orders to mobilize and I see no reason to rush it.'

'It is not up to us to ask questions. We are soldiers. These are our orders. We obey them.'

'But don't you think—?'

'No, I don't think. I am confirming your orders. Mobilize the Vercors immediately.'

'But how do you intend that I should defend the plateau once it is closed? I have neither sufficient men nor sufficient arms.'

'I know that as well as you. We will get reinforcements. I have been formally promised them from Algiers. It is now up to us to do what they expect of us.'

Later, when Descour met Chavant, *le Patron* echoed Huet's reservations. But Descour insisted. The fate of the Vercors was sealed at the moment Descour gave his order and Huet, good soldier that he was, obeyed, even against his better judgement. As Huet said after the war, 'My job was simply to execute the orders I was given.'

Asked after the war why Descour had insisted on this fateful decision, Roland Costa de Beauregard said he thought that the experience of the Glières plateau had played a part. According to de Beauregard, Descour had no doubts about the wisdom of the redoubt strategy. He believed rather that the operation on the Glières had failed because the order to mobilize came too late for the Maquis to take advantage of the arms which the Allies had parachuted on to the plateau. He was determined that the Vercors would not make the same mistake by hesitating too long again.

Explaining his decision, Descour himself wrote after the war, 'The visit of Chavant to Algiers influenced me decisively ... Since the arrest of General Delestraint, I continually asked if the Plan Montagnards was still valid. I expressed my doubts on this score to Chavant who remained firm in his conviction that it was and even had a tendency, in common with many others, to criticize us career Army officers for what he regarded as an excessively "wait and see" attitude. I saw him again in Lyon ... on his return from Algiers when he showed me the famous instruction signed by Soustelle confirming the validity of Plan Montagnards. From this moment onwards it was not open to me to doubt ... I had received an order ... direct from de Gaulle himself. Naturally we could not imagine that de Gaulle could have been left in ignorance of the date of the landings [in the south].'

In fact, though Descour was not to know it, the date for Operation Anvil, the southern landing, had only been finally decided by 'Jumbo' Maitland Wilson on the previous day, 7 June, when the British General had written to Eisenhower informing him that 'The target date at which I am aiming is 15 August.' From Montagnards onwards, all plans for the Vercors had agreed on one thing; the plateau could hold out for three weeks – no more. Now, though no one on the plateau knew it, they would have to hold out for more than two months.

With the date for Anvil fixed, Maitland Wilson's headquarters got down to preparing and planning for the southern invasion. Francis Brooks Richards' men in their Nissen huts and twenty-five tents moved on to an active-service footing on 8 June and started to produce a daily Situation Report which was circulated round the Algiers headquarters at 09.00 every morning. This gave a summary of the main events in southern France over the last twenty-four hours. Their report for 9 June noted, with a degree of premature optimism, 'German troops in Isère invisible. Shut in their barracks ... Maquis ... are installed in Barcelonnette ... they have sealed off the Ubaye Valley but owing to lack of arms are unable to annihilate the German garrisons. If arms not received soon they will have to evacuate.'

Henri Zeller, who left Lyon for Barcelonnette on this day, also noted the absence of Germans on the roads: 'I left on 9 June for Barcelonnette using what transport I could. All normal forms of transport were completely disorganized. Throughout my journey I noticed the demoralized and panicky state of the Germans, some of whom had been killed outside the villages through which I passed. I also noticed that the Resistance had taken over as the authorities in some towns and villages, without putting in place any basic system of security. Between Digne and Barcelonnette I didn't see a single German or encounter a single roadblock and all along the way the inhabitants, some of whom were armed, were coming out openly for the Resistance.'

In his Saint-Martin-en-Vercors headquarters, François Huet spent the night of 8 June writing and dispatching movement and mobilization orders to his commanders. On the military side, these consisted of Geyer commanding the southern plateau and de Beauregard commanding the northern plateau. The 'volunteer' side of Huet's command was made up of the five 'underground' companies, which had been lying low in the communities around the plateau, waiting for the call to rise. When this came, they were told to leave home quickly and gather at a predetermined rendezvous for what, they were assured, would be a short holding operation until paratroop reinforcements were dropped on to the plateau.

Huet's plan was to mobilize these companies and deploy them to key positions on the plateau. The Compagnie Fayard, recruited from the Royans area and commanded by Louis Bourdeaux, would be mobilized and take up defensive positions in the Forêt de Lente along the southern half of the plateau's eastern rim. The Compagnie Brisac, recruited mostly from Grenoble and commanded by Paul Brisac, would also be deployed to defend Saint-Nizier, the vulnerable north-eastern gateway to the plateau. Here they would be reinforced by the Compagnie Goderville, which, commanded by Jean Prévost, was an already formed unit made up from the *réfractaires* who had come to the plateau over the last two years. The Compagnie Philippe, commanded by Henri Ullman, was, like Jean Prévost's company, already formed, and would be deployed to defend the northern half of the eastern Vercors rim. Finally the Compagnie Abel, commanded by Fernand Crouau and drawn mostly from the communities of Romans, Bourg-de-Péage and Saint-Donat, would be mobilized to defend the Gorges de la Bourne at La Balme-de-Rencurel.

The orders which Huet sent out to these 'hidden' companies that night, together with those who would come up to the plateau spontaneously over the next weeks, would, over time, have the effect of tripling the Resistance strength on the Vercors to nearly 3,000.

The following morning, Paul Brisac, commander of Compagnie Brisac, arrived in his office at the electrical engineers Merlin-Gerin to find a handwritten note waiting for him: 'Order No. 1. 8 June. Midnight. Mobilize your company immediately. Carry out the mission already assigned to you [closing off the Saint-Nizier entrance to the Vercors] on the morning of 10 June. Send your representative to meet me at 06.00 at the Pont de la Goule Noire for further details. H.' Brisac started moving his men, around 160 of them, out of Grenoble and up to Saint-Nizier by bus and mountain tram that morning. Arriving at their destination, the volunteers found their arms waiting for them – a handful of rifles, a few Stens and some grenades to be shared out between them all.

Jean Prévost met the new recruits he would soon be taking to war as they arrived at Saint-Nizier: 'They were in civilian clothes, many in just white open-necked shirts. On their left arms they wore an FFI armband with the Croix de Lorraine [the Free French symbol]. Most wore mountain boots and carried only a pullover. The vast majority were simple, ordinary young men, full of enthusiasm but with absolutely no combat experience. Most had never touched a firearm in their lives.'

At midday, Fernand Crouau, the commander of the Compagnie Abel, was handed a similar slip by a motorcyclist: 'Headquarters midnight. Immediate mobilization. Your mission is to close off La Balme-de-Rencurel and Rencurel. Send a representative at 06.00 to the Pont de la Goule Noire. Huet.' At 17.00, the volunteers of Crouau's Company, numbering some 400 men, mostly shoemakers from nearby factories, began gathering at the tram station in Bourg-de-Péage. 'We leave this evening,' wrote young Nicolas Bernard of Bourg. 'It's 9 June, the Allies landed at Normandy 3 days ago … for months now we have been meeting regularly in the Café de Marseille, where we have learnt how to use automatic arms and in particular how we may have to leave our homes at the rush – in no more than half an hour – saying goodbye to our families and our jobs. I only have the time to return home, say goodbye to my wife, hitch up my rucksack and rejoin my colleagues on foot.'

On his way to his rendezvous, Bernard bumped into a German convoy held up behind one of their trucks which had broken down: 'The lorries are bursting with German soldiers in helmets, their sub-machine guns in their hands ... they look like the kind of fighters one would prefer not to meet again in a hurry. My problem now is how to get past the blockage and make the rendezvous with a very obvious Maquisard's sack on my back. I nip back home and bury my rucksack in a bag of potatoes which I put on the back of my wife's bicycle and set off again. We all meet together in the streets surrounding the tram station. At 6 p.m. a huge truck arrives. The back is full of men crouching down to remain hidden and there are even some women sitting together at the rear of the vehicle. Some of them are weeping softly.'

For Nicolas Bernard and most of his colleagues, there was adventure ahead. But not for the wives they left behind. 'In many ways they have more courage than we have,' he wrote. 'Little circles of citizens form spontaneously on the streets, talking and worrying. Some say: "Was this all not too early? They will all be massacred." But our wives have to say nothing. Because no one can know that their husbands have left to join the Maquis. Tomorrow they will explain: "He has left for Paris" – or Grenoble – or somewhere else.'

While this new flood of raw recruits were being transported up to the plateau in trucks, Jean Prévost's son-in-law Roland Bechmann was out with a group of volunteers armed with picks, shovels and a large quantity of explosive, mining the bridges, tunnels and culverts of the main Vercors approach roads. That evening, Prévost himself was in Saint-Nizier supervising the deployment of men into defensive positions on the Charvet ridge, overlooking the road up from Grenoble. Here he was joined by his son Michel who, despite instructions to stay at home, had walked from the family house at Valet farm near Saint-Agnan to join his father's company. Prévost, who understood only too well the full implications of the fateful decision to mobilize the plateau, was in sombre mood. 'It's a strange thing indeed', he said to Michel, 'to have your son as a brother-in-arms.'

All that day arms were being pulled out of secret hiding places – a cow shed near Romans, the back room of a pharmacy in Grenoble, behind a turbine in the saw-mill at Villard-de-Lans. Even some of the local Gendarmes helped, albeit in ways which could be made to look excusable to their superiors afterwards. In Lans 'Lieutenant' Francisque

Troussier, a local hotelier turned Maquis chief, deliberately led his Maquis to the town Gendarmerie. 'Cut the telephone wires and surround the building,' he ordered. As his commands were being carried out, the Gendarmes came to the windows to watch. Troussier shouted, 'On parade!' and the Gendarmes meekly filed out, their arms in the air. This charade enabled them to claim afterwards that they had given assistance to the Maquis only 'under duress'. The same thing happened at Moirans just north of the plateau where the Gendarmerie commander and his eight Gendarmes claimed to have been attacked by thirty Maquisards who had forced their cooperation before disappearing 'in an unknown direction'.

At the far end of the plateau, near the Ferme d'Ambel, André Valot recorded the same atmosphere. 'It was the end of having to hide, the end of the clandestine life. Madame Eynard's café was jam-packed with the young. A group near the door sang the "Marseillaise" … All day long the lorries passed filled with young men. The whole population was in holi-day mood. Only some of the better-known Milice were gloomy. We rounded them all up that night, except for one or two who, spotting how the wind was blowing, had dashed off with their families to ask for protection from their friends, the Germans.'

In the early hours of 10 June, Halifax bombers flew over the plateau and dropped containers full of weapons and equipment to the Coupe-Papier parachute site 2 kilometres north of Saint-Martin. These were swiftly gathered up and used to complete the arming of Jean Prévost's and Paul Brisac's companies in Saint-Nizier.

After the heavy rainstorms of two days previously, the morning of 10 June 1944 was bright and still, with a thick mist hanging over the Grésivaudan valley. At sunrise, the men of de Beauregard's units, who had been marching all night, found themselves on the high ground around the Tunnel d'Engins overlooking Sassenage, where their task was to protect the tunnel and the north-eastern gateway to the plateau. Suddenly, after the best part of a year spent in the inhospitable, stony isolation of the Plénouse plateau, they were back in civilization again. Through the mist, which was already being sucked up by the morning sun, they could see glimpses of Grenoble, laid out at their feet, its roads busy with traffic and hurrying people. It was as if they had suddenly re-entered the twentieth century from some more primitive age.

Then the mist broke to reveal the whole valley lying below with the snow on the peaks of the Belledonne range and the Chartreuse Massif sparkling in the sun.

After their enforced isolation, de Beauregard's men found their new duties guarding access to the Vercors through the Tunnel d'Engins most congenial. From early in the morning, *gazogène* lorries, cars of all types, motorbikes, bicycles and even pedestrians started streaming up the mountain. It was the start of several weeks of a spontaneous influx of young and middle-aged men who had heard of the mobilization and were determined to join those on the 'free territory', *là-haut* on the Vercors plateau, and strike a blow against the hated German occupier. The Germans were still notable by their absence. Some even wondered if this was a deliberate German tactic to get all the 'terrorists' gathered together in one place.

During the day tourists from Grenoble joined the throng: 'The curious came to observe what we were up to. "Ah – so *you're* the dissidents," they commented, surprised that we appeared quite so ordinary,' one of de Beauregard's men, Gilbert Joseph, later wrote. 'They gave us cigarettes and sweets and asked us all sorts of questions … [later] on Sunday they came up in their Sunday best: parents, brothers, sisters, friends, lovers. One by one their loved ones came down the steep path which led to the front of the tunnel to meet them, creating a little throng at the edge of the ravine …'

François Huet, too, was on the move this morning. He had left his headquarters in Saint-Martin early on the Peugeot 750cc motorbike which was his preferred means of transport on the plateau, arriving in good time for the 06.00 meeting he had arranged at the Pont de la Goule Noire with the representatives of the companies he had mobilized the previous day.

Huet did not have to stand for long on the narrow little bridge across the roaring torrent, in the deep shadows and cool airs at the bottom of the Gorges de la Bourne. Soon the liaison agents began arriving, saluting their new commander and making their reports. Fernand Crouau himself came up from La Balme-de-Rencurel, complaining about the need for more weapons. For the rest, the reports were given by representatives of the various company commanders. In Jean Prévost's case, a pretty young girl in a beret came spinning down to the bridge on her bicycle from the direction of Villard-de-Lans. After the last report, Huet roared off on his motorbike, the echoes reverberating behind him in the canyon. He spent the rest of the day inspecting positions around the plateau.

Chavant too was busy this day. The closure of the plateau and the huge influx of Resistance volunteers had caused major administrative problems. Meetings were held all day in the Hôtel Breyton in Saint-Martin to ensure that services on the plateau, such as water, telephones, mail, petrol (where it could be obtained) and of course charcoal for *gazogène* lorries could be maintained. There was also the problem of how to feed all these new arrivals.

Down the road from Saint-Martin, Lieutenant Bob Bennes, now installed in La Britière as the commander of the small detachment of wireless operators, oversaw the dispatch of the first of many coded messages which would be transmitted from the crowded little ex-creamery. It was addressed to Jean Constans in Algiers: 'Remind you of the urgent need for arms and men to be parachuted to the Vercors area. We can receive at least a parachute regiment. Mobilization is completed but quantity of arms in the Vercors very inadequate. We could not resist if attacked. We lack both light and heavy arms for 2,000 to hold the Vercors as a bastion. It is very urgent to arm and equip us. Our parachute sites are open day and night.'

Bennes' operators quickly followed this with a second message, this time from Descour personally: 'In the Vercors have 2,000 volunteers to arm. Enthusiasm fading because of lack of arms. Urgent you send men, arms, petrol and tobacco within 48 hours. Possible the Germans will attack in force. Impossible to hold them effectively in present conditions. Failing to do so would be followed by terrible reprisals. Disastrous for Resistance in region.'

Algiers however had its own preoccupations including, among other crises, the developing situation in Barcelonnette, where Henri Zeller was now installed preparing to defend the Ubaye valley against strong German columns reportedly moving in his direction.

Bennes waited and waited for an answer to the earlier appeals to Constans for the urgent dispatch of arms and reinforcements. But none came. Instead a bombshell arrived from London. It was a telegram from Koenig: 'Curb to the maximum all guerrilla activity. Impossible at present to supply you with arms in sufficient quantities. Break off contact with the enemy as much as possible to permit reorganization. Reform in small isolated groups.'

Koenig, who repeated this order in messages sent out on 14 and 16 June, was of course doing no more than he said he would do when told that Eisenhower wanted to mobilize the whole of France on D-Day – pull back in the areas most distant from the Normandy beaches as soon as possible. His orders to 'break off contact with the enemy' would have been feasible forty-eight hours before, if Descour had not insisted on mobilizing the Vercors. But now that the newly mobilized Maquisards had been called away from their homes, it was impossible – in reality, suicidal – for them to go back.

Bennes took Koenig's signal up to Descour in his Rang des Pourrets headquarters, where the commander of the R1 region convened a meeting with Dom Guétet, Huet and Chavant – the latter two summoned urgently from Saint-Martin. The four men were bewildered by Koenig's orders – how could he ask them, as they saw it, to send the men back home, having been the person who, only a few days before, had told them to rise? It did not take long for them to decide that they could not conform with Koenig's orders without risking both the lives of the young men who had been called up and consequent reprisals against the civilian population on the plateau.

The meeting did not take long to reach its conclusion. They would disobey the French Commander-in-Chief. The preparation of Fortress Vercors would continue.

THE FIRST BATTLE OF SAINT-NIZIER

On 7 June 1944, Francis Cammaerts intercepted a message from an unknown French source ordering the men of his networks in the eastern Alps to go immediately to Barcelonnette in the Ubaye valley, where they were to help defend the newly established 'Free Republic' against an impending German attack. Furious, Cammaerts swiftly countermanded the order and demanded an apology. Cammaerts duly got his way together with orders from London to go to the beleaguered town himself where he was to act as SOE's liaison officer to Henri Zeller.

Arriving in Barcelonnette, Cammaerts went straight to the Mairie, outside which flew a huge tricolour emblazoned with the Croix de Lorraine. There were two guards on the door in full uniform who saluted him as he entered. Inside he met Zeller, accompanied by his small staff and a British officer, Captain Alastair Hay, who had been parachuted in a few days before. Zeller ('dry, precise of speech beneath a benevolent moustache', as Cammaerts later described him) explained the situation; he had been ordered to establish, in Cammaerts' words, redoubts in the 'plateau and mountain areas [which would be] held as permanent bases, e.g. Barcelonnette, Vercors and parts of the Ain and Jura … he explained that this plan was the result of discussions in Algiers and London. They were to establish strong points to be held at all costs and which were to serve for receiving personnel, large scale drops and to be used as divisional headquarters.'

Cammaerts knew nothing of any such immediate orders. He explained to Zeller that London had explicitly instructed him not to bring his men out into the open yet and to concentrate instead on clandestine sabotage. Thanks to lack of clarity, muddled instructions and a failure of communication, the French and the British had sent contradictory post-D-Day instructions to their networks. The British had told their people to lie low and wait. The French had told theirs to come out and fight.

Zeller's second claim was even more startling. While in Algiers in April, he had been given instructions to use the Vercors as a redoubt, instructions similar to those which Chavant had been given by Soustelle. And then, immediately after D-Day, Algiers had ordered him to hold on to Barcelonnette at all costs because the southern invasion force would land in less than a week. Shocked, Cammaerts asked, 'What assurances do you have for that, Colonel?'

'Algiers' message was delivered to me by Captain Hay when he parachuted in a few days ago,' Zeller replied.

Hay confirmed that this was indeed the message Algiers had asked him to deliver to the Colonel. Zeller and Hay demanded that Cammaerts should now hand over all the weapons he had recently received for his own networks and order his men to concentrate on the Ubaye valley to help them beat off the impending attack by the German columns approaching Barcelonnette. Cammaerts refused – he could not withdraw weapons which had only just been issued and were now scattered all across the eastern Alps. 'You don't take a bone away from a ravenous dog which has just been given it,' he remarked tartly. Furthermore, even if his men could get to the valley in time, he would not order them to do so. Quite simply, Barcelonnette could not be held against the superior German forces now advancing on the valley. He would not ask his men to walk into a death-trap. He had ordered them to continue to lie low after D-Day, waiting for their time to come, and he would not expose them now for an enterprise which was obviously doomed.

Zeller's first reaction was angry – he even accused Cammaerts of cowardice. But eventually after a heated discussion it was agreed that the only sensible action was to disperse before the German ring closed. Zeller and Cammaerts left Barcelonnette on 11 June and arrived, via Die and the Col de Rousset, at Descour's headquarters on the Vercors late that same day. The 'Free Republic of Barcelonnette' fell shortly afterwards. Alastair Hay died in the fighting. Some captured Maquisards were shot and the Germans began preparing for reprisals by rounding up members of the civilian population.

Barcelonnette was, after the risings on the Mont Mouchet and the Glières plateau, the third costly failure of the redoubt strategy. It should have been plain to all by now that trying to establish mountain fortresses protected by fixed defences in the face of German will and military power was folly of a high order. Unhappily no such lesson appears to have occurred to those, senior and junior, who were now involved in planning, directing and executing Resistance operations in southern France. The great 'aircraft carrier' of the Vercors continued to plough its way steadily towards the rocks.

Zeller's arrival on the Vercors meant that the plateau was now home and headquarters to the three most important Resistance commanders in southern France, the commander of the Vercors (Huet), the commander of the region (Descour) and the commander of the whole of south-eastern France (Zeller himself). Francis Cammaerts, who controlled most of the key SOE networks in south-eastern France, now also had his base there. La Britière, which accommodated all their wireless sets and operators, was getting very crowded. There can be little doubt that the Germans, whose radio-tracking stations would have identified all these wirelesses, were now well aware of just how important the plateau was becoming to the Resistance in southern France.

Pflaum's first move against the plateau was a cautious one. At 09.00 on 11 June, the telephone rang in Costa de Beauregard's forward headquarters just outside Saint-Nizier, guarding the Grenoble gateway to the plateau. 'They're coming!' a voice said, urgently.

De Beauregard's defensive position was strung along the steep-fronted, 3-kilometre-long Charvet ridge, which looks down on Grenoble and performs the function of a shelf on which the town of Saint-Nizier sits. The ridge itself is bounded on the south by three towers of rock called Les Trois Pucelles and to the north by some cliffs bordering the village of Le Charvet (see map on page 209). For the Germans, the best axis of approach ran from La Tour-sans-Venin (a pointed rock pillar, topped by the ruins of a castle, beside the main road on the outskirts of Grenoble), to a rock outcrop north of and slightly above the Charvet farm. If the Germans could establish machine guns at this point above the farm, they could lay down enfilade fire covering the entire northern half of de Beauregard's line, making the Charvet farm area the crucial weak point for its defenders.

It was easy to see German troops and vehicles deploying around La Tour-sans-Venin from the ridge that morning, but the German assault seemed half-hearted and consisted of little more than sporadic exchanges of small-arms fire, which lasted throughout the day. When the Germans pulled back at dusk into the city, the younger Maquisards declared a victory – if this was what war was like, what was all the fuss about? But older hands knew that the Germans' intention that day had not been to mount a serious assault on the plateau but to carry out a 'reconnaissance in force', designed to establish the strength and disposition of de Beauregard's line and especially the weight and position of his chief armaments, such as mortars and machine guns.

During gaps in the action and in the rear areas, the young raw Maquisards were given some basic weapons training, chiefly to show them how a Sten worked and how to throw a hand grenade. But no one thought to start digging trenches – or prepare proper fire positions – or clear the low scrub and long summer grass, so as to improve fields of fire.

For Gilbert Joseph and his comrades in the next valley north, guarding the Engins tunnel and the road up from Sassenage, 11 June was relatively quiet – though they could occasionally hear the firing from Saint-Nizier 2 kilometres away. Not long after dawn that morning, three figures suddenly emerged out of the mist walking towards the tunnel. The sentry mistook them for Germans and called the alert. Before the Maquisards could open fire, the figures started shouting in heavy foreign accents: 'Don't shoot. We have come to join you. We are Spanish Republicans. We spent the night in the local cemetery.' It was the beginning of another day when men of all ages and backgrounds flooded up the road to join the fight.

The highlight of Gilbert Joseph's day was a visit by Eugène Chavant, who called his unit together and told them of his visit to Algiers and the promises he had been given – parachutists would be arriving any day now, he assured them. Chavant was accompanied by a small wiry man who, Joseph learnt later, was a baker or a pastry chef. The newcomer spent the day skipping busily through and round the Engins tunnel, saying to the small team who were with him, 'put one here … and one here … and one here', as he tapped the tunnel's sides and poked at points on its concrete entrances. It was only later when a team of explosive experts turned up that Joseph realized that they were discussing how and when to blow up the tunnel. François Huet also called in on Gilbert Joseph's position a little after Chavant, distributing compliments to all and sundry as he was shown the unit's defensive positions.

The wireless operators in La Britière were busy again this day, coding and sending messages, including more urgent requests for arms to Constans: 'We gave the order to mobilize strictly against assurances that we would receive these arms. A failure to honour these promises will produce a very serious situation on the Vercors. With best wishes.' The following morning, finally, Constans in Algiers, replied: 'The only obstacle at the moment is weather conditions. We are doing our best in the face of restrictions of air transport resources. Best wishes.' But this telegram crossed with another desperate appeal from La Britière: 'Send material with maximum urgency to each of our parachute sites on the Vercors. We lack machine guns, mortars and if possible anti-tank weapons.'

The next day, 12 June, was also quiet on the plateau, much of it spent giving the new raw recruits of the Compagnie Brisac more basic training and weapon handling. But, again, no work was done to bolster the front line defending the Charvet ridge – no trenches dug, no fire positions strengthened, no brush and grass cleared to improve fields of fire.

In Grenoble, however, all the signs now pointed to an imminent second German attack. The city was placed under a virtual siege; all access and exit roads were closed off and a curfew was imposed between 20.00 and 06.00. The roads were crowded with the movement of German armoured vehicles and lorries carrying troops to the eastern edge of the city at the foot of the escarpment below the Charvet ridge. Fieseler Storch reconnaissance aircraft (*mouches*), which had been active these last few days circling above the positions at Saint-Nizier and the Engins tunnel, seemed to be even busier today, flying at times so low over the positions that the Maquis took to shouting at them: 'Bastards! Come and have a look here! Come down a little more and we'll show you what's what!'

Gilbert Joseph, guarding the Engins tunnel, reported: 'At one stage quite late in the day an elderly couple came up to our guard post. "We are worried for you," they whispered. "Things are beginning to move in Grenoble" … Some of the old men who had fought in the last war approached us later on and told us, "Dig trenches. Make yourselves shelters." We replied patronizingly, "Thank you, Grandfather." What did they know, these leftovers from another generation? They think they are still in Verdun.'

That night, Roland Bechmann, Jean Prévost's son-in-law, accompanied by a little troop of sappers and miners, slipped through the French lines and made his way down the hill, past La Tour-sans-Venin and almost into the outskirts of Grenoble. Later he wrote: 'Under the "relative" protection of two comrades with Stens, we dug holes for explosive in the railway ballast on the bridge which carried the little mountain tram over the main road and at the same time also placed a large amount of explosive in one of the water culverts under the main road leading up from Grenoble ... The Germans' plan was to attack later that morning, but they arrived after we had finished our work. We only understood the following day the reason for the growling of engines we could hear occasionally, somewhere behind us, while we were making it back up on to the plateau in our wheezing and spluttering *gazogène* lorry. We made it, despite the fact that our driver, exhausted or drunk, almost put us in the ditch, forcing me to take over the wheel to get us back safely. At 04.00, exhausted, I fell into my bed in the Hôtel du Moucherotte in Saint-Nizier.'

The sun rose into a perfect blue sky on 13 June 1944, the day of Jean Prévost's forty-third birthday. The early edition of the Grenoble daily *Le Petit Dauphinois* announced: 'The Grenoble electric tramway company informs its clients that service on the line to Saint-Nizier is temporarily suspended.'

Above the city, at Saint-Nizier, de Beauregard had deployed, in all, some 700 men strung out along the 3,000-metre defensive line of the Charvet ridge. The Compagnie Brisac, made up almost exclusively of young and totally inexperienced men from Grenoble, covered the right (southern) half of the line, leading up to the foot of Les Trois Pucelles. Jean Prévost's Compagnie Goderville, made up of more hardened but still untried men who had come up to the plateau as *réfractaires*, were deployed on the more vulnerable left (northern) half of the line. There were also a small number of others who had come with de Beauregard from the camps in Plénouse.

De Beauregard himself had his headquarters in a roadside villa at Les Guillets, a small hamlet just east of Saint-Nizier; the house had a substantial balcony with a panoramic view. He must have known that, apart from the weakness of his right flank and the failure to prepare defensive positions such as trenches, his situation had three crucial deficiencies – all due to a lack of manpower. First, his position had no depth; he had to rely on purely linear defence – once the Germans broke through anywhere, they could turn the rest of the line, everywhere. Second, he had no forward pickets to warn him of the enemy's approach – he must have calculated that this was not a huge deficiency, as he could see anything moving below – except, of course, at night. And third, he had no reserves to move around to fill gaps and reinforce points where he was under pressure. This last deficiency was the most crucial. The fact that the Germans were about to attack was hardly a secret. Huet must have understood the inherent weakness of the Saint-Nizier position and the fact that de Beauregard had insufficient manpower to cover the kilometre-and-a-half breach between Les Trois Pucelles and the Charvet cliffs. So it is perhaps surprising that Huet took no steps to give his local commander a few extra men to act as a mobile reserve to plug gaps where necessary.

De Beauregard's men on the Charvet hill were not the only ones up early that morning. In his house below the plateau, Pierre Tanant kissed his wife goodbye at 06.00 and started the long journey on his bicycle up to the Vercors, where he had been ordered by Descour to take up the post as François Huet's Chief of Staff. This was to be Tanant's first day in his new post and it would be a baptism of fire.

The thirty-four-year-old Tanant, another French Alpine soldier, had first come to the Vercors in March. A decent and straightforward man, he was above all a professional soldier who saw the world only through a professional soldier's eyes. One observer described him as 'Too heavy and rather too portly for the life of a Maquisard ... He had the enthusiasm of a young officer just out of Saint-Cyr.* Always governed by the rules, always attentive to the forms of external military discipline, always imbued with the ancient traditions of the army, he was a man who was most at home in uniform and most lost when out of it.'

Tanant arrived at Descour's headquarters at Rang des Pourrets at a little after 09.30 to be told that the Germans had launched an attack on Saint-Nizier. In fact, the first inkling of the German attack came at about 09.00 when farmers working the fields below Saint-Nizier told the Compagnie Brisac that they had seen a column of 300–400 German soldiers manoeuvring at the bottom of the hill.

Sure enough, very soon afterwards de Beauregard's forward lookouts reported seeing tiny *feldgrau*† figures at the foot of the hill, marching up towards them in column. The news was swiftly reported by telephone to

---

* The French equivalent of Sandhurst and West Point.

† Field grey – the colour of the German uniforms.

the headquarters in Saint-Martin. Huet jumped on his motorbike and raced off to Saint-Nizier, arriving at de Beauregard's command post at around 10.30. He pushed his way through the little crowd of runners waiting for de Beauregard's orders and joined his local commander on the balcony. 'How many are there?'

'About 400,' de Beauregard answered, his binoculars still trained on the column marching up the lower slopes of the hill. 'Perhaps a little less, they're still quite a way off.'

'No artillery?'

'Heavy machine guns that they are manhandling. They've left their transport at the Tour-sans-Venin.'

As they watched, the Germans broke column and fanned out on the slopes on either side of the road. 'They're heading for Charvet hill – or possibly the mountain tram track. Or maybe both,' de Beauregard concluded. It was clear, even this early, that the Germans were not intending a direct frontal assault. They would try to outflank de Beauregard's line to the north or the south. They knew as well as de Beauregard that these were the vulnerable points.

Huet, quickly realizing that the German attack was serious, returned to Saint-Nizier to telephone his headquarters and order up reinforcements from Geyer's units stationed near their base in La Rivière, midway between Saint-Martin and Saint-Agnan. An old bus was quickly found and Sergeant-Major Abel Chabal was swiftly dispatched from his base at Revoulat farm in the Loscence valley to Saint-Nizier with twenty of his men.

Huet returned to de Beauregard's headquarters to tell him that reinforcements were on their way. By this time, the battle had been properly joined with a German heavy 13.7mm machine gun opening up from a sandbagged position near the Charvet farm. This was serious for, if the machine gun got properly established, it could lay down suppressing fire for almost the full length of de Beauregard's front line, forcing the defenders to keep their heads down while the Germans positioned themselves for a frontal assault. Prévost's men tried desperately to deal with the new threat, firing from behind the banks and walls of Charvet farm and engaging the German position with Compagnie Goderville's one light mortar. De Beauregard, looking through his binoculars, could see the bullets sending up little spurts of dust as they struck the sandbags round the German position. But the enemy gun still kept firing. So he ordered one of Compagnie Brisac's sections to do what they could to give assistance.

It must have been about this time that someone thought to wake the exhausted Roland Bechmann, sleeping in his room in the Hôtel Revoulat at Saint-Nizier after his night spent planting explosive charges. Later he wrote: 'I leapt out of bed, buckled on my belt, pistol and bandolier of ammunition and dashed the 300 metres down to our headquarters where I found ... François Huet talking to de Beauregard. I could already hear the first exchanges of machine-gun fire. I asked Huet if I should blow the charges we had placed the previous night. He replied that it was pointless since the enemy had already long passed that point on the road.' Bechmann, his primary role now overtaken by events, took charge of a bazooka and joined up with a few men commanded by an old veteran, Sergeant Itier, known to all because of his antique blue uniform and the little terrier who was always at his heels.

Roland Bechmann was not the only person who was surprised by the speed of the German advance that morning. France Pinhas, a nurse, had been looking after a sick friend in the Hôtel Touristique in the little village of Les Michalons, close to the main Saint-Nizier–Grenoble road just below the Charvet ridge. She later wrote: 'I was deeply shocked when, early in the afternoon, I saw German soldiers among the trees with machine guns ready to fire. I was very worried. I knew what the Germans were capable of. Shortly afterwards they surrounded the building. They looked like beasts, full of hate and terror ... One set up a machine gun firing from one of the rooms of the hotel. The noise was simply terrible. We were all very afraid and decided to take shelter in the cellar.'

The weapon which opened up from France Pinhas' hotel was a second 13.7mm heavy machine gun, whose fire was now raking the Maquisard line from the south, its heavy thumping filling the valley and its bullets ricocheting off the walls and slicing the leaves from the trees in the garden of de Beauregard's headquarters. The Germans tried to use the fire from the two machine guns to push a column up the road towards the centre of de Beauregard's line, but they were stopped by Gammon grenades thrown from the higher ground and the bazooka manned by Roland Bechmann and Sergeant Itier, his devoted terrier still jogging at his heels.

De Beauregard, increasingly pinned down, decided it was time to find another command post and, with Huet following, dashed across the road. 'I ran of course, bent double,' he later said. 'But Huet would never bend. I think he thought it undignified. He marched across the road with his head held high. Unhappily he slipped on the tarmac, which rather spoiled the effect.'

It was now around 14.30 and Huet felt he needed to report on the situation to Descour. He took off on his motorbike, heading for Rang des Pourrets. But just outside Saint-Martin he ran into Descour, Geyer and the newly arrived Tanant in two cars coming from the opposite direction. There was a hurried roadside conference, as Huet briefed his senior officer on the situation at Saint-Nizier. Suddenly the little group saw a strange, heavily laden convoy heading towards them. A young officer jumped down from the lead vehicle and reported that he had four 25mm Hotchkiss anti-tank guns, together with ammunition and other equipment, on board. What would Huet like him to do with them?

It transpired that, at 05.00 that morning, the Maquis in the Chambarand forest, west of the Vercors, had 'requisitioned' the guns from an old French military camp in the area after 'neutralizing' the French Commandant and his staff. The guns, together with a small tracked store-carrying truck, a good deal of ammunition and other useful military equipment, were loaded on to eight lorries which made their way in plain daylight towards the Vercors. Unhappily, in one of the narrow roads which run through Pont-en-Royans, one of the trucks broke down. There followed a nervous wait while it was mended; the Germans conducted frequent patrols through the town, which had been bombarded only two days previously because of German suspicions that the town harboured 'terrorists'. The townspeople, however, seemed wholly unconcerned by the danger and brought the drivers and the Maquis unit guarding the convoy baskets of cherries. Fortunately, the broken lorry was soon fixed and the convoy completed its journey to Huet's headquarters in Saint-Martin without further mishap. Huet immediately dispatched one of the guns, together with its ammunition, to Saint-Nizier.

While all this was going on, a bus sped by carrying Chabal and his twenty reinforcements to Saint-Nizier with as much speed as its *gazogène* engine would allow. The group at the side of the road watched as it disappeared in a cloud of charcoal smoke, the sound of the 'Marseillaise' being lustily sung by its passengers echoing after it.

When Descour got back to Rang des Pourrets he drafted a report on the situation for Bob Bennes' team to send to Algiers: 'We have been attacked by heavy forces coming from Grenoble. We cannot contemplate leaving the local population compromised and without defence. The situation is now critical because of lack of arms and munitions. We are begging you to help us soon with massive parachute drops on all Vercors sites. A battalion of parachutists would help us save the situation. Papier Gommé [the parachute site near Saint-Martin] is ready. Best wishes.'

By the time Chabal reached Saint-Nizier, the battle had been going on for more than six hours and was reaching its climax. The German machine gun at Charvet farm was still in action. Unless it was taken out quickly there was a real danger that one of the German assaults would break de Beauregard's line. Chabal led his men along a covered farm track and then, after an audacious dash across open ground, set up his own machine gun on a small hill behind the German position, forcing them to pull out. The greatest danger to de Beauregard's line had been removed. Chabal then tried a second assault on a German position behind the embankment of the mountain tramway. But this failed under intense fire from the Michalons machine gun.

Suddenly, with dusk approaching, the Germans started to pull back. It was at this moment that the newly 'requisitioned' 25mm Hotchkiss cannon from Chambaran arrived. It was too late for the main battle, but, with the Germans now withdrawing, the gun was taken down the road to a point where it could fire on the retreating German vehicles. The absence of a proper aiming sight on the Hotchkiss made accuracy difficult and the best that could be achieved was when a solid shot from the gun fell so close to one German vehicle that it made the driver swerve, and another shot which passed harmlessly through the canopy of one of the enemy lorries. Those on the plateau nevertheless cheered.

That night at the Hôtel du Moucherotte in Saint-Nizier there was a combined victory celebration and forty-third birthday party for Jean Prévost. It was Prévost's company around the Charvet farm who had borne the brunt of the German attacks. Huet sent a message to them: 'Bravo, Goderville. You have shown of what mettle you are made.'

Descour sent a message to Algiers expressing the same sense of jubilation, along with his usual pleas for more arms and a good deal of exaggeration when it came to estimating the size of the German attack: 'Vercors attacked by a battalion. The enemy was forced to abandon the attack after 12 hours. We expect a renewed attack after a brief delay. We have 8 dead and four wounded. We need arms. We ask you to redouble your efforts to help us. The population has risen *en masse* against the enemy. Bazookas have done marvellous work. Best wishes.'

But everyone knew the celebrations were premature. Late in the evening, there was a meeting between Huet, Descour, Chavant, Dom Guétet, Zeller and Cammaerts at Rang des Pourrets to assess the situation. All agreed the Germans would be back. Next time they would come with more troops and they would, as today, go for the north and south wings of de Beauregard's line to try to turn the French position.

The Germans, too, had to reassess the situation. The truth was that Pflaum had underestimated the strength and determination of French resistance. He would need to mount a more heavyweight attack, with proper supporting fire, if he was to succeed.

Despite the fact that Algiers had sent almost no responses to the increasingly desperate pleas coming from the Vercors, things were in fact moving in the North African capital. During the afternoon, Fernand Grenier, de Gaulle's Communist Minister for Air, received assurances from one of his subordinates that 'Bombers from Britain and Italy would be dropping "the necessary" ... [to the Vercors] tonight. The Allies had promised that they were doing – and would continue to do – the maximum possible to support the French Resistance.'

But Grenier was not relying only on the Allies. He knew that little more could be hoped for from the Americans and British, bogged down as they were in the 82-kilometre-long but still only 24-kilometre-deep Normandy bridgehead, which had been struck by a fierce summer storm only the previous day. All available Allied aircraft were now employed helping the British and Canadians extricate themselves from the 'meat grinder' of Caen, while at the same time supporting the Americans in their crucial push to take Cherbourg.

Grenier decided to use the antiquated French bombers, fighters and training aircraft left behind on abandoned bases in Syria and Morocco, which he intended to deploy in what he christened 'Plan Patrie'. The idea was to form a squadron of these ancient aircraft which could be used to fly missions for the French Resistance.

There was one small practical problem with Grenier's plan and one large political one. Practically, the range of the superannuated French aircraft was so limited that, although they had enough fuel to get to the south of France, they did not have enough to get back again afterwards. Nothing daunted, another French Air Force officer, Lieutenant Colonel

Morlaix, an ace with twenty-five enemy 'kills' to his name, had already recruited two dozen volunteer French pilots who were prepared to make the one-way trip to help their comrades, parachuting into France after their mission was over. Grenier's political problem was de Gaulle. He would have to get the General's approval and, as he was a Communist, this would not necessarily be easy.

Meanwhile, in London, General Koenig on this day issued instructions to his planning staff to draw up plans for 'developing the Massif Central into a large controlled area, supported by airborne troops'. His timing seems curious, given that there was already one of these struggling to survive in the Vercors. It was even more curious since, only the previous day, the Germans had finally and brutally put down the rising in the Mont Mouchet in the middle of the Massif Central.

After dark that night, with the Germans now gone from the Hôtel Touristique at Les Michalons, France Pinhas led her fellow guests and their children in a little column up the road towards Saint-Nizier shouting 'Don't shoot, don't shoot. We're French' at the tops of their voices. They were terrified because the Saint-Nizier defenders were nervous and fired at every sound. But their cries were heard and a patrol came out to meet them and escorted them back to safety behind the French lines.

At 22.15 that night, true to the promises given to Grenier, the BBC's evening broadcast carried two code phrases, 'Le petit chat est mort' and 'Gloire et honneur à ce cochon de popotier'. At 03.00 the following morning, the exhausted defenders of Saint-Nizier, lying out under the stars, were woken by air-raid sirens in Grenoble, followed shortly afterwards by the roar of British Halifax bombers flying overhead. In the moonlight they could even pick out the white blossoms of the parachutes as the bombers dropped containers with fresh arms and ammunition at the Sous-Main site at Méaudre and at another drop at the Rayon site near La Maye farm in the Loscence valley, west of La Chapelle.

THE SECOND BATTLE OF SAINT-NIZIER

The Germans spent 14 June recovering from their repulse on the Charvet ridge and assembling their forces to try again. This time Karl Pflaum was taking no chances. He ordered artillery pieces and mortars to be set up in the Parc Bachelard in the western outskirts of Grenoble and reinforcements to be called up from Gap and Lyon. His force for the second Battle of Saint-Nizier numbered about 1,000 and consisted of those engaged in the attack of 13 June reinforced by other elements of his division and some Milice units.

Meanwhile, up on the plateau, Huet made use of the day's respite to rearm his troops and reinforce the weak points in his line, especially its two extremities. Chabal's men were moved in to strengthen the Charvet farm, a picket was placed on the high ground on La Grande Moucherotte mountain, above Les Trois Pucelles, and one of Geyer's units, together with 60 men drawn from the Compagnie Abel, were moved in to reinforce the centre of the line, around the point where the road from Grenoble crosses the Charvet ridge. When they left La Balme the new reinforcements had almost no arms and only three grenades each. They received arms and more ammunition for the battle ahead only as they moved through Saint-Nizier on their way to the front line.

Despite these reinforcements, Huet's options were still severely constrained by lack of manpower and the size of the area he had to defend. He had a total of perhaps 3,000 men to defend the whole plateau, nearly a third of whom were now committed to defending the 3-kilometre line on the Charvet ridge, leaving only 2,000 to cover the remaining 200 kilometres of the Vercors perimeter. What if the German attack was a feint designed to draw him into deploying the bulk of his forces in the north of the plateau, while the enemy suddenly attacked in the south, where his headquarters and main parachute and landing sites lay? Once again he had to rely largely on a purely linear defence. Once again he was not able to find enough troops to form an adequate reserve. Once again, if the Germans managed to break the French line at any point, the battle would be lost and the only option would be retreat.

Though there is no record of it, it seems certain that Huet, as a good commander, must have been making contingency arrangements for the fall of Saint-Nizier. He would have known that he could not withstand a determined and properly resourced German attack on the town. He had, we know, long held the view that the northern plateau was *in extremis* indefensible. It would therefore be unwise, if the Charvet line was broken, to contest the rest of the plateau inch by inch. Better to pull back early and in good order before his losses were too great, and take up new positions which would be more easily defensible around the shorter perimeter of the southern plateau.

Huet spent the day on his motorbike visiting and inspecting his main defensive positions around the rims of the northern and southern plateaus, starting with Saint-Nizier. He returned to his headquarters in Saint-Martin that night confident that his men were as ready as they could be to face the German attack wherever and whenever it came.

Saint-Nizier buzzed with activity that morning as weapons and ammunition were distributed and troops moved backwards and forwards to the front line. Below the Charvet ridge a patrol stopped two men in civilian clothes behaving suspiciously. They turned out to be Milice and were later executed.

Chavant had attended the parachute drops of the previous night and insisted that the containers were immediately cut free of their parachutes and driven in trucks at full speed to the main square in Saint-Nizier. Here a team unpacked the new weapons which were hurriedly degreased and assembled before being distributed to the front line. There was some disappointment. The drop had contained a few Browning light machine guns, which would be useful. But there was only a limited amount of ammunition to serve them. There were also some heavy and cumbersome old First World War Hotchkiss 8mm machine guns, but again with too little ammunition.

Others, helped by volunteers from among the citizens of Saint-Nizier, ferried food down to the defenders who had now spent the best part of thirty-six hours non-stop in the front line. The lack of large containers in the town made this a laborious and time-consuming business. Meanwhile, the coffins of the eight dead from the previous day's fighting, each covered with a tricolour, were laid out on trestles in Saint-Nizier church, where a considerable crowd lined up to pay their last respects.

Bob Bennes and his signallers in La Britière used the day to continue transmitting a stream of messages to Algiers repeating their need for ammunition, mortars, machine guns. In the morning Henri Zeller, the experience of Barcelonnette still fresh in his mind, sent a message to Algiers: 'I strongly support the pleas from Descour. It would be terrible if the zones liberated by the Resistance, which will be invaluable in the context of a southern invasion, are allowed to fall to the enemy one by one.'

Also among the signal traffic this day was a second message from General Koenig in London, ordering all Maquis units to disengage from the enemy, break up into small groups and disperse into the forests. It is not difficult to imagine how this was received by Huet and his commanders, bracing themselves for a second German assault.

In the evening of 14 June, the brief respite ended with some forty artillery and mortar shells falling in the Saint-Nizier area. Miraculously these caused neither casualties nor substantial damage and stopped at dusk. They were almost certainly ranging shots, so that the guns could be ready to support the main event when it started. Now everyone knew what everyone had feared; this time there would be artillery support for the German assault. This time it would not be just the front line along the Charvet hill which would be exposed to attack, but also the units positioned out of the direct line of fire on the reverse slopes as well. And, without artillery or mortars with which to respond, there was absolutely nothing the French could do about it.

De Beauregard slept that night on the balcony of his headquarters while his men grabbed what sleep they could out in the open along the Charvet front line. The night was star studded, calm and warm. Every noise from the city below drifted up to the defenders on a light breeze. A truck changing gear; the shunting of a train in the station; something heavy and powerful grinding up the hill towards them; a fox barking in a wood below. A young Maquisard, Ferdinand Sallier, recalled afterwards: 'Up to now we had been accommodated, for good or evil, in barns and sheds which were often leaky and in a piteous state. But these days and nights [in front of Saint-Nizier], which were full of constant alerts, we spent lying out in our holes, waiting for the Boches. The courier from headquarters never stopped carrying messages on little slips of paper – put this machine gun here, move that section over there …'

The second battle of Saint-Nizier opened abruptly on 15 June. This time there was no long, leisurely approach by the enemy. No preceding skirmishes. A little before dawn there was a fierce forty-five-minute artillery barrage, including heavy 155mm guns firing from somewhere deep in the city below. When dawn broke that morning at around 05.00, de Beauregard discovered to his horror that a German heavy machine gun had already established itself under cover of darkness on the hill overlooking Charvet farm and was now subjecting the whole of the left half of his line to fierce enfilade fire. On his other wing, under Les Trois Pucelles, the situation was little better. At first light the men on Compagnie Brisac's right wing saw a group of 'comrades' approaching them through the mist. They were wearing French Resistance armbands and calling out in French that they were a returning patrol. But as they got close to the French lines the 'comrades' suddenly opened up with machine guns and were beaten back only with difficulty. They were in fact Milice who had infiltrated the woods below Les Trois Pucelles overnight.

Shortly afterwards another German heavy machine gun which had infiltrated through the French lines overnight opened up from a position among the jumble of rocks at the foot of Les Trois Pucelles – behind the Compagnie Brisac. De Beauregard was paying a heavy price for not putting forward pickets out in front of his lines.

The French, too, had machine-gun positions interspersed all along their line. But many of these were equipped with the ancient 8mm Hotchkiss guns dropped in two nights previously. These proved very difficult to fire by troops untrained to their special ways. The lack of cleared fields of fire also inhibited the effectiveness of the French response. At 07.20 a mortar round fell on a sack full of grenades, causing a massive explosion and cutting the young Maquisard lying alongside it to ribbons.

De Beauregard, on the back foot from the start, was never able to recover the initiative. In some places his men had to resort to hand-to-hand fighting, as they struggled desperately to hold the line. More worrying, without any form of wireless communications, he found it more and more difficult to get his messages through by courier to his

THE BATTLE OF SAINT-NIZIER

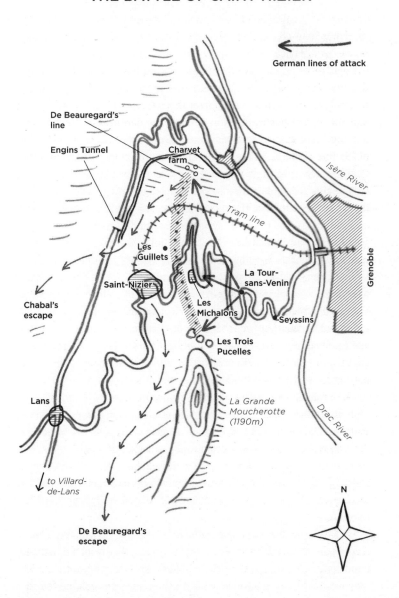

German lines of attack

De Beauregard's line

Engins Tunnel

Charvet farm

Isère River

Tram line

Les Guillets

La Tour-sans-Venin

Saint-Nizier

Les Michalons

Grenoble

Chabal's escape

Les Trois Pucelles

Seyssins

Lans

La Grande Moucherotte (1190m)

Drac River

to Villard-de-Lans

De Beauregard's escape

N

forward commanders, Prévost and Brisac. He was in severe danger of losing control as his line began to disintegrate. As the battle raged, a message was being furiously tapped out to Algiers: 'Being attacked in force. Beg you to act quickly – we are on the [parachute] sites. You have contributed to this catastrophic situation because ammunition now running out. You bear the responsibility for us being unable to resist.'

France Pinhas had spent the last thirty-six hours helping the wounded with another nurse, Mme Royannez. As soon as she heard the firing she rushed to the front line: 'I took my little medical case containing several bandages and tried to get as close to the place where the men were fighting ... When the men threw themselves down on the ground because of an incoming shell, I did the same thing. But each time when they got up, I immediately dashed further forward. One young man who wanted to be called "Jesus" told me that he had been shot through the stomach ... I did not think he would make it, but hastily patched him up with a temporary bandage to make him feel more comfortable.'

De Beauregard's line was already beginning to waver. 'I was by now used to war and to weapons firing,' France Pinhas continued. 'The men were running backwards and forwards and it was impossible to understand what was going on. One of them was angry to find me there and told me to go back to the rear area. Why? I didn't think it was because the retreat had started yet ... but he pulled me back by my nurse's apron and made me return to the village. Back at the Hôtel Belvédère I found several wounded being attended to as well as was possible under the circumstances by Mme Royannez and Dr Ullmann while other young medical orderlies bandaged wounds and administered injections ...'

By around 09.45, it was all over. Huet, realizing that the line could not be held and determined to withdraw in good order with the minimum of losses, gave de Beauregard the order to break off contact with the enemy and start pulling back. Sergeant Itier in his antique blue uniform stayed behind trying to cover the retreat with his bazooka. He was felled by a burst of machine-gun fire and bled to death on the ground, his faithful terrier whimpering by his body and licking his wounds.

France Pinhas found herself in the middle of the mêlée: 'It is impossible to describe the atmosphere in Saint-Nizier ... Some men had to pull back, but others continued to stay and fight. We were very worried. The Germans had more men than we did and they were forcing us to flee. The village and the neighbouring farms were now in total panic. Men were fleeing in trucks and many of the farm families were trying to get away in heavily loaded carts with the farm animals following behind. We left with the wounded, driving first to Autrans where I was redirected on to Vassieux. There was a long line of trucks streaming out of Saint-Nizier heading for the southern plateau … [Eventually] we arrived in Saint-Martin and stopped outside the hospital. It was only then that I had my first meal of the day … before joining the doctors and three other nurses who were already at work there …'

Most of de Beauregard's men pulled back through Saint-Nizier and were among those France Pinhas saw in the convoy of trucks heading for Villard. On the way they were cheered and fêted with wine by the local population as though they were the victors, not the vanquished. They passed through Villard and moved on to the relative safety of the southern plateau.

Others, however, continued fighting despite the order to withdraw. Geyer's men, who had been moved down from Les Trois Pucelles to reinforce de Beauregard's centre, held their position against successive attacks along the road as the rest of the French line disintegrated around them. Eventually they too were forced to pull back in order to avoid being encircled. One man volunteered to remain with a machine gun to cover his comrades' withdrawal. But he was soon overwhelmed and killed.

Abel Chabal refused no fewer than three orders to withdraw. Only when he and his men were almost totally encircled in the early afternoon did he finally pull out with a risky dash under intense fire across open ground. This was brave but irresponsible. It could make no difference to the outcome of the battle, but it placed his men at unnecessary risk.

De Beauregard waited to ensure that most of his men got away and then slipped into the woods behind Saint-Nizier and made his way to safety through the forest east of Villard. Paul Brisac took the same escape route but got lost in the forest and only managed to link up with his unit at the Col de Rousset three days later. Chabal, who left his position too late to escape south down the Lans valley, led his men instead south-west across the mountain to the gorge of the River Furon. Crossing this, he headed for Autrans and then turned south to the Gorges de la Bourne and on to the southern plateau.

Gilbert Joseph's section, guarding the Engins tunnel in the next valley, heard the thump of every bullet and the fall of every shell as the battle raged, unseen, on the other side of the hill. He and his comrades finally received the order to withdraw at 14.00. It was not a moment too soon, for by then they could clearly see the line of German troops advancing towards them on the other side of the Furon gorge, no more than 500 metres away.

In all de Beauregard lost sixteen men killed in the second Battle of Saint-Nizier. German reports put their own casualties at six killed and fifteen wounded. The French losses would have been much higher had it not been for the early and, mostly, disciplined withdrawal of the bulk of the French troops and the fact that the Germans, who should have given hot pursuit, allowed themselves to be distracted instead by the burning and pillaging of Saint-Nizier. Forty-three out of Saint-Nizier's ninety-three houses were burnt, as were a number of farms in the area. Most inhabitants had fled before the German arrival, but not the local vicar, the veteran Abbé Lambert, who valiantly guarded his church. But he could not stop the Germans taking away the coffins of the Maquisards killed in the first battle and throwing them into a burning house.

In the early afternoon in the pouring rain, the Germans pressed on to Villard. The Maquisards had passed through the town at around midday leaving its streets deserted. 'We heard the firing, at first far off and then getting closer and closer,' noted Janina Lamenta, a young student at the Cyprian-Norwid Polish school in the town. 'And then the Germans arrived. They put a machine gun opposite the Hôtel du Col de l'Arc and searched the rooms of the hotel. Among the Germans were some Silesian Poles based in Grenoble who reassured us all would be OK.'

A few arrests were made and one house burnt – the garage owned by the Huillier family who, as co-founders of the Organisation Vercors, were well known to have put their substantial transport and haulier business at the service of the Resistance on the plateau. The Germans arrested the only member of the Huillier family they could find there, Louis Huillier, who was later deported to a concentration camp in Germany and never seen again.

If the Germans had decided to press their advantage this day they could probably have swept through the southern plateau almost unimpeded. With Huet's forces in full flight, the road to his headquarters in Saint-Martin now lay dangerously open, despite a small detachment of Geyer's men which Huet had sent at 15.00 hours to block the road by the little deserted village of Valchevrière, the most vulnerable point of entry into the southern plateau. But the Germans, who had had their fingers badly burnt in the first Battle of Saint-Nizier, uncharacteristically opted for caution and pushed no further south. At nightfall they pulled out of Villard and consolidated around Saint-Nizier, where they began digging trenches, giving Huet time to reorganize and redeploy his troops around the now shorter perimeter of the southern plateau.

That night Pierre Tanant led a reconnaissance patrol back to Saint-Nizier to probe the new German positions. 'We assembled our patrol from volunteers at Saint-Martin ... and collected our arms: machine guns and grenades. I found a truck, which I commandeered, and we set off ... The air was fresh and cold as it nearly always is at this altitude ... on the way we met Chavant coming in the other direction. He told us that we could safely drive in the lorry as far as Lans ... When we reached the Lans town square we jumped down from the truck and started to make our way on foot to Saint-Nizier seven kilometres away. The patrol split into two columns on either side of the road. It was a long monotonous march through the night – though we were accompanied by an abandoned cow which wandered along ahead of us as though acting as our guide. When we were about 1,500 metres from the village a voice suddenly shouted *Halt!* We dropped flat by the side of the road as the bullets whizzed over our heads ... ricocheting off the rocks around us. There was no point in pressing on – the Germans had been alerted and we had got the information we came for. The enemy were in possession of Saint-Nizier. For the first time they had not limited their action to one day before returning to their quarters at nightfall. This time they were holding the territory they had taken overnight. What could this mean? We made our way back to Lans over the next hour and then returned in the truck to Rang des Pourrets where I met Huet, who had come to see Descour to get new orders.'

In the early hours of the next morning, as if by way of consolation, there was a substantial parachute drop of weapons at the Taille-Crayon site at Vassieux, one of the first of many that would come to this site over the next few weeks.

Five days after the fall of Saint-Nizier *Le Petit Dauphinois* announced that the Grenoble–Saint-Nizier tramway had been reopened for business. But now the Germans were in permanent occupation of the town. Pflaum was in no hurry to go further. He had captured the key gateway to the plateau and for the moment that was good enough.

The second battle had another lasting effect on the situation in the Vercors, recorded by André Valot, who noted that, although the combat had the effect of increasing the morale and zeal of the Maquisards, the effect on the civilian population of the plateau was rather different: 'Up to now they had always shown us the utmost cordiality, albeit tinged with the usual peasant scepticism ... they considered us ... a bit mad perhaps – but harmless. They mostly took the view that they should help us if they were in a position to do so, provided it didn't cost them too much. But Saint-Nizier made them think again. It was us partisans who had caused the Germans to come to the plateau ... Now their houses were burnt, their farm animals killed or taken away and their harvest damaged ... would it not have been better not to have provoked the Germans? ... Better to make sure everyone knew that they were staying out of it – "We are not for the Germans, of course ... but we are not for the Maquis either. We are just for the quiet life."'

Huet's Chief of Staff, the ever-optimistic Pierre Tanant, summed up the day's work in characteristically Panglossian terms: 'Taking everything into account this first battle did not end unsatisfactorily for us. We had some losses, but the enemy had more. One of our towns was burnt, but we could soon reconstruct it. We lost territory, but we held on to the most important part of the plateau. Our fortress had suffered a violent shock. But the result was that the interior wall which we had to protect was now shorter and easier to defend.'

Huet himself was more realistic and more sombre: 'It should have been possible ... to hold on to Saint-Nizier. But this position was vital to the Germans and they were prepared to throw whatever was needed at us in order to capture the town. We would have had quite high losses, as we did not have heavy weapons on the same scale as the enemy – artillery and aircraft especially. Our Partisans were astonishing – but they weren't made for extended battle. Their arms, equipment and training were just not up to the task.'

Huet's assessment is almost certainly accurate. But it prompted the key question. If indeed his forces were best suited for the swift actions of guerrilla warfare rather than the drawn-out conflict of extended battle, then why did the entire French military leadership on and beyond the Vercors continue to base their strategy, not on what Huet's Maquisards could do well (guerrilla warfare), but on a Saint-Nizier-style fixed defence which they didn't have the arms, equipment or training to undertake at all? The answer to the fall of Saint-Nizier should have been to adopt a more mobile defensive strategy.

As it happens, those directing the Vercors didn't have to look very far to find one. Saint-Nizier was not the only place under strenuous German attack on this day. A hundred and fifty kilometres north of the Vercors plateau, a mixed German force of 2,500 had been engaged for the previous four days in a major attack on Henri Romans-Petit's forces around Oyonnax, in the southern Jura. As Huet's forces were being beaten back from a burning Saint-Nizier, Romans-Petit's men 'withdrew ... in perfect order' into the forests, leaving the Germans with no one to attack.

The date of the second Battle of Saint-Nizier, 15 June 1944, was also a significant day for the little village of Saint-Donat-sur-l'Herbasse, 20 kilometres west of Pont-en-Royans. At 08.30, without any warning four Messerschmitt 109s made repeated low passes over Saint-Donat, indiscriminately machine-gunning anything that moved in the village's streets, houses and gardens. In their wake three German armoured columns swept into the town from the west. After several long bursts of fire, German soldiers moved in to pillage houses and shops alike. They soon discovered that the Maquis they were looking for had withdrawn from the area some time previously. At midday, having told all the inhabitants to go indoors, the Germans assembled eighty-three hostages of all ages in the town square. After savage beatings and interrogations, six were taken away to Valence.

Then the Germans let loose their Eastern Troops – the Asiatic units that they had recruited on the eastern front, known by the French as the Mongols. What happened next, before the Germans finally pulled out at 17.00, was later recorded by the local doctor:

> I the undersigned swear and certify that on 15 June 1944 I was called to some 25 women and young girls who had been raped by German soldiers. The age of these women ranged from 13 to 50. Each had been raped several times by the soldiers under threat of death and after being brutally beaten.
>
> My colleague Dr Nicolaides had to deal with a similar number of cases.

Dr Lémonon
2 October 1944

The following day, three of the six prisoners taken from Saint-Donat were released, but the remaining three were taken to Montluc prison in Lyon where they were shot on 8 July 1944.

It may be that this recent German activity on and around the edges of the Vercors was the result of rising German concern about the possibility of airborne landings deep in southern France ahead of a landing on the Mediterranean coast. A German signal decrypted at 06.45 on this day by British codebreakers at Bletchley Park, read: 'Admiral south coast France informed by [superior command of] definite signs that operations are intended against south coast France. Possibility of parachute operations and of airborne landings.'

Pierre Dalloz, back in London, read about the defeat at Saint-Nizier in the English papers three days afterwards and immediately contacted André Manuel, the number two in de Gaulle's London headquarters: 'What I have read in the British papers is gravely worrying. The Vercors has been mobilized far too early. It seems to have been given a role greatly in excess of the forces it has at its disposal. It cannot hold on for weeks, let alone months. There will be no element of surprise when we carry out the southern landing. In fact, there will be no more Vercors!'

RESPITE AND REORGANIZATION

If 15 June 1944 was a day of tragedy and loss on the Vercors, the day which followed was one of farce and stupidity. Following the infiltration of the Milice in Maquisard disguise at the second battle of Saint-Nizier, orders were given to tighten up controls at all the main entry points to the plateau. No one was to leave or enter without the proper papers.

In the evening of 16 June, Eugène Chavant's Citroën, taking *le Patron* to Pont-en-Royans for a meeting, was stopped at the checkpoint run by Narcisse Geyer's men at the entrance to the Grands Goulets tunnels, near Les Barraques. Chavant's driver was asked for documents. He replied that they didn't have any – couldn't the guard see it was *le Patron*? The guard responded that without documents they couldn't proceed – they must turn back. Chavant stuck his head out of the window so that the guard could see him and demanded to pass. The row swiftly escalated, ending with the arrest of Chavant and his driver, who were transported as prisoners to Geyer's headquarters at La Rivière.

The word flew round that *le Patron* had been taken by the military, and a small armed group of civilian Maquis soon set off for Geyer's head-quarters at Buget farm at La Rivière. Here they arrested the headstrong cavalry commander and brought him back to Saint-Martin under armed guard. It took all the diplomatic skills of Huet, Descour and Zeller to defuse the situation and get things back on track. The immediate crisis soon passed, but the embers still smouldered and could be – would be – easily fanned back to life again.

The personal relations between Chavant and Geyer had long been strained, but civil and military structures on the plateau, fed especially by a strong anti-militarist sentiment among the volunteer Maquisard companies, had also been deteriorating for weeks. 'Unbridled accusations unsupported by evidence created an increasingly explosive atmosphere between the civil and the military …' noted Gilbert Joseph. 'We

believed the [military] officers were keeping for themselves the chocolate and cigarettes which had been dropped by parachute and not
distributing them to the Maquisards. One matter caused special indig-
nation. Military trousers and battledress tops came with every para
drop. These were much better than the flimsy stuff with which we were
supplied by Tanant [Huet's Chief of Staff]. The foreign uniforms were
strong and light and flexible and had large pockets and were just what
we Maquisards needed. We sent [one of our people] to demand that
these be distributed ... but he reported back that Tanant had refused,
saying that French soldiers couldn't be dressed in foreign uniforms.'
There were also rumours that money from the parachute drops had gone
missing ...

For François Huet, the Chavant/Geyer affair must have been extremely
tiresome on a day when he was fully occupied redeploying his forces in
the light of the loss of Saint-Nizier. 'Our three options were as follows,'
wrote Roland Costa de Beauregard after the war. 'To retake Saint-Nizier;
to retreat fully to the southern plateau, beyond the Gorges de la Bourne;
or to maintain a light presence on the northern plateau. Of the three
options, only the first had to be rejected as impossible ... The second
option was not necessary because the enemy showed no signs of wanting
to occupy the northern plateau. So we chose the third, since this enabled
us to continue to make use, if necessary, of the substantial parachute and
landing zones on the northern plateau around Autrans and Correçon.'

Huet used the respite which followed the Saint-Nizier battles to redeploy his forces, ordering a halt to all operations while this was in
progress. 'This is not the moment to provoke the Boches,' he instructed.
He divided his area into four zones, each under the command of one of
his senior commanders.

De Beauregard's units would continue to occupy those areas of the
northern plateau which were free of Germans, leaving a strip of no man's
land around Saint-Nizier. His main towns were Méaudre, Autrans and
Villard-de-Lans. But he was also responsible for the defence of the most
vulnerable point in the natural barrier surrounding the southern plateau,
the little winding mountain road which runs from Villard past deserted
Valchevrière village to Saint-Martin. De Beauregard placed the
Valchevrière area under the command of his most trusted commander,
Jean Prévost, who, together with his ubiquitous portable typewriter,
books and scripts, set up his headquarters in a large, white-painted farm-

house in the middle of the Herbouilly valley, just behind the Valchevrière ridge.

De Beauregard was well aware that, with the Germans already camped out in Saint-Nizier, his position on the northern plateau was more exposed than those in the southern half of the Vercors, so, thinking as a good guerrilla commander should, he started seeking out isolated refuges for his men to disperse to if things turned suddenly bad.

The north-west of the plateau, around the Presles forest, was defended by a 'battalion' commanded by Henri Ullman, the south-west covering the Forêt de Lente by Louis Bourdeaux, and the remainder, including the Col de Rousset, Vassieux, Saint-Agnan, La Chapelle, Saint-Martin and the entire eastern wall of the plateau, by Narcisse Geyer and his cavalrymen.

In addition to repositioning his troops inside the Vercors, Huet moved to create a defensive buffer around the plateau. On 16 June, Zeller called in one of Cammaerts' key Resistance leaders in the area, Pierre Raynaud, who led an 800-strong Maquisard group in the area south of Die, guarding the southern gateway to the plateau. Zeller instructed Raynaud to prepare ambushes to impede German movements along the main roads running east–west through Die at the southern edge of the Vercors. The Combovin plateau south-west of the Vercors was protected by another Drôme Maquis, numbering some 1,700. A third Maquisard unit, the Compagnie de Trièves, covered the eastern and south-eastern approaches to the Vercors' eastern ramparts.

Meanwhile the radios of La Britière were also busy on 16 June. A message arrived from General Koenig repeating for the third time his earlier instruction to all Resistance units in southern France to disperse. Koenig also sent a second signal saying that the order of priority for future arms supplies would 'correspond to the importance of the area concerned, to the development of the current battle for liberation' (that is, the north of France would get the weapons first). For the third time, the Vercors commanders briefly considered Koenig's order to disperse – and for the third time ignored it.

Cammaerts sent a signal that day to Brooks Richards in SPOC, re-inforcing the complaints about the urgent need for heavy weapons. Zeller also sent a message to Algiers addressed to Constans: 'I repeat previous requests that small detachments of paratroops should be parachuted into "liberated zones". The effect on morale would be very beneficial and this

HUET'S DISPOSITIONS AND EARLY GERMAN PROBES

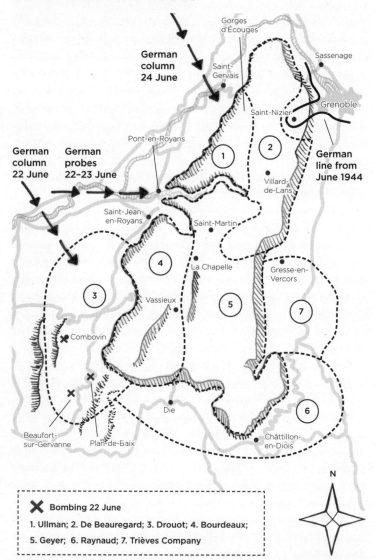

Gorges d'Écouges

Sassenage

German column 24 June

Saint-Gervais

Saint-Nizier

Grenoble

Pont-en-Royans

German column 22 June

German probes 22–23 June

German line from June 1944

1

2

Villard-de-Lans

Saint-Jean-en-Royans

Saint-Martin

4

La Chapelle

Gresse-en-Vercors

3

Vassieux

5

7

Combovin

Die

Beaufort-sur-Gervanne

Plan-de-Baix

6

Châtillon-en-Diois

N

✗ Bombing 22 June

1. Ullman; 2. De Beauregard; 3. Drouot; 4. Bourdeaux;
5. Geyer; 6. Raynaud; 7. Trièves Company

would have the effect of preserving these zones, which are currently under threat, for future use.' During his visit to Algiers, Chavant had asked for 2,000 paratroops. Constans had insisted on promising 4,000. Now all the plateau was asking for was 'small detachments'.

Zeller's demand for parachutists was very far from being an unreasonable request. In May 1943, a French parachute regiment had been formed from the remnants of two parachute units disbanded when the Armistice Army was dissolved. In addition, the Allies were at this time separately training 100 French paras a month for use in France. In April 1944, the newly reconstituted French parachute unit, numbering some 1,800 men, moved to an airbase at Trapani, at the western extremity of Sicily. There they had stayed for the last ten weeks, with nothing to do – they joked that they weren't so much 'parachutists' as 'paratourists'. They were desperate for action, and the Vercors was desperate for help. Surely sensible minds could bring the two together?

Now, however, to add to the general confusion, a demarcation dispute broke out between London and Algiers about exactly who was responsible for the Vercors. Up to this point, the vast bulk of assistance given to the plateau had come from Algiers, who, through Maitland Wilson's headquarters, regarded themselves as responsible for the support and operational direction of the plateau. Now Koenig, on the eve of being confirmed by Eisenhower in his position as commander of all French forces in France, asserted his authority and sent a telegram to Algiers: 'The Vercors, whether it be that portion in the Drôme or in the Isère, is to be considered part of the north and not the south of France (and therefore under the command of London, not Algiers).'

On the Vercors plateau itself, Huet had more practical problems to deal with. With some 3,000 men to command and more coming up to the plateau every day, he decided that, as well as reshaping his forces on the ground, he also needed to reorganize his headquarters in Saint-Martin. Initially these had been set up on the ground floor of the Hôtel Breyton, with Chavant's civil administration occupying the whole of the first floor. But the Breyton was becoming very crowded. So Huet found a new base in an Alpine-styled house called the Villa Bellon on the outskirts of Saint-Martin. The house suited Huet's needs perfectly. There is a garage on the ground floor, above which are the main rooms consisting of a library, a sitting room, a dining room which, for Huet, doubled as a conference facility, a substantial room used as a secretariat and another which Huet and Tanant shared as an office. The entire frontage of the first floor is served by a large balcony facing the peaks of the Vercors' eastern wall. On the second floor, there are several bedrooms, one of which is also east facing and has a balcony. This Huet used for his bedroom. In front of the house there is a low stable block alongside a front entrance closed by a stout gate.

Huet's new headquarters housed some fifty officers, nearly all of whom were professional soldiers, many having come to the plateau to join Huet only in the weeks since D-Day. One of these, René Bousquet, was appointed by Descour to act as Huet's second-in-command. Tanant, as Huet's Chief of Staff, set up the Villa Bellon HQ on the classic four-bureaux model of a modern French Army headquarters – the 1st Bureau was responsible for the direction of the four 'battalion' commands Huet had established across the plateau, the 2nd Bureau for intelligence, the 3rd Bureau for operational planning and the 4th Bureau for transport and logistics including the reception of parachute drops. In addition a supply, rations and maintenance unit was established in nearby La Chapelle.

The Villa Bellon also housed a guard post at the front gate and a 'command section' which was accommodated in the garage under the main building and consisted of a number of orderlies who were responsible for looking after the personal needs of the officers. Inside Huet's headquarters, all was uniforms and saluting and shiny shoes and polished leather belts and formal military discipline. The Villa was, in short, a little island of unreality in the midst of a guerrilla war – a tiny microcosm of the French Army which would become, many hoped, the seed from which that proud organization would be rebuilt: 'The Headquarters buzzed with activity like a beehive. All the comings and goings of different uniforms, officers from every corner, foreign missions, secretaries, runners carrying messages, scurrying orderlies and regular inmates, all of whom passed through the formal procedures of the guard post under the mocking gaze of the older Maquisards ...'

Satellite headquarters were also established at Saint-Agnan and La Chapelle, as were a number of other linked military departments. According to one estimate, the staff needed to run this administrative empire amounted to between 10 and 15 per cent of Huet's total disposable manpower.

The Villa Bellon staff wasted no time in getting to work. Security on the plateau was a priority and Huet appointed the ex-Professor of

Mathematics from Romans and founder of the Compagnie Abel, André Vincent-Beaume, to oversee it. In his late forties, lanky and manically energetic, Beaume flung himself into his task. A census was swiftly instigated, which involved carefully noting down the names of all those in the military and Maquisard units on the plateau.

There was also an attempt to establish a judicial system. A military tribunal, comprising two lieutenants who were also jurists and a civilian much respected for his fairness and judgement, sat in the elementary school in Saint-Martin on 14 June, where it heard the cases of a number of Miliciens captured at Saint-Nizier. Proper decorum was observed. 'The words "La République Française" and "Tribunal Militaire du Vercors" were displayed on a black cloth, flanked by two red flags.' The cases of two of the accused were held over for judgement after the Liberation. But three others were condemned to death. They were executed in the presence of Descour, Huet and Chavant, who were determined to demonstrate that the new French authorities on the Vercors followed the due processes of a civilized state and not the barbaric practices of the Germans. One of the condemned men asked to see his father before execution and this request was granted. Father and son embraced for the last time. 'Adieu, mon père,' said the young man, as his father was led away in tears, 'I have allowed myself to be deceived and I am paying for it.' The three were then shot in accordance with French official regulations: a glass of rum, a last cigarette and the final absolution of a priest.

Although there were instances of summary execution by individual Maquis groups on the Vercors, these were rare – numbering no more than twenty according to an official post-war inquiry. The Military Tribunal was later replaced by a Commission of Inquiry which, after similar due process (including, on one occasion, importing an advocate from Paris to defend an accused), also passed a limited number of death penalties against Milice and other spies and collaborators.

On 23 June a prison was established in a holiday centre in Auboyneaux just outside La Chapelle (it was later moved to the nearby Loscence valley). With the exception of eight German prisoners and several Miliciens, many of those detained in what soon became known locally as the 'concentration camp' were held purely on suspicion or because someone had a grudge against them – like the unpopular seventy-year-old Marquis de Jarente and a doctor who was intensely disliked in his local community. This caused some disquiet, evoking in many minds the much discredited 'Law of the Suspects' which had been a central part of the 1793 Terror. The reputation of the 'concentration camp' soon became so bad that Huet had to act: 'The concentration camp has become the dumping ground for the region. It has not been effective. This has contributed to the lowering of morale, which is having a damaging effect on the battle in which we are engaged. This state of affairs must cease.'

It was not just the military headquarters that were expanding. Chavant's civil structure now numbered more than fifty and began to resemble a mini-version of a classic French *préfecture*. Departments were established to manage the forests and water sources of the 'free' parts of the plateau, ensure the supply of charcoal to power *gazogène* vehicles, look after public health, coordinate a rudimentary system of public transport and administer the supply of food and other essentials. In an attempt to make a visible break with the Vichy government, there was even discussion about minting special Vercors money and stamps, on which the hated portrait of Marshal Pétain would be replaced by the figure of Marianne, the famous French symbol of liberty.

A hospital was set up in a large building previously used as a holiday centre on the outskirts of Saint-Martin. It was, by all accounts, well staffed and well equipped. One Resistant remembered: 'Two brilliant Parisian surgeons, Fischer and Ullmann, ran [the] very well-appointed country hospital. They practised under the direction of an older surgeon from Romans, Dr Ganimède, who was there with his wife and teenage son. About forty wounded men were being treated there, including ten Germans. They were astounded by the care they were being given. They thought that "terrorists" like us would have massacred them or left them to croak. It was hard for them to free themselves from the propaganda to which they had been subjected. The Germans, on the other hand, tortured and finished off all of our wounded men they captured alive.'

A telephone exchange covering all the 'free' Vercors was set up in La Chapelle and a special newspaper *Vercors Libre* (later *Le Petit Vercors*) was published about three times a week, complete with editorials, news, jokes, cartoons and gossip. A regular mail service to and from the plateau was established, along with four 'official' points of exit and entry, where documents were checked (though many unofficial trips were still made to the plateau by anxious relatives using unregulated mountain paths to pay a visit to a loved one in the camps).

With what Pierre Tanant later reported was something akin to a 'mass uprising' of new recruits arriving daily on the plateau, food soon became a real problem. A system of rationing was ordained which limited the daily consumption of bread (all locally baked) to 500 grams for each soldier and 200 grams for each civilian. Arrangements were made with suppliers outside the plateau for the provision of flour, vegetables and fruit, which were brought up the mountain in daily convoys of lorries, seemingly without interruption from the Germans.

Civil penalties were imposed for infringements of the law. Commercial establishments, such as a café in Tourtres, were closed for failing to obey regulations, and officials were removed where they failed properly to carry out their duties. These latter included the Mayor of Saint-Julien, who was suspected of having supplied food to the Milice, and the Mayor of Vassieux, who was sacked for abandoning his post at a crucial moment.

Where adequate supplies of essential items could not be found on the plateau, they were acquired through raids into the valley. Thirty tonnes of sugar were purloined from a derailed train in mid-June. At Chavant's request, the Groupe Vallier carried out an armed hijack of nine lorries and four cars on the main Grenoble–Valence road, managing to get them up to the plateau just ahead of their German pursuers. Two hundred litres of petrol and 80 litres of oil were stolen from a local water-works in an operation which was carried out by six of Abel Chabal's men, who timed their raid to coincide with *midi*, the sacred French lunch period when no one works. A tanker full of wine destined for German consumption was purloined and driven up to the plateau, to general rejoicing.

Despite the loss – and losses – of Saint-Nizier, there was an air of routine, even gaiety, on the plateau in the latter half of June and the early weeks of July: 'There was a buzz about life in La Chapelle. People led their usual lives, just as they did in the old days. The shopkeepers contin-ued to sell their normal range of goods, even if the prices were – and for good reason – kept lower than usual by the civil authorities. One of the strangest things was to see, mixed among the drab garb of the Maquisards, the brilliant uniforms of the cavalry officers, and little flocks of women, for the most part young and some of them beautiful, dressed up in all their finery. La Chapelle felt like one huge office. All those working in the various services and departments were put up in the local hotels and could always be found at *midi* in the communal dining room in the Hôtel Bellier, where a mixed company of thirty or so [of the plateau's most important functionaries] would meet and talk and eat. At 2 o'clock, just as in normal times, they would all return to their offices scattered throughout the village.'

A new 'normality' was being created. From Huet and Chavant to the lowest Maquisard and the simplest young man struggling up to the plateau, all subscribed to the belief that, despite the overwhelming German power all around them, despite the tragic examples of Glières, the Mont Mouchet and Barcelonnette, this new reality could still survive; the old shame could be erased; a new *gloire* could emerge. Here in the Vercors, a tiny patch of France could, by their will and sacrifice, be created fit enough for de Gaulle to return to – worthy enough to be the true birthplace of the new Fourth Republic.

In this lies the answer to the central conundrum of the Vercors. Why did so many intelligent, decent, dedicated and honourable men suspend rational judgement and subscribe to such military unwisdom? The answer was that they considered it their sacred duty never to give up on the mighty promise they believed they had been given – that they would play a key role in the rebirth of their nation and would not be abandoned.

Unhappily, Algiers did not see it in the same way. On 16 June, the day after the fall of Saint-Nizier, Charles de Gaulle returned to Algiers, where, in his absence, work had been in progress to develop Plan Caïman, the French proposal to establish a redoubt which could be used as a base for action to liberate territory and for the support of the coming southern invasion.

Despite the fact that the rising on the Mont Mouchet in the Massif Central had been swiftly snuffed out, the French authorities in London and Algiers decided for reasons which seem to have more to do with the politics of liberation than with military good sense that 'they were no longer interested in [developing redoubts in] the Alps and would from now on concentrate on the Massif Central'. Henceforth, the main focus of de Gaulle's government-in-exile would be to persuade the Allies to support a plan, not for the reinforcement of the Vercors redoubt which was desperate for help, but for the creation of a new 'redoubt' in the Massif Central, where little remained of structured resistance beyond the smoking ruins of the recent German reprisals.

Some in Algiers did, however, realize that the policy of redoubts could place those on the ground in extreme danger. A French report, dated Algiers 17 June, examined the lessons to be learnt from Barcelonnette, and concluded: 'Given the disproportionate weakness of both armament and the capacity of the units involved, following a policy of fixed defence proved fatal.' The report proposed that a better strategy would have been one of mobile defence, avoiding frontal battle and relying instead on 'rapid movement to attack flanks', followed by dispersal when confronted by superior force. It ended with a recommendation that the lessons of Barcelonnette should be sent to all commanders on the ground.

SOE in London were getting alarmed, too, having heard rumours (presumably from Cammaerts) about a secret Algiers instruction sent to the Vercors which countermanded Eisenhower's instructions to concentrate on clandestine sabotage and to delay 'uprisings'. On 16 June, Brigadier Eric Mockler-Ferryman, the SOE Director for western Europe, wrote to Colonel Dewavrin in de Gaulle's headquarters: 'You asked us at a meeting the other evening to investigate whether any of the messages from Algiers given out among our "action messages" over the BBC could account for the wide-spread outburst of guerilla activity in southern France. I have … found that our … Algiers messages [were] the same as those from here. These were, as you know, confined to specific activities of a sniping character, far smaller in scope than the flare-up which has actually taken place … it seems probable … that pent up enthusiasm burst all bounds … However it does appear that there is also a more sinister explanation … certain orders appear to have been secretly sent from Algiers which may account for some … outbursts … particularly … the undertaking given to the Vercors purporting to be on a plan originating with General Delestraint.'

Across London, in Richmond Terrace opposite Downing Street, David Astor, whose influence and circle of contacts was far more extensive than his formal daytime job on the Public Relations Staff of Combined Operations would suggest, forwarded a report to his chief, the head of Combined Operations, Brigadier Robert 'Lucky' Laycock. This warned in the starkest terms of the impending tragedy in the Alps if something was not done: 'Thousands of men assembled in these areas are very poorly armed. At best they have only light weapons and explosives sent for sabotage and "underground" warfare. They have practically no arms suitable for open warfare such as have been supplied to the guerrillas in Jugoslavia [sic] ... without such arms these men are at the mercy of the Germans should they decide to wipe them out by the use of heavily armed units and reconnaissance aircraft ... Should this occur the Allies will lose the potential valuable assistance of a guerrilla army in the rear of the enemy ... The consequence of a massacre of thousands of men in the Maquis areas due to inadequate provision of suitable arms by the Allies would be very grave and would continue long after the war ... As regards armaments, there are undoubtedly enough machine guns, anti-tank guns of various types and field service rifles at the disposal of Britain and America for arming 100,000 or considerably more French guerrillas ... if the Allies meet this need they will earn ... deep gratitude ... if they fail they will never be forgiven.'

Astor's fears about German plans to deal with the Maquis were well founded. On 18 June, the day after Astor's letter, the codebreakers at Bletchley Park decrypted another Japanese diplomatic telegram, this time reporting on a visit by the Japanese Ambassador to Gestapo head-quarters in Paris: 'According to information obtained by the German police authorities, Eisenhower expected that, immediately after the land-ings, all the German armies would be concentrated in the north and ... he appears to have believed that there would be a general Maquis rising on a large and long-term scale. Actually, however, the German military authorities detailed three divisions for the express purposes of subduing the Maquis ... here, too the enemy has miscalculated.'

There was, however, one man in Algiers who was still working on a practical plan to help the Vercors. On the morning of 18 June, one of Fernand Grenier's subordinates met Jean Constans to discuss Grenier's plan to create a French squadron made up of old unwanted aircraft which would provide rudimentary support to the Resistance. The two men agreed to put the wheels in motion by starting to gather the aircraft together. Three days later, on 22 June, Soustelle rang Grenier: 'I presented your plan to General de Gaulle. He said he was fully in favour of the principle and asked me ... to instruct you to press ahead with this plan to help the Resistance.' The following day, Soustelle confirmed the substance of his telephone call by a written message marked 'Most urgent, personal and secret'.

The day after this, Grenier submitted his proposal to the General. The matter was scheduled for discussion on 27 June at a meeting which included several ministers and the three French service chiefs, with de

Gaulle in the chair. But, the day before, Grenier was astonished to find that his plan was not on the agenda. He dashed off a long note to de Gaulle expressing his surprise. 'I think certain of our senior officers are not at all convinced of the effectiveness of the battles being undertaken by the [Resistance]. Nothing in their military background equips them to understand this aspect of modern warfare.' Grenier went on to propose to de Gaulle that he should, among other measures, urgently send the 1,800 French 'paratourists' kicking their heels in Trapani to reinforce Resistance strongpoints in southern France.

The next day, 29 June, Grenier submitted two papers on his plan to de Gaulle for final signature. Then Grenier waited – and waited – and waited, while the General delayed and delayed and delayed. On 3 July, de Gaulle left for his long-planned visit to Washington, with Grenier's papers still lying unsigned on his desk.

When de Gaulle returned from Washington in mid-July, Grenier tried again. This time the General flatly rejected the plan with the terse note: 'insufficiently detailed'. In truth, Grenier's plan was (and in more ways than one) a pretty ramshackle, not to say desperate, affair. But it was at least designed to help those fighting for their lives on the ground in southern France. In the end, however, his idea was quietly shunted off into the French decision-making structures in Algiers, where it was quietly strangled to death by political wrangling, delay and lack of interest.

But it was not just de Gaulle and his government who were putting political considerations and personal preferences before Allied unity in these weeks. Churchill was also active during this period trying to undermine Anvil in favour of almost any alternative which did not mean landing Allied troops on the Mediterranean coast of France. While his preference remained for an invasion across the Italian passes, he proposed numerous alternative schemes, including, variously, landings near Saint-Nazaire, on the Médoc peninsula near Bordeaux and on the beaches of the Gulf of Gascony.

On 22 June, the British War Cabinet met and reluctantly (but not yet irreversibly) agreed to Anvil, provided it was on a reduced scale. At precisely the same time as French authorities in Algiers were deciding to abandon the Alps and the Rhône Valley in preference for the Massif Central, the British Cabinet envisaged 'An attempt ... to boost activities of the Maquis in the area of the Rhône valley by assistance from the air in supplies and perhaps airborne units'.

On 6 July, Eisenhower attempted to put a stop to the Churchill-driven uncertainty about Anvil by issuing the formal instruction to Maitland Wilson to go ahead with the operation, with a target date of 15 August. Churchill was furious when he heard, telling his Chief of Staff, 'I hope you realise that an intense impression must be made on the Americans that we have been ill-treated. Do not let any smoothings or smirchings cover this fact … The [US Chiefs of Staff are] … one of the stupidest strategic teams ever seen.' Having made his anger plain, Churchill continued to ignore Eisenhower's decision and went on suggesting alternatives to Anvil. On 4 August – just ten days from the target date of the southern landings – he wrote to Eisenhower. 'Instead of landing a considerable force before the guns of the enemy at their strongest point', he proposed an invasion in Brittany that would be 'the decisive blow which would deliver France to a victorious Eisenhower by the shortest route'.

Despite his determined attempts to undermine Anvil, preparations for the operation continued. Troops were assembled, training intensified, and the landing, support, command and supply vessels which would make the crossing to the French coast were gathered and made ready. Allied airbases in Corsica (the main bases used to provide air support to southern France) were closed while runways were lengthened and resurfaced in preparation for the operation ahead.

By 26 July US troops in Cherbourg and British and Canadian troops in Caen were at last beginning to make progress in breaking out from the Normandy beachhead. By the end of the month, all available air power was deployed to assist in the breakout towards Paris.

Amid all this clamour of arms and quarrelling between the Titans, and with a French government more interested in the new possibilities of the Massif Central than in old plans for the Vercors, the increasingly desperate calls for help from the plateau were little more than the plaintive cries of an orphan, trying to be heard among giants who were all determinedly looking in the opposite direction.

25

A DAMNED GOOD SHOW

Despite Huet's orders, offensive action on the plateau continued. On the morning of 17 June 1944, Henri Rosencher, a newly arrived explosives expert, was sent to sabotage the railway tunnel just below the Col de la Croix Haute at the south-east corner of the Vercors massif. After laying the charges, Rosencher and the local Maquisards settled down in expectation. They did not have to wait long before a train full of German soldiers made its way up to the Col. 'The train entered the tunnel. We waited until it had fully disappeared and then added another minute before setting off the charges. Boulders flew and huge chunks of earth cascaded in a thunderous burst; a huge mass completely covered the entrance. Then we heard one – then two more huge explosions [from the other end of the tunnel]. The train had been imprisoned. The 500 "feldgraus" inside weren't about to leave, and the railway would be blocked for a long, long time.'

Due to the short summer hours of darkness, parachute drops from the UK to the plateau began to decline in the second half of June. Now only the single RAF squadron based on Blida airfield outside Algiers could get to the plateau and back during the hours of darkness. To make matters worse, Algiers' containers were very badly packed. On 16 June an angry telegram was sent to Maitland Wilson's headquarters, complaining about the previous night's drop. 'Around two out of every three submachine guns [in the drop] were unusable. The containers opened during their descent or were not attached to their parachutes. As soon as the weather clears, drop to us day and night.'

In fact, though no one on the Vercors could have known it, the possibility of daylight parachute drops had been under discussion for some time. The French in London had already approached the British to see if, because of the short nights, they might be prepared to carry out daylight drops. The British refused, in part because they did not have the air resources to provide daylight fighter cover, but mostly because they believed these would be too risky, not just for pilots, but also for reception parties on the ground.

In mid-June, the French turned to the commander of the US Eighth Air Force, General Kinner, who showed 'a much greater comprehension of our needs and a much more open approach [than the British]' to the idea. Some of this American enthusiasm may have been a reaction to criticism from the French earlier in the year that the British were doing much more than the Americans to help the Resistance. Some may have resulted from the fact that the breakout from Normandy had now released US air assets for other tasks. But much was also undoubtedly due to a new understanding by Eisenhower of the potential of the Resistance. He wrote at the time, 'In the landings on the South of France we should reap the fruits of the action which can be taken by the French Resistance whose results exceeded my hopes [in Brittany] and which is particularly strong in the South.' On 18 June, instructions were issued for Operation Zebra, the first daylight parachute drop to France. This was to be carried out by US Flying Fortresses on four sites including Vassieux on the Vercors.

Meanwhile, on 19 June Descour reported to Algiers on the overall situation in his area: '[Our] troops have fallen back to cover the northwest approaches to the [southern] Vercors plateau. In the centre troops occupy solid position …' But he added ominously, 'Armoured cars and 22 tonne tanks reported at [Valence] including an SS Panzer section.' It was the beginning of the end of the brief respite after the fall of Saint-Nizier.

The following day, German raiding parties supported by armoured vehicles began a series of attacks on the Combovin plateau, which formed a buffer zone around the south-western corner of the Vercors. A post-war history of the Vercors explained: 'From 20 June onwards, the Germans made frequent incursions on to the plateau, supported by tanks and aircraft which bombarded local villages. Their attacks took the form of brief raids which achieved little effect as our men just dispersed in front of them and returned after they had left.' (See map on page 220.)

The Maquis force on the Combovin plateau numbered around 700 and were part of the Drôme Maquis, whose headquarters were in a large farmhouse near the village of Combovin at the western edge of the Combovin plateau. Soon after the attacks started, the Maquis commander ordered a withdrawal south on to the plateau, leaving only a few guards and a team of radio operators in the farmhouse.

Early on the morning of 22 June, Lilette Lesage, one of Descour's couriers who happened to be staying in the farm, was woken suddenly by the sound of heavy explosions near by. She looked out of the window to see a dozen or so German aircraft bombing and strafing the neighbouring villages of Plan-de-Baix and Beaufort. She watched in horror as the planes abruptly turned and flew straight for Combovin village and the farm in which she was staying. Several men were wounded in the bombing which followed, which reduced the main farmhouse and several outbuildings to smoking ruins. Looking down the valley after the planes had left, Lilette saw a German armoured column making its way up the hill. She bundled as many of the wounded into the back of the old ambulance she used as cover for her journeys round the plateau and tried to escape east towards the Vercors. But the spotter planes flying overhead directed the Germans to intercept her. Just before the Germans reached her position, Lilette got all the wounded out and hid them in the scrub alongside the road. But the Germans soon found them and killed them all, leaving Lilette herself for dead with a bullet in her thigh. Altogether the raid cost eleven civilians, three Maquis and one radio operator killed. The surviving wounded, including Lilette Lesage, were taken that evening to the hospital in Saint-Martin. It was the first time the Germans had used aircraft to support their anti-partisan operations.

On 21 June, the second day of the German attacks on the Combovin plateau, there was a plenary meeting of all the heads of Maquis units in the Drôme which was held in the school room at La Chapelle. They concluded that an attack on the Vercors was imminent and called on all Resistance units within a 60-kilometre radius of the Vercors to ask for volunteers to reinforce the plateau. The response was almost nil. Two days later, on 24 June, the Maquis commander who covered the southern access to the plateau from Die asked one of his Maquis leaders to take his men up to the Vercors. The reply was: 'If you order me personally to go, I will go. But I will not ask my men to go. The Vercors is a trap. When the Germans decide to encircle it and attack, they will do so.'

A few Maquis units, though not willing to go up on to the plateau, did commit to helping if the Vercors was attacked. On 28 June the Mens platoon of the Compagnie de Trièves, who had agreed to guard the Vercors' south-eastern passes, made the long ascent on to the plateau by the Pas de la Ville and then marched across country to a large mountain hut called Pré Grandu. Here they joined a line of other Maquis units, queuing up to receive their new arms and equipment before returning to the valley.

In the days following the Combovin attack, German air activity over the Vercors plateau, especially by spotter planes, intensified and several of their patrols were sent into the Gorges de la Bourne to probe Huet's defences.

Descour saw these German moves as the beginning of an attack on the Vercors itself. He sent a message to London and to Constans in Algiers on 22 June: 'The Vercors is about to be attacked from the north-east and the south. We will not be able to hold on unless we are helped immediately. The magnificent opportunities offered by the Vercors for future operations will be lost.'

It seems much more likely, however, that the Germans' real intention had more to do with the protection of both the main roads running down the Rhône and the important airport of Chabeuil, on the outskirts of Valence and close to the western rim of the Vercors. There had been several reports of a build-up of German fighters and light bombers on the airfield, including an eyewitness account from Francis Cammaerts describing gliders with parachutes attached to their tails being assembled on a small airport 'near Montelimar'. Descour, cheered by a signal from Algiers on 22 June promising that paratroops would be sent on the night of 23/24 June, sent a full report on the Combovin action to Maitland Wilson's headquarters the next day, ending with an appeal that would be repeated many times in the weeks ahead: 'Request with extreme urgency Allied bombing of Chabeuil airport. There are currently 60 aircraft on the airfield and dispersed in the little woods near by.'

That night the young of the Vercors gathered around bonfires for the traditional midsummer celebration of St John's Eve. Among them were signal fires, lit to welcome the promised paratroops. But in the event, only weapons were dropped – no paratroops. This time however there was a good reason for the disappointment. The 'parachute unit' promised by Algiers was in fact two English SOE officers, Captains Desmond Longe and John Houseman, who, together with their radio operator André Pecquet, were the advance party of the special mission to the Vercors first recommended by Thackthwaite back in May.

Longe and Houseman were, in many ways, an odd pair to send on such a vital and delicate operation. The 6-foot 4-inch, thirty-year-old Longe, who was the Mission head, was an ex-Barclay's Bank employee, with extensive knowledge and contacts in South America but little experience of France beyond holiday visits. He could, however, speak some rudimentary French. His Mission colleague John Houseman could speak none. Houseman, at twenty-nine, was an ex-land agent from High Wycombe who seemed to have only one quality which fitted him for this mission – he was a close regimental friend of its leader, Desmond Longe. According to his SOE personal file, before being parachuted into France on this operation Houseman had spent the grand total of '2 weeks in France' on holiday, rather less time than he had spent on holidays in Italy, Spain or Switzerland. When asked, on his SOE joining form, which areas of the world he knew best, he answered with disarming honesty, 'The Home Counties'. Judging from the backgrounds and qualifications of the two men, it is difficult not to conclude that they volunteered for this mission because they believed the war would soon be over and they didn't want to miss the fun. Why SOE chose them is more difficult to determine.

Longe and Houseman had been briefed for their mission, codenamed Eucalyptus, in London and then flown to Algiers on 15 June. Here, shortly before midnight on 23 June, they had, together with Pecquet, boarded a Halifax at Blida airfield and taken off for Vassieux.

Along with the three SOE passengers, the Halifax also carried a load consisting of eleven packages and fifteen containers. Among the latter were several canisters packed with some of the heavy weapons for which the Vercors had been begging for weeks – but not, unfortunately, mortars. These were still being withheld because of the unresolved problem of accidentally exploding ammunition. Instead, there were a number of Hotchkiss heavy machine guns with ammunition and also two small motorbikes called Wellbikes which were ideally suited to the rugged terrain of the Vercors. Walkie-talkie, short-range radio sets would have been better. But since these did not appear to be available, Wellbikes were the next best thing. They would give the Vercors commanders a greatly enhanced capacity to communicate with their forward troops quickly, rather than relying on human runners.

Over Majorca, the outside engine on the Halifax's starboard wing caught fire and the plane started to lose height alarmingly. The pilot gave orders to jettison the containers. Longe asked that they should start with the standard containers first. This done, the plane stabilized and they managed to limp back to Blida. But here it became clear that the aircraft would have to do a forced landing and the pilot ordered the remaining containers – the ones with the precious Hotchkiss machine guns and the Wellbikes – to be ditched over the desert before the plane could make a safe landing.

The Eucalyptus Mission could try again. But what about their precious cargo?

Dawn the following morning, 24 June, broke clear but cold on the Vercors. The sun on what promised to be a bright day had as yet only reached the summit of the Vercors peaks when the Maquis sentry post at the top of the cliff face at the Gorges d'Écouges on the north-west corner of the Vercors spotted movement on the road running through a wood far below them. This road, which descends to the plain down one side of the Gorges d'Écouges, is the most dramatic of all the Vercors' dramatic mountain roads. After descending on a long incline from the Col de Romayère the road enters a tunnel, carved through the tortured rock formations that characterize this north-western end of the Vercors plateau. The road emerges from this tunnel seemingly into the void at the top of a sheer cliff hanging over the gorge and the valley below. From here it drops vertiginously to the valley floor by way a dizzying tracery of zig-zags carved – sometimes, it seems, impossibly – out of the vertical rock face.

This was no Saint-Nizier. It was easy to defend. The cliff road is at best only one lorry wide. A single bazooka would have been sufficient to hold it. At the top of the gorge and overlooking the foot of the road below, there is plenty of cover among the rocks and boulders. And crucially, given the German habit of sending their Gebirgsjäger to outflank fixed positions, both flanks of the Écouges gorge are protected by sheer cliffs.

As the light of the coming day flooded into the valley below, the watchers on the cliff could clearly see what they did not expect to see: a long column of some twenty field-grey trucks carrying up to 300 men, accompanied by armoured vehicles approaching the foot of the cliff below them. Through binoculars it was possible to establish that the convoy also included a number of mountain artillery pieces. The forward sentries warned the Maquis section guarding the gorge from a position above the tunnel on the Pont Chabert. They in turn sent swift word to their headquarters a short way back from the forward positions. At this stage, the only weapon the forward positions had to guard the gorge was an ancient French FM 24/29 machine gun from the 1920s, which had little ammunition and a disconcerting habit of jamming when overheated. The Pont Chabert guard had been relieved at 06.00 that morning by a new detachment which included two Russian Maquisards – both seasoned soldiers who had fought on the eastern front before being captured, forced into the German Army and defecting to the Resistance after their arrival in France.

Back at the Maquisards' headquarters, the only reinforcements which could be found were five Maquisards with rifles and an American 0.5 inch Browning machine gun with just four belts of ammunition. These were rushed forward under the command of one of Geyer's young trainee officers. The Browning was quickly mounted and the Maquisards took their positions in the rocks and bushes around the Pont Chabert waiting for the Germans to come into view. As the bull nose of the first truck emerged from the wood at the foot of the cliff, the two machine guns high above them opened fire – carefully and sparingly in order to conserve ammunition on one and avoid overheating on the other. The Maquis riflemen joined in, picking their targets as the Germans jumped down from the lorries to look for cover at the side of the road.

The key strategic point in the battle was a short stretch of open ground which lay on the German side of the Pont de la Cascade, at the foot of the cliff. If the Germans succeeded in crossing this and the bridge they would reach safety in a patch of dead ground which lay out of sight of the Maquis positions above. From here, they would be able to advance up the road with impunity and attempt to force the tunnel when they reached the top. Over the next two hours, the Germans made several attempts to cross the open ground to the Pont de la Cascade, but were always driven back by intense and accurate French fire from above.

Under cover of the opening exchanges of fire, the Germans set up their mountain guns and mortars on a patch of open ground out of range of the defenders. Their opening salvoes were rather haphazard as the German artillery tried to find the French fire positions among the rocks. But finally they found their targets and shells started bursting all round the little group of Maquisards, sending splinters of rocks flying in all directions.

'It was like the worst tempest you can imagine breaking over us, as suddenly all the German weapons opened in unison,' Geyer's young officer wrote later. 'An infernal racket crashed around our heads, seeming to burst out of every fissure in the rock face and submerge us in a veritable torrent of flying metal and rock. Thinking that we were positioned on the crests, the Germans hosed us down with bullets (some even fell as far away as Autrans) ... we did our best to respond, but then our ammunition ran out. Now we had just one last, desperate resort left – blow up the road in front of us ... At a little before 11 a.m., there was a sudden increase in the German fire as they threw everything at us. We thought this was it – their final assault ... In fact it was their last salvo. They started withdrawing under the cover of their mortars and we saluted their retreat with the last rounds of our machine guns.'

The Maquis once again celebrated a victory. But it was, as before, only an armed reconnaissance to determine the strength and dispositions of the French defenders. The Germans withdrew, not because they had been beaten back, but because they had got the information they came for.

This was not the only 'victory' which the Vercors Maquis scored that day. A week or so before the Écouges battle, the Vercors commanders had begun to receive information about a group of fifty-three captured French 'Senegalese' colonial troops in Lyon. An audacious plan was hatched to ambush the lorry which took them every morning to the German officers' mess where, dressed in their original French sky-blue uniforms with red fezzes, they were put to work waiting at table. Two covered lorries carrying a troop of Maquisards were sent to Lyon where they intercepted the African soldiers on their way to work and brought them triumphantly back to the plateau. Here they exchanged waiting in a German officers' mess, for acting as guard of honour at Descour's headquarters at Rang des Pourrets, giving much satisfaction to visiting Army officers with their smart blue uniforms, fezzes and skill at presenting arms and saluting.

For the military leaders of the Vercors, the German assaults at Écouges and on the Combovin plateau were firm evidence that the next German assault would be on the plateau itself. On 24 June, Zeller, still anxious about the aircraft on Chabeuil airfield, signalled Algiers about 120 troop-carrying lorries gathering in Valence. He again asked that the aircraft on Chabeuil should be attacked as soon as possible. However, concerned that action against the lorries in Valence presented too much risk for the townspeople he initially asked for only the airfield to be attacked, a position he revised later in the day in a second signal predicting an 'impending' attack and asking for the lorries to be attacked, even while in Valence, but 'with maximum precision to avoid civilian losses'.

Both of Zeller's requests got as far as being mentioned in the next day's Situation Report at Maitland Wilson's headquarters in Algiers. But they got no further. The airfields in Corsica, from which any attack would have to have been mounted, were closed for resurfacing ahead of Anvil.

That night, Francis Cammaerts sent a second message full of urgency and dark warnings to London: 'I have been in contact with Zeller. It is vital that you send me as soon as possible your plan for the use of strong points [redoubts]. The Resistance cannot function unless they are supplied with the right equipment. The southern Drôme is engulfed in constant fighting. We may have to let them fall back to the Vercors. They need Piats [shoulder-fired anti-tank grenades], heavy machine guns, rifles, Gammon grenades but NO Stens. At the least 20% of supplies and munitions have been damaged during the drops. Need 10 million Francs immediately and if possible a parachute company. The Allied high command has led the French to think that a landing in the south-east will happen in the next 15 days. The effect of these messages is pushing them towards premature action. We will not be able to save them except by supplying them with the weapons and resources they need. In the absence of this the entire Resistance organisation in the south east will be wiped out.'

What he did not know was that his hopes for a huge increase in resources were in the process of being fulfilled. Even as his message was being tapped out from La Britière 120 3-ton lorries were criss-crossing the roads of southern England. By the day's end, they had transported in all 11,664 containers full of arms and equipment from five container-packing stations around London to the operational airfields which had been selected for Operation Zebra. On each airfield squadrons of B17 Flying Fortresses stood waiting for their loads. The operational instructions for the following day's drop called for thirty-seven aircraft to drop at Vassieux, eighty-four at Châteauneuf in the Haute-Vienne, thirty-eight near Nantua in the Ain and another thirty-eight at Charette on the Côte-d'Or in Burgundy.

Two of the Flying Fortresses destined for the Vercors did not make it. One was shot down by German fighters. The other, though damaged by flak, managed to limp back to the coast and make a successful crash landing on the Normandy beaches. The remaining thirty-five arrived over the plateau, under a clear, blue and cloudless sky, at a little before 10.00. By 10.17, a total of 420 containers had been dropped. The Flying Fortresses turned for home.

Strangely, there appears to be no eyewitness account from the ground of this extraordinary event. But it is not difficult to imagine the effect that the sudden appearance of such overwhelming Allied might would have had on the beleaguered fighters on the Vercors. They must have marvelled at the sight of thirty-five huge American bombers appearing over the ridge of the plateau, the flock of circling fighters glinting in the sun above them, the ground trembling with their power as they flew overhead, the majesty of their progression as they swept over in perfect order to deliver largesse packed specially for them by the unseen hands of friends so far away. With such mighty allies, why should the Vercors any longer fear the occasional pair of German Messerschmitts or the haphazard visitation of *mouche* spotter planes? Surely this was evidence, if any were needed, that they were not alone – and would not be abandoned?

With the sound of the Flying Fortresses fading away, the reception team at Vassieux got to work. Four hundred volunteers and all the available carts and lorries in the area had been assembled to collect the containers, which were taken mostly to the school house at Chabottes. Here the weapons were unpacked, degreased and assembled.

It was a gigantic task – in all there were seventy-four Bren guns with ammunition, some 650 rifles, more than 750 Sten guns, 545 9mm pistols, nearly 4,000 hand grenades, 1.5 tonnes of high explosive, complete with detonators, fuses and primers, almost half a million rounds of assorted ammunition, thirty-six bazookas with more than 500 rockets and just short of 3,000 first-aid battle dressings. SOE estimated that the drop to the Vercors alone on this day was enough to arm 1,500 Maquisards. The Vercors was now self-sufficient in arms (though still grievously lacking heavy weapons) and had enough left over to act as a store and distribution point for weapons and equipment for the other Maquis organizations throughout the Isère and Drôme.

As the work progressed through the afternoon, crowds of curious spectators gathered around the edge of the drop site. Some passing Maquisards not involved in gathering in the sudden harvest opportunistically helped themselves to a share of the spoils. 'In the afternoon we thought we would go to the drop site to see what we could pick up,' recalled one of Geyer's men later. 'We organized ourselves as a patrol so as not to look suspicious. Soon we found two containers and emptied them of the rifles inside. Not content with our plunder we searched the area and found another container in which there were some wonderful American pistols, some bandages and some grenades. On our way back to our position we were spotted by some blokes in a car who shouted at us. Our officer went over to talk to them while the rest of us scarpered … They asked him if he had seen anyone stealing rifles. He answered that he had seen no one.'

Chavant, Huet, Zeller, Descour and the other senior leaders of the Organisation Vercors were not on the Vassieux site on this day. They were at the little church in Saint-Martin, attending a Sunday memorial service for the dead of Saint-Nizier. The ceremony was dominated by the military, with little or no recognition for the part played in the battle by the civilian Maquisard companies. Huet looked imposing in full uniform, his belt and boots glinting in the sun. Geyer was resplendent in full uniform and kepi, riding his horse at the head of a guard of his cavaliers, their prominent fleur de lys* standard giving deep offence to the republican sentiments of onlookers and the few Maquisards present.

The high point of the service was when the Abbé Gaston, one of the most enthusiastic of the Vercors priests, with great dignity and solemnity blessed the standards and weapons of the reconstituted French Army units who were present. The Maquisards, ragged, standardless and in their drab fighting clothes, looked uncomfortable, embarrassed, cross and out of place. Jean Prévost was furious and had refused to allow his men to attend. 'If that's what is going on,' he said to his fellow Maquisard commander at Saint-Nizier, Paul Brisac, 'I won't send any of my men to the ceremony and you shouldn't either. The excellent work our Maquisards did at Saint-Nizier has been simply pushed to one side.' But Brisac did attend and noted that, when Huet read out the list of those killed, the names of the dead from his and Prévost's companies were not included.

Among the Bletchley decrypts delivered to 10 Downing Street that night for the British Prime Minister to read in the morning, sitting up in bed

---

* The fleur de lys was the Royalist symbol.

in his silk dressing gown, the wreckage of his breakfast surrounding him and his favourite cat Mauser purring on the bedclothes, was the following extract from the German summary of air activities over France for that day, 25 June: 'About 150 four engined aircraft in four formations with fighter protection from the north-west flew over Aix les Bain, Annecy, Ambérieu, Grenoble, Montélimar, Lyon, St Etienne. Target not ascertained.'

Operation Zebra had caught the Germans completely by surprise. They thought the US aircraft were on bombing raids. By the time the Germans realized that the American bombers had been supplying the Resistance, it was too late to react. They would not be caught like that again. The size of this drop also did much to reinforce the German view that the Allies placed great importance on the Vercors in the context of the coming southern invasion, which was by now occupying much of their thinking.

Late that night, a coded message reached London from France. It was addressed to General Kinner, the commander of the US Eighth Air Force: 'The Maquis thank the U.S. Air Force for a damned good show! When is the next?'

MIXED MESSAGES

The mood of euphoria on the plateau which followed the mass daylight drop by US Flying Fortresses did not last long. Within days the Vercors had lapsed back into its previous normality. Bob Bennes' operators sent more signals asking for yet more arms 'and, for the radio operators, money, tobacco and soap'. Descour reported 'all rail traffic cut on the Grenoble–Chambery and Grenoble–Valence lines. Enemy casualties 48 killed and 51 wounded … All telephone and telecommunications cut.' The French delegate for medical affairs for south-east France arrived to make an assessment of the plateau's needs, sending a long list of medical requirements for up to 3,000 troops to Algiers through La Britière.

But beneath this apparently placid surface real doubt was now gnawing at the confidence of the Vercors leadership. Chabeuil was still there, still menacing. And Algiers still seemed complacent about its threat. On 27 June Francis Cammaerts sent an angry signal – the substance of which was later repeated by Zeller – to Algiers: 'You must immediately bomb Chabeuil. It is absolutely certain that there are 110 planes … with a lot of equipment. The planes are in the woods around the airfield … this is the main threat to the Vercors. This is absolutely essential. Very big stock of bombs not yet placed in the woods. Firmly demand aircraft over target.'

Cammaerts' signal crossed with one from Jean Constans in Algiers: 'Chabeuil aerodrome … is included in the Mediterranean Allied Air Forces programme. Action will be taken from here within several days.' Perhaps Constans intended his message to be reassuring, but the phrase 'within several days' did not seem to Cammaerts to indicate that Algiers understood the urgency he had been pressing for. He was right. British and American leaders in Algiers were at this moment thinking of only one thing – and it wasn't the Vercors, it was preparing for Anvil.

There were a few in Algiers pushing for help for the Vercors, but their voices did not carry much weight. The Minister for Air, Fernand Grenier, found himself suddenly excluded from the circulation list of those who saw incoming messages from the Vercors and he only got to know of the true situation on the plateau on 28 June. Meanwhile Jean Constans' ambivalent position within Maitland Wilson's headquarters meant that his pleas had little or no impact on those who actually disposed of resources. The same was true of Constans' senior colleague, Air Force General Gabriel Cochet, who had been appointed by de Gaulle to ensure that Resistance action was coordinated with Anvil planning. His position was described in cruelly dismissive terms in a post-war report: 'Actually General Cochet exercised no control over French Resistance since all orders to France went out over Allied controlled radio links and all policy matters were planned and approved by [Maitland Wilson's] Allied Forces Headquarters.'

At the lower level, however, the message was that the Vercors was still a central part of Allied planning in Algiers. On the evening of 28 June, Constans dispatched a signal to the plateau saying that due to 'the primordial importance of the Vercors' it had been decided to send the thirty-one-year-old airfield expert Jean Tournissa to create a landing strip on the flat meadow at the Vassieux parachute site.

That same evening, two Halifax bombers took off from Blida airfield outside Algiers. They carried between them thirty-seven containers, thirteen packages and nineteen agents – the largest parachute drop of personnel which the Vercors had so far seen. But what really caused excitement on the plateau that night was the fact that among the nineteen parachutists who landed were fifteen American commandos. Commanded by Lieutenant Vernon Hoppers, the new arrivals were members of an OSS mission codenamed Justine. De Gaulle's government may not have been able to provide the French paras which Algiers had promised – but the Americans had sent some of their own. Surely that must confirm that Eisenhower had indeed great things planned for the Vercors?

Also parachuted in that night were the delayed Desmond Longe, John Houseman and André Pecquet of the Eucalyptus Mission – together with a second wireless operator for the Eucalyptus team. After giving the password for the night, 'Voici le cheval de Troie,'* the Eucalyptus four

_____

* 'Here is the Trojan horse.'

were taken to a nearby farmhouse where, as Desmond Longe recorded in his diary, they found 'all the world ... gathered. The Americans ... like us were a little overwhelmed at being hugged and kissed by men and women alike. We were given bread, wine and hot milk and the Allies were toasted time and time again ... Finally ... we are ushered into two cars ... and moved off amid tremendous excitement ... toward Vassieux. But [our] driver ... forgot to maintain control of the car and drove us straight into a ditch turning us over. I really thought we had had about enough for one night. We climbed through the broken windows and ... walked into the village.'

That night Longe, as the Eucalyptus commander, was accommodated in the Mayor's house in Vassieux. The others were found a bed in one of the other houses in the village. But they did not get much sleep, for in the early hours of the morning Cammaerts and another newly arrived SOE officer, Neil Marten, burst unannounced into their bedroom. Cammaerts, incensed because he had had no prior warning of the arrival of Eucalyptus or of its mission, woke the three men and demanded, in no uncertain terms, to know what was going on. It was the start of a tense relationship between Cammaerts and the new arrivals, whom Cammaerts clearly considered little more than unprofessional voyeurs in someone else's war, insisting that he was the senior officer in charge and that they should report to him.

When the containers from the previous night's drop were unpacked, it was discovered that Pecquet's wireless and personal kit had been lost. And – more seriously – the promised replacement machine guns and Wellbikes for those abandoned to the desert when Eucalyptus' first Halifax had caught fire had not been included. Instead Algiers had sent yet more Stens.

A briefing session was held for the new British and American arrivals at the Villa Bellon in Saint-Martin the following day. This was attended by Huet, Zeller, Cammaerts, Marten, Hoppers and the Justine and Eucalyptus teams. Huet, chain-smoking as always, his cigarette held delicately between his long fingers, stood before a large map of the plateau pointing out his positions and the main enemy forces surrounding them, as he explained his defensive strategy.

Afterwards there was a welcoming lunch accompanied by elaborate toasting and mutual expressions of the indissoluble amity between the Allies. This did not, however, stop more squabbling breaking out among the British contingent, to the considerable embarrassment of the others present. Later there was a kind of truce when it was agreed that the Eucalyptus team would assist Huet, while Cammaerts would be assigned to Zeller – but not until Cammaerts had signalled London protesting that he had not been warned about the new arrivals and asking for it to be confirmed that, as 'Chief Allied Liaison Officer' to Zeller, he was the senior British officer on the ground.

At one stage in the Villa Bellon briefing, Longe asked Huet whether, if he got all the weapons he had asked for, he could hold on against a German attack. After a long pause Huet replied: 'Provided we got the equipment, we could fight off a division – say ten to fifteen thousand men. If they come at us with more, well …' Huet's answer trailed off at this point into a pause, ending with 'Then I think it will be dubious.'

Vernon Hoppers commented after the briefing that he found Huet 'aggressive and intelligent' and was amazed to find that the plateau was 'no longer a Maquis headquarters, but the headquarters of a republic with an organized army of 5,000 men'.

One of Huet's first actions after the Villa Bellon lunch was to assign two local Resistants to help Eucalyptus with liaison and interpreting and a local girl, Léa Blain, to assist André Pecquet with coding and decoding messages.

The instructions given to Longe as head of Eucalyptus when he was still in London were to do his best to slow down and, if possible, reverse everything the Vercors leadership had been encouraged by Algiers to achieve in the month since D-Day. He was to inform the plateau's leaders that: 'The Vercors is not given a high priority at the present time … it is your duty to advise the local leaders to undertake small operations aimed principally at interfering with enemy communications … [and] avoid open fighting with the enemy.' The Vercors commanders should not 'accept more men than it will be possible to arm adequately'. As for the plateau's constant appeals for heavy weapons, the Vercors leaders should understand that 'True guerrilla tactics do not require the employment of heavy weapons.'

It is difficult to read Eucalyptus' instructions, in which the echoes of General Koenig's earlier orders to disperse can clearly be heard, and not marvel at how out of touch London were with what was happening on the plateau – and how out of tune they were with what the French in Algiers had been saying, not least the message from Constans only the previous day, which had referred to the plateau's 'primordial importance'. The next day – 30 June – Longe, Houseman and Huet began a three-day tour of the defences of the Vercors. Longe is silent on whether he ever tried to persuade Huet along the lines London had instructed; but if he did, it had – unsurprisingly – precisely no effect.

Hoppers' men spent what remained of the night of their drop billeted in Vassieux. The following morning they were taken to the hamlet of Les Berthonnets where they set up their base and spent the rest of the day unpacking and cleaning their weapons. The next day, Hoppers divided his force into seven pairs who were each sent out with interpreters to train Maquis units around the plateau in the use of American and British weapons.

Hoppers' mission, as Justine's commander, was more straightforward and realistic than that given to Longe and Eucalyptus: 'To strengthen the Maquis in the Vercors region and to conduct guerrilla warfare against enemy lines of communications and telecommunications'. The Germans would have been much reassured if they had known the limited tasks set for Justine. When they heard of the little force's arrival though their spy network, they concluded that Hoppers' fifteen Americans were in fact a whole battalion of Canadian paratroops.

Some time during the last days of June, a middle-aged man of rather anodyne appearance, with heavy glasses, an unruly mop of white hair and a luxuriant moustache to match, arrived at Descour's headquarters at Rang des Pourrets, to the accompaniment of much stamping of feet and presenting of arms from the blue-coated, fez-hatted Senegalese guard of honour. Yves Farge, forty-five years old but now looking a good ten years older because of the pressures of clandestine life, had come a long way since, as the foreign editor of the *Progrès de Lyon* newspaper, he had lunched with Paul Dalloz in a Lyon restaurant in the first months of 1943. In April 1944, Farge had been appointed by de Gaulle as one of seventeen civilian Commissioners of the Republic covering the whole of France. Farge's role was to set up what was, in effect, a provisional republican government in the Lyon region, charged with taking 'all necessary measures to ensure the security of the French and Allied armies, to provide for the administration of the territory, to establish republican legality and to satisfy the population's needs'. Insignificant though he appeared at first sight, Farge was energetic, dedicated and a highly capable and subtle politician. As the personal representative of de Gaulle, he was also the supreme civil authority in the area, empowered to pass decrees, issue death sentences and install civil and governmental institutions.

Farge's first act was to convene a meeting of the Committee for the Liberation of the Vercors, the over-arching body which dealt with all civilian and military matters on the plateau. He later wrote that the main purpose of the meeting, which was held in a classroom of the Saint-Martin secondary school, was to 'find the best way to overcome the tensions between the civil and military structures' of the Vercors.

It was the beginning of an entirely new phase which would see the plateau turned from hopeful fortress against attack into France's first fully fledged, formally constructed and officially recognised 'République', charged with nurturing the shoots of freedom from which the new Fourth Republic of France would grow. That, at least, was the dream.

THE REPUBLIC

Winston Churchill's attempts to halt or divert Operation Anvil finally ended on 2 July 1944 when the combined American and British Chiefs of Staff told the US General designated to command the operation, Alexander Patch, that Anvil was confirmed. The landings would take place on the Mediterranean coast of France, as planned, on 15 August. With just six weeks left now before the 'southern D-Day', Algiers became a hive of activity as all arms and headquarters stumbled over themselves to make the final, frantic preparations for the landings.

This was the moment for which de Gaulle had been preparing. If the Caïman Plan for a French-led landing in the Massif Central was to happen, it could do so only as part of Anvil. It had already been agreed that the General should visit Washington and meet Roosevelt in the first ten days of July. Prior to his departure, de Gaulle sent one copy of the full Caïman plan to Maitland Wilson and another to the President's Chief of Staff, General George Marshall. In a covering letter, General Koenig told Marshall (erroneously) that Eisenhower had already approved the plan and asked Marshall to do so too, so that 'de Gaulle could be informed of this during his US visit'.

The final, detailed Caïman Plan was astonishingly ambitious – and astonishingly expensive in resources. It proposed an air invasion of the Massif Central, 200 kilometres west of the main Anvil area of operations, involving some 9,000 men (in contrast to the 400 men which the Vercors had requested) and requiring an airlift, which, among other assets, called for eighty-four gliders and 852 sorties by American Dakota C47 aircraft – than the entire available Allied air transport resources in Algiers.

The troops for the Caïman force (to be known as Force C) were to consist of one British, one French and one American airborne brigade, under the overall command of de Gaulle's close ally Colonel Pierre Billotte, with Jacques Soustelle acting as Billotte's political adviser.

Among the French forces earmarked for Force C were the Trapani 'para-tourists' – who had by now moved to Staoueli airfield north of Algiers. The remainder of the French airborne brigade was to be made up of two battalions of paratroops from Britain, a regiment of mountain artillery and a squadron of light tanks.

Despite the massive commitment of troops and air resources required by the French plan at precisely the time that Maitland Wilson was trying to scrape together enough of both to carry out Anvil, George Marshall in Washington welcomed the proposal in a letter to Eisenhower on 8 July, two days after de Gaulle's arrival in the US.

Eisenhower replied to Marshall on 10 July. Although careful to leave the final decision to Maitland Wilson as the theatre commander, it is not difficult to detect Eisenhower's own views on Caïman from his letter: 'Plan Caïman … bears little relation to operational requirements and practicabilities … The … support of resistance forces should always be in proportion to the ability of the resistance to assist planned operations … I do NOT feel … that it is practicable for us to furnish air-lift and supplies … It is for General Wilson to comment on whether Caïman … as it now stands is either practicable or of assistance to Anvil … however any plan worthy of our support must have as its principal objective the assisting of military operations and NOT merely the liberation of terri-tory to come under French command.'

On 11 July, Marshall received a cable from Maitland Wilson referring to discussions he had had with General Eaker, the Commander-in-Chief of the Mediterranean Allied Air Forces: 'We have examined [Caïman] thoroughly and are opposed to it … To attempt to lift forces [in this way] … would be hazardous and unacceptable … much better to hold French airborne forces as can be made available outside Anvil … to be dropped where and when the situation … may dictate.'

That should have been the end of the matter. But, probably in an attempt to soften the blow to de Gaulle, who was in the US at the time, it was agreed with the French that there would be further discussion on the issue in Algiers on 20 July. Until this date, both Plan Caïman and the French units earmarked to take part in it were placed in a state of limbo. And so, over the next crucial weeks when the Vercors was crying out for help as German forces gathered, the 'paratourists' in Staoueli were forced to spend more time kicking their heels while waiting for the final but inevitable decision on Caïman to be taken in Algiers in the third week of July.

At 16.00 on the day before General Alexander Patch received the final go-ahead for Anvil, Gabriel Cochet made yet another attempt, his third, to persuade the Allies to bomb Chabeuil with urgency.

That same day (1 July), Cammaerts asked SOE for a Lysander to fly Neil Marten back to Algiers, following up the next day with a request that he should return with Marten in order personally to clarify Algiers' intentions for the Vercors and other Resistance units in the south in the context of Anvil: 'The necessity for seeing that the south-eastern resistance plan was in line with actualities is very great.' London replied on 4 July telling Cammaerts to stay put, but instructing him to give a detailed brief of his concerns to Marten.

By now, however, the Vercors commanders had decided not to rely solely on an air attack to put Chabeuil airfield out of business, but to look at the possibility of mounting a ground attack themselves. During the morning of 1 July, leaving the bulk of his men to continue with their training duties, Vernon Hoppers and one of his corporals, Delmar Calvert, were driven to Louis Bourdeaux's headquarters on the western edge of the plateau. The pair arrived at Bourdeaux's base at Gaudissart, near Saint-Jean-en-Royans, in the late afternoon and were entertained to a lavish dinner that night. Hoppers' orders were to carry out a reconnaissance of Chabeuil in order to assess the possibility of a ground attack on the airfield. But it appears that, some time during that day, his original itinerary changed, possibly because he received intelligence that a German convoy was moving up to the Combovin plateau on the following afternoon.

The next day, Hoppers, Calvert and eight Maquisards led by one of Bourdeaux's officers set an ambush on the main road from Valence to Léoncel about 3 kilometres west of the village of La Vacherie. They did not have long to wait. At 16.00, a German convoy consisting of troop-carrying lorries protected by armoured cars came grinding up the hill. Hoppers' ambush was set up where the road, climbing from the steep-sided valley below, is forced to avoid a buttress of rock by turning through a sharp left-hand bend with a bank some 20 metres high on one side and open ground on the other. The ambush was sprung by a bazooka fired at the lead armoured car as the German convoy passed below Hoppers' men, hidden in the scrub on the bank above the road. The rest of the damage was done by Gammon grenades dropped on to the soft canopies of the lorries and into the open hatches of the armoured cars.

Those trying to escape the carnage were cut down by Sten and machine-gun fire. Two German armoured cars were destroyed and eighteen of their soldiers killed. 'We wanted to save the flag on the leading car as a battle token,' Hoppers wrote in his report afterwards, 'but the largest piece we could find was only two inches square.'

On the opposite side of the Vercors the Germans started the process of 'cleaning up' Resistance strongpoints and clearing main roads around the edge of the massif with an operation to seize the strategic Col de la Croix Haute, close to the little village of the same name at the south-eastern corner of the plateau. At the same time, a column of German bicycle troops carried out a sweep of the nearby Trièves and Mens areas.

After his success in the La Vacherie ambush, Hoppers spent the whole of the following day (3 July) watching Chabeuil airport from a ridge south-west of the village of Combovin, 'observing through field glasses and discussing a plan to attack the field. There were about sixty planes on the field at the time.' Late that afternoon, his task completed, Hoppers headed back to his base.

At Saint-Martin that morning an important ceremony, presided over by Yves Farge in his role as Commissioner of the Republic, had been held in the town. Farge, flanked by members of the Committee for National Liberation, stood in the shade of the magnificent old lime tree which dominates the Saint-Martin square. Before him lay a French tricolour emblazoned with the Croix de Lorraine with the letter V at its base (symbolizing the Vercors), ready to be raised. Facing the official party on the other side of the square, Narcisse Geyer, complete with kepi, white gloves and sword, sat erect on his horse. And behind Geyer, in a space so cramped that the front rank had to endure being swished by the tail of his horse, stood three rather ragged ranks of uniformed soldiers, each with a rifle.

Curious onlookers lined the walls of the square and hung out of upstairs windows, while a little posse of girls in their Sunday-best dresses stood in the full glare of the midday sun alongside the last of the three ranks of soldiers. The tricolour was raised, the 'Marseillaise' played, Geyer, with due flourish, saluted with his sword and the soldiers presented arms. Then Commissioner of the Republic Yves Farge stepped forward into the sunlight to read the proclamation declaring the formal founding of the 'Free Republic of the Vercors'.

REPUBLIQUE FRANÇAISE
LIBERTE EGALITE FRATERNITE

To the population of the Vercors
As from 3 July 1944, the French Republic is officially restored on the Vercors.

On this date decrees passed by Vichy are abolished, all its laws cease to have effect and the laws of the Republic shall again be in force from this day onwards. The Committee for National Liberation on the Vercors has been formally invested with its functions and with wide powers by the Commissioner for the Republic.

Charged with the implementation of these decisions, the Committee seeks to carry out its administrative functions in a manner consistent with the principles of justice, but also of firmness, relying on the dedicated assistance and the common sense of the people of the Vercors who, during the entire period of clandestine resistance, have shown levels of courage and loyalty to France which are beyond all praise.

Our region is under siege. The Committee for National Liberation therefore asks the population to be prepared to do all that is possible and more, as we ourselves shall do, to place every available means at the disposal of the military command who have the daunting task of protecting us against a barbaric enemy.

People of the Vercors, it is our privilege to be the site of our great Republic's rebirth. You should be proud of this fact. We are certain that you will do all in your power to defend it. We intend that the 14th of July will be for the Vercors a moment when we shall be able to celebrate, more than ever before, our faith in the Republic and our loyalty to our great country.

Long live the French Republic!
Long live France!
Long live General de Gaulle!

For the Committee for National Liberation
The President: Clément

After the ceremony, specially printed notices carrying the formal declaration signed by Chavant were posted on noticeboards, trees and other public sites around the plateau (see first plate section).

In London that day, a report by the British Joint Intelligence Committee contained a summary of the latest situation in France, which included a paragraph reporting that the Germans in southern France 'fear a landing is imminent. Force of circumstances has led them to place tired Divisions in the area.' In fact, at the time Pflaum's 'tired' division was in the process of launching a full-scale and energetic offensive using 3,500 troops against the Maquis in the Bauges mountains 25 kilometres north-east of the Vercors.

The early-morning Situation Report to Maitland Wilson's headquarters in Algiers on 4 July included yet another request from the Vercors for the bombing of Chabeuil airfield, stressing that 'The position is so urgent that they are themselves planning a ground attack on the airfield.' Later in the day, however, Constans in Algiers sent Zeller a telegram which not only flatly contradicted the information from Hoppers' reconnaissance of the previous day, but also hinted that the Vercors may have exaggerated the Chabeuil threat: 'Allied aerial photographs of the area [of Chabeuil] can only find indications of 10 aircraft. We have now received [from you] three different map co-ordinates of this target. Please confirm the true co-ordinates as soon as possible.'

That night, probably in response to Yves Farge's request to patch up strained relations between the military and the civil organizations on the plateau, Narcisse Geyer invited Eugène Chavant to a full-scale regimental dinner at the cavalryman's headquarters at La Rivière, south of Saint-Martin. No description survives of what must have been, given Geyer's love of military ceremony and Chavant's Socialist dislike of it, a pretty tense affair.

It seems that about this time – towards the end of the first week of July – the thought began to take root in the minds of the Vercors leaders that, despite all the promises and the parachute drops, the fate of the plateau was not a first – or even high – priority in either Algiers or London. The maximum time the plateau was supposed to hold out for was three weeks. But it was now almost a month since the Vercors had mobilized. Meanwhile there was every sign that the Germans were preparing to move on to the offensive and no sign whatever of the promised Allied southern landing. There was no sign either that Algiers was prepared to take action against the greatest immediate threat to the plateau – air attack from Chabeuil airfield.

On 5 July, both Huet and Cammaerts produced what were almost certainly coordinated reports for their superiors on the state of the Vercors. Cammaerts gave his report to Marten, who left that day at the start of the journey to the Lysander that would fly him to Algiers. Huet's report was carried to London by courier and incorporated into a later paper on resistance in the south-east of France.

Huet, cool and analytical, concludes his report with an appeal for clarity about the Vercors' role in the context of the southern invasion and for the resources to carry out his mission – especially money, uniforms, outdoor clothing, heavy weapons, small special force teams (underlined) and rapid Allied air support when required. He ends: 'It is only by these means that we can counteract the very high level of disillusionment which has been caused by the premature launching of open resistance (I do not know who is responsible for this) which places thousands of ordinary people in a situation which is critical.'

Where Huet was cool, Cammaerts was angry and characteristically blunt. He started with a broadside of excoriating criticism for the confusion of messages which had caused the disaster of Barcelonnette, holding 'Someone in the High Command responsible for reprisals against the civilian population … and for the reduction of 70% of [our] efficacy'. Then he turns to the Vercors: 'You must treat us as a serious military force. E.G. bombing of Chabeuil. Answers are so slow that the tendency is growing to exaggerate in order to get half what we ask. If the High Command do not agree to these plans they will have on their consciences the unnecessary deaths of Allied troops and French civilians … do not let the French down again. My report coupled with my name and accompanied by a list of all the unnecessary casualties should be published in red and hung in every office so that the responsible person should know the result of his actions.'

That same day, Henri Zeller, probably at the prompting of Cammaerts, added his concern about the lack of clarity of the Vercors mission by sending a signal to Algiers: 'it is very desirable for me to make a quick visit to either Algiers or London to clarify my instructions and orders'. Algiers refused the request. But Constans did send what appeared to be a helpful signal to Descour (at this time in Lyon) promising to send three

American 75mm mountain guns and ammunition. The guns never arrived.

Other new arrivals did, however, make it through to the Vercors during these days. In the early hours of 7 July (the night of the full moon), Algiers dropped three men and a woman on to the Taille-Crayon drop site outside Vassieux: Jean Tournissa, the promised expert who had orders from Jacques Soustelle to create a landing strip at Taille-Crayon; Francis Billon, an ex-French Army officer who had volunteered to be dropped into the Vercors to train Maquisards; and Yves Morineaux, one of Tournissa's team. The fourth agent parachuted in that night was arguably the most successful and certainly one of the most extraordinary of all SOE women agents of the Second World War. The name by which she was known to her SOE colleagues was Christine Granville. But her true name was Krystyna, the Countess Skarbek.

Born in Poland, Krystyna Skarbek was probably a British MI6 agent before the war. After her country had been occupied, she made clandestine trips over the snow-covered Tatra mountains when others died in the attempt and later delivered the microfilm to MI6 which gave London the first evidence of German troops massing on the Polish border before Operation Barbarossa, Hitler's invasion of Russia. She finally escaped to Cairo with the Gestapo hot on her heels in May 1941.

Beguilingly beautiful, extraordinarily courageous and enthusiastically promiscuous (Vera Atkins, the terrifying 'Mother Superior' of the SOE, once commented that nothing in trousers was safe in her presence), she was, some claim, one of Ian Fleming's lovers after the war and the inspiration for Vesper Lynd in his first book, *Casino Royale*.

After spending some time kicking her heels in Cairo, the twenty-nine-year-old Christine Granville was recruited by SOE, who originally intended to parachute her into Hungary. When this operation was cancelled, she was asked if, in view of her near-flawless French, she would be prepared to be parachuted into France. Of course Christine, the inveterate adventurer, immediately agreed and was sent to the SOE North African training school at the Club des Pins, in the sand dunes north of Algiers. Although she proved adept at the skills required to be a good courier, she had no aptitude as a wireless operator and was regarded as too headstrong for an extended mission in France. For this reason 'It was decided that her courage was best restrained until nearer the time of liberation.'

Furious and frustrated at being idle, she took matters into her own hands. At the end of a dinner specially arranged to introduce her to the new regional head of SOE, General Stawell, she persuaded the General to accompany her into the nearby sand dunes. When the General returned he was 'visibly knocking at the knees and said she had better go to France'.

In a subsequent assessment of her suitability carried out by Francis Brooks Richards, it was recorded that Christine Granville had 'made it quite clear that she was quite prepared for cover purposes to become fictitiously married to somebody'. Brooks Richards immediately thought of Francis Cammaerts, who was in desperate need of a courier after his previous one had been arrested by the Gestapo. And so it was that Christine Granville, dressed, under her voluminous SOE jumpsuit, in a smart but simple shirt, skirt and jacket cut to a French pattern by a tailor in London, parachuted out of a moonlit sky into the Vercors. Along with a revolver and false identity documents in the name of Jacqueline Armand, she also carried 5 million francs for Cammaerts.

Although Christine Granville's real-life exploits were, even unembellished, the stuff of legend, she was not averse to embroidering for greater effect. And so it was on this night. She later described being blown off course by a strong wind and landing several kilometres from the landing site, hitting the ground so hard that she damaged her coccyx and broke the revolver in her back pocket. According to this version, she quickly buried her parachute and jumpsuit, and, when found the following morning by a search party, looked like any other young woman out for a country stroll – though, she claimed, they were surprised at her ability to swear in French. In fact, according to Robert Bennes who was in charge of the reception party that night, she landed, with the others on the Vassieux site, without mishap. One element of Christine Granville's story was accurate, however. There was indeed a high wind that night which resulted in Jean Tournissa landing on a roof in Vassieux town, from where he was extricated with some difficulty. More seriously, it also caused Francis Billon to break his arm and fracture his skull. He was sent straight to Dr Ganimède's hospital at Saint-Martin.

When, the following day, Descour sent a signal to Algiers reporting the safe delivery of the new arrivals, he added a cryptic postscript to his message: 'No more Stens.'

Jean Tournissa wasted no time getting to work on his airstrip. During the morning of 7 July, he inspected the area of the Taille-Crayon site and chose a long flat meadow on the south side. It was perfect in terms of approach and exit flight paths. But an electric supply line which crossed the site had to be dismantled and there was good deal of work to be done flattening out and removing stones and boulders from the grass runway. That afternoon a workforce made up of volunteer labourers from neighbouring villages, prisoners, Polish students from Villard-de-Lans and Vincent-Beaume's 'discipline section' started work on the strip, which was now protected by three heavy machine guns and a detachment under the command of Captain Pierre Haezebrouck.

The arrival of Jean Tournissa gave another huge boost to morale on the plateau, especially among the Vercors' leaders. Surely now, whatever their previous doubts, they could feel reassured? Surely the arrival of this man, with this task set by the very highest in Algiers, must mean that the Allies were indeed coming; that they did indeed see a major role for the plateau; that Montagnards was still alive; that they were not going to be abandoned?

On 8 July, the pace of events on and around the plateau started to quicken. During the day, Jean Tournissa reported to Algiers that he would need six days to create a landing strip 1,050 metres long and 140 metres wide. Algiers responded almost immediately: 'Reiterate the site must be suitable for a Dakota. We do not have Hudsons available. Moreover only the Dakota will be able to deliver the matériel envisaged for this operation.'

Algiers' signal was a blow to those hoping for the earliest possible landing of supplies and heavy weapons – and perhaps even troops – on the Vassieux site. The Dakota needed a longer landing strip than the Hudson, which meant more work and more time to prepare the strip. With the extra work now required to make the Taille-Crayon strip ready for Dakotas, steps were taken on 8 July to enlist the assistance of a tractor and large roller owned by Victor Boiron from Vassieux and to expand the workforce on the site to around 400. Fortunately, a settled period of good weather dominated the south of France over these first weeks of July 1944, giving long hours of daylight and clear blue skies to work under. But this was a mixed blessing. For it also meant good conditions for the *mouches*, the German Fieseler Storch observation planes which were now in near-constant, inquisitive attendance above the

Vassieux site, circling, inspecting and photographing every detail of the activity below.

In the early afternoon of 8 July, the Germans blew up the road up to the Vercors from Saint-Nazaire-en-Royans. They were beginning to shut off minor access roads to the plateau.

Also that day, Generalleutnant Heinrich Niehoff, the German military commander for the south of France, issued a report on the situation in his area: 'The concentration of powerful enemy forces in the Vercors area, their growing amount of equipment including heavy weapons, the fact that they have probably been reinforced by Canadian parachutists and are preparing for more reinforcements by airborne forces lead us to believe that, in the event of a southern landing, the enemy will attempt a strong thrust into our area with the aim of occupying Valence, the Rhône valley and perhaps even the city of Grenoble … the 157th Division will therefore immediately take all steps under the codename Operation Bettina to assemble all operational units under its authority in the Grenoble area.'

At the time, three of the Gebirgsjäger units of Pflaum's division were engaged as part of a 5,000-strong assault on Henri Romans-Petit's bases in the Jura mountains. The operation had begun only the day before (7 July) and was not planned to end until 19 July. Pflaum would therefore have to wait before launching the Vercors operation ordered by Niehoff. But the planning and mobilization of forces for Bettina began immediately. On the same day that Niehoff gave the orders for Operation Bettina, the Luftwaffe's anti-partisan squadron also received new orders: 'do something quickly about the enemy airfield at Vassieux-en-Vercors, 16 km north of Die'.

With the German forces gathering on the plateau and around its rim, the Vercors was now being slowly drawn towards an ineluctable destiny.

28

ACTION AND EXPECTATION

On 7 July, Huet called Lieutenant Vernon Hoppers into his headquarters at the Villa Bellon to brief him on intelligence he had just received: a large German troop column would move north on the main road from Aspres-sur-Buëch, 15 kilometres south of the Vercors, to the Grenoble area in a couple of days. The two men spent the day planning an ambush by a combined force made up of Hoppers' men and a detachment of Maquisards. The spot they chose was a horseshoe bend, flanked on one side by a high bank, just below the Col de la Croix Haute at the south-eastern corner of the plateau. That same day, Hoppers called his men in from their instruction duties across the plateau and told them to prepare for action the following afternoon.

At 15.00 the next day, a combined force made up of fourteen Americans under the command of Hoppers and seventeen Maquisards under the command of Maurice Bourgeois climbed on to lorries and set off for the Col de Menée, some 8 kilometres north-west of Hoppers' chosen ambush position. Here they were dropped off to complete the journey on foot. It cannot have been an easy night's march as Hoppers' route took him across rough terrain and over several high exposed ridges.

Hoppers and Bourgeois arrived at their destination, an abandoned railway station at the highest point of the Col de la Croix Haute, in the small hours of the morning. Here they met guides from the local Maquis who were to lead the two officers down to the ambush point about 800 metres away on the north side of the Col. Hoppers told his men to grab what sleep they could in a deserted railway shed and went forward with Bourgeois to reconnoitre the ambush position.

Even in the darkness, Hoppers could see that the spot he and Huet had chosen was near perfect for a road ambush. Small rocky cliffs backed by thick forest for easy getaway dominate the entry and exit of the

300-metre-long horseshoe bend on its closed western side. On the other side of the road the slope drops sharply away to a ravine leading down to a stream. Hoppers' plan was to place a bazooka and a machine gun on each of the rocky points dominating the two horns of the horseshoe. The trap would not be sprung until the leading lorry of the convoy had reached the far (northern) end of the ambush position when it would be stopped by bazooka and machine-gun fire. The bazooka at the far end would then destroy the rear vehicle of the convoy trapping all the others in the killing ground.

At 07.00 the following morning, only a few minutes after Hoppers' men had taken up their positions, a lorry drove round the corner into the ambush killing ground. It turned out to be a friendly Maquisard who told Hoppers and Bourgeois that the German convoy, consisting of six trucks carrying about 120 men, was an hour or so away and heading in their direction.

What happened next is best described in Hoppers' own words: 'An hour and twenty minutes later our look-out spotted the convoy. When the first truck had passed the ambush spot to a point even with the bazooka at the far end, Sgt. Richman ... stopped the truck with his first shot. He thought this truck would block the road but the second truck speeded up and started around the first. The machine gun located to the left and rear of the bazooka for just such an emergency opened up and stopped the second truck. The third truck was hit by the bazooka at the far end of the trap and the machine gun supporting him went to work on the fourth vehicle which was a bus. In the meantime when the first bazooka round was fired every man started to work with grenades and rifles to liquidate the men in the rear of the trucks. We used Gammon grenades, filled with one pound of plastic and one pound of scrap iron. These grenades did a thorough job on the men closely packed into the rear of the trucks. On the second shot with his bazooka Sgt. Harp, who was firing at the cab of the third truck, caught the driver in the chest as he tried to get out of the door. The upper part of his body disappeared and his legs fell forward upon the road. The men in the two trucks which were not caught in the ambush, unloaded and set up a mortar and a light machine gun. Three German teams were shot off that one gun before they moved to a new position. On a given signal we moved out from the ambush spot and started off for the assembly point which was about ten miles across country ... we arrived at the rendezvous to find everyone there but two Maquis. One Maquis we knew was dead, the other we waited for.'

Joseph Picirella, one of Bourgeois' men, later gave a Maquisard's description of the action: 'I lay behind a hastily constructed wall of stones on a rocky promontory overlooking the road ... we heard the sound of engines and saw the first vehicle appear. I opened fire on it and heard another Maquisard fire a bazooka he had been given by the Americans. I had three trucks in my field of fire ... The Germans returned fire with the machine guns mounted above the drivers' cabins. Others were leaping from the rear of the truck and taking cover ... I missed a German who leapt out and took cover under the truck, but got the man who followed him – or so I thought. He lay still for a moment or so, and then rolled into cover and started returning fire. His bullet pierced my shelter and wounded me in the hand. But I still had 200 bullets left so I laid down covering fire ... A German tried to pull a wounded comrade beneath the truck ... another German jumped out, was hit and lay in the roadway covered in blood ... moving closer to the first truck I could see men lying under it and threw two American hand grenades at them ... Some cries and groans, then an awful silence ...'

Picirella was now on his own, the rest of the ambush party having withdrawn. 'I tried to recover Picard's body. He had been killed by mortar shrapnel right in the heart ... he had only come with us because he was bored with work in the kitchen. By coincidence, I knew his mother who sold eggs to mine in the market. In the uncanny silence I made my escape picking up food and ammunition which had been abandoned by the Americans. Catching up with them, I and my comrades helped to carry the Americans' weapons and other burdens, as they were unused to the mountains.'

The missing Maquisard who did not make the rendezvous after the attack was Jean Gayvallet. Wounded, he was captured by the Germans and taken back up to the Col, where a railway bridge crosses the road just below the deserted station in which he and his comrades had spent the previous night. Soon buses arrived carrying the inhabitants of the nearby town of Lalley, whom the Germans had rounded up to help gather up their wounded and dead. Among them was Mme Fernande Battier, who later described the fate of the twenty-year-old Maquisard: 'They took him down to where the dead and the wounded were lying to show him what he had done. Then they bundled him, hands tied, into the ravine where he was beaten again and his limbs broken. We could hear him crying "Mercy! Mercy!" from where we were standing on the road. It was terrible. Then he was dragged up to the road and tied to a tree, where he was beaten by some and shot by others. They kept him tied in this position for a long time. Then the ambulances arrived and parked in front of him blocking our view. We heard five pistol shots and that was the end for him.'

The following day, two Maquisards came in a car to collect Gayvallet's body, reporting to Hoppers that, after his eyes had been gouged out and his tongue torn off, he had been bayoneted to death – but there are no independent witnesses for this. Later it was also reported to Hoppers that the Germans had suffered sixty killed, twenty-five wounded and three trucks destroyed – but this toll too is almost certainly a considerable exaggeration. Contrary to everyone's expectations, the nearby villages of Lus-la-Croix-Haute and Lalley did not suffer reprisals because, the Germans said, it was foreign troops not local Maquisards who had been responsible for the killing.

Three days later, on 11 July, Huet and Chavant signed a joint order which was posted in every commune and village, calling up all young men on the plateau aged between twenty and twenty-four who had not yet joined up. This raised the total under Huet's command to well over 3,000 in all. Pierre Tanant, Huet's Chief of Staff, euphemistic as ever, claimed a high-minded motive for the call-up: 'In a spirit of justice and to mark the total union which reigned in our little republic, the military and civil chiefs decided to mobilize those young men on the plateau who had not so far responded to the patriotic call and also all those who lived in "no man's land" in Villard who risked, given their age, being arrested by the Germans.'

The truth was probably more prosaic. Huet was dangerously short of men to defend the perimeter of his territory. Some units were very strung out, especially on the eastern flank of the plateau, where only a handful of men – usually no more than ten – guarded each of the passes. Whatever the motive, the call-up was not popular so close to harvest time when young hands were badly needed at home and in the fields. There were complaints from some villages and a number of young men 'forgot' to register, notably in Villard-de-Lans. Those who did register for service were rushed through rudimentary military training.

Back in London, General Koenig, unable to send Allied aircraft to bomb Chabeuil, sent the next best thing – a cheering message: 'On D-Day you took up arms and have resisted the assaults of the enemy with great heroism. By so doing you have caused the Tricolour and the emblems of liberty to fly again in a small corner of the soil of France. To you, the fighters of the Free French Forces of the Interior and to the courageous population of the Vercors who support you, I send my warmest congratulations together with the hope that your success will spread rapidly across the whole of our homeland.' It is not known how many saw the signal – or, if they did see it, how many felt better as a result.

That night Jean Tournissa too was on the airwaves reporting that his strip would be ready 'for landing Dakotas very soon'. Algiers responded the following day with a message which seemed encouraging in its urgency: 'We will take care of everything as soon as possible. Please organize a row of campfires able to provide night landing in case we need to supply you. We are being delayed by constant bad weather conditions in your area. But we consider it very important that we take the first opportunity we can.'

Later that day, 12 July, true to their habit of shutting the stable door after the horse had bolted, Supreme Allied Headquarters in London issued a directive 'intended for General Cochet' in Algiers. Once again, it is possible to hear the sentiments, if not the language, of Koenig in the text: 'It is impractical to build up the Free French forces to a strength capable of engaging the enemy in open combat due to logistical limitations … you must avoid decisive combat … you will therefore restrict operations to sabotage and guerrilla warfare … the concentration of forces in large bodies and formations is to be avoided.' Once again London was showing how out of touch they were with the realities on the ground, which they among others had helped to create. Perhaps SHAEF's signal was a desperate attempt to change course before it was too late – or perhaps it was an attempt to distance London from the consequences of the events which were now beginning to unfold.

We know that, by this time, Allied command were aware of the likelihood of an impending German attack on the plateau, because on 11 July US General Eugene Caffey, Maitland Wilson's Chief of Staff, breezily told Cochet about this when the two men bumped into each other in Algiers that day. 'Here is some information which should interest you,' the

American General told the Frenchman. 'German aircraft have been taking aerial photos over the Vercors. And they are also pulling troops back from the Midi [southern France] which makes us think they are going to use them against the plateau.'

Cochet wasted no time in getting this information through to the plateau, following this up by sending one of his staff, Captain Delmas, to Naples to act as his liaison officer at the headquarters of General Ira Eaker, the Commander-in-Chief of Mediterranean Allied Air Forces. Cochet's instructions to Delmas were to do all he could to extract just a few of the 5,000 aircraft Eaker had under his command to help the Vercors: 'You must plead their cause constantly with [Eaker] and do what you can to obtain the most assistance you can for them … by making clear the urgency of the situation and the necessity of providing support.'

That day, Koenig in London intervened on the airwaves again: 'General Koenig draws attention to the fact that the Vercors is part of the northern zone of France and, as such, it is his responsibility alone to issue orders to the Vercors.' Apart from getting in the way and sowing confusion, this demand had precisely no effect and appears again to have been ignored by all concerned.

At 20.00 hours on 12 July, the Germans launched their first air attack on the plateau, dropping 500-pound bombs on La Chapelle, Malleval, Cognin and Vassieux, and then machine-gunning everything they saw moving in the four villages. Damage was slight and injuries few, but it marked the beginning of a new phase on the plateau.

There were also signs of German interest in the plateau's landing sites. At about this time, according to Desmond Longe's diary, Huet received what appeared to be a clandestine note from a German pilot offering to defect with his aircraft and suggesting that he should be shown where to land. Huet, with a characteristic mix of politeness and caution, replied that the offer was welcome but that the pilot would have to take his chances where he could. A little time later a German fighter flew up and down the plateau looking for signs, but when none appeared, decided instead to carry out a little random machine-gunning.

Since early July, Huet's Chief of Staff, Pierre Tanant, had been pressing his commander to complete the process of militarization of the plateau by incorporating all civil Maquis companies into formal Army units. On 13 July, Huet agreed, issuing an 'Order No. 1' whose flowery language hints that it had been drafted by Tanant himself: 'For the last two years, the flags, standards and pennants of our regiments and battalions have lain sleeping. Now France, in all her spirit and glory, rises once again against the invader. The old Army of France, with its centuries of illustrious history on every battlefield, must now take its rightful place again in the great institutions of our nation. From today Major Huet, the Commander of the Vercors, has decided that all units under his command will again take up the glorious names and traditions of the old units of our region.'

All the autonomous Maquisard groups on the plateau were immediately incorporated into four 'battalions' and two 'regiments', each named after units in the pre-war Army of the Alps. Each new unit commander was instructed to make precise lists of those under his command which were to be submitted without delay to the Villa Bellon – where in due course they would prove much more valuable to the Germans than they ever were to the French. On 13 July, the lists in Huet's headquarters indicated that his total strength was 3,909 'soldiers', including 169 officers and 317 non-commissioned officers.

Pierre Tanant, ever the military romantic, regarded Huet's order as a way of raising fighting spirit among the Maquisards. 'I saw regimental history as a means by which we could raise our *esprit de corps*. I believed that the French soldier is proud of his regimental insignia and fights far better as part of a unit with regimental traditions than as a member of some anonymous and amorphous body. So I proposed that we should adopt the numbers and traditions of the regiments and battalions which were garrisoned in our area before the war.'

Some of the young Maquisards did indeed welcome being treated as regular soldiers. But many didn't. 'We were incorporated *en bloc* into [a cavalry unit] under the command of Narcisse Geyer. He was young and pleasant enough – but overly impressed with his own importance … He was always impeccably turned out, right down to his gleaming cavalry boots, and was most often driven from place to place in an open-topped car with two black bodyguards in the back seat. For these stupid affectations we had to give up our comfortable farmhouse. We really missed our old barn draped with parachutes and our soft, comfortable straw-stuffed mattresses.'

Gilbert Joseph, one of de Beauregard's Maquisards, was more caustic: 'The opening sentence [of Huet's order] "For the last two years, the flags, standards and pennants of our regiments and battalions have lain sleeping" was unintentionally comical as it acknowledged that the French Army collapsed almost without a fight ... As in the past it was we civilians – we Resistants – who had restored the Army's glory, not the other way round – and indeed been killed while doing it.' Others after the war saw this decision 'as an attempt to exorcize the military defeat of the 1940s'.

In fact Huet's 'Order No. 1' was probably inspired more by the need for discipline and a proper command structure than by any romantic notion of recreating the old units of the Army of the Alps. With his units spread so thinly over so wide an area, and dependent as he was on human couriers as his only means of communication, Huet had no alternative but to create effective structures through which he could pass on his orders. And, given his concerns about the reliability of the newly arrived Maquisards under enemy fire, incorporating the novices in units alongside more experienced soldiers seems a perfectly sensible military move.

Tanant's focus now turned to the lack of uniforms in his newly formed units: 'Our Maquisards have the air of bandits, not soldiers.' This deficiency was quickly put right when a daring (and, in the circumstances, highly risky) foray into the old Army of the Alps' stores in the Alma Barracks in Grenoble netted 350 French uniforms which were spirited back to the plateau under the noses of the Germans. This haul permitted Tanant to provide some with proper uniforms. One of the first to get the new uniforms were the soldiers of the Command Section who looked after the personal needs of the officers at the Villa Bellon.

During that day, 13 July, Descour reported to Algiers that the German garrisons in Valence and Romans, under the western edge of the plateau, had been reinforced by some 1,500 troops, among them units which had special expertise in anti-partisan warfare; a new general and his headquarters had arrived in Romans; some seventy-five aircraft were gathered on Chabeuil airfield and aerial reconnaissance *mouches* were ever more present in the skies above the plateau. With Descour's intelligence update in his hand, Cochet in Algiers tried again with Eaker, sending a pleading message to the American General's headquarters in Italy. In reply he was advised to approach Eaker's British deputy, Air Marshal Sir John Slessor. But Slessor was as unhelpful as Eaker's headquarters had been, telling Cochet that Vassieux was a matter to be considered after and not before Anvil had been launched.

In London, the Chief of Staff at the French headquarters added his bit by writing that same day to Koenig, appealing to him to intervene at the highest level to get Chabeuil bombed without delay: 'The Vercors commanders have asked three times for the bombing of Chabeuil, from where enemy aircraft have attacked the plateau on many occasions. We have passed these requests on to SHAEF without any success ... I request now that you intervene personally and urgently with SHAEF to get this airfield bombed as soon as possible.'

At 19.00 hours that evening, Focke-Wulf 190s from Chabeuil again bombed Vassieux and La Chapelle. This time, five were killed in Vassieux. While the Focke-Wulf attack was in progress, one of Bob Bennes' radio operators received a message from London: there was to be another mass daylight drop by US Flying Fortresses the following day (14 July – the national day of France) at Vassieux.

It would be a busy night – the plateau was already expecting a drop at Vassieux in the early hours of the next morning by ten Halifaxes from Algiers. Later that evening, in their regular 'Messages personnels' broadcast, the BBC sent the message of confirmation to indicate that the following day's mass drop was on. By 04.00 the next morning, the Vassieux site had been cleared of the 150 containers and fifteen packages dropped by the night visitors from Algiers and three bonfires had been constructed 200 metres apart, in the shape of a triangle. A fleet of lorries, ready to carry away the expected largesse, was assembled in garages in Vassieux and two of Bob Bennes' radio operators were already on site, one to help vector in the expected aircraft and the other to report directly to London on the progress of the drop.

All was ready for the great day.

BASTILLE DAY: 14 JULY 1944

The 14th of July – Bastille Day – broke clear and cloudless on the Vercors. The sawtooth line of crests on the plateau's eastern ramparts stood out black against the glow of the rising sun. The ground was moist from recent rain and the grass wet with dew. As colour seeped into the sky, the shadows already gathered on the Taille-Crayon drop site took form and substance in the morning brightness and the grey shapes of Vassieux resolved themselves into sturdy buildings sheltering under the protection of the village church. Already a scurry of people filled the streets. The word had gone round about the big event promised for France's national day.

The Germans had probably heard it too, through their network of spies. Or perhaps they already had their own plans to mark this special day – a restaurateur on the plain had recently reported overhearing German officers commenting over dinner, 'They'll certainly remember 14 July on the Vercors.'

Across the Vercors and in the towns and villages around it, this was to be a day of celebration. The biggest of these on the plateau was a military parade, with Huet taking the salute, to be held during the morning in La Chapelle, followed by a lunch in the Hôtel Bellier. Before the parade started, a fraternal delegation from the Committee for National Liberation of the Isère, among them Alain Le Ray, was received by Chavant with all due solemnity in Saint-Martin. Meanwhile, in Die, a grand march-past of 400 Maquisards, presided over by Henri Zeller and Yves Farge, was planned for midday, despite persistent warnings that the near-constant presence of German *mouches* over the town during previous days made this a hazardous undertaking.

In the small hours of that morning, a congratulatory message addressed to Eugène Chavant as President of the Committee for National Liberation on the Vercors arrived from Algiers: 'On this 14th of July, the day of liberty, we wish to pass on to you and those around you our expressions of admiration and good wishes. Your friends from Algiers.'

At around 09.30, the plateau began to reverberate with a distant thunder which grew louder and louder till it shook the summer air and made the ground tremble in sympathy. A faint dark line began to appear above the rim of the plateau. Onlookers crowded on to the streets of the Vercors' towns and villages. Looking up, their hands shielding the sun from their eyes, they saw what appeared to them an inconceivable multitude of four-engined bombers protected by Mustang fighters, which appeared as little shards of sunlight, flashing and twinkling against the clear blue sky.

Nicolas Bernard, who had left his Maquisard camp at 04.00 that morning to help with the drop, was in a truck approaching Vassieux when he saw them: 'A huge formation of American Flying Fortresses flew over us at very low altitude … We jumped for joy and shouted and sang the Marseillaise and wept with emotion at the giant birds carrying help from our friends from far away. And then they turned and began releasing their treasure – over a thousand parachutes of all colours floated to earth just a few hundred metres away. It was a magnificent – an unbelievable spectacle on this national day of 14th July.'

The spectacle was enhanced by the fact that the parachutes were red, white and blue, the colours of the French tricolour. In reality this was nothing to do with the Bastille Day – it was colour-coding to indicate the nature of each parachute load (red for ammunition and so on). But it increased the sense of wonder and emotion among those watching.

Operation Cadillac had in fact begun in the UK at 04.00 that morning when 320 American Flying Fortresses took off from nine airfields across the south of England, shattering the early-morning silence. After forming up in a single body, they crossed the French coast at around 04.30 and flew on to Blois where they divided into seven groups, each heading for different drop sites in southern France. The largest group of seventy-five aircraft headed for the Vercors, where they planned to drop nearly 900 containers carrying a total of almost 95 tonnes of arms and munitions.

An SOE observer in one of the rear Flying Fortresses wrote in his report afterwards: 'The bonfires were first visible to the pilot at a range of … 25 miles … the dropping was extremely accurate – 90% within a mile of the fires and, of this, 90% were so close to the dropping point that they formed almost a solid mass of parachute canopies.'

But this time the Germans were waiting.

Because the drop took twenty minutes longer than planned, the protective screen of US fighters, short of fuel, had to turn for home before it had finished. The Flying Fortresses, now without protection, were immediately pounced on by twelve German fighters from Chabeuil. In the running battles which ensued, two of the American aircraft were damaged and had to limp towards home, finally landing at an airfield near the Normandy bridgehead. Fortunately the Germans did not press home their attack on the unprotected American formation. It was not really the Americans they were interested in; it was the Vassieux site.

As soon as the US bombers had left, two German Focke-Wulf 190s began machine-gunning the mounds of parachutes and containers. The accuracy of the American dropping actually made this easier for the German pilots, as the clustered parachutes provided a perfect aiming marker. By this time, a small fleet of lorries had driven on to a nearby wheatfield and were already beginning to load the containers. There was a mad scramble to find cover behind and underneath the lorries, as the whole area began to erupt with little spurts of dust kicked up by machine-gun bullets. Bob Bennes' radio operator, reporting to London from the Taille-Crayon site, just had time to close his transmission with the words 'Being machine-gunned' before throwing himself under a lorry. The two aircraft made several low-level passes, their machine guns chattering venomously, before withdrawing. After the wounded had been sent in a lorry to Dr Ganimède's hospital outside Saint-Martin, the business of collecting containers continued.

Earlier, at around 08.30 that morning, Christine Granville and her friend Sylviane Rey, a nurse, had travelled down from the plateau to Die. Perhaps they wanted to be present for the evening parade. But more probably they were on their way to a prearranged meeting with Francis Cammaerts, whom Christine had not met yet. We know that Cammaerts returned to the Vercors that day after an extended tour of his Resistance networks in the Digne area. We know, too, that he met Christine before going up to the plateau. And we know, finally, that he was in Die in time to see the drop on the plateau, for he commented that it was 'bloody stupid' to drop by daylight when 'the parachutes were clear as hell against the sky'. So it is reasonable to suppose that he arrived in Die, probably by train, in the early morning. Piecing together the various accounts, it seems most likely that Cammaerts had arranged for Sylviane Rey, with whom he was rumoured to be romantically attached, to pick him up from Die station and that Christine came along to meet her new chief.

Cammaerts later described his first impressions of his new courier: 'I saw a beautiful, slender dark-haired young woman. Even in those rough conditions, I was impressed by her features and bearing. Her face was sensitive and alert ...' Later he noted that, while 'structurally very beautiful', she was an 'actress' who could 'pass completely unnoticed' as easily as she could draw people's eyes 'with tremendous magnetism'.

Cammaerts and the two women stayed in Die waiting for the midday parade, which was to be led by one of Cammaerts' Maquis leaders, Pierre Raynaud. The town was in a state of high fête. Everyone was in their Sunday best. Flags hung in every window and Maquis vehicles and columns marched to and fro in every street. Even Hoppers and his men were there. Before the parade, the VIPs, including mayors of the villages in the area, gathered on the patio in the town square and toasted Bastille Day in Clairette de Die, the sparkling white wine for which the little medieval market town is famous. Then there was a lunch, after which the parade was to be held. Just as the last course was being served, two German fighters roared low overhead. It was quickly decided that the parade and presentation of medals should be held without delay. That completed, Farge stood on the fountain in the town square and delivered his address – though he may not have been heard as well as he might have hoped. The townspeople had been instructed not to stand in the square but to remain hidden under the plane trees and in the doorways of the houses that surround it.

Up on the plateau, the respite after the initial machine-gunning of the Taille-Crayon site did not last long. Forty minutes after they left, the fighters returned with reinforcements – Heinkel bombers which started methodically pounding Vassieux. The bombardment went on until 17.00 and included high explosive, incendiary bombs and *chapelets* (canisters) full of small grenades which were released at about 100 metres from the ground and scattered over a wide area before going off. After an hour, all external communications with Vassieux were cut and the approach roads to the village became too dangerous to use. In the early hours of the afternoon, the church was hit. By evening, only four out of the eighty-five houses in the village remained unscathed and half were totally destroyed.

While the second air attack was in progress, Bob Bennes, Jean Tournissa and Pierre Haezebrouck met in the shelter of one of the ruins and agreed that it would probably be followed by an assault by paratroops. The defences around the site were reorganized and strengthened, especially on the high ground east and south-east of the village where a number of machine-gun posts were established, covering the approaches to Vassieux and Tournissa's half-completed landing site.

With the Germans fully occupied attacking Vassieux, Huet judged, in his typically unflappable way, that the 11.00 parade of arms in La Chapelle could go ahead. At the appointed hour, the ceremony duly took place, complete with marching columns, regimental standards, pennants and even music – above which the distant sound of the bombing of Vassieux could, nevertheless, still distinctly be heard.

After the parade in La Chapelle had finished, everyone filed into the Hôtel Bellier for the celebration lunch. In the hotel dining room, decked out with tricolours, Union Jacks, Stars and Stripes and red, white and blue bunting, Vincent-Beaume, holding the lapels of his coat, stood to give the speech of welcome. But he got no further than 'Mesdames et Messieurs' when his voice was drowned out by a huge explosion as the first German 200-kilo bomb fell on the town. Everyone instinctively stood up, sang the 'Marseillaise' and then dispersed to deal with the fires and rescue people from collapsing buildings. One man, however, refused to leave. A minor hindrance like a German bomb was not going to deprive him of a free lunch. He sat there, an uncorked bottle of wine in front of him, and calmly finished his meal in the midst of the dust, the chaos and the noise.

Huet appears to have decided that he should return to his headquarters at the Villa Bellon, where he had planned a lunch of his own. Longe and Houseman were there and were astonished by his sangfroid. By now the Germans had turned their attention to Saint-Martin. As Focke-Wulf 190s roared past outside, their machine guns hammering away and their wing tips level with the dining-room window, Huet completely unperturbed went, laboriously and with great deliberation, through a seemingly endless series of toasts. After each one, everyone pushed back their chairs, stood to attention, raised their glasses and solemnly repeated their Colonel's* words as though they were all at a great Paris banquet and not at imminent risk of obliteration by a German bomb: 'Vive la République Française' – 'Vive l'Angleterre' – 'Vive l'Amérique' – 'Vive les Alliés' – 'Je vous donne la victoire'.

That evening, Yves Farge, his duties in Die finished, made his way up to the plateau. Arriving at Vassieux he saw 'the skeletons of houses which had been destroyed by the flames or were or being devoured by them. The flames seemed the only thing alive in the immense solitude of the mountain.' Later he visited the church, and found himself filled with a terrible wonder: 'I've never seen anything so grand, so beautiful as the flames that enveloped the roof, that took possession of the great wooden beams beneath it, that devoured and illuminated the choir stalls in a last but magnificent rite. We leapt out of the church into the square … At that moment the whole roof collapsed and millions of red sparks whirled towards the sky.'

Farge went on to La Chapelle, where he found Eugène Chavant grimy with soot, smoke and sweat having spent the afternoon helping the village firemen. In the immediate aftermath of the bombing, Chavant had been shocked to find that looters had been out in the village, but he had soon restored order.

It appears that Francis Cammaerts, Christine Granville and Sylviane Rey may have reached Vassieux while it was still light and before the bombing had ended, for there is a description of Cammaerts and Christine helping to recover parachutes while Sylviane Rey, in her starched white nurse's apron, cared for the wounded.

Returning from Vassieux that evening, Bob Bennes dropped in to see a dishevelled Chavant, who was by then in his headquarters in Saint-Martin. *Le Patron* proposed a glass of Clairette de Die. But no sooner had they filled their glasses than a nearby explosion dislodged a shower of plaster from the ceiling, which fell into their newly poured wine. They swiftly recharged their glasses and continued their private celebration of the French national day. Later that evening, Bennes returned to La Britière and sent a sarcastic signal to London: 'Received daytime parachute drop 14th. About seventy-two planes. Very successful. Have been machine-gunned ever since departure Allied aircraft. Thanks.'

---

* Huet had been promoted just days previously.

At dinner at the Villa Bellon that night, one of Hoppers' men, the Canadian Lieutenant Chester Myers, suddenly complained of feeling nauseous and of suffering from an excruciating pain in his side. He was rushed to Dr Ganimède at the Saint-Martin hospital who swiftly diagnosed appendicitis. The bombing had cut the electricity supply line to Saint-Martin, so Ganimède did not have enough light to operate. He packed the Canadian's side with ice and operated early the following morning before the air raids restarted, using chloroform, the only anaesthetic available on the plateau.

At midnight, a meeting between Huet, Chavant and Farge was held at Villa Bellon to discuss the situation. The three men now had to face up to the fact that it was no longer a question of whether the Vercors would be attacked by the Germans, but when; that it was now a race between the Allies and the enemy as to who would reach the plateau first.

It was time to make contingency plans. Orders were given for a new 'outpost' hospital to be set up for serious, non-ambulant patients in the woods near the little village of Tourtres a few kilometres from Saint-Martin; André Vincent-Beaume's prison at Auboyneaux on the outskirts of La Chapelle was to move to the more isolated Loscence plateau; the telephone exchange would be repositioned, transferring from La Chapelle to the nearby hamlet of Les Drevets; work on Tournissa's strip was reorganized to take place at night – as was the collection of the remaining containers still lying on the Taille-Crayon site. There is also some evidence that it was at this time that Huet began to give thought to a 'dispersal plan' for all his units, if the worst were to happen.

Cammaerts was not at the Villa Bellon meeting. He spent the night with Christine Granville 'in a burning hotel at St Agnan. It was the first time we made love. We were absolutely certain we were going to die the next day; it was all over, this was the end – the hotel was on fire, bombs were falling, troops were gathering on the side of the mountain … we simply went into each other's arms. In the morning, we were standing at the window and a fighter with a bomb slung beneath it made straight for us. We could see the pilot's face. I said – if he releases it now, we've had it – and on the word "now", he fired. The bomb skidded across the roof and buried itself in the ground behind the hotel without exploding. Christine gripped my hand and laughed – "They don't want us to die."'

Many on the plateau (including Bennes and Cammaerts) blamed the day's attacks on the American daylight drop. While it seems likely that the attack on the Taille-Crayon site immediately after the mass drop by the first two Focke-Wulf 190s was a spontaneous reaction, the scale of the air offensive which followed seems to indicate a carefully planned German operation designed, perhaps, to mark, in their own way, the French national day.

But the day's mass drop of arms, which were now being used to provision Resistance groups throughout the Isère and Drôme areas, deepened German worries about the threats which were building up to their main communication routes when the southern invasion was launched. While the plateau was preoccupied, for better or worse, in the celebrations of Bastille Day, French intelligence reported a German bicycle company and eight lorryloads of troops moving into Saint-Nizier. The following day, General Niehoff's headquarters in Lyon ordered two of the Gebirgsjäger regiments from Pflaum's division to be withdrawn prematurely from the Jura and to proceed immediately south, by forced march, to the Vercors.

PFLAUM'S PLANS
AND PEOPLE

The plans drawn up by the German staff for what was now known as
Operation Vercors were based on the classic 'surround, attack, annihilate, destroy' model employed on the Glières, at Malleval and on the
Mont Mouchet. But the scale was very different. With a total force
(excluding air resources) of up to 10,000 men, this was to be, by a factor
of two, the largest German anti-partisan operation carried out in western Europe in the Second World War.

The central aim of Operation Vercors was first to capture and destroy
Huet's headquarters, then to clear the Vercors of 'terrorists' and finally to
render the plateau unusable as a future base for Resistance operations.
The officer in overall charge of the operation was to be the German
commander of occupation forces in southern France, Heinrich Niehoff.
But the tactical commander on the ground was the 157th Reserve
Divisional commander, General Karl Pflaum.

The forces deployed in Operation Vercors included almost all the
units of Pflaum's division, some of which by now had the reputation of
being the most experienced and effective anti-partisan unit in France.
Pflaum's Alpine regiments had, between them, conducted five separate
operations since early February and many of their component units had
been in constant contact with the enemy for two weeks by the time they
were withdrawn from the Jura on 15 July and ordered to march on the
Vercors. Other units earmarked for the operation included a specialist
airborne unit, an armoured battalion and a variety of specialized bodies
including police and security units and various Eastern Troop elements
(the so-called Mongols).

The plan for Operation Vercors was divided into two distinct parts.
The first part involved the positioning of an encirclement force, whose
role was to cordon off the plateau. The northern element of this cordon
was to be set up in a continuous line running along the foot of the

Vercors from Grenoble around the northern point of the massif to the village of Combovin at the plateau's south-western extremity. This line would be manned by troops posted in fixed positions a kilometre apart, who would operate constant patrols along the roads. A second cordon was set up to block the exits from the south-eastern corner of the plateau, centred on the Col de la Grimone and the Col de la Croix Haute. The remaining exits from the plateau did not need to be closed off, as these were to be used by the assaulting troops.

The attack element of Operation Vercors consisted of four 'columns', or *Kampfgruppen*, each named after its commander. These were to attack the plateau simultaneously from four different points, so as to keep the enemy's forces dispersed and unable to concentrate on any single threat.

The three largest of these columns were to be land based. The first, under the command of Oberst Alfred Seeger, was to attack from Saint-Nizier in the north, with the aim of first clearing the northern plateau and then breaking through Huet's defensive line in the Valchevrière sector, which was protected by Jean Prévost's Compagnie Goderville. Seeger was an artillery officer who had never commanded such a unit on anti-partisan operations before and had just returned from sick leave in Germany. Taciturn and aloof, he was regarded as a competent but unexceptional commander in the field.

The second column, which included a number of armoured cars and personnel carriers, was commanded by Major Zabel (his first name is unknown) and would launch from the Romans area. Its aim was to sweep aside the Drôme Maquis units protecting the Vercors' southern access, capture Die, seal off the southern escape route from the plateau and then be ready to turn north to break into the plateau by forcing Huet's defensive line at the Col de Rousset.

The main fighting elements of Pflaum's third column, commanded by Oberst Franz Schwehr, were two Alpine battalions, supported by mountain artillery and engineers. Their task was to break through the thinly held defensive positions holding the passes on the Vercors' forbidding eastern ramparts and then drive towards the centre of the Vercors, where all three columns would meet and secure the plateau.

The forty-five-year-old Schwehr had finished the First World War as a second lieutenant but had been forced to leave the Army, enduring considerable poverty during the German depression of the 1920s. He rejoined the Army in 1935 and was sent to the Russian front in 1941.

Here Schwehr appears to have had some kind of nervous breakdown and, like his commander General Pflaum, was declared medically unfit for front-line duty and posted to France. An accomplished mountaineer and physically strong, Schwehr was – following the operations in the Ain and Jura – one of the foremost experts in anti-partisan operations in mountainous areas in the whole of the Wehrmacht. An able and respected officer among his German colleagues, Schwehr had, nevertheless, over recent months, gained a reputation for brutality in the conduct of his operations.

Pflaum would have known that the troops assembling for these three land-based thrusts into the plateau could not be hidden from the eyes of the network of French observers who fed the Resistance intelligence networks in the area. He had to assume, therefore, that the French commanders would have a very good idea of the broad shape of his intentions. He sought to regain the element of surprise by simultaneously inserting a fourth, airborne column in twenty-two assault gliders right into the heart of the Vercors citadel itself. This part of the operation was to be carried out by men of a Luftwaffe airborne unit which specialized in anti-partisan operations under the command of Oberleutnant Friedrich Schäfer. Many in Schäfer's unit had joined to gain 'redemption by combat' as an alternative to military punishment, and for some, this operation would be their first taste of action.

At twenty-five years old, Schäfer himself, however, was a veteran of glider-borne air assaults. He had participated in all the major German airborne operations, starting with Crete. A highly decorated officer, he came from a working-class family in Germany's industrial heartland in the Ruhr valley and was a committed supporter of the Nazi Party. Keen, loyal, energetic and highly ambitious, he had been quickly recognized for his bravery and aggression and had risen fast through the ranks before receiving his commission as an officer.

Pflaum's plan called for Schäfer's gliders to attack in two waves half an hour apart. Each glider would carry nine men as well as the pilot, and was equipped with a medium machine gun on the canopy with which the pilot could provide covering fire. The gliders were also fitted with parachutes and retro rockets which enabled the little aircraft to land in just 9 metres (less than the length of the gliders themselves). The decision to land Schäfer's men in two waves is curious, as it left the first wave very exposed until the second arrived. The normal rule for airborne

PFLAUM'S PLAN

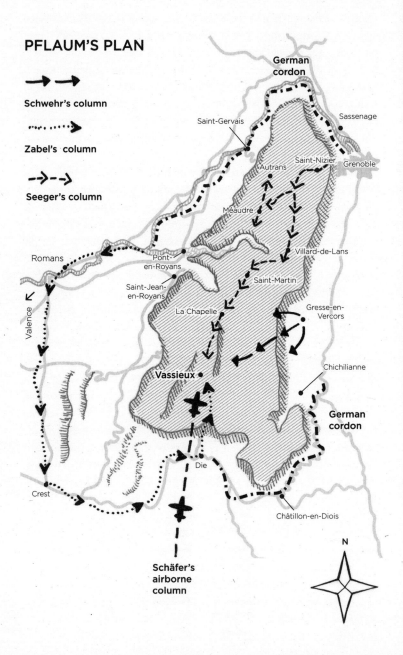

Schwehr's column

Zabel's column

Seeger's column

German cordon

Sassenage

Saint-Gervais

Autrans

Saint-Nizier

Grenoble

Méaudre

Villard-de-Lans

Romans

Pont-
en-Royans

Saint-Martin

Saint-Jean-
en-Royans

Gresse-en-
Vercors

La Chapelle

Valence

Chichilianne

Vassieux

German
cordon

Die

Crest

Châtillon-en-Diois

**Schäfer's
airborne
column**

N

Grenoble from the Charvet ridge

Francis Cammaerts, SOE

Christine Granville (Krystyna Skarbek), SOE

Lieutenant Vernon Hoppers, US Special Forces

Desmond Longe, SOE

John Houseman, SOE

Jean Tournissa

Operation Cadillac 14 July 1944

Generalleutnant Heinrich Niehoff

Generalleutnant Karl Ludwig Pflaum

Oberst Franz Schwehr

Oberleutnant Friedrich Schäfer

Schäfer's men gather on Lyon-Bron airport, dawn 21 July 1944

German DFS 230 assault gliders in flight

Roland Costa de Beauregard

Abel Chabal

Compagnie Abel in action

The dead at Vassieux

Atrocities at La Mure

Grotte de la Luire circa 24 July 1943 (the figure of Père Montcheuil just visible front right)

Bob Bennes leads his Maquisards at the victory parade at Grenoble, 22 August 1944

operations is to get as many people on to the ground as quickly as possible. It may be that Schäfer's options were limited by the lack of available towing aircraft. After both waves had landed, Schäfer would have, in total, 220 men with which to secure the site and beat off counter-attacks before reinforcements and heavy weapons could be flown in by heavy-lift resupply gliders.

Schäfer's part in Pflaum's operation was highly sensitive to weather conditions. If the weather was bad at the time scheduled for his landing, he would have to delay. If it went bad after he landed, his troops would be desperately exposed to French counter-attack until conditions improved sufficiently to bring in the reinforcements. This meant that close air support from the bombers and fighters from Chabeuil airport would be vital, as would logistic supply by German air transport specialist units.

Each of Pflaum's attack columns was to be accompanied by specialist Sipo/SD so-called 'Gestapo' units and, in the case of columns led by Schäfer and Zabel, reinforced by a detachment of Eastern Troops. Their job was to carry out the interrogation of prisoners and conduct reprisals against the civilian population, as directed by the head of the Sipo/SD in the Lyon area, SS Obersturmbannführer Werner Knab. It was decided that Knab himself would accompany Schäfer and his men on board a glider in the second of the initial assault waves. This was highly unusual and seems to indicate the importance of Operation Vercors, compared with the anti-partisan operations which had preceded it.

Once the plateau had been secured by Pflaum's four attack columns, other units, including the Eastern Troops, were to be moved up to the plateau to carry out punishment and reprisals with the aim, not just of wiping out the Vercors Maquis, but also of making the plateau unusable as a base for future Resistance operations.

By July 1944, any feeling of 'softness' towards the French civilian population had long since vanished. At this stage of the war, the Germans felt themselves to be in an alien country surrounded by enemies on all sides. The year's earlier operations had largely inured most of Pflaum's force to the 'necessity' of summary executions and reprisals as part of the normal conduct of anti-partisan warfare. By now all except the most fanatical of Pflaum's troops would have realized that Germany was not going to win the war. This, combined with a fear that every house, boulder and bush hid an enemy, made for a mood of desperation and nervousness which tended to produce erratic and brutal responses. It is not difficult to imagine, for instance, how German losses in Hoppers' successful ambush at the Col de la Croix Haute would have resulted in a thirst for revenge among Pflaum's forces, fed no doubt by exaggeration and hyperbole on the German side, just as it had been on that of the French.

There were other recent 'terrorist' incidents which would have added to this sense of anger. On 12 June, after a battle at Virieu-la-Grande, north-west of Aix-les-Bains, several Germans were taken prisoner. The exact number involved is disputed – Germans defending themselves at war crimes trials in Grenoble after the war claimed there were thirty. After the battle and in confusing circumstances, the German prisoners were all executed by firing squad. What really happened is of less import-ance than what was believed to have happened, even at the highest levels of Pflaum's division. Given these factors, many in Pflaum's force, gather-ing for Operation Vercors around the rim of the plateau, would have been in uncompromising mood about the battle ahead.

Up on the plateau, Huet's options, as he watched Pflaum's forces gath-ering below, were far more limited than those of his German adversary. Having chosen a static defence, his dispositions were now dictated more by topography than by any other factor. The walls of his 'fortress' were the cliffs, crests and crags which delineated the edges of the southern plateau. But this meant trying to defend a line 150 kilometres long with only 4,000 men, 1,000 of whom were not yet fully armed – and even more untried, untested and untrained.

As a consequence of this almost impossible overstretch, Huet was forced to make risky tactical decisions in order to provide some semblance of cover for the whole of his line of defence. One of these was to defend the half-dozen key passes along the Vercors' eastern ramparts with, in some cases, fewer than ten men each. Even then, his units cover-ing the most likely axes along which the enemy would attack (for exam-ple, the winding mountain road from Villard-de-Lans through Valchevrière) would have to defend a front extending over more than 10 kilometres with just 250–300 men.

As in Saint-Nizier, Huet had no defence in depth, and almost no reserves beyond the troop of Senegalese guarding Descour's headquar-ters and those who could be spared from his headquarters at Villa Bellon. As a result he had no serious ability to counter-attack, except by transferring forces from some other part of his line, which would therefore be left unguarded.

This shortage of manpower also confirmed his previous decision not to defend the northern plateau. The wide, open valley leading from Saint-Nizier to Villard offered a near-perfect terrain for the Germans to use their full range of heavy weapons such as artillery, machine guns and mortars, of which they had so many and Huet so few. The French commander therefore, very sensibly, ordered the forces led by de Beauregard and Ullman on the northern plateau to ambush any advancing German column but not seriously to oppose them and, at the appropriate moment, to pull back without major loss behind the line of the Gorges de la Bourne into the southern plateau.

THE RISING STORM

On 15 July 1944, in London, David Astor wrote another manuscript letter to his friend and chief Brigadier 'Lucky' Laycock, the head of Combined Operations. Astor attached some papers, which were 'intended to open the eyes of SHAEF'. These included a signal sent to SOE in London (probably from Cammaerts) on 3 July warning that 'It is the duty of the Commandant of French Forces and the Allies to make every effort to send heavy matériel and men. Failure on their part will cause the massacre of the population and would lead to grave political internal and external situations.'

In his letter, Astor appealed to Laycock to intervene in SHAEF's failure to reinforce Resistance 'fortresses', reporting that there was a 'general feeling' in SOE that 'A very great opportunity [in France] is being neglected and mishandled and the consequences will not only be the unnecessary loss of Allied lives but also bad feeling between us and our nearest neighbours which will last for years – and which is also unnecessary … The military arguments for using the huge areas behind the enemy are overwhelming …'

An Algiers report (from SPOC) also dated this day made an assessment of the strength of the Resistance in southern France. It described the Vercors in terms which would have surprised those on the plateau who were desperately trying to alert the North African capital about their increasingly vulnerable situation: 'Perhaps … the most powerful area of all is the Vercors … its strength is about 6,000 men. They are organised into military formations of light and heavy companies.'

At least, on this the first day of the official countdown to Anvil, Algiers was now beginning to think seriously how these centres of Resistance strength in southern France could be used in the coming operation. Another SPOC paper reported: 'It is planned to commence landing operations in the Vercors in the August moon period [25 July

to 10 August] … 24 operations [will be carried out] by DC3 aircraft …
loaded with heavy weapons from Italy … on the return journey they
will transport wounded … the use of gliders is also suggested as a means
to increase the supply of heavy weapons.' This was of course exactly
what Pierre Dalloz had in mind when he first thought of Plan
Montagnards.

At about this time also and perhaps with the same intention,
Cammaerts seems to have resurrected his leapfrogging plan, because
another Algiers document (again from SPOC) dated 15 July reported
that 'An agent who has great experience … is prepared to put the former
[Operation] Dagenham project into operation at 70 hours' notice; this
involves seizing the plateau of Valensole [by] gliders and paratroops [and
moving on to] the Vercors.'

Both Maitland Wilson in Algiers and Niehoff in Lyon were now
becoming increasingly aware of the opportunities and dangers posed by
the 4,000 men planted behind enemy lines on the Vercors plateau. The
question was, could the plateau hold out until the Allied landing planned
for the moon period beginning on 25 July? It may be safely assumed that
the Germans were just as aware of the significance of 25 July as were the
staff officers in Algiers and the labourers wielding picks and shovels on
Tournissa's strip.

But, even now, by no means everyone in Algiers was thinking along
the same lines. This same day, General Jean de Lattre de Tassigny, the
man due to command the French forces on Anvil, met with Maitland
Wilson's Chief of Staff, General Eugene Caffey, to discuss the southern
landing. Caffey told de Tassigny that the overall commander of Anvil,
General Patch, intended to drop French parachutists on to the Vercors.
De Tassigny was strongly opposed. 'It would be far more effective for
these troops to be employed in the Massif Central. From there they
could strike south towards the advancing invasion troops.' Caffey pointed
out that, for aircraft coming from Corsica, the Vercors was in range but
the Massif Central was not. De Tassigny insisted, saying that if the
Caïman operation could not be carried out now, the troops should be
held on stand-by until the moment when it would become possible –
perhaps a week or ten days after the Anvil landing.

Later that day, Caffey announced in Algiers that Chabeuil had at last
been bombed – but it turned out to be misinformation. Muddled signals
had led Algiers to confuse the German bombing of the Vercors from

Chabeuil the previous day with an attack of their own on the German airfield.

Meanwhile that day at Caserta, north of Naples, Maitland Wilson held a meeting with Ira Eaker, the Commander-in-Chief of the Mediterranean Allied Air Forces, to consider Caïman. The French were deliberately not invited. But Pierre Billotte, nominated by de Gaulle to lead the operation, somehow got to hear of the gathering, flew to Naples in a specially requisitioned French plane and burst unannounced into the middle of the discussions.

Billotte immediately launched into a blistering attack, accusing the Allies of having 'taken no account of the huge and growing possibilities currently offered by the French Resistance. In the face of German atrocities, it is not only the Resistance, but the whole population of [the Massif Central area] who burn with impatience to rise against their occupiers. All the authority of General de Gaulle has been needed to contain their actions to that of sabotage and harassment of the Germans, in conjunction with the promise that they will, at a set time and with the necessary support, free themselves, thus giving the most efficient and timely assistance to Allied operations. If this backing is not given to them they will feel deeply deceived, and will rise anyway, resulting almost certainly in massacre, disorder and squandered operational opportunities. To misunderstand this situation is to provoke just such a dramatic outcome. I do not envy the person who ends up taking responsibility for this.'

Despite Billotte's outburst Maitland Wilson wrote to de Gaulle rejecting Caïman the following day: 'I have carefully considered Operation "C" [Caïman] … In the first place practically all the troops which you propose to use for this operation have already been allotted to Anvil … for this reason I should find it difficult to justify a recommendation to the Chiefs of Staff that troops … considered essential to Anvil … should be … allotted to another operation.'

Allied tensions were, however, by no means just between the French on the one side and the British and Americans on the other. Koenig wrote to Bedell Smith earlier in the day complaining that it had been 'impossible up to now to exercise my actual command effectively because I don't have either the resources or the means to do this under my control'. But this did not stop him once again seeking to exercise his authority over the Vercors, sending another signal that day to Gabriel Cochet in Algiers: 'General Koenig reminds you that the Vercors is a part of the Northern Zone. All orders for the Vercors must be sent from General Koenig.' The instruction was so patently ridiculous that it was, again, simply ignored in Algiers.

While the Allies were busy squabbling, the Germans were progressively tightening their grip on the plateau. The Bastille Day bombings had marked a significant shift in German activity on the Vercors. Their fighters were now constantly present in the skies over the plateau, machine-gunning targets wherever they saw them. German records show that the Luftwaffe's anti-partisan unit flew fifteen sorties on this day – most of them directed at La Chapelle, which was almost as heavily bombed and badly damaged on 15 July as Vassieux had been the day before.

Resistance sources reported a new German battalion moving into Saint-Nizier where work was in progress strengthening and expanding the trench system protecting the town. The Germans were, in fact, active all around the plateau. Pflaum's forward divisional headquarters was being established at the village of Seyssins, at the foot of the Charvet ridge, beneath Saint-Nizier. To the north, the Engins tunnel was blown, denying access from Sassenage at the north-west corner of the plateau. On the western flank of the plateau, bridges on several small roads were destroyed, most notably east of Pont-en-Royans. In Grenoble, road-blocks were reinforced, and there were reports of the impending arrival of Alpine troops and artillery.

The leaders of the Organisation Vercors were also not idle on this Sunday. At dawn, a convoy of Resistance lorries filed into Villard-de-Lans to round up all the young men who had not yet joined up. Yves Farge was there directing operations, as was Jean Prévost, whose men carried out armed house searches for those who tried to hide. Many parents pleaded for their sons to be spared the call-up, especially in view of the need to bring in the harvest. But the pleas were in vain. When the convoy left the town, it contained about 150 of Villard's youth for immediate conscription into Huet's forces. Among them were twenty-eight Poles, including twelve students from the Villard Polish school and five of their teachers, nearly all of whom were sent to join the workforce on Tournissa's strip at Vassieux.

As dawn broke on 16 July, a small group of heavily armed Maquisards suddenly appeared in the little town of Saint-Marcellin, under the western flank of the plateau. Having cut all telephone lines to the village, they swiftly laid siege to the local Gendarmerie, where 'coincidentally' all the Gendarmes had been gathered together the previous night to deal with an 'alert'. The Maquis raiders demanded that all the Gendarmes come out with their hands up and drove the 'captured' men off to the plateau under armed guard. In fact, the whole 'battle' was a carefully arranged piece of theatre, right down to smears of animal blood to suggest to the Germans that a fierce battle had taken place so, it was hoped, protecting their families from reprisals.

The following morning, Franz Schwehr received his movement orders for Operation Vercors. His two Gebirgsjäger battalions were to march south to their start positions under the eastern wall of the plateau, while his mountain artillery were to travel by train. The German movements were closely tracked by the Resistance intelligence service, who reported three columns of around a hundred cavalry, two Alpine battalions and a dozen artillery pieces moving south towards Grenoble.

As Schwehr's men marched towards Grenoble, covered heavy lorries were making their way to Lyon-Bron airport by back roads, hoping not to be observed by French watchers. Each carried one of the small German assault gliders. Meanwhile, under cover of darkness, more covered lorries were making their way from Lyon to Chabeuil carrying more assault gliders and a number of heavy resupply gliders.

The next day, 18 July, three trainloads of German Alpine soldiers were spotted by Resistance watchers embarking on trains at Goncellin at the head of the Grésivaudan valley. Other reports detailed a column of Alpine troops arriving at the Pont-de-Claix in the southern outskirts of Grenoble, a battalion headquarters settling into some old barracks at Eybens, another HQ in temporary residence at Échirolles in the same area and concentrations of armoured vehicles at La Paillasse on the banks of the Drôme, 40 kilometres west of the Vercors. During that day the first of the German glider transporters also started arriving at Lyon-Bron airport, where 'the glider leaders were briefed about the operation [on the Vercors] and the details of the terrain with the help of aerial photographs'.

Meanwhile, in Algiers, the daily Situation Report included a message from the Eucalyptus Mission on the Vercors: 'Enemy now firmly entrenched north of [Villard-de-]Lans. 2nd line south of St. Nizier which is being prepared as base for action against the Vercors.'

That evening, Huet and Pierre Tanant met in the Villa Bellon for their usual conference to sum up the day's events. Tanant told his chief that he could feel the battle coming and 'it would be a very tough one'. Huet replied, 'I think we will be all right so long as the Germans don't land airborne troops right in the middle of the plateau.'

The morning of 19 July broke under a clear blue sky, with a slight mist lying in the valleys – a welcome relief after the last few days of unsettled weather and rain on the plateau.

In Algiers, one of Eisenhower's senior advisers, Lieutenant Colonel Robert Alms, who had been sent to the North African capital to help deal with the Caïman issue, signalled the Supreme Commander: 'Arrived Algiers Tue 11 July … Wilson regards plan Caiman as of NO assistance to Anvil operations. He is seeing de Gaulle tomorrow … to point out again that Caiman is not a feasible operation to carry out at the present time … Wilson is considering dropping 1 or 2 French airborne battalions in the Vercors area … Decision will have to wait until after the conversation with de Gaulle. On the Billotte question … the scope of the operation would be such as to require the appointment of a more senior and experienced officer than Billotte.'

At 09.45 the same day, Pierre Dalloz arrived at the Algiers French headquarters for a meeting with Jean Constans. The night before, at Constans' request, Dalloz had left him a bundle of reports on the Vercors calling for urgent action. Given his previous attempts to get his views noticed in both London and Algiers, Dalloz was, to say the least, surprised to be told by Constans: 'From your reports I have come to understand things which had previously been unclear to me. What a pity you didn't arrive here three months ago. Things might have taken a different turn.' Dalloz, not knowing what a bad turn things actually had taken on the plateau, left for Oran to finish his translation of the *Treatise* of St Bernard, believing that, at last, his warnings were getting through. On his way out of Algiers, he noticed how many French parachutists could be seen idling through the city's souks and took this to be a good sign.

During this day, Pflaum's four assault columns received their orders for Operation Vercors. The objective Pflaum gave to each of his commanders was to break through as fast as possible in order to relieve Schäfer's airborne troops with the minimum of delay. Each set of orders was accompanied by a detailed map showing the positions of Huet's troops, including headquarters, observation posts and main defensive lines. In one key point, however, German intelligence were wrong – they believed Huet's headquarters were in either Vassieux or La Chapelle, not in Saint-Martin.

On the plateau, Huet too was preparing for battle as more information came in pointing to an imminent attack. Desmond Longe, writing in his diary, gives a flavour of the atmosphere in the Villa Bellon as the tension built up: 'Necessary to watch the sky every time you left the building – sometimes dodging from tree to tree to avoid machine-gunning. Enemy patrols in contact with our out-posts. Huet maintaining extraordinary calm … Signs of nervousness among the junior officers – John [Houseman] and I trying hard not to show signs of alarm, even when a German plane passed the dining room window as I was swallowing a spoonful of soup. Martial law proclaimed throughout the Vercors – all units in battle positions. La Chapelle burned out by constant air attack, ambulances making constant journeys … to the hospital with the wounded … We kept our rucksacks packed – all expected an emergency at any moment. The tension is beginning to tell …'

The previous day, at Mens in the south-east corner of the plateau, the Trièves platoon received their orders for action from their commanders. They were to go to the Vercors to help strengthen the defenders on the eastern passes. Having spent the night in a hut in the forests close to Mens, they were told this morning to return home to say their goodbyes and be ready to move up on to the plateau in the afternoon.

In Villard-de-Lans, a rumour flew round that the Germans were about to mount a punitive expedition. The few young men still taking refuge in the town left hurriedly.

That evening the weather changed, leaving the troops of Seeger's northern column to march up from Grenoble to Saint-Nizier in heavy rain. They spent the night under bivouac in the forest around the town.

Other reports reaching Huet from Resistance sources that evening reported mobile artillery on the move from the Lyon area and small units, forty strong, being distributed at regular intervals along the main road from Grenoble through Sassenage and round the northern end of the plateau as far as Romans. There were also some reports about the possibility of an airborne assault. The assumption in the Villa Bellon was that this would be an attack by parachutists on the Saint-Martin valley since that was the administrative and military centre of the Organisation Vercors. Hoppers' men were instructed to move the four 0.5-inch heavy machine guns they had positioned at Vassieux only two days previously into defensive positions around Saint-Martin and to be on stand-by to man these on a twenty-four-hour basis.

Early on the morning of 20 July the Compagnie de Trièves, now fully laden with weapons, ammunition and provisions, started the long ascent from the hamlet of La Richardière up to the plateau where they were to guard the Pas de l'Aiguille, one of the most frequented passes through the eastern wall. It was fortunate that they left early, for not long after their departure, Resistance watchers saw Schwehr's Alpine units starting to occupy the little villages spread along the bottom of the eastern wall.

At about 16.30, Zabel's column, which had, the previous day, begun to fight its way through stiff opposition around the south-western corner of the Vercors, arrived in the centre of Crest having taken the village without combat. Witnesses say that about twenty 'reprisal troops' were let loose. According to one suspiciously over-coloured report, these 'Mongols' were 'Sinister individuals, who had skin the colour of lemon juice, braided pigtails and gold rings in their hair'. They pillaged the houses and violated the women of the village. A more measured account by two local doctors and the village priest (which does not mention 'Mongols' at all) estimates that there were forty cases of rape committed in the village that afternoon, fifteen involving young girls.

Meanwhile, at the south-eastern corner of the Vercors, a 1,500-strong German column coming from the north occupied the Col de Menée, the Col de la Grimone and the Col de la Croix Haute, sealing off that quadrant of the plateau before pushing on to reach the little town of Châtillon-en-Diois before nightfall. The Maquis units in the area did what they could to hold back the advance but found it impossible to cope with the German Alpine troops, who constantly outflanked their positions by using the forest tracks.

At the Villa Bellon this was a day of alarms and final preparations for Huet and his 4,000 Maquisards. In Huet's operations room, the telephone rang incessantly as reports came in from the network of Resistance watchers: the Germans were on the Grenoble–Romans road; they were at Saint-Gervais; at Saint-Romans; at Izeron; at Saint-Quentin; a horse-drawn artillery company had crossed the Drac river; a column of Georgian and Turcoman 'Mongols' had arrived in Valence; Saint-Nazaire had been pillaged; suspicious Morse messages were being sent from somewhere close to Saint-Royans – coloured pins on the wall map in Huet's operations room began to sprout from all corners of the plateau. Some reports from the watchers were especially disturbing. One related the warning given by the German commander who occupied Izeron on the western flank of the plateau: 'No harm will come to the population if you behave correctly. But at the first act of hostility, we will burn the whole village and shoot all its inhabitants. You have been duly warned ...'

Huet spent the day checking and adjusting his troop deployments. He gave the order to be ready to blow up the Pont de la Goule Noire, which had been mined with explosives for days, and instructed his second-in-command René Bousquet to make contact with the Drôme Maquis commander in order to coordinate their actions around the south-western corner of the plateau. Jean Prévost, at his headquarters on the Herbouilly high pasture, also toured his positions. Apart from a small reserve force at Herbouilly made up of Senegalese guards with-drawn from Descour's HQ, he had units deployed as a forward screen in Autrans and Méaudre, while Abel Chabal (promoted to lieutenant after Saint-Nizier) and his men defended the little winding mountain road through Valchevrière, the key point of access to the southern plateau.

Meanwhile, high on the western wall of the plateau, Ferdinand Sallier watched through binoculars as the Germans moved towards Saint-Jean-en-Royans and thought of his dead relative Louis lying in the village cemetery: 'Sleep well my dear Louis, you who fell before the same enemy in 1914. Your sacrifice confirms the sanctity of our cause. Sleep peacefully you heroes of the Great War. Your sons have risen in the mountains to carry on the fight where you left off. And so it is across the whole of France. In the factories they await the signal. From Marseille to Verdun, the French are rising again against the Boches. Sleep well our sacred dead. The enemy will not for much longer desecrate your graves. Very soon we will all suffer and death will come to some of us in the ranks of the Vercors Maquis. But we, who the Vichy traitors called "terrorists", we whom they treated as bandits, will save the honour of our country and our region.'

A hundred and twenty kilometres north of the Vercors, in the southern Jura, Henri Romans-Petit once more ordered his Maquis to disperse into the forests. When the German assault troops reached their objectives, they again found nothing to attack.

Early that evening, 20 July, the fifty-one-year-old retired French Army General Jacques Humbert took a decision at his home in Seyssins, below Saint-Nizier. He had always been strongly opposed to the idea of a redoubt on the Vercors. Now, as he watched the Germans taking up their positions, he knew that the battle for the plateau was imminent and that he must join it: 'An active General cannot stand idly by within a few hours' march, while his comrades are in bloody combat.' He dressed in his hiking clothes, filled a rucksack, kissed his wife goodbye and headed up the mountain to join the fight. He managed to catch the last tram up to Saint-Nizier before it was shut by the Germans and then headed into the forests on the eastern side of the Lans valley, making his way along forest tracks for the southern plateau.

Throughout the day an increasingly frantic to and fro of messages flowed through La Britière, where Robert Bennes' operators and coders, who had worked non-stop for the previous thirty-six hours, were completely exhausted, often falling asleep over their Morse keys. Henri Zeller to Jean Constans in Algiers: 'In view of the clear threat to the Vercors, I repeat my demand for the bombing of Saint-Nizier 7 km west Grenoble. Send a strong force of parachutists. Send money ... keen to return to London or Algiers to brief you on the current situation.' That afternoon a telegram in English from the Vercors arrived at the OSS headquarters in Algiers: 'If you want to save the Vercors, you had better act fast and fulfil our demands in full including the bombing of St. Nizier and Chabeuil.'

Late that afternoon Jean Constans in Algiers sent reassurance: 'All our information indicates the total enemy forces facing you are not more than three regiments. The total German forces deployed between the Rhône and the Isère ... is 10,000 men, repeat 10,000 men ... at present none of our paratroop units will be ready for battle in less than fifteen days ... Requesting sorties for tomorrow on enemy columns north of Lans ... all our information leads us to believe decline German morale.' And then again, later in the evening, he sent what he hoped would be even more encouraging news: 'For Huet. The following will be sent to you starting from the night of July 22–23. 2 French Commando units of 15 men each, including officers and NCOs. 6 bazookas and ammunition. 20 PIATS. Ammunition for the American mortars already dispatched. 15 heavy 0.5 inch machine guns as already sent. 90 light British mortars. Tools and repair kits for arms. Medical equipment. Indicate which ones you can receive and where they should be dropped. Courage!' The problem was that, because of coding and transmission problems in Algiers, Constans' signal, which seems clearly to indicate that Dakota landings on Tournissa's strip at Vassieux would begin in two days, did not reach the Vercors until late the following morning.

That afternoon Huet sent out a carefully drafted final order to his men: 'Soldiers of the Vercors, the time has come for you to show what you are made of. It is the hour of battle. We will fight from our posts. We will engage the enemy wherever he is at all times and, above all, when he least expects it. We will harass him without ceasing … the eyes of the whole country are fixed on us. We have right on our side … the ideal that has motivated us and unites us will enable us to win.'

In the early hours of the morning of 21 July Zeller dispatched a further signal: 'A strong [German] attempt to take the Vercors is about to be launched. Without immediate assistance, the result is uncertain. Request with urgency that a battalion be parachuted and that you send mortars. Also request the immediate bombing of Saint-Nizier and Chabeuil. A simultaneous ground attack is impossible at the moment. Help us by every means you can. Good day!'

Others, too, were sending signals on this evening. In his regular evening report to Berlin, the German Commander in the West, Field Marshal Gerd von Rundstedt, noted: 'Deployment of our forces for the operation to take place in the region of the Vercors complete, evening 20 July', adding, 'The success of this operation, the most important in France against the terrorists, is, up to now, not yet assured.'

On Tournissa's strip outside Vassieux, a young Polish student called Edward Renn was more optimistic: 'The landing site … was by now almost finished … everyone seemed well pleased with the progress we had made. We were all now thinking of the Allied landing which would soon take place on our strip. We young Poles were rather looking forward to it because now we would be able to use our English and that would make us more useful than just being labourers. I even silently revised my last six years' English courses while I worked. When I went to bed that night, I took comfort from the fact that my knowledge of the language would give me a better chance of getting through this.'

Near Algiers, on Blida airfield, the pilots of 624 Squadron RAF were relaxing. Operations for 21 July had been cancelled 'due to continued bad weather in France'. But the German meteorologists had spotted something different in the weather patterns over the Vercors: 'The first cold front that reached Central France yesterday has fully dispersed during the day. The second of the cold fronts moving east from the Atlantic … is expected to weaken as it moves further east. Signed Widenbauer – Central meteorological service group.' The Germans knew what the Allies had not spotted. The next day there would be a brief break in the bad weather over the plateau, beginning a little before dawn and lasting until the early hours of the afternoon.

THE END OF DREAMS:
FRIDAY 21 JULY 1944

Jean Tournissa mopped his brow and packed up his theodolite. It had been a good night's work, despite the torrential downpours which had left everyone soaked to the skin. Another twenty-four hours or so and the airstrip should finally be complete. The old tractor-drawn roller, driven by M. Boiron from the village, could return to agricultural tasks and the 400 workers could be released. There was even talk of a grand parade attended by all the Vercors dignitaries, to mark the end of their labours and the opening of the little airfield.

Nevertheless Tournissa was worried. Over the last few days the daylight hours had never been free of visits from German fighter-bombers attempting to undo the work his labourers had done with sweat and shovels the previous night. And always circling away busily above them were the *mouches* – ever present, ever observant, ever photographing and marking each new cleared patch of earth, gun emplacement, trench and troop position.

Tournissa looked towards the rim of the mountains marking the eastern ramparts of the Vercors and watched for a few moments as they became etched in darker relief against the red glow of an angry dawn. At least the rain had stopped. Looking at his watch, he noted it was a little before 05.00; in an hour or so it would be fully light and the German fighters would be back. Sure enough, and right on time, a few moments after 05.00 the first *mouche* of the day came skimming over a low ridge and let loose several bursts of machine-gun fire, sending most of Tournissa's men scurrying back to the cover of Vassieux. Tournissa himself did not join the others. Instead he walked over to take command of new defensive positions guarding the east of the strip, leaving the command of those to the west, closest to the village, to his colleague Pierre Haezebrouck.

Among those running back to the relative safety of their quarters in a barn close to the Vassieux Mairie was Kazimir Siebeneichen, one of the

Polish students from Villard. He remembered: 'Our work on the strip was nearly finished and our bosses told us that soon we would be able to play our part in defeating the enemy with arms, rather than shovels.'

As dawn turned to morning, Vassieux settled down to another day of German bombing and strafing. Around the perimeter of the airstrip, Haezebrouck's men took up their positions under a sky which, though clear now, was heavy with the possibility of more thunder. In the barns, shelters and houses of the village, the night workers made themselves as comfortable as they could and hoped for a good day's sleep. Someone commented that the German fighters were later than usual that day.

Then, at shortly before 09.00, they heard the low rumble of approaching aircraft to the south. Not the high-pitched whine of fighters – something very different. A few rushed out on to the streets to see a line of distant black dots emerging from the cloud base and descending towards them over the But de Nève on the Vercors' southern rim. They were coming from the same direction as the American bombers which had dropped all those arms on 14 July. Someone shouted 'Les Amerlots!* Les Amerlots!'

But Maquis units in the Drôme forests south of the Vercors knew that these were not the Americans. Twenty minutes earlier at 09.00 they had seen a large number of Dornier bombers lumbering over, their noses tilting awkwardly skywards to counter the drag of the glider each towed behind them. Not having direct contact with the Vercors, an immediate message was sent to Algiers to warn the plateau of the approaching armada. There it joined a queue of signals and was not decoded until two days later.

Friedrich Schäfer had assembled his men beside their assault gliders on the tarmac at Lyon-Bron as a misty dawn broke that morning. His final orders were brief and brutal. One of his men was later to describe them: 'Hit hard and fast, don't wait to find out who's who. He who hesitates is lost.' They would be outnumbered, he explained, so they must shoot on sight and without discriminating between civilians and combatants. Any building which could harbour partisans ('terrorists' he called them) should be burnt without concern for who was inside. The only way to win was speed, shock and total ruthlessness. Once they had secured the area, reinforcements and heavy weapons would be flown in. Their job was to hold the perimeter at all costs until these arrived.

* Slang for 'Americans'.

Then Schäfer loaded his men, ten to a glider, each sitting tightly packed with weapons and equipment, one behind the other on a long metal bench along the centre line of the tiny aircraft. After take-off from Lyon, the Dorniers flew downstream along the Rhône, swinging first east at Orange then north to head for the Vercors plateau.

It cannot have taken long for those in Vassieux to realize that it was not their saviours who were about to descend upon them from the morning sky but their pitiless enemy. Jerzy Delingier, another Pole, was in the middle of peeling potatoes for lunch when he heard the noise of the approaching armada – and knew it for what it was. He remembered the sound of Dornier bombers flying over his parents' house in Lyon. 'It's not Americans!' he shouted to his friends. 'It's the Germans!' Soon black crosses on glinting wings became visible, sending many scurrying for cover and – those who had them (the Polish students were unarmed) – for their weapons. But some just watched, stunned and mesmerized, as, at a height of 2,500 metres and 10 kilometres out from their targets, the first nine gliders detached from their parent aircraft and headed straight for Vassieux. After about six minutes' flight, they split into four groups.

Two gliders headed for an isolated farm called Les Chaux astride the main road a thousand metres east of Vassieux; two more for the hamlet of Le Château positioned at a crossroads 1½ kilometres north-east of the town; a further two gliders flew over Vassieux as they headed for the farmsteads gathered around a small promontory at La Mure, commanding the road from La Chapelle, 2 kilometres to the north. The final three gliders swung off to the west and, skimming over the village roofs, headed for a collection of houses around the hamlet of Josseau, which lay across the road down from the Col de la Chau.

As they began their final run-in to their targets, the gliders, in almost perfect unison like some precision aerial ballet, suddenly tipped down at an angle of 60 degrees, appearing to the watchers to be flying almost vertically at the ground. At a height of 300 metres, small circular khaki-coloured brake parachutes flowered from their tails. And then, very close to the ground now, they levelled out, fired retro rockets from their noses like snorting fiery dragons and landed with astonishing precision in just a handful of metres.

It had taken the cunning little craft only eight minutes to reach their targets since releasing from their parent aircraft. Only eight minutes for a sleepy Vassieux to rush to arms and meet the assault which was now upon them. Even before the gliders had bumped to a halt, their occupants were out, firing and running for the nearest shelter while their pilots gave them covering fire from the machine guns mounted on each aircraft roof. At the same time smoke grenades were dropped from the air to give the assailants extra cover as they sprinted across the open ground.

Within only a few minutes, all the approach roads to Vassieux were cut and Schäfer, who was in the second wave, was able to fly in with his main force of fifteen gliders, landing in and around Vassieux village and astride the airstrip on its south-east edge. By now, the defenders' stunned surprise had turned to furious action. Haezebrouck's machine guns opened up and two gliders were hit, crashing and killing their pilots and seven of Schäfer's men, including the unit medical officer. But the Germans had the momentum – and heavy air support. Now the air was full of Focke-Wulf 190 fighter-bombers roaring overhead, providing close support to Schäfer's furious assault. In a storm of grenades and automatic fire, the German troops soon had full command of the village, but not without significant casualties. One of the earliest of these was the Sipo/SD chief Walter Knab, who took a bullet in the leg.

From the start, the French were on the back foot. Pierre Tanant later described what happened: 'For the most part our men didn't have the time to react and were cut down even before they could mount a defence. Some, however, were magnificent. Victor Vermorel threw himself on a heavy machine gun and fired without stopping for a quarter of an hour, hitting two of the gliders. His shoulder broken by an enemy bullet, he grabbed a sub-machine gun and continued firing until, his ammunition exhausted, he took refuge in an uninhabited farm.'

A young Maquisard, Claude Forget, was at the edge of a wood just outside the immediate battle zone: 'We fired at everything we could see. But the Germans supported their people on the ground with heavy air attacks. It seemed as though a stream of fire was falling unceasingly from the sky. We just couldn't move an inch.'

General Descour's son Jacques perished in the initial assault. His commander, Pierre Haezebrouck, was also killed with eleven others when the counter-attack Haezebrouck launched straight after the landing was stopped by German fire at the edge of the village. Tournissa, who had taken a bullet through his left ear, another which grazed his right temple and a third which shattered his left shin bone, was dragged to a small cave at the edge of the town which had previously been equipped

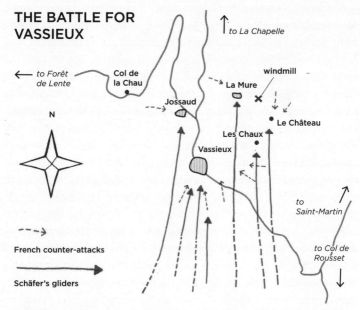

THE BATTLE FOR VASSIEUX

↑ to La Chapelle

← to Forêt de Lente

Col de la Chau

windmill

La Mure

Jossaud

N

Le Château

Les Chaux

Vassieux

to Saint-Martin

to Col de Rousset

- - -→   French counter-attacks

——→   Schäfer's gliders

as a first-aid centre. Six of the Polish students in the barn close to the Mairie were mowed down as they tried to run, as were up to forty of Vassieux's civilian population.

In the assault on La Mure, north of Vassieux, the first two gliders, carrying a twenty-man assault team, landed on fields just below the farm owned by Aimé and Antoinette Algoud, who happened to be visiting Vassieux at the time. The Germans' first target was a nearby farm building in which a group of thirty Maquis of Compagnie Philippe were still asleep, having arrived, singing, the night before at the end of a long march over the mountains from Saint-Agnan. Caught unawares, they were all killed. Then Schäfer's men turned their attention to the civilians living in the two farms situated on the bluff above the main road. All the inhabitants, numbering around a dozen, were rounded up, herded together in an underground cellar and killed with grenades – they included a mother with her eighteen-month-old baby and eighteen-year-old daughter. Then the farms were burnt. That night, the Germans at La Mure took up defensive positions in the shells of the farms they had destroyed and in the ruins of a neighbouring stone-built windmill.

No detailed plan of Schäfer's attack on Vassieux has yet come to light. But with a force, now numbering only around 220, dispersed in small groups so widely spread that they could not provide fire support for each other, it must have been his original intention that the third wave with reinforcements and heavy weapons would fly in to consolidate his position in the course of the day. Given the size of the area enclosed by Schäfer's positions at Vassieux, Jossaud, La Mure, Le Château and Les Chaux, it is tempting to speculate that these were originally intended to act as a perimeter force to protect a landing ground for parachutists who would form the main body of the third wave.* In the afternoon, however, just as predicted by the meteorologists, the weather broke, ushering in another prolonged period of thunder and heavy rain. Without any possibility of support, reinforcement or resupply from the air, Schäfer's force was now heavily outnumbered, dangerously dispersed and highly vulnerable to counter-attack.

As dusk fell Schäfer prepared for a long night. He positioned a machine gun in Vassieux's church tower from where it could command all the approaches to the town and ordered his men to take up interlocking fire positions in the ruined buildings around the edge of the town. Then it was just a case of waiting under the teeming rain for the counter-attacks to start. His report to headquarters at the end of the day listed twenty-two killed and twenty-nine wounded – at 23 per cent, an unusually high casualty rate, even by the standards of an airborne operation.

Elsewhere, the Germans' four-pronged assault on the Vercors was progressing much more smoothly. In the very early hours of the morning of 21 July, having been told of the impending German attack the night before, a 170-strong company of Costa de Beauregard's 'Battalion' were nearing the end of a long night march across the mountains through heavy rain to an ambush position designed to cut off the road from Lans-en-Vercors over the Col de la Croix Perrin to the Autrans valley.

One of them, Gilbert Joseph, later wrote: 'Suddenly we saw below us in the blackness of the Lans valley, between the sheets of rain, an endless ribbon of lights and lanterns winding their way down the valley parallel to us and about four hundred yards away as the crow flies. The thunder alternated with the crash of a distant bombardment as the Germans rained shells on the valley below. The lightning mixed in with the

---

* There are persistent reports (not least from Joseph Picirella and in the post-war French film *Au Coeur de l'Orage*) that parachutists were dropped at Vassieux. These are erroneous – no parachutists were deployed in the German attack.

incandescent illumination shells the Germans fired to light the sky as they marched inexorably closer and closer to our position. Despite the terrible din, this conjunction of natural and artificial elements, each multiplying the effect of the other, only served to deepen the personal silence into which each of us retreated in an attempt to fortify our courage for the battle ahead.'

It was Seeger's column advancing on Villard-de-Lans and the road to the Autrans-Méaudre valley, the first objectives of their northern strike into the plateau. 'We estimated that the enemy troops were passing down the valley from Saint-Nizier at the rate of 500 men an hour,' Gilbert Joseph continued. 'Among them were trains of mules carrying heavy cases of ammunition and dismantled artillery pieces, their harnesses glinting in the early-morning sun. From these we knew that their plan was not just to use the roads but the high passes and the mountain tracks as well.'

The German column split into two just below Gilbert Joseph's position, the larger continuing their march towards Villard-de-Lans, while the smaller one, numbering around 100, swung north-west towards the Maquisard ambush, which they hit at about 08.00.

'The signal for the ambush, a pistol shot, was given,' Gilbert Joseph recounted, 'and we all loosed off one or two magazines from our Sten guns. The firing had only gone on for about a minute when the order was given to pull out. We just had time to look back to see the mules weighed down with their heavy loads standing alone in the middle of the road as their handlers as the rest of the enemy soldiers jumped over a fence and dashed for cover in a neighbouring field. We had scarcely run a few steps up the mountain before the enemy unleashed his response, firing wildly in all directions. Soaked with sweat, our lungs bursting, we jumped from rock to rock and tree to tree, using what natural cover we could as bullets and flying shrapnel cut the branches and leaves from the trees all round us. Then the mortars and heavy machine guns joined in, punctuating the din with the regular chatter of their firing, the clatter of bullets and the crump of explosive all around us. Now there was no hiding. We could only run and hope for the best …'

Having brushed aside the ambush, Seeger's column advanced up the road to the Col de la Croix Perrin, above the Autrans-Méaudre valley. Here they should have been challenged again by Henri Ullman's severely understrength unit. But Ullman decided not to oppose the superior German force and fell back into the dense Forêt des Clapiers, which borders the western side of the Autrans valley. By 17.00 that evening, both Autrans and Méaudre were in German hands.

The second arm of Seeger's column meanwhile pushed on to Villard, to their surprise finding almost no opposition. François Huet's decision not to contest the valley and the town meant that Villard was spared reprisals. At 10.30, a little before the Germans arrived in Villard, Jacques Humbert came down from the ridge above the town to find it completely deserted. Hearing mortar and artillery fire advancing up the valley, Humbert pushed on to Corrençon, where he met up with the members of Prévost's company defending the town.

The Germans too, finding Villard empty, pressed on to Corrençon, which nestles in a bowl surrounded by high mountains and deep forests. Here the Maquis, holding the high ground, put up fierce resistance, which it took Seeger's men six hours to suppress; even after nightfall Maquisard units in the woods were still engaging the Germans in the town. For the moment, this German advance into the plateau was halted. But the entire northern half of the Vercors was now firmly in their hands.

At about the same time as Seeger's forces were entering Corrençon, high above and some 15 kilometres to the south-east a different kind of battle was beginning. During the night of 20/21 July, Schwehr's 1,200-strong column had deployed in four company groups along the south-eastern flank of the Vercors, between the villages of Chichilianne and Gresse-en-Vercors.

Above them, defending the passes, were the 150 men of the Compagnie André, commanded by Lieutenant Louis Kalck. Kalck's task was to defend the six key passes which formed the main corridors through the southern half of the eastern wall of the Vercors rim. From north to south these were the Pas de Berrièves, the Pas de la Ville, the Pas des Chattons, the Pas des Bachassons, the Pas de la Selle and the Pas de l'Aiguille. With so few men, Compagnie André, whose headquarters were in an old shepherd's hut called La Grande Cabane 2½ kilometres back from the main ridge line, could only deploy between ten and twenty lightly armed Maquisards to defend each pass. Given their meagre numbers it is surprising that, again, no proper defensive positions such as trenches or rock-protected firing positions were prepared. Perhaps the Maquisards believed that the steep approaches to the passes so favoured defence that these were unnecessary. It was a misjudgement which would cost them dear.

During the morning and afternoon of 21 July, Schwehr's column swept the lower slopes for Maquis positions which might threaten their unprotected supply lines once the main attack had started. In the process, they burnt some houses which had given shelter to Maquis units in the village of La Bâtie. The sky that day was overcast, but, with a cloud base a little higher than the Vercors peaks, the burning buildings and German activity must have been clearly visible to the Maquisards on the passes 450 metres above them. In the late afternoon, the Gebirgsjäger turned their faces to the mountain and started to climb, their heavy weapons following in a long trail of mules behind them. There is some evidence that they may have had French guides. Two hundred metres below the passes, well out of Sten-gun range, Schwehr's men deployed for battle.

The conflict at the Pas de la Selle was typical of those fought elsewhere along the eastern rim of the Vercors that late afternoon. This pass was the objective of a Gebirgsjäger company commanded by Leutnant Stefan Ritter. Shortly before Ritter's men reached the summit, the French defenders began to pour a withering fire on them from above, pinning down the two forward German platoons and preventing the third platoon from moving forward. Ritter's men waited for an hour or so while their mortars and heavy machine guns were brought up and then, under a barrage of well-placed fire, forced the Maquisard defenders to retreat. The Germans occupied the Pas de la Selle at 21.15 that evening. The company's diarist recorded: 'At the top of the pass, the company took up a position of all-round defence, made camp and spent a fairly cold and rainy night. Torrential rain beat down incessantly. The medics were ordered to take our wounded down into the valley, helped by a group of pioneers, a few radio operators and some French civilians – there were not enough helpers to carry the 5 wounded on improvised stretchers. It was very difficult for them – it was pitch-dark, the rain was beating down and no one really knew the way. After a descent of seven hours the column with our wounded comrades finally arrived safely at the Regimental First Aid Post.' Overall, Ritter's losses in this operation – one killed and six wounded – were extraordinarily light, given that he was attacking uphill against an enemy in established positions.

The two neighbouring passes to the north of the Pas de la Selle – the Pas des Chattons and the Pas des Bachassons – also fell that night. The Germans had broken through the centre of Compagnie André's line. However, despite heavy use of mountain artillery and machine guns, the

BATTLE OF THE PASSES

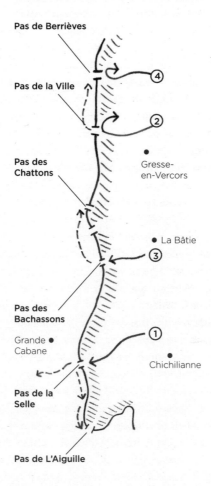

Pas de Berrièves

Pas de la Ville

④

②

Pas des
Chattons

● Gresse-
en-Vercors

● La Bâtie

③

Pas des
Bachassons

Grande ●
Cabane

①

● Chichilianne

Pas de la
Selle

Pas de L'Aiguille

① 3 Kompanie, Reserve Gebirgsjäger
Batallion 1/98

② 1 Kompanie, Reserve Gebirgsjäger
Batallion 1/98

③ 7 Kompanie, Reserve Gebirgsjäger
Batallion 11/98

④ 8 Kompanie, Reserve Gebirgsjäger
Batallion 11/98

two most northerly passes, the Pas de Berrièves and the Pas de la Ville, held out till nightfall, forcing the Germans to spend an uncomfortable night out on the exposed slopes of the mountain in the teeming rain.

Further to the south at the Pas de l'Aiguille the Trièves Maquisards had time to settle into their new position, making use of two nearby caves to store their food and ammunition. Although they could hear fighting to the north and see German planes attacking shepherds' cabins on the deserted plateau, they had no clear idea of what was happening.

Despite the minor setbacks, German commanders must have felt well pleased with Schwehr's achievements during the day. Thanks to superior training and the extensive use of heavy weapons, they had broken through the centre of the French line of defence and could now circle round and cut off the remaining passes from the rear. And all this at a total cost of just two killed and seventeen wounded.

Meanwhile, south-west of the plateau, Zabel's column, after fierce battles against some determined resistance and much pillaging and burning of houses, finally reached a point within striking distance of Die on the evening of 21 July. The town was hastily abandoned, leaving the wounded to the mercy of the Germans.

By the end of 21 July, the first day of the battle for the Vercors, Pflaum's southern strike into the plateau from Die was ready to be launched. His northern and eastern columns had broken through. And he held, albeit precariously, a key position at Vassieux, right at the heart of the plateau. If Schäfer could hold on till the bad weather cleared, Pflaum could use his possession of Vassieux to block any Allied reinforcement from the air, while he flew in his own forces for a breakout across the plateau.

The French, on the other hand, were reeling from the shock of the German attack. One young Maquisard described the feeling: 'We felt like hunted men. It was a curious sensation, almost hallucinatory, the consciousness that an invisible enemy was all around us, on all sides and all the time. Like a hydra which had us in its tentacles, squeezing us to death slowly and without us being able to do anything. We imagined a "Fritz" behind every tree whenever there was the merest rustling of leaves.'

For Huet, in particular, this day must have been terrible as his plans for the static defence of the plateau collapsed about him. Nevertheless, all reports of his demeanour testify to his calmness, perhaps even resignation. The first news of the German attacks would have reached him around dawn that day, with reports of the progress of Seeger's column down the Lans valley towards Villard and their subsequent breakthrough over the Col de la Croix Perrin into the Autrans valley. Then, in mid-morning, the news from Vassieux came in a brief, broken telephone call to Narcisse Geyer's headquarters in La Rivière: 'Haezebrouck is probably killed and Tournissa is wounded –' Then the line went dead.

Eugène Chavant heard the rumble of aircraft over Vassieux while sipping his morning coffee at his usual table outside the Hôtel Breyton. '*Le Patron*'s first response on hearing the approaching planes', a witness later reported, 'was that, at last, the Allies had honoured the promises given him in Algiers – which he had always believed they would.' But then, when he heard that they were in fact Germans, his usual quiet, stolid demeanour broke down and he 'roared with pain. I had never seen him before in such an emotional state and it was a terrible sight. He pounded the café table with his fist, swearing that he had been betrayed.'

At a few minutes after 11.00, André Pecquet, transmitting from the radio shack at La Britière, sent an urgent flash message to London: 'Under attack from parachutists. We are defending ourselves. Farewell.' At the SOE wireless station at Grendon Hall in Buckinghamshire, Rachel Millard, who had christened Pecquet 'Le Rex' because of his clean Morse technique, was on duty that day: 'I was working. Le Rex was having difficulty getting my messages through because of terrible interference. It was very worrying as we had to change frequency not once but twice and it wasn't until the early afternoon that we finally got through. Then to my great consternation he started to send messages "en clair" … in plain English … I shall never forget the gist of the contents to the effect that 400 enemy paratroops were attacking Vassieux, request to bomb Chabeuil and something about a bridge.'

Soon afterwards, François Huet called La Rivière and asked for Geyer. The conversation, resonant with the mutual tension, even hostility, between the two men, was overheard by the telephone operator at the little exchange at Les Drevets, outside La Chapelle. 'Enemy troops have landed at Vassieux,' said Huet. 'I want you to assemble all the forces you need to surround the enemy and attack.'

'I am aware of the situation, Colonel,' Geyer replied coldly. 'I have already issued the necessary orders.' Huet started to question his junior commander, but Geyer cut him short. 'I repeat, Colonel, it's all in hand.'

Huet, who was perfectly within his rights to discuss the tactics of such a vital attack, backed down. 'Well, I have faith in you, Geyer. Keep me informed.'

It was already clear from the early reports that the intensity of fire coming from Schäfer's men was too heavy to permit a successful counter-attack by the French forces already in Vassieux. They would have to be reinforced. But Geyer's problem was that, with so few men available and so much information coming into his headquarters about attacks developing from all directions, he could not afford to deploy more men to Vassieux than the threat demanded without depleting his resources so much that he could not respond to other attacks. He had to find out the actual enemy strength at Vassieux before deciding on the scale of the counter-attack required. But with Vassieux occupied and all telephone lines down, how was he to get the information he needed?

He gave instructions for messages to be passed to the scattered French units around Vassieux to do all they could to keep the enemy pinned down. Then he telephoned his local commander guarding the Col de Rousset, south of Vassieux, and ordered him to carry out an immediate reconnaissance and report back to him as soon as possible.

During this morning Vernon Hoppers was instructed, probably by Huet, to get his men to Vassieux as quickly as possible. According to Hoppers' subsequent report, at around 15.00 hours he and his men, armed with two Browning light machine guns, two 7.62mm machine guns, three mortars and two bazookas, arrived in Vassieux where they joined up with seventy-five Maquisards, 'most of whom were untrained recruits who had been mobilized just two days previously'. That night, Hoppers set up his base in some farm buildings on a rise a couple of hundred metres west of Vassieux and, just after dark, carried out a reconnaissance for the counter-attacks he planned to launch on Schäfer's positions.

Back in Saint-Martin, Huet's headquarters swarmed with staff taking reports and assessing and reassessing the constantly deteriorating situation. In due course, Huet decided that he should send an emissary to attempt to persuade the Maquis forces in the Oisans range, east of the Vercors, to mount an attack on the German rear in an attempt to draw them off. He explained the situation to Lieutenant Adrien Conus, a former big-game hunter from Chad and late arrival to the Eucalyptus Mission. Conus cheerfully agreed to do what he could and set off with one other officer to Jean Prévost's headquarters at Herbouilly. There, on Huet's instructions, the two men were given guides to take them over the mountains and, they hoped, through the German cordon. It was a desperate throw, but Huet knew he had to do something to wrest back the initiative he had lost that day.

It must have been in the late afternoon that Geyer heard from Louis Kalck that Schwehr's column was now attacking the passes. It was clear that sooner or later they would break through somewhere. Geyer had to keep enough reserves uncommitted to plug the gap when this happened. Kalck, now aware of the Vassieux landings, reported, 'There's a strange lull in the fighting.' This was almost certainly the hour's lull below the Pas de la Selle while the Germans brought up their heavy weapons. 'Do you think they are planning an airborne operation near the Grande Cabane?' Geyer agreed it was possible and added, 'I'll try to get some men to you. Keep alert for paratroops. Hold the passes at all costs. Even if you are forced to withdraw, stay in close contact with the enemy and counterattack when you can.'

Geyer telephoned his commander in the western sector of the plateau, where, so far, things had been quiet, and ordered him to send men to reinforce the Compagnie André on the passes. But it would take them hours to get there. Geyer's task, as the tactical commander responsible for most of the southern half of the plateau, was not made easier that day because Kalck's reports on the situation on the passes were much more positive than they should have been. As night fell, Kalck reported to Geyer that all passes were still in French hands, when in fact the three key centre ones had already fallen to the Germans.

Meanwhile, news was coming in to Huet's headquarters that German forces were encircling the plateau in the south-east and another German attack was developing from the north-west, close to the recently destroyed village of Malleval. When Geyer tried to speak to the commander in Malleval, he was too busy fighting to answer the telephone.

Towards evening, the report on the reconnaissance Geyer had ordered on Vassieux was phoned through to his La Rivière headquarters. The German forces were not strong and were deployed in four scattered positions ringed round the plain to the north of the village. But they were well dug in and prepared for a fight. Geyer concluded that they could be dislodged if he were to mount three simultaneous counter-attacks under cover of darkness. He ordered Maquis forces to move up from Les

Barraques and prepare a counter-attack on La Mure, repositioned a second force to prepare an attack on Jossaud and left Hoppers and his seventy-five raw recruits to attack Vassieux itself.

He might have been better advised to concentrate all his forces on Vassieux, for, if that fell, the other pockets could be individually cleaned up later. Schäfer's position that night was very vulnerable, with his severely outnumbered forces so widely dispersed that they could not support each other. He had suffered heavy casualties and had many wounded to care for. Sitting in the dark, in the pouring rain, he would doubtless have been much reassured if he had known that Geyer was not intending to capitalize on the Germans' weakness, but to replicate it by dividing the French forces too.

At 21.15 that night, Geyer's men and Hoppers' commandos attempted the first counter-attack against Schäfer's positions at Vassieux. It seems to have been a rather half-hearted affair, which was brought to an end when Hoppers called a halt to the attack without, according to one record, 'having himself taken much part in the action'.

At 22.00, Huet called an urgent meeting of all the Vercors leaders at the Villa Bellon. Present were Henri Zeller, Francis Cammaerts, André Vincent-Beaume, Eugène Chavant, Desmond Longe, John Houseman, Pierre Tanant and Huet's second-in-command, René Bousquet. As the rain beat down incessantly, Huet, chain-smoking as always and haggard from loss of sleep, but nevertheless calm and rational, opened the discussion. 'Gentlemen, we must face the facts. Short of a miracle our lines will break – perhaps tomorrow, maybe the day after … In my opinion, we have only one course of action: to disperse in small groups into the forests, from where we can attempt to break out of the Vercors and continue the fight in the neighbouring mountains.' Huet finished his opening words with one of his characteristic gestures, a wave of the hand and a fatalistic shrug of the shoulders. 'We may die, of course. But we shall die with our weapons in our hands.'

René Bousquet was the first to respond. He was opposed – and angry. 'Don't you think we have had enough of these nonsenses? All these head-quarters we have created as though we were organized as a classic division? It has been a monstrous mistake. There is only one solution. Evacuate the Vercors – break out as an organized fighting force. The way is still open east of Die. I was there myself this morning. [Pierre] Raynaud has plenty of men and will keep the exit open for us at all costs.'

Chavant agreed with Bousquet – an organized breakout was the only answer. Bousquet then proposed another possible option. Perhaps they could organize the breakout through Villard-de-Lans where they would not be expected? Henri Zeller intervened supporting Bousquet's latest proposal.

Huet turned to him: 'If that's your opinion, why don't you take command of the Vercors yourself?'

Zeller backed off. 'You know very well that I have other responsibilities to fulfil elsewhere in the region.'

Cammaerts spoke, agreeing with Huet. The French knew the forests and the secret paths. The Germans disliked being off the main roads. In the forests they could be safe and slip out of the German ring when it became possible to do so.

Huet pointed out the impracticality of disengaging his force while they were in contact with the enemy and forming them into an organized column to break out. Without wirelesses it was impossible. Besides, the enemy would never give them the time or space to reorganize into columns; and even if Huet's men could manage this, they would only be creating better targets for the German fighter-bombers. Conscious that his force was the only thing which stood between the civil population and the terrible reprisals which would ensue when the fighting was over, Huet added, with some emotion: 'I have accepted the responsibility to defend the Vercors and defend it I will. If they must kill me they will kill me.'

There followed a brief discussion about holding on to the last man, but this was soon dismissed as futile. Finally, as the fug of cigarette smoke in the room thickened, an agreement of sorts was hammered out. They would fight on in all sectors for as long as they could, but when defeat was inevitable, Huet would give the order to disperse and everyone would head for the forests in small parties and wait for the Germans to pull out. Someone said that they never normally stayed longer than three days after these operations.

As the meeting closed, Bousquet turned to Huet: 'I have put forward my proposal. But it has not prevailed. I regret that. But that's the way things are. You're the boss. I am with you.'

Three supplementary decisions were taken that night after the Villa Bellon meeting. Zeller and Cammaerts, accompanied by Christine Granville, would leave the plateau in the early hours of the morning so that Zeller could continue to coordinate his Resistance units in other parts of the region. The prisoners in Loscence would be released at the same time as Huet gave the order for the final dispersal. And the wounded in Ganimède's hospital would be immediately taken down to the Catholic hospital in Die that night, before the Germans closed the circle.

After the meeting, private preparations began for a fast withdrawal when the moment came. Longe and Houseman packed their kit and André Pecquet began to collect together his heavy wireless equipment with a view to moving it in the morning. At La Britière, Bob Bennes installed a system of all-round defence.

After the meeting Chavant dictated an angry message for Pecquet to send to Algiers: 'La Chapelle, Vassieux, Saint-Martin bombed by German aircraft. Enemy troops parachuted on to Vassieux. Request immediate bombardment. We had promised that we would hold on for three weeks. The time which has passed since we established our organization is now six weeks. We need urgent resupply of men, food and matériel. Morale of the population excellent. But it will quickly turn against you if you do not fulfil these needs immediately. We would then agree with them that, in London and Algiers, you have no idea of the situation in which we are placed and are therefore to be considered criminals and cowards. We repeat criminals and cowards.'

Later that evening, Huet, standing at the window of the Villa Bellon and looking out into the inky blackness of the night as driving rain beat against the windowpanes, said to Pierre Tanant: 'You know, Pierre, we are launched on a great – a very great – enterprise. I've always believed that no more than one out of ten of us will get out of this alive. Nevertheless it is our duty to follow our orders.'

FIGHTING ON:
SATURDAY 22 JULY 1944

There were few on the Vercors who got any sleep on the night of 21/22 July 1944. It was especially dark and the rain fell incessantly all through the hours of darkness. Shortly after nightfall on the previous evening, the Maquis units above Corrençon were ordered to pull back behind the perimeter of the southern plateau.

Jacques Humbert went with them: 'Marching in silence and soaked to the skin, we stumbled through the darkness along the rocky forest path over the Pas de la Sambue. A little after midnight, as we descended down the other side, we bumped into a small party coming in the opposite direction. By the light of a torch, I recognized Jean Prévost leading two [sic] men from an inter-Allied Mission.* He was accompanied by a man dressed in a white windcheater jacket who carried an ice-axe ... Not long afterwards, we slipped and slid down the last grassy slope under torrential rain to arrive at Prévost's headquarters in Herbouilly ... In a large room in the farmhouse lit by flickering acetylene lamps was a collection of officers and soldiers in all sorts of uniforms, their weapons and ammunition piled around them within easy reach. It was quite like a headquarters on the front in the First War. We had a brief meal made from American rations and I was given Jean Prévost's bed to sleep in. Prévost's books were piled on a table near by: "Les Fleurs du Mal", "Les Essais" in "La Pléiade". Once a writer ever a writer.'

Down in the valley at La Rivière, the corridors of Narcisse Geyer's headquarters at Buget farm were filled with runners patiently waiting for orders, their wet clothes steaming in the warm atmosphere. Inside Geyer's operations room the air was thick with cigarette smoke and filled

---

* Almost certainly Conus, accompanied by Léon Jaille (alias Olivier), 'Chief Scout' of the Vercors, and one other, who were on the mission Huet had given them to get help from Maquis outside the plateau.

with the staccato orders and the insistent ringing of telephones. At 01.40, the commander of the engineering unit, which had been part of Huet's headquarters but had now been turned into a twenty-strong impromptu machine-gun section, came to ask for orders. At the same time, one of Geyer's commanders rang in to report that he was leaving Saint-Martin with a platoon of raw recruits and a 25mm cannon to reinforce Vassieux. An hour later, at 02.50, a runner arrived from Louis Kalck's headquarters at La Grande Cabane; he needed a telephone line laid by 06.00 to enable him to communicate directly with Geyer. At 05.00 news reached Buget farm that German columns were closing in on Die from both east and west. An hour later, a report came in from one of the labourers on Tournissa's landing strip who had managed to escape the German assault: the Germans had shot everyone they found in the village; both Vassieux and La Chapelle were being bombed by German aircraft and were in flames.

A few kilometres away, at the hospital in Saint-Martin, Fernand Ganimède, his two fellow doctors Ullmann and Fischer and eight nurses, spent the last hours of 21 July preparing the wounded for the long, jolting journey down from the plateau to the seventeenth-century Catholic hospital in Die, where the nursing Mother Superior had been warned of their probable arrival the previous afternoon. The wounded who were fit enough to walk were released back to their units, while Ganimède loaded up the remainder for the journey to Die. Dr Fischer went to collect the more seriously wounded from the newly set up auxiliary hospital at Tourtres. He was to follow Ganimède down the mountain later. But what was to be done with three wounded Wehrmacht soldiers who were also being cared for in Saint-Martin? Huet worried that, if they were sent to Die, they might divulge to the Germans the information they had gathered while on the plateau. So it was decided that the enemy wounded would be kept in Saint-Martin and released when Huet gave the order to disperse.

At 04.00 the first little convoy left Saint-Martin. It consisted of Ganimède leading in a car, followed by buses for the wounded and a lorry carrying medical equipment and food. As dawn broke on the way down, they were attacked by a German fighter but managed to reach Die largely unscathed. The Mother Superior of the hospital was astonished to see them. The town was in the process of being heavily machine-gunned by German aircraft and their troops were expected any moment.

Die's Maquis defenders had left hours previously. The Mother Superior had already taken steps to hide her wounded and simply could not take more.

Ganimède had no alternative but to reload his wounded and go back up the mountain. He telephoned the guard post at the Col de Rousset and arranged for Dr Fischer's convoy to be stopped. He was to be instructed to go to the village of Rousset where he should wait for Ganimède. On his way back up to the plateau, Ganimède's convoy met the car with Zeller, Cammaerts and Christine Granville travelling in the opposite direction. There was a brief roadside conference before Zeller and his party drove on down the mountain towards Die, while Ganimède and his wounded made their way back up to the Vercors.

Not long after this chance encounter, Zeller, Cammaerts and Christine Granville abandoned their car at the side of the road and completed their journey on foot. 'Trying to make no noise, we stumbled down through the undergrowth,' Cammaerts later said. 'It was not easy because it was very steep and we had heavy gear, radios and all our personal equipment.' Eventually the little party reached the main road just west of Die where they slipped passed the German cordon and made their way south to join up with the Drôme Maquis.

When Ganimède met Fischer at Rousset, the two men decided that they should propose to Huet that the best place to hide the wounded was in the Grotte de la Luire, a large open-mouthed cave screened by woods 4 kilometres outside the village of Rousset on the Saint-Agnan road. A little time later, Huet paid Ganimède a visit and agreed that, although conditions were rough, the cave, which had its own water supply, was well hidden and would be suitable as a temporary field hospital.

It took Ganimède and his team most of the next day and some of the following evening to carry the wounded and all the medical equipment and supplies over the rough path through the woods to the cave. In the evening a Red Cross flag was laid out in front of the cavern entrance so that it would be the first thing which would be seen if they were discovered. Huet decided that the three enemy wounded could join Ganimède and his team in the cave, which now housed, including medical staff and stretcher bearers, 116 people. Huet, worried that Ganimède would not have enough food, also arranged for extra supplies from the store houses at Saint-Martin.

One of the nurses, Maud Romana, described what it was like to move the wounded along the rough forest path that day: 'We began to transport the wounded during the night and in total silence. When I look back I am amazed at the efforts we made. My companions and I stumbled at almost every step, pushing and pulling until we eventually succeeded. I remember especially the incredible courage of the wounded as they held back their cries, despite the terrible pain. In the end we got everything into the cave: the patients, the medical supplies and instruments and all the food. We laid our worst wounded on their stretchers on the rocks. For the rest we had to move the stones on the floor to make spaces for them to lie on the ground as comfortably as possible, trying to avoid the drips which fell constantly from the roof above. We maintained total silence day and night so that we weren't heard outside. Somehow [we] were able to look after our wounded as well as humanly possible. Their bandages were changed every day and everything was done in the best manner possible – all the time hoping that somehow, in the end, we would be able to win through.'

At Vassieux at 03.00 that morning, Hoppers' men, now reinforced by the newly arrived recruits sent by Geyer, who had arrived with their 25mm gun half an hour earlier, started to move forward for their second counter-attack against Schäfer's diminished and rain-sodden force, dug in among the ruins of the village. The attack started well enough, but petered out at the edge of the village where, in Hoppers' words, 'we were driven off by automatic weapons in position on the outer perimeter of the town and were forced to withdraw by German aircraft which arrived as soon as it was light enough to see. All during the day we were bombed and strafed by the planes but managed to keep the Germans' heads down enough for the survivors amongst the civilian population to escape towards St Martin.'*

Holed up in the ruins of Vassieux and La Mure, these were difficult hours for Schäfer's men too. Surrounded by superior forces, constantly under fire from higher ground, they had no way to evacuate their wounded and little shelter from the incessant rain. Despite this and the appalling weather, a courageous Fieseler Storch pilot managed to carry some wounded from La Mure to Vassieux, where they were placed with the other casualties. A German account for this day, 22 July, reads: 'The

---

* The survivors included Jean Tournissa.

day was marked by further attacks of Resistance fighters who had received more reinforcements during the night. However, heavy rain and low cloud prevented support from the air, including resupply.'

At Saint-Martin, the Villa Bellon started to empty in the early hours of 22 July – despite the fact that Huet had not yet given the order to disperse. Not long after midnight, instructions were issued to close down La Britière and hide the radios installed there. André Pecquet arranged for his radios to be taken to a cave – 'little more than a rabbit hole and running with water' – at Le Briac above Saint-Martin.

Before he left that morning, Henri Zeller ordered Bob Bennes to accompany him off the plateau and act as his wireless operator. Bennes refused and, insisting that his place was on the Vercors, asked Huet what he could do to help, now that he no longer had a radio. Huet ordered him to take charge of the units at the Forestry Cabin at Pré Grandu, the main gateway from the Saint-Martin valley to the eastern plateau.

During the following hours, Huet stripped his headquarters of all unnecessary officers and troops, forming them into a 'commando' and sending them up to the woods behind the hamlet of Les Michalons east of Saint-Martin. Here they were to act as a counter-attack force if the Germans attempted a parachute assault on Saint-Martin. This newly formed Commando, numbering around twenty, left the Villa Bellon at 07.00. Passing the Eucalyptus Mission's base in Saint-Martin school on their way out of the village, Gustave Boissière, English-speaker, speleologist and the Eucalyptus Mission's interpreter and liaison officer, halted the column while he called in to see Houseman and Longe; did they want to join the Commando and leave as well? The two Englishmen, who had packed their kit ready for quick flight hours earlier, said they did.

Although there were perfectly sound tactical reasons for Huet to strip down his headquarters in order to form a unit that he could use as a counter-attack force, there may have been more to his decision than meets the eye. General Jacques Humbert finally arrived at Huet's headquarters at 09.00 that morning. After breakfast, Huet briefed him on the situation, telling the General, among other things, that the German attack had caused something close to panic in his headquarters the previous evening: 'the mood of depression had been so profound that he had felt it right to allow those who wished to leave to do so'. After the war, Longe and Houseman were to be severely criticized for abandoning Huet at this crucial moment.

High above Saint-Martin, dawn broke misty and damp on the passes of the eastern wall. The night had been cold enough to produce a light dusting of snow on the Grand Veymont and around the Pas de la Ville, which was still in French hands. Having broken through the French line the night before, however, the Germans were now able to make use of the high ground to attack the defenders from above and sweep round to cut them off from the rear. At 09.30, Geyer received a phone message from Kalck reporting that one of the defenders on the Pas de la Ville had been wounded by a German attack mounted from the summit of the Grand Veymont. At the Pas de la Balme, on the northern end of the line of passes, a small Maquis group drafted in from Romans were fighting to drive off a frontal assault from the valley, when they were suddenly attacked from the rear by a group of Schwehr's men who had circled round behind them. They were all killed.

From about 10.30 onwards the precise chronology of the battle for the passes becomes confused. What is clear, however, is that by the early evening of this day all the passes had, with a single exception, been cleared of French defenders. Stefan Ritter's company diarist takes up the story of the final mopping up of the French positions: 'When the fog lifted on the morning of the 22/7, our observation posts noticed that terrorists were going in and coming out of a cabin 3km south of the Pas de la Selle (La Grande Cabane). 25 terrorists were counted. Lt Ritter received the order to attack the terrorist nest with 2 mountain infantry platoons … and some heavy weapons. The other platoon of our company was positioned on the right, with the order to bypass the cabin in a wide sweep to prevent the terrorists from escaping to the south. One platoon, the grenade launcher unit, the heavy machine group and the company leader and his headquarters advanced along the ridge towards the cabin. Enemy observers appeared to have noticed our intentions, because the terrorists tried to escape individually in a south-easterly direction in order to reach the woods. But our marksmen made their lives difficult. When the area was secured, the task force advanced to the cabin. But it was empty.'

Comparing the French and German reports of this battle, two points are clear.

Conditions for the young French Maquisards on the passes may have been a factor in the fall of the passes. There are several entries in Geyer's unit log recording complaints from the defenders that they had neither shelter nor, in some cases, adequate supplies of food. The French detachments on the passes were, moreover, small, isolated, under-armed and led chiefly by inexperienced junior officers, and had not, in the main, made any serious attempts to strengthen their positions with rocks or protected fire positions.

In spite of all this, however, there is no doubt that some of the French defenders fought with great tenacity and courage, despite their lack of experience and the inadequacy of their weapons. Thanks to these stout hearts, Schwehr's troops had to spend more time securing the eastern wall than they had planned and were, in consequence, delayed in their central aim of pushing as fast as possible across the eastern plateau to relieve Schäfer in Vassieux.

The single exception to the German clean sweep of the passes on 22 July was the Pas de l'Aiguille at the southern end of the eastern wall. This pass was originally to be defended by the whole Compagnie de Trièves, who spent a quiet day on 21 July, bringing food and ammunition up from the valley – though they could hear the sound of gunfire from the passes to their north and knew that it was only a matter of time before the battle reached them. During the morning of 22 July, the group was split in three. Two parties were sent to support a planned counter-attack to recover the Pas des Chattons and the Pas de la Selle, leaving only some twenty-five men from the Mens platoon to defend the Pas de l'Aiguille under the command of Lieutenant Paul Blanc.

The layout of the Pas de l'Aiguille consists of a gateway through the pass that is some 250 metres wide. In the middle of this sits a grassy hump dominating the pathway from the valley. This was, at the time, crowned by a wooden sheep pen. A few metres further into the pass, on the northern side, there is a substantial shepherd's hut, above which are two caves that overlook the main path up from the valley. Paul Blanc's men used the larger cave, which consists of a broad entrance leading to a deep cleft in the rocks, to store their food and spare ammunition. Seventy metres away to the east lies the second, smaller cavern, whose opening is difficult to see from a distance. This cave opens out from a narrow mouth just big enough for two men to scramble through to an interior which is some 3 metres deep, 5 wide, and, at its highest point, big enough for a man to stand up in. The front lip of the cave mouth is in the form of a natural rock parapet providing a near-perfect protected firing position overlooking the main track below.

Even with so few men, the natural features of the Pas de l'Aiguille provided Paul Blanc with a strong defensive position from which to deal with an attack from the valley, but a very vulnerable one in the case of an assault from the high ground to the north of the pass. Apart from an occasional runner bringing rather muddled messages of the progress of the battles on the passes to the north, the morning and early afternoon of 22 July were quiet. Then suddenly, at 16.00, Blanc's sentry on the high ground to the north of the pass fired a long burst on his machine gun – the agreed signal that the Germans were approaching.

We have two accounts of what happened next: one from the French and one from the Germans. According to the French account, there was a rush of action as the Germans came down from the high ground firing at anything that moved. The local shepherd, accompanied by his dog, was tending to his flock of sheep on the grassy hump. He started to run but was almost immediately cut down in a hail of fire. As he lay bleeding on the grass, his dog howling over his master's body, Blanc's men grabbed what they could and dashed for the protection of the little cave. Twenty-three of them made it, cramming themselves into the tiny space with their weapons and rucksacks. But one, Blanc's second-in-command, Martial Kaufmann, was killed as he ran from the large cave. The valley flooded with German soldiers who unleashed a torrent of fire at the mouth of the little cave. After a few minutes, there was a lull and an officer walked forward calling on the Maquisards to surrender. He was met with a hail of fire and grenades. The Germans scattered, some twenty of them falling under the fire. Over the next hours until nightfall, the Germans threw everything they could at the Maquisards, but without success. Although they made several attempts to hurl hand grenades into the cave mouth, Blanc's men managed to prevent them from getting close enough to succeed. By nightfall the little cave was still in French hands and the Germans were still unable either to kill them or persuade them to leave. The Maquisards settled down to a terrible night, never knowing when the next attack would be unleashed, or when a grenade would suddenly fly through the entrance and fall among them, huddled together in the inky blackness.

The German version of what happened was written up later by Ritter's company diarist: 'When we climbed down the mountain, we were suddenly under fire from a large rock hole approx. 200m north of the cabin. After a request to leave the cave immediately, a terrorist came out with raised hands. After that the company approached the cave led by the company leader. Nobody believed that there was any more danger. However, just above the large cave a small hole in the rock was discovered and, at the same time, we came under fire from machine guns and hand grenades. As our men were on the downward slope, there was nothing they could do but find cover. The leader and some of his men were wounded. The men were forced to remain here until nightfall. We were ordered to stay behind to prevent the terrorists escaping from the cave. The ... wounded were transported after dark to the Pas de la Selle in a three-hour march ... On this day, our comrade Gustl Steube was killed in action. As nearly always, he had been near the Company Commander as a runner.'

Although the defenders of the Pas de l'Aiguille had not yet been fully suppressed, the battle for the eastern passes was now effectively over, leaving the bulk of Schäfer's men free to push on foot across the eastern plateau, heading for Vassieux. In all, the battle had cost the Germans ten killed and thirty-one wounded. The French had lost between forty and fifty killed – there were no French wounded as they, together with any prisoners, were summarily shot by Schwehr's men.

Ten kilometres to the south of the Pas de l'Aiguille, off the southern edge of the plateau, German forces were now closing in on Die from both sides. Not long after Ganimède had left Die hospital, Zabel's column rolled into the town. Finding the Maquis gone, they searched out as many prisoners as they could find and shot them all before turning north and heading for the Vercors. They should have been held up at the little town of Chamaloc at the foot of the Vercors escarpment, but Pierre Raynaud's Maquis had abandoned their positions, leaving the German column to continue their journey north, unimpeded. Because Schwehr's forces had been held up on the eastern passes, Zabel's force was now most likely to be the first to break through to relieve Schäfer's beleaguered men in Vassieux. Huet's Maquisards quickly recognized the threat and prepared to blow up the tunnel at the top of the Col de Rousset. The interior of the tunnel, however, was stacked full of arms, food and vital ammunition from the mass daylight drop of 14 July. A race ensued between Huet's men trying to empty the tunnel of vital supplies before blowing it up and Zabel's forward elements rushing to get there before this happened. Huet's Maquisards won – just. As the first of Zabel's armoured vehicles turned the last bend before the Col de Rousset, there was a mighty explosion and the whole hillside collapsed over the tunnel entrance. Zabel's column now had no option but to park their vehicles and continue their journey on foot to Vassieux.

Pflaum's northern column, Kampfgruppe Seeger, having been held up by the unexpected tenacity of the Maquis forces above Corrençon, spent most of 22 July in cautious probes. This was the enemy thrust which Huet feared most. If the Germans managed to break through into the Herbouilly valley, it would take them less than an hour to reach the heights above Saint-Martin. Then it would all be over.

Seeger had a choice of two possible corridors for his assault on Prévost's forces guarding the north-eastern corner of Huet's line. He could either put his infantry along the forest paths leading over the Pas de la Sambue. Or he could push a mixed infantry and vehicle column up the winding mountain road from Villard-de-Lans, past Valchevrière and then on to Saint-Martin. He decided that his main force would take the Valchevrière route, while a smaller column on foot would attack the Pas de la Sambue.

Prévost, anticipating that the most likely German attack was along the road, gave the task of defending this area to his best commander and his strongest force. Altogether Lt Abel Chabal, the hero who had saved the day in the first battle of Saint-Nizier, had eighty-two men, many of them raw recruits, with whom to try and stop an assault by Seeger with a force of not fewer than 1,200 fully armed and equipped men. Chabal, thirty-four years old, tall, fit and with a finely chiselled face, was greatly respected by his men for his aggression, even foolhardiness in battle and his refusal to submit, even when the odds against him seemed impossible. But his unit was, as ever, crucially hampered by lack of mortars and heavy machine guns. His men were armed with British No. 4 rifles, Sten guns, British grenades, a few Gammon grenades, some light machine guns and two bazookas.

During 21 and 22 July, Chabal's men did what they could to strengthen the natural defences along the length of the Valchevrière mountain road with roadblocks made from pine trunks and protected by minefields on either side. Chabal paid particular attention to a lookout platform, the Belvedere, positioned by the side of the road 200 metres or so from the ruins of Valchevrière and at the gateway to the final low pass which crosses the ridge above the Herbouilly valley. This position, which is protected from the north by steep slopes leading down to the Gorges de la Bourne, was strengthened with tree trunks and boulders to make it into a strongpoint covering the road from Villard-de-Lans. As a defensive position, the Belvedere has, however, one crucial deficiency. It is completely dominated by a bluff and cliff face which tower over it on the southern side of the road.

At 15.00 on the afternoon of 22 July, Seeger pushed a column up the road. It was intended not as a serious attack but as reconnaissance in force. There was an exchange of fire with Chabal's forward positions, who fell back a little so that the Germans could be engaged by a second, larger Maquisard group behind them.

At Herbouilly, itself now receiving sporadic incoming German mortar fire, Prévost wrote a brief message on a sheet of his notebook, tore it out and gave it to a runner with instructions to take it to Huet: 'Strong attack on Chabal. Three of his posts have had to pull back. I am sending a reserve section forward to support him.' This was followed fifteen minutes later by a second: 'Success at Valchevrière. Chabal has pushed the enemy back and inflicted serious casualties.' It was, of course, premature. The Germans had found out what they wanted to know about the strengths and dispositions of Chabal's forces defending the road. They would return in the morning.

Huet spent the day at the Villa Bellon trying to dispose his forces as best he could to meet the multiple threats which now confronted him. He knew that sooner or later the fatal thrust would come at Valchevrière. But as long as Chabal held, the priority was to make every attempt possible to deal with the situation at Vassieux. They might still stand a chance if they could remove this threat before either the weather cleared enough to bring in reinforcements, or one of Pflaum's column was able to break through to relieve Schäfer.

That morning, Huet called in one of his remaining staff officers, Lieutenant d'Anglejan, and instructed him to go to Vassieux and coordinate another counter-attack, to take place that evening. D'Anglejan's plan was for simultaneous counter-attacks to be launched on Vassieux from several directions at 21.30 that night. The signal to attack was to be given by firing three rounds from the 25mm gun brought up that morning from La Rivière. The gun was duly fired at the appointed hour but, for some reason, perhaps the lashing rain or the constant exchange of fire which went on all night, no one heard the three shots above the din. It was decided to delay the attack until dawn the following morning. Back in Saint-Martin, Huet knew that this would almost certainly be his last throw.

In the late afternoon, André Pecquet left the Villa Bellon and climbed the hill to the cave at Le Briac where his radio equipment was hidden. With some difficulty he managed to extract his small suitcase wireless, strung the aerial between the branches of the beech trees that surround the cave and tapped out a message to London: 'Our link with Algiers is down. Retransmit our messages to Algiers. We need fighter aircraft urgently. Send what you can to Vassieux, which remains in our hands. Our positions on the Col de Rousset have been outflanked by parachutists. We are being heavily attacked from the air across the whole area. Bomb Chabeuil and Saint-Nizier.'

At 12.15 that day Jean Constans walked into Jacques Soustelle's office in Algiers and showed him Eugène Chavant's 'criminals and cowards' telegram of the previous day. Soustelle immediately picked up his telephone and rang Gabriel Cochet, demanding that a French airborne Commando should be sent to the Vercors urgently. But there was disagreement with the proposal in the French Ministry of Defence, so no action was taken that day.

Elsewhere, something close to panic was breaking out in Algiers. At 20.00 Cochet sent a signal to Huet and Zeller: 'We are making the maximum effort to provide the staff and matériel left out on the list you have already sent us. But we are being held back by bad weather. In accordance with a message sent by Pecquet through London, we will parachute this to the Taille-Crayon site unless we hear from you to the contrary. Giving advice to you from here is very difficult. But preserving your men is more important than holding territory ...'

At 21.30 Cochet followed up with a telegram to the headquarters of Mediterranean Allied Air Forces: 'It is absolutely necessary to bomb Chabeuil and Saint-Nizier. Do not attack Vassieux which appears to be still held by French forces. German machine-gun column moving up the Vercors escarpment towards the Col de Rousset. Carry out a daylight reconnaissance to identify positions of friendly forces.'

At the same time he sent the following to Koenig in London: 'Please pass us any information you have on the exact position in the Vercors and on their plans. We are considering an air operation to support them on Sunday evening [that is, the next day] or on Monday during the day. Please send all information you have with maximum urgency.' Koenig responded by return: 'All the information we have has already been passed to [you in Algiers]. Please make your parachute drops at Saint-Martin … as requested in the last telegram from Longe and arrange the maximum direct assistance you can for the Vercors, especially against airfields.'

While London and Algiers did all they could to close the stable door even as the horse was furiously bolting, Gerd von Rundstedt was sending his regular nightly report to the Supreme Command of the Armed Forces in Berlin: 'Southern France: Operation Vercors going to plan. Air-landed own troops, supported by the Luftwaffe, in hard combat against superior enemy in Vassieux and La Mure.' Perhaps aware that Operation Vercors was in fact running behind schedule, he added a last sentence in which there is a hint of surprise at the tenacity of his French opponents: 'Current impression of the enemy: opponent engages in battle.'

34

THE FINAL BATTLES: SUNDAY 23 JULY 1944

At 04.00 on 23 July 1944 Pierre Tanant was rudely woken from a fitful sleep by a large explosion in the garden behind the Villa Bellon. It was a stray German shell meant for Prévost's headquarters which had overshot its target and fallen into the valley below. Looking out of the window he noted that the rain had at last stopped and the first light of morning was just beginning to smudge the eastern ridgeline above a misty valley.

An hour or so later, as dawn was breaking, Hoppers and Bourgeois launched the final French counter-attack on Vassieux. 'At dawn, the time set for the assault, the section started to move forward,' wrote Hoppers in his report; 'some of the Maquis who were to our left started forward also. We were almost into the edge of the village before we realised that there was no-one with the section but six maquis and again we had to retreat to the woods.'

Elsewhere, in the French reports of this action there are hints at demoralization and lack of offensive spirit among the attackers: 'The attack got within 200 metres of the north-west of Vassieux in coordination with the other attack which was mounted from the south and east. Intense fire from the enemy prevented any further progress. The fighting spirit of our men was diminished by their physical state and the fact that they had been under constant enemy air attack and without shelter or food for 48 hours.'

These must have been truly terrible days for the raw young Maquisard recruits engaged in the battle for Vassieux. Few would have handled weapons for more than a few days, fewer still would have experienced the terrors of close-quarter battle and many would probably not have spent more than a tiny handful of nights out of their own beds in their whole short lives. Wet, dejected, hungry, sleepless, under constant air attack and facing an implacable enemy, it is scarcely surprising that their 'fighting spirit' was diminished. In the official SOE history of the Resistance in France there is a brief reference to the summary execution of deserters: 'During the Vercors fighting, certain men who had abandoned their positions were immediately shot.' If these things did happen, it would have been on such days and nights as those faced by Geyer's young recruits desperately trying to recapture the ruins of Vassieux under the teeming rain.

The Germans, meanwhile, lost no time in capitalizing on the good weather, for which they had been praying for two days. At 07.30 they flew in the long-awaited resupply and reinforcements including some heavy weapons and a detachment of Eastern Troops. With the siege of Schäfer's men in Vassieux broken, the Germans could now move on to the offensive under the cover of close air support. Meanwhile Fieseler Storch observer planes began to collect the German wounded from outlying positions, flying them to Tournissa's strip where, later in the day, a Junkers 52 three-engine cargo plane (the German equivalent of the Dakota) was able to land and fly them off the plateau. It was the first sizeable plane to land on Jean Tournissa's painstakingly constructed strip. Among the heavy weapons landed from one of the cargo gliders that morning was a 20mm anti-aircraft gun which was immediately brought into action: 'In an hour this gun destroyed all the key Maquis positions, including a stone house on a slope below the forest to the north, forcing all the French to pull back into the shelter of the trees.'

Hearing of the failure of the dawn counter-attack on Vassieux, Huet ordered his exhausted men back to their base at La Rivière at 11.00 and sent Pierre Tanant by motorbike to the western edge of the plateau where there had been no fighting. His orders were to put together a scratch force and take them to Vassieux where they were to attempt a further counter-attack. It was another desperate throw. And it was too late. By the time Tanant gave the order, the remaining French forces around Vassieux had been neutralized and the Germans were already moving north on La Chapelle and south towards the Col de Rousset to exploit their success.

At Blida airport, near Algiers, 624 Squadron's Halifax bombers again stayed on the ground all day. Air operations 'again had to be cancelled due to continued bad weather in Southern France'.

For Abel Chabal and his men, blocking the Route d'Herbouilly from Villard to Saint-Martin past Valchevrière, the day began with a mortar bombardment which started even before the early-morning mist had been sucked away by the July sun.

As soon as the mortar fire lifted, Seeger's column began to grind up the narrow mountain road. It was not long before they bumped into Chabal's forward position at the little settlement at Bois Barbu. In a brief silence shortly after the opening exchange of fire, a Maquisard from Alsace who could speak good German went forward a few metres and shouted, '*Kameraden!* Go back. We are too strong for you. The Allies have landed in the south. There has been an attempt on the Führer's life and a revolution has been launched in Germany. The Third Reich cannot win the war!' There was a moment of puzzled silence; then the firing began again with renewed vigour. The Alsatian tried to run back to the Maquisard line but was caught in a hail of fire. 'I am done for!' he shouted. 'I've been hit hard! My wife won't see me again! Oh shit!'

Over the next four and a half hours the Germans pushed relentlessly up the road. Every time they were stopped by a French roadblock, the Gebirgsjäger took to the forest, outflanking the French positions and forcing them to withdraw. Then the roadblock was pushed aside by an armoured vehicle and the column pressed on.

At 10.30 the Germans finally arrived in front of Chabal's position on the Belvedere. There followed a brief pause. The defenders could hear the cracking of branches as the Germans moved through the forest south of

THE BATTLE OF VALCHEVRIÈRE

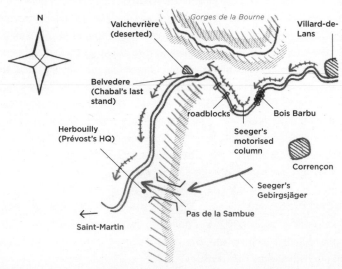

the road. Then a wild and desperate battle broke out for the last impediment to the German's breakthrough on to the Herbouilly plateau. Chabal sent a note back to Prévost: 'I am completely surrounded. We are preparing for a Sidi-Brahim.* Vive la France.' Prévost immediately dispatched a small force with instructions to attack the enemy's flank in the hope they would pull back. But they found the Germans too strong. Prévost sent a note instructing Chabal to withdraw.

It was too late. At first, Abel Chabal and his small group of remaining Maquisards, firing from positions behind the tree-trunk barricade at the Belvedere, were able to hold up the German advance along the road. But soon sharpshooters managed to climb the bluff looking down on the Belvedere. From here they picked Chabal's men off one by one. Eventually Chabal himself was mortally wounded. His last act was to throw his notebook over the parapet of the Belvedere, some say because it contained not only his orders but also the names of his men.

At his headquarters Prévost was now dealing with two simultaneous German thrusts: one up the road from Valchevrière and another threatening the Pas de la Sambue. This was defended by a unit under the command of Jean Veyrat, Chavant's companion on his late-May trip to Algiers. Among Veyrat's men were the Senegalese from Descour's disbanded headquarters who were especially dispirited, having found the cold and rain of the previous days hard to bear. At around 14.00, the Pas de la Sambue fell to Seeger's Gebirgsjäger. Prévost tried desperately to assemble a force for a counter-attack, but he had no reserves left. Nothing now could stop Seeger's men from reaching Saint-Martin.

Jacques Humbert spent that whole day at the Villa Bellon with Huet: 'Saint-Martin was pretty well deserted. It was a Sunday. But even the Priest had left the village and the church stood empty and desolate … Though the telephone … was still operating. Huet knew that the fall of Valchevrière would mean that nothing could stop the enemy marching on Herbouilly, outflanking our men on the Pas de la Sambue and dominating the Saint-Martin Valley.'

At 10.00 came the news that 'Valchevrière could not hold for much longer.' 'Not having any reserves left, Huet sent orders to all units …

---

* Chabal was referring to a battle in 1845 when eighty-two French soldiers were encircled by 10,000 Algerian Berbers. Only sixteen managed to break out, of whom eleven survived their wounds.

[saying that] if the Herbouilly line broke then all those engaged in that area should disperse and survive in small groups into the forest until such time as it was possible to resume operations [that is, after the Germans had left the plateau]. All other units should remain in position until the order to disperse was given. He also gave orders for the Pont de la Goule Noire – the only remaining means of road communication between the northern and southern plateau – to be blown. Huet's decisiveness and calm authority in giving his orders and in facing the difficulties that confronted us was absolutely remarkable.'

In the course of the morning matters got worse. Humbert recorded: 'We were kept in regular touch with the situation on the Herbouilly front through situation reports from Prévost who also seemed calm and professional throughout. At 14.00 we heard finally from Prévost that Valchevrière had fallen ... and that Chabal had died, his weapon in his hand. "It's over. We have had it," Huet said sadly. He telephoned each of his commanders to say that, as of 16.00, his headquarters at the Villa Bellon would cease to exist and instructed that his orders should be placed in previously agreed "letter boxes" for stragglers and those not on the telephone. Then, in calm good order we started to pack up the headquarters, burning or hiding all papers, while everyone collected as much food and ammunition as they needed. Already the first random shells were falling on Saint-Martin.'

Each of Huet's dispersal orders was specific for the unit to which it was addressed, instructing its members exactly where they should hide. On the Col de Gaudissart, above Saint-Jean-en-Royans at the western edge of the plateau, André Valot did not receive his order until 17.00, when a motorcyclist rode up and handed him a piece of paper: 'General headquarters, Vercors. Order of Colonel Huet. Our lines have broken. To avoid being encircled you are to break contact with the enemy immediately. Hide the weapons you cannot carry and make your way, as far as possible under cover, to the Col de la Rama. You are to find a place to hide in this area. But you should maintain regular contact with your Squadron Commander, Geyer. Signed Huet.'

When Huet issued the dispersal order, he also gave instructions to release the prisoners at Loscence. Some were killed by the Maquisards as they tried to get away, but most escaped to safety. During the afternoon one of Huet's remaining staff officers blew up the ammunition store, the sound of the explosion reverberating around the Saint-Martin valley.

At 10.00 in Algiers that morning, de Gaulle asked his Chief of Staff for

Defence, General Béthouart, to find what could be done to help the Vercors. Béthouart reported back that plans were in hand to send a French Commando and heavy weapons, notably 37mm cannon, twenty Browning heavy machine guns and some British mortars.* At the same time and not far away, Jacques Soustelle was in conference working out if he could get three French Commando units of 400 men each to the plateau. The problem was that the French units were equipped only with rifles and would need machine guns, which hadn't been supplied. Soustelle was told they couldn't be ready in less than forty-eight hours after they had received the new weapons. Meanwhile Gabriel Cochet grabbed a handful of the latest telegrams from the Vercors and leapt on a plane for Sicily to make a last-minute personal appeal to the Allied air forces to act.

During the day, there was a constant stream of messages coming in to Algiers from Henri Zeller and the Drôme Maquis reporting as best they could what was happening on the plateau. At 07.20 Zeller sent this appeal: 'Due to the absence of mortars, we are unable at the moment to dislodge the Germans who have landed by glider. Parachute these to any Vercors parachute site, except Vassieux. Urgently. Also send parachutists. What the Germans can do, the British ought to be able to do.'

The only messages coming from inside the plateau were being sent by André Pecquet transmitting to London on his little suitcase wireless from his 'rabbit hole' cave in the grove of beech trees near Le Briac. But being away from the Villa Bellon, he had only a vague idea of what was going on. At 08.05, still working on the previous night's information, he reported: 'Attack continuing in the Vercors. The Germans are contained. The Vercors is subdividing into autonomous Maquis groups. We are being very heavily attacked by German aircraft. Send fighters.'

He followed this up at 13.15: 'Situation in the Vercors. The Boches are encircled at Vassieux. Not having mortars we have been unable to prevent them from landing. They are attacking all points on our periphery. We are doing our best to resist. Communications with the outside world impossible. We are being constantly attacked by aircraft. If you don't send fighter aircraft we will all be sacrificed. We have no news of Zeller and Tournissa is probably dead. Things are so desperate that our radio operators have all had to join fighting units. Farewell.'

---

* Probably the weapons and troops referred to in Constance's signal of 20 July (see page 293).

Then Pecquet packed up his little wireless and returned with it to the Villa Bellon, where he had a late lunch with Huet. This was interrupted by a telephone message saying that they should leave immediately as German troops had been seen on the summit of Roche Rousse, a prominent cliff opposite Saint-Martin. But Huet first wanted to visit Geyer in La Rivière to check that he had received the dispersal signal. La Rivière was empty. Geyer's men had moved out at 17.00.

While Huet was away Pecquet sent a last message to London, dictated by Huet before he left: 'We have held on for 56 hours against 3 enemy Divisions ... the troops have fought with courage but also desperation because they are physically exhausted and almost out of ammunition. Despite our repeated requests we have received no help at all since this combat started. The situation will at any moment become desperate. Then terrible tragedies will come to the Vercors. We have done our duty. But we are full of sadness at the weight of responsibility which must be borne by those who, deliberately and from afar, have led us into this situation.'

By now it was nearly 18.00. The remaining men at the Villa Bellon headquarters had already left by vehicle for Les Barraques, where they would begin their journey into the forest hiding place Huet had already chosen for them. As he waited, Pecquet watched Hoppers and his men moving off into the forest. When Huet returned, he said to Pecquet, 'Well, André, we will now go and meet the men at Les Barraques.' The first organized salvoes of German shells were already falling on the village as the car carrying the two men, Pecquet's suitcase wireless and his pedal battery charger coughed and wheezed its way up the hill from Saint-Martin. At Les Barraques, his pack on his back and his rifle slung over his shoulder, Huet led the sixty men from his headquarters up a forest track and into hiding.

At about the same time, Gerd von Rundstedt reported on the day's work: 'Carried out own air landing near Vassieux, La Mure and Le Château. Air-landed group has taken up a position of all-round defence in La Mure–Vassieux; ammunition supply carried out. Heavily fortified villages of St Martin and St Julien bombed by the Luftwaffe. To date 220 enemy dead. Own casualties to date: 29 dead, 20 wounded.'

What neither Huet nor von Rundstedt knew was that, even at this last desperate hour, some of the French had still not given up fighting. Up on the Pas de l'Aiguille, Paul Blanc and his twenty-two Maquisards, crammed into their tiny dark cave, were still holding out.

During the afternoon and evening of 22 July, the Germans had thrown everything they could at the cave mouth, but because of the lie of the land they were firing upwards which meant that their bullets struck the cave roof rather than the Maquisards sheltering behind the parapet. Nevertheless Blanc, concerned that his enemy might be able to get grenades and mortar bombs through the mouth of the cave, told his men to fill their rucksacks with the stones and rocks lying on the cave floor. He piled these up in the cave mouth in order to reduce the size of the open-ing to that required for a single machine-gunner. All through the evening of 22 July, Blanc's men maintained a sufficient return of fire, accompanied by volleys of grenades, to keep the Germans at a safe distance.

At 23.00 there was a brief lull in the shooting from outside and Blanc thought about making a dash for it. But a renewed burst of firing, accom-panied by grenades exploding round the mouth of the cave and illumin-ation shells which lit up the entire valley, made him think again. By now, with little food and almost no water, the pains of hunger and especially thirst were adding to fear and exhaustion, gnawing at the morale of Blanc's men.

Eventually after a seemingly endless night the first glimmers of dawn began to seep into the cave. Looking out as daylight broke the Maquisards saw the shepherd's dog, which had howled most of the early part of the night, lying dead in a pool of blood by its master's side. Paul Blanc's men had now held out for twelve hours without a single casualty. How much longer could they last?

At 09.00 the Germans recommenced the battle with a furious fusil-lade. Then some mortars, newly installed in the valley overnight, started firing ranging shots at the cave mouth, adjusting the fire after each salvo. The Maquisards watched in horror as the salvoes crept closer and closer to them. Suddenly, inevitably, one found the pile of rock-filled rucksacks at the mouth and exploded with a deafening crash, showering shrapnel into the cave. The man guarding the cave mouth fell wordlessly to the floor, a piece of shrapnel through his head. Although many in the cave were wounded, only two had serious injuries. The dead man's body was covered with a blanket and laid down at the back of the cave where the roof slopes down to meet the floor. The two wounded men, having been bandaged as well as could be managed, were also carried to the back of the cave and laid on the floor close to their dead colleague.

At 10.00 there was a second fusillade of fire, though curiously this did not include the mortars. Suddenly there was a huge explosion right in the middle of the cave. Initially Blanc thought it was grenade, but in fact the Germans had detonated a large explosive charge which they had lowered into the mouth of the cave from above. Miraculously, although some suffered light wounds, there were no serious casualties. Shortly afterwards the inside of the cave reverberated with another loud report. Was it another explosive charge? The answer came when someone at the back of the cave shouted that one of the two men wounded in the first mortar attack had shot himself. His body was laid alongside that of his dead comrade.

Around midday Blanc saw another charge being lowered into the cave mouth from above. He coolly threw himself at the package and yanked it hard. Unprepared for this, the German above let go and Blanc was able to throw the pack of explosive down the hill where it exploded harmlessly. Over the next hours the Germans tried the same trick two or three more times, but on each occasion the Maquisards managed to cut the cord on which the charges were lowered before they could be detonated.

By evening, at around the same time Huet was leaving the Villa Bellon for the last time, Blanc's sentry manning the machine gun in the cave mouth suddenly fell backwards into the cave without uttering a sound. He had been shot clean through the head. They laid him next to his two dead comrades at the rear of the cave. By now the wounded Maquisard lying next to the three dead bodies was delirious, screaming with pain and begging to be killed. At around 19.00 the Germans finally succeeded in throwing a grenade through the cave mouth. Again there were mostly only light injuries. One of the defenders, however, received a large piece of shrapnel in his thigh and was losing a lot of blood. He was bandaged and carefully carried, groaning with pain, to the back of the little cave.

The frustration on the German side at being held up by this handful of 'terrorists' is evident from the description given by Stefan Ritter's company diarist: 'Marksmen were used; however, the success was limited as they could not make a frontal approach to the cave. A demolition charge was also attempted. But due to the terrain, these were very difficult to attach. We had no success.'

As day turned into another night in the cave, Blanc knew that they could not hold out for much longer. He had done an outstanding job of leadership maintaining the morale of his men in the cramped space, under constant attack, with one of their number delirious with pain, another seriously wounded and three lying dead just feet away from their comrades. Thirst, more than fear, was now their greatest torture. Hunger too. And their ammunition stocks were also running dangerously low. Blanc suggested that their only chance, however slim, was to make a run for it in the night. His men agreed. Better to die outside than like rats in this airless black hole.

That night a damp mist rolled down the mountainside and filled the little valley. Worried that this could be used by the Germans to get close to the cave, Blanc decided to make his break in the early hours of the morning. But what to do with the two badly wounded men? According to later accounts both begged to be shot rather than fall into German hands. Instead, so the record suggests, Blanc let them have his revolver and they shot themselves.

Finally, after more than sixty hours, without food or water, holding out against a greatly superior force, Paul Blanc led his men to the parapet at the front of the cave, gave them a rendezvous to meet at if they survived and counted to three: they all dashed out into the night, the less wounded helping those who were more hurt. Against the odds, all eighteen of the survivors made it and over the next few days were able to return to their homes in the valley.

There is an intriguing postscript to this well-documented story. According to Ritter's diarist, the siege at the Pas de l'Aiguille ended quite differently: 'Marksmen and heavy machine guns are used again. More demolition charges are thrown into the cave, finally the terrorists are destroyed completely. At 06:30 hours the first of our soldiers enter the cave. They retrieve: 2 light machine guns with 20 magazines, 5 submachine guns and large amounts of ammunition. Between 22 July and 24 July, 21 terrorists were killed. The access to the pass is finally free. Towards the evening the two platoons return to the rest of the company and set up camp on the Pas de la Selle with all-round protection.'

If, as seems reasonable given the evidence, we believe the numerous French accounts of the Pas de l'Aiguille story, then we can only conclude that, having failed to stop Paul Blanc and his men when they made a dash for it, the two German platoons responsible for 'cleaning up' the last 'terrorists' on the Pas de l'Aiguille returned to their parent unit and claimed a success that they had never achieved.

Paul Blanc and his men were the last Frenchmen fighting on the Vercors, and the first to make it home through the German cordon that ringed the plateau.

RETREAT AND REFUGE

On 24 July 1944, just a few hours after the last French position on the plateau fell, at Pas de l'Aiguille, sixty American B-24 Liberator heavy bombers finally attacked Chabeuil airfield. The Situation Report circulated in Algiers two days later listed the damage as 'About 30 aircraft destroyed; important losses in personnel; petrol dumps destroyed; AA guns untouched.' That afternoon, Algiers sent a telegram to the Drôme Maquis base just south of the Vercors: 'Please indicate urgently on which drop site you could receive 44 French parachutists which we will drop to you after 25 July.' The French commandos were eventually dropped on to a parachute site at Comps, 30 kilometres south of the Vercors on 30 July.

Given the fact that this day, 25 July, was the date on which the window opened for Maitland, Wilson's plan to 'commence landing operations in the Vercors' (see page 284) with Dakotas and gliders, it seems reasonable to speculate that the Chabeuil bombings of 24 July, and the French commandos to be dropped after 25 July, were originally planned as support operations for an Allied airborne landing on the Vercors plateau on, or soon after, 25 July.

On 28 July, five days after the fall of the Vercors, Colonel Georges Gauthier of the French Air Force took off from the Allied base in Bastia, northern Corsica, with eleven P-47 Thunderbolt fighters on the first combat mission to the Vercors. Gauthier and his colleagues flew over the plateau for nearly an hour. Failing to identify anything to attack, they flew on to the Pô valley in northern Italy to strafe opportunity targets and then returned to Bastia.

Any one of these initiatives, especially the bombing of Chabeuil, would have been useful – perhaps even life-saving – before 23 July. But the only things which concerned Huet and his men now were concealment and survival on the plateau. On 23 July, shortly after entering the forest west of Les Barraques, Huet's headquarters column of sixty split into two groups, one of which headed north, while Huet led the other west along little-used forest paths. At dusk, Huet's group arrived at a clearing where he called a halt. The food, enough to last two weeks, was scrupulously shared out for the evening meal and then the fugitives settled down under the stars for the night. Already thirst was becoming a problem as few of them had water bottles and summer water sources on the limestone plateau are extremely rare.

Shortly before nightfall, a group of twenty of Chabal's men who had escaped from Valchevrière were discovered in a clearing near by. Demoralized and dejected, they had thrown away their weapons and were intent on fleeing the plateau to the west. Huet told them that this would be seen as desertion and ordered them to report to him in the morning when he would attach them to his group.

On the morning of 24 July a thick, penetrating mist hung over the whole plateau. It was scarcely possible to see more than 10 metres. In silence Huet's group packed their rucksacks and prepared to move off. A little while before they left, the twenty fugitives from Valchevrière arrived. Huet took them to one side out of earshot of the others and told them that their duty now was to stay with him. He promised that he would not abandon them and would always ensure that they had an equal share of the group's food.

Huet was about to move off at the head of his column, now number-ing fifty, when suddenly a group of Senegalese appeared out of the forest, led by a white officer in a parachute smock. Huet instructed them also to join his column, again promising that they would have equal shares of the food. With a column numbering close to 100, the food supplies were now sufficient for only four days, causing some grumbling about the Colonel's generosity. Huet silenced the complaints with a well-known French aphorism, 'Aux petits des oiseaux …'*

That day Huet pushed on west towards the Pas du Gier, again by little-used tracks. This was a tough day's march. The column had to stop frequently to allow those from the headquarters, who were less used to the rigours of the Maquisard life, to catch up. André Pecquet, who was

---

* Literally 'God gives food to the bird's young' – roughly, the equivalent of our 'God tempers the wind to the shorn lamb.' The phrase comes from the play *Athalie* (Act II, scene 7) by Racine: 'Dieu laissa-t-il jamais ses enfants au besoin?/Aux petits des oiseaux il donne leur pâture,/Et sa bonté s'étend sur toute la nature.'

by this time suffering from dysentery as well as being weighed down by his heavy radio set, found it especially hard and begged to be left behind. Huet refused, redistributed Pecquet's load and pressed on. That evening a food party was sent out to a local farm, returning with the carcass of a sheep, pails of milk and some flagons of water.

The next day Huet decided that his column was too big to be easily hidden from the German aircraft now constantly circling over them and the enemy patrols which, he judged, would soon be scouring the area for fugitives. He instructed that the group should be divided into three independent parties who would find their own refuge where they could.

Two parties pushed south, deeper into the Forêt de Lente, while Huet with his twenty-five men turned north, heading into the deserted forest area on the Montagne de l'Arp, overlooking Sainte-Eulalie-en-Vercors on the western edge of the plateau. This he decided would be his base until it was time to gather his forces and move on to the offensive again. That day's march, too, was a difficult one for the stragglers. They were, however, able to obtain some food, including eggs from a farm in the area.

Around 17.00 on 25 July, Huet's group finally arrived at the place he had chosen as their base for the next few days. At 01.00 the following morning the first message from Huet since the fall of the plateau was received at the SOE listening station at Grendon Hall in Buckinghamshire. It had been tapped out by André Pecquet from a small clearing 1,000 metres up, deep in the Vercors forest: 'The Vercors' defences were penetrated on 23 July at 16.00 after 56 hours of combat. I ordered all units to disperse into small groups until conditions are right for us to start the fight again. Everyone fought with courage in what was a desperate fight. We feel it tragic to have had to cede under the force of numbers and to have been abandoned to fend for ourselves at the height of combat. Huet.'

Pecquet, who could retune his little radio so as to pick up the BBC news, was able this day to announce to Huet and the little group camped in their isolated forest clearing the excellent news that General Patton's tanks had at last begun their breakthrough of the German lines at Saint-Lô. After six weeks of hard, bloody fighting, the Normandy stalemate was coming to an end. Soon the breakout towards Paris could begin. Surely now the southern invasion could not be far way?

The following day, 26 July, Gerd von Rundstedt included the following in his daily report to the Supreme Command of the Armed Forces in

Berlin: 'During a large operation between Grenoble and Valence, enemy resistance collapsed. Terrorist camps and villages were hastily cleared, leaving behind weapons, ammunition and equipment. Enemy tries to cross boundary line in the north-west in small groups.'

Narcisse Geyer's men in La Rivière had started dismantling his headquarters at 15.00 on 23 July, even before Huet had formally sent his dispersal order. They burnt all papers, buried surplus ammunition and weapons, along with two containers of film which a Resistance film crew had been taking in the Vercors. Then they drove to La Chapelle, where they picked up charcoal for their *gazogène* vehicles. The first German columns from Vassieux must have arrived in La Chapelle no more than half an hour after Geyer's convoy passed through. Leaving La Chapelle, Geyer continued west to the wood-covered, cliff-faced Rochers de Pionniers ridge above the little village of Bouvante-le-Bas at the western edge of the plateau. This was to be Geyer's main base until it was safe to move out again. At Bouvante-le-Bas, Geyer's group met up with the wounded Jean Tournissa, who had escaped from Vassieux on the night of the German landing and had been installed in a cave close to Geyer's camp to recuperate.

Others among Huet's main unit commanders similarly dispersed into the forests, taking as many of their men with them as possible. Roland Costa de Beauregard returned to the Plénouse plateau at the northern end of the Vercors, where, at the slightest whiff of danger, he could quickly spirit his men away into the *lapiaz* pavements of the Plateau de Sornin. Here, on Plénouse, de Beauregard's men had access to one of the few precious sources of water in the area, the Fontaine de Plénouse.

Henri Ullman took his men to the Forêt de Coulmes which runs along the north-west edge of the plateau. Unlike de Beauregard, however, he did not stay with his men, but abandoned them and took refuge in a small farm by himself. Although he was quickly replaced, his departure was followed by a spate of desertions – over 24 and 25 July, half of those in Ullman's company deserted to try and make their way back to the Romans area. Most were killed in the attempt.

Georges Jouneau, the head of what had been the Vercors Motor Transport Depot, led his men in the opposite direction, finding them hiding places in the forests of the eastern plateau.

Eugène Chavant and several of his closest colleagues found refuge in the woods on a steep hillside above the Ferme le Paradis, north of Pont-en-Royans. Here the farmer risked his life and that of his family by supplying food to *le Patron* and his little group. If the Germans were not about, then the lights were left on in the farm, signalling that it was safe to come down to eat. If the lights were out, the coast was not clear and a pitcher of milk accompanied by a bundle containing bread, pâté and cheese would be left (almost invariably by a female member of the farmer's family) at a prearranged spot at the corner of a wood, to be collected after dark.

When Vernon Hoppers arrived back at his base at Les Berthonnets west of Saint-Martin after the failed Vassieux counter-attacks of 23 July, he discovered that, overnight, his second-in-command, Chester Myers, recovering from his appendicitis operation, had been moved with the other patients to the Grotte de la Luire. He also found that in his absence some of the equipment, clothes, food and stores that he had left behind at Les Berthonnets had been pillaged. Hoppers collected his remaining men and as much food as he could find and headed north out of Saint-Martin to the high wooded plateau of Choranche above the Bourne gorges. He spent the following day watching for activity on the roads along the Gorges de la Bourne and then during the night dropped down the steep slopes, crossed the Bourne river and climbed up the other side to the Presles plateau. Here he met up with a guide from Ullman's group, who the following day led the American commandos down the western escarpment of the plateau to the banks of the Isère river.

Hoppers' report picks up the story: 'The entire Isère valley was guarded by one German every 50 metres. The German intention was that no-one should escape the Vercors alive. That evening 400 Germans moved into our area. For 11 days the section lay in one spot while German patrols scoured the woods and fired into the underbrush trying to scare the Maquis into the Isère valley, where many were shot trying to escape and many others drowned trying to swim across the river. For 11 days we ate nothing but raw potatoes and occasionally a little cheese. Not more than one man moved at a time and then never more than fifty feet away from where we lay. The men were never allowed to speak above a whisper. The food we did get was stolen at night from a farmer who lived close to the woods in which we were hiding. On the night of 6 August we received word from a Maquisard that the bridge outside Saint-Marcellin was no longer guarded. We moved down from the plateau and force marched 40 kilometres [away from the Vercors] into the Isère Department ... I lost 37lbs, three of my men were not able to walk for almost two weeks and some of them had dysentery which lasted for a month.'

The privations suffered by Hoppers' men were by no means unusual, as the following extract from a Maquisard's diary illustrates:

31 July – Cornflour brought back by a patrol cooked in bad water in a washing boiler. Those who managed to eat this mess are ill.
1 August – Several comrades poisoned by eating leaves. A little milk taken from an abandoned cow which we found after hours of searching.
2 August – Found several chickens – cooked on a spit in the forest.
10 August – Eating raw carrots found in a field – also some apples we found.
11 August – Stripped a cherry tree of all its fruit.

Some also took their chances to the east. These included Adrien Conus, the former big-game hunter charged by Huet with asking the Resistance east of the Vercors to try to draw off the German assault by attacking their rear. After crossing the Pas de la Sambue in the pouring rain on the night of 21 July, Conus and his two guides climbed to the Pas de la Balme. Here one of his guides stepped on a mine. Though himself quite severely concussed, Conus pressed on with his second guide, Léon Jaille. The two men spent the next day resting up in the shepherd's hut on the Pas de la Balme. In the early hours of the third day, in thick fog, they made the long steep descent of the eastern wall into the valley. On several occasions the two men found themselves almost bumping into German columns moving through the mist in the opposite direction – towards the eastern passes. By 10.00 the following morning, entering the little town of Gresse-en-Vercors they suddenly stumbled into the middle of a German ambush. They were taken prisoner and handed over to the Gestapo, who interrogated the two men under torture. Conus, his hands tied behind his back, both shoulders dislocated, some fingers broken and severely beaten, said nothing. So they led him to the edge of a ravine and placed him at the right end of a line of kneeling men. A Gestapo officer walked down the line from the far end shooting each man in the back of the head. Just before it was his turn, Conus launched himself into the ravine. By some miracle he survived and was not found by the ensuing search party. He eventually reached a local Maquis headquarters and, using their radio, signalled London: 'Captured, interrogated, tortured, shot. In good health. Conus.'

Jean Prévost's Compagnie Goderville had been scattered to the four winds by Seeger's assaults at Valchevrière and the Pas de la Sambue. His men had to find their own refuge, singly or in small groups, as best they could. Prévost himself, together with a small group including Jean Veyrat and Léa Blain (rumoured to be Prévost's lover at the time), were led by Paul Borel, a twenty-year-old local Maquisard, from Herbouilly to a cave which only he and his cousin knew about called the Grotte des Fées, near the summit of the ridge which dominates the eastern side of the Saint-Martin valley. Vercors legend has it that Prévost took with him the small portable typewriter which was his constant companion, carefully burying it near a cave which the group passed on the journey.

Difficult to reach, little known, well hidden and permanently supplied with its own source of fresh water, the Grotte des Fées was in many ways a perfect hiding place. Nevertheless, according to accounts, Prévost became increasingly depressed at spending day after day in the cave and at his inability to sustain his morale in comparison with his younger companions. The closed atmosphere and forced idleness did not suit his active personality. While the fugitives could occasionally sit outside the cave and see almost everything that moved in the Saint-Martin valley, the frequency of German patrols in the area made it necessary for them to spend most of their time in hiding, trapped in their cave and waiting to be betrayed or discovered.

Eventually, on 31 July, unable to bear the inactivity and claustrophobia any longer, Prévost left the Grotte des Fées, accompanied by his six companions. He headed north for Pierre Dalloz's house, La Grande Vigne, in Sassenage. One of their number split off to go to Méaudre to see his family. Léa Blain, whose bleeding feet made it difficult for her to keep up with the men, also left the group somewhere before Villard-de-Lans. A young Maquisard volunteered to accompany her and it was agreed that the two would make their own way off the plateau and meet up with the others later.

Early on the morning of 1 August, Léa and her companion came down from the woods above Villard, heading for a crossroads of forest paths called La Croix des Glovettes. Here they ran headlong into a German patrol. The precise circumstances of what happened next are unclear, but some say Blain and her colleague, finding themselves trapped, tried to fight their way out and were swiftly killed. In the account written by André Pecquet after the war, he reports that, either before or after her death, Léa Blain was terribly mutilated. But no corroborating evidence for this atrocity has come to light in recent years.

Early on the same morning that Léa Blain met her death at La Croix des Glovettes, Jean Prévost and his remaining four colleagues were coming down a well-used forest track alongside the Furon gorge above Sassenage. No one knows precisely why Prévost decided to use this much frequented path from the plateau – some say he had been encouraged to do so after a conversation with a local farmer, who told him the way was clear. Prévost and his colleagues were certainly not expecting trouble – their Stens were packed away in their rucksacks. As the little group walked out of the mouth of the Furon gorge, the town of Sassenage now laid out before them in the sunshine and La Grande Vigne in plain sight, they were cut down by a German ambush. Prévost appears to have tried to escape by jumping over a wall into the torrent below, for his bloodied body was found lying among the rocks later that day by locals. The day before Prévost's death, his friend and fellow writer the Air Force pilot Antoine de Saint-Exupéry disappeared on a mission over the Mediterranean. France had, tragically, lost two of her greatest young writers within the space of twenty-four hours.

Houseman and Longe had better luck. They left their 'Commando' in the woods opposite Saint-Martin on 24 July. With Gustave Boissière as their guide, the two Englishmen, after some difficult physical trials and many inter-personal squabbles and tribulations, managed to cross to the northern plateau, where they left Boissière. They then joined up with a local Maquis unit, who saw the two foreigners safely off the plateau and across the Isère, from where they made their way, with the help of various Maquis groups, to Switzerland and safety.

Of all the odysseys of escape and evasion in the weeks after the fall of the Vercors, the long march undertaken by a large group of Maquisards under the leadership of Bob Bennes is perhaps the most remarkable.

At 22.00 on the night of 23 July, Bennes gathered together all the stragglers who had ended up after the day's battles at the forestry hut at Pré Grandu, the key gateway to the eastern plateau. There were seventy-three of them in all, ranging from wireless operators through administrative staff from Descour's abandoned headquarters (including some of his Senegalese guard of honour) to those who had fled when the eastern

FLIGHT AND REFUGE

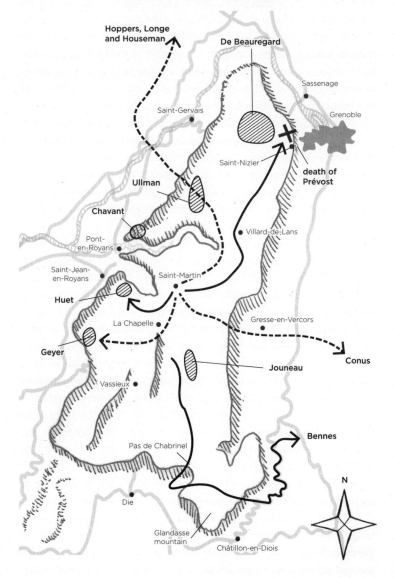

Hoppers, Longe
and Houseman

De Beauregard

Sassenage

Grenoble

Saint-Gervais

Saint-Nizier

death of
Prévost

Ullman

Chavant

Villard-de-Lans

Pont-
en-Royans

Saint-Jean-
en-Royans

Saint-Martin

Huet

La Chapelle

Gresse-en-Vercors

Geyer

Conus

Jouneau

Vassieux

Bennes

Pas de Chabrinel

Die

N

Glandasse
mountain

Châtillon-en-Diois

passes fell, including Lieutenant Louis Kalck. Reasoning that the Germans might not yet have had time to close the south-eastern exits from the plateau, Bennes led his column towards the Pas de Chabrinel, close to the Glandasse mountain. After about an hour's march, stumbling along the uneven path on what was a very dark night, there was a sudden rifle shot in the middle of the column. One of the Maquisards, whose mind had become unhinged after a mortar round had fallen next to him at the Pas de la Ville, had shot himself. Later Bennes discovered that in the darkness the back of the column had somehow become separated from the front. It eventually turned out that the exhausted Louis Kalck had fallen asleep on the march and, by the time his comrades were finally able to wake him, the front of the column had vanished into the night. The two groups were reunited by chance midway down the 1,000-metre rocky descent from the Pas de Chabrinel to their destination for that night, some woods close to the twelfth-century Abbey of Valcroissant. Here they lay up during the following day.

In the evening Bennes led his group 1,200 metres up to the summit of the Glandasse mountain. Many of them were carrying equipment weighing as much as 50 kilos, including machine guns. The following morning they had to find a way down the 200-metre Archiane cliffs, which the column negotiated without losing a single person or item of equipment. On 1 August, the day Prévost was killed in the north of the plateau, Bennes' column, now swollen with stragglers collected on the way, finally reached the top of the Col de Saint-Sébastien, 5 kilometres north-east of Mens, where they were picked up by Resistance transport. In all Bennes had marched his fully loaded rag-tag column on very little water and only occasional food, 75 kilometres in eight days over some of the most rugged terrain anywhere in Europe – and had lost not a single man. This was, by any standards, an outstanding feat of leadership and endurance by Robert Bennes and his men.

In the main, those lucky enough to be part of an organized and properly led group survived the German manhunt which followed the fall of the Vercors. By far the safest option during these terrible weeks was to take refuge in the deep forests of the plateau, which by and large the Germans feared to enter because of Maquis ambushes. But of course this was not understood by panicked, terrified and inexperienced young men, left leaderless and isolated from their companions. Their first instinct was to get as far and as fast as they could away from the horrors they had experienced. For many, the pull of hearth and home in the valley was irresistible. Some were lost for days as they wandered without maps or anyone to guide them. A number, driven mad by thirst, were shot as they approached one of the few natural water sources on the plateau – or while trying to beg water or food from a farmhouse. Fifteen-year-old Gilbert Carichon saw two young men, scarcely older than himself, gunned down as they left the woods above the village of Rousset, heading for the back door of a local farm. Their bodies were left where they fell in the farmer's back garden – until the Germans gave permission for them to be buried. Many made it down to the valley only to be caught in the German cordon and summarily shot, sometimes in sight of their home villages on the plain. Some drowned trying to swim across the Isère river. The bodies of a few may still lie where they fell, bewildered and exhausted, in some undiscovered spot deep in the forests of the plateau.

THE HARROWING
OF THE VERCORS

On 27 July 1944 General Niehoff promulgated the following order:

> The Resistance groups which existed in the Vercors have been
> dislodged by the attacks of Schwehr, Seeger and Schäfer. They have
> now broken up into small groups and are trying to slip through our
> lines and out of the Vercors. We do not any longer have to worry
> about a serious threat from the French Resistance except in the
> south.
>
> It is now necessary to harrow the Vercors methodically in order
> to seek out and annihilate the terrorists in their hiding places and to
> find and destroy their ammunition, their food stocks, their
> equipment and their repair centres. Our aim is to ensure that the
> terrorists will never again be able to set up their bases on the
> Vercors …
>
> The male population of the Vercors between the ages of 17 and 30
> who have neither been in nor supported the French Resistance are to
> be arrested and formed into labour squads for the removal of mines,
> the reconstruction of bridges and the transport of booty into our
> possession … Houses used by the terrorists are to be burned … To
> prevent the Vercors again being used as a base by the French
> Resistance, you will leave in each farm only the animals, cows and
> pigs etc. that are necessary for the survival of legitimate inhabitants.
> After slaughtering sufficient for their own requirements, units will
> ensure that all additional livestock will be rounded up by the
> inhabitants and driven into marshalling areas.
>
> Orders for transporting booty, the treatment of civilian prisoners
> and the transport of livestock will be given later.

In fact Niehoff's order had already been in informal operation since the main body of Schäfer's men had marched out of Vassieux at around midday on 23 July. At about that time, the Eastern Troops, who had been flown in that morning, established themselves in the now ruined farm complex at La Mure, where, according to French sources, they began an orgy of bestiality among the seventy-two prisoners, both military and civilian, who were delivered to them shortly after their arrival.

In attempting to reconstruct what happened during these horrors, it is necessary to try to separate fact from fiction. What is fully documented is that these Eastern Troops were well practised in especially sadistic forms of killing which had been used widely on the Russian front. One of these was to hang a man from the branch of a tree in such a way that only his toes touched the ground. As long as the victim could stand on tiptoe he could prevent himself from strangling. But as his muscles became too weak to maintain this position, he progressively strangled himself. A variant of this involved tying up one leg. The victim was then forced to stand for as long as he could on his remaining leg, before again this gave way and he strangled himself. Another was to place a beam across the crock of a tree and hang a tiptoeing man at each end, so that the one who weakened first effectively strangled his colleague before being strangled himself. There are seemingly believable reports – and photographic evidence – that these practices were carried out at La Mure, some say in the presence of German officers eating their lunch.

On the other hand, it is also incontestable that attempts were made after the war to heighten the horror by claiming that band saws were used for even greater atrocities. Some clearly doctored photographs were produced which purported to show examples of this. No contemporary or other objective evidence has yet come to light which supports these particular claims. Nevertheless horrors enough were perpetrated at La Mure and elsewhere, even if some elements were, as always happens in war, exaggerated.

Schäfer's men arrived in La Chapelle at around midday on 23 July, burning many dwellings and especially farmhouses on their march from Vassieux. Shortly after they arrived, they were joined by forward elements of Schwehr's column, the unit which was supposed to have relieved them a day earlier in Vassieux. Some French sources claim that, during that afternoon, the two units celebrated their victory with a beer-drinking session in La Chapelle cafés. In mid-afternoon, elements of the Eastern

Troops at La Mure also entered the town, having burnt, on their way, all those houses which Schäfer's men had spared earlier. During the afternoon, La Chapelle was systematically looted.

It must have been at about this time that the priest of La Chapelle, Abbé Pitavy, approached two German officers sitting at a table in front of the town fountain enjoying a bottle of Clairette de Die: 'I am the curé of this town and I am offering myself as a hostage, so that the town and its people can be spared.' He was invited to sit down with the two officers and then politely but firmly interrogated about the presence of the Resistance in the town. The curé insisted that they had all left and anyway La Chapelle had never been a great Resistance centre. He was then made to accompany the German officers on a search of houses, during which a Sten gun and the magazine for a Colt automatic pistol were found. Again Abbé Pitavy denied knowledge of any Resistance in the town. Angered, the Germans took him to the square where the townspeople had been assembled in three groups: one for men between seventeen and forty; one for men above forty and one for women and children. The priest was ordered to take his place in the older men's group.

There followed an inspection of identity cards, after which the older men and women were instructed to go home and get what they needed for the night. On their return, they were all marched to the La Chapelle school where they were to spend the night. As they were marched away, Abbé Pitavy noticed that the guard on the group of younger men, now numbering some fifteen, had been noticeably strengthened. At 17.00 that night, the Germans started methodically burning La Chapelle. Later, at around 21.45, several bursts of automatic fire were heard, even above the loud cracking and crashing of burning houses.

In the early hours of the following morning, one of the older men held in the school slipped out and made his way through the darkness to the courtyard of a farm near the centre of the village, where, to his horror, he found his son lying among a pile of bodies. Early the following day, Abbé Pitavy visited the courtyard and was able to identify the bodies of sixteen of his young parishioners strewn about the blood-spattered courtyard.

On that same day, 23 July, Schwehr's Gebirgsjäger came down off the plateau to occupy the towns and villages in the Saint-Martin valley, among them Saint-Agnan. From here, the German unit commander sent a patrol to investigate the neighbouring village of Chabottes. The first

Chabottes resident to spot the approaching Germans was in his garden tending his vegetables and later commented how nervous they seemed to be, firing constantly into the bushes and woods even though there was no one there. It was not long before the Germans discovered that the Chabottes school house had been used as a weapons store and repair depot. The villagers were told to gather together and a German officer asked for the name of the school head. The local teacher, Rose Jarrand, stepped forward. She was arrested and, a little later, bundled into a black car with two 'Gestapo' officers and driven off. No one heard any further news of her until, two days later, a man collecting milk early in the morning saw her dead body lying by the side of the road. The presumption was that, after interrogation, she had been shot and her body pushed out of the car in Saint-Agnan to act as a deterrent to others. She was thirty-five years old and the mother of a little girl.

Not to be left out, the Milice also played their part, executing nineteen Maquisards from the plateau at Beauvoir-en-Royans, on the banks of the Isère river, on 25 July. Some French sources claim that Mireille Provence was present at these executions, but there is no reliable evidence for this.

All over the Vercors, during the last week of July, the air was thick with the smell of burning farms and the sound of summary executions. Nicolas Bernard, hiding in the forest above Rencurel, remembers that the two sounds which characterized these terrible, bright, still summer days was the screaming of unmilked cows and the rattle of the machine guns floating up from the valley below.

On 25 July, the Germans started pulling back some of their combat troops and repatriating their dead. One of the glider pilots wrote: 'In the early hours of 25 July the majority of the paratroopers and the pilots having marched off in the direction of Grenoble, the mountain infantry finally arrived to relieve us. They had advanced into the plateau without encountering the enemy and were now surprised to see such signs of combat. We had covered our dead with tarpaulins because of the enormous heat and the burning rays of the sun. In the afternoon two Junkers 52 landed without any problems on the landing strip ... We loaded the dead on to one of the planes and then we left for Lyon in the second Ju 52, saying goodbye to the plateau which had brought death to so many comrades and also to many French people.'

The next day, 26 July, Niehoff, Pflaum and Knab (presumably now recovered from his wounds) flew in to Vassieux for a tour of inspection.

It appears that Niehoff and Knab strongly criticized Pflaum and his troops for being too lenient to 'terrorists' and civilians alike. It may be that it was a result of this visit and his disappointment at what he saw as the lack of severity of the German reprisals that Niehoff wrote his field order of 27 July (see the start of this chapter). The toughening up that Niehoff ordered may even have been a factor in what some regard as the defining atrocity of the whole Vercors tragedy.

The day after Niehoff's visit, Seeger's and Schwehr's Gebirgsjäger were ordered to begin a sweep across the eastern plateau and the neighbouring valleys. Each unit had a defined area to search. In the course of these operations, Descour's old headquarters at Rang des Pourrets was blown up, as were Geyer's headquarters at Buget farm in La Rivière (but, curiously, not Huet's headquarters at Villa Bellon in Saint-Martin). We do not know which unit was assigned to the Rousset area but we do know that, at around 17.00 on the day after the sweep started, a Gebirgsjäger patrol found Ganimède's hospital at the Grotte de la Luire.

Some days previously, Ganimède and Fischer had taken the decision that only the most gravely wounded should stay in the cave. The rest were dispersed into the forests, some to a smaller cave about a mile away. By 27 July, there were thirty-six wounded left, including twenty-eight Maquisards (among them one Senegalese), two civilian women casualties from the bombing at Vassieux, four wounded Polish Wehrmacht soldiers, Chester Myers who had had his appendix out and Lilette Lesage, who was herself a Red Cross nurse and was being tended for the bullet she had received in her thigh when the Germans had attacked the Combovin plateau a month previously. In addition there were three doctors, seven nurses and a Jesuit priest, Father Yves de Montcheuil. Father Yves, renowned throughout France as a theologian and thinker and a man of extraordinary spiritual calm and presence, had come to the Grotte de la Luire on the first day to comfort the wounded and administer the last rites to the dying. Though he had been advised to go when the walking wounded had dispersed a few days previously, he had insisted on staying in the cave with those who were most in danger.

'In the afternoon a German aircraft flew over the cave mouth several times and then fired a white flare,' Dr Ganimède stated in his war crimes testimony after the war. 'Three of our wounded climbed up on to a rock so they could see anyone coming. It was 16.50 and everyone was resting. I had written the names of the last three wounded to have arrived on a piece of paper. Fearing the worst I swallowed it. Suddenly the sounds of gunfire echoed round the valley and all of us in the cave fell absolutely silent. A little afterwards 5 or 6 silhouettes appeared, the sun behind them, on the path leading to the cave mouth. One gave a whistle and others surged after them firing and telling everyone to stand up with their hands in the air. They called for the person in charge. I came forward with my wife and son which they did not take kindly to at all … All those who could stood against the wall with their arms in the air while they pointed their guns at us. At this stage the 4 Polish (Wehrmacht) soldiers, who were afraid that we were all about to be shot, shouted "Don't shoot, don't shoot" in German. They explained that they had been well looked after by us … Then the Germans began pillaging the cave. All the packets of medicines etc were opened. Anything they didn't want was kicked away. My wallet was taken from my pocket with the dexterity of a pickpocket. They missed nothing.'

Apart from Chester Myers, who had continued to wear his US uniform and insignia, Ganimède had previously ensured that none of the other wounded wore anything that hinted of military clothing, insisting that these should all be exchanged for old clothes borrowed from local farmers. He had also taken the trouble to arrange for all the wounded to have false local identity papers. Now he tried to convince the German officer in charge that this meant that his patients were ordinary locals and not Maquisards. But the German was not fooled: 'These are all false papers and you are all terrorists.'

Fortunately the Germans did not notice that, in the confusion, two of the more ambulant wounded had managed to slip out of the cave and into the forest, while one quietly disappeared into the deeper tunnels of the cave where he stayed for three days in the bitter cold before emerging and making good his escape.

The Germans then divided the wounded into three groups: the ambulant, the semi-ambulant and the stretcher cases. Those in the ambulant group were pushed and shoved out of the cave with the encouragement of rifle butts. In the course of this, one of the Germans spotted Myers' US uniform and demanded he identify himself. Myers confirmed that he was indeed a US soldier and was led a way to a nearby house as a prisoner of war. Once they were beyond the woods which hid the cave, the first group, which included the doctors and all but one of the nurses, were marched under armed guard to Rousset where the Germans had a first-aid post. One commonly believed version of this journey relates that, on the way to Rousset, the wounded Senegalese soldier made some comment that offended one of the German escorts, who shot him dead on the spot.*

Those in the second, semi-ambulant group were each assigned a German soldier to help them from the cave along the path which led, after 200 metres, to a road. Here they were loaded on to ox-carts and left for Rousset, past burning farmhouses and destroyed outbuildings. As they looked back, they saw the third group being carried out of the cave. This element consisted of the most severely wounded on six stretchers, accompanied by nurse Anita Winter who had volunteered to stay with them to look after their needs. The stretchers were laid out in the sun on a grassy bank in front of the woods which hid the cave.

The German officer in charge then left for Rousset to get his orders, while his soldiers sat in the sun eating their lunch. When the officer returned, he ordered one of his soldiers to take Anita Winter under armed guard to the burning farm buildings near by and began interrogating Lieutenant Francis Billon, who had broken his leg when parachuting in with Jean Tournissa on 7 July. When she reached the burning buildings, Anita Winter turned to see Billon being carried after her on a stretcher. Shortly after dark, the two, together with a third wounded civilian, were put in a car and driven to Rousset. As they left, they heard five or six long bursts of machine-gun fire.

When the first two groups arrived in Rousset, they were segregated and herded into an abandoned farmhouse in the centre of the village, the men on the first floor and the women on the ground floor. Here Anita Winter and Francis Billon joined them after dark.

That night, the young Gilbert Carichon was hanging around near the abandoned farmhouse watching an elderly, fat German sentry marching up and down in his hobnailed boots. The young man, using broken German and hand signals, asked what was going on. The sentry replied, 'Terroristen – Grotte – kaput!' making a slicing sign across his throat. When, later, the locals were able to return to the Grotte de la Luire they discovered that the six stretcher cases Anita Winter had been forced to abandon had been machine-gunned to death. Their corpses were found in a heap at the bottom of a small ravine near by.

---

* This story is, however, not substantiated in witness evidence.

The following day at around midday, after dressing the wounded and having a brief meal, the three doctors, the seven nurses, Dr Ganimède's family, Lilette Lesage and Father Montcheuil were loaded on to a lorry and driven away to Grenoble. As they left, they looked back to see the remaining walking wounded paraded in the village square from where they were taken one by one for interrogation.

In the early afternoon of that day, 28 July, all eight of these wounded men were marched (or in Billon's case probably carried) out of the village to a meadow not far away – and shot. According to one account, a local couple on their way to collect milk from the village were forced to watch the executions. Another report claims that, before they were shot, the condemned men were forced to dig their own graves – but there is no hard evidence for this, and the usual German practice was not to bury those they executed, but to let them lie where they fell as a warning to others.

Of those taken to Grenoble, Lilette Lesage, Mme Ganimède and her son managed to escape, or were allowed to leave on their arrival. Later Dr Ganimède himself was also able to escape in the confusion of an Allied air raid. Chester Myers was put in a German prisoner-of-war camp and subsequently liberated by the Russians. But Drs Fischer and Ullmann, together with Father Montcheuil, were interrogated by the Gestapo and subsequently executed by firing squad in the Polygone de l'Artillerie in Grenoble. All seven nurses were deported to Ravensbrück, the infamous German camp for women, where one of them, Odette Malossane, died. The others survived the war and returned to France.

On 14 August, at the Cours Berriat in Grenoble, under the eastern lee of the Charvet hill, twenty young Maquisards, many from the Villard and Saint-Nizier area, were also executed by firing squad.

Among the horrors of this period there were a few bright lights. A German driver, taking some condemned men to be shot, deliberately set them free in the middle of a wood. A German soldier offered food to a starving Maquisard and then, turning his back, allowed him to flee. Saint-Martin was apparently spared the reprisals meted out to other villages because of a particular, unnamed Bavarian officer who intervened to stop the brutal treatment of prisoners and to save the village and church from being burnt.

'The Germans arrived at my house in Saint-Martin,' wrote local doctor Michel Blanche later, 'and ordered me to join a group of about 40 men, who were then herded into the church. I protested that I was a doctor and had gravely ill patients to see. Eventually I was allowed to leave – on foot because my car, my motorbike and my bicycle had all been stolen [by the Germans]. Apart from the pregnant women in the village I also had a badly wounded man with several bullets in his stomach to care for. The fact that we weren't all shot was entirely thanks to the German commander in Saint-Martin, who was a Bavarian and a Catholic.' Vercors folklore has it that the 'good German of Saint-Martin' was shot after leaving the Vercors because of his complicity in the plot against Hitler.

For the most part, however, the attitude of the German soldiers involved in the three weeks of the 'harrowing of the Vercors' was that of 'Rudolf', who appears to have been at the Grotte de la Luire and whose unposted letter to his parents was found on his dead body three weeks later: 'How savagely those people were killed by us. We completely exterminated a hospital of partisans with doctors and nurses … but those dogs deserved nothing more.'

The total German casualties from both the conflict and 'harrowing' phases of the battle on the Vercors are estimated as sixty-five killed, 133 wounded and eighteen missing. On the French side, the figures have been estimated at 201 civilians and (including those executed) 639 Maquisards killed. The number of French wounded is unknown. As for damage and losses, the French post-war estimate was that over 500 houses were burnt, a further 650 severely damaged and some 700 cattle driven from the plateau. The Germans lost forty-three assault gliders, three heavy-stores gliders and a small number of fighter-bombers and Fieseler Storch observation planes.

RESURGENCE
AND REVENGE

In the late afternoon of 26 July 1944 two tall, gaunt figures walked un-announced out of the mist into Huet's forest camp at the Pas du Gier. They were Marcel Descour and Dom Guétet.

While many others were trying by any means to leave the Vercors, Descour, who had only recently learnt of the death of his son Jacques, led a small group back on to the plateau and managed to find where Huet was hiding. He told Huet that he was shocked by the inaction of his forces and had already instructed Geyer immediately to assemble a force to take back Vassieux and La Chapelle. Huet, who had already allowed his better judgement to be overruled by Descour on the fatal 8 July decision to mobilize the Vercors, patiently told his boss why this was, at the moment, absolute folly. The time would come, but it was not now. Huet persisted and eventually Descour backed off. The following morning, Huet sent a runner to Geyer's camp on the Rochers de Pionniers ridge, countermanding Descour's orders. By the time Geyer received the message, however, two of his squadrons had already left to carry out Descour's orders.

Huet's decision was a wise one. For, far from being able to attack the Germans, Geyer now found he had to deal with a serious German threat to his own position. Earlier, he had sent one of his cavaliers off on horse-back to liaise with Huet on a different matter. When his emissary did not return, Geyer himself led a search party. He found the young cavalier lying dead alongside his horse, having been ambushed by a German patrol. Geyer brought the body back to camp, slung behind him on the back of his horse.

On 30 July, Geyer tried, in revenge, to ambush a German raiding party intent on burning a farm. Though the ambush backfired due to some Senegalese soldiers opening fire too early, appreciable losses were inflicted on the Germans. But this limited success was achieved at a price

– Geyer had given away his position. The Germans now encircled the ridge on which he had his base and started sweeping it in force. Geyer was trapped. He took the only way out, leading his men – without ropes – down an almost vertical cliff face into the valley below, leaving his horses in a wood under the guard of two cavaliers, and the wounded Jean Tournissa in the cave in which he was recuperating. Fortunately the Germans found neither. As soon as their sweep had passed through, Geyer took his men up the mountain again and reoccupied his base.

Geyer began to feel increasingly concerned that he had not heard anything from the two squadrons sent out to attack German positions around Vassieux on Descour's instructions. Eventually, one of the squadrons returned exhausted. Its leader reported that the foray had been a disaster. The leader of the second squadron had been killed and around 100 men lost.

In the last days of July, at his headquarters deep in the forest, Huet began to hear the distant thunder of the Allies' preparatory aerial bombardments which, he concluded, must be the prelude to the southern invasion. There were also now clear signs that the German grip on the plateau was weakening. On 2 August, just twenty days after he had fled Saint-Martin, Huet decided that the time had come to move on to the offensive.

On 6 and 7 August, Huet travelled across the plateau, at considerable personal risk, visiting his commanders and regrouping them for offensive operations. On 7 August, not knowing that Jean Prévost was already dead, Huet sent him a note: 'Regroup your forces in the forest in two regions: Darbonouse and Pré Grandu. Recover your arms from their hiding places. Split your men into small well-led guerrilla groups of 25–30. The ideal for each group should be 1 Officer, 3 NCOs. Armament: 3 Light Machine Guns, 1 or 2 Bazookas and the rest rifles or sub-machine guns and Gammon grenades. You are to move on to the attack through ambushes and small raids.'

The following day, 8 August, de Beauregard's men claimed twenty-seven Germans killed in ambushes on the Col de la Croix Perrin, Saint-Nizier and the Gorges de la Bourne. So much for Niehoff's boast of less than two weeks previously that Operation Vercors had been so successful that 'We do not any longer have to worry about a serious threat from the French Resistance.'

On 11 August, Huet moved his headquarters to Combe Laval over-looking Saint-Jean-en-Royans so as to be ready to break out on to the Isère plain to assist the Allied advance when the moment arrived. Two days later, on the 13 August, Geyer moved his squadrons off the plateau to La Beaume-d'Hostun close to the banks of the Isère. On 15 August the Allies finally launched Operation Dragoon (as Anvil was now called). A combined force of nearly 200,000 men, including glider-borne assault troops and parachutists, supported by a force of 1,300 heavy bombers, landed all along the French coast from the mouth of the Rhône to Nice. Although there were some strenuous engagements, the German defences, many of them manned by Eastern Troops, swiftly collapsed, enabling Allied motorized columns to break out of their bridgeheads and start advancing up the Rhône valley and along the Route Napoléon towards Grenoble. Cammaerts' Resistance groups were closely engaged with the Allied advance, enabling General Patch to reach Grenoble in days rather than the weeks which the Anvil planners had expected. Coincidentally, on the day the Allies landed Huet, ignorant of the great event taking place to the south, moved his headquarters down from the Vercors, choosing the little town of Notre-Dame-de-l'Osier on the far, western bank of the Isère as the best place from which to coordinate ambushes on the main communications routes running up the Rhône valley. On the following day, the 16th, Geyer claimed twenty-five Germans killed in an ambush on the highway running from Valence to Grenoble. Huet's men were now firmly back on the offensive and ready to assist the Allied advance now pressing fast towards them.

Over the following days, most of Huet's commanders met up with Allied forces as they drove the Germans back along the routes passing below the eastern and western edges of the Vercors plateau. Many of them were present, fighting alongside the main battle units of the Allies, when on 20 August the first US troops reached the oustkirts of Grenoble. On the 22nd, the last German stand was overcome at the Voreppe narrows at the northern end of the Vercors plateau, where, four years previously, the old French Army of the Alps had fought their final engagement before surrender. On that same day, when Grenoble was formally liberated, the young Maquisards of the Vercors units were right at the front of the victory parade.

The following day, 23 August, British codebreakers at Bletchley Park decoded a signal from German units still operating south of Grenoble:

'According to reports from the 157th division, Gebirgsjäger Battalion II/98 was cut to ribbons on 23 August by superior forces with tanks.' Just a month after Schwehr's men had used overwhelming force and superior weapons to destroy the Vercors Maquisards on the eastern passes, they in their turn were destroyed by the overwhelming force and superior weapons of the Allies.

After the war, many have sought to justify the tragedy on the Vercors by claiming that Huet's men held down '10,000' troops which would otherwise have been used to strengthen German units in Normandy. This is inaccurate. All the German forces used in Operation Vercors were reserve units who were unsuited and unequipped for front-line battles of the sort that were being fought around the Normandy beaches – as the swift destruction of Pflaum's most capable unit, the Alpine infantry of his Gebirgsjäger battalions, amply showed.

The truth is much simpler. The Germans did not win on the Vercors. They lost.

Despite their overwhelming numbers (they probably had a superiority of close to 4 to 1 over Huet's men), despite their superior training, despite their greatly superior weapons, despite the massive expenditure of both resources and blood, Niehoff and Pflaum achieved not one of the aims they had set out in the orders for Operation Vercors. Their primary aim was to destroy Huet's headquarters. But they misjudged where this was and left him free to withdraw intact into the forests until it was time to strike back. Their second aim was to destroy the Vercors Maquis. But they failed to do more than dislodge them for perhaps three weeks. The main Resistance units on the Vercors remained largely intact and, as the Germans found to their cost, highly effective when they needed to be, during the Allied push north to Grenoble. The Germans also set out to ensure that the Vercors would never again be home for the French Resistance. Niehoff even boasted he had achieved this. Instead, even before the Germans had fully packed their bags, the Maquis were out of the forests, their weapons in their hands, killing Germans almost at will.

Huet and his men had rolled magnificently with the German punch. He had preserved both his ability to control his forces and the battle effectiveness of his men and units as a guerrilla force. In fact, as Alain Le Ray pointed out after the war: 'Proportionally, the loss of men in the Vercors, despite the fact that they were untrained and in many cases not well led, was far less than French units suffered in [some battles] in Italy or which the British and Americans experienced in the assault on Monte Cassino. It was, in reality, not greater than would have been perfectly normal for ordinary conventional operations.'

Many criticisms may be made of the conduct of the battle of the Vercors – the most serious being the decision to adopt a fixed defence. But when the Vercors Maquis returned to what they did best – operating as guerrillas – they were able to turn a terrible reverse into a significant success.

In the end, the Maquisards of the Vercors did not suffer a defeat – they won a very special kind of victory, albeit a bloody and cruel one.

38

AFTERMATH
AND AFTERLIVES

On 20 July 1944, the very last moment when the Allies could have helped the Vercors before Pflaum's assault on the following day, Maitland Wilson met de Gaulle in Algiers. The subject for discussion was not the desperate plight of the 4,000 Resistance fighters on the Vercors plateau, but Operation Caïman, de Gaulle's plan for an airborne invasion of the Massif Central. In a tetchy exchange, Maitland Wilson repeated that his air resources were only enough for Anvil (now renamed Dragoon) and that the huge commitment of aircraft required for Caïman was therefore out of the question.

That should have been the end of the matter. The air and paratroop resources 'frozen' for Caïman should have been immediately released. But de Gaulle refused to accept Maitland Wilson's decision. The British General, sensing that de Gaulle would appeal over his head to Eisenhower, sent a telegram to the Supreme Commander on 22 July, the day before the Vercors fell, in which he made his position clear: 'The Caiman Plan cannot be carried out as part of Anvil and is therefore unacceptable as such.'

In fact, de Gaulle went higher still, appealing to General Marshall in Washington for a reinstatement of Caïman. On 1 August, SHAEF responded bluntly to Marshall's request for guidance: 'The Caiman Plan is unacceptable.' Bedell Smith backed this up with a simultaneous cable direct to de Gaulle saying that any decision on Caïman was for Maitland Wilson alone, having regard to available air resources, adding tartly: 'You are therefore requested to plan your operations with this limiting factor in mind.'

De Gaulle tried again on 27 July, this time with a personally signed letter to Maitland Wilson: 'I appeal to you one more time to reconsider this matter so that everything can be done to enable the Free French forces to play the full role of which they are capable in the coming battle.'

On 4 August, Maitland Wilson replied, repeating that Caïman was 'impractical'. This conclusion should have been plain to all for the previous month – and probably longer. But once again diplomacy and politics trumped military common sense. The result was that vital resources were set aside for a plan which was never going to happen, instead of being used to try to save the Vercors from the pall of misery, destruction and ruin which now hung over it.

The news of the fall of the Vercors leaked out only gradually in Algiers. On 25 July, de Gaulle, recently returned from his trip to the US and Canada, gave a speech in Algiers in which he deliberately concealed the fact that the battle for the Vercors was over and the plateau had fallen two days previously: 'Vast areas, sometimes as big as whole departments, find themselves, at one time or another, entirely under the control of French troops operating in daylight. The enemy has had to dispatch major military forces in an attempt to re-establish control. At this very moment they are attacking the Vercors with a force including all arms, powerfully supported from the air ... France is only too well aware of the cost to itself of this kind of warfare which will be paid in human lives and ruined buildings. It will be for the Government to ensure, as far as possible that the losses are appropriately apportioned ...'

The following day, 26 July, Pierre Dalloz returned from Oran, where he had been working on the *Treatise* of St Bernard, and paid a call on Jean Constans. 'How are things on the Vercors?' he asked. 'The Vercors is finished,' Constans replied.

Fernand Grenier, de Gaulle's Communist Minister for Air, claims that he was fully informed about what had happened on the plateau only on 27 July, four days after Huet had given the order to disperse. Grenier, never short of a conspiracy theory, was later to claim that the reason he was told of the tragedy so late was because this would make it easier to blame the fall of the plateau on the inaction of a Communist minister.

Perhaps following the principle that attack is the best form of defence, Grenier swiftly called a press conference at which he released his letter of immediate resignation to de Gaulle. This contained a thinly veiled accusation that the General and his government had been responsible for the catastrophe on the plateau: 'For my part I do not intend to be associated with a criminal form of politics which has had at its disposal the means to help our French brothers who are at risk of their lives, but did not use them.' However, at a meeting of the government's Council of Ministers the following day, de Gaulle forced Grenier into a humiliating climbdown which included formally withdrawing both his resignation and his letter.

In London too, the fall of the plateau caused some worried soul-searching at the highest levels. On 26 July, three days after Huet had left Saint-Martin for the forest, Brigadier Mockler-Ferryman, the head of SOE operations in the whole of western Europe, wrote a one-line minute to Maurice Buckmaster, the head of SOE's F Section: 'Please submit a full report regarding the Vidal [Montagnards] controversy.'

SOE's liaison officer in Koenig's headquarters responded the same day in terms which make it clear that the principal high-level British concern was less about the fate of the plateau and its people than about ensuring that the Allies should not get blamed: 'It is my ... opinion that the premature attempt to seize territory was caused by wishful thinking on the part of certain Resistance leaders, brought about by injudicious and incorrect interpretation of Allied intentions ... If it comes at any time to a trial on the question of responsibility, I cannot see that this can be properly apportioned without further knowledge of facts, which are only in the possession of sources not now available.'

While Algiers and London were squabbling about who was to blame for the fall of the Vercors, others were dealing with its dreadful aftermath. In the last days of July, Maurice Rouchy, one-time Chief Scout of France and Director of the youth leader school at the Château de Chamarges near Die, called for volunteers to bury the dead at Vassieux. He wrote an on-the-spot report of what he saw. 'Even while we were still several kilometres from the village, the smell of decomposing corpses made us retch. Soon we began to pass the remnants of farmhouses, all of them lying in ruins, having been looted and burnt. Everywhere lay the bloated carcasses of animals – many had been tied up in their barns before they were set alight. The sight of their torn, burnt and mutilated flesh was terrible. The first human corpse we saw was a farmer who had been machine-gunned and left lying half in a water trough. Beyond that a couple in their seventies lay, the man's arm around his wife as though to protect her. Further on we found some youngsters lying where they had been cut down at the entrance to a farm ... When we were 500 metres from the pile of ruins that used to be the village, the smell became overpowering. A terrible silence lay over the whole of the Vassieux plain.

All around the village lay the burnt-out carcasses of the German gliders, like birds of death.'

As Rouchy's party approached the village 'we came to an old woman of maybe 90 lying on her back, her arms flung out, so that her body seemed to form some kind of ghastly crucifix warning us not to go further. By now the smell was so terrible that we could stand it only if we held handkerchiefs soaked in lavender eau de cologne over our noses and mouths. A little further on we found seventeen bodies lying in a heap where they had fallen among the ruins. We learnt later from their papers that these were the young workers who had just returned from helping to reconstruct the airstrip, when they had been surprised and machine-gunned as they ran. Further still were two old men crouched together in the corner of a wall as though they had squatted down to sleep. There were bodies all over the village – in the streets, in the ruins, in the cellars, lying on the footpaths. Everywhere, everywhere, there was only death.'

The little town of Vassieux, home to 400 souls, had been reduced to a stinking Golgotha among the ruins. That night, Maurice Rouchy and his volunteers tried to get some sleep in the remains of one of the farmhouses. But they found it difficult to cope with the terrible smell, the noise of dogs fighting over human carcasses and the ghostly screeching of corrugated iron flapping in the wind on broken roofs.

The next day the nightmare continued. They found sixty-five corpses in a nearby field, among them some men who had been castrated. Others had had their skulls smashed in with rifle butts. A group of jumbled cadavers on a dung heap turned out to be former Italian soldiers who had defected to the Maquis after the Italian Armistice earlier in the year. In a cellar they found the bodies of three children aged between eight and ten who had been sheltering with their mother; they had been cut to pieces with grenades. In Le Château, north-east of the village, were the bodies of an entire family, including a baby of sixteen months, machine-gunned where they had huddled together in the family pigsty.

Next door, the courageous priest of Vassieux, Abbé Gagnol, discovered a twelve-year-old girl, Arlette Blanc, still alive, trapped under a fallen beam in the house where her whole family had died around her. Raging with thirst in the summer heat, she had begged for water from passing German soldiers, who had only mocked her in return. She was taken gently from the ruins, but died four days later.

Travelling on to La Mure, they found the terrible decomposing remains of those who had been systematically tortured and then delivered to the vilest of deaths by the 'Mongols' under the gaze of their German superiors.

All around Vassieux, corpses lay in the fields and woods where they had fallen, rotting in the hot summer sun. No other village or community on the Vercors had suffered as badly as Vassieux. But all had suffered in one way or another. Luftwaffe bombing and the subsequent burning and pillaging by the first German troops to occupy the town had reduced most of the centre of La Chapelle to little more than smoking ruins. Elsewhere hundreds of farms and houses had been burnt and almost everywhere with a connection to the Vercors Maquisards had been dynamited.

The reconstruction of the Vercors began in the winter of 1944 with a labour force consisting of 330 German prisoners of war and some 700 French labourers. In all 1,185 houses and 126 farms had to be completely reconstructed. By the first anniversary of the German attack, 615 buildings had been rebuilt. Although the Route des Grands Goulets was reopened for traffic in September 1945, the Col de Rousset tunnel remained closed until May 1946.

At the Nuremberg war crimes trials which followed the peace in 1945, the German actions in the Vercors were cited in the main indictment against those charged with major war crimes: 'The defendants wantonly destroyed cities, towns, and villages and committed other acts of devastation without military justification or necessity. These acts violated Articles 46 and 50 of the Hague Regulations, 1907, the laws and customs of war ... Entire villages were destroyed in France, among others Oradour-sur-Glane, Saint-Nizier and, in the Vercors, La Mure, Vassieux, La Chapelle-en-Vercors ...'

Although this and more detailed supporting evidence of the Vercors atrocities was submitted by the French against major war criminals and contributed, in several cases, to the establishment of their guilt, no German soldier who had seen action in the Vercors was individually indicted at Nuremberg. However, after the war, several were tried for their crimes in Grenoble. These included Karl Pflaum, who could not attend his case in person due to illness. On 22 June 1959, the French judge ruled that Pflaum's case should not be pursued – presumably because of his ill-health and the fact that his personal complicity in individual crimes could not be reliably established. He died in 1972.

Werner Knab was also tried in Grenoble and condemned to death in his absence. But the sentence was never carried out, because he was believed to have been killed in an air raid on Germany in February 1945.

The commander of the Milice raid on Vassieux in April 1944, Raoul Dagostini, was tried in Lyon on 6 September 1944, condemned to death and shot at Saint Jean prison in Lyon the following morning. His mistress, Maude Champetier de Ribes, was tried ten days later and shot at Fort Montluc in Lyon on 17 September. Mireille Provence, who had also spied for the Milice before the April raid, was tried on 11 October and condemned to death. But three weeks later her sentence was commuted to life imprisonment with hard labour by de Gaulle, perhaps because she was pregnant at the time.

Nearly all the French commanders in the Vercors later went on to glittering careers. Marcel Descour and Henri Zeller retired as five-star generals. Henri Zeller stayed out of politics, but his brother André, also a five-star general, was one of the leaders of the Generals' Coup against de Gaulle in 1961, as was Jacques Soustelle, who turned against his old chief over the issue of Algeria and was forced to live in exile before receiving a pardon from de Gaulle in 1968. Alain Le Ray, who ended up as a four-star general, served in Vietnam and Algeria, where he had to learn how to fight guerrillas, rather than be one. Roland Costa de Beauregard did two tours in Vietnam and also retired as a general with four stars on his shoulder.

Though strongly criticized after the war for his handling of the Vercors, François Huet maintained his silence, never directly responding to his accusers, beyond producing a simple point-by-point refutation of some of the most egregious 'charges' laid at his door. He fought as a divisional commander in Algeria, retiring as a four-star general. He died in 1968, much loved by his family and much respected by those with whom he had served.

The only Vercors commander who was not promoted to high rank afterwards was Narcisse Geyer, who retired with the relatively humble rank of lieutenant colonel.

Eugène Chavant was offered the prestigious post of Préfet of the Isère Department but refused it. He never forgot or forgave those who he believed had abandoned the Vercors at its most desperate hour. He died on 28 January 1969, just a year after Huet.

Adrien Conus, the big-game hunter who survived being 'captured, interrogated, tortured and shot', moved first to the Far East and then to Central Africa where he died in 1947.

Jean Tournissa recovered from his wounds but was then killed with Victor Boiron, the tractor driver from Vassieux, in a German ambush near Saint-Nazaire-en-Royans on 28 August 1944.

Many of the French Vercors dead are buried in what is now a national memorial site on Charvet ridge, more or less at the centre of the French line defending the plateau in the battles of Saint-Nizier. Here too lie the bodies of Eugène Chavant, François Huet and many of the other leaders who died in the post-war years. An annual commemoration service is held here every year on 21 July, the anniversary of the start of the Battle of the Vercors.

By contrast, all the German commanders during Operation Vercors sank into obscurity. Two became teachers in Bavaria. One became an artist in New York. Franz Schwehr committed suicide in the 1950s. Heinrich Niehoff fell into Russian hands near the end of the war and was never seen again. The highly decorated Friedrich Schäfer ended up as a humble sales representative.

Francis Cammaerts was recognized after the war as one of the most successful of all SOE agents in France – 'our star turn' as he was described in his personal file. He received the DSO from the British, the Légion d'Honneur and the Croix de Guerre from the French and the Medal of Freedom from the US. He revisited the Vercors with his wife every year to attend the annual memorial event at Saint-Nizier and, for a few years, lived near the plateau at the little village of Grane, 10 kilometres west of Crest. In 1952, he returned to his old profession of teaching, taking up posts as diverse as head of Rolle College in Exmouth in Devon and Professor of Education in Nairobi. He died in 2006. He always said that he would much prefer to be remembered as an educationalist than as a war hero.

After the war, Christine Granville was awarded the George Medal for a daring rescue of Francis Cammaerts not long after the couple left the Vercors. She also received the Croix de Guerre from the French authorities for her work with the Resistance. But she found it impossible to cope with the boredom of peace when it came. Turned down for a job in the British Civil Service because she wasn't a British citizen, she worked as a stewardess on passenger liners. She occasionally saw Cammaerts and some of her other wartime colleagues, but otherwise lived a quiet and rather lonely life. On 15 June 1952, she was tragically murdered in the Shelbourne Hotel, Earl's Court by a man who had become obsessed with her from the time the two had first met, working on a passenger liner.

Following criticism, not least by Cammaerts, the SOE held an official inquiry in December 1944 into the departure of Houseman and Longe from the Vercors. Among those who were asked to submit evidence were Cammaerts, Thackthwaite, Huet, Zeller, Descour, Boissière, Pecquet, two of his fellow radio operators, Conus and Chavant. Although Cammaerts, reflecting the view of many in the SOE, was critical, all the key French witnesses were either supportive or non-committal. In its findings, the inquiry exonerated the two men and congratulated them for the initiative they had shown in reaching Switzerland. After the inquiry, John Houseman was awarded the MBE and Desmond Longe an MC.

The redoubtable Peter Ortiz, the US Marine dropped in with the Union Mission, returned to London after Thackthwaite. He led a second mission into France (Union II) and was parachuted on to the plateau of Les Saisies (now a ski resort) in what was the largest parachute drop of personnel and equipment of the war. Captured by the Germans, he was treated as a prisoner of war and spent the remaining months of the conflict in a PoW camp. After the war he returned to California where his friend the director John Ford gave him bit parts in several John Wayne movies. His unmistakable features can still be seen by sharp-eyed enthusiasts for these old cowboy epics. He died on 16 May 1988.

In the post-war years, the Vercors story swiftly assumed the status of legend – even myth. Some went so far as to complain that it smothered out the stories and achievements of lesser-known Resistance groups. What had happened on the plateau and who was to blame became a political *cause célèbre* which sent shockwaves through the French establishment for the next three decades and more. There were inquiries both informal and official. There were conferences and exposés, new theories were put forward and old facts revisited. The left blamed the right. The Communists blamed de Gaulle and the Army. The right blamed the left, and particularly the Communists. Both blamed the Allies. There were even some who believed it was all the result of a KGB conspiracy.

It is only in recent years that the overlay of French politics on the story has begun to diminish in favour of a more objective view. Even so, what happened on the plateau retains an important position, perhaps second only to Oradour-sur-Glane, in the pantheon of modern French history, as a living testament to the sacrifices made during the years of resistance. Evoking the spirit of Vercors can still play a part in French politics at the highest level. In 1994, President Mitterrand, whose own history in the Resistance had been the subject of controversy, ordered that an impressive Memorial to the Resistance in the form of a museum be constructed, at considerable expense, at the top of the Col de la Chau, above Vassieux. Presidential candidate Lionel Jospin in his turn declared, 'France was in London or in the Vercors, she was not in Vichy,' in the course of his campaign in 2002. More recently, Nicolas Sarkozy went out of his way to associate himself with the Vercors spirit in a speech in La Chapelle during his 2012 Presidential election campaign. This was originally intended to be a speech on agriculture in mountainous areas, but was changed at the last moment into a highly controversial speech on the nature of national identity.

Meanwhile, there is scarcely a town of any size in France that does not remember the 'Vercors' in the name of one of its streets, squares or public places. As for the historical record, in addition to the more impressive Memorial museum decreed by President Mitterrand above the town, there is a more homely one containing artefacts and photographs which was founded by one of the Vercors' combatants in the village of Vassieux itself.

There have also been more than thirty factual books published, many of them by former combatants, together with eight works of fiction, innumerable pamphlets and papers and four films, all based on the events of 1941–4. Each of these tells the story of the Vercors from a particular viewpoint – often overlaid with the personal politics of the narrator. Curiously, none of them places this extraordinary human epic within the wider context of Allied and Gaullist strategy and decision-making.

39

POSTSCRIPT

There are no simple explanations for the misjudgements, miscalculations and sometimes downright stupidities which led to the tragedies on the Vercors. Like all great tragedies, the causes are complex and multiple.

After the war, Francis Cammaerts said: 'It was obvious that Plan Montagnards had an enormous amount to commend it and I backed it as hard as I could. However, in the minds, particularly, of the French command in North Africa, it got twisted into a way of flying the flag – of acquiring a little panache, a little *gloire*.' There is truth in this. But it is not the whole truth.

It is correct to say that the redoubt idea became one of the means by which de Gaulle and the Free French in London, having been excluded from D-Day planning, were able to seek a part in the liberation of their own country, while at the same time creating 'facts on the ground' which would make it more difficult for the Allies to impose an Allied Military Government in Occupied Territories on France. But, as the Allied/ French Overlord planning meetings in late May 1944 show, by the time D-Day came, the concept of the mountain redoubt which could be held for a short period until reinforced by paratroops was no longer just a French idea, it was Allied policy. Cammaerts himself had proposed just such a strategy with his leapfrogging plan, as early as January 1944.

In the same way, although the Allies were not part of the arguably unreal promises given by Soustelle and Constans to Chavant during his visit to Algiers in May 1944, they were aware of these at the time and considered that the plan was 'practicable and that an enduring base could be established'. We need only look at the concern which reverberated around SOE just two days after the plateau fell to see that the highest Allied circles in London felt a sense of responsibility for what happened. The French authorities in Algiers and London may have been in charge of the day-to-day direction of matters on the Vercors. But what they were doing was known about – and approved of – at the highest levels in Allied command. If there is blame to be attached for making promises which were not subsequently fulfilled, it is not borne by the French alone but is shared by the Allied high command as well.

It is not difficult to see why and for what purpose the redoubt concept was invented. It is much more difficult to see why, after the brutal obliteration of the Resistance in the Glières, Mont Mouchet and Barcelonnette risings, the idea continued to be part of Allied strategy. Cammaerts was very clear about the dangers of repeating the mistakes of Barcelonnette and warned London about these. If these were plain to him, why were they invisible to both London and Algiers?

The redoubt strategy, which was strongly opposed by local Maquis commanders such as Henri Romans-Petit and Albert Chambonnet, depended on three presumptions: first, that untrained, inexperienced and lightly armed Maquisards could, if attacked, successfully conduct a static defence; second, that the Germans could not muster the troops to challenge these concentrations; and third, that, even if the Germans could find the troops, they did not have the will to carry it through. To have been brutally disabused of these misjudgements once at Glières, without understanding that the strategy was flawed, was bad enough. To have failed to learn the lesson even after the third occasion represents the triumph of boundless hope over bloody experience on a grand scale. But here again the blame for this lies not just with the French, but also with Allied planners who, even beyond D-Day, continued to plan for redoubts.

One of the most puzzling and unresolved conundrums of this story is why, despite very clear instructions issued by SHAEF on 21 May 1944 that the *only* action to be taken on D-Day should be clandestine sabotage, these orders were, for the most part, simply ignored. As late as 4 June – just two days before the landings – junior staff in SHAEF were still holding meetings and producing papers on the conduct and formation of redoubts after D-Day.

A second unresolved question is why the messages sent to the British-led SOE networks in France limiting post D-Day actions to sabotage contradicted those sent to the French-led networks. When Francis Cammaerts met Henri Zeller in Barcelonnette on 10 June 1944, he discovered that, although he had received instructions from SOE in London to keep his men hidden for at least six weeks after D-Day, Zeller (and, it seems, Descour too) had been told exactly the opposite. Their instructions from Algiers were to mobilize and defend 'permanent bases … to be held at all costs'. Did the Algiers French authorities not get the message? Did they decide to continue with their own plans, nevertheless? Or did SOE deliberately keep its (British) networks hidden, while encouraging the French to expose theirs?

By far the most likely answer is, none of the above. As so often in war, conspiracies are far less likely to be the cause of disasters than cock-ups. The truth was that the *ad hoc*, ramshackle and politically charged systems of liaison between the French in Algiers and London and their Allied partners was simply incapable of coping effectively with the fast-moving – and fast-changing – events in the lead-up to D-Day. This was not, however, a problem which existed only between the French and the Allies. Internally, Koenig's headquarters in London was famously dysfunctional – as indeed were the systems of coordination and control in that 'basket of crabs', Algiers. None of this was improved by the fact that, as we have seen, there was a running French turf war between the two capitals as to who was in charge in southern France (and the Vercors in particular).

This confusion was not just a matter of systems, however; it came from the top. De Gaulle, who had invested so much in ensuring that any 'national uprising' would be carefully calibrated and controlled, then made an incendiary 'call to arms' on D-Day instructing French men and women that 'wherever they are and whatever they are, [their] simple and sacred duty is to fight the enemy by every means in their power'. Eisenhower, meanwhile, who had earlier given instructions for 'tout le monde à la bataille', warned the French people of the dangers of a premature rising, instructing them to 'Be patient, prepare' in his D-Day address.

It is debatable whether it would ever have been possible to restrain the people of France from intemperate action when the moment they had waited for so long finally arrived. But, in the face of the unclear, even contradictory messages they received from their leaders on and after D-Day, it is scarcely surprising that the majority did what they wanted to do most – come out into the open and strike back against their hated occupiers.

And so it was that, in the face of self-evident civil and military sentiment on the plateau and sustained by what he believed were orders originating from de Gaulle himself, Marcel Descour overruled the caution of his local commander, François Huet, and insisted on the fateful decision from which there was no way back – to mobilize and close off the Vercors on 8 June.

But was there really no way back? All the Vercors leaders, from Descour through Chavant to Cammaerts, summarily dismissed as unworkable Koenig's order of 10 June (repeated frequently afterwards) to disperse because they believed that it meant sending recently mobilized young men back to their communities, which would have been tantamount to sending them back to the firing squad. But there was another alternative – indeed the alternative Koenig had actually proposed and the Vercors Maquis themselves were forced to adopt when the plateau finally fell – to disperse 'in small groups' into the forests of the plateau and sit it out until the southern invasion. It is easy to see why this would have been unappealing to Chavant and Huet, who both felt a high sense of responsibility for protecting the civilian population of the plateau from the reprisals which would have inevitably followed – and in due course did follow. Furthermore, what made the position of the Vercors Maquisards different from those in the nearby Jura and Bauges ranges was that, while the plateau was big enough to provide substantial areas of forests in which to hide, it was also small enough (just) to be surrounded.

No doubt a dispersal into the forests on 10 June would have meant a long period of great discomfort and trial for encircled Maquisards trying to obtain food from a local population which would have been subject to terrible reprisals by German forces determined to starve the 'wolves' out of the woods. But would it really have been worse than what happened in the end? Particularly since the Germans would not have been able to devote the kind of forces necessary for complete subjugation of the plateau for the seven weeks between D-Day and the southern invasion.

These are, however, much easier judgements to make with the benefit of hindsight and from a distance of seventy years than they would have been at the time. They also take no account of the fact that the Vercors leaders believed – and with good reason – that they had cast-iron promises of support and a sacred duty to establish, sustain and defend what they understood would be the first French-controlled liberated area of their country and possibly even the seat of the nascent government and leader of the Fourth Republic.

This raises the question of the role of Operation Caïman in the ulti-
mate fate of the Vercors plateau. It is not open to doubt that, whatever
the Vercors leaders thought, de Gaulle's hope was to establish his new
power base inside France, not on their plateau, but on the Massif Central.
Some have claimed that this was because the French leader believed that
the plateau was a hotbed of revolutionary socialism, even communism.
This is wholly incorrect. No doubt there were some radical idealist
Maquisards. But in its leadership, its direction and its structures, the
Organisation Vercors was Gaullist almost to a man.

The reasons for de Gaulle's preference for the Massif Central over the
Vercors were purely political and sprang from what he was trying to
achieve at the time. De Gaulle's success in recreating, upholding and
sustaining the concept of France as a great power is truly extraordinary.
He took a France that had been humiliated, broken and disregarded – and
moreover which had contributed very little to either the final victory or
even to her own liberation – and, by his obstinacy, cunning, political skill
and ability to concentrate on the things that mattered, ensured that she
emerged from the war with her great-power status largely unscathed.
What is more, he managed to achieve this without any significant assets
to bring to the table and against the sometimes virulent and very personal
opposition of the world's most powerful man – President Roosevelt.

Although it seems incontestable that the Algiers French did abandon
the Vercors in favour of Caïman, given the political aims outlined above,
it is impossible to conclude that de Gaulle was wrong to do this. He had,
in fact, no option but to pursue the possibilities, however slim, of
Caïman, even if it meant sacrificing the Vercors. The reasons for this are
obvious. Caïman would have given the French leader a French-led invasion to be counted alongside the British and American-led ones. It would
have given him a political foothold in France which was not only
geographically central, but also purely and demonstrably French. It
would have provided him with a military base which in strategical terms
was perfectly positioned between the Allied pushes east from Normandy
and north up the Rhône valley. Above all, it would have established
French 'facts on the ground' in the centre of France, which would have
made an Allied interim government impossible. The Vercors could offer
few of these advantages – and none on the same scale.

If there was a mistake in the handling of the Caïman question, it does
not alone lie with de Gaulle for pursuing it right up to the final 'no', but

also with the Allies – and perhaps especially Maitland Wilson – for taking so long to make up their minds. If Allied command had spent less time spinning out, in the interests of diplomacy, what they must have known was an inevitable rejection, the French parachute units might have been deployed earlier, instead of arriving, just south of the Vercors, only a few days after the fall of the plateau.

Finally, we must consider the human question. Who were the heroes and who were not? I leave it to others to make these judgements – with three exceptions. The first is François Huet. He was heavily criticized after the war for his conduct of the defence of the Vercors; in my view most unjustly so. As a soldier he carried out his duty, obeyed his orders even where he thought them wrong and behaved with honour and intelligence throughout.

With the single exception of the decision to mobilize the plateau on 8 June – which he opposed – and possibly the rejection of Koenig's order to disperse 'in small groups' into the forests on 10 June, all of Huet's decisions were right. He was right not to contest the northern plateau after the fall of Saint-Nizier. His judgements about the dispositions of his very limited forces afterwards were justifiable. He was right to resist a breakout in force, in favour of dispersal, when it became probable that the plateau would fall. The timing of his decision on dispersal on 23 July was finely and accurately judged. He held his forces together magnificently and preserved their effectiveness in the period of refuge in the forests. He was right to resist Descour's orders to return to the offensive prematurely, judging with some skill the moment when it was proper to do this. And he was, in consequence, able to play a significant role in harassing the Germans as they left the plateau and in the liberation of Grenoble afterwards.

It is also necessary to recognize the key role played by the communities of the Vercors. Of course, not all supported the Maquisards, and many, like the agricultural community after the fall of Saint-Nizier, just wanted 'the quiet life'. But there would have been no refuge for the *réfractaires*, no camps and therefore no Vercors Resistance without the active complicity and support of the vast majority of those who lived on the plateau. Among these it is perhaps especially important to record the role of the women. After the war Francis Cammaerts went out of his way to stress the vital part played by what one notable historian called 'The woman at the doorway'. It was the women who carried the burden of sustaining and holding together families in the absence of their menfolk and maintaining silence in the face of the inquisitiveness of their neighbours and the interrogation of both the Germans and the Milice. It was they who, often at the same time, acted as couriers, liaison agents, Resistance activists and, in one case, even a Maquis leader. In the final terrible days of refuge in the forests, it was more often than not the women who, at risk of their lives, carried the little baskets of food to the starving fugitives in the forest, or placed the bundle of cheese and pâté at the prearranged corner of a wood or in the rafters of a barn. The Vercors' communities, and perhaps especially their women, were in the front line quite as much as the Maquisards – and of course, when it came to suffering the consequences, they bore more than their fair share of the horrors and the pain.

Finally there are the Maquisards themselves. I am astonished at the raw courage of the vast majority of these young, inexperienced, often inadequately led, under-armed and massively outnumbered fighters. It was their tenacity which beat back the German's first serious attack on Saint-Nizier; inflicted appreciable casualties on Schäfer's beleaguered paratroopers in Vassieux; significantly delayed Schwehr's forces on the eastern passes and Zabel's armoured columns at Valchevrière. And when all was lost, it was their stalwart endurance during the days of refuge and privation in the forests which denied the Germans the success they most sought – the destruction of resistance on the plateau, in the end, enabling Huet to return to the offensive in a way which turned what seemed unavoidable defeat into a final, if bitter, victory.

If there are heroes in this story, they can be found among these extraordinary young men, some of whom had lived a hunted life for two hard years, winter and summer, on the plateau, while others went to war still in the clothes they left home in only days previously. Not all of them were brave. Not all of them died well. Not all of them acted as they should have done. How could we expect otherwise, given their motley backgrounds and how unready they were for the terrible trials they had to face?

Those who understand the terrors of war will find it extraordinary that so many of these men were ready, when the moment came, to stand up and take on, face to face, the gathered might of the German Army, in what they genuinely believed was the glorious cause of the liberation of their country.

ANNEX A

NOTE ON THE POSSIBLE USE OF THE VERCORS FOR MILITARY PURPOSES (ISÈRE AND DRÔME) BY PIERRE DALLOZ*

Nowhere in France is there a natural citadel comparable to that of the Vercors. This region comprises roughly the high plateau of Autrans, of Villard-de-Lans and of La Chapelle-en-Vercors, situated at an altitude of a thousand metres. On its north, east and south sides it is protected by an almost continuous mountain chain (with summits of from 1,600 to 2,300 metres) which presents to the outside a series of steep limestone slopes with a drop of several hundred metres. Towards the west beside the lower valley of the Isère, there are some gaps which correspond to rock falls. But even there the rim of the plateau seen from the outside is a sheer drop.

Several roads use these natural gashes in the cliffs. They are well known to tourists. These are the roads of Combe-Laval, of the gorges of La Bourne, of Grands Goulets and of the Écouges. Their names bring to mind memories of tracks cut into the rock above precipices of several hundred metres, and of overhangs and tunnels. In fact, as we shall show later, an analysis of the defensive value of the rare passageways which allow penetration into the Vercors shows that the citadel would be easier to *protect on its western side than on its eastern side*.†

Here are the dimensions of the fortress area, which by the way could easily be reduced if needed.

---

* Translation by Charles Forman.

† This is probably a misprint. The plateau was easier to protect from the east than the west.

- 55km from north to south
- 10 to 20km from east to west in the southern half
- 10 to 15km from east to west in the northern half

The central area of the Vercors is in the form of broad longitudinal valleys running north–south, rather like the valleys of the Jura. The valley floor is filled with crops and especially by pastures. The crests around them are covered in forests.

These high valleys are few in number. We can pick out among them:

- The plateau from Lans to Villard-de-Lans
- The valley of Méaudre and Autrans
- The long plateau which includes Saint-Martin-La-Chapelle and Saint-Agnan-en-Vercors

One ought to mention other natural characteristics of the Vercors in so far as they could influence decisions as to the suitability of the area for military purposes.

The Vercors is a veritable sponge, pierced as it is by underground rivers, caves and potholes which are known locally as *scialets*. The inhabitants of the plateau know little or nothing of this underground network. However, it is well known and would be usable by the author of these lines.

The Vercors is a land of pastures, thus of livestock and of dairy produce. A large body of men could quite easily live off the land.

Finally, the Vercors is an area in which the population lives in groups. Immense spaces separate villages and well-defined hamlets. Its people, who sent socialist representatives to parliament, are in fact mainly republicans, so very much pro-Allies.

PROGRAMME OF IMMEDIATE ACTION

We are constituting in secret a small committee with only a few members. We have a few thousand francs in hand to cover the study period. We also have several sets of the 1/20,000 series of maps of the region.

Several of us, as reserve officers, know the region perfectly as well as the general conditions for waging mountain warfare.

Some of us have vehicular transport along with official documents enabling us to justify our presence at any place in the region at any given moment.

We propose to study a plan for complete protection of the Vercors, that is to say:

- The creation of one or more voluntary corps (number, command structure, strength, armament, quarters, siting [of units])
- Plans for defensive fire covering each access route

The men for the volunteer corps would be provided by recruitment from the local populace.

We are aware of a certain amount of Gaullist agitation among the young of the area. We intend not to make contact with these elements unless forced to do so by necessity, in which event we would proceed little by little, acting with due care and circumspection. We shall nevertheless establish a list of persons considered sure and potentially useful.

We also propose:

- To reconnoitre and render usable a small number of clandestine airstrips. Several suitable sites exist in the Vercors. We are ready to welcome and act as guides for any experts sent to evaluate these sites.
- To gather up and put in safe places the arms, explosives and tools needed for the carrying out of these projects.
- To welcome and accompany any allied agents who might be deposited or dropped by parachute.
- To bring in, in similar conditions, any persons that the Allied Command would like to see escaping from France.

Later, and when the order has been given to do so, to proceed with the training of our volunteers.

PROGRAMME FOR ACTION AT A LATER STAGE

This part of our plans can obviously take place only within the framework of occupation of France by the Allies. Under protection from a set of patrols and defensive positions which we would have organized, the

Allies would have the possibility of carrying out airborne troop landings and parachute drops in the Vercors.

Thus they could create, behind the enemy's lines and in a dangerous position for him, a strong fortress from which could be launched, in the best of conditions, raids on industrial regions and highly important communications networks.

We mentioned above the clandestine airstrips. In the event of massive occupation of the Vercors, there are other even better pieces of land which could be used, in particular the magnificent flat plain to the south of Lans.

Among objectives which would be vulnerable to attack from the Vercors, one can mention:

In the north:
- The SNCF railway line from Grenoble to Lyon (10km west as the crow flies).
- The SNCF railway line from Grenoble to Valence via Moirans (5 to 6km as the crow flies).
- The bridges over the Drac or the Isère (of Veurey, of Saint-Quentin, of Tullins, of Romans).

On the eastern side:
- The region of Grenoble – the industrial areas of Pont-de-Claix and of Vizille, chemical industries (10km as the crow flies).
- The point where high-tension lines join up from the dams at Sautet and Chambon.
- A very important line, with several big bridges, runs from Pont-de-Claix to Bec de l'Echaillon, and penetrates right into the Vercors. It would become very easily and seriously vulnerable at several points.
- The SNCF railway line from Grenoble to Marseille via Veynes, the so-called Alpine Line. It runs along the eastern edge of the Vercors through very rough terrain and is only 6 to 7km as the crow flies from the line of crests of the mountains. It comprises numerous engineering works: tunnels, viaducts.

To the south:

- The SNCF railway line from Livron to Veynes and Briançon via Die. Numerous vulnerable engineering works, 10km as the crow flies from the Col du Rousset.

To the west:

- The industrial regions of Romans and Bourg-de-Péage (20km as the crow flies).
- Valence and the SNCF railway line Paris–Lyon–Marseille (40km as the crow flies from the forests of Léoncel and of Bouvante).

It is clear that by virtue of its situation, its possibilities for defence and the facilities it could provide for the launching of raids, the Vercors could represent an excellent means for disturbing any enemy in the event that the latter found themselves in a critical situation.

Before going beyond the first stage of our plans, we should very much like to know the following:

- In what measure our programme for immediate action would be of interest to the Allied Command.
- Same question for the programme of action proposed for a later stage.
- To what extent we would receive support: arms, tools, etc.
- What means of liaison we would have available.
- The assistance on which we could rely in the event our organization came under suspicion.

Important Note: The above project is obviously only feasible under conditions of surprise and with an enemy in an advanced state of disorganization.

It should be noted that at the moment there is a garrison of Alpini at Grenoble and that these elements of German artillery (anti-aircraft) also occupy the town.

The occupation of Villard-de-Lans by an Italian company would seriously affect our projects.

December 1942

ANNEX B

PIERRE DALLOZ'S RECONSTRUCTION FROM MEMORY OF LE RAY'S MILITARY STUDY OF 1943 (MADE WHILE HE WAS IN ALGIERS IN 1944)*

THE FIVE SUB-SECTORS

Le Ray defined five sub-sectors each comprising three local commands. Broadly speaking, each command corresponded to an infantry battalion (500 men, 50 automatic rifles, 50 sub-machine-guns, with the remainder in individual weapons, automatic pistols or old-model artillerymen's short rifles).

For each command we indicate P.C.'s (command posts), drop zones, assembly areas, supplies of anti-tank weapons and mortars along with remarks as appropriate.

I SUB-SECTOR FURON/SAINT-NIZIER

This is the weak point of the defences. Two good defensive positions† from which to impede an attacking enemy: d1 at the Engin gorges then d2 and d3 up at the Bruyant gorges. The latter two are separated by a distance of 7 kilometres. Unfortunately the first one mentioned, d1, could be

---

* Translation by Charles Forman.

† Translator's note: I know of no exact equivalent English word for *verrou*, which usually refers to an ambush-type position placed for example in narrow, rock-strewn river valleys or gorges. The translations used – 'defensive positions' or 'prepared defensive positions' – are my interpretation of what was appropriate in the context. In particular, the word 'prepared' does not in itself imply any construction work, strongpoint, blockhouse or similar.

outflanked from the south (Charvet plateau) where the natural defences are relatively weak; the others, d2–d3, could be as well, this time from the north (eastern slope from point 1710). We have taken on the option of defending these positions.

Special provisions of resources for this sub-sector:

- 3 sections of scouts (90 men, 9 light machine guns, 9 sub-machine guns)
- 5 anti-tank weapons
- 4 mortars

Command post at Volant (just south of Saint-Nizier):

1 Command Merciers (E3): drop zone in P2 (the plain of Lans); assembly area in R21 (at Jaume); command post at Merciers.
2 Command Charvet (E2): command post near point 1120; drop zone in P2 (plain of Lans); assembly area in R22 (at Bernards).
3 Command Volant-Bruyant (E1): command post at Donnets (point 1119); drop zone in P2 (plain of Lans); assembly area in R22 (at Bernards).

II SUB-SECTOR AUTRANS

Command post at Autrans.

This sector is very fortunate to have a fine landing ground for parachutes, i.e. the long, broad plain between Autrans and Méaudre (5km long, 1km wide): no steep slopes in the immediate area. An electric cable which crosses the site should be removed altogether (it is only a distribution line bringing current to Gonnets).

(I was somewhat surprised to learn from Le Ray that this site had not been retained by the inspection commission which came to look at the plateau during the summer. Since this could be due to an error of some sort I shall point out for the three commands of the sub-sector two parachute landing and assembly areas, the first in the Autrans-Méaudre plain and the second in the plain at Lans.)

The first line of defence (resistance) for the Autrans sub-sector corresponds in its southern part to a line drawn through the summit of

Roche-Chalve, the Col de Romeyère and point 1478. Before it, that is to the west, lies a vast wooded plateau, the Plateau des Presles, where possible enemy infiltration would be a risk. These would put at risk:

- The d5 defensive position among the rocks called Rochers du Rang.
- The power station at La Goule Noire which is vital for us.
- The safety of the road from La Goule Noire to Saint-Julien, which provides the sole connecting route between the northern and southern halves of the Vercors. For an enemy firing from Rencurel it would be within range and could thus be pinned down.
- This is why we decided to defend the Plateau des Presles by placing a certain number of scouts there (A4). Personally I would prefer to increase their numbers, if need be withdrawing some men from less vulnerable areas.

Resources reserved from this sub-sector:

- 4 sections of scouts, at least, for the Plateau des Presles (120 men, 12 light machine guns, 12 sub-machine guns);
- 3 mortars (1 each per command).

1 Command Écouges (A1): command post at Écouges farm … drop zone in P1 (Autrans-Méaudre plain); assembly area in R11 (at Autrans).

Alternative solution: drop zone in P2 (plain of Lans); assembly area in R21 (at Jaume); itinerary: Col de la Croix Perrin (10km of road between Jaume and Autrans).

2 Command Royemère (A2): command post near the Col; drop zone in P1 (Autrans/Méaudre plain); assembly area in R12 (Gonnets).

Alternative solution: drop zone in P2 (plain of Lans); assembly area in R23 (at Geymonds); itinerary: Villar-de-Lans, Les Jarrands, gorges of the Bourne, Rencurel, Col de Romeyère (20 km of road from Geymonds to the Col).

3 Command Roche-Chalve (A3): command post at Roche-Chalve; drop zone in P1 (Autrans-Méaudre plain); assembly area in R13 (at Méaudre).

Alternative solution: drop zone in P2 (plain of Lans); assembly area in R23 (at Geymonds); itinerary: Villard-de-Lans, Les Jarrands, Méaudre (11km of road).

III CENTRAL SUB-SECTOR

Command post at Saint-Julien.

Well placed for Commands B1 and B2, much too far from B3.

It is in any case bad for a chief to have to face enemy units coming from opposite directions. In these circumstances it would be better to make B3 an autonomous command to which one could entrust (with the help of sections of scouts) the guarding of the crests running from Moucherotte to the foot of La Balme.

Resources reserved for this sub-sector:

- 4 sections of scouts (120 men, 12 light machine guns, 12 sub-machine guns) for B3;
- 4 mortars (for B1 and B2, so as to fire down on and around the demolitions d5 and d7).

1 Command Allier (B1): command post on the high ground to the west of Janis; drop zone in P2 (plain of Lans); assembly area in R23 (at Geymonds); itinerary: Villard-de-Lans, Les Jarrands, bridge at Goule Noire, Saint-Julien (11km of road from Geymonds to Saint-Julien).
2 Command Guignon (B2): command post at Barraques-en-Vercors; drop zone in P3 (Vassieux plain); assembly area in R42 (at Le Château) (16km of easy road between Vassieux and Barraques-en-Vercors).

(I had foreseen, for B1 and B2, parachute drop zones and assembly areas on the same spot, on the vast open terrain south of Saint-Martin-en-Vercors. I do not know why these were not retained.)

3 Command Cornaflon (B3): command post at Eymards (Col de l'Arc); drop zone in P2 (plain of Lans); assembly area in R24 (at Eymards).

IV SUB-SECTOR MANDEMENT OR LENTE

An area which is on very rough terrain, very wooded, far from everything. Little in the way of resources. Difficult forestry roads.

Command post either at the Mandement farm or the Lente chalet.

Resources reserved:

- 2 mortars for C1 and C2.

1 Command Echarasson (C1): command post at Col de la Machine; drop zone in P3 (Mandement meadows); assembly area in R31 (Lente chalet).
2 Command Pionnier (C2): command post at the farm or forestry lodge at Pionnier (first crossroads east of the Pas de l'Échelle); drop zone in P3 (Mandement meadows); assembly area in R23 (Lente farm).
3 Command Gagère (C3): command post at Col de Lachaux; drop zone in P4 (Vassieux plain); assembly area in R41 (Vassieux).

V SUB-SECTOR VERCORS

Forest of Vercors, a difficult region, at some distance away. Only one point of access by road, the Col du Rousset.

Command post at Rousset.

Resources reserved:

- 3 sections of scouts (90 men, 9 light machine guns, 9 sub-machine guns);

(These sections are to form the link between Pas de la Balme and B3 command)

- 2 mortars for D1.

1 Command Rousset (D1): command post situated at a point between the tunnel and the But-Sapiau, where one could see all the hairpin bends in the road; drop zone in P4 (Vassieux plain); assembly area in R41 (Vassieux), 8km of road from Vassieux to the Col du Rousset.
2 Command Tourte-Barreaux (D2): command post somewhere near the Pas de Chabrinel; drop zone in P4 (Vassieux plain); assembly area in R42 (Le Château). 13km of road from Le Château to the hamlet of Rousset via the Col de Saint-Alexis: a short cut from the Col de Saint-Alexis to Rousset should enable a saving of 8km; from Rousset to the Pas de Chabrinel, a difference in altitude of 700m; more than 8km are actually mule paths.

Le Ray considers that this sector would be rather permeable.

3 Command Veymont (D3): command post at La Grande Cabane; drop zone and assembly areas as for D2. Access itineraries (by Rousset) comparable in time and distance to those of D2.

SUMMARY

1. STRENGTH
- 15 Command centres – 7500 men
- Scouts – 450 men

2. ARMS
- Light machine guns – 795
- Sub-machine guns – 795
- Pistols, short-barrel light rifles – 6360
- Anti-tank weapons – 5
- Mortars – 15

3. MUNITIONS
Ten times the weight of the weapons.

(If we have to reduce the number of these we would economise on D3, D2, C3, C2 and A1.)

4. DROP ZONES AND ASSEMBLY AREAS
(on approved landing areas only)

- Jaume (plain of Lans) – E3, A1
- Les Bernards (ditto) – E2, E1
- Les Geymonds (ditto) – A2, A3, B1
- Les Eymards (ditto) – B3
- Vassieux (Vassieux plain) – C3, D1
- Le Château (ditto) – D2, D3, B2
- Mandement meadows – C1, C2

It is important to check with Capt. Le Ray on the exact location of these assembly areas.

5. DROP ZONES (CLANDESTINE)
- Arbounouze – N1
- Léoncel – N2

6. DEMOLITIONS
- Supplies of dynamite as at September 1943 – 21.5 tonnes
- For detonators and fuse-cord, see Capt. Le Ray

Mining staff and materials to be supplied *in situ* by the Bridges and Highways Service. Their chief engineer is one of us.

7. PLACING OF PREPARED DEFENSIVE POSITIONS (map reading as per Michelin map no. 77)

Road from Sassenage to Jaume
- d1 at the place [on the map] where it says Gorges du Furon. Road above, path below.
- d2 at the letter B of les Gorges du Bruyant

Road from Saint-Nizier to Lans
- d3 by the letter 'n' in Bruyant

Road from Saint-Gervais to Rencurel
- d4 just at the tunnel, under the star indicating the waterfall

Road from Choranche to Villard-de-Lans
- d5 by the letter 'n' in Rts-de-Rang
- d6 demolition of secondary importance: bridge at La Goule Noire

Road from Sainte-Eulalie to Barraques-en-Vercors (Grand Goulets)
- d7 by the letter 'e' in Grand Goulets
- d8 by the letter 'C' in Combe-Laval
- d9 demolition or blocking by the infantry just to the north of the Col de l'Écharasson

Road from Col de la Croix or Chalet de Lente, known as the Pionnier route
- d10 under the two letters 'll' in Pas de l'Échelle

Road of the Col du Rousset
- d11 under the letter 'g' of Refuge (the last hairpin bend when going up the road towards the tunnel).

ANNEX C

CAVES USED BY THE MAQUIS IN THE VERCORS

Grotte de la Luire, Saint-Agnan, Hospital, July 1944.

Grotte du Pas de l'Aiguille, Pas de l'Aiguille, Fighting position, July 1944.

Grotte des Fées, Above Saint-Martin, Refuge for Jean Prévost, Léa Blain etc. July 1944. Position lat. 44.9789608016585, long. 5.45337185031601, height 1,267m.

Barme Chinelles, Saint-Martin, Depot for parachuted arms, 1944. Position lat. 45.041146707554, long 5.42898503309844, height 968m.

Grotte Albert, Saint-Martin, Depot for shoes. Position lat. 45.045042580915, long. 5.43287047315212, height 914m.

Grotte Tournissa, Above Revoulat, Convalescence of Capt. Tournissa, July/August 1944.

Grotte de l'Ours, Col de la Sarna, Arms depot, November 1943.

Grotte de Loscence, East of Col de Maupas Arms depot, 1944.

Grotte des Boeufs, Presles-Le Faz, Arms depot, 1944.

Scialet des Pacons, Briac, Saint-Martin, Pecquet's depot for radio, July 1944. Position lat. 45.0272404196669, long. 5.42003117783819, height 1,021m.

Scialet du Boutin, Combettes, Refuge, July/August 1944.

Roche-Abri de Richebonne, Vassieux, Refuge during Vassieux attack, July 1944.

Trou Peyrou, East of Saint-Martin, Refuge for Morel family, July 1944.

Grotte des Ferrières, Cime du Mas, Refuge for local families.

ACKNOWLEDGEMENTS

They say that fools rush in where angels fear to tread. The truth is that when I decided, three years ago, to try to write this story I had no idea of the scale of the task, or of the extent of my own deficiencies in tackling it. Most authors in their Acknowledgements thank those who have helped to make their book better. In my case I have to thank some without whom this book would possibly never have been finished, or at least never finished in this form.

Chief among these is Sylvie Young, who two years ago volunteered, out of the blue, to help me. Since then she has been the implacable protector of her native France and the spirit of France in everything I have written. Her research has uncovered sources I would have missed. She has opened doors, particularly French doors, which I would never have been able to open. She has gone down caves I couldn't find. She has interviewed witnesses I couldn't reach. She has acted as an occasional interpreter of those passages with which I had difficulty in the more than sixty French books and hundreds of documents which I have read in the course of my research. She has corrected mistakes in my French, read and re-read my texts more times – almost – than I have and acted as interlocutor with French contributors where, for lack of time, I could not give them the attention they deserved. She has been utterly indomitable – sometimes even very annoying – in her insistence on the greatest accuracy and proper sourcing of everything, even down to the smallest detail. She has criticized, cajoled and encouraged. In short her contribution to this book is simply incalculable, as indeed are my thanks to her and to her family, Gordon and Margaux, who have been so tolerant in accepting her near obsession with perfection – or at least the nearest approximation to it that she could insist on.

I have also been especially fortunate to have had the assistance of four distinguished historians – all of them foremost experts in their field; all of them busy with their own works; all of them generous to a fault in the time they have given to this book and to ensuring that I am guided towards accuracy and away from errors which would otherwise have littered this work in profusion. They are the distinguished French historian of the Second World War, Jean-Louis Crémieux-Brilhac, the author of many books on the Resistance (among other matters) who, as a young man, himself played a part in de Gaulle's Free French organization in London; Gilles Vergnon, arguably the most knowledgeable expert on the Vercors tragedy; Rod Kedward, the doyen of British historians of the Resistance; and Peter Lieb, who has written several highly regarded books on the Germans and the Resistance in southern France and who, as well as correcting my many mistakes on German matters, has allowed me generous access to a number of original German texts which he has uncovered.

Others who have provided invaluable help have been Dame Janet Smith, who has been my Nitpicker-in-Chief, correcting and improving my English text; and Linda Siegle, who provided huge help in managing and recording the many hours of research we spent together in the National Archives, while also conducting valuable research of her own into the Vercors and the Nuremberg war crimes trials.

I have also been greatly assisted by the staff of the various archives I have consulted. These include Julie Lennard and Neil Cobbett of the National Archives in Kew; Pascal Gallien and André Rakoto of the Service Historique de l'Armée de Terre at the Château de Vincennes in Paris; Commandant Perpezat and Lieutenant Cianéa of the Division des Affaires Pénales Militaires in Le Blanc, France; Pierre-Louis Fillet, Director of the Musée de la Résistance in Vassieux; Gerard Estève, Director of the Mémorial de la Résistance en Vercors; Patricia Gillet and Nicole Even of the Archives Nationales in Paris; Richard Hughes of the sound archives section of the Imperial War Museum, London; Jeff Walden of the BBC's Written Archives Centre at Caversham; Philippe Leroux-Martin for his assistance in retrieving documents from US National Archives; Youssef Elkei and Ambassador Bob Beecroft for their advice and help in accessing documents from the Dwight D. Eisenhower papers at Johns Hopkins University; Dr Steve Bell, Head of HM Nautical Almanac Office, UK Hydrographic Office; and Joan Self and Mark Beswick of the Met Office National Meteorological Archive.

Others have helped me in very practical ways, like Charles Forman, who has placed his formidable translation skills at my disposal for official French documents and joined me when I interviewed the Chavant family in Grenoble; Paul-Yves Belette and his partner Miha, both speleologists from La Chapelle who took me and Sylvie Young down a number of the caves on the Vercors used by the Maquis; Bernard Monréal, who accompanied me down the Grotte des Fées; Philippe Huet, who provided me with invaluable information on his remarkable father; Mike Fox, who sent me his TV documentary on Francis Cammaerts; Joanna Wey, Cammaerts' daughter, for insights on her father; Max Hastings, author of *Das Reich* among many other exceptional historical works, for his generous advice and insights into the Resistance; Robert Gildea for his early encouragement and research advice; Clare Mulley for her help and advice on Christine Granville, about whom she has written a notable biography; Rachel Millard, who gave me access to her account of life as an SOE radio operator at Grendon Hall; David Harrison for his invaluable help with advice, SOE files and information on Francis Cammaerts; Steven Kippax for giving me access to his comprehensive collection of SOE files; Julia Chalkley and Martine Pattin for allowing me to see and use the journal of Nicolas Bernard; Christine Tochtermann for her translations of German documents; my friend and close colleague on my last book Dr Tom Keene for his advice on this text and help with details of SOE; my talented goddaughter Harriett McDougal, who has once again drawn the fine maps in this book; and Dr Jack Sheldon, André Chavant, Yves Baudrier, Guillaume Dalloz, the late Serge Saint-André, Mayor of La Chapelle, Patricia Villard of the Mairie in Saint-Martin-en-Vercors, Guy Bonnel, Jean-Luc Descombes and Angela and Martyn Jones for their kindnesses during the several visits my wife and I paid to the Vercors plateau.

I have also been lucky to have a wonderful team of readers who, apart from many of those mentioned above, have included Ellen Dahrendorf, Stephanie Bailey, Rosemary Billinge, Steve Radley and Hamish Norbrook. Their encouragement, comments, criticisms and amendments have been of immense assistance to me. To this list must be added Olly Grender, who, although she has not as far as I know read a word of my book, has shown great patience in putting up with its pervasive and no doubt often annoying background presence in the office we share (she also lent me her red pen).

Since I am an enthusiast and have to know everything before I write anything, the first draft of this book was very long and over-burdened with unnecessary detail. It needed tough and intelligent editing, and thankfully got just that from my editor Arabella Pike of William Collins. I am hugely grateful to her for helping me to stay on the story rather than galloping off after my many geekish enthusiasms. As someone who can at times be rather sloppy about attention to detail and, I regret, even grammar, when carried away by my subject, I also owe a considerable debt to my miraculously painstaking copy-editor, Peter James, and to Stephen Guise of William Collins, who carried the main burden of the book's production.

Finally, I want to express my gratitude once again to my agent Michael Sissons for his advice and encouragement and, as ever, to my long-suffering wife Jane, who together with my family has had to tolerate my obsession with this project over the last three years. Special thanks to my grandchildren, both French and English: to Loïs and Matthias for their occasional help with stubbornly difficult translations from their mother tongue and to Annie-Rose Ashdown, the best ticker-off in the whole world (precisely what that means is a secret between her and me). And of course to her younger sister Josie, who despite her enthusiasm for my shredding machine managed not to shred any of my chapters that *really* mattered.

To all of these I owe my acknowledgement and thanks. To none should be ascribed any faults and infelicities which remain in these pages. In a work this complex it is inevitable there will be errors. But there would have been immeasurably more without the help of those mentioned above. Those that remain are mine alone.

NOTES

Abbreviations
ADD   Archives Départementales de la Drôme, Valence
ADR   Archives Départementales du Rhône, Lyon
AN   Achives Nationale, Paris
BA-MA   Bundesarchiv-Militaerarchiv, Bundesarchiv, Freiburg
DCAJM   Depôt Central des Archives de la Justice Militaire, Le Blanc
IWM   Imperial War Museum, London
NARA   National Archives and Records Administration, College Park, Maryland
SHAT   Service Historique de l'Armée de Terre, Château de Vincennes, Vincennes
TNA   The National Archives, Kew

A Note on Usages
Greenwich Mean Time: Dr Steve Bell, HM Nautical Almanac Office, email to the author, 28 June 1943.

Prologue
the Grésivaudan valley: This valley, which takes its name from Grenoble, consists chiefly of the plain of the Isère river and runs north to Albertville.
'morning of Austerlitz!': Gilbert Joseph, *Combattant du Vercors*, Grenoble: Éditions Curandera, 1994 (1st edn, Paris: Fayard 1992), p. 133.

Chapter 1: The Vercors before the Vercors
the name 'Vercors' itself: Abbé Fillet, *Essai Historique sur le Vercors (Drôme)*, Valence: Lantheaume, 1888, p. 21.
'defence against foreigners': Jules Michelet, *Tableau de la France* (first published 1861), Paris: Bibliothèque de Cluny, Librairie Armand Colin, 1962, p. 38 (http://classiques.uqac.ca/classiques/michelet_jules/tableau_de_la_france/michelet_tableau_france.pdf).
An Englishman who will play a small part in this story: Sir Francis Brooks Richards.
small funicular tramway: The tramway which started at Fontaine in Grenoble actually went beyond Saint-Nizier to Villard-de-Lans. It closed in 1951.
of the Drôme: Most French departments are named after the major rivers that run through them.
langue d'oïl: Fillet, *Essai Historique sur le Vercors*, p. 34.
by film stars: Such as the glamorous Michèle Morgan.

Chapter 2: France from the Fall to 1943: Setting the Scene
not be extinguished: http://www.charles-de-gaulle.org/pages/l-homme/dossiers-thematiques/1940-1944-la-seconde-guerre-mondiale/l-appel-du-18-juin/documents/l-appel-du-18-juin-1940.php.
6 million radios: Jean-Louis Crémieux-Brilhac, *L'Appel du 18 juin*, Paris: Armand Colin, 2010, p. 64.
almost 70,000 casualties: These figure break down as 55,500 casualties during the actual campaign and 10,400 in the 'Drôle de Guerre' which preceded it. German casualty figures

for the French campaign were in comparison 30,000. Jean Quellien *et al.*, *La France pendant la seconde guerre mondiale: Atlas historique*, Paris: Fayard/Ministère de la Défense, 2010. I am grateful to Gilles Vergnon for drawing my attention to these figures.

Special Operations Executive (SOE): SOE's birth and short wartime life were complex, dogged by politics and subject to constant attacks and rivalry from Britain's other clandestine organizations, especially MI6 – the Secret Intelligence Service.

his own clandestine organization: The Bureau Central de Renseignements et d'Action (BCRA).

Colonel André Dewavrin: Alias Passy.

'the "revolutionary war"': Jean-François Muracciole, 'La France Libre et la lutte armée', in François Marcot (ed.), *La Résistance et les Français: Lutte armée et maquis*, Colloque International de Besançon 15–17 June 1995, Paris: Annales Littéraires de l'Université de Franche-Comté, Diffusion Les Belles Lettres, 1996, p. 161.

as the Préfet: The administration of France is divided into departments, each of which has its own *préfet* representing the French state.

'determined their objectives': François-Georges Dreyfus (ed.), *Unrecognized Resistance: The Franco-American Experience in World War Two*, New Brunswick: Transaction Publishers, 2004, p. 37.

of the southern zone: Combat (Henri Frenay), Libération (Emmanuel d'Astier de La Vigérie), Franc-Tireur (Jean-Pierre Lévy).

a single body: Mouvements Unis de la Résistance (MUR).

back to Britain: Freddy Clark, *Agents by Moonlight*, London: Tempus Publishing, 1999, p. 130.

'territory of France': SHAT 1 K 374/3; TNA HS 6/332.

'General of the Secret Army Vidal': Official history of the FFI, TNA HS 7/132, p. 21.

Marcel Descour: In October 1943, Colonel Marcel Descour became the Chief of Staff of the Armée Secrète of the Rhône-Alpes region.

equipment a month: Christian Wyler, *La Longue Marche de la Division 157: Contre les maquis et les partisans 1942–1945*, Paris: Grancher, 2004, p. 39.

Minister for Labour: His formal title was General Plenipotentiary for Labour Deployment (Generalbevollmächtigter für den Arbeitseinsatz).

'"agent, Gauleiter Sauckel"': Pierre Bot, *La Bataille du Vercors*, Valence: Éditions Peuple Libre, 2008, p. 9.

away to Germany: Jean Sauvageon, Gilles Vergnon and Jacki Vinay, *1939–1945: Et se leva le vent de la liberté: Entre Drôme des collines et Vercors*, Guilherand-Granges: ANACR, 2012, pp. 28, 62 and 243.

12 March 1943: RF Section diary, TNA HS 7/247, for these dates.

Chapter 3: Beginnings

in March 1941: There is some dispute about this date. In Dalloz's book *Vérités sur le drame du Vercors* he relates that this incident took place on the day that the news broke that the aircraft carrying a senior Vichy official, Jean Chiappe, had been accidentally shot down by Italian fighters. If this is correct, this meeting would have taken place, not in March 1941, but around 27 November 1940. Pierre Dalloz, *Vérités sur le drame du Vercors*, Paris: Éditions Fernand Lanore, 1979, p. 11.

one-time government servant: He had served in the office of Jean Giraudoux, the Minister of Information, in France's pre-fall government of 1939–40.

'behind the enemy lines': Dalloz, *Vérités sur le drame du Vercors*, p. 33.

'rather than me': *Ibid.*, p. 35.

'of limestone rock': Paul Dreyfus, *Histoire de la Résistance en Vercors*, Paris: Arthaud, 1980, p. 12.

and medical stores: History of the ORA by Colonel Augustin de Dainville, SHAT 1 K 89/8.

one of the chief smugglers: Louis Nal.

'sat holding court': Pierre Vial, *La Bataille du Vercors 1943–1944*, Paris: Presses de la Cité, 1991, p. 15.

of all types: Dreyfus, *Histoire de la Résistance en Vercors*, p. 13.

wait and see: Referred to by the French as *attentisme*.

Rue du Polygone: The area was completely demolished and redeveloped after the war. It now consists of modern high-rise flats, a trade centre and hotels serving the station. The Rue du Polygone, which led to the Artillery Park of the same name where many Resistants were executed, has been renamed the Rue des Martyrs.

the railway workers: *Cheminots*.

but also Masons: In France the Masonic movement was and remains much more left wing than its counterpart in Britain. Many members of the Socialist Party at the time also belonged to a Masonic lodge.

local shoe factory: Neyret Bellier.

of a restaurant: Le Grand Café on the nearby Île Verte (interview with André Chavant, 6 June 2013, Grenoble).

a railway worker at the station: Paul Deshières.

a garage owner: Eugène Ferrafiat.

establishment in the town: Association Mémoire du Lycée Polonais Cyprian-Norwid, *Des résistants polonais en Vercors: La saga du lycée polonais Cyprian-Norwid: Villard de-Lans 1940–1946*, Grenoble: Presses Universitaires de Grenoble, 2012, p. 28.

the Villard-de-Lans area: Jean Sauvageon, Gilles Vergnon and Jacki Vinay, *1939–1945: Et se leva le vent de la liberté: Entre Drôme des collines et Vercors*, Guilherand-Granges: ANACR, 2012, p. 268.

the south as well: The first census of Jews took place in the area on 21 July 1941 (*ibid.*).

origin, Dr Samuel: Alias Ravalec and Jacques.

of his pharmacy: The Pharmacie du Parc.

of a hotelier: Théo Racouchot.

local tax inspector: Marius Charlier (alias Florentin).

the Banque Populaire: Édouard Masson.

the Villard group: Other members were Jo Beaudoingt, Baptiste Converso, Marcel Dumas, Jean Galudas, Raymond Piqueret.

one of their number: Théo Racouchot.

'the Vercors started': Sauvageon *et al.*, *1939–1945: Et se leva le vent de la liberté*, p. 268.

'and a fortress': AMLPC-N, *Des résistants polonais en Vercors: La saga du lycée polonais Cyprian-Norwid*, p. 15.

Chapter 4: The Army Goes Underground

Hôtel de la Division: This impressive seventeenth-century building, also known as Hôtel des Troupes de Montagne de Grenoble, is not a hotel but the Army headquarters in Grenoble.

from his superior: General Picquendar.

previously Italian units: 20th Alpine Group of the Italian 5th Alpine 'Pusteria' Division.

to occupy Grenoble: *La Guérilla n'aura pas lieu … La Bataille du Vercors 1940–1944*, Paris: CDEF/DREX/Bureau Recherche, 2010 (http://www.cdef.terre.defense.gouv.fr/…la…/la-bataille-du-vercors-1940-1944), p. 19.

the Pont de la Boucle: Now renamed the Pont Winston Churchill.

'have replaced me': Paul Dreyfus, *Histoire de la Résistance en Vercors*, Paris: Arthaud, 1980, p. 27.

towards the forests of the Savoie: There are many stories surrounding Geyer's exit from Lyon and entry into the clandestine life. Some appear to belong more in the realm of legend than history. For this one I am indebted to the account in Paul Dreyfus' excellently researched *Histoire de la Résistance en Vercors*.

a rubber hammer: Pierre Vial, *La Bataille du Vercors 1943–1944*, Paris: Presses de la Cité, 1991, p. 44.

life as a Maquisard: There are also rather more prosaic legends of Geyer's flight from Lyon into the maquis. According to the residents of the village of Le Grand Serre, the dashing cavalry commander took the regular bus from Lyon and got off at the village terminus, spending his first night as a Maquisard in the local hotel, the Hotel Brenier, before moving into the nearby Thivolet farm. Andrew Bunney email to the author, 12 November 2014.

iron-studded gate: Lieutenant Stephen (André Valot), *Vercors, premier maquis de France*, Grenoble: Association Nationale des Pionniers et Combattants Volontaires du Vercors, 1991 (1st edn, Buenos Aires: VIAU, 1946), p. 70.

'playing at soldiers': Vial, *La Bataille du Vercors 1943–1944*, p. 83.

much loved commander: Albert de Seguin de Reyniès, the commander of 6th Battalion of Chasseurs Alpins (6th BCA).

'as a fighting unit': SHAT T 1167, 6th BCA.

called Dom Guétet: Alias Commandant Lemoine.

'on the Crusades': The words of Captain Pierre Tanant. Gilbert Joseph, *Combattant du Vercors*, Grenoble: Éditions Curandera, 1994 (1st edn, Paris: Fayard, 1992), p. 162.

draft of his plan: See Annex A.

'resolution and hope': Pierre Dalloz, *Vérités sur le drame du Vercors*, Paris: Éditions Fernand Lanore, 1979, p. 36.

Chapter 5: Camps and Plans

Jean Veyrat: Alias Raymond.

On 17 December: I am indebted for the details of this description to Patrice Escolan and Lucien Ratel, *Guide-mémorial du Vercors résistant*, Paris: Le Cherche-Midi, 1994, p. 54. Some sources put the date of the Brun/Samuel visit as 19 December 1943.

La Ferme d'Ambel: The farm and its outbuildings were burnt down by Vichy security forces in April 1944. The main farmhouse was rebuilt as a mountain refuge after the war. The outbuildings have disappeared.

most active partners: Victor Huillier and his brother-in-law, André Glaudas.

a hardware shop: The Quincaillerie Allemand.

by two sympathizers: Louis and Lilly Allemand.

Place Verdun in Grenoble: I am indebted for the details in this passage to the descriptions of this process given by Fernand Rude, 'Vercors', in Pierre Bolle (ed.), *Grenoble et le Vercors: De la Résistance à la Libération 1940–1944*, Lyon: La Manufacture, 1985, p. 100, and Aimé Pupin's in Pierre Dalloz's *Vérités sur le drame du Vercors*, Paris: Éditions Fernand Lanore, 1979, p. 340.

the main street: Rue des Lesdiguières.

Louis Bourdeaux: Alias Fayard.

in quick succession: Lieutenant Stephen (André Valot), *Vercors, premier maquis de France*, Grenoble: Association Nationale des Pionniers et Combattants Volontaires du Vercors, 1991 (1st edn, Buenos Aires: VIAU, 1946), p. 30.

Yves Farge: Alias Bessonneau and Grégoire.

a nearby restaurant: The Brasserie du Tonneau.

on 29 January: As it happens, Moulin and Delestraint had been waiting in the Château de Villevieux in the Jura for a pick-up on 27 January. But the pick-up was cancelled and the two men left by bus for Lyon on 28 January, so they would probably have been in Lyon on 29 January. Laure Moulin, *Jean Moulin: Biographie*, Paris: Presses de la Cité, 1982, p. 293.

should be supported: Although the original of this courier message cannot be found, its existence and a broad idea of its contents are referred to in an SOE minute (Plans 325/221 of 10 April 1943) in TNA HS 8/284, Military and other Projected Targets. I am indebted to Steven Kippax for drawing my attention to this important document.

paid Dalloz: Now equipped with the alias Senlis.

'will meet you': Dalloz, *Vérités sur le drame du Vercors*, p. 55.

their contact 'Alain': Daniel Cordier, who was at the time secretary to Jean Moulin and later his biographer.

'the newspaper *Signal*': A German-edited illustrated weekly.

an insurance company: The offices of M. Fornier, the Bourg representative for Union Insurance. Fornier (alias Bob) was, with his brother, one of the key architects of the Resistance in the Ain Department of France and was later arrested and deported. The house, marked by a plaque recording its role in the Resistance, remains exactly as it was in 1943.

Charles Delestraint: Alias Vidal.

General Desmazes: Alias Richard.

'the Plan Montagnards': Dalloz, *Vérités sur le drame du Vercors*, p. 58. The title 'Montagnards' was probably taken from the nickname used by the Democratic Party in the 1791 Republican Assembly.

RAF's 161 Squadron: Flown by Flight Lieutenants Vaughan-Fowler and McCairns.

in the Jura: http://www.plan-sussex-1944.net/anglais/pdf/infiltrations_into_france.pdf.

including in the Vercors: Dalloz, *Vérités sur le drame du Vercors*, p. 71.

'the Allied Command': Charles de Gaulle, *The War Memoirs*, vol. 2: *Unity 1942-1944*, New York: Simon & Schuster, 1959, p. 102.

'on their own': Plans 325/221 to D/R (SOE's French Regional Controller, Robin Brook), 10 April 1943, in TNA HS 8/284, Military and Other Projected Targets.

the head of the Department for Water and Forests on the Vercors: Rémi Bayle de Jessé.

an ex-commander of the Mountain Warfare School at Chamonix: Marcel Pourchier.

Alain Le Ray: Alias Rouvier and Bastide.

three fellow ex-officers: Lieutenants Jeannest, Régnier and Roland Costa de Beauregard.

Roland Costa de Beauregard: Alias Durieu.

to the ground: The remains of the farmhouse are still visible in the middle of the Herbouilly pasture.

Chapter 6: Exodus and Folly

door behind him: I am indebted for the details in this passage to the descriptions of this process given by Fernand Rude, 'Vercors', in Pierre Bolle (ed.), *Grenoble et le Vercors: De la Résistance à la Libération 1940-1944*, Lyon: La Manufacture, 1985, p. 100, and Aimé Pupin's in Pierre Dalloz's *Vérités sur le drame du Vercors*, Paris: Éditions Fernand Lanore, 1979, p. 328

the same again: Taken largely from the evidence of Fernand Rude, 'Vercors', p. 100.

rose to eighty-five: *La Guérilla n'aura pas lieu … La Bataille du Vercors 1940-1944*, Paris: CDEF/DREX/Bureau Recherche, 2010 (http://www.cdef.terre.defense.gouv.fr/…la…/ la-bataille-du-vercors-1940-1944), p. 24, and Jean-Marc Collavet, *Chronique du Vercors*, Valence: Éditions Peuple Libre, 1994, p. 18.

'We needed arms': Collavet, *Chronique du Vercors*, p. 18.

eight new *réfractaire* camps: C1 was Ambel; C2 was housed in a specially constructed cabin at Puits des Ravières, near Corrençon; C3 was in the forestry cabin at Gèves, above Autrans; C4 was on the plateau at Cournouze; C5 was at Gros Martel above Méaudre; C6 was first at Laragnole but moved later to Col de Lachau near Vassieux; C7 (a Combat camp) was on the Plateau Saint-Ange; C8 was at Piarrou near Vassieux. Other camps were also established: C9, 10 and 11 were all military camps, the last being at the Monastery of Esparron in the Trièves south-east of the edge of the plateau. A twelfth camp, C12, was at the Chalet Bellier and, at the end of May, a final camp was set up by the Valence Military School near La Chapelle.

some 400 men: This figures varies according to the sources used, due probably to turnover in the camps. Pierre Dalloz gives 400, the register of the Vercors Pioneers gives 392, Henri Jaboulay gives 560 and Fernand Rude 325. Gilles Vergnon, *Le Vercors: Histoire et mémoire d'un maquis*, Paris: Les Éditions de l'Atelier, 2002, p. 64.

from Ambel (C1): The camps in the Isère had even numbers and those in the Drôme uneven ones. Pierre Montagnon, *Les Maquis de la Libération*, Paris: Éditions Pygmalion/Gérard Watelet, 2000, p. 67.

eastern regions of France: Vergnon, *Le Vercors: Histoire et mémoire d'un maquis*, p. 65.

'our time fully': Collavet, *Chronique du Vercors*, p. 27.

collected from contacts: They were called Rosenfeld and Lévy – Aimé Pupin's evidence in Dalloz, *Vérités sur le drame du Vercors*, p. 329.

'and resistance movements': Colonel Passy (André Dewawrin), *Souvenirs*, vol. 2: *10, Duke Street, Londres (Le BCRA)*, Paris: Raoul Solar, 1948, p. 309; also Laure Moulin, *Jean Moulin: Biographie*, Paris: Presses de la Cité, 1982, p. 266.

Plan Montagnards alone: Moulin, *Jean Moulin*, p. 266.

Moulin's deputy: Daniel Cordier.

budget proposals for March: TNA HS 7/247, p. 174.

1.75 million francs: In her biography of her brother, Laure Moulin quotes an even larger figure – 3.2 million francs – for the size of the London subvention going into the Vercors in the spring of 1943. Moulin, *Jean Moulin*, p. 383.

'François Tirard': There was in fact no such person, François Tirard being a play on the name of the Resistance organization Franc-Tireur.

branch in Villard: Michael Pearson, *Tears of Glory: The Betrayal of the Vercors*, London: Pan Books, 1978, p. 14.

'to get money': Interrogation of Procureur (Capt. Thackthwaite), 13 May 1944, TNA HS 6/359.

Darbonouse: Also spelt d'Arbonouze.

Their commander: Gaston Cathala, alias Grange.

'the Resistance is judged': Pierre Vial, *La Bataille du Vercors 1943–1944*, Paris: Presses de la Cité, 1991, p. 48.

sheep in the area: *Ibid.*

'improving their tans': Vial, *La Bataille du Vercors 1943–1944*, p. 54

its commander: Pierre Dunoyer de Ségonzac.

château of Murinais: It had at one time belonged to the 'The knight without fear or reproach', Pierre Terrail de Bayard, from whom Marcel Descour took his *nom de guerre*.

flying squads: *Équipes volantes.*

in Morse code: Albert Renier (alias Vauban) taught Morse in the semi-military camp which was founded on the plateau Saint-Ange. Vial, *La Bataille du Vercors 1943–1944*, p. 28.

a small booklet: Bernard Comte, 'Uriage et la Résistance', in Bolle (ed.), *Grenoble et le Vercors*, pp. 31 and 170 *et seq.*

Fabien Rey: Alias Blaireau (badger) and Marseille.

any visitor who called: Much of this description of Rey is drawn from Dalloz, *Vérités sur le drame du Vercors*, p. 65.

In February 1943: Collavet, *Chronique du Vercors*, p. 18.

From now on: There is some uncertainty about exactly when this was formed for the first time and who was on it. Dalloz speaks of a 'Committee of three', formed on 23 May 1943, which consisted of himself, Pourchier and Pupin. Le Ray (who calls this a 'Comité de Combat') says it was formed in early March and consisted of six members: Dalloz, Pourchier, Farge, Bayle de Jessé, Le Ray and Pupin. See Vergnon, *Le Vercors: Histoire et mémoire d'un maquis*, p. 51.

Combat Committee: Comité de Combat.

pay for the camps: Dalloz, *Vérités sur le drame du Vercors*, p. 330.

by a sympathizer: Marcel Gay.

'parachuted from the sky': Dalloz, *Vérités sur le drame du Vercors*, p. 64.

fourteen other core members: Demeure, Veyrat, Claude Lévy, Loulou Chabas, Robert Brunte, Rigaudin, Marcel and René Fraisse, Batelli, Gavet, Portaluppi, Clet, Visantin and Mme Ruggiero.

Chapter 7: Expectation, *Nomadisation* and Decapitation

his Lysander's: A Westland Lysander Mark II, Registration number V9367 according to http://www.ww2aircraft.net/forum/aviation/squadron-161-lysander-mk-iii-31062.html.

pointing to the right: I am indebted to Pierre Lorain, *Secret Warfare*, London: Orbis, 1983, for much of the detail in this description.

his wheel rims: John T. Correll, 'The Moon Squadrons', *Air Force Magazine*, July 2012, http://www.airforcemag.com/MagazineArchive/Pages/2012/July%202012/0712moon.aspx.

one other Resistance agent: Christian Pineau (alias Francis) of the Phalanx Resistance network.

village of Melay: There is an error on one of the websites giving details of this landing (http://www.plan-sussex-1944.net/anglais/pdf/infiltrations_into_france.pdf) which positions the landing site 1.3 kilometres north-west of Saint-Yan. There is a magnificent red marble memorial marking this operation and the arrival of Jean Moulin and Charles Delestraint back in France on the canal side near the hamlet of Bagneau, less than a kilometre east of Melay.

22.44 hours: 20.44 UK time. Most of the details on Sirène II in this description come from Bridger's post-operational report in file TNA AIR 27/1068, entry for Lysander operations, 19/20 March 1943.

after sunset: Sunset was at 18.09 this evening.

'the journey was uneventful': TNA AIR 27/1068.

Pierre Delay: Alias Var and Joseph. See http://www.memoresist.org/spip. php?page=oublionspas_detail&id=10.

a previous SOE landing: At nearby Saint-Yan; see *ibid.*

a landing on this site: In fact Delay had previously suggested that this landing should take place at Loyettes in the Ain Department, but London had insisted that an alternative site should be found.

Les Français parlent aux Français: Unfortunately no BBC broadcast messages from this early in the war survive at the BBC Archives in Caversham (Jeff Walden email to the author, 21 June 2013).

he had a cousin: M. Burdin.

north of the landing site: In the village of Marcigny.

local garage owner: Claude Commerçon.

on these occasions: http://www.memoresist.org/spip.php?page=oublionspas_detail&id=10.

'apathy and despair': SOE memorandum, 'The Function of Resistance Groups in France', p. 2, TNA HS 6/322.

On 18 March: Rod Kedward, *France and the French: A Modern History*, Woodstock and New York: Overlook Press, 2006, p. 297.

the Légion des Montagnes: On 23 September 1793, the Revolutionary Convention Nationale called for four battalions to be formed in the Pyrenees, under the name Légion des Montagnes, to protect the French/Spanish border from invasion.

'Allied action was imminent': François Marcot, 'Le Service national maquis: Structures, pouvoirs et stratégies', in François Marcot (ed.), *La Résistance et les Français: Lutte armée et maquis*, Colloque International de Besançon 15–17 June 1995, Paris: Annales Littéraires de l'Université de Franche-Comté, Diffusion Les Belles Lettres, 1996, p. 212.

'[the French] clandestine services': *Ibid.*, p. 213.

'the Allied landings': Instructions to Vidal, SHAT 1 K 374/3.

'burning for action …': Jean-Marc Collavet, *Chronique du Vercors*, Valence: Éditions Peuple Libre, 1994, p. 27.

Gestapo: The name comes from the first letters of their long name *Geheime Staatspolizei* (State Secret Police).

'might be imminent': Paper dated 20 August 1943 analysing the Japanese Ambassador's telegram of earlier in the year (precise date unknown, but probably in late June), TNA HS 6/339.

in the summer: Report from Mackerel Major, 30 April 1944, TNA HS 7/247.

'ten metres way': Witness evidence and illustration from Association Nationale des Pionniers du Vercors, *Le Vercors raconté par ceux qui l'ont vécu*, Valence: Imprimerie Nouvelle, 1990, p. 148.

'as long as possible': Pierre Vial, *La Bataille du Vercors 1943–1944*, Presses de la Cité, 1991, p. 59.

the young Maquisards: Jean Moulin had lent one of his radios and a radio operator (Scalare) to the Vercors. See Laure Moulin, *Jean Moulin: Biographie*, Paris: Presses de la Cité, 1982, p. 328.

'thwarting the attack': Message from 'Scalare via Volga', 21 May 1943, TNA HS 7/247.

Col de Rousset: It is today the Col de Rousset ski station, and Mémé Bordat's café – reconstructed after being destroyed during the war – is still there.

'friends [the Germans]': Lieutenant Stephen (André Valot), *Vercors, premier maquis de France*, Grenoble: Association Nationale des Pionniers et Combattants Volontaires du Vercors, 1991 (1st edn, Buenos Aires: VIAU, 1946), p. 58.

'to the French police': Cammaerts' post-operational report, p. 10, TNA HS 6/568.

1.6 million francs: Moulin, *Jean Moulin*, p. 384.

a further 40 million: London estimated that the cost of funding a single Maquisard for one
   month was between 700 and 1,000 francs.

his work across France: Entry for 11 April 1943, TNA HS 7/247.

on Jean Moulin's instructions: Moulin, *Jean Moulin*, p. 328.

'Lyon would fall': Pierre Dalloz, *Vérités sur le drame du Vercors*, Paris: Éditions Fernand
   Lanore, 1979, p. 73.

'mountainous part of the Vercors': There are two versions of this conversation. One is given in
   Paul Dreyfus, *Histoire de la Résistance en Vercors*, Paris: Arthaud, 1980, p. 61, and the other
   in Yves Farge, *Rebelles, soldats et citoyens*, Geneva: Éditions Grasset, 1948, p. 94. The author
   has combined these here.

'took refuge here': Dalloz, *Vérités sur le drame du Vercors*, p. 334.

'land in France': Dreyfus, *Histoire de la Résistance en Vercors*, p. 60.

after the Allied landings: Dalloz, *Vérités sur le drame du Vercors*, p. 335.

'the great nations again': Jacques Soustelle, *Envers et contre tout*, 3 vols, Geneva: Éditions de
   Crémille, 1970 (1st edn, Paris: Robert Laffont, 1947–50), vol. 3, p. 70.

a nearby government depot: The depot for the Chantier de Jeunesse at Saint-Laurent-du-Pont.

across the plateau: Many decomposing pairs of men's and ladies' shoes of the era can still be
   found in the Grottes Albert (lat. 45.045042580915, long. 5.43287047315212), a cave above
   Saint-Martin. These may be the unwanted shoes from this raid. Author's visit with Pierre-
   Yves Belette, 29 May 2013.

'it was hopeless': Collavet, *Chronique du Vercors*, p. 27.

known Resistance sympathies: André Fluchaire. His garage was in Mens, south-east of the
   plateau.

eleven armed Maquisards: Baptiste Converso (driver), Captain Virel, Simon Samuel, Jo
   Beaudoingt, Ackerman, Magnat, Ollech, Nallet, Piqueret and two mechanics.

its Resistance sympathies: The Bar Sully.

the leader of the Villard Commando: Captain Virel.

four other key Resistance organizers: Marius Charlier, the two Glaudas brothers and the
   forestry chief, Rémy Bayle de Jessé.

dynamite hidden near by: Michael Pearson, *Tears of Glory: The Betrayal of the Vercors*,
   London: Pan Books, 1978, p. 15.

possession of the house: Interview with Guillaume Dalloz, 6 June 2013, La Grande Vigne.

from all military action: TNA HS 7/247.

'or we don't live': Dalloz, *Vérités sur le drame du Vercors*, p. 81.

a village west of Grenoble: Chamrousse. Dreyfus, *Histoire de la Résistance en Vercors*,
   pp. 76 –8.

a restaurant in Lyon: At 46 Rue Tête d'Or.

Jean Prévost: Now with the alias Goderville after the town in which he was born in Normandy.

the Alma-Marceau exit of the Métro: Chez Francis and its terrace are still there on the Place de
   l'Alma and look much as they must have looked at the time, allowing for wartime
   circumstances.

another Resistance leader: Joseph Gastaldo.

'is to cease': Scalare's signal via Red Perch, 29 June 1943, TNA HS 7/247.

seven other key Resistance leaders: Jean Moulin, Emile Schwartzfeld, Raymond Aubrac,
   André Lassagne, Bruno Larat, Albert Lacaze, Henri Aubry. An eighth person was also
   present, René Hardy, who is believed by some to have been the person who betrayed
   Moulin to the Germans.

tortured to death: He died on 9 July 1943.

the Alpes-Maritimes: TNA HS 7/247.

'organisation were arrested': TNA CAB 66/56/20 WP (44) 570, 13 October 1944.

a secret French source: Probably Gabriel Cochet.

'[the notorious Gestapo prison in Paris]': Report of 29 July 1943, TNA HS 6/328.

Chapter 8: Retreat, Retrenchment and Reconstruction

survived the summer purges: Daniel Cordier.

odyssey out of France: Pierre Dalloz later recorded in his book *Vérités sur le drame du Vercors* (Paris: Éditions Fernand Lanore, 1979, p. 113) that over the next six months of his flight, he slept in more than seventy different beds.

Place des Postes: Now known as the Place Dr Léon Martin, after the man in whose pharmacy the Grenoble group was established (see Chapter 3).

the Château de Murinais: This was the home of the flying squads which were made up from the remaining elements of the École de Uriage. See Chapter 6.

A second Combat Committee: Its full membership was Jean Prévost, Eugène Chavant, Eugène Samuel, Chevalier, Tarze, Charlotte Mayaud and Geneviève Blum-Gayet. Jean-Marc Collavet, *Chronique du Vercors*, Valence: Éditions Peuple Libre, 1994, p. 36.

the 'Organisation Vercors': Gilles Vergnon, *Résistance dans le Vercors: Histoire et lieux de mémoire*, Grenoble: Glénat, 2002, p. 66.

two administrative sub-units: The head of the northern half was Eugène Samuel, while the southern half was placed under the control of Benjamin Malossane.

controlling the north: His deputy was André Bordenave (alias Dufau).

another of his officers: Lieutenant Jeannest (alias Gay).

each of the Maquis groups: Paul Dreyfus, *Vercors: Citadelle de la liberté*, Romagnat: De Borée, 2007 (1st edn Paris: Arthaud, 1969), p. 81.

four secret Maquisard companies should be raised: Two companies in Grenoble, Compagnie Brisac (after its leader Paul Brisac) and Compagnie Philippe (after the alias of its leader Henri Ullman), a company in Villard-de-Lans (led initially by Francisque Troussier) and Compagnie Vincent, which became Compagnie Abel – see below.

André Vincent-Beaume: Alias Sambo and Vincent. Vincent-Beaume recruited a group of Socialist fellow teachers to help with the early 'political' instruction of the new recruits. These included seven teachers and three professors, among whom were André Archinard, Louis Ferroul, Raymond Machon, Gustave Ferlin and Henri Vergnon. See Vergnon, *Résistance dans le Vercors: Histoire et lieux de mémoire*, p. 61.

One of these companies: For the information in these paragraphs, I am indebted to the pamphlet *Le Pionnier du Vercors: La Compagnie Abel 1943–1944*, Grenoble: Association Nationale des Pionniers et Combattants du Vercors, Special number 2012.

Abel Company: Named after its leader, another local teacher, Fernand Crouau (alias Abel).

a local factory owner: Justin Bonardel.

divided into four sections: One for each of the three cantons of Bourg-de-Péage, Romans and Saint-Donat and one section specially for 18–20-year-olds drawn from across the three towns.

the south-west quadrant of the plateau: Broadly speaking from the Combe Laval to the Col de Rousset.

a water bottle: Witness evidence of André Vincent-Beaume, ADD, 9J5. Also quoted in Vergnon, *Résistance dans le Vercors: Histoire et lieux de mémoire*, p. 61.

at the entry to Mens: Albert Darier, *Tu prendras les armes*, Valence: Imprimerie Nouvelle, 1983, p. 74. Darier relates the event described in these paragraphs as having taken place in January 1943, but the order to form civil companies was not made until June of that year.

the Bonnet de Calvin: At 1,937 metres high, the unusual shape of the Bonnet de Calvin (Calvin's Hat) is easily identified as the key geographical feature of the Trièves region and marks the fact that, in the era of the French wars of religion, this area was strongly Protestant.

Albert Darier: Alias Félix.

a shepherd's hut: The original building was destroyed by the Germans but was rebuilt after the war and still stands on the same spot.

'Great Day': 'Journée grandiose'. Pierre Vial, *La Bataille du Vercors 1943–1944*, Paris: Presses de la Cité, 1991, p. 55.

Tents stolen from the valley: From the Chantiers de la Jeunesse Française (CJF) – a Vichy-founded youth organization which progressively passed over to the Resistance.

of 14 July 1790: See Dreyfus, *Vercors: Citadelle de la liberté*, p. 86.

many of the heads: Bourdeaux, Vincent-Beaume, Chosson, Ferlin, Machon among them.

the newly formed Maquisard companies: Known as *compagnies civiles*.

'highly mobile groups of thirty': Known as *trentaines*.

'our best defences': Vial, *La Bataille du Vercors 1943–1944*, p. 55.

'hedgehog': *Hérisson*.

bystanders to the main action: Vergnon, *Résistance dans le Vercors: Histoire et lieux de mémoire*, p. 63, quoting Vincent-Beaume.

'been so united': Paul Dreyfus, *Histoire de la Résistance en Vercors*, Paris: Arthaud, 1980, p. 80.

an SOE 'circuit': All SOE networks were known as 'circuits'. The French equivalent was *réseaux*. Churchill's circuit was 'Donkeyman'.

'Grands Pieds' (as he was quickly christened by Chavant): His other local Vercors nickname was 'Le Diable Anglais'.

'a couple of the military chaps': Given Cammaerts' importance, one of these would almost certainly have been Alain Le Ray.

'such as the Vercors]': Cammaerts also mentions two other areas, the Valensole plateau in the south of France and Beaurepaire north-west of the Vercors, where the same thing could happen, enabling what he referred to as a 'leapfrogging' operation with Allied troops moving north from the Mediterranean coast.

'in combat trim': IWM sound archives, Interview with Francis Cammaerts, Session No. 11238, Reel 3 at 15' 40" *et seq.*

Marcel Roudet: Alias Raoul.

Chief of Police in Lyon: René Cussonac, who was executed in September 1945 by the post-war Tribunal in Lyon for collaboration.

himself a heroin addict: Interview with Gilbert Carichon, 2 June 2013, at Chalet Fleuri, Rousset, Vercors.

'in his pocket': Witness statement dated 1945 from Geneviève Blum-Gayet. Dalloz, *Vérités sur le drame du Vercors*, p. 344.

'on the street': Darier, *Tu prendras les armes*, p. 92.

Another 'freelance' Maquis: They were known as *Groupes Francs*.

the Groupe Vallier: They were also known as *les hommes aux chapeaux mous* (literally 'the men in the soft hats'), referring to their love of the felt hats made famous by 1930 American gangster movies.

Paul Gariboldy: Alias Vallier. Some of the aliases of others in the Groupe Vallier are known. They included Bayard, Fratello, Riquet, Pierre, César, Christian and Barratta. See Pierre Tanant, *Vercors, haut-lieu de France*, Grenoble: Arthaud, 1948 and 1950, p. 104.

'how to stop': Gustave Estadès. Claude Muller, *Dauphiné 1939–1945: Les Sentiers de la liberté*, Romagnat: De Borée, 2003, p. 109.

under central control: Marcel Roudet's Raoul Maquis maintained a degree of autonomy right through to mid-1944.

Paulette Jacquier: Alias Marie-Jeanne and La Frette.

in their own right: La Frette carried out some highly successful ambushes for which Marie-Jeanne received the Croix de Chevalier of the Légion d'Honneur from de Gaulle after the war. See Tanant, *Vercors, haut-lieu de France*, p. 102.

Charlotte Mayaud: Alias Charlotte. It was unusual but not unheard of to use forenames as aliases.

Geneviève Blum-Gayet: Alias Germaine.

Gaby Lacarrière and Jacqueline Gröll: Jacqueline was Pierre Dalloz's sister-in-law.

her new husband Robert: Alias Filou.

'Bishop in France': Pierre Giolitto, *Grenoble 40–44*, Paris: Librairie Académique Perrin, 2001, plates.

Abbé Pierre: Father Henry Grouès. He was the founder of the Emmaus movement.

direct communication with London: Pierre Lassalle and Raymond Muelle, *La Liberté venait des ondes*, Paris: Grancher, 2001, p. 129.

'who served them': Joseph, *Combattant du Vercors*, p. 182.

one of the local priests: Abbé Georges Magnet, known as 'Le Barbu'.

'half a dozen [hand] grenades': Desmond Longe's diary, TNA, HS 6/361, p. 25. Also Michael Pearson, *Tears of Glory: The Betrayal of the Vercors*, London: Pan Books, 1978, p. 137.

Chapter 9: Pressure and Parachutes

'[for the Communists]': Charles de Gaulle, *The War Memoirs*, vol. 2: *Unity 1942–1944*, New York: Simon & Schuster, 1959, p. 159.

south towards Grenoble: Paul Dreyfus, *Vercors: Citadelle de la liberté*, Romagnat: De Borée, 2007 (1st edn Paris: Arthaud, 1969), ch. 10.

in Place Grenette: Jean-Pierre Andrevon, *La Forteresse sacrifiée*, Paris: Éditions Nathan, 2006, p. 11.

the Gestapo arrived in the city: They were commanded by Hauptstürmführer Paul Heimann, forty years old, a Prussian and a committed Nazi.

'France is free': Pierre Giolitto, *Grenoble 40–44*, Paris: Librairie Académique Perrin, 2001, p. 220.

a local engineer: André Abry.

'against the [German] oppression': Giolitto, *Histoire des groupes francs grenoblois*, p. 169.

'as if from a signal': *Ibid.*

the Diables Bleus monument: The monument, a magnificent affair of bronze and marble constructed in 1936 to mark the victories of France's elite Alpine troops, still stands at the western edge of the Parc Paul Mistral. The name 'Les Diables Bleus' has become more widely adopted by the city and is for instance the name of the Grenoble American Football Club.

never seen again: Giolitto, *Histoire des groupes francs grenoblois*, p. 175. Also the witness statement of Jacques Breton, Affaire, DCAJM, Box Deporte-Patrie.

the Grenoble St Bartholomew's Day massacre: Referring to the St Bartholomew's Day massacre of French Protestants of 1572.

a French couple: Antoine and Édith Girousse.

'weeks of blood': *semaines rouges*.

'three days later': Ray Jenkins, *Pacifist at War*, London: Hutchinson, 2009, p. 104, quoting from Denise Domenach-Lallich's book *Demain il fera beau: Journal d'une adolescente (novembre 1939–septembre 1944)*. There is confusion about the date of this diary entry, which may have been made in the summer of 1944.

raid on a camp: C8.

'the Grand Veymont': Jean-Marc Collavet, *Chronique du Vercors*, Valence: Éditions Peuple Libre, 1994, p. 53.

foraging in the woods: http://www.11eme-cuirassiers-vercors.com/11eme.php?sp=7&ssp=d.

in October 1943: The full moon was on 13 October.

one of the Tempsford RAF squadrons: 138 Squadron RAF. TNA AIR 20/8459.

a Halifax bomber: The pilot was Squadron Leader T. C. S. Cooke.

other missions: e.g. Operation Cadillac. See Chapter 29.

for parachute drops: TNA HS 8/444.

'the "Messages personnels" section': This would probably have been the 19.30 shortwave broadcast on 49 or 41 metres.

'"Nous avons visité Marrakech"': Some other later publications use the phrase 'Nous irons visiter Marrakech' (Paul Dreyfus, *Histoire de la Résistance en Vercors*, Paris: Arthaud, 1980, p. 83) and 'Nous revenons de Marrakech' (Joseph Parsus, *Malleval-en-Vercors dans la Résistance*, Valence: Éditions Peuple Libre, 2011, p. 83). But Valot has this right. The code phrase which appears among those used for the November 1943 moon period in SOE's records (TNA HS 8/444) is the one quoted here by Valot.

'"make the arrangements"': Lieutenant Stephen (André Valot), *Vercors, premier maquis de France*, Grenoble: Association Nationale des Pionniers et Combattants Volontaires du Vercors, 1991 (1st edn, Buenos Aires: VIAU, 1946), pp. 50–5.

taken charge of the drop site: Collavet, *Chronique du Vercors*, p. 55.

'a silent and empty sky': This is artistic licence. The moon that night did not set until 10.43 the following morning on an azimuth of 294.1 degrees – that is, at a point just a little north of east on the compass.

the still invisible aircraft: There were four Halifaxes from 161 Squadron on this drop.

shaped like torpedoes: A more or less complete collection of the various containers dropped to the Vercors during 1943 and 1944 has been assembled by M. Guy Bonnel, who is contactable on bonnel.guy@free.fr. M. Bonnel lives in a house on the plateau which was originally the location of one of the key headquarters in the final battle.

and woollen wear: Joseph Parsus in *Malleval-en-Vercors dans la Résistance*, p. 84, also lists chocolate, corned beef, K rations, blocks of plastic explosive and cigarettes.

'isolated, abandoned and alone': Stephen, *Vercors, premier maquis de France*, pp. 50–5.

the parachutes and containers: There is dispute about the total numbers of containers dropped. The journal of the 11th Cuirassiers lists fifteen containers and six packages (http://www.11eme-cuirassiers-vercors.com/11eme.php?sp=2). Paul Dreyfus in his *Histoire de la Résistance en Vercors*, p. 84, says it was 'a hundred or so'. Given the wide distribution of arms the latter figure appears more likely.

others the detonators: In Camp C2 above Autrans, according to Parsus, *Malleval-en-Vercors dans la Résistance*, p. 85.

the Grotte de l'Ours: This lies by the side of the track which runs through the Col de la Sarna, one of the main access points to the Darbonouse. Though in no way a hiding place, this could have provided convenient cover from the elements until the matériel was distributed.

in the village presbytery: The journal of the Maquis de Malleval, Fonds Privés, SHAT 1 K 907.

his plans to hold the Valensole and the Vercors plateaux: Arthur L. Funk, *Hidden Ally: The French Resistance, Special Operations, and the Landings in Southern France, 1944*, New York: Greenwood Press, 1992, p. 23

'if possible, be initiated': Paul Gaujac, *La Guerre en Provence 1944–1945*, Lyon: Presses Universitaires de Lyon, 1998, p. 49. This passage was retranslated back from the French. The original English version appears not to be available.

the codename Anvil: Later renamed Dragoon.

two clandestine radios: Robert Bennes, 'Mémoires de guerre', 2010, p. 59, by kind permission of the author.

Gaston Vincent: Alias Commandant Azur and Pierre.

Pierre Bouquet: Alias Mississippi and Charly.

the Office of Strategic Services (OSS): Established in 1943.

the owner of Les Berthonnets: M. Trappier.

within which the Vercors fell: R1 military area comprised the Dauphiné, the Savoie, the Bugey, the Bresse, the Lyonnais and the Vivarais areas – what is now known as the Rhône-Alpes Region.

all the military commanders: These included Louis Mangin, de Gaulle's Military Delegate for the whole of the old Zone Libre, and Maurice Bourgès-Maunoury, the Regional Military Delegate for the R1 Region.

criticizing Le Ray for 'feudalism': Fernand Rude, 'Vercors', in Pierre Bolle (ed.), *Grenoble et le Vercors: De la Résistance à la Libération 1940–1944*, Lyon: La Manufacture, 1985, p. 103.

'suspicions of the unidentified': Pierre Vial, *La Bataille du Vercors 1943–1944*, Paris: Presses de la Cité, 1991, p. 66.

'Resignation accepted!': François Broche, *François Huet, chef militaire du Vercors: Une vie au service de la France*, Paris: Éditions Italique, 2004, p. 160, and other sources.

under overall military control: Broche, *François Huet, chef militaire du Vercors*, p. 161.

near Saint-Julien-en-Vercors: Michael Pearson, *Tears of Glory: The Betrayal of the Vercors*, London: Pan Books, 1978, pp. 10–18.

near Bourg-de-Péage: Jean Sauvageon, Gilles Vergnon and Jacki Vinay, *1939–1945: Et se leva le vent de la liberté: Entre Drôme des collines et Vercors*, Guilherand-Granges: ANACR, 2012, p. 278.

150 French civilians: Andrevon, *La Forteresse sacrifiée*, p. 24, and Joseph La Picirella, *Témoignages sur le Vercors*, Lyon: Imprimerie Rivet, 1976, p. 67.

railway locomotives: An SOE report for the year June 1943 to May 1944 listed total railway sabotage in France in the period as 1,822 locomotives severely damaged, 200 passenger coaches damaged and 1,500 destroyed, 2,500 freight cars destroyed and 8,000 damaged. Sabotage in France 1943–44, TNA HS 7/130.

at Portes-lès-Valence: La Picirella, *Témoignages sur le Vercors*, p. 68.

30 million francs' worth of damage: Demolitions by Resistance, TNA HS 7/130.

the Valence-to-Grenoble railway: Parsus, *Malleval-en-Vercors dans la Résistance*, p. 89.

sabotaged at Vercheny: Sauvageon *et al.*, *1939–1945: Et se leva le vent de la liberté*, p. 279.

Sainte-Croix, Pontaix and Barsac: *Ibid.*

the mid-levels of the plateau: Parsus, *Malleval-en-Vercors dans la Résistance*, p. 86.

at the Ferme d'Ambel: Collavet, *Chronique du Vercors*, p. 61.

the texts of Karl Marx: Rude, 'Vercors', p. 123.

Pierre Godart: Alias Raoul, but not to be confused with the corrupt Lyon policeman (see Chapter 8).

the Bishop: Alexandre Caillot.

'outside the law of God': In this somewhat uncharitable attitude, he was doing no less than obeying Vatican policy, which prohibited priests from holding mass for the Maquis.

the great churchman's response: Parsus, *Malleval-en-Vercors dans la Résistance*, p. 93.

a priest: Father Fraisse, a Jesuit from Grenoble.

Communist and atheist alike: Description based on that in Parsus, *Malleval-en-Vercors dans la Résistance*, pp. 95 *et seq.*

'sweetness of home': The diary of the Marquis de Malleval, SHAT 1 K 907. There is also a description drawn from this account in Parsus, *Malleval-en-Vercors dans la Résistance*, pp. 95 *et seq.* The description given here may have been somewhat rose coloured.

Chapter 10: The Labours of Hercules

the Tehran Tripartite Conference: Codenamed Eureka, the conference ran from 28 November to 1 December 1943.

from Algiers (Anvil): Churchill was at one time so peeved by the US insistence on Overlord at the expense of his Balkan ambitions that he even briefly threatened to deny the Americans the use of British bases and the Channel for the invasion. David Irving, *The War between the Generals*, London: Penguin Books, 1981, pp. 19 *et seq.*

'the right way home': *Ibid.*, p. 435.

when it came to partisans: 'He thought all his geese were swans', as Colonel Buckmaster, the head of SOE's F Section, put it. See Max Hastings, *Finest Years: Churchill as Warlord 1940– 45*, London: William Collins, 2010, p. 437.

the US and Russian colossi: In January 1944, the US had 11 million troops under arms, while the British only had 4.5 million. Roosevelt was fond of commenting that, even in January 1944, the US had more troops stationed in Britain than Britain had in total worldwide and an air force stationed on British soil which was one and a half times bigger than the entire RAF. Irving, *The War between the Generals*, pp. 15–16.

for her own liberation: See Hastings, *Finest Years: Churchill as Warlord*, for more on this.

'European allies put together': Charles de Gaulle, *The War Memoirs*, vol. 2: *Unity 1942–1944*, New York: Simon & Schuster, 1959, p. 114.

the Allied invasion of North Africa: The British followed Roosevelt's lead in this.

in Königstein Castle, escaped: Cammaerts' opinion was that, thanks to evidence revealed after the war, 'We know now that Giraud had been let out of prison by the Germans to stick something against de Gaulle.' IWM sound archives, Interview with Francis Cammaerts, Session No. 11238, Reel 3 at 5' 15".

a submarine picked him up: HM Submarine *Seraph*.

'of that at all': G. Ward Price, *Giraud and the African Scene*, New York: Macmillan, 1944, p. 260.

'except through de Gaulle ...': IWM sound archives, Interview with Francis Cammaerts, Reel 3 at 4' 27".

'after the Liberation': Jean-François Muracciole, 'La France Libre et la lutte armée', in François Marcot (ed.), *La Résistance et les Français: Lutte armée et maquis*, Colloque International de Besançon 15–17 June 1995, Paris: Annales Littéraires de l'Université de Franche-Comté, Diffusion Les Belles Lettres, 1996, p. 160.

bloody guerrilla warfare: Irving, *The War between the Generals*, p. 21.

It put France as third strategic priority: TNA CAB 80–68, Serial 154.

of that year: Jean-Louis Crémieux-Brilhac, 'Les Glières', *Vingtième Siècle: Revue d'Histoire*, vol. 45, no. 1, January–March 1995, p. 57.

A Cabinet paper: Paper of 31 March 1944, War Cabinet Minutes, TNA CAB 80–68.

numbering 220,000: Those in Poland and Czechoslovakia numbered 143,000 and 110,000 respectively.

'net male population': Measured as the estimated total male population aged between nineteen and fifty after deducting the number required to maintain essential services.

'total reorganisation and reformation': SOE report of 26 June 1943, TNA HS 6/339.

One of these missions: The Musc Mission headed by Jean Rosenthal and Richard Heslop. It was charged with assessing Resistance strengths in the Isère, Ain, Jura, Haute-Savoie and Savoie regions.

'difficult conditions, good morale': Fernand Rude, 'Vercors', in Pierre Bolle (ed.), *Grenoble et le Vercors: De la Résistance à la Libération 1940–1944*, Lyon: La Manufacture, 1985, p. 102.

what they had in mind: Though de Gaulle was briefed on Anvil on 27 December 1943 by US staff officers in Algiers and received assurances that French troops would be used on both Anvil and Overlord. See Arthur L. Funk, *Hidden Ally: The French Resistance, Special Operations, and the Landings in Southern France, 1944*, New York: Greenwood Press, 1992, p. 5.

furious at the snub: See de Gaulle, *The War Memoirs*, vol. 2, p. 239.

a special planning unit: This took over and greatly expanded on the planning duties previously carried by French Air Force General Gabriel Cochet. Reading the files in the National Archives in Kew (which were of course secret in 1943) it seems almost certain that Cochet, if not formally a British agent, was at least a much valued British confidential source and agent of influence in the Free French hierarchy in London and Algiers.

'of France as well?': De Gaulle, *The War Memoirs*, vol. 2, p. 165.

Miksche produced a study: 'Military Conditions for a Landing in France' produced on 20 January 1944, TNA HS 7/132, p. 76.

landing points was Normandy: Miksche's report, *ibid.*, suggested four possible landing points, between the Escaut and Somme river mouths (that is, broadly speaking either side of Calais), the Normandy/Brittany beaches, the Aquitaine Atlantic coast in south-west France and the Mediterranean coast in southern France.

'help in the landing': *Ibid.*, p. 77.

'for the enemy': *Ibid.*, p. 76.

lines of communication: 'Paraphrase of incoming cable', 13 November 1943, TNA HS 6/376.

a London-based French Army officer: Lieutenant Colonel Pierre Fourcaud.

'a little before, D-Day': TNA HS 6/324.

'and thus controlled': 'Controlled Areas – Ref. DRM/2024 of 31/12/43', TNA HS 6/378.

one of de Gaulle's most senior advisers: Louis Joxe, the General Secretary of the Comité Français de la Libération Nationale (CFLN).

one of London's 'mission leaders': Jean Rosenthal of the Musc Mission – see above.

'an impregnable fortress': Alain Dalotel, *Le Maquis des Glières*, Paris: Plon, 1992, p. 127.

Chapter 11: January 1944

Emmanuel d'Astier de La Vigérie: Alias Commandant Bernard.

senior member of de Gaulle's government-in-exile: He was Commissioner for Internal Affairs.

on 15 January 1944: In his book *Les Dieux et les hommes*, Paris: Julliard, 1952, p. 18, d'Astier claims that meeting was on 14 January. But this must be a mistake as Churchill was in Gibraltar on that date – see below.

'Duff Cooper': He was the British Ambassador in Algiers.

as was Macmillan: Harold Macmillan was Minister Resident at Allied Force Headquarters.

Clementine and Mary Churchill: The Prime Minister's wife and youngest daughter.

Diana Cooper: Duff Cooper's wife. She was one of the great beauties of the day.

'and put it out)': D'Astier de La Vigérie, *Les Dieux et les hommes*, pp. 19–20.

silk pyjamas: Jacques Baumel, *La Liberté guidait nos pas*, Paris: Plon, 2004, p. 165.

Chiefs of Staff Committee of the War Cabinet: Those included Admiral Sir John Cunningham, Major General Leslie Hollis and General Sir Henry Maitland Wilson.

and the Haute-Savoie: In this Churchill may well have been right – several post-war studies identified the decision to choose the south of France for a landing over a continued Allied push through Italy into France as the Western Allies' greatest strategic mistake of the war.

'to pre-Tehran dimensions': War Cabinet, Chiefs of Staff Committee, Prime Minister's Conference at Gibraltar, 4 p.m. 14 January 1944, TNA CAB 80/78, p. 159.

'Ventimiglia': In Italy, at the French border.

The next substantive meeting: Though the two men had informally dined together the night before, but the subject was de Gaulle's government not assistance to the Resistance. D'Astier de La Vigérie, *Les Dieux et les hommes*, p. 43.

All the British Prime Minister's key advisers: Among the attendees were Lord Selborne, the minister in charge of SOE, together with Brigadier Eric Mockler-Ferryman of SOE, Georges Boris of the French National Committee, Churchill's influential personal adviser Desmond Morton, Air Marshal Sir Charles Portal, General Sir Hastings Ismay and Archibald Sinclair, the Secretary of State for Air.

'I aided Mihailovic': Draža Mihailović was the nationalist/royalist partisan leader in Yugoslavia opposed to Tito.

'of a political nature?': On 10 February, when d'Astier had his first meeting with the famously direct General Montgomery the latter put exactly the same question: 'I want to be assured that if we give an order to the Resistance to carry out a mission required by Allied command, it will be transmitted and executed without delay.' Jean-Louis Crémieux-Brilhac, 'Une Stratégie militaire pour la Résistance: le Bloc Planning et l'insurrection nationale', *Revue Espoir*, no.139, June 2004, p. 42.

'the French patriots': D'Astier de La Vigérie, *Les Dieux et les hommes*, p. 48.

'to the Allied strategy': War Cabinet papers, Minute of a meeting held at No. 10 Downing Street, 27 January 1943, TNA CAB 80/78, pp. 321–4.

of February 1944: Jean-Louis Crémieux-Brilhac, 'Les Glières', *Vingtième Siècle: Revue d'Histoire*, vol. 45, no. 1, January–March 1995, p. 58.

some 425,000 Maquisards: Crémieux-Brilhac, 'Une Stratégie militaire pour la Résistance', p. 43.

'WSC 4.3.44': Minute from Morton, 3 March 1944, TNA HS 6/597.

a landing site at Eymeux: Codename Agonie. The Resistance reception site commander was Jean Farroul.

Henry Thackthwaite: Alias Procureur.

Peter Ortiz: Alias Chambellan and Jean-Pierre.

a French radio operator: Lieutenant Camille Monnier (alias Magyar).

since the fall in 1940: The Ortiz file on the website of the Californian State Military Museum (http://www.militarymuseum.org/Ortiz.html), quoting M. R. D. Foot.

probably fairly accurate: This translation, which I have substantially altered to remove inaccuracies, is based on André Valot's description of the Union visit in Lieutenant Stephen (André Valot), *Vercors, premier maquis de France*, Grenoble: Association Nationale des Pionniers et Combattants Volontaires du Vercors, 1991 (1st edn, Buenos Aires: VIAU, 1946), p. 57.

'[Ortiz carried]': Ortiz was a larger-than-life character and true soldier of fortune. A member of the French Foreign Legion, he was captured in 1940 and escaped from Germany after three attempts. Returning to America he joined the US Marines and fought in the Pacific and Tunisia before joining the US clandestine services. He was famous during his time in France for, so the legend says, entering restaurants where Germans were dining and, wearing the full uniform of a US Marine officer, pulling out his Colt 45 and assassinating them.

'coast of France materialised': Précis of Procureur's report, March 1944, TNA HS 7/252.

one blanket between them: Given that, so far as we know, the only other visit made in the Vercors after Union's visit to Ambel was to Geyer's headquarters, this may well refer to Geyer himself since it reflects views that were held also by others, including of course Chavant.

'necessary for the Vercors': RF Section history, TNA HS 7/252.

almost spring-like, weather: Evidence taken by the author from Gilbert Carichot in Rousset village, 2 June 2013. The story of the ambush of the German car in Rousset, of which he was an eyewitness, is also taken from this interview.

on 17 January: Pierre Vial, *La Bataille du Vercors 1943–1944*, Paris: Presses de la Cité, 1991, p. 83.

Les Combes: The Germans subsequently blew up the farm. There is little now left beyond a few stones overgrown with forest and a small plaque to mark the spot today.

'sign of discipline': Attributed to Geyer by one of his senior lieutenants, Yves Moine. Vial, *La Bataille du Vercors 1943–1944*, p. 84.

an advance party of staff: Led by Captains Guigou and Oschwald. Among the other radio operators were Mario Montefusco (alias Titin and Argentin).

Pierre Lassalle: Alias Benjamin and Bolivien.

the inhabitants of Peyronnet Farm: The Callet family.

'twiddling radio dials': Pierre Lassalle and Raymond Muelle, *La Liberté venait des ondes*, Paris: Grancher, 2001, p. 109.

instructed the owner: M. Badois.

an ambush position: The ambush was under the command of Lieutenant Lositski (alias François) and consisted of two machine guns and a number of soldiers.

(the Maquisards called them *mouches* – flies): SHAT 1 K 907.

all anti-partisan operations: Geoffrey J. Thomas and Barry Ketley, *KG 200: The Luftwaffe's Most Secret Unit*, Crowborough, East Sussex: Hikoki Publications, 2003, p. 104.

'the supreme Allied Command': Gilles Vergnon, *Résistance dans le Vercors: Histoire et lieux de mémoire*, Grenoble: Glénat, 2002, p. 68.

one of the delegates: Pierre Flureau (alias Pel) representing the Communist Party.

'more than a trap': Paul Dreyfus, *Histoire de la Résistance en Vercors*, Paris: Arthaud, 1980, p. 95.

an ex-Alpine regimental commander: Albert de Reyniès.

his old unit: The 6th Battalion of Alpine Chasseurs (6th BCA).

'do not recognize petitions': Joseph Parsus in *Malleval-en-Vercors dans la Résistance*, p. 110.

a local man: Louis Revolle.

a Jewish woman refugee: Gertrude Blümenstock. Her husband was Dr Moses Blümenstock, also a Jew. He too was at Malleval and tended to the wounded. He was not shot on the spot but was taken away for interrogation and then, according to reliable reports, executed. *23 mois de vie clandestine*, Conférences de l'Information 1945, 23 April 1945, Paris: Imp. Curial-Archerau, 1945, p. 363.

Chapter 12: Of Germans and Spies

Gestapo chief Klaus Barbie: Responsible for torturing Jean Moulin to death (see Chapter 7), Barbie was tried and found guilty of war crimes after the war and was sentenced to life imprisonment, dying of cancer in prison in 1991.

to do with the death: Pierre Vial, *La Bataille du Vercors 1943–1944*, Paris: Presses de la Cité, 1991, p. 72. Lecuy was also believed to have connections with the famous Soviet ring, the Red Orchestra.

Villemarest relinquished his job: He returned later to take command of the Groupe Vallier. Charlotte Mayaud was subsequently denounced, arrested and deported first to the Natzweiler-Struthof concentration camp and then to Ravensbrück. She escaped thanks to the help of a French guard who had fallen in love with her and managed to escape with him to South America. In 1989 she finally received the Légion d'Honneur from the French government for her Resistance activities.

captured and executed: Vial, *La Bataille du Vercors 1943–1944*, p. 143.

a patriotic duty: Pierre Flaureau, 'Le Comité de Libération de l'Isère', in Pierre Bolle (ed.), *Grenoble et le Vercors: De la Résistance à la Libération 1940–1944*, Lyon: La Manufacture, 1985, p. 85.

stealing side-arms: *Ibid.*, p. 88.

SIS: The Secret Intelligence Service, also known as MI6.

his death in June 1944: From natural causes.

brothel keepers, barbers and barmen: Clare Mulley, *The Spy Who Loved: The Secrets and Lives of Christine Granville, Britain's First Female Special Agent of World War II*, Macmillan, 2012, p. 200.

used as agents provocateurs: Union Report, TNA HS 6/359.

'worked for the Gestapo': André Paray's report, RF Section diary, SHAT 1 K 907, p. 1445.

Guy Alexander Kyriazis: Alias Guédot among many others.

'were intercepting messages': Kyriazis file, TNA KV 27/49.

sent by the French: The order also applied to other governments-in-exile in London.

use British or US codes: Minutes of the 11th meeting of 1944 War Cabinet Chiefs of Staff Committee, 3.30 p.m., 13 January 1944, TNA CAB 79/69.

'outrage and an insult': Charles de Gaulle, *The War Memoirs*, vol. 2: *Unity 1942–1944*, New York: Simon & Schuster, 1959, p. 249.

An SOE report: TNA HS 6/336.

provide reason for punishment: Der Militärbefehlshaber in Frankreich. Ia Nr. 558/44 g.Kdos v. 12.2.1944. Betr.: Banden-und Sabotagebekämpfung, BA-MA, RW 35/551.

'before the enemy landing': 'Geheime Kommandosache', 12 February 1944, BA-MA, RW 35/551. Courtesy of Peter Lieb.

not combat but training: Until 1942, the training of new recruits was done in Germany. But because of German overstretch and lack of manpower it was decided to send new recruits to train in post in the 'Reserve Divisions' in occupied countries.

his area of responsibility: For this and much of the other information in this chapter I am indebted to Peter Lieb and especially his paper: 'La 157e division de réserve et la lutte contre le Maquis dans le Jura et les Alpes françaises', in Bernard Garnier, Jean-Luc Leleu and Jean Quellien (eds), *La Répression en France, 1940–1945*, Actes du colloque, Caen, 8, 9 et 10 December 2005, Caen: Centre de Recherche d'Histoire Quantitative, 2007, pp. 289–301.

because of heart disease: For the greater part of the information in the paragraphs that follow, I am indebted to Peter Lieb and his outstanding pamphlet *Vercors 1944: Resistance in the French Alps*, Botley, Oxford: Osprey Publishing, 2012; also his chapter in *L'Engagement Résistant dans l'Ain*, Bourg-en-Bresse: Édition Conseil Général de l'Ain, 2012, p. 102.

Supreme High Command of the German Army: Oberkommando des Heeres (OKH).

his elite Alpine Gebirgsjäger Regiment: This was Reserve Gebirgsjäger Regiment 1, which consisted of two support companies and four Gebirgsjäger battalions – Gebirgsjäger Battalions I/98, II/98, 99 and 100.

'more experienced soldiers': Colonel Defrasne at the post-war commission looking into the history of the Vercors, Commission d'Histoire du Vercors, 72 A 588, at the Institut d'Histoire du Temps Présent (IHTP), Paris. Also quoted in *La Guérilla n'aura pas lieu ... La Bataille du Vercors 1940–1944*, Paris: CDEF/DREX/Bureau Recherche, 2010 (http://www.cdef.terre.defense.gouv.fr/...la.../la-bataille-du-vercors-1940-1944), p. 33.

A German historian of the period: Roland Kaltenegger.

'of the Second World War': Christian Wyler, *La Longue Marche de la Division 157: Contre les maquis et les partisans 1942–1945*, Paris: Grancher, 2004, p. 81.

a French agent: Jean Rosenthal.

'corrupt and miserable': Procureur's report, TNA HS 6/359.

anti-partisan operations: Notably Operation Korporal in the Ain Department which ran from 5 to 13 February 1944.

elements of Pflaum's forces: Signal to London, 17 March 1944, TNA HS 6/359.

'Eastern Troops': *Osttruppen*. Also known as the *Ost Volk* or Eastern Peoples and by the Waffen SS as the Eastern Legions.

their nation of origin: See SHAT 1 K 89/15.

These included Slovenes: The Allies mistook these as Czechs as a result of the reports from Cammaerts and Rosenthal, among others. In fact there were few if any Czechs in Pflaum's command.

'join us on D-Day': Procureur's report, TNA HS 6/359.

the Sipo/SD: Sicherheitspolizei und Sicherheitsdienst.

Security Police: Sicherheitspolizei.

the Security Department: Sicherheitsdienst.

in the Lyon area: Knab's direct superior was the Higher SS and Police Leader for all France (Höherer SS und Polizeiführer Frankreich) SS-Gruppenführer Carl Albrecht Oberg.

'mobile killing units': Einsatzgruppe C.

hostile to it: Wyler, *La Longue Marche de la Division 157*, pp. 38–9 and 67.

Chapter 13: February 1944

Pflaum launched 2,000 men: Operation Korporal.

Henri Romans-Petit: His real name was Henri Petit. After the war he adopted his alias – Romans – and added it to his surname. He is now almost universally referred to as Romans-Petit.

explosive were stolen: TNA HS 7/130.

the station at La Mure: Not to be confused with the hamlet of La Mure, close to Vassieux, on the Vercors.

and winding gear: TNA HS 7/130.

a dozen or so locomotives: NARA, Historian Jockey Licensee – OSS Report, F Section, Western Europe, vol. 3, Jockey Circuit, p. 41. This operation was carried out by Francis Cammaerts' Jockey circuit and was one of three simultaneous attacks which were carried out in Veynes, Avignon and Miramas. In these, Cammerts reported, his agents had immobilized thirty-six locomotives for a period of between three and six months.

Paul Adam: Alias Le Fauve.

with a friend: Maurice Cornu.

'in our haversacks': Association Nationale des Pionniers du Vercors, *Le Vercors raconté par ceux qui l'ont vécu*, Valence: Imprimerie Nouvelle, 1990, pp. 109–11.

Jean Sadin: Alias Pédago.

'the monastery building behind us': ANPV, *Le Vercors raconté par ceux qui l'ont vécu*, pp. 109–11.

easier to defend than the Vercors: Jean Rosenthal's view.

one of London's agents: Probably Jean Rosenthal.

'aid and assistance': The telegram was sent by Marcel Descour and shown to Churchill by d'Astier de La Vigérie at a meeting.

'whole of the Resistance': The words here are d'Astier's.

on the … Plateau': Cantinier's report, 27 February 1944, TNA HS 7/252.

'citadel of the Glières': Cantinier signal, TNA HS 7/252.

'when D-Day comes': Jean-Louis Crémieux-Brilhac, 'Les Glières', *Vingtième Siècle: Revue d'Histoire*, vol. 45, no. 1, January–March 1995, p. 61.

'"Freedom or Die"': TNA HS 7/252.

to discuss overall strategy: Thackthwaite's report, 17 December 1944, TNA HS 6/355.

his report of 20 January: See Chapter 10.

'his flanks without mercy': *La Guérilla n'aura pas lieu … La Bataille du Vercors 1940–1944*, Paris: CDEF/DREX/Bureau Recherche, 2010 (http://www.cdef.terre.defense.gouv.fr/…la…/la-bataille-du-vercors-1940-1944), p. 34.

'locked up and neutralized': Jean-Marc Collavet, *Chronique du Vercors*, Valence: Éditions Peuple Libre, 1994, p. 72; and *La Guérilla n'aura pas lieu … La Bataille du Vercors 1940–1944*, p. 52.

a representative from London: Jean Rosenthal.

'have to reckon with': The words of Jean Guidollet quoted in Douglas Boyd, *Blood in the Snow, Blood on the Grass*, Stroud: The History Press, 2012, p. 46.

'their own considerable defects': Minute from Morton to Selborne, 14 February 1944, TNA HS 6/597.

'feel very deflated': Lieutenant Stephen (André Valot), *Vercors, premier maquis de France*, Grenoble: Association Nationale des Pionniers et Combattants Volontaires du Vercors, 1991 (1st edn, Buenos Aires: VIAU, 1946), p. 95.

'on a lonely farm': Ray Jenkins, *Pacifist at War*, London: Hutchinson, 2009, pp. 115–16.

Cammaerts' orders: NARA, Historian Jockey Licensee – OSS Report, F Section, Western Europe, vol. 3, Jockey Circuit, p. 38. The orders included 'We have informed you that Allied Force Headquarters [AFHQ] in Africa have warmly approved your project for seizing and holding the Valensole Plain for the reception of airborne troops.'

Chapter 14: March 1944

'to unjustifiable risks': RF Section diary, TNA HS 7/252. Text altered slightly to make it more readable.

five Stirling light bombers: TNA HS 7/252.

codenamed Gabin: It was later given a different codename – Coupe-Papier (paper knife).

in an open valley surrounded by woods: Approximately between La Matrassière and Les Morands

Pilot Officer Caldwell: From 161 Squadron RAF.

Operation Bob 149: Flight reports 15/16 March, TNA AIR 20/846. The operation was also known as Torrent.

half an hour after midnight: The moon rose in the Grenoble area on 16 March 1944 on a bearing of 113 degrees at 00.18 hours. http://www.world-timedate.com/astronomy/ moonrise_moonset/moonrise_moonset_time.php?month=3&year=1944&city_id=1578.

Bren light machine guns: Known as LMGs.

a drop site called 'Cavalier': Another name for Coupe-Papier. Joseph La Picirella, *Témoignages sur le Vercors*, Lyon: Imprimerie Rivet, 1976, p. 97.

ammunition, boots and socks: Fourcaud's signal, 21 March 1944, RF Section diary, TNA HS 7/252.

the mortar ammunition: Referred to as 'bombs'.

on impact with the ground: Union II briefing, TNA HS 3/37, and Eucalyptus briefing, p. 1441, SHAT 1 K 907.

pleas for them from the plateau: According to Paul Dreyfus, *Histoire de la Résistance en Vercors*, p. 107, Thackthwaite was told that mortars weren't dropped to the Resistance because there weren't enough for the British Army, let alone others. In his book *Eastern Approaches* (London: Penguin Books, 1991; 1st edn, London: Jonathan Cape, 1949), Fitzroy Maclean lists (p. 461) 1,380 mortars and 324,000,000 mortar bombs as being dropped to the partisans over the course of the Yugoslav guerrilla campaign. However, there is reason to believe that at least some of these may refer to the PIAT anti-tank weapon, which is also for some reason referred to by Maclean as a 'mortar'. In his book *Envers et contre tout* (3 vols, Geneva: Éditions de Crémille, 1970; 1st edn, Paris: Robert Laffont, 1947–50), Jacques Soustelle lists (vol. 3, pp. 188–9) 138 mortars having been dropped to the French Resistance in the month of April 1944. It may even be that the mortar ammunition dropped this night landed safely because its impact was cushioned by the covering of snow. The British mortar-bomb problem was finally resolved around the end of August 1944, by which time this story had run its course.

cave of Barme-Chenille: This cave, with its entrance as big as a small garage forecourt, lies in the woods at lat. 45.041146707554, long. 5.42898503309844, some 300 metres or so from the edge of the drop zone. The remains of an old track which could have been usable by carts is still visible on the approach to the cave. The wide entrance of the cave funnels down to a narrow throat at which point it is still possible to see iron hinges that could have supported an iron or steel door used to lock the entrance to the deeper chamber of the cave, where the weapons would probably have been stored.

by a local priest: Patrice Escolan and Lucien Ratel, *Guide-mémorial du Vercors résistant*, Paris: Le Cherche-Midi, 1994, suggest that a local priest known by the Gestapo as 'the Vercors Priest' was responsible. Pierre-Louis Fillet (Curator of the Vassieux Resistance Museum) confirms this in an email to the author, 8 June 2013.

lower pastures of the Vercors: This account draws on those given in Pierre Tanant, *Vercors, haut-lieu de France*, Grenoble: Arthaud, 1948 and 1950; Jean-Marc Collavet, *Chronique du Vercors*, Valence: Éditions Peuple Libre, 1994; Gilles Vergnon, *Résistance dans le Vercors: Histoire et lieux de mémoire*, Grenoble: Glénat, 2002; Pierre Vial, *La Bataille du Vercors 1943–1944*, Paris: Presses de la Cité, 1991; and TNA HS 7/252.

'our driver': Julien Chabert.

for her pains: Fourcaud's signal, 21 March 1944, TNA HS 7/252.

Peyronnet farm: Owned by the Callet family.

destroyed with explosive: The remains of Geyer's headquarters at Combe farm can still be seen, little more now than a few stones overgrown by moss and brambles in the middle of what is now forest. There is, however, a plaque marking the ruin's previous role.

taking two prisoners: Boutin and Garcia, two charcoal makers who had come to the plateau from Alsace-Lorraine.

six Maquisards: Captain Marc Oschwald (aged 30), Second Lieutenant Jean Simon-Perret (22), André Coudart (21), Roger Guigou (34), Hubert Levacque (33) and Marc-Henri Leroy (21).

three civilians: Henri Borel, Julien Callet and a Miss Bonnier aged forty-one.

with more Stens: Fourcaud's signal, 22 March 1944, TNA HS 7/252.

a former French military inspector: Robert Ducasse (alias Vergaville).

'currently in charge there': Fernand Rude, 'Vercors', in Pierre Bolle (ed.), *Grenoble et le Vercors: De la Résistance à la Libération 1940–1944*, Lyon: La Manufacture, 1985, p. 105.

to be used for D-Day: Confidential report from a French source – possibly Cochet – of 11 April 1944, TNA HS 6/376.

Four Maquisards: Lieutenant Ruetard, Cavaliers Bilcke, Briant and Broyer.

near a village: Beauregard-Baret.

close to Romans: There are several versions of this event, all rather more heroic than this one. I have chosen to base this version of events on that given in Collavet, *Chronique du Vercors*, which seems to conform most closely to the brief details on this affair given in the RF Section diary in TNA HS 7/252.

caught in a Milice ambush: Pierre Giolitto, *Histoire des groupes francs grenoblois*, Grenoble: Presses Universitaires de Grenoble, 2003, p. 69.

one of the Vercors' summits: La Grande Moucherotte

a nearby hotel: The Hôtel Polycand.

two Maquisards dead: Jean Bocq (alias Jimmy), Gariboldy's close friend and number two, and Henri Tarze (alias Bob).

two wounded: George Ravinet and Gaston Petitpas.

this piece of 'gangsterism': Vial, *La Bataille du Vercors 1943–1944*, p. 144.

tobacco and shoe depot: Journal of Louis Rose, 11eme-cuirassiers-vercors.com/11eme.php?sp=7.

a wave of Maquisard attacks: TNA HS 7/252.

at Bourg-en-Valence: Jean Sauvageon, Gilles Vergnon and Jacki Vinay, *1939–1945: Et se leva le vent de la liberté: entre Drôme des collines et Vercors*, Guilherand-Granges: ANACR, 2012, p. 282.

for good measure: NARA, Historian Jockey Licensee – OSS Report, F Section, Western Europe, vol. 3, Jockey Circuit, p. 42.

another twenty locomotives: TNA HS 9-258/5/1.

'shootings and hangings': Cammaerts' report, 26 March 1944, TNA HS 9/258/5.

'of the French Resistance': 'The Military Role of the French Resistance', 6 March 1944, TNA HS 6/375.

'and strong points': SOE paper 'Resistance in South East France', 22 March 1944, TNA HS 6/330.

be conducted simultaneously: TNA CAB 70/72.

'some time after D-Day': Cipher telegram to Massingham, 16 April 1944, TNA HS 6/340.

'in the name of this Government': Forest C. Pogue, *The United States Army in World War II: The European Theater of Operations: The Supreme Command*, Washington, DC: Office of the Chief of Military History, Department of the Army, 1954, p. 146 (http://www.history.army.mil/html/books/007/7-1/CMH_Pub_7-1.pdf).

'the single French Army': M. R. D. Foot, *SOE in France: An Account of the Work of the British Special Operations Executive in France 1940–1944*, London: HM Stationery Office, 1966, p. 360.

'on a national uprising': Jean-Louis Crémieux-Brilhac, *La France Libre II: De l'appel du 18 Juin à la Libération*, Paris: Gallimard, 2014, p. 1147.

two secret couriers: This was the mission codenamed Clef and was very important to de Gaulle. The two couriers were Colonel Ely (alias Algèbre) and Lazare Rachline (alias Socrate).

the Military Delegates: Délégués Militaires de Zone (DMZ).

the Military Delegate for the southern zone: Maurice Bourgès-Maunoury.

'effective forces in the area': Courrier to Polygone, 31 March 1944, TNA HS 7/132.

work already done in London: For example, the paper produced by Ferdinand Miksche of Bloc Planning dated 6 March 1944 and entitled 'The Military Role of the French Resistance', TNA HS 6/375.

Chapter 15: Weapons, Wirelesses, Air Drops and Codes

The weapons dropped: Jacques Soustelle, *Envers et contre tout*, 3 vols, Geneva: Éditions de Crémille, 1970 (1st edn, Paris: Robert Laffont, 1947–50), vol. 3, pp. 188–9.

some 14 tonnes: Arms deliveries, April Moon, TNA HS 6/597.

a special hunting rifle: In the case of Captain Adrien Conus (alias Volume).

'percentage through breakages': Cammaerts' post-operational report, TNA HS 6/568.

a parachute operation: Codenamed Centipède.

'my God I do': Cammaerts' telegram to Massingham, 19 April 1944, TNA HS 9/258/5.

'side of the mountain': Fourcaud's signal, 25 March 1944, TNA HS 7/252.

'wasn't his fault': François-Georges Dreyfus (ed.), *Unrecognized Resistance: The Franco-American Experience in World War Two*, New Brunswick: Transaction Publishers, 2004, p. 88. Pérouse was born in Albi.

pre-war Czech design: The name is a combination of *Br* for Brno, the city in Czechoslovakia where the weapon was first produced, and *en* for Lee-Enfield.

anyone within 25 metres: Although the British Army said an early and unlamented goodbye to the Sten shortly after the war, it is testimony to the longevity and efficacy of the Mark 4 rifle, the Bren and the Mills grenade that all three were used by the author on operational service right up to the early 1960s.

an old creamery at La Britière: It was owned by the Arnaud family.

and their operators: Those who worked at one time or another from La Britière included Bob Bennes (alias Bob), Pierre Lassalle (alias Benjamin and Bolivien), André Lacourt (alias Joseph), Juste Winant (alias Olivier), Mario Montefusco (alias Argentin and Titin), Jean Cendral (alias Lombard).

a small team of local volunteers: The main team of cipher assistants at La Britière were Patrick Garnot (alias Patrick), Jacques Jouanneau (alias Sammy) and Marie-Louise Dragol – see Robert Bennes, 'Mémoires de Guerre', p. 61, by kind permission of the author.

one-time code pads: These are pads consisting of pages of randomly produced letters and symbols, each assigned to a letter of the alphabet. Each page is used once and then discarded.

three assistants: André Pecquet who was assisted by two men called Ricard and Sebastini and a young girl called Léa Blain. SHAT 1 K 907.

Augustin Deschamps: Alias Albert, Deschamps, Floiras and Saddler.

SOE operator: See TNA HS/9 Floiras A. He received the OBE from the British and the Croix de Guerre from the French after the war.

from a 'Pedalator': These sets were still in regular service when the author was in the British Special Boat Service and he can still well remember the pain in his thighs caused by long periods pedalling in the middle of some hide or other, while trying to get an urgent signal through.

four times a day: At 13.30, 14.30, 19.30 and 21.15.

long, medium and short waves: TNA HS 6/609. The wavelengths were 1500 metres (long wave), 373, 285 and 261 metres (medium wave) and 49 and 41 metres (short wave).

in Bari in Italy: See letter MSC/BBC/92 of 14 October 1943, TNA HS 8/444.

listen to operational messages: RF Section diary, SHAT 1 K 907. See also TNA HS 7/252.

pre-prepared regional sabotage plans: Plan Vert – sabotage against strategic railway lines; Plan Tortue – sabotage against strategic roads; Plan Bleu – sabotage of electrical installations; Plan Violet – sabotage of long-distance telephone and telecommunications; Plan Rouge – sabotage of ammunition dumps; Plan Jaune – attacks on key enemy headquarters; and Plan Noir – sabotage of petrol dumps. Other plans, such as Grenouille, targeting railways signalling systems, were also established as sub-sets of these main plans. Later on, Plans Rouge, Jaune and Noir were regrouped into Plan Guérilla.

Chapter 16: April 1944

everyone thought she had come from Paris: Interview with La Chapelle Mayor, Serge Saint-André, 31 May 2013.

numbering some 5,000: The declaration of Maude Champetier de Ribes, Court Martial paper dated 16 September 1944, ADR 394 W2.

'like a film star': Jean Sauvageon, Gilles Vergnon and Jacki Vinay, *1939–1945: Et se leva le vent de la liberté: entre Drôme des collines et Vercors*, Guilherand-Granges: ANACR, 2012, p. 121.

one of the Maquisard leaders: Ferdinand Sallier (alias Christophe).

other Vichy security forces: Groupes Mobiles de Réserve (GMR).

burnt it to the ground: Lieutenant Stephen (André Valot), *Vercors, premier maquis de France*, Grenoble: Association Nationale des Pionniers et Combattants Volontaires du Vercors, 1991 (1st edn, Buenos Aires: VIAU, 1946), p. 97.

'you will die': Sauvageon *et al.*, *1939–1945: Et se leva le vent de la liberté*, p. 121.

'Leave it': *Ibid.*, pp. 120–1.

one of Geyer's men: Lieutenant Moine.

Another of Geyer's men: Lieutenant Louis Rose.

gave him the slip: Journal of Louis Rose, entry for 10 April 1944, http://11eme-cuirassiers-vercors.com/11eme.php?sp=6.

four agents: Jean Paris (alias Egyptien), W. T. Henri Benhamou (alias Andalou), Roger Olive (alias Hache) and Commandant Henri Guillermin (alias Pacha). Tentative of History of In/Exfiltrations into/from France during WWII from 1941 to 1945, http://www.plan-sussex-1944.net/anglais/pdf/infiltrations_into_france.pdf.

90 million francs: The money was hidden in the tunnel of a nearby canal at Saint-Thomas-en-Royans. http://www.11eme-cuirassiers-vercors.com.

a restaurant owner: M. Fusch.

an operation involving 'major forces': Pierre Vial, *La Bataille du Vercors, 1940–1944*, Paris: Presses de la Cité, 1991, p. 136. Also Jean Abonnenc, *Il n'est pas trop tard pour parler de Résistance*, Die: Imprimerie Cayol, 2004, p. 144.

One camp: Camp C12.

Jacques Dugé de Bernonville: De Bernonville was infamous for tracking down and executing Maquisards and assisting in the deportation of French Jews.

Raoul Dagostini: A former French Colonial Officer, Dagostini had served on the eastern front where he had been accused of excessive cruelty against the inhabitants of a village. Arrested by the Germans for the crime, he was sentenced to death. But the sentence was commuted and he was posted back to France instead.

'A veritable amazon': The words of Serge-Henri Moreau. Michel Germain, *Histoire de la Milice et des forces du maintien de l'ordre en Haute-Savoie 1940–1945*, Montmélian: La Fontaine de Siloé, 1997, p. 217. Translation by Charles Forman.

no firm evidence to support this: Mireille Provence study provided by M. Pierre-Louis Fillet, Curator of the Vassieux Resistance Museum.

'I could not speak': Association Nationale des Pionniers du Vercors, *Le Vercors raconté par ceux qui l'ont vécu*, Valence: Imprimerie Nouvelle, 1990, pp. 138 *et seq.*

'fomenting revolution …': *Ibid.*

three condemned men: Lieutenant André Doucin, a pharmacist's assistant from Saint-Jean-en-Royans, Casimir Ezingeard, a postman from Omblèze, and Paul Mially, a farmer from Upie.

in front of two haystacks: Jeanne Barbier, *Ici, jadis, était un village de France*, Die: Imprimerie Cayol, 2001, p. 69.

'plummeted even further': Patrice Escolan and Lucien Ratel, *Guide-mémorial du Vercors résistant*, Paris: Le Cherche-Midi, 1994, pp. 228–9. Also quoted in François Broche, *François Huet, chef militaire du Vercors: Une vie au service de la France*, Paris: Éditions Italique, 2004, p. 162.

dissatisfied with the Milice performance: Peter Lieb, *Vercors 1944: Resistance in the French Alps*, Botley, Oxford: Osprey Publishing, 2012, p. 35.

a captured German document: TNA HS 6/341.

when D-Day happened: This report was almost certainly an exaggeration. The measures listed applied only in the combat zones such as Normandy and were listed on a 'Combat poster' (*Kampfplakat*) which it was planned would be posted in villages in the affected area. However, these 'rules' proved to be impractical and were suspended. Peter Lieb email to the author, 8 September 2013.

was also planned: Extract from London Group Intelligence summary No. 1, 20 April 1944, TNA HS 6/324.

an OSS agent: Captain Pierre Maurice Martinot.

The first job: Bourne Patterson report, TNA HS 7/122.

he was betrayed: Martinot was sent to Dachau but survived the war. TNA HS 9/998/8.

the Allied leapfrogging plans: See also http://www.reseaugallia.org/wiki/wiki.php.

in preparation for the attack: At this stage it was known as Operation Bergen.

'make the same mistakes': Cammaerts' report, 16 April 1944, TNA HS 9/2585.

the Resistance leader of the Maquis in the Auvergne/Massif Central area: Émile Coulandon (alias Gaspard).

nearby Mont Mouchet: Gilles Lévy, 'La Genèse du groupe "Auvergne" du Réduit du Massif Central (avril–août 1944)', http://lesamitiesdelaresistance.fr/lien28/p23-50_la_genese_du_groupe_auvergne.pdf, p. 27.

On 17 April: Two days earlier, on 15 April, he had written to Selborne proposing the use of gliders to help the French partisans and asking that French pilots should be trained as glider pilots for this purpose. Note on the utilization of gliders for the supply of Resistance Groups after D-Day, TNA HS 6/597.

'to attack Resistance forces': Emmanuel d'Astier de La Vigérie, *Les Dieux et les hommes*, Paris: Julliard, 1952, p. 73–4.

'able to satisfy them': *Ibid.*

camps on the plateau: Broche, *François Huet, chef militaire du Vercors*, p. 166.

Huet was later to claim: *Ibid.*

what it was all about: Extract of a passage from Eugène Chavant's 'black book'. By kind permission of M. André Chavant, who let me look at his father's journal on a visit to see him in Grenoble on 6 June 2013. Translated by Charles Forman.

Chapter 17: A Basket of Crabs

'out of Washington': John N. Bradley, *The Second World War*, vol. 1: *Europe and the Mediterranean*, New York: Square One Publishers, 2002, p. 258.

'You are a man': Arthur L. Funk, *De Gaulle, Eisenhower et la Résistance en 1944*, http://www.charles-de-gaulle.org/pages/l-homme/dossiers-thematiques/1940-1944-la-seconde-guerre-mondiale/la-france-libre-et-les-allies/les-etats-unis/de-gaulle-eisenhower-et-la-resistance-en-1944.php.

'a case on them': Hull to US Ambassador, London, 11 May 1944, SHAEF SGS 092 France, French Relations, I. Roosevelt to Eisenhower, W-36054, 13 May 1944; Marshall to Eisenhower, W-36189, 13 May 1944. Both in Eisenhower personal file, referred to in Forest C. Pogue, *The United States Army in World War II: The European Theater of Operations: The Supreme Command*, Washington, DC: Office of the Chief of Military History, Department of the Army, 1954 (http://www.history.army.mil/html/books/007/7-1/CMH_Pub_7-1.pdf), p. 148.

the French Committee for National Liberation: Comité Français de la Libération Nationale (CFLN).

the Military Action Committee: Comité d'Action Militaire (COMIDAC). The committee was known as COMIDAC until May 1944 when de Gaulle reduced its power and changed its name.

the French Special Forces Directorate: Direction Générale des Services Spéciaux (DGSS).

the National Defence Committee: Comité de Défense Nationale (CDN). This was created on 22 June 1944.

the French hero: Koenig had been the commander at the Battle of Bir Hakeim when French forces had, at considerable loss, held an old Turkish fort against superior German and Italian forces as part of the Battle of Gazala at the end of May 1942.

body for all special forces operations in France: Special Forces Headquarters (SFHQ).

Club des Pins: At the time this was based at a seaside holiday 'camp' on the shores of the Mediterranean and housed not just a training school but also the main centre for the reception and decoding of messages from France. The area, much developed but still called the Club des Pins, is today the site of a large Sheraton Hotel.

Lieutenant Colonel Jean Constans: Alias Saint-Sauveur.

his representative in Algiers: Arthur L. Funk, *Hidden Ally: The French Resistance, Special Operations, and the Landings in Southern France, 1944*, New York: Greenwood Press, 1992, p. 32.

'we were subordinated': *Ibid.*, p. 41.

'cold-shouldered by the others': IWM sound archives, Brooks Richards statement, Accession 9970/13, Recorded 21 September 1987. In the written transcript of this, Constans is spelt 'Constant'. One wonders whether this was deliberate on Brooks Richards' part.

dedicated special forces units: 2671st Special Reconnaissance Battalion.

in Algiers during April: NARA, Report of OSS Activities with 7th Army, 14 October 1944 (RG 226, E99, Box 741, Folder 1473, Summary Report).

'irresponsible and also underhand': Minute from CD to SC, 3 March 1944, TNA HS 6/336.

a wooden mess hall: Funk, *Hidden Ally*, p. 32.

near the Villa Magnol: In Chemin cheikh Bachir el Ibrahimi, El-Biar, Alger. The building has been demolished to make way for the US embassy.

in Baker Street: Rachel Millard, 'Two Years in World War Two'. By kind permission of the author who was herself a radio operator receiving Vercors signals at Grendon Hall.

Maitland Wilson's Algerian headquarters: For a fuller description of this process see Fernand Rude, 'Le Dialogue Vercors–Algers (juin–juillet 1944)', *Revue d'Histoire de la Deuxième Guerre Mondiale*, no. 49, January 1963, pp. 79–110, and Paul Dreyfus, *Histoire de la Résistance en Vercors*, Paris: Arthaud, 1980, p. 155.

their final destination: Funk, *Hidden Ally*, p. 36.

'supposed to serve them': Jacques Soustelle, *Envers et contre tout*, 3 vols, Geneva: Éditions de Crémille, 1970 (1st edn, Paris: Robert Laffont, 1947–50), vol. 3, p. 119.

'bain de haine': Letter to Dalloz. Pierre Dalloz, *Vérités sur le drame du Vercors*, Paris: Éditions Fernand Lanore, 1979, p. 275.

'panier de crabes': Interview with André Chavant, 6 June 2013, Grenoble.

Chapter 18: May 1944

warning messages: *Messages d'alertes*.

a Hudson light bomber: From 161 Squadron RAF.

flew them back to Britain: The Hudson, piloted by Flight Lieutenant Affleck, carried one of the most valuable and unusual loads of any clandestine flight of the war. Apart from

Thackthwaite and Rosenthal, the passenger list included Mme Fleury with her very young baby, Maurice Bourgès-Maunoury (alias Polygone), the DMR for the region which covered the Vercors, Francis Closon (alias Vincent) and Paul Rivière (alias Marquis).

'first hand of conditions': Minute of 4 May 1944, TNA HS 6/340.

mortars and anti-tank guns: M. R. D. Foot, *SOE in France: An Account of the Work of the British Special Operations Executive in France 1940–1944*, London: HM Stationery Office, 1966, p. 144.

'misunderstanding and obstruction': Fernand Rude, 'Vercors', in Pierre Bolle (ed.), *Grenoble et le Vercors: De la Résistance à la Libération 1940–1944*, Lyon: La Manufacture, 1985, p. 106.

'the military side either': *Ibid.*, p. 124.

'broader role above him': Michael Pearson, *Tears of Glory: The Betrayal of the Vercors*, London: Pan Books, 1978, pp. 10–11.

'Vercors for very long': François Broche, *François Huet, chef militaire du Vercors: Une vie au service de la France*, Paris: Éditions Italique, 2004, p. 166.

the process initiated in March: See Chapter 14.

The first iteration: There were two versions of the Caïman Plan, which were very different in form and content but are often confused. This version is often referred to as Caïman I. Caïman II is described in detail in Chapter 24.

'Ici commence La France libre': Harry R. Kedward, *In Search of the Maquis*, Oxford: Clarendon Press, 1993, p. 167.

'airborne forces could operate': TNA HS 6/607; and SHAT 1 K 374/3.

a coordinated attack on the French railway system: Plan Vert.

an attack on underground long-distance telecoms cables: Plan Violet.

the sabotage of electricity supply lines: Plan Bleu.

attacks on Wehrmacht convoys: Plan Tortue.

guerrilla actions against German command posts, petroleum facilities and ammunition dumps: Plan Guérilla.

'guerrilla plan into effect': SHAEF HQ to Maitland Wilson, 'Role of the Resistance in the South of France', 21 May 1944, Annex E, TNA WO 204/2030B.

what he had agreed to: TNA HS 6/337.

the Provisional Government of France: Officially announced on 3 June 1944.

'for some time': Cammaerts' signal to SPOC and London, 26 May 1944, TNA HS 9/258/5.

finally arrived in Algiers: We do not know the full story of Chavant's trip to Algiers, but it appears that the original plan may have been for the Free French submarine *Casabianca* to pick him and Veyrat up by rubber boat near the Cap Camarat on the night of either 22/23 or 23/24 May. The logbook of the *Casabianca* shows that the submarine's Captain, Lieutenant Henri Bellet, received orders on 18 May to embark on a secret mission to pick up agents between 22.00 and 01.00 on these two nights. It appears, however, that for the second time the rendezvous failed. Eventually the two men were collected by a US motor torpedo boat and taken to the port of Bastia on the north-eastern coast of Corsica, from where they were bundled on to an aircraft and flown on to Algiers.

only a few days previously: Interview with Robert Bennes, 10 November 2103, Castres.

'Signed Chavant': TNA HS 6/340.

the Regional Military Delegate: At the time this was Paul Leistenschneider (alias Carré) who had recently taken over from Bourgès-Maunoury.

on behalf of General de Gaulle: Soustelle confirmed to Fernand Rude after the war that de Gaulle had personally authorized Soustelle to sign on his behalf having seen and approved the order. Rude, 'Vercors', p. 108.

Jacques Soustelle: Ibid.

During this meeting: For a description of this meeting see Gilles Lévy, 'La Genèse du groupe "Auvergne" du Réduit du massif Central (avril–août 1944), http://lesamitiesdelaresistance. fr/lien28/p23-50_la_genese_du_groupe_auvergne.pdf, p. 41.

'advised of these decisions': SHAT T 1160, Pouget de Nadaillac papers.

not arrive in London until 8 June: According to http://11eme-cuirassiers-vercors.com/index. php, the full Constans report arrived in London on 8 June.

'seem excellent project …': TNA HS 6/340.

London replied swiftly: That is, Special Forces Headquarters (SFHQ).

'of 1,000 paratroops …': TNA HS 6/340.

a one-line coded message: See Chapter 15 for details of this alert message.

'l'eau dans le gaz': TNA HS 8/444.

for further developments: The message, along with the alert messages, was sent out at 21.00 on
1 June 1944 and repeated at the same time on 2 and 3 June. Letter from Alain Le Ray to
Jean-Louis Crémieux-Brilhac of 24 September 1999 (by kind permission of the recipient).
In this letter Le Ray makes clear that he could not be certain that 'Le chamois des Alpes
bondit' was ever sent.

Chapter 19: The First Five Days of June 1944

'one felt totally free': Pierre Tanant, Vercors, haut-lieu de France, Grenoble: Arthaud, 1948 and
1950, p. 56.

Pierre Tanant: Alias Laroche.

his three children: Michel, the eldest, had just finished his baccalauréat in Lyon and cycled to
the plateau to join his father and stepmother.

pure, 'vertical' quality: Jérôme Garcin, Pour Jean Prévost, Paris: Éditions Gallimard, 1994, p.
158.

7 tonnes of tungsten: TNA HS 7/130.

Miss M. P. Hornsby-Smith: Pat Hornsby-Smith DBE, PC (1914–85) was PPS to Lord Selborne
and later became an MP and baroness.

'he noted on the latter': In handwriting.

'"Good. Press on"': TNA HS 6/597.

'the Department of the Isère': Which includes the northern half of the Vercors.

'are increasing constantly': Paul Dreyfus, Histoire de la Résistance en Vercors, Paris: Arthaud,
1980, p. 118.

Brigadier Mockler-Ferryman: Director for SOE operations in western Europe.

'Tout le monde à la bataille': Foch at the Battle of the Marne, 18 July 1918.

when the Allies could not help them: Jean-Louis Crémieux-Brilhac, 'Une Stratégie militaire
pour la Résistance: Le Bloc Planning et l'insurrection nationale', Revue Espoir, no. 139, June
2004, pp. 41–57.

de Gaulle's Resistance directorate: The BCRA.

an impromptu cocktail party: M. R. D. Foot, SOE: The Special Operations Executive 1940–
1946, London: Pimlico, 1989 and 1999, p. 322.

'the French government exists': Jonathan Fenby, The General: Charles de Gaulle and the France
He Saved, London: Simon & Schuster, 2010, pp. 241–2.

the speech that it was proposed he should deliver: Composed by the Psychological Warfare
Division of Supreme Allied Force Headquarters (SHAEF).

'treason at the height of battle': Antony Beevor, D-Day: The Battle for Normandy, London:
Penguin, 2012, p. 21.

that he should be flown back to Algiers: The letter carrying Churchill's instructions for the
forcible expulsion of de Gaulle was only finally burnt at three o'clock on the morning of
D-Day. See François Kersaudy, De Gaulle et Churchill, Paris: Éditions Perrin, 2010,
p. 363.

'in chains if necessary': Beevor, D-Day: The Battle for Normandy, p. 21.

two Westland Lysanders: From 148 Squadron.

Among the arrivals: The other arrivals were Lieutenant Hubert Gominet (alias Alouette) and
another passenger who can be identified only by his alias, Soutane. There were six outgoing
passengers: Dr Tibor Revesz-Long (alias Thibaud), Jean-Francois Clouët des Pesruches
(alias Galilée), Toubas (alias Seigneur), Perret and Michel Pichard (alias Pic). The Lysander
pilots were Captain Vaughan-Fowler and Flight Lieutenant Attenborrow. Hugh Verity, We
Landed by Moonlight: Secret RAF Landings in France 1940–1944, Wilmslow: Air Data
Publications, 1995, p. 209.

a safe house: Owned by the Abbé Boursier.

'both men and arms': Pierre Dalloz, *Vérités sur le drame du Vercors*, Paris: Éditions Fernand Lanore, 1979, p. 236.

'and from what direction': Michael Pearson, *Tears of Glory: The Betrayal of the Vercors*, London: Pan Books, 1978, p. 36.

'only from the north': *Ibid.*, p. 132.

'withdraw from combat': *Ibid.*

the needless deaths of many Resistance fighters: Jean-Louis Crémieux-Brilhac, *Georges Boris: Trente ans d'influence*, Paris: Gallimard, 2010, p. 285.

warning Miksche of the tragic consequences: Dreyfus, *Histoire de la Résistance dans le Vercors*, p. 120.

'the south coast of France as well': Koenig letter to Dreyfus, quoted in *ibid.*, p. 132.

SHAEF produced instructions: In practice this was Special Forces Headquarters (SFHQ).

'a stiffening framework': TNA HS 6/330.

the Tunnel d'Engins: The tunnel no longer exists. It was blown up by the Germans and is now an open passage.

commented unkindly afterwards: Pearson, *Tears of Glory*, p. 39.

Huet inspected with due seriousness: I am indebted for many of the facts in this account to Michael Pearson's research: *ibid.*, pp. 37 *et seq.*

'a real French aristocrat': *Ibid.*, p. 39.

according to some witnesses: Pierre Vial, *La Bataille du Vercors 1943–1944*, Paris: Presses de la Cité, 1991, p. 151; Gilbert Joseph, *Combattant du Vercors*, Grenoble: Éditions Curandera, 1994 (1st edn, Paris: Fayard, 1992), p. 94.

'meet our requests': Dwight D. Eisenhower, *Crusade in Europe*, London: William Heinemann, p. 273.

the SS Main Security Office: SS-Reichssicherheitshauptamt.

where they had expected it: Peter Lieb email to the author, 30 September 2013; Vial, *La Bataille du Vercors 1943–1944*, p. 148

'Les sanglots longs des violons d'automne': 'The long sighs of the violins of autumn'. The broadcast message did not faithfully follow Verlaine's line in his poem 'Chanson d'automne', which was 'Les sanglots longs des violons de l'automne'.

'Bercent': The BBC broadcast misquoted Verlaine in this line too. The original of the Verlaine uses the French verb *blesser* (to wound), not *bercer* (to rock, as in a cradle). Verlaine's phrase is more poetic – 'The long sighs of the violins of autumn wound my heart with a monotonous longing' rather than 'cradle my heart'. A popular post-war singer also used these lines from Verlaine, adopting the form 'Bercent'.

one SOE circuit: The F Section Ventriloquist circuit.

four messages: 'Le premier accroc coûte deux cents francs' – launch Plan Vert (sabotage of railways); 'Qu'un sang impur abreuve nos sillons' – launch Plan Guérilla (attacks on German command posts, ammunition dumps and petroleum facilities); 'Que serait ce si vous portiez une maison' – launch Plan Tortue (attacks on German military convoys); 'La voix humaine est morte' – launch Plan Violet (cut underground long-distance telecommunications cables). BBC Caversham Archives, French scripts, June 1944.

one further noteworthy fact: I am grateful to my colleague Sylvie Young for first identifying this new and startling fact.

British-run circuits: That is F Section circuits.

'D-Day took place': Cammaerts' report, TNA HS 9/258/5, p. 19.

get back to sleep: François Broche, *François Huet, chef militaire du Vercors: Une vie au service de la France*, Paris: Éditions Italique, 2004, p. 169.

Chapter 20: D-Day: 6 June 1944

René Piron: Alias Daniel.

'made leaving much easier …': Journal of Daniel, http://11eme-cuirassiers-vercors.com/11eme.php?sp=3&ssp=b.

whose alias was Yvon: Real name not known.

'doing our duty': Journal of Yvon, http://11eme-cuirassiers-vercors.com/11eme.
    php?sp=3&ssp=b.

'On the evening of 5 June': Jean Dacier, *Ceux du maquis*, Grenoble and Paris: Arthaud, 1945,
    pp. 79 *et seq.*

'blew up the railway line': A British Cabinet report on Resistance action around D-Day
    estimated that, in all, 480 rail lines were cut and 180 German trains derailed in the
    immediate post-D-Day period. SOE Assessment of Overlord, TNA CAB 66/56/20.

'Not more than twenty': Dacier, *Ceux du maquis*, p. 86.

their way up to the Vercors: François Broche, *François Huet, chef militaire du Vercors: Une vie
    au service de la France*, Paris: Éditions Italique, 2004, p. 170.

a new Maquis group: The Groupe Baudet. Jean Abonnenc, *Il n'est pas trop tard pour parler de
    Résistance*, Die: Imprimerie Cayol, 2004, p. 165.

'defend against the Boches': Pierre Vial, *La Bataille du Vercors 1943–1944*, Paris: Presses de la
    Cité, 1991, p. 161.

'hospital at Saint-Martin': Association Nationale des Pionniers du Vercors, *Le Vercors raconté
    par ceux qui l'ont vécu*, Valence: Imprimerie Nouvelle, 1990, p. 309.

'it seemed impregnable': Michael Pearson, *Tears of Glory: The Betrayal of the Vercors*, London:
    Pan Books, 1978, p. 41 – translated from Paul Dreyfus, *Vercors citadelle de Liberté*, Paris,
    Arthaud, 2007, p. 147.

to the echo as they passed: Association Mémoire du Lycée Polonais Cyprian-Norwid, *Des
    résistants polonais en Vercors: La saga du lycée polonais Cyprian-Norwid: Villard de-Lans
    1940–1946*, Grenoble: Presses Universitaires de Grenoble, 2012, p. 86.

'no orders to mobilize the plateau': In saying this Huet seems tacitly to concede that he had
    not heard, or heard reliable proof of, 'Le chamois des Alpes' being received.

'ready to leave Algiers': Pearson, *Tears of Glory*, p. 43.

'have some sport!': Dreyfus, *Histoire de la Résistance en Vercors*, p. 124.

'the enemy from France': Pearson, *Tears of Glory*, p. 43; and Dreyfus, *Histoire de la Résistance
    en Vercors*, p. 158.

'discipline and honesty': Vial, *La Bataille du Vercors 1943–1944*, p. 153.

Chavant intervened: Interview with his son André Chavant, 6 June 2003.

Rang des Pourrets: There are no more than a few moss-covered stones amid the forest to mark
    the site today.

parachuted into France: His false identity was M. Suchet.

Georges Jouneau: Alias Georges. Also Commandant Georges.

Motor Transport Depot: Dreyfus, *Histoire de la Résistance en Vercors*, p. 126; and Robert
    Bennes, 'Mémoires de guerre', 2010, p. 45, by kind permission of the author.

18.31: 17.31 UK time.

'greatness is now reappearing': BBC Caversham Archives, French scripts for 6 June.

Eisenhower's broadcast in English: Which Eisenhower had actually recorded before de Gaulle
    had even arrived in London.

'by the French Command': Charles de Gaulle, *The War Memoirs*, vol. 2: *Unity 1942–1944*, New
    York: Simon & Schuster, 1959, pp. 256 and 316.

Chapter 21: Mobilization

'a suitable house': Michael Pearson, *Tears of Glory: The Betrayal of the Vercors*, London: Pan
    Books, 1978, p. 46.

'a fervent and practising Catholic': Jean-Marc Collavet, *Chronique du Vercors*, Valence:
    Éditions Peuple Libre, 1994, p. 87.

the Maquis took over the Corrèze town of Tulle: Led by Jean-Jacques Chapou.

'driver taken prisoner …': Max Hastings, *Das Reich: The March of the 2nd Panzer Division
    through France, June 1944*, London: Pan Books, 2000, p. 76.

his son Jacques: Alias Flèche.

one of Geyer's men: Lieutenant Louis Rose.

he left Lyon by car: Journal of Louis Rose, http://11eme-cuirassiers-vercors.com/index.php.

the local Departmental Liberation Committee: Comité Departemental de Libération.

'will come later': Pierre Vial, *La Bataille du Vercors 1943–1944*, Paris: Presses de la Cité, 1991, p. 155.

with 1,545,000 francs: TNA HS 6/342 and HS 7/130.

'appropriated' for Maquis use: Vial, *La Bataille du Vercors 1943–1944*, p. 186.

under some pressure from Hitler's headquarters: Mainly from Hitler's Chief of Operations, General Alfred Jodl.

'population in the future': Von Rundstedt's war diary (KTB/Ob. West, XIII-f Anl. 159 et XIV-f), http://fr.academic.ru/dic.nsf/frwiki/17734.

the Geneva Convention: Several commanders of German units in France requested clarity on the status of FFI forces. Von Rundstedt published his decision (including to the French public) on 11 June 1944. Meanwhile on 9 June, de Gaulle had declared FFI as part of his own forces. But his government had not yet been internationally recognized as the official French government (according to law the French government was still in Vichy). So Eisenhower, in an attempt to get round this problem, declared on 15 July that the FFI was part of his expeditionary force. Von Rundstedt gave his response on 26 July reaffirming his previous position. Internally there had been meanwhile some debates among the Germans; Stülpnagel seems to have been in favour of recognizing the FFI as lawful combatants. In early August von Rundstedt's Chief of Staff, Blumentritt, pointed out the contradiction in the German arguments: the Germans demanded that FFI behave according to the laws, but Germans themselves denied FFI combatant status. This resulted in a change of combatant status for the FFI, but only on 17 September, i.e. when most of France had already been liberated. An interesting opinion on this matter was also given by SHAEF's Psychological Warfare Division in a document of 31 January 1945: 'The Germans cannot be blamed for taking strong measures against these [Resistance] groups … As for the Maquisards themselves, as well as the members of the resistance, they expected to be shot if caught and they do not protest on this score.' The report continued: 'But the Nazi method of dealing with the situation was to punish the innocent. Finding that operations against the Maquis were costly and unfruitful, they adopted the policy of reprisals.' Peter Lieb, *Konventioneller Krieg oder NS-Weltanschauungskrieg? Kriegführung und Partisanenbekämpfung in Frankreich 1943/44*, Munich: Oldenbourg, 2007, pp. 245–54, quotation from p. 254. I am indebted to Peter Lieb for his help in making sense of this complex situation.

'treated as guerrillas': Luftwaffe Field Marshal Hugo Sperrle. Lieb, *Konventioneller Krieg*, p. 246.

still bear terrible testimony: The village has been preserved in the state that the Das Reich left it as a memorial to this horror.

'These are our orders': Francis Cammaerts was later to confirm that he agreed with this judgement: 'Every other message for general mobilisation had been received, including mine … so there was no serious ambiguity.' See Pearson, *Tears of Glory*, p. 49.

'what they expect of us': There are several versions of this crucial conversation, which differ in minor details but agree about the general substance. This one is taken from Paul Dreyfus, *Histoire de la Résistance en Vercors*, Paris: Arthaud, 1980, p. 129, supplemented by the account given in François Broche, *François Huet, chef militaire du Vercors: Une vie au service de la France*, Paris: Éditions Italique, 2004, p. 172.

'I was given': Fernand Rude, 'Vercors', in Pierre Bolle (ed.), *Grenoble et le Vercors: De la Résistance à la Libération 1940–1944*, Lyon: La Manufacture, 1985, p. 111.

the experience of the Glières plateau: Roland Costa de Beauregard, 'Le Vercors juin 1944: Projets et réalités', *Revue Historique de l'Armée*, no. 4, 1972, p. 106.

'landings [in the south]': Letter Descour to Dalloz, May 1973, Pierre Dalloz, *Vérités sur le drame du Vercors*, Paris: Éditions Fernand Lanore, 1979, p. 218.

'aiming is 15 August': Pearson, *Tears of Glory*, p. 81. Wilson had to wait until the fall of Rome, which liberated troops he would need for the assault.

a daily Situation Report: Sitrep.

'have to evacuate': TNA WO 204/1947.

'openly for the Resistance': SHAT T 1160, Fonds Ziegler, Pouget de Nadaillac folder.

drawn mostly from the communities: See Chapter 8.

'for further details. H': Vial, *La Bataille du Vercors 1943–1944*, p. 156.

'in their lives': Broche, *François Huet, chef militaire du Vercors*, p. 175.

Fernand Crouau: Alias Abel.

'to the Pont de la Goule Noire. Huet': *Le Pionnier du Vercors: La Compagnie Abel 1943–1944*, Grenoble: Association Nationale des Pionniers et Combattants du Vercors, Special number 2012, p. 8. Huet used his alias, Hervieux.

'or somewhere else': 'Les Résistants dans le Vercors, 9 Juin–7 Août 1944: Témoignages de Nicolas Bernard', by kind permission of his daughter Martine Pattin and her friend Julia Chalkley.

Roland Bechmann: Alias Lescot. Bechmann was married to the daughter of Prévost's second wife Claude.

'as a brother-in-arms': Jérôme Garcin, *Pour Jean Prévost*, Paris: Gallimard, 1994, p. 160.

'in an unknown direction': Vial, *La Bataille du Vercors 1943–1944*, pp. 156 *et seq.*

'their friends, the Germans': Lieutenant Stephen (André Valot), *Vercors, premier maquis de France*, Grenoble: Association Nationale des Pionniers et Combattants Volontaires du Vercors, 1991 (1st edn, Buenos Aires: VIAU, 1946), pp. 103–4.

the parachute site: Papier Gommé.

north of Saint-Martin: De Beauregard, 'Le Vercors juin 1944: Projets et réalités', p. 111.

'up on the plateau …': Based on *ibid.*, pp. 136–43.

a young girl in a beret: Probably Léa Blain.

detachment of wireless operators: Bennes only occasionally sent messages himself, concentrating on coding and decoding. Interview with Robert Bennes, 10 November 2013, Castres.

'open day and night': Fernand Rude, 'Le Dialogue Vercors–Algers (juin–juillet 1944)', *Revue d'Histoire de la Deuxième Guerre Mondiale*, no. 49, January 1963, p. 82.

'for Resistance in region': Ibid.

'small isolated groups': Pearson, *Tears of Glory*, p. 58.

Chapter 22: The First Battle of Saint-Nizier

Captain Alastair Hay: Alias Edgar.

'a benevolent moustache': Ray Jenkins, *Pacifist at War*, London: Hutchinson, 2009, p. 142.

'used as divisional headquarters': Cammaerts' post-operational report, TNA HS 9/258/5.

on clandestine sabotage: Paul Dreyfus, *Histoire de la Résistance en Vercors*, Paris: Arthaud, 1980, p. 131.

given by Soustelle: Cammaerts' interview with Professor Rod Kedward, Reel 1' 32", 13 March 1991, by kind permission of Professor Kedward.

'a few days ago': *Vercors 1944: Un officier britannique dans la tourmente*, http://www.benchart.net/benchart/arnaud-duret/textes/article.doc.

'the local cemetery': Pierre Vial, *La Battaile du Vercors 1943–1944*, Paris: Presses de la Cité, 1991, p. 171.

of explosive experts: Roland Bechmann was probably one of this team.

'We gave the order': Unless otherwise stated all subsequent messages are taken from Fernand Rude's study 'Le Dialogue Vercors–Algers (juin–juillet 1944)', *Revue d'Histoire de la Deuxième Guerre Mondiale*, no. 49, January 1963, pp. 79–110.

'show you what's what!': Vial, *La Bataille du Vercors 1943–1944*, p. 169.

'still in Verdun': Based on conversations reported in Joseph, *Combattant du Vercors*, pp. 136–43, and Vial, *La Bataille du Vercors 1943–1944*, p. 169.

Hôtel du Moucherotte: Run by M. and Mme Revollet. The other hotel at the time was the Hôtel du Belvédère run by Mme Royannez. See Association Nationale des Pionniers du Vercors, *Le Vercors raconté par ceux qui l'ont vécu*, Valence: Imprimerie Nouvelle, 1990, p. 314.

'in Saint-Nizier': Philippe Hanus and Gilles Vergnon, *Vercors: Résistance en Résonances*, Paris: L'Harmattan, 2008, p. 40.

'when out of it': Dreyfus, *Histoire de la Résistance en Vercors*, p. 158.

'Or maybe both': Michael Pearson, *Tears of Glory: The Betrayal of the Vercors*, London: Pan Books, 1978, p. 1.

a direct frontal assault: The German force consisted of a company of 157th Division's Reserve Grenadier Battalion, reinforced by the Reserve Artillery Abteilung (Detachment) acting in the infantry role. See Peter Lieb, *Vercors 1944: Resistance in the French Alps*, Botley, Oxford: Osprey Publishing, 2012, p. 36.

Revoulat farm: Though later largely destroyed by the Germans, the remains of the farm, with its extensive outbuildings, can still easily be found at the north-western end of the Losence valley.

Compagnie Goderville's one mortar: Probably a light 2-inch mortar.

'point on the road': Hanus and Vergnon, *Vercors: Résistance en Résonances*, p. 40.

'shelter in the cellar': Evidence of France Pinhas, ANPV, *Le Vercors raconté par ceux qui l'ont vécu*, p. 312.

'spoiled the effect': Pearson, *Tears of Glory*, p. 66.

A young officer: Second Lieutenant Michel Perotin (alias Fressinat).

store-carrying truck: Called a *chenillette de ravitaillement*. See http://beaucoudray.free.fr/vercors4.htm, journal entry for 13 June.

baskets of cherries: Evidence of Pierre Deveaux, ANPV, *Le Vercors raconté par ceux qui l'ont vécu*, p. 266.

its ammunition, to Saint-Nizier: Evidence of Pierre Deveaux, *ibid.*, p. 266.

'you are made': Jérôme Garcin, *Pour Jean Prévost*, Paris: Éditions Gallimard, 1994, p. 160.

Descour sent a message to Algiers: This was actually sent early the following morning.

one of his subordinates: General Lasserre.

'support the French Resistance': Fernand Grenier, *C'était ainsi (souvenirs)*, Paris: Éditions Sociales, 1959, p. 201.

his planning staff: Bloc Planning.

'supported by airborne troops': TNA HS 6/378.

Chapter 23: The Second Battle of Saint-Nizier

in the Parc Bachelard: François Broche, *François Huet, chef militaire du Vercors: Une vie au service de la France*, Paris: Éditions Italique, 2004, p. 177. This space is still a park.

numbered about 1,000: French estimates of the German strength ranged from 1,200 to 2,000.

other elements of his division: Including elements of Reserve Grenadier Regiment 157 and Reserve Engineer Battalion 7 acting in an infantry role. Peter Lieb, *Vercors 1944: Résistance in the French Alps*, Botley, Oxford: Osprey Publishing, 2012, p. 36.

one of Geyer's units: Commanded by Lieutenant Point (alias Payot).

100 men drawn from the Compagnie Abel: Under the command of Lieutenant Chapus. See *Le Pionnier du Vercors: La Compagnie Abel 1943–1944*, Grenoble: Association Nationale des Pionniers et Combattants du Vercors, Special number 2012, p. 22.

three grenades between them: Jean Sauvageon, Gilles Vergnon and Jacki Vinay, *1939–1945: Et se leva le vent de la liberté: Entre Drôme des collines et Vercors*, Guilherand-Granges: ANACR, 2012, p. 152.

on his motorbike: Broche, *François Huet, chef militaire du Vercors*, p. 177.

were later executed: Douglas Boyd, *Blood in the Snow, Blood on the Grass*, Stroud: The History Press, 2012. One of those captured and executed was Cémoi (see Chapter 12).

too little ammunition: Michael Pearson, *Tears of Glory: The Betrayal of the Vercors*, London: Pan Books, 1978, p. 73.

'the enemy one by one': Fernand Rude, 'Le Dialogue Vercors–Algers (juin–juillet 1944)', *Revue d'Histoire de la Deuxième Guerre Mondiale*, no. 49, January 1963, p. 84.

'that section over there …': Sauvageon *et al.*, *1939–1945: Et se leva le vent de la liberté*, p. 123.

a mortar round fell: Joseph La Picirella, *Témoignages sur le Vercors*, Lyon: Imprimerie Rivet, 1976, p. 153.

to his forward commanders: Pierre Vial, *La Bataille du Vercors 1943–1944*, Paris: Presses de la Cité, 1991, p. 177.

'and administered injections …': Association Nationale des Pionniers du Vercors, *Le Vercors raconté par ceux qui l'ont vécu*, Valence: Imprimerie Nouvelle, 1990, p. 316.

six killed and fifteen wounded: Lieb, *Vercors 1944: Resistance in the French Alps*, p. 36.

According to the German estimates, the French killed numbered twenty-four, but this figure probably includes the eight killed in the first battle.

houses were burnt: SHAT 1 K 907, p. 1446.

'all would be OK': Association Mémoire du Lycée Polonais Cyprian-Norwid, *Des résistants polonais en Vercors: La saga du lycée polonais Cyprian-Norwid: Villard de-Lans 1940–1946*, Grenoble: Presses Universitaires de Grenoble, 2012, p. 86.

into the southern plateau: Journal of Louis Rose, http://11eme-cuirassiers-vercors.com/11eme.php?sp=7&ssp=d.

'to get new orders': Pierre Tanant, *Vercors, haut-lieu de France*, Grenoble: Arthaud, 1948 and 1950, pp. 73–5.

'"just for the quiet life"': Lieutenant Stephen (André Valot), *Vercors, premier maquis de France*, Grenoble: Association Nationale des Pionniers et Combattants Volontaires du Vercors, 1991 (1st edn, Buenos Aires: VIAU, 1946), p. 122.

'easier to defend': Tanant, *Vercors, haut-lieu de France*, Grenoble: Arnaud, 1948 and 1950, pp. 75–6.

'not up to the task': *Ibid*.

'withdrew … in perfect order': NARA, Box 740, Folder 1466, Special Maquis Missions, Cantinier-Xavier Mission.

Germans with no one to attack: Romans-Petit's withdrawal did not prevent reprisals against civilians in the area. Twenty-four hostages were shot in the village of Dortan on 13 July.

a similar number of cases: Joseph La Picirella in *Témoignages sur le Vercors*, p. 155, lists the number of rapes as fifteen.

Dr Lémonon: http://www.resistance-familles.com/wp-content/uploads/la-drome-en-armes.pdf, and La Picirella, *Témoignages sur le Vercors*, pp. 155–6.

the remaining three: Émile Gay, seventy-three years old, Gendarme Louis Nau and Albert Bernard aged twenty.

'of airborne landings': Ultra decrypt, 15 June 1944, TNA HW 1/2361.

André Manuel: Alias Pallas and Marnier.

Chapter 24: Respite and Reorganization

In the evening of 16 June: There is dispute about this date with some sources putting this event on 26 or 27 June. Dreyfus in *Citadelle de la Liberté*, p. 176, puts the date at 29 June.

was stopped at the checkpoint: The man who stopped him was Roger Rabatel.

transported as prisoners: One post-war report by a French agent who arrived later in the Vercors even claimed Chavant was beaten up – but there is no evidence for this. Report by A. E. Paray, p. 9, TNA HS 6/361.

'dressed in foreign uniforms': Joseph, *Combattant du Vercors*, p. 177.

'Autrans and Corrençon': General Costa de Beauregard, 'Le Vercors juin 1944: projets et réalité', *Revue Historique de l'Armée*, no. 4, 1972, p. 113.

'provoke the Boches': François Broche, *François Huet, chef militaire du Vercors: Une vie au service de la France*, Paris: Éditions Italique, 2004, p. 181,

if things turned suddenly bad: Pierre Vial, *La Bataille du Vercors 1943–1944*, Paris: Presses de la Cité, 1991, p. 191.

Pierre Raynaud: alias Alain.

running east–west through Die: The N93 from the Col de Grimone at the south-eastern corner of the Vercors to Crest, south-west of the plateau.

the southern edge of the Vercors: Raynaud's report, TNA HS 6/586.

another Drôme Maquis: Commanded by Jean Drouot (alias Hermine).

numbering some 1,700: Fernand Rude, 'Le Dialogue Vercors–Algers (juin–juillet 1944)', *Revue d'Histoire de la Deuxième Guerre Mondiale*, no. 49, January 1963, p. 85.

'current battle for liberation': Jean-Marc Collavet, *Chronique du Vercors*, Valence: Éditions Peuple Libre, 1994, p. 97.

Cammaerts sent a signal: TNA HS 6/568.

'for future use': Rude, 'Le Dialogue Vercors–Algers', p. 85.

100 French paras a month: Telegram of 28 May 1944, Bedell Smith to General Gammell, TNA WO 204/1959.

the newly reconstituted French parachute unit: 1st Battalion of the French Régiment de Chasseurs Parachutistes (1st RCP).

as 'paratourists': SHAT 12/P 88.

asserted his authority: It seems likely that Koenig's attempt to regain control over the Vercors was not an isolated act. Since May he had been fighting a strenuous battle with Soustelle in Algiers as to who controlled the southern Resistance networks. See Philippe André, *La Résistance Confisquée?*, Paris: Éditions Perrin, 2013, p. 188.

'(and therefore under the command of London, not Algiers)': Rude, 'Le Dialogue Vercors–Algers', p. 85.

called the Villa Bellon: The house, which was owned by the family Bellon from Valence, is still standing and appears much as it would have been in 1944.

shared as an office: Pierre Tanant, *Vercors, haut-lieu de France*, Grenoble: Arthaud, 1948 and 1950, p. 83.

closed by a stout gate: Villa Bellon remains today almost totally unchanged from the time when it was Huet's HQ.

René Bousquet: Alias Chabert.

four-bureaux model: Up to the defeat of France in 1940, French military headquarters were organized in a five-bureaux model. But from that date the 5th and 2nd Bureaux (both of which dealt with intelligence matters) were combined into a single 2nd Burueau.

the 1st Bureau: Commanded by Lieutenant Picard.

the 2nd Bureau: Commanded by Captain Vincent-Beaume; this was stationed at La Chapelle, where there was more space.

the 3rd Bureau: Commanded initially by Pierre Tanant, then by Lieutenant d'Anglejan and finally by Captain de Nadaillac.

the 4th Bureau: Commanded initially by Lieutenant d'Alchansky and later by Captain Pierre de Montjamont.

a supply, rations and maintenance unit: Commanded by Lieutenant Beauchamp.

a 'command section': Commanded by Lieutenant Coquet.

'the older Maquisards …': Patrice Escolan and Lucien Ratel, *Guide-Mémorial du Vercors résistant*, Paris: Le Cherche-Midi, 1994, p. 267.

other linked military departments: A detention facility, a military police and provost section, an accommodation unit, an investigation section, a census and personnel records section, a traffic section, a military intelligence section, two vehicle parks, one at Saint-Martin and one at La Chapelle, complete with drivers and mechanics, an armoury, an ammunition dump, an engineer section, an archives department, a Military Tribunal.

total disposable manpower: Joseph, *Combattant du Vercors*, p. 169.

Security on the plateau: This included the police, the prison, the intelligence service, the military tribunal and the census service.

comprising two lieutenants: Meyer and Lipschitz.

and a civilian: Elie Revol.

'two red flags': Michael Pearson, *Tears of Glory: The Betrayal of the Vercors*, London: Pan Books, 1978, p. 97.

two of the accused: Vincent and Kuhn.

'paying for it': Conversation reported to Michael Pearson by Vincent-Beaume. Pearson, *Tears of Glory*, p. 97.

absolution of a priest: Gilles Vergnon email to the author, 2 June 2013. According to witnesses, the three men were shot on the slope below where the Musée de la Résistance stands today and their bodies were buried on the spot.

an official post-war inquiry: A 1946 Gendarmerie investigation into summary executions on the plateau established that the total number of these was likely to be less than twenty. I am indebted to Gilles Vergnon for this information.

a holiday centre in Auboyneaux: The building has been destroyed and the space built on.

the nearby Loscence valley: The building was later destroyed.

'affairs must cease': Vergnon, *Le Vercors: Histoire et mémoire d'un maquis*, Huet's order no. 2 of 13 July, p. 100.

a classic French *préfecture*: It was from about this time that Chavant also started to be known informally as the 'Préfet du Vercors'.

previously used as a holiday centre: The building, marked with a commemorative plaque explaining its previous purpose, is still there and largely unchanged. It is the last building on the left as you leave Saint-Martin on the Saint-Julien road.

'they captured alive': Henri Rosencher, *Le Sel, la cendre, la flamme*, Paris: Éditions du Félin, 2000, p. 272.

four 'official' points of exit and entry: Col de Rousset, Les Barraques, La Balme and the Pont de la Goule Noire.

'mass uprising': Tanant, *Vercors, haut-lieu de France*, p. 77.

daily convoys of lorries: *Ibid.*, p. 80. The provision of food to the plateau was managed by Benjamin Malossane.

'scattered throughout the village': Vergnon, *Le Vercors: Histoire et mémoire d'un maquis*, pp. 98 –9, quoting the personal archives of Pierre de Saint-Prix.

the French authorities in London and Algiers: Effectively Colonel Billotte, Jacques Soustelle in Algiers and Colonel Armand Sémidei in London.

'the Massif Central': Gilles Lévy, 'La Genèse du groupe "Auvergne" du Réduit du Massif Central (avril–août 1944)', http://lesamitiesdelaresistance.fr/lien28/p23-50_la_genese_du_groupe_auvergne.pdf, Paul Ricoeur, p. 45.

the creation of a new 'redoubt': See *ibid.* for more details.

A French report: Signed by General Caffey. TNA WO 204/1959.

'with General Delestraint': Letter from Mockler-Ferryman to Colonel Passy, 16 June 1944, TNA HS 6/332.

David Astor: David Langhorne Astor, educated at Eton and Oxford, was the son of the owner of the *Observer* newspaper (which he eventually edited for twenty-seven years) and was very well connected in the highest London circles.

'will never be forgiven': Minute to CCO from Astor, 17 June 1944, attaching a report written by Lieutenant Colonel Broad, TNA DEFE 2/1151.

'the enemy has miscalculated': TNA HW 3.

one of Fernand Grenier's subordinates: Lieutenant Colonel Morlaix.

'to help the Resistance': Paul Dreyfus, *Vercors: Citadelle de la liberté*, Romagnat: De Borée, 2007 (1st edn Paris: Arthaud, 1969), p. 261. Soustelle was later to claim that he was the original author of Opération Patrie.

at a meeting: The Committee for National Defence (CDN).

included several ministers: Commissioners André Diethelm (Army), Louis Jacquinot (Navy) and Grenier (Air).

the three French service chiefs: General Leyer for the Army, Admiral Lemonnier for the Navy and General Bouscat for the Air Force.

'aspect of modern warfare': Dreyfus, *Vercors: Citadelle de la liberté*, p. 262.

'perhaps airborne units': TNA CAB 79/76.

his Chief of Staff: General Ismay.

'stupidest strategic teams ever seen': Pearson, *Tears of Glory*, p. 129.

'by the shortest route': Dreyfus, *Vercors: Citadelle de la liberté*, p. 322 – translation back into English from the French translation of the original text.

breaking out from the Normandy beachhead: Operation Cobra.

Chapter 25: A Damned Good Show

Henri Rosencher: Alias Toubib (this may be more of a nickname than an alias – 'Toubib' is also a French colloquial name for a medical doctor).

'a long, long time': Henri Rosencher, *Le Sel, la cendre, la flamme*, Paris: Éditions du Félin, 2000, p. 271.

the single RAF squadron: 624 Squadron.

were very badly packed: Italian prisoners of war did most of the packing and were not averse to minor acts of sabotage.

'day and night': Fernand Rude, 'Le Dialogue Vercors–Algers (juin–juillet 1944)', *Revue d'Histoire de la Deuxième Guerre Mondiale*, no. 49, January 1963, p. 85.

The French in London: Henri Ziegler of BCRA.

'more open approach [than the British]': SHAT T 1097, Fonds Ziegler.

'my hopes [in Brittany]': Eisenhower was referring to an extensive programme of Resistance sabotage and ambushes coordinated with the Normandy landings. It was credited with helping impede the free movement of German troops in their rear areas and especially the deployment of their reinforcements to weak parts of the German line.

'strong in the South': Paul Gaujac, *La Guerre en Provence 1944–1945*, Lyon: Presses Universitaires de Lyon, 1998, p. 66. Gaujac cites *The Papers of Dwight David Eisenhower: The War Years*, ed. Alfred D. Chandler Jr, Baltimore: Johns Hopkins University Press, 1970, vol. 3, but does not give a page number.

US Flying Fortresses: They were from 3rd Bombardment Division of the US Eighth Air Force.

four sites including Vassieux on the Vercors: The others were near Nantua in the Ain, near Charette, 30 kilometres east of Beaune in Burgundy, near Châteauneuf in the Haute Vienne and twin drops on Chaudes-Aigues and the Barrage de l'Aigle in the Cantal area. This last had to be cancelled at the last minute because they were under heavy attack by the Germans. NARA, Report of OSS Activities with 7th Army, 14 October 1944 (RG 226, E99, Box 741, Folder 1476, OSS Massive supply drops to the French Resistance, Operation Zebra).

'an SS Panzer section': SPOC Sitrep, 30 June 1944, TNA WO 204/1947. The 'SS Panzer section' was in fact a battle group of the 9th Panzer Division, which the French often confused with the SS because of the black uniform and death's-head insignia both had in common. It is also very likely that the 'tanks' were in fact armoured personnel carriers. Peter Lieb email to the author, 29 October 2013.

'after they had left': SHAT T 1160, Fonds Ziegler, Zeller report, p. 50.

a large farmhouse: Owned by the Belle family.

heavy explosions near by: Michael Pearson, *Tears of Glory: The Betrayal of the Vercors*, London: Pan Books, 1978, p. 85.

one radio operator killed: The report of this action in TNA HS 7/131 puts the Maquis losses at six radio and telephone operators, but this is probably an exaggeration.

reinforce the plateau: Gilbert Joseph, *Combattant du Vercors*, Grenoble: Éditions Curandera, 1994 (1st edn, Paris: Fayard, 1992), p. 186.

the Maquis commander: Pierre Raynaud.

one of his Maquis leaders: Paul Abonnenc.

'they will do so': Jean Abonnenc, *Il n'est pas trop tard pour parler de Résistance*, Die: Imprimerie Cayol, 2004, p. 190.

new arms and equipment: Albert Darier, *Tu prendras les armes*, Valence: Imprimerie Nouvelle, 1983, p. 149.

a message to London: Addressed to Colonel Lejeune (alias Delphin).

'near Montelimar': Ray Jenkins, *Pacifist at War*, London: Hutchinson, 2009, p.153. This may have been Chabeuil.

St John's Eve: The eve of the feast of St John is celebrated in many Catholic countries and especially in rural areas as being in effect midsummer eve. The tradition is to light bonfires and jump over them to mark the passing of the mid-point of the year. There are several accounts of the celebration of this event on this night in 1944 in the Vercors.

dropped – no paratroops: TNA AIR 27/2142.

Desmond Longe: Alias Réfraction.

John Houseman: Alias Réflexion.

André Pecquet: Alias Paray (by which name he was known even after the war) and Bavarois.

an ex-Barclay's Bank employee: Desmond Longe's personal file, TNA HS 9/937/8.

a close regimental friend: Both had been in the Royal Norfolk Regiment.

'The Home Counties': John Houseman's personal file, TNA HS 9/749/1.

motorbikes called Wellbikes: A light, portable, folding motorcycle, specially designed by SOE for parachute operations.

caught fire: Desmond Longe, TNA HS 6/361, p. 9. The fire was in fact extinguished, but in the process one of the engine's oil pipes was ruptured.

make a safe landing: Major D. Longe's report, TNA HS 6/425.

two Russian Maquisards: Paul Borisov and George Morosov.

one of Geyer's young trainee officers: Cadet Francisque Troussier.

'our machine guns': Troussier's evidence, Association Nationale des Pionniers du Vercors, *Le Vercors raconté par ceux qui l'ont vécu*, Valence: Imprimerie Nouvelle, 1990, pp. 252–3.

group of fifty-three: In fact, of the fifty-three Africans, only seven were Senegalese. Among the remainder were Africans from Sudan, Gabon, the Ivory Coast, Guinea, Dahomey and Mali. These troops were specially chosen for their size and were very often used on ceremonial parades. See Jean-Marc Collavet, *Chronique du Vercors*, Valence: Éditions Peuple Libre, 1994, p. 97. See also Association Nationale des Pionniers du Vercors, *Le Vercors raconté par ceux qui l'ont vécu*, Valence: Imprimerie Nouvelle, 1990, pp. 171–3.

The airfields in Corsica: There were in all four old airfields in Corsica. But new ones had to be built to accommodate the needs of Anvil. Huge amounts of ammunition and weapons were also stocked on the island, ready for Anvil – amounting in all to some 136,000 bombs and 3.5 million rounds of ammunition. See http://www.ibiblio.org/hyperwar/AAF/III/AAF-III-12.html.

'will be wiped out': *Vercors 1944: Un officier britannique dans la tourmente*, http://www.benchart.net/benchart/arnaud-duret/textes/article.doc; and Rude, 'Le Dialogue Vercors–Algers (juin–juillet 1944)', p. 86.

3,000 first-aid battle dressings: NARA, Report of OSS Activities with 7th Army, 14 October 1944.

'Our officer': Captain Jury.

'seen no one': Evidence of Aspirant Bertie, ANPV, *Le Vercors raconté par ceux qui l'ont vécu*, p. 245.

the reconstituted French Army units who were present: Most notably at this parade, the 6th Bataillon de Chasseurs Alpins (6th BCA).

'pushed to one side': Pierre Vial, *La Battaile du Vercors 1943–1944*, Paris: Presses de la Cité, 1991, p. 194. See also Paul Brisac, 'Souvenir du Vercors', Archives Départementales de l'Isère, ADI 57J53.

were not included: Paul Dreyfus, *Histoire de la Résistance en Vercors*, Paris: Arthaud, 1980, p. 146.

'Target not ascertained': TNA HW 5/520.

'When is the next?': NARA, Report of OSS Activities with 7th Army, 14 October 1944.

Chapter 26: Mixed Messages

'tobacco and soap': Fernand Rude, 'Le Dialogue Vercors–Algers (juin–juillet 1944)', *Revue d'Histoire de la Deuxième Guerre Mondiale*, no. 49, January 1963, p. 89.

'telephone and telecommunications cut': *Ibid.*

The French delegate for medical affairs: Dr Rozans (alias Raoul).

later repeated by Zeller: Zeller's signal was sent on 29 June and said, 'I repeat our request for the bombing of Chabeuil, which I have already asked for three times.' Rude, 'Le Dialogue Vercors–Algers (juin–juillet 1944)', p. 89.

'aircraft over target': Michael Pearson, *Tears of Glory: The Betrayal of the Vercors*, London: Pan Books, 1978, p. 113. See also *Vercors 1944: Un officier britannique dans la tourmente*, http://www.benchart.net/benchart/arnaud-duret/textes/article.doc; and Rude, 'Le Dialogue Vercors–Algers (juin–juillet 1944)', p. 89.

Mediterranean Allied Air Forces: MAAF.

'within several days': Pearson, *Tears of Glory*, p. 113.

the true situation on the plateau: Paul Dreyfus, *Vercors: Citadelle de la liberté*, Romagnat: De Borée, 2007 (1st edn Paris: Arthaud, 1969), p. 265. Soustelle later denied this.

Allied Forces Headquarters: AFHQ, History of Special Forces Operations, TNA WO 204/2030B.

Jean Tournissa: Alias Paquebot.

the Vassieux parachute site: Taille-Crayon (pencil sharpener).

two Halifax bombers: 624 Squadron.

an OSS mission codenamed Justine: OSS units such as these were known as Operational Groups, or OG, which normally numbered thirty men. Justine was therefore technically known as a 'Half OG'.

the Americans had sent some of their own: In his book *Envers et contre tout* (3 vols, Geneva: Éditions de Crémille, 1970; 1st edn, Paris: Robert Laffont, 1947–50), Jacques Soustelle claims that these were French Paras sent by him – see vol. 3, p. 240.

a second wireless operator: Yves Croix (alias Pingouin).

'walked into the village': Desmond Longe, TNA HS 6/361, p. 17.

Neil Marten: Marten had been parachuted into the Beaurepaire area west of the plateau some days earlier. He was head of the Veganin Mission to the Beaurepaire plateau and was therefore under Cammaerts' command.

unprofessional voyeurs: According to Robert Bennes, André Pecquet also had a low opinion of the two Englishmen. Interview with Robert Bennes, 10 November 2013, Castres. It should be recorded, however, that when the conduct of Houseman and Longe was the subject of a post-war inquiry, Pecquet in his evidence did not criticize them.

A briefing session: Marcel Descour left the plateau that day to deal with a crisis in Lyon following the arrest of his chief Resistance organizer.

'it will be dubious': Pearson, *Tears of Glory*, p. 132.

'aggressive and intelligent': *Ibid.*

'of 5,000 men': *Ibid.*

two local Resistants: Ricard and Bourdon. There was also a cook, Louis Sebastini.

The instructions given to Longe: Pearson, *Tears of Glory*, p. 132.

'with the enemy': M. R. D. Foot, *SOE in France: An Account of the Work of the British Special Operations Executive in France 1940–1944*, London: HM Stationery Office, 1966, p. 344.

'of heavy weapons': *Ibid.*

'of communications and telecommunications': NARA, Box 741, Folder 1473, Summary Report.

Commissioners of the Republic: Commissaires de la République.

the population's needs: Charles de Gaulle, *The War Memoirs*, vol. 2: *Unity 1942–1944*, New York: Simon & Schuster, 1959, p. 198.

the Committee for the Liberation of the Vercors: Le Comité de Libération du Vercors.

'the civil and military structures': Fernand Rude, 'Vercors', in Pierre Bolle (ed.), *Grenoble et le Vercors: De la Résistance à la Libération 1940–1944*, Lyon: La Manufacture, 1985, p. 113.

the new Fourth Republic of France: The Vercors was not unique in believing this. For instance, the Fourth Republic was also declared in Oyonnax on 6 June 1944. Gilles Vergnon email to the author, 16 January 2013.

Chapter 27: The Republic

'during his US visit': Top Secret memo to Marshall from SHAEF, 9 July 1944, TNA HS 6/605.

American Dakota C47 aircraft: TNA WO 204/10188B; and Pierre Billotte, *Le Temps des armes*, Paris: Plon, 1972, p. 298.

Colonel Pierre Billotte: Billotte was appointed on 2 July just before de Gaulle left for the United States. He started to assemble his staff for Caïman immediately. Billotte, *Le Temps des armes*, p. 294.

the Trapani 'paratourists': 1st Battalion of the RCP (Régiment de Chasseurs Parachutistes).

George Marshall in Washington welcomed the proposal: See SHAEF OPD 381 TS Memos, 8 July to 5 Aug., in *The Papers of Dwight David Eisenhower*, ed. Alfred D. Chandler Jr, Baltimore: Johns Hopkins University Press, 1970, vol. 3, p. 1993.

'under French command': Memo to Marshall, 10 July 1944, *The Papers of Dwight David Eisenhower*, vol. 3, p. 1992.

'the situation … may dictate': Telegram BX-13550, 11 July 1944, TNA HS 6/605.

to persuade the Allies to bomb Chabeuil: He left a handwritten note dated 1 July to this effect on the desk of Maitland Wilson's Chief of Staff, Eugene Caffey.

fly Neil Marten back to Algiers: There are some hints in SOE files and other documents that Marten, who had arrived only three weeks previously, was being sent back because he was finding clandestine life difficult in France. He had been, it was said, greatly affected by the fact that his British wireless operator had been killed because of a parachute malfunction when they had both been parachuted in to a drop site near Beaurepaire on 9 June 1944.

After the war he became Conservative MP for Banbury in Oxfordshire and held two ministerial posts under Mrs Thatcher (Aviation and Overseas Development).

'is very great': NARA, Signal A 2466/8, 2 July 1944, OSS report – Jockey Circuit, p. 457.

of 1 July: There is dispute about this date, with some sources saying that Hoppers left on 30 June. I have taken the chronology for what follows from NARA, Justine Mission, Hoppers' report, Box 741, Folder 1473.

one of Bourdeaux's officers: We only have his alias, Captain Durard.

open ground on the other: The hairpin bend on which Hoppers placed his ambush is still easily identifiable some 1,500 metres west of the col at Les Limouches on the D68.

Trièves and Mens area: Albert Darier, *Tu prendras les armes*, Valence: Imprimerie Nouvelle, 1983, p. 166.

'at the time': It seems very likely that Hoppers' reconnaissance of the Chabeuil was connected with a plan which Cammaerts had drawn up for an attack on the airfield which was to be carried out by the Drôme Maquis under cover of an RAF bombing raid. The raid, however, never materialized and the attack was called off. See *Vercors 1944: Un officier britannique dans la tourmente*, http://www.benchart.net/benchart/arnaud-duret/textes/article.doc, p. 11.

the magnificent old lime tree: Known as 'L'arbre de la Liberté', this famous tree was planted on the orders of Maximilien de Béthune, first Duke of Sully, who was one of the chief ministers of Henry IV of France.

sat erect on his horse: Boucaro, the horse which Geyer 'liberated' when the Armistice Army was disbanded, was one of the regiment's stallions. However, during the period that Geyer was commander of the Vercors one of his men, Beseau, stole a beautiful chestnut mare from the German commandant in Romans and gave it to Geyer, who rode it for the rest of his time in the Vercors, including at the 3 July 1944 parade when the Vercors Republic was inaugurated.

a full-scale and energetic offensive: Peter Lieb, *Vercors 1944: Resistance in the French Alps*, Botley, Oxford: Osprey Publishing, 2012, p. 29.

'on the airfield': TNA WO 204/1947.

'as soon as possible': Fernand Rude, 'Le Dialogue Vercors–Algers (juin–juillet 1944)', *Revue d'Histoire de la Deuxième Guerre Mondiale*, no. 49, January 1963, p. 91. Zeller responded the next day confirming both Hoppers' numbers for aircraft on the Chabeuil field and the precise map coordinates of where they were. On 10 July, Constans sent a signal promising that the RAF would bomb Chabeuil, adding, 'But the FFI should consider the dispersed aircraft round the airfield as objectives for ground attack. This is an order from the Supreme Allied Command.' Neither the RAF attack nor the FFI one ever materialized – *ibid.*, p. 91.

a full-scale regimental dinner: Journal of Louis Rose, http://11eme-cuirassiers-vercors.com/.

almost certainly coordinated reports: Huet's document refers to the verbal report given by Cammaerts to Marten.

Cammaerts gave his report: It seems likely that that the report Cammaerts originally gave to Marten was an oral one, because Huet refers in his submission to a verbal report. However, Cammaerts' file contains the actual report which arrived in Algiers and this is dated 7 July 1944 – two days after Marten left the plateau. Given that Marten did not get out until 12 July, it is probable that Cammaerts thought better of trusting such a vital message to oral communication and wrote his report two days after Marten left the Vercors and had it delivered to him by hand before he left. Once back in Algiers, Marten was told he could not return to France because he knew too much about future operations.

Huet's report: AN BCRA 3 AG 2/478. I am indebted to Gilles Vergnon for sight of this document.

'of his actions': Cammaerts' report, 7 July 1944, TNA HS 9/258/5.

'my instructions and orders': Rude, 'Le Dialogue Vercors–Algers (juin–juillet 1944)', p. 91.

Jean Tournissa: He carried false identity documents in the name of Jean-Étienne Trémoulet, a quantity surveyor. In fact Tournissa and his team had tried to get in the night before but the Halifax that was carrying them couldn't find the DZ. See the evidence of Yves

Morineaux, Association Nationale des Pionniers du Vercors, *Le Vercors raconté par ceux qui l'ont vécu*, Valence: Imprimerie Nouvelle, 1990, p. 197.

Francis Billon: Alias Tartane.

to train Maquisards: TNA HS 9/152/6.

Yves Morineaux: Alias Bateau.

Christine Granville: Alias Pauline.

'the time of liberation': Douglas Dodds-Parker, quoted in Clare Mulley, *The Spy Who Loved: The Secrets and Lives of Christine Granville, Britain's First Female Special Agent of World War II*, London: Macmillan, 2012, p. 173.

'go to France': Douglas Dodds-Parker, quoted in *ibid.*, p. 179.

'married to somebody': *Ibid.*

his previous one: Cecily Lefort (alias Alice).

5 million francs for Cammaerts: Interview with Robert Bennes, 10 November 2013, Castres.

without mishap: *Ibid.* Bennes distinctly remembers seeing her ('a most handsome woman') on the landing site that night. This is confirmed in Desmond Longe's diary (p. 24, TNA HS 6/361) in which he records that, although Christine did drift, she was found unhurt and joined the others that night.

with some difficulty: Evidence of François Morineaux, ANPV, *Le Vercors raconté par ceux qui l'ont vécu*, p. 194.

'No more Stens': The words Descour used, 'Plus de Stens', can actually be read in French two quite contradictory ways – either 'More Stens' or 'No more Stens'. But given the number of Stens already on the plateau and their poor reputation among the Maquisards, there can be no doubt about his intended meaning.

'discipline section': Those under punishment for minor offences such as stealing.

three heavy machine guns: Interview with Robert Bennes, 10 November 2013, Castres. Bennes' memory was a little vague: he said that there may have been only two machine guns on the site.

Captain Pierre Haezebrouck: Alias Hardy. Paul Dreyfus, *Vercors: Citadelle de la liberté*, Romagnat: De Borée, 2007 (1st edn Paris: Arthaud, 1969), p. 208.

boost to morale: Roland Costa de Beauregard, 'Le Vercors, juin 1944: Projets et réalités', *Revue Historique de l'Armée*, no. 4, 1972, p. 113.

'for this operation': *Ibid.*, p. 114.

prepare the strip: Algiers' insistence that the Vassieux site had to be able to accommodate a Dakota was probably connected with an event which took place that night on a flat field at Izernore in the Ain Department, 120 kilometres north of the Vercors. Here, in the early hours of 9 June 1944, Colonel Clifford J. Heflin USAF landed the first Dakota in occupied France and unloaded a jeep, a large load of mortar bombs and other ammunition and eleven passengers, including three, Adrien Conus, Gaston Peliat and Pierre Gaillard, who, as the second half of the Eucalyptus Mission, were destined for the Vercors. The three were driven up to the plateau on 11 July, in a disguised Milice truck.

Victor Boiron: Journal de Marche du 11e Régiment de Cuirassiers, 23 July 1944, http://11eme-cuirassiers-vercors.com/11eme.php?sp=7.

period of good weather: Darier, *Tu prendras les armes*, p. 177.

blew up the road: Journal of Louis Rose, http://11eme-cuirassiers-vercors.com/.

'in the Grenoble area': BA-MA, Document RW 35/47, quoted in Gilles Vergnon, *Résistance dans le Vercors: Histoire et lieux de mémoire*, Grenoble: Glénat, 2002, p. 121, and *Le Pionnier du Vercors: La Compagnie Abel 1943–1944*, Grenoble: Association Nationale des Pionniers et Combattants du Vercors, Special number 2012, p. 27.

5,000-strong assault: Codenamed Operation Treffenfeld.

for Bettina: Bettina is the codename often used for the whole Vercors operation. But this may be an error. There is good reason to believe that Bettina was just the movement order to get the troops into position. The Germans always referred to the operation itself as Operation Vercors. Peter Lieb email to the author, 18 February 2012.

the Luftwaffe's anti-partisan squadron: Kampfgeschwader Bongart. This unit was formed on 5 April 1944 as an anti-partisan unit and named after Oberst Hermann Freiherr von dem

Bongart. See Geoffrey J. Thomas and Barry Ketley, *KG 200: The Luftwaffe's Most Secret Unit*, Crowborough, East Sussex: Hikoki Publications, 2003, for more details.

'north of Die': Andrew Arthy, *Luftwaffe Anti-Partisan Operations in France, June–September 1944*, http://www.thescale.info/news/publish/luftwaffe-Anti-Partisan.shtml, p. 6.

Chapter 28: Action and Expectation

the main road from Aspres-sur-Buëch: At the time the D1075. Now the N75.

in a couple of days: Although the intelligence of this movement appears to have arrived with Huet on the day before Niehoff issued orders for Operation Bettina, it seems very likely that it was in fact connected with it.

to prepare for action: NARA, Box 741, Folder 1473, Justine Mission, Hoppers' report. It is worth noting that Hoppers' report, which was written after he left the Vercors, is for some reason inaccurate in its dates. Hoppers, who seems to have lost two days in his chronology of all these events, puts the initial briefing on 5, not 7, July.

Maurice Bourgeois: Alias Bataille.

the 300-metre-long horseshoe bend: There is a stone plaque marking the event on a rock close to the centre of Hoppers' killing ground.

'The machine gun': A Browning Automatic Rifle (BAR), an American light machine gun.

'One Maquis we knew was dead': Louis Picard, a cook

'we waited for': Hoppers' report, Box 741, Folder 1473.

'unused to the mountains': Joseph La Picirella, *Mon journal du Vercors*, Lyon: Imprimerie Rivet, 1982, pp. 63–8.

'the end for him': Evidence of Fernande Battier of Lalley, Association Nationale des Pionniers du Vercors, *Le Vercors raconté par ceux qui l'ont vécu*, Valence: Imprimerie Nouvelle, 1990, p. 241.

a considerable exaggeration: German sources indicated fifteen dead. Peter Lieb email to the author, 11 January 2014.

well over 3,000: 3,200 according to M. R. D. Foot, *SOE in France: An Account of the Work of the British Special Operations Executive in France 1940–1944*, London: HM Stationery Office, 1966, p. 345.

'arrested by the Germans': Pierre Tanant, *Vercors, haut-lieu de France*, Grenoble: Arthaud, 1948 and 1950, p. 98.

rudimentary military training: *Le Pionnier du Vercors: La Compagnie Abel 1943–1944*, Grenoble: Association Nationale des Pionniers et Combattants du Vercors, Special number 2012, p. 25.

'of our homeland': Jean-Marc Collavet, *Chronique du Vercors*, Valence: Éditions Peuple Libre, 1994, p. 101.

'Dakotas very soon': Fernand Rude, 'Le Dialogue Vercors–Algers (juin–juillet 1944)', *Revue d'Histoire de la Deuxième Guerre Mondiale*, no. 49, January 1963, p. 93.

'opportunity we can': *Ibid*.

'is to be avoided': SHAEF/17245/6/5/2/Ops, TNA HS 6/337, 12 July 1944.

'against the plateau': Rude, 'Le Dialogue Vercors–Algers (juin–juillet 1944)', p. 94.

Cochet wasted no time: See Rude, 'Le Dialogue Vercors–Algers (juin–juillet 1944)', p. 94.

to Naples: Eaker's headquarters later moved to Corsica.

the 5,000 aircraft: 3,000 on Corsica alone.

'of providing support': Rude, 'Le Dialogue Vercors–Algers (juin–juillet 1944)', p. 93.

in the four villages: SPOC Sitrep, 12 July 1944, TNA WO 204/1947.

Desmond Longe's diary: TNA HS 6/361, p. 27.

'units of our region': Joseph Gilbert, *Combattant du Vercors*, Grenoble: Éditions Curandera, 1994 (1st edn, Paris: Fayard, 1992), p. 199.

each named after units: The 11th Cuirassiers under Narcisse Geyer, the 6th BCA (Bataillon de Chasseurs Alpins) under Roland Costa de Beauregard, 12th BCA under Henri Ullman and 14th BCA under Louis Bourdeaux. The Senegalese made up a section of their own, as did the 4th Régiment de Génie (4th Engineering Regiment) and the 2th Régiment d'Artillery, a 'virtual unit' formed in anticipation of the arrival of the American mountain guns which were promised but never arrived.

his total strength: There is some scepticism among Vercors historians (e.g. Gilles Vergnon) about these figures – which do not anyway differentiate armed men from unarmed. *Vercors 1944: Un officier britannique dans la tourmente*, http://www.benchart.net/benchart/arnaud-duret/textes/article.doc.

'before the war': Tanant, *Vercors, haut-lieu de France*, pp. 92 –3.

'[a cavalry unit]': 11th Cuirassiers.

'straw-stuffed mattresses': Evidence of Aspirant Bertie, ANPV, *Le Vercors raconté par ceux qui l'ont vécu*, pp. 245–6.

'killed while doing it': Gilbert, *Combattant du Vercors*, p. 200.

'of the 1940s': Patrice Escolan and Lucien Ratel, *Guide-mémorial du Vercors résistant*, Paris: Le Cherche-Midi, 1994, p. 265.

'bandits, not soldiers': Tanant, *Vercors, haut-lieu de France*, p. 94.

at the Villa Bellon: See *ibid.*, p. 96.

aerial reconnaissance *mouches*: One of these was shot down on this day by a unit of Compagnie Abel at La Balme. See *Le Pionnier du Vercors: La Compagnie Abel 1943–1944*, p. 25.

above the plateau: Dreyfus, *Vercors: Citadelle de la liberté*, p. 181.

the Chief of Staff at the French headquarters: Colonel Vernon.

'as soon as possible': EMFFI 53, Letter Vernon to Koenig, London, 13 July 1944, SHAT 1 K 374/3.

one of Bob Bennes' radio operators: Jean Cendral (alias Lombard).

the 150 containers and fifteen packages: http://11eme-cuirassiers-vercors.com/.

in garages in Vassieux: Robert Bennes, 'Mémoires de guerre', 2010, p. 54, by kind permission of the author.

one to help vector in the expected aircraft: Pierre Lassalle.

and the other: Mario Montefusco, alias Titin and Argentin.

Chapter 29: Bastille Day

'on the Vercors': Michael Pearson, *Tears of Glory: The Betrayal of the Vercors*, London: Pan Books, 1978, p. 151.

a fraternal delegation: Fernand Rude, 'Le Vercors', in Pierre Bolle (ed.), *Grenoble et le Vercors: De la Résistance à la Libération 1940–1944*, Lyon: La Manufacture, 1985, p. 159.

a hazardous undertaking: Jean Abonnenc, *Il n'est pas trop tard pour parler de Résistance*, Die: Imprimerie Cayol, 2004, p. 218. See also TNA HS 7/131, p. 103. There is a disagreement on the time of the parade. This book quotes 17.00 but Farge's account in his book, *Rebelles, soldats et citoyens* (Geneva: Éditions Grasset, 1948) gives midday. I have taken Farge's account as the timings of this day.

'Your friends from Algiers': Fernand Rude, 'Le Dialogue Vercors–Algers (juin–juillet 1944)', *Revue d'Histoire de la Deuxième Guerre Mondiale*, no. 49, January 1963, p. 95.

'national day of 14th July': 'Les Résistants dans le Vercors, 9 Juin–7 Août 1944: Témoignages de Nicolas Bernard', by kind permission of his daughter Martine Pattin and her friend Julia Chalkley.

320 American Flying Fortresses bombers: Again from the 3rd Bombardment Division of the US Eighth Air Force.

different drop sites: Apart from the Vercors, with 75 aircraft dispatched, these were east of Salornay in the Saône-et-Loire (38 aircraft), near Mauriac in the Cantal (67 aircraft), north of Pleaux in the Cantal (36 aircraft), near Argentat in the Corrèze (40 aircraft), near Veyrac in the Lot (53 aircraft) and near Domps in the Haute-Vienne (40 aircraft). Drops were also planned near Nantua in the Ain, but because of Operation Treffenfeld these were cancelled. There was, in addition, a 'spare' site near Bourganeuf in the Creuse which was never used.

almost 95 tonnes: The detailed breakdown of arms was 3,895 pounds of explosive, 691 Stens, 1.15 million rounds of 9mm ammunition, 1,040 Mills grenades, 470 Gammon grenades, 130 pistols, 186 Bren light machine guns, 1.5 million rounds of .303 ammunition, 999 rifles, twenty-one PIAT anti-tank launchers, 420 rounds of PIAT ammunition.

'of parachute canopies': Operation Cadillac, TNA HS 6/606.

two German Focke-Wulf 190s: From Kampfgeschwader Bongart.

Bob Bennes' radio operator: Mario Montefusco.

'Being machine gunned': Robert Bennes, 'Mémoires de guerre', 2010, p. 59, by kind permission of the author.

in the Digne area: NARA, Historian Jockey Licensee – OSS Report, vol. 3, p. 459.

'against the sky': Ray Jenkins, Pacifist at War, London: Hutchinson, 2009, p. 170.

romantically attached: Interview with Cammaerts' daughter Joanna Wey, 13 May 2013, House of Lords.

'sensitive and alert ...': E. H. Cookridge, They Came from the Sky, London: Corgi Books, 1976 (1st edn, London: Heinemann, 1965), p. 129. Quoted in Clare Mulley, The Spy Who Loved: The Secrets and Lives of Christine Granville, Britain's First Female Special Agent of World War II, London: Macmillan, 2012, p. 194. Also Jenkins, Pacifist at War, p. 166.

'with tremendous magnetism': Wladimir Ledóchowski, 'Christine Skarbek-Granville', p. 216, quoted in Mulley, The Spy Who Loved, p. 194.

Pierre Raynaud: Abonnenc, Il n'est pas trop tard, p. 104.

to remain hidden: The details of this account are taken from Farge, Rebelles, soldats et citoyens, p. 110.

half were totally destroyed: Peter Lieb, Vercors 1944: Resistance in the French Alps, Botley, Oxford: Osprey Publishing, 2012, p. 38.

met in the shelter: Interview with Robert Bennes, 10 November 2013, Castres.

the chaos and the noise: Paul Dreyfus, Histoire de la Résistance en Vercors, Paris: Arthaud, 1980, p. 151.

'donne la victoire': Pearson, Tears of Glory, pp. 154–5.

'solitude of the mountain': Dreyfus, Histoire de la Résistance en Vercors, p. 151.

'towards the sky': Pearson, Tears of Glory, pp. 155–6.

soon restored order: Ibid.

there is a description: Mulley, The Spy Who Loved, p. 212.

recharged their glasses: Interview with Robert Bennes, 10 November 2013, Castres.

'Allied aircraft. Thanks': Rude, 'Le Dialogue Vercors–Algers (juin–juillet 1944)', p. 95.

the telephone exchange: No sign of this building remains. The site and the area around it are now home to an equestrian centre.

a 'dispersal plan': See Paray's report in TNA HS 6/424. The prevailing thinking on the plateau was that if they were occupied by the Germans, then as with other similar 'occupations' it would last for three days or so.

'want us to die"': Jenkins, Pacifist at War, p. 172.

the Isère and Drôme areas: See Vercors 1944: Un officier britannique dans la tourmente, http://www.benchart.net/benchart/arnaud-duret/textes/article.doc, p. 13.

eight lorryloads: SHAT 1 K 89/15, 'Les Operations du Vercors'.

Chapter 30: Pflaum's Plans and People

the largest German anti-partisan operation: For details of German forces in this chapter, I am greatly indebted to Peter Lieb and his book Vercors 1944: Resistance in the French Alps, Botley, Oxford: Osprey Publishing, 2012.

Pflaum's Alpine regiments: Reserve Gebirgsjäger Regiment 1 consisting of Gebirgsjäger Battalions I/98, II/98, 99 and 100 as well as some regimental units.

a specialist airborne unit: No. 7 Company, Kampfgeschwader 200 (known as KG 200).

an armoured battalion: No. 2 Battalion of the 10th Panzergrenadier Regiment.

police and security units: SS-Polizei Regiment 19, Sicherungs Regiment 200.

Eastern Troop elements: Osttruppen from the Freiwilligen-Stamm-Division.

Oberst: Colonel.

twenty-two assault gliders: German DFS 230 gliders.

a Luftwaffe airborne unit: No. 7 Company of Kampfgeschwader 200 (KG 200).

a medium machine gun: The German MG15.

resupply gliders: GO (Gotha) 242 gliders.

bombers and fighters: From Kampfgeschwader Bongart.

air transport specialist units: Luftlandegeschwader (LLG, Airborne Wing) 1 and 2.

would accompany Schäfer: There is some suggestion that Knab was considered by many of his colleagues to have an aversion to being too close to action. It may be that his decision to fly in with Schäfer's men was an attempt to answer this criticism. Peter Lieb email to the author, 14 January 2014.

claimed there were thirty: See DCAJM, Pflaum's defence documents, Box 1999. Translation by Christine Tochtermann.

not yet fully armed: See Eucalyptus estimate given in SPOS Sitrep of 14 July 1944, TNA WO 204/1947.

Chapter 31: The Rising Storm

'and external situations': Astor's letter to Laycock, 15 July 1944, TNA DEFE 2/1151.

'light and heavy companies': Plan for the Use of Resistance in Support of Operation Anvil – Present Situation by Regions, TNA WO 204/1959.

DC3 aircraft: Dakota.

'supply of heavy weapons': TNA WO 204/1959.

'[Operation] Dagenham project': Cammaerts' leapfrogging plan (see Chapter 13) had now been given the codename Dagenham.

'on to] the Vercors': TNA HS 6/605.

'advancing invasion troops': Michael Pearson, *Tears of Glory: The Betrayal of the Vercors*, London: Pan Books, 1978, p. 163.

Muddled signals: Fernand Rude, 'Le Dialogue Vercors–Algers (juin–juillet 1944)', *Revue d'Histoire de la Deuxième Guerre Mondiale*, no. 49, January 1963, p. 96.

'responsibility for this': Pierre Billotte, *Le Temp des armes*, Paris: Plon, 1972, pp. 298 *et seq.*

'to another operation': Letter Maitland Wilson to General de Gaulle, 16 July 1944, TNA WO 204/5750.

'under my control': Jacques Soustelle, *Envers et contre tout*, 3 vols, Geneva: Éditions de Crémille, 1970 (1st edn, Paris: Robert Laffont, 1947–50), vol. 3, p. 223.

to Gabriel Cochet: Cochet had himself still not received the formal letter confirming his appointment as head of FFI forces in North Africa.

'from General Koenig': Rude, 'Le Dialogue Vercors–Algers (juin–juillet 1944)', p. 94; and Jean-Marc Collavet, *Chronique du Vercors*, Valence: Éditions Peuple Libre, 1994, p. 106.

the Luftwaffe's anti-partisan unit: Kampfgeschwader Bongart.

fifteen sorties: Andrew Arthy, *Luftwaffe Anti-Partisan Operations in France, June–September 1944*, http://www.thescale.info/news/publish/luftwaffe-Anti-Partisan.shtml.

Alpine troops and artillery: SHAT 1 K 907, p. 1451.

heavily armed Maquisards: Commanded by Lieutenant Bagnaud.

a carefully arranged piece of theatre: SHAT 1 K 907, p. 1451. For further details see Pierre Vial, *La Bataille du Vercors 1943–1944*, Paris: Presses de la Cité, 1991, p. 158.

travel by train: They were instructed to embark at Goncellin at the head of the Grésivaudan valley, where Schwehr had also positioned his temporary headquarters. SHAT 1 K 89/15.

south towards Grenoble: *Ibid.*

in the same area: *Ibid.*

'of aerial photographs': Georg Schlaug, *Die deutschen Lastensegler-Verbände 1937–1945: Eine Chronik aus Berichten, Tagebüchern, Dokumenten*, Stuttgart: Motorbuch, 1985, pp. 212–15. Translation by Christine Tochtermann.

'middle of the plateau': François Broche, *François Huet, chef militaire du Vercors: Une vie au service de la France*, Paris: Éditions Italique, 2004, p. 194.

rain on the plateau: Albert Darier, *Tu prendras les armes*, Valence: Imprimerie Nouvelle, 1983, p. 200.

'officer than Billotte': Cable Alms to Eisenhower, 19 July 1944, TNA HS 6/605.

'a different turn': Pierre Dalloz, *Vérités sur le drame du Vercors*, Paris: Éditions Fernand Lanore, 1979, p. 203.

'beginning to tell …': Longe's diary, SHAT 1 K 907. Note that Longe seems to have lost two days in his account (see also TNA HS 6/361) in which the dates as given are two days earlier than those confirmed by other sources. Curiously Vernon Hoppers also lost two days in his after-action report (see Chapter 28).

their commanders: Lieutenants François Sotty (alias Simonot) and Paul Blanc (alias Jean-Paul).

say their goodbyes: Darier, *Tu prendras les armes*, p. 202.

left hurriedly: Association Mémoire du Lycée Polonais Cyprian-Norwid, *Des résistants polonais en Vercors: La saga du lycée polonais Cyprian-Norwid: Villard de-Lans 1940–1946*, Grenoble: Presses Universitaires de Grenoble, 2012, p. 95.

as far as Romans: SHAT 1 K 89/15.

twenty-four-hour basis: NARA, Justine Mission, Hoppers' report, Box 741, Folder 1473.

occupy the little villages: SHAT 1 K 89/15. The detailed unit positions were reported as: headquarters at Cognelle, 7th Company at Saint-Martin-de-la-Cluze, 8th Company at Les Jails, 9th Company at Benetz, 10th Company at Pigeonnier. 20th Company continues the march towards Clelles and bivouacs at Chaffaud, Clelles and Saint-Martin-de-Clelles.

'rings in their hair': Paul Dreyfus, *Vercors: Citadelle de la liberté*, Romagnat: De Borée, 2007 (1st edn Paris: Arthaud, 1969), pp. 223–4.

A more measured account: The evidence of Father Folte and Drs Pierre Fabre and Schaeffer. DCAJM, Crest file.

using the forest tracks: See Raynaud's reports, TNA HS 6/586.

his 4,000 Maquisards: The final best estimate for Huet's numbers was 3,909 men of whom 169 were officers and 317 NCOs.

'been duly warned …': Dreyfus, *Vercors: Citadelle de la liberté*, p. 195.

the Drôme Maquis commander: De Lassus.

'and our region': Jean Sauvageon, Gilles Vergnon and Jacki Vinay, *1939–1945: Et se leva le vent de la liberté: Entre Drôme des collines et Vercors*, Guilherand-Granges: ANACR, 2012, p. 130.

'in bloody combat': SHAT T 1167, Fonds Ziegler, Humbert's account.

'the current situation': Rude, 'Le Dialogue Vercors–Algers (juin–juillet 1944)', p. 98.

'St. Nizier and Chabeuil': *Ibid.* Translated back from the French. The telegram was addressed to Colonel Bill Davis' second-in-command, Captain Piolenc.

'enable us to win': Pearson, *Tears of Glory*, p. 173.

'Good day!': *Ibid.*

'evening 20 July': Geoffrey J. Thomas and Barry Ketley, *KG 200: The Luftwaffe's Most Secret Unit*, Crowborough, East Sussex: Hikoki Publications, 2003, p. 111.

'not yet assured': Fernand Rude, 'Vercors', in Pierre Bolle (ed.), *Grenoble et le Vercors: De la Résistance à la Libération 1940–1944*, Lyon: La Manufacture, 1985, p. 116.

'getting through this': AMLPC-N, *Des résistants polonais en Vercors: La saga du lycée polonais Cyprian-Norwid*, p. 99.

'bad weather in France': TNA AIR 27/2142.

'Central meteorological service group': Vol. 69 of the German wartime weather reports – by kind permission of the British Meteorological Archives.

Chapter 32: The End of Dreams: Friday 21 July 1944

driven by M. Boiron: Journal de Marche du 11e Régiment de Cuirassiers, 23 July 1944, http://11eme-cuirassiers-vercors.com/11eme.php?sp=7.

the little airfield: Gilbert Joseph, *Combattant du Vercors*, Grenoble: Éditions Curandera, 1994 (1st edn, Paris: Fayard, 1992), p. 229.

to the cover of Vassieux: Geoffrey J. Thomas and Barry Ketley, *KG 200: The Luftwaffe's Most Secret Unit*, Crowborough, East Sussex: Hikoki Publications, 2003, p. 111.

his colleague Pierre Haezebrouck: *Ibid.*

'rather than shovels': Association Mémoire du Lycée Polonais Cyprian-Norwid, *Des résistants polonais en Vercors: La saga du lycée polonais Cyprian-Norwid: Villard de-Lans 1940–1946*, Grenoble: Presses Universitaires de Grenoble, 2012, p. 99.

two days later: Jean Abonnenc, *Il n'est pas trop tard pour parler de Résistance*, Die: Imprimerie Cayol, 2004, p. 227.

'hesitates is lost': Gilles Vergnon, *Le Vercors: Histoire et mémoire d'un maquis*, Paris: Les Éditions de l'Atelier, 2002, p. 106; and Philippe Hanus and Gilles Vergnon, *Vercors: Résistance en Résonances*, Paris: L'Harmattan, 2008, p. 128.

the Dorniers flew downstream: Georg Schlaug, *Die deutschen Lastensegler-Verbände 1937–1945: Eine Chronik aus Berichten, Tagebüchern, Dokumenten*, Stuttgart: Motorbuch, 1985, pp. 212–15.

'It's the Germans!': AMLPC-N, *Des résistants polonais en Vercors: La saga du lycée polonais Cyprian-Norwid*, p. 103.

killing their pilots: Unteroffiziers Rink and Pyritz.

the unit medical officer: Dr Max Burkard.

'an uninhabited farm':: Pierre Tanant, *Vercors, haut-lieu de France*, Grenoble: Arthaud, 1948 and 1950, p. 122. Also quoted in Jean-Marc Collavet, *Chronique du Vercors*, Valence: Éditions Peuple Libre, 1994, p. 107.

'move an inch': Paul Dreyfus, *Vercors: Citadelle de la liberté*, Romagnat: De Borée, 2007 (1st edn Paris: Arthaud, 1969), p. 212.

the edge of the village: Thomas and Ketley, *KG 200*, p. 113; and Jean Sauvageon, Gilles Vergnon and Jacki Vinay, *1939–1945: Et se leva le vent de la liberté: Entre Drôme des collines et Vercors*, Guilherand-Granges: ANACR, 2012, p. 131.

his left shin bone: Journal de Marche du 11e Régiment de Cuirassiers.

Aimé and Antoinette Algoud: Interview with Mme Algoud, 15 September 2012, La Mure.

an unusually high casualty rate: Thomas and Ketley, *KG 200*, p. 113.

a 170-strong company: Under the command of André Bordenave.

'the battle ahead': Joseph, *Combattant du Vercors*, p. 227.

'mountain tracks as well': *Ibid.*

the smaller one: Made up chiefly of Reserve Gebirgsjäger Battalion 100. For this information, together with many of the other facts relating to the composition and movements of German forces during this operation, I am much indebted to Peter Lieb's publication *Vercors 1944: Resistance in the French Alps*, Botley, Oxford: Osprey Publishing, 2012.

'hope for the best …': Joseph, *Combattant du Vercors*, pp. 224–5.

the Compagnie André: Sometimes also referred to (e.g. in the journal of the 11th Cuirassiers after the battle of the passes) as Compagnie Henry, after Lieutenant Henry, alias Champon. Henry was a close friend of Kalck.

Lieutenant Louis Kalck: Alias André.

'the village of La Bâtie': Joseph, *Combattant du Vercors*, p. 234.

a Gebirgsjäger company: Reserve Gebirgsjäger Battalion II/98's No. 8 Company.

the two forward German platoons: Platoons Wilhelm and Hilche.

the third platoon: Commanded by Oberleutnant Hans Schlemmer.

from moving forward: Lieb, *Vercors 1944: Resistance in the French Alps*, pp. 51–5.

'Regimental First Aid Post': AN, Diary of 8. Kompanie Reserve Gebirgsjäger Bataillon II/98. Courtesy of Peter Lieb.

'rustling of leaves': François Broche, *François Huet, chef militaire du Vercors: Une vie au service de la France*, Paris: Éditions Italique, 2004, p. 199; also quoted in Dreyfus, *Vercors: Citadelle de la liberté*, p. 215.

the line went dead: Michael Pearson, *Tears of Glory: The Betrayal of the Vercors*, London: Pan Books, 1978, p. 179.

the Hôtel Breyton: Now the Hôtel Saint-Martin.

a witness: Vincent-Beaume.

'had been betrayed': Pearson, *Tears of Glory*, p. 180.

flash message to London: This message did not reach Cochet in Algiers until 14.20 that afternoon.

'something about a bridge': Rachel Millard, 'Two Years in World War Two', p. 11, by kind permission of the author.

'Keep me informed': Pearson, *Tears of Glory*, p. 180.

his local commander: Gaston Cathala.

'two days previously': Taken from a French translation of Hoppers' report in the OSS archives in Washington, given to the author by Gilles Vergnon, August 2012.

some farm buildings on a rise: Probably Le Foulet.

'lull in the fighting': Pearson, *Tears of Glory*, p. 183.

'when you can': *Ibid.*, p. 182. See also the Journal de Marche du 11e Régiment de Cuirassiers, http://11eme-cuirassiers-vercors.com/.

'part in the action': Journal de Marche du 11e Régiment de Cuirassiers, http://11eme-cuirassiers-vercors.com/.

'they will kill me': Broche, *François Huet, chef militaire du Vercors*, p. 201. This dialogue is an amalgam of those reported in this book, in Tanant, *Vercors, haut-lieu de France*, and in Pearson, *Tears of Glory*.

all-round defence: Interview with Robert Bennes, 10 November 2013, Castres.

'criminals and cowards': Fernand Rude, 'Le Dialogue Vercors–Algers (juin–juillet 1944)', *Revue d'Histoire de la Deuxième Guerre Mondiale*, no. 49, January 1963, p. 100. Thanks to (probably deliberate) delays in the Algiers systems, Gabriel Cochet first saw this embarrassing signal five days after it had been sent.

'follow our orders': Tanant, *Vercors, haut-lieu de France*, p. 115; also Pearson, *Tears of Glory*, p. 173.

Chapter 33: Fighting On: Saturday 22 July 1944

'Les Fleurs du Mal': Charles Baudelaire.

'Les Essais': Michel de Montaigne.

'La Pléiade': 'La Pléiade', or more correctly 'La Bibliothèque de la Pléiade', is the name of a prestigious leather-bound Bible-paper collection of works in French (literature, history, etc.) published by the Éditions Gallimard publishing house.

'ever a writer': SHAT T 1167, Fonds Ziegler, Humbert's account.

one of Geyer's commanders: Maurice Bourgeois.

were in flames: http://11eme-cuirassiers-vercors.com/.

three wounded Wehrmacht soldiers: They were actually Poles.

'our personal equipment': Ray Jenkins, *Pacifist at War*, London: Hutchinson, 2009, p. 178.

When Ganimède met Fischer: The details of this are taken from Dr Ganimède's witness statements. DCAJM, Grotte de la Luire Box.

to the cave: The cave and access are today much as they would have been in 1944, though it is now a memorial site.

'able to win through': Evidence of Maud Romana, Association Nationale des Pionniers du Vercors, *Le Vercors raconté par ceux qui l'ont vécu*, Valence: Imprimerie Nouvelle, 1990, p. 341.

'the survivors amongst the civilian population': Including the wounded Jean Tournissa. See Michael Pearson, *Tears of Glory: The Betrayal of the Vercors*, London: Pan Books, 1978, p. 179.

'escape towards St Martin': NARA, Justine Mission, Hoppers' report, Box 741, Folder 1473.

'and air supplies': Georg Schlaug, *Die deutschen Lastensegler-Verbände 1937–1945: Eine Chronik aus Berichten, Tagebüchern, Dokumenten*, Stuttgart: Motorbuch, 1985, pp. 212–15.

'running with water': Paray's report, TNA HS 6/425.

at Le Briac above Saint-Martin: Le Scialet des Pacons: lat. 45.0272404196669, long. 5.42003117783819, height 1,021 metres. The cave is still there, though difficult to find. Visit by Sylvie Young and Pierre-Yves Belette's partner and speleologist Miha, 28 August 2013.

to the eastern plateau: Interview with Robert Bennes, 10 November 2013, Castres.

Gustave Boissière: Alias Bois.

'to leave to do so': SHAT T 1167, Fonds Ziegler, Humbert's account, p. 17.

The night had been cold enough: Interview with Robert Bennes, 10 November 2013, Castres.

on the Pas de la Ville: http://11eme-cuirassiers-vercors.com/. The report actually quotes the message as coming from the Pas des Chattons, but this must be incorrect as that pass had fallen the night before.

They were all killed: ANPV, *Le Vercors raconté par ceux qui l'ont vécu*, p. 209.

'coming out of a cabin': La Grande Cabane – Kalck's headquarters.

Lieutenant Paul Blanc: Alias Jean-Paul.

a grassy hump: The French word for this type of feature is a *mamelon*, which shares its roots with the English word 'mammary'.

crowned by a wooden sheep pen: Today a memorial to those who fought and fell in the battle for the Pas de l'Aiguille stands on this spot.

a substantial shepherd's hut: La Cabane des Chaumailloux.

According to the French account: Albert Darier, *Tu prendras les armes*, Valence: Imprimerie Nouvelle, 1983, pp. 233 *et seq.*

Martial Kaufmann: Alias Martial.

continue their journey on foot: They would have used the Chemin de Mondrin to the But de Nève, 3 kilometres to the west, and thence turned north for Vassieux.

'forward to support him': Paul Dreyfus, *Vercors: Citadelle de la liberté*, Geneva: Famot, 1975, vol. 2, p. 234.

Lieutenant d'Anglejan: Alias Arnolle.

'Bomb Chabeuil and Saint-Nizier': Fernand Rude, 'Le Dialogue Vercors–Algers (juin–juillet 1944)', *Revue d'Histoire de la Deuxième Guerre Mondiale*, no. 49, January 1963, pp. 102 *et seq.*

'than holding territory …': *Ibid.*

'positions of friendly forces': *Ibid.*

'with maximum urgency': *Ibid.*

'Vassieux and La Mure': BA-MA, RH 19 IV/137. Ob West. Ic Nr. 5087/44 geh. v. 23.7.1944, kindly supplied by Peter Lieb.

Chapter 34: The Final Battles: Sunday 23 July 1944

'retreat to the woods': NARA, Justine Mission, Hoppers' report, Box 741, Folder 1473.

'for 48 hours': Captain Roland, Journal de marche de 11e Régiment de Cuirassiers, http://11eme-cuirassiers-vercors.com/.

'were immediately shot': SOE, Participation of the FFI in the Liberation of France, ch. V, p. 188, TNA HS 7/131.

'shelter of the trees': Association Nationale des Pionniers du Vercors, *Le Vercors raconté par ceux qui l'ont vécu*, Valence: Imprimerie Nouvelle, 1990, p. 206.

'in Southern France': TNA AIR 27/2142.

a Maquisard: We only know his alias, Mülheim – probably an association with his home town.

'Oh shit!': Paul Dreyfus, *Vercors: Citadelle de la liberté*, Romagnat: De Borée, 2007 (1st edn Paris: Arthaud, 1969), p. 75.

'Vive la France': *Ibid.*, p. 76.

hard to bear: See Pierre Tanant, *Vercors, haut-lieu de France*, Grenoble: Arthaud, 1948 and 1950, p. 137.

'We have had it': The actual phrase used by Huet was 'C'est cuit' – 'We're cooked'.

'falling on Saint-Martin': SHAT T 1167, Fonds Ziegler, Humbert's account, p. 21.

'Signed Huet': Lieutenant Stephen (André Valot), *Vercors, premier maquis de France*, Grenoble: Association Nationale des Pionniers et Combattants Volontaires du Vercors, 1991 (1st edn, Buenos Aires: VIAU, 1946), p. 146.

tried to get away: See Michael Pearson, *Tears of Glory: The Betrayal of the Vercors*, London: Pan Books, 1978, p. 207.

one of Huet's remaining staff officers: Pierre de Montjamont.

'able to do': Fernand Rude, 'Le Dialogue Vercors–Algers (juin–juillet 1944)', *Revue d'Histoire de la Deuxième Guerre Mondiale*, no. 49, January 1963, p. 103.

'Send fighters': *Ibid.*

'fighting units. Farewell': *Ibid.*

'into this situation': Jean-Marc Collavet, *Chronique du Vercors*, Valence: Éditions Peuple Libre, 1994, p. 110.

'at Les Barraques': Paray's report, TNA HS 6/425.

'29 dead, 20 wounded': BA-MA, Ob. West (Supreme Commander West) Ia no. 5932/44 RH 19
  IV. Courtesy of Peter Lieb. The signal was sent on 23 July 1944. Peter Lieb email to the
  author, 12 January 2013.

The man guarding the cave mouth: Gilbert Galland (alias Francis).

only two had serious injuries: Jean Moscone (alias Soulier) and Gaston Nicolas (alias
  Ramuntcho).

Blanc's sentry: René Simiand (alias Joseph).

One of the defenders: Xavier Boucard (alias Bachus).

According to later accounts: Albert Darier, *Tu prendras les armes*, Valence: Imprimerie
  Nouvelle, 1983, p. 269.

they shot themselves: It is not difficult to imagine how, after the war, the story of the end of
  this remarkable siege might have been amended to protect the feelings of the families
  involved and the reputation of the survivors. In the Second World War, as in previous
  conflicts, it was not wholly unknown for commanders to kill their wounded rather than let
  them fall into the hands of a pitiless enemy (the British are said to have killed their
  wounded before retreating across the Irrawaddy River, rather than let them fall into
  Japanese hands). I know of no case, however, where the wounded killed themselves in these
  circumstances.

'all-round protection': AN, Diary of 8. Kompanie Reserve Gebirgsjäger Bataillon II/98.
  Courtesy of Peter Lieb.

Chapter 35: Retreat and Refuge

'30 aircraft destroyed': According to Peter Lieb this is almost certainly an exaggeration.

'AA guns untouched': 26 July Sitrep, TNA WO 204/1947.

'after 25 July': Fernand Rude, 'Le Dialogue Vercors–Algers (juin–juillet 1944)', *Revue d'Histoire
  de la Deuxième Guerre Mondiale*, no. 49, January 1963, p. 106.

a parachute site at Comps: Jean Abonnenc, *Il n'est pas trop tard pour parler de Résistance*, Die:
  Imprimerie Cayol, 2004, p. 261.

returned to Bastia: Association Nationale des Pionniers du Vercors, *Le Vercors raconté par
  ceux qui l'ont vécu*, Valence: Imprimerie Nouvelle, 1990, p. 198.

more than 10 metres: Most of the details which follow are taken from SHAT T 1167, Fonds
  Ziegler, Humbert's account.

a white officer in a parachute smock: Almost certainly Lieutenant Yves Moine.

'height of combat. Huet': Rude, 'Le Dialogue Vercors–Algers (juin–juillet 1944)', p. 107.

the breakout towards Paris: Michael Pearson, *Tears of Glory: The Betrayal of the Vercors*,
  London: Pan Books, 1978, p. 219.

'in small groups': BA-MA Ob. West (Supreme Commander West) Ic no. 5161/44 RH 19 IV.
  Courtesy of Peter Lieb.

two containers of film: The film was subsequently shown under the title *Au coeur de l'orage*.
  Extracts from it can still be found on YouTube.

Geyer's main base: Details from Journal de Marche du Régiment de 11e Cuirassiers,
  http://11eme-cuirassiers-vercors.com/.

he was quickly replaced: By Fernand Crouau (alias Abel).

Most were killed in the attempt: 'Les Résistants dans le Vercors, 9 Juin–7 Août 1944:
  Témoignages de Nicolas Bernard', by kind permission of his daughter Martine Pattin and
  her friend Julia Chalkley, pp. 11 *et seq*.

Georges Jouneau: Pierre Tanant, *Vercors, haut-lieu de France*, Grenoble: Arthaud, 1948 and
  1950, p. 178.

collected after dark: Interview with André Chavant, 6 June 2013, Grenoble.

'lasted for a month': NARA, Justine Mission, Hoppers' report, Box 741, Folder 1473.

'of all its fruit': Paul Dreyfus, *Vercors: Citadelle de la liberté*, Romagnat: De Borée, 2007 (1st
  edn Paris: Arthaud, 1969), p. 295.

Conus and his two guides: The full details of this extraordinary story can be found in Conus'
  evidence to ANPV, *Le Vercors raconté par ceux qui l'ont vécu*, p. 393.

'In good health. Conus': Pearson, *Tears of Glory*, p. 208.

a small group: Charles Loysel, André Julien du Breuil (one of the Eucalyptus team), Alfred Leitzer, Léa Blain, Jean Veyrat, Simon Nora and René Lifschitz.

led by Paul Borel: Interview by telephone by Sylvie Young with Mme Anne-Marie Borel, Paul Borel's widow, August 2013.

a cave: Said to be close to the Grotte de l'Ours, near the Col de la Sarna.

the Grotte des Fées: Lat. 44.9789608016585, long. 5.45337185031601, height 1,267 metres. The author visited this cave on 22 May 2013 in the company of the speleologist Pierre-Yves Belette. Access is by a steep bank which precedes a near-vertical incline. Ropes to approach the entrance of the cave are not strictly necessary but advisable for safety. Inside there are many perfectly preserved crayon signatures of visitors going back to the late nineteenth century (one comments on the Dreyfus affair). On his visit the author discovered that among these is one which says 'Trotsky 1934' in handwriting which appears, from comparisons, to be that of Leon Trotsky. Trotsky is known to have hired a villa in Grenoble in 1934 and to have spent much of his time walking with his mistress in the region. But there is no mention of this expedition either in either Trotsky's book, *Journal d'exil*, which covers in some detail most of his Alpine walks, or in the later work of the late P. Broué, the leading expert on Trotsky's time in France.

according to accounts: See for example Jérôme Garcin, *Pour Jean Prévost*, Paris: Gallimard, 1994; Patrice Escolan and Lucien Ratel, *Guide-mémorial du Vercors résistant*, Paris: Le Cherche-Midi, 1994; and Simon Nora's preface to Jean Prévost, *L'Amateur de poèmes*, Paris: Gallimard, 1990.

on 31 July: There is dispute about this date which some sources say was 29 July. This date is taken from Escolan and Ratel, *Guide-mémorial du Vercors résistant*, p. 307.

One of their number: Simon Nora.

A young Maquisard: René Lifschitz.

with the others later: Escolan and Ratel, *Guide-mémorial du Vercors résistant*, p. 307.

La Croix des Glovettes: The place is now a car park close to some winter-sports flats on the northern outskirts of Villard-de-Lans.

the mouth of the Furon gorge: The actual location is alongside a small pedestrian bridge called the Pont de Charvet.

a mission over the Mediterranean: The remains of his aircraft and his identity disc were discovered by a fisherman off Riou Island near Marseille in September 1998.

to Switzerland and safety: They arrived at the Swiss frontier on 9 August 1944 – see Desmond Longe's report, TNA HS 6/361.

One of the Maquisards: Adrien Martin.

fallen asleep on the march: Exhausted and on a dark night, it is far easier to do this than might be imagined. The author has experienced the same problem on several occasions.

Abbey of Valcroissant: This isolated abbey, with its magnificent rose window, sits in the midst of meadows at the foot of the towering slopes of the Glandasse mountain and is currently being restored.

to be buried: Author's interview with Gilbert Carichon, 2 June 2013, Rousset.

Chapter 36: The Harrowing of the Vercors

'will be given later': Jean-Marc Collavet, *Chronique du Vercors*, Valence: Éditions Peuple Libre, 1994, p. 120. See also Paul Dreyfus, *Vercors: Citadelle de la liberté*, Romagnat: De Borée, 2007 (1st edn Paris: Arthaud, 1969), p. 283.

according to French sources: Author's interview with Mayor Serge Saint-André of La Chapelle, 1 May 2013, La Chapelle. See also Mayor Saint-André's speech of 22 September 2012.

on 23 July: This date is contested. The evidence in witness statements in the Dépôt Central des Archives de la Justice Militaire in Le Blanc suggest that German troops did not arrive in La Chapelle until 25 July. But La Chapelle sources (e.g. Mayor Saint-André) indicate 23 July, and this date seems to fit better with the fact that the fighting in Vassieux was effectively over by 11.00 on 23 July, after which Schäfer's men moved out.

'can be spared': DCAJM, Evidence of Abbé Pitavy, La Chapelle Box.

the courtyard of a farm: The Ferme Albert.

sixteen of his young parishioners: Philippe Saint-André (aged 36), Maurice Rolland (17), Léopold Rolland (19), Jean Allouard (18), Aimé Bouvet (17), René Bayoud (19), Pierre Benevène (36), Georges Borel (37), René Chabert (18), Jules Fontanabona (23), Nello Fontanabona (20), Paul Morin (19), Robert Rochas (19), Fernand Rome (37), Roger Revol (28), Stanislas Sitarz (38).

blood-spattered courtyard: This account is taken largely from evidence of Abbé Pitavy, DCAJM, La Chapelle Box. The courtyard is preserved as a memorial in La Chapelle.

deterrent to others: Details from the author's interview with Yves Baudrier, Saint-Agnan teacher, 5 June 2013. The local school in Saint-Agnan is now named for Rose Jarrand, and the students there have produced an excellent pamphlet on the story of her death.

executing nineteen Maquisards: Gilles Vergnon, *Résistance dans le Vercors: Histoire et lieux de mémoire*, Grenoble: Glénat, 2002, p. 129. See also Collavet, *Chronique du Vercors*, p. 118.

Some French sources: Bernard Coliat, *Vercors 1944: Des GI dans le maquis*, Bourg-lès-Valence: Imprimerie Jalin, 2003, p. 203.

from the valley below: 'Les Résistants dans le Vercors, 9 Juin–7 Août 1944: Témoignages de Nicolas Bernard', by kind permission of his daughter Martine Pattin and her friend Julia Chalkley, p. 21.

'many French people': Georg Schlaug, *Die deutschen Lastensegler-Verbände 1937–1945: Eine Chronik aus Berichten, Tagebüchern, Dokumenten*, Stuttgart: Motorbuch, 1985, pp. 212–15.

Niehoff and Knab strongly criticized Pflaum: Peter Lieb, *Vercors 1944: Resistance in the French Alps*, Botley, Oxford: Osprey Publishing, 2012, p. 69.

Buget Farm in La Rivière: Curiously the Germans did not blow up Huet's HQ at Villa Bellon.

The rest: Among them Marie Roblès, an auxiliary nurse, who was asked to leave the cave because she was married. All the other nurses were single. She stayed in the forest with others until 7 August. Marie Roblès is now 100 years old and still lives in Romans. Interview by Sylvie Young, 26 August 2013, Romans.

three doctors: Ullmann, Fischer and Ganimède, who was accompanied by his wife and twenty-one-year-old son, Jean.

seven nurses: Maud Romana, Cécile Goldet, Anita Winter, France Pinhas, Suzanne Siveton, Rosine Bernheim and Odette Malossane.

'a German aircraft': Almost certainly a Fieseler Storch *mouche*.

'5 or 6 silhouettes appeared': According to the witness evidence of one of the nurses, Anita Winter, the Germans numbered about twenty-five, were Gebirgsjäger led by an SS officer and were taken to the spot by a local man – DCAJM, Grotte de la Luire Box.

'They missed nothing': DCAJM, Evidence of Dr Ganimède, Grotte de la Luire Box.

'you are all terrorists': *Ibid*.

dead on the spot: This story is, however, not substantiated in witness evidence held at DCAJM.

When the officer returned: There is some uncertainty about who was the senior officer who gave the order to shoot the wounded. Some claim he was Maximilian Kneitinger, commander of Reserve Grenadier Regiment 157 of 157th Reserve Division, but there is strong circumstantial evidence that he was at the south-west of the plateau at the time. The two other possibilities are Schwehr himself, or Graf Clement Rességuier de Miremont, the commander of Gebirgsjäger Battalion II/98. Some French documents also point the finger at a Lieutenant Anton Büttner. Peter Lieb email to the author, 1 June 2013.

five or six long bursts: The detail here is taken from Anita Winter's witness statement. DCAJM, Grotte de la Luire Box.

'Terroristen – Grotte – kaput!': Interview with Gilbert Carichon, 2 June 2013, Rousset.

all eight … were marched: The eight were Ahmed Abdesselem, Albert Baigneux, Francis Billon, René Bourgond, Fernand Delvalle, Édouard Hervé, Victorio Marinucci and Georges Robert.

forced to watch the executions: Interview with Gilbert Carichon, 2 June 2013, Rousset.

twenty young Maquisards: A prominent monument marks the spot today.

'a Bavarian and a Catholic': Collavet, *Chronique du Vercors*, p. 111.

the plot against Hitler: *Ibid*.

'deserved nothing more': Unposted letter found on a dead German. It is dated Aix-les-Bains, 13 August 1944, and was from 'Rudolf' to his family. Referred to in Gilles Vergnon, *Le*

Vercors: Histoire et mémoire d'un maquis, Paris: Les Éditions de l'Atelier, 2002, p. 152. Cf. letter of a German soldier to be found in Philippe Hanus and Gilles Vergnon, *Vercors: Résistance en résonances*, Paris: L'Harmattan, 2008, p. 112.

On the French side: Lieb, *Vercors 1944: Resistance in the French Alps*, p. 71. There is some scepticism about the accuracy of these figures which may be exaggerated or otherwise inaccurate (e.g. by double-counting corpses). Gilles Vergnon email to the author, 16 January 2014.

three heavy-stores gliders: Schlaug, *Die deutschen Lastensegler-Verbände 1937–1945*, pp. 212–15.

Chapter 37: Resurgence and Revenge

one of his cavaliers: Lieutenant Yves Beseau.

Its leader: Captain Bagnaud. Christian name and alias not known.

The leader of the second squadron: Captain Yves Chastenet de Géry (alias Roland).

the prelude to the southern invasion: François Broche, *François Huet, chef militaire du Vercors: Une vie au service de la France*, Paris: Éditions Italique, 2004, p. 215.

'ambushes and small raids': *La Guérilla n'aura pas lieu … La Bataille du Vercors 1940–1944*, Paris: CDEF/DREX/Bureau Recherche, 2010 (http://www.cdef.terre.defense.gouv.fr/…la…/la-bataille-du-vercors-1940-1944), p. 55.

twenty-seven Germans killed: This is probably an exaggeration.

So much for Niehoff's boast: See Chapter 36.

'superior forces with tanks': TNA HW 1/2361.

'ordinary conventional operations': *La Guérilla n'aura pas lieu … La Bataille du Vercors 1940–1944*, p. 48.

Chapter 38: Aftermath and Afterlives

In a tetchy: Pierre Billotte, *Le Temps des armes*, Paris: Plon, 1972, p. 301.

'unacceptable as such': Cable Maitland Wilson to Eisenhower, 22 July 1944, 22.00 hours, TNA HS 6/605.

'The Caiman Plan is unacceptable': SHAEF signal to Marshall and Wilson, TNA WO 204/1959.

'factor in mind': *Ibid*.

'the coming battle': Letter de Gaulle to Maitland Wilson, 27 July 1944, TNA WO 204/5750.

Caïman was 'impractical': Letter Maitland Wilson to de Gaulle, 4 August 1944, TNA WO 204/5750.

'losses are appropriately apportioned …': Fernand Rude, 'Le Dialogue Vercors–Algers (juin–juillet 1944)', *Revue d'Histoire de la Deuxième Guerre Mondiale*, no. 49, January 1963, p. 108.

was fully informed: Fernand Grenier, *C'était ainsi (souvenirs)*, Paris: Éditions Sociales, 1959, p. 206.

a Communist minister: Pierre Dalloz, *Vérités sur le drame du Vercors*, Paris: Éditions Fernand Lanore, 1979, p. 262.

'not use them': Rude, 'Le Dialogue Vercors–Algers (juin–juillet 1944)', p. 109; and also Michael Pearson, *Tears of Glory: The Betrayal of the Vercors*, London: Pan Books, 1978, pp. 222–4.

'Vidal [Montagnards] controversy': AD/E to Lieutenant Colonel Buckmaster, 26 July 1944, TNA HS 6/342.

'not now available': EMFFI to AD/E of 28 July 1944, TNA HS 6/342.

'there was only death': Paul Dreyfus, *Vercors: Citadelle de la liberté*, Romagnat: De Borée, 2007 (1st edn Paris: Arthaud, 1969), pp. 286 *et seq*.

Arlette Blanc: Her age is variously given in different sources as seven, eight, ten and twelve. Her gravestone indicates that her age was twelve – as does the photograph of her first communion.

closed until May 1946: *La Guérilla n'aura pas lieu … La Bataille du Vercors 1940–1944*, Paris: CDEF/DREX/Bureau Recherche, 2010 (http://www.cdef.terre.defense.gouv.fr/…la…/la-bataille-du-vercors-1940-1944), p. 61.

'La Mure, Vassieux, La Chapelle en Vercors …': *Trial of the Major War Criminals before the International Military Tribunal, Nuremberg, 14 November 1945-1 October 1946: Nuremberg Trial Proceedings*, vol. 1, Indictment: Count Three, War Crimes, Section (G) (Yale University Avalon Project), http://avalon.law.yale.edu/subject_menus/imtproc_v1menu.asp.

Raoul Dagostini: I am indebted to Charles Forman on whose research in the archives in Grenoble this information is based.

pregnant at the time: Provence had been captured in La Chapelle in early July and placed in Loscence prison by the Vercors French authorities. Here she revealed that she was pregnant, a fact confirmed by a local doctor. She was released when Huet ordered all the Loscence prisoners to be set free on 23 July. Recaptured, she was tried and condemned to death at Grenoble on 11 October 1945, but her sentence was commuted to life imprisonment with hard labour by de Gaulle on 31 October. I am indebted to Pierre-Louis Fillet, Director of the Musée de la Résistance in Vassieux, for this information.

killed with Victor Boiron: A roadside memorial marks the spot where the two men were killed. Lat. 45.06569, long. 5.23806.

a national memorial site: The Vercors Nécropole.

Two became teachers: Kolb and Kneitinger.

One became an artist: Graf Clement Mirement de Rességuier.

a humble sales representative: I am indebted to Peter Lieb's *Vercors 1944: Resistance in the French Alps*, Botley, Oxford: Osprey Publishing, 2012, p. 90, for this information.

'our star turn': TNA HS 9/258.

than as a war hero: David Harrison email to the author, 31 December 2013.

two of his fellow radio operators: Yves Croix and Pierre Saillard.

supportive or non-committal: During my research I have been struck by the mutual solidarity of all those who actually went through the trials of June, July and August 1944 on the Vercors. No matter what the grounds, they are almost without exception extremely reluctant to criticize anyone else who went through the same experiences.

the inquiry exonerated the two men: Findings of Court of Enquiry, 2 December 1944, TNA HS 6/425.

MBE: Member of the British Empire.

MC: Military Cross.

lesser-known Resistance groups: See Le Ray's Preface to Patrice Escolan and Lucien Ratel, *Guide-mémorial du Vercors résistant*, Paris: Le Cherche-Midi, 1994.

'France is the Vercors': Gilles Vergnon, *Résistance dans le Vercors: Histoire et lieux de mémoire*, Grenoble: Glénat, 2002, p. 8.

one of the Vercors' combatants: Joseph Picirella.

in the village of Vassieux: Musée de la Résistance, Vassieux-en-Vercors.

Chapter 39: Postscript

'a little *gloire*': IWM sound archives, Interview with Francis Cammaerts, Session 11238, Reel 3 at 15' 55".

an Allied Military Government in Occupied Territories: AMGOT.

the Allied/French Overlord planning meetings in late May 1944: For example, the 20 May 1944 meeting at Finchampstead.

promises given by Soustelle: On behalf of de Gaulle. See Chapter 18.

his visit to Algiers in May: It is an often overlooked fact that Zeller was given exactly the same promises on a visit to Algiers earlier in the year – see Cammaerts' post-war interview in the IWM sound archives.

'could be established': TNA HS 6/340. See Chapter 18.

the concern which reverberated around SOE: See Chapter 38.

instructions issued by SHAEF on 21 May 1944: See Chapter 18.

met Henri Zeller in Barcelonnette: See Chapter 22.

'held at all costs': Cammaerts' post-operational report, TNA HS 9/258/5.

'basket of crabs': See Chapter 17.

'in their power': BBC Caversham Archives, French scripts for 6 June 1944.

'Be patient, prepare': http://www.bbc.co.uk/schoolradio/…/speeches/eisenhower.

in his D-Day address: See Chapter 20.

to disperse 'in small groups': See Chapter 21.

'the quiet life': See Chapter 23.

'The woman at the doorway': Professor Harry R. Kedward. See his *In Search of the Maquis*, Oxford: Clarendon Press, 1993, p. 89.

even a Maquis leader: Paulette Jacquier (alias Marie-Jeanne and La Frette).

Annex A

possible use of the Vercors: Gilles Vergnon, *Le Vercors: Histoire et mémoire d'un maquis*, Paris: Les Éditions de l'Atelier, 2002, p. 211.

Annex C

Caves Used by the Maquis in the Vercors: SHAT 1 K 907, supplemented by information from Pierre-Yves Belette.

LIST OF ILLUSTRATIONS

BIBLIOGRAPHY

23 mois de vie clandestine, Conférences de l'Information 1945, 23 April 1945, Paris: Imp. Curial-Archerau, 1945

Abonnenc, Jean, *Il n'est pas trop tard pour parler de Résistance*, Die: Imprimerie Cayol, 2004

Albertelli, Sébastien, *Les Services secrets du général de Gaulle: Le BCRA 1940–1944*, Paris: Éditions Perrin, 2009

André, Philippe, *La Résistance Confisquée?*, Paris: Éditions Perrin, 2013

Andrevon, Jean-Pierre, *La Forteresse sacrifiée*, Paris: Éditions Nathan, 2006

Arthy, Andrew, *Luftwaffe Anti-Partisan Operations in France, June–September 1944*, http://www.thescale.info/news/publish/luftwaffe-Anti-Partisan.shtml

Association Mémoire du Lycée Polonais Cyprian-Norwid, *Des résistants polonais en Vercors: La saga du lycée polonais Cyprian-Norwid: Villard de-Lans 1940–1946*, Grenoble: Presses Universitaires de Grenoble, 2012

Association Nationale des Pionniers du Vercors, *Le Vercors raconté par ceux qui l'ont vécu*, Valence: Imprimerie Nouvelle, 1990

Azéma, Jean-Pierre, *De Munich à la Libération (1938–44)*, Paris: Éditions du Seuil, 1980

Balzarro Anna, *Le Vercors et la Zone Libre de Alto Tortonese: Récits, mémoires, histoires*, Paris: L'Harmattan, 2002

Barbier, Jeanne, *Ici, jadis, était un village de France*, Die: Imprimerie Cayol, 2001

Baumel, Jacques, *La Liberté guidait nos pas*, Paris: Plon, 2004

Beevor, Antony, *D-Day: The Battle for Normandy*, London: Penguin, 2012

Billotte, Pierre, *Le Temps des armes*, Paris: Plon, 1972

Bolle, Pierre (ed.), *Grenoble et le Vercors: De la Résistance à la Libération, 1940–1944*, Lyon: La Manufacture, 1985

Bot, Pierre, *La Bataille du Vercors*, Valence: Éditions Peuple Libre, 2008

Bourdet, Claude, *L'Aventure incertaine*, Paris: Stock, 1975

Boyd, Douglas, *Blood in the Snow, Blood on the Grass*, Stroud: The History Press, 2012

Bradley, John N., *The Second World War*, vol. 1: *Europe and the Mediterranean*, New York: Square One Publishers, 2002

Broche, François, *François Huet, chef militaire du Vercors: Une vie au service de la France*, Paris: Éditions Italique, 2004

Chalou, George C. (ed.), *The Secret War: The Office of Strategic Services in World War II*, Washington, DC: National Archives and Records Administration, 1992

Chauvy, Gérard, *Histoire sombre de la Milice*, Brussels: Ixelles Publishing, 2012

Clark, Freddy, *Agents by Moonlight*, London: Tempus Publishing, 1999

Coliat, Bernard, *Vercors 1944: Des GI dans le maquis*, Bourg-lès-Valence: Imprimerie Jalin, 2003

Collavet, Jean-Marc, *Chronique du Vercors*, Valence: Éditions Peuple Libre, 1994

Comte, Bernard, 'Uriage et la Résistance', in Pierre Bolle (ed.), *Grenoble et le Vercors: De la Résistance à la Libération 1940–1944*, Lyon: La Manufacture, 1985

Cookridge, E. H., *They Came from the Sky*, London: Corgi Books, 1976 (1st edn, London: Heinemann, 1965)

Correll, John T., 'The Moon Squadrons', Air Force Magazine, July 2012 (http://www.airforcemag.com/MagazineArchive/Pages/2012/July%202012/0712moon.aspx)

Costa de Beauregard, Roland, 'Le Vercors juin 1944: Projets et réalités', Revue Historique de l'Armée, no. 4, 1972

Crémieux-Brilhac, Jean-Louis, 'Les Glières', Vingtième Siécle: Revue d'Histoire, vol. 45, no. 1, January–March 1995, pp. 54–66

Crémieux-Brilhac, Jean-Louis, La France Libre: De l'appel du 18 Juin à la Libération, Paris: Gallimard, 1998

Crémieux-Brilhac, Jean-Louis, 'Une Stratégie militaire pour la Résistance: Le Bloc Planning et l'insurrection nationale', Revue Espoir, no. 139, June 2004, pp. 41–57

Crémieux-Brilhac, Jean-Louis, Georges Boris: Trente ans d'influence, Paris: Gallimard, 2010

Crémieux-Brilhac, Jean-Louis, L'Appel du 18 juin, Paris: Armand Colin, 2010

d'Astier de La Vigérie, Emmanuel, Les Dieux et les hommes, Paris: Julliard, 1952

Dacier, Jean, Ceux du maquis, Grenoble and Paris: Arthaud, 1945

Dalloz, Pierre, Vérités sur le drame du Vercors, Paris: Éditions Fernand Lanore, 1979

Dalotel, Alain, Le Maquis des Glières, Paris: Plon, 1992

Darier, Albert, Tu prendras les armes, Valence: Imprimerie Nouvelle, 1983

de Gaulle, Charles, The War Memoirs, vol. 2: Unity 1942–1944, New York: Simon & Schuster, 1959

Delpla, François, Pourquoi Mandel n'est pas allé en Angleterre?, Paris: L'Archipel, 2008

Delpla, François, Churchill et les Français: Six hommes dans la tourmente, Septembre 1939–Juin 1940, rev. edn, Paris: François-Xavier de Guibert, 2010

Dereymez, Jean-William (ed.), Les Militaires dans la Résistance: Ain, Dauphiné, Savoie, 1940–1944, Avon-les-Roches: Éditions Anovi, 2010

Dewavrin, André Passy (Colonel), Souvenirs, vol. 2: 10, Duke Street, Londres (Le BCRA), Paris: Raoul Solar, 1948

Dreyfus, François-Georges (ed.), Unrecognized Resistance: The Franco-American Experience in World War Two, New Brunswick: Transaction Publishers, 2004

Dreyfus, Paul, Histoire de la Résistance en Vercors, Paris: Arthaud, 1980

Dreyfus, Paul, Vercors: Citadelle de la liberté, Romagnat: De Borée, 2007 (1st edn, Paris: Arthaud, 1969)

Eisenhower, Dwight D., Crusade in Europe, London: William Heinemann, 1948

Ellis, Major L. F., The War in France and Flanders 1939–1940, History of the Second World War, United Kingdom Military Series, http://www.ibiblio.org/hyperwar/UN/UK/UK-NWE-Flanders/

Escolan, Patrice, and Lucien Ratel, Guide-mémorial du Vercors résistant, Paris: Le Cherche-Midi, 1994

Farge, Yves, Rebelles, soldats et citoyens, Geneva: Éditions Grasset, 1948

Fenby, Jonathan, The General: Charles de Gaulle and the France He Saved, London: Simon & Schuster, 2010

Fillet, Abbé, Essai Historique sur le Vercors (Drôme), Valence: Lantheaume, 1888

Flaureau, Pierre, 'Le Comité de Libération de l'Isère', in Pierre Bolle (ed.), Grenoble et le Vercors: De la Résistance à la Libération 1940–1944, Lyon: La Manufacture, 1985

Fleutot, François-Marin, Des royalistes dans la Résistance, Paris: Flammarion, 2000

Foot, M. R. D., SOE in France: An Account of the Work of the British Special Operations Executive in France 1940–1944, London: HM Stationery Office, 1966

Foot, M. R. D., SOE: The Special Operations Executive 1940–1946, London: Pimlico, 1989 and 1999

Foot, M. R. D., and Jean-Louis Crémieux-Brilhac, Des Anglais dans la Résistance: Le service secret britannique d'action, SOE en France, 1940–1944, Paris: Éditions Tallandier, 2011

Frenay, Henri, La Nuit finira: Mémoires de résistance 1940–1945, Paris: Robert Laffont, 1973

Funk, Arthur L., De Gaulle, Eisenhower et la Résistance en 1944, http://www.charles-de-gaulle.org/pages/l-homme/dossiers-thematiques/1940-1944-la-seconde-guerre-mondiale/la-france-libre-et-les-allies/les-etats-unis/de-gaulle-eisenhower-et-la-resistance-en-1944.php

Funk, Arthur L., *Hidden Ally: The French Resistance, Special Operations, and the Landings in Southern France, 1944*, New York: Greenwood Press, 1992 (http://www.6thcorpscombatengineers.com/docs/RichardFietz/HiddenAlly.htm)

Garcin, Jérôme, *Pour Jean Prévost*, Paris: Éditions Gallimard, 1994

Gates, Eleanor M., *End of the Affair: The Collapse of the Anglo-French Alliance (1939–40)*, London: Allen & Unwin, 1982

Gaujac, Paul, *La Guerre en Provence 1944–1945*, Lyon: Presses Universitaires de Lyon, 1998

Germain, Michel, *Histoire de la Milice et des forces du maintien de l'ordre en Haute-Savoie 1940–1945*, Montmélian: La Fontaine de Siloé, 1997

Giolitto, Pierre, *Grenoble 40–44*, Paris: Librairie Académique Perrin, 2001

Giolitto, Pierre, *Histoire des groupes francs grenoblois*, Grenoble: Presses Universitaires de Grenoble, 2003

Grenier, Fernand, *C'était ainsi (souvenirs)*, Paris: Éditions Sociales, 1959

Hanus, Philippe, and Gilles Vergnon, *Vercors: Résistance en Résonances*, Paris: L'Harmattan, 2008

Hastings, Max, *Das Reich: The March of the 2nd Panzer Division through France, June 1944*, London: Pan Books, 2000

Hastings, Max, *Finest Years: Churchill as Warlord 1940–45*, London: William Collins, 2010

Heslop, Richard, *Xavier: The Famous British Agent's Dramatic Account of his Work with the French Resistance*, London: Rupert Hart-Davis, 1970

Irving, David, *The War between the Generals*, London: Penguin Books, 1981

Irwin, Lt Col. Will, *The Jedburghs: The Secret History of the Allied Special Forces, France 1944*, New York: Public Affairs, 2005

Jenkins, Ray, *Pacifist at War*, London: Hutchinson, 2009

Joseph, Gilbert, *Combattant du Vercors*, Grenoble: Éditions Curandera, 1994 (1st edn, Paris: Fayard, 1992)

Kedward, Harry R., *In Search of the Maquis*, Oxford: Clarendon Press, 1993

Kedward, Rod, *France and the French: A Modern History*, Woodstock and New York: Overlook Press, 2006

Kersaudy, François, *De Gaulle et Churchill*, Paris: Éditions Perrin, 2010

Krivopissko, Guy, *La Dernière Lettre: Paroles de résistants fusillés en France*, Paris: Magnard, 2011

La Guérilla n'aura pas lieu … La Bataille du Vercors 1940–1944, Paris: CDEF/DREX/Bureau Recherche, 2010 (http://www.cdef.terre.defense.gouv.fr/…la…/la-bataille-du-vercors-1940-1944)

La Picirella, Joseph, *Mon journal du Vercors*, Lyon: Imprimerie Rivet, 1982

La Picirella, Joseph, *Témoignages sur le Vercors*, Lyon: Imprimerie Rivet, 1976

Lacouture, Jean, *De Gaulle*, vol. 1: *Le Rebelle (1890–1944)*, Paris: Éditions du Seuil, 1984

Lassalle, Pierre, and Raymond Muelle, *La Liberté venait des ondes*, Paris: Grancher, 2001

L'Engagement Résistant dans l'Ain, Bourg-en-Bresse: Édition Conseil Général de l'Ain, 2012

Le Pionnier du Vercors: La Compagnie Abel 1943–1944, Grenoble: Association Nationale des Pionniers et Combattants du Vercors, Special number 2012

Lévy, Gilles, 'La Genèse du groupe "Auvergne" du Réduit du Massif Central (avril–août 1944)', http://lesamitiesdelaresistance.fr/lien28/p23-50_la_genese_du_groupe_auvergne.pdf

Lieb, Peter, *Konventioneller Krieg oder NS-Weltanschauungskrieg? Kriegführung und Partisanenbekämpfung in Frankreich 1943/44*, Munich: Oldenbourg, 2007

Lieb, Peter, 'La 157e division de réserve et la lutte contre le Maquis dans le Jura et les Alpes françaises', in Bernard Garnier, Jean-Luc Leleu and Jean Quellien (eds), *La Répression en France, 1940–1945*, Actes du colloque, Caen, 8, 9 and 10 December 2005, Caen: Centre de Recherche d'Histoire Quantitative, 2007, pp. 289–301

Lieb, Peter, *Vercors 1944: Resistance in the French Alps*, Botley, Oxford: Osprey Publishing, 2012

Lorain, Pierre, *Secret Warfare*, London: Orbis, 1983

Maclean, Fitzroy, *Eastern Approaches*, London: Penguin Books, 1991 (1st edn, London: Jonathan Cape, 1949)

Manierre, Carter, *Pop's War*, private publication, n.d.

Marcot, François (ed.), *Dictionnaire historique de la Résistance: Résistance intérieure et France libre*, Paris: Robert Laffont, 2006

Marcot, François (ed.), *La Résistance et les Français: Lutte armée et le Maquis*, Colloque International de Besançon, 15–17 June 1995, Paris: Annales Littéraires de l'Université de Franche-Comté, Diffusion Les Belles Lettres, 1996

Marcot, François, 'Le Service national maquis: Structures, pouvoirs et stratégies', in François Marcot (ed.), *La Résistance et les Français: Lutte armée et maquis*, Colloque International de Besançon, 15–17 June 1995, Paris: Annales Littéraires de l'Université de Franche-Comté, Diffusion Les Belles Lettres, 1996

Marks, Leo, *Between Silk and Cyanide: A Codemaker's War 1941–45*, London: Touchstone, 2007

Masson, Madeleine, *Christine: A Search for Christine Granville*, London: Hamish Hamilton, 1975

Masson, Madeleine, *Christine: SOE agent and Churchill's Favourite Spy*, London: Virago, 2005

Michelet, Jules, *Tableau de La France* (first published 1861), Paris: Bibliothèque de Cluny, Librairie Armand Colin, 1962 (http://classiques.uqac.ca/classiques/michelet_jules/tableau_de_la_france/michelet_tableau_france.pdf)

Montagnon, Pierre, *Les Maquis de la Libération*, Paris: Éditions Pygmalion/Gérard Watelet, 2000

Moulin, Laure, *Jean Moulin: Biographie*, Paris: Presses de la Cité, 1982

Muller, Claude, *Dauphiné 1939–1945: Les Sentiers de la liberté*, Romagnat: De Borée, 2003

Mulley, Clare, *The Spy Who Loved: The Secrets and Lives of Christine Granville, Britain's First Female Special Agent of World War II*, London: Macmillan, 2012

Muracciole, Jean-François, 'La France Libre et la lutte armée', in François Marcot (ed.), *La Résistance et les Français: Lutte armée et maquis*, Colloque International de Besançon 15–17 June 1995, Paris: Annales Littéraires de l'Université de Franche-Comté, Diffusion Les Belles Lettres, 1996

Nal, Commandant Louis, *La Bataille de Grenoble*, Paris: Éditions des Deux Miroirs, 1964

The Papers of Dwight David Eisenhower: The War Years, ed. Alfred D. Chandler Jr, Baltimore: Johns Hopkins University Press, 1970

Parsus, Joseph, *Malleval-en-Vercors dans la Résistance*, Valence: Éditions Peuple Libre, 2011

Pearson, Michael, *Tears of Glory: The Betrayal of the Vercors*, London: Pan Books, 1978

Pogue, Forest C., *The United States Army in World War II: The European Theater of Operations: The Supreme Command*, Washington, DC: Office of the Chief of Military History, Department of the Army, 1954 (http://www.history.army.mil/html/books/007/7-1/CMH_Pub_7-1.pdf)

Pontaut, Jean-Marie, and Eric Pelletier, *Chronique d'une France Occupée*, Neuilly sur Seine: Éditions Michel Lafon, 2008

Prévost, Jean, *L'Amateur de poèmes*, Paris: Gallimard, 1990

Quellien, Jean, et al., *La France pendant la seconde guerre mondiale: Atlas historique*, Paris: Fayard/Ministère de la Défense, 2010

Romans-Petit, Col. Henri, *Les Obstinés*, Lille: Janicot, 1945

Rosencher, Henri, *Le Sel, la cendre, la flamme*, Paris: Éditions du Félin, 2000

Rude, Fernand, 'Le Dialogue Vercors–Algers (juin–juillet 1944)', *Revue d'Histoire de la Deuxième Guerre Mondiale*, no. 49, January 1963, pp. 79–110

Rude, Fernand, 'Vercors', in Pierre Bolle (ed.), *Grenoble et le Vercors: De la Résistance à la Libération 1940–1944*, Lyon: La Manufacture, 1985

Ruffin, Raymond, *Ces chefs de Maquis qui génaient*, Paris: Presses de la Cité, 1980

Sauvageon, Jean, Gilles Vergnon and Jacki Vinay, *1939–1945: Et se leva le vent de la liberté: Entre Drôme des collines et Vercors*, Guilherand-Granges: ANACR, 2012

Schlaug, Georg, *Die deutschen Lastensegler-Verbände 1937–1945: Eine Chronik aus Berichten, Tagebüchern, Dokumenten*, Stuttgart: Motorbuch, 1985

Soustelle, Jacques, *Envers et contre tout*, 3 vols, Geneva: Éditions de Crémille, 1970 (1st edn, Paris: Robert Laffont, 1947–50)

Stephen, Lieutenant (André Valot), *Vercors, premier maquis de France*, Grenoble: Association Nationale des Pionniers et Combattants Volontaires du Vercors, 1991 (1st edn, Buenos Aires: VIAU, 1946)

Tanant, Pierre, *Vercors, haut-lieu de France*, Grenoble: Arthaud, 1948 and 1950

Tentative of History of In/Exfiltrations into/from France during WWII from 1941 to 1945, http://www.plan-sussex-1944.net/anglais/pdf/infiltrations_into_france.pdf

Thomas, Geoffrey J., and Barry Ketley, *KG 200: The Luftwaffe's Most Secret Unit*, Crowborough, East Sussex: Hikoki Publications, 2003

Vallette d'Osia, Jean, *Quarante-deux ans dans de vie militaire*, Lyon: Lyonnaises d'Art et d'Histoire, 1994

Vercors 1944: Un officier britannique dans la tourmente, http://www.benchart.net/benchart/arnaud-duret/textes/article.doc

Vercors, *The Battle of Silence*, Austin, Texas: Holt, Rinehart & Winston, 1968

Vergnon, Gilles, *Le Vercors: Histoire et mémoire d'un maquis*, Paris: Les Éditions de l'Atelier, 2002

Vergnon, Gilles, *Résistance dans le Vercors: Histoire et lieux de mémoire*, Grenoble: Glénat, 2002

Verity, Hugh, *We Landed by Moonlight: Secret RAF Landings in France 1940–1944*, Wilmslow: Air Data Publications, 1995

Vial, Pierre, *La Bataille du Vercors 1943–1944*, Paris: Presses de la Cité, 1991

Vistel, Alban, *La Nuit sans ombre: Histoire des mouvements unis de résistance, leur rôle dans la libération du sud-est*, Paris: Fayard, 1970

Ward Price, G., *Giraud and the African Scene*, New York: Macmillan, 1944

Wieviorka, Olivier, *Histoire du débarquement en Normandie: Des origines à la Libération de Paris 1941–1944*, Paris: Éditions du Seuil, 2007

Williams, Charles, *The Last Great Frenchman: A Life of General de Gaulle*, San Francisco: Jossey Bass, 1997

Wyler, Christian, *La Longue Marche de la Division 157: Contre les maquis et les partisans 1942–1945*, Paris: Grancher, 2004

Web Sites

11th Cuirassiers in the Vercors – also includes tab for German activity as well as regimental history re Vercors and Thivolet, http://11eme-cuirassiers-vercors.com/index.php

The web site of the Resistance museum in Vassieux, http://www.museedelaresistanceenligne.org

The web site of Resistance Memorial (museum) in the Vercors, http://www.memorial-vercors.fr/fr_FR/index.php

Nuremberg trials, http://www.loc.gov/rr/frd/Military_Law/pdf/NT_Vol-I.pdf

De Gaulle's appeal, D-Day June 1946, http://www.charles-de-gaulle.org/pages/l-homme/dossiers-thematiques/1940-1944-la-seconde-guerre-mondiale/l-appel-du-18-juin/documents/l-appel-du-18-juin-1940.php

Lysander Squadron details, http://www.ww2aircraft.net/forum/aviation/squadron-161-lysander-mk-iii-31062.html

Resistance memorials, http://www.memoresist.org/spip.php?page=oublionspas_detail&id=10

California Military Museum, http://www.militarymuseum.org

Historical sun and moon rise and set and other astronomical details for 1944, http://www.world-timedate.com/astronomy/moonrise_moonset/moonrise_moonset_time.php?month=3&year=1944&city_id=1578

Amicale Mémoire du Réseau Gallia, http://www.reseaugallia.org/wiki/wiki.php

Von Rundstedt's war diary (KTB/Ob. West, XIII-f Anl. 159 et XIV-f), http://fr.academic.ru/dic.nsf/frwiki/17734

Information on Resistance in the Vercors, http://beaucoudray.free.fr/vercors4.htm

Resistance witness statements in the Département du Drôme, http://www.resistance-familles.com/wp-content/uploads/la-drome-en-armes.pdf

Information and details on Operation Dragoon, http://www.ibiblio.org/hyperwar/AAF/III/AAF-III-12.html

Film *Au Coeur de l'orage* made in the Vercors, June–July 1944, http://www.ina.fr/histoire-et-conflits/seconde-guerre-mondiale/video/AFE00003041/au-coeur-de-l-orage.fr.html

The Fondation de la Résistance – this web site gives details on all French Resistance networks, including radio operators, major sabotage events, parachute operations and historical development, http://www.fondationresistance.org/pages/accueil/les-reseaux-action-france-combattante_publication6.htm

624 Squadron RAF records and information, The Unsung Heroes of 624 RAF (Special Duties) Squadron, http://www.624squadron.org Paris

INDEX

Chavant, 157; Churchill invites to London from Algiers, 161, 163; opposes Roosevelt's plans for French post-war government, 84, 161; anger at Roosevelt, 163; disputes with Churchill, 163; D-Day broadcast, 167–8, 177–9, 372; and Descour's order to mobilize, 184; and Grenier's plan to fly planes from Algeria to France, 204; returns to Algiers (16 June 1944), 226; rejects Grenier's plan to mobilize old aircraft, 228–9; appoints Commissioners of the Republic, 247; and Caïman Plan, 249–50, 374; meets Roosevelt, 249; influence on French population, 286; enquires about help for Vercors, 330–1; disagreement with Maitland Wilson over Caïman Plan, 361; speech on battle for Vercors, 362; reverses Grenier's statement and resignation, 363; and redoubt strategy, 370

Gauthier, Colonel Georges, 336

Gayvallet, Jean, 262–3

Gendarmerie: attitude to Resistance, 67, 187–8

German Troops: Eastern ('Mongols'), 70, 106–7, 215, 277, 281, 291, 327, 348; Seventh Army, 168; Fifteenth Army, 168; Das Reich Division, 181–3; 157th Reserve Division, 105, 259, 277; Alpine Gebirgsjäger Regiment, 105–61, 113, 259, 276, 288, 304, 349, 351, 359

Germany/Germans: defeats France (1940), 9–10; reprisals and terror tactics, 15–16, 78, 97–8, 108, 113, 121, 182, 215–16, 281, 314, 348–55; demands on French production and manpower, 16, 38; in Italy, 68; occupies Grenoble, 68–9; detector vans in Vercors, 75; intelligence networks and gathering, 101–3, 120; offensive actions against Maquis, 104–6, 109–11, 117–20, 122, 252; morale of troops in France, 106; casualties, 107–8, 355; plans strategy against D-Day, 138–40; plan of Mediterranean defence system captured, 142; postpones attack on Vercors, 150; anti-partisan activities after D-Day, 182; advance on Saint-Nizier, 194–200; raids on Combovin plateau, 232–3; use aircraft against

partisans, 233–4; surprised by US parachute drop, 242; convoys attacked by Hoppers, 251–2, 260–1; blow up access roads to Vercors, 259; air attacks on Vercors, 265, 268; Operation Vercors against partisans, 277–8; alienation of troops from French civilians, 281–2; troop movements for Operation Vercors, 288; dead recovered, 350

Gestapo: penetrates Resistance movement, 48; arrests, 55; captures Maquis leader in Saint-Jean-en-Royans, 70; in Saint-Martin, 75; and Sipo/SD, 107

Geyer, Lieutenant Narcisse ('Thivolet'): qualities, 27–9, 77; as Maquisard, 29; Descour appoints to replace Le Ray, 77, 151; moves troops to Les Combes, 96; prepares for German attack, 113; Combe HQ destroyed, 118; objects to Gariboldy's Grenoble Post Office raid, 121; differences with Chavant, 141–2, 151, 156, 217; D-Day actions, 175; Huet outranks, 176; and mobilization order, 185; reinforces Saint-Nizier, 199; Huet briefs on Saint-Nizier, 201; and second battle of Saint-Nizier, 205, 211; men block road to Saint-Martin, 212; and arrest of Chavant, 217; defensive area, 219; attends memorial service for Saint-Nizier dead, 241; at proclamation founding Free Republic of Vercors, 252; invites Chavant to formal dinner, 254; and incorporation of Maquis units into army, 266; conversation with Huet on counter-attack at Vassieux, 307–8; told of fall of Vassieux, 307; attempt to recover Vassieux, 309–10; HQ at La Rivière, 313–14; and battle of the Passes, 318; and dispersal of units, 330; evacuates La Rivière, 332, 339; continues actions against Germans, 356–8; Descour instructs to recover Vassieux and La Chapelle, 356; moves to La Beaume-d'Hostun, 358; later career and retirement, 366

Giraud, General Henri, 83–5, 86, 144–5

Glaudas, Denise, 117

Glières plateau, 89, 100, 111–13, 122, 140, 193, 371

Godart, Pierre, 79, 98, 99